Fodor's

ESSENTIAL BELGIUM

Welcome to Belgium

Bordered by the Netherlands, France, Germany, and Luxembourg, it's not hard to spot Belgium's cultural influences. Half the country speaks Dutch (Flanders), the other French (Wallonia), and even a tiny portion converse in German (East Cantons). In the middle, there's cosmopolitan capital Brussels. The medieval cities of Ghent and Bruges offer gateways to the coast and World War I battlefields, while couture reigns supreme in Antwerp. And, of course, expect plenty of beer, chocolate, and frites wherever you wander.

TOP REASONS TO GO

★ **Medieval wonders:** The fairy-tale cobbles of Bruges and Ghent are like stepping into the Middle Ages.

★ **Battlefield tours:** Napoléon's final stand and the most important battles of the 20th century all happened here.

★ **Great trails:** Walk the lush forests of the Ardennes or pedal in the tire tracks of Tour of Flanders legends.

★ **Best brews:** Well-stocked bars, heritage breweries, and heavenly stews—Belgian beer unites them all.

★ **Historic art:** From Flemish Primitives to the finest Surrealist of them all, there's plenty of art to discover.

★ **Sweet tooth:** This is the land of waffles and chocolate—it would be wrong not to indulge.

Contents

1 EXPERIENCE BELGIUM 6
14 Ultimate Experiences 8
What's Where 14
Belgium Today 16
What to Eat in Belgium 18
Belgium's Best Beers 20
Best Castles in Belgium 22
Best Museums in Belgium 24
What to Watch and Read 26
Belgium with Kids 28

2 TRAVEL SMART 29
Know Before You Go 30
Getting Here and Around 32
Essentials 37
Contacts 43
Great Itineraries 44
On the Calendar 49
Helpful Phrases in French 52
Helpful Phrases in Flemish 54

3 BRUSSELS 57
Welcome to Brussels 58
Planning 61
Lower Town 65
Upper Town 79
Cinquantenaire and Schuman 88
Ixelles and Saint-Gilles 95
Laeken and Schaerbeek 104
Day Trips from Brussels 110

4 ANTWERP AND THE NORTHEAST 121
Welcome to Antwerp and the Northeast 122
Planning 125
Oude Stad and Het Eilandje 128
Meir, Diamond Quarter, and Centraal Station 141
South of the Center 150
Mechelen 155
Lier 158
Limburg Province 159

5 GHENT AND THE LEIE 163
Welcome to Ghent and the Leie 164
Planning 166
Ghent 169
Leiestreek Villages 186
Dendermonde 192
Vlaamse Ardennen 196
Kortrijk 202

6 BRUGES AND THE COAST 207
Welcome to Bruges and the Coast 208
Planning 211
Bruges 213
Damme 231
Knokke-Heist 233
De Haan 235
Oostende 236
Koksijde 239
Ypres 240

7 WESTERN WALLONIA 245
Welcome to Western Wallonia 246
Planning 249
Mons 251
Tournai 261
Ath 267
Lessines 271
Nivelles 272
Waterloo 273
Louvain-la-Neuve 277
La Louvière 278

Binche ... 282
Charleroi ... 285
Chimay ... 290

8 THE MEUSE AND THE ARDENNES ... 293
Welcome to The Meuse and the Ardennes ... 294
Planning ... 296
Liège ... 298
Spa ... 308
Huy ... 311
Hautes Fagnes ... 312
Malmedy ... 313
Stavelot ... 315
Namur ... 316
Dinant ... 323
Rochefort ... 326
Bastogne ... 328
Durbuy ... 331
La Roche-en-Ardenne ... 332
Bouillon ... 334

9 LUXEMBOURG ... 337
Welcome to Luxembourg ... 338
Planning ... 340
Luxembourg City ... 343
Esch-sur-Alzette and the Redlands ... 357
Remich and the Moselle ... 361
Echternach and Little Switzerland ... 365
Luxembourg Ardennes ... 368

INDEX ... 377

ABOUT OUR WRITERS ... 384

MAPS

Lower Town ... 66–67
Upper Town ... 82–83
Cinquantenaire and Schuman ... 90–91
Ixelles and Saint-Gilles ... 96–97
Laeken and Schaerbeek ... 106
Day Trips from Brussels ... 110
Oude Stad and Het Eilandje ... 130–131
Meir, Diamond Quarter, and Centraal Station ... 144–145
South of the Center ... 151
Ghent ... 170–171
Bruges ... 214–215
The Coast and Nearby ... 232
Mons ... 252–253
Western Wallonia ... 282
Liège ... 300–301
The Ardennes ... 315
Namur ... 318–319
Luxembourg City ... 344–345

Chapter 1

EXPERIENCE BELGIUM

14 ULTIMATE EXPERIENCES

Belgium offers terrific experiences that should be on every traveler's list. Here are Fodor's top picks for a memorable trip.

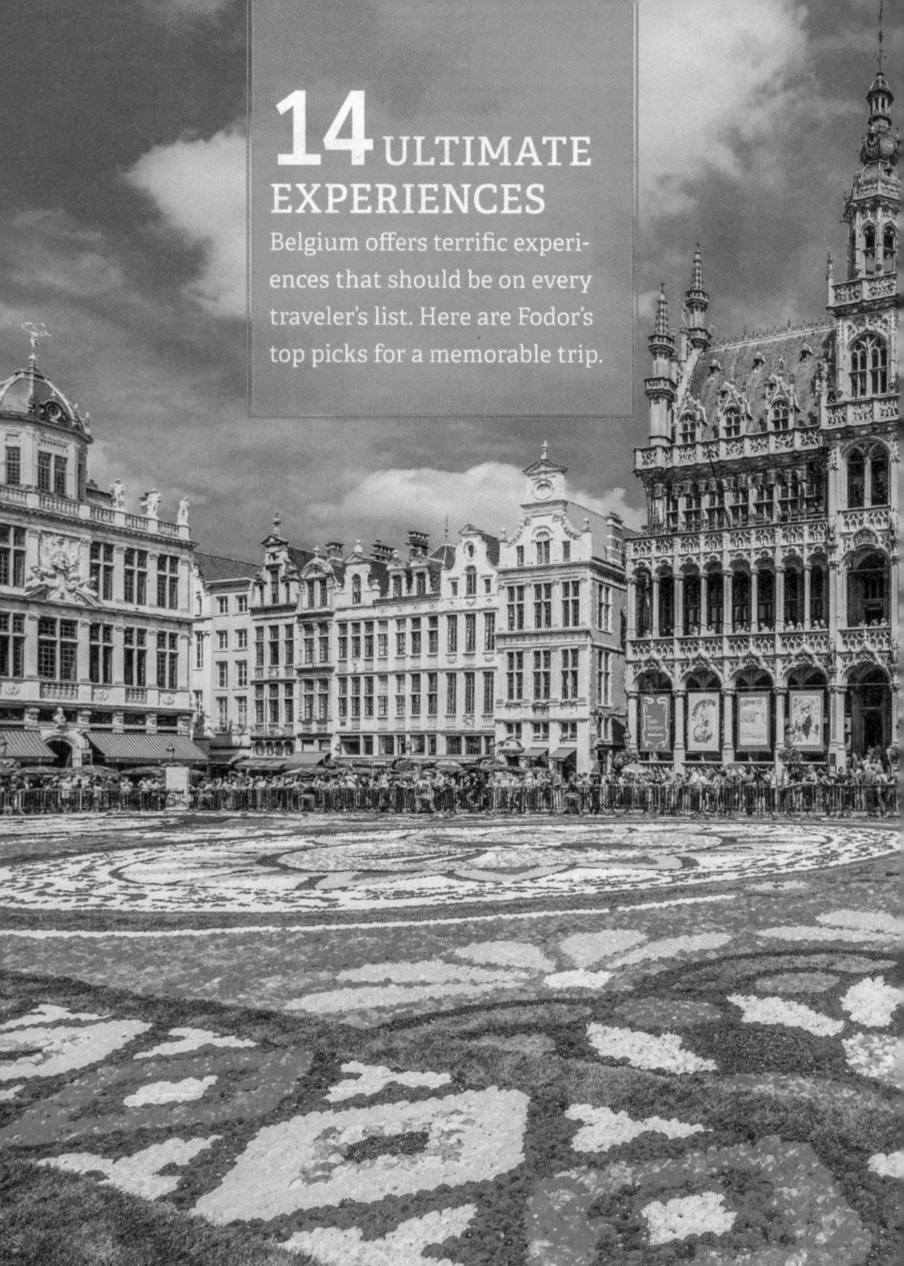

1 Marvel at the Grand Place

Brussels's Grand Place is one of the grandest squares in Europe. Its gold-flecked guild houses and 15th-century Gothic town hall are lit up in nightly displays during winter, and every two years its cobbles host a magnificent giant carpet of flowers (August). *(Ch. 3)*

2 Paddle and Hike the Ardennes

The Meuse River winds its way through Namur and down into the vast forests of the Ardennes. Kayak and SUP are a great way to explore here. *(Ch. 8)*

3 See the Famous Ghent Altarpiece

Ghent's St. Bavo's Cathedral is home to one of Europe's most prized artworks: the *Adoration of the Mystic Lamb* by Jan and Hubert van Eyck. *(Ch. 5)*

4 World War I and II Battlefields

Some of the most important battles in modern European history were fought in Flanders Fields (World War I) and in the Battle of the Bulge, near Bastogne (World War II). *(Ch. 6, 8)*

5 Stroll Art Nouveau Districts

Brussels's Ixelles and Saint-Gilles areas are the best places to see Art Nouveau architecture, not least the home of iconic architect Victor Horta, who used the capital's streets as his canvas. *(Ch. 3)*

6 Go Shopping in Antwerp

Its reputation as Belgium's couture capital is not without foundation. Nationalestraat is the playground of the designer set, while the hip crowd head to Kammenstraat for something more edgy. *(Ch. 4)*

7 Discover the Flemish Masters

From the early realism of the Flemish Primitives to the Italian-influenced Brueghels and 17th-century Antwerp masters, their work scatters galleries and churches across the cities. *(Ch. 4, 6)*

8 Visit Waterloo

Climb the Lion's Mound, commemorating the site of the 1815 showdown between Napoléon and the Duke of Wellington, then tour the surrounding battlefields. *(Ch. 7)*

9 Enjoy Carnival Season in Wallonia

Belgium's carnivals are some of the most unusual in Europe—from the mask-wearing *gilles* of Binche to the carrot-nosed *blanc moussis* pranksters of Stavelot. *(Ch. 7, 8)*

10 Embrace Medieval Belgium

Medieval belfries, beguinages, and religious buildings scatter the land here, with Antwerp, Ghent, Bruges, and Tournai home to some of the greatest examples. *(Ch. 4, 5, 6, 7)*

11 Read a Comic Book

It's not just nostalgia. Belgium's *bandes dessinées* (comic books) are woven into culture here, and are found everywhere, including the streets of Brussels where a trail of murals wraps the city. *(Ch. 3)*

12 Learn about Belgian Brewing

Belgian brewing is a subject as dense as its history. And while most Trappist abbey breweries don't allow visitors, plenty of others do, including Halve Maan in Bruges and Cantillon in Brussels. *(Ch. 3, 4, 5)*

13 Stock up on Chocolate

Belgian chocolate is world-famous. Some shops date back to the late 19th century, when brands like Neuhaus opened in Brussels but, for sheer density of chocolate shops, Bruges is king. *(Ch. 3, 6)*

14 Visit a Medieval Castle

Belgium is filled with castles. Some of the finest are found in the Ardennes and Western Wallonia, where Beloeil Castle is often likened to France's Versailles. *(Ch. 7, 8)*

WHAT'S WHERE

1 Brussels. Brussels is a cosmopolitan capital filled with history. Flâneurs are well rewarded here, as the modern office blocks of the EU Quarter give way to Gothic spires and Art Nouveau town houses. At its heart is one of the greatest city squares in Europe, best enjoyed with a cone of salty frites.

2 Antwerp and the Northeast. This historic port city shines as bright as the diamonds it so famously trades. As Brussels's cooler cousin, it is known for its couture and techno, yet boasts a medieval center and art history to rival even Bruges. To its east lies Belgium's oldest town, Tongeren.

3 Ghent and the Leie. In the 15th century, Ghent was among the richest cities in Europe, sprouting opulent merchants' homes and cathedrals that survive today. Around them now bustles a lively university town. On its outskirts, pretty villages dot the Leie Valley.

4 Bruges and the Coast. Once a powerful medieval city, Bruges attracted some of the greatest Flemish artists of the era.

Today, its center is still etched in labyrinthine cobbles, canals, and Gothic flourishes. Beyond lies the coastline and the World War I trenches of Flanders Fields.

5 Western Wallonia. Some travelers' experience of Western Wallonia is a brief stop at the budget airport of Charleroi. It's a shame. They miss out on a region filled with medieval towns, abbey breweries, and the site of the Battle of Waterloo.

6 The Meuse and the Ardennes. The great forests of the Ardennes spill from France into southern Belgium and on to Luxembourg. The Meuse Valley is arguably the most beautiful section. Farther east, the symbol of Walloon independence and pride is the city of Liège.

7 Luxembourg. One of the smallest countries in Europe nestles snugly between France, Belgium, and Germany. The capital is arguably the star here. Beyond, scenic villages scatter the borderlands from the wine country of the Moselle Valley to Müllerthal's "Little Switzerland."

Belgium Today

WHO NEEDS A GOVERNMENT? THE GREAT DIVIDE

In 1830, the regions of Dutch-speaking Flanders and French-speaking Wallonia, allied over their shared Catholicism, broke away from William I's Protestant Netherlands to form Belgium. It has always been an uneasy alliance. Past French rule had ensured theirs was the language of the upper classes, clergy, and the lawmakers; Dutch, despite being spoken by the majority, belonged to those who served. It sparked a Flemish nationalist movement that still burns bright. Recent years, in particular, have seen separatist parties dominate the polls in Flanders. French, Dutch, and also German (spoken in the East Cantons of Wallonia) may be the three official languages here, but the national conversation over who and what is Belgian never goes away.

THE NEW OLD

While the late-2022 reopening of Antwerp's renovated Royal Museum of Fine Arts has been hotly anticipated, another recent unveiling in the city was met with a colder response. The Steen is a 12th-century port-side castle that once guarded access to the important Scheldt River. Over the years it has housed a prison and numerous museums, but a recent blockish new addition, home to an information center for tourists, prompted angry petitions upon its completion. It isn't the first time the castle has had a radical new look; in 1890, the facade was given its current fairy-tale revamp to house a museum of archaeology. Form your own opinion when you visit.

THE BEAUTIFUL GAME

Soccer is king here, but rarely has the country been so good at it. Now is Belgium's golden age on the pitch. The national team, known as Les Diables Rouges (The Red Devils), ranked number one in the world FIFA rankings during 2020 and 2021. It's a monumental achievement for such a small nation. And while they didn't actually win anything (such is the eccentricity of FIFA rankings), the last decade has spawned memorable wins, and heroes such as Eden Hazard, Kevin de Bruyne, and Romulu Lukaku. Catch a game at the King Baudouin Stadium in Laeken, Brussels, to see a footballing nation in its pomp.

MORE TO DO ...

Most folk festivals in Belgium are joyous affairs with carnival atmospheres. A small handful, however, are problematic. These often feature offensive colonial imagery and have become a source of often heated debate. In 2019, repeated public complaints finally saw Aalst's carnival stripped of its UNESCO status due to its refusal to remove anti-Semitic images, while Ath's Giants' Parade sparked similar protests over its *"sauvage"* (savage) character. As large gatherings return post-COVID, traditional folk festivals may face a long-overdue reckoning.

BYE-BYE TO CARS

Cars are increasingly unwelcome in Belgium's cities. Ghent banished vehicles from its historic center in 2017, Bruges is so difficult to drive in that it's practically car-free by default, and Antwerp is planning on emptying the motoring heart of the city by 2024. But Brussels has the biggest plans of all and is slowly freeing up its center, having paved the once-busy Bourse and Boulevard Anspach. It now claims the second-largest pedestrianized area in Europe, even if locals grumble this has increased traffic on the already jammed outskirts. Now, in the place of cars, e-scooter apps and city bikes whisk visitors around its Art Nouveau streets.

NATURAL SELECTION

While beer is still everything in Belgium, the popularity of natural wine, made without additives or pesticides, has been rising in recent years. In Brussels, especially, new dedicated bars are cropping up all the time, with Titulus, in the Matonge area, one of first and still the largest. It opened in 2011 and now imports its own label, made in France's Loire Valley. But, finally, there is some real choice for natural wine fans. Raise a glass to change.

RISE OF THE SLEEPER TRAIN

The sleeper train is on the rise in Europe, as travelers become more conscious of their carbon footprint. In 2022, services on RegioJet's night train are due to start, connecting Belgium to Berlin, Amsterdam, and Prague, while ÖBB's Nightjet route between Brussels and Vienna, via Liège, increased in frequency post-COVID. There are even rumors of a new "Transeurope Express" route, which originally ceased operating in the 1980s, cutting across Belgium. Great news for those on an old-fashioned European rail tour.

ADDRESSING THE PAST

Much of Belgium's 20th-century wealth was torn out of Africa's Congo region in a long, bloody period from the late 1800s on. Only today are its museums arguably coming to terms with this. The recent renovation and reopening of the Royal Museum for Central Africa in Tervuren came with an abrupt about-face in how it presents its collection. In previous years, it had been strongly criticized for concentrating on the ephemera of colonialism over the lives of the several million Congolese who died during the occupation. Even the building was complicit, built by King Leopold II as a propagandist tool for his 1897 World's Fair. It bore a memorial to the Belgian colonialists who lost their lives, but no African names. Now the museum has sought to change its approach, going so far as to engrave the names of the Congolese who died at the fair in 1897 into the walls. For the first time, in unflinching detail, it is shining a much-needed light on a murky period of history.

What to Eat in Belgium

GENTSE WATERZOOI

This Ghentish creamy stew is comfort food at its finest. Usually bulked out with thinly sliced carrots, leek, and chicken, it was traditionally prepared with burbot (a codlike freshwater fish) from the Leie and Scheldt rivers. As fish stocks declined meat was often substituted.

BOULET À LA LIÉGEOISE

Boulettes (meatballs) are common across Belgium. In Flanders they usually come drizzled in a heavy tomato sauce. But in Wallonia's Liège they are raised to new heights in the form of the *boulet à la liégeoise*. This consists of typically one or two large pork meatballs drowned in a deep meaty gravy.

MOULES

Mussels (*moules* in French; *moulessen* in Dutch) are a Belgian staple. Like all good things, this was once peasant food, a cheap, easy-to-find substitute for when fresh fish was hard to come by. They are usually steamed in white wine and served with frites—the two are almost inseparable.

CHICON AU GRATIN

This very Belgian take on the simple gratin starts with ham-wrapped chicory and smothers it in a Gruyère-pumped béchamel sauce. It's a gooey, cheesy indulgence that was traditionally served in winter, though you'll find it year-round. It's best finished with a piece of crusty bread, dabbing at the last moist corners of sauce without repent.

WAFFLES

The scent of Belgian waffles invades everywhere you find tourists. Its effect is Pavlovian; it's hard not to want one after you've smelled it. Sprinkle on simple icing sugar for a classic taste, or top with any manner of heart-stopping ingredients (usually chocolate sauce and whipped cream). For an alternative, try the humble *stroopwaffel*—a delicious Dutch biscuit popular here, made with two waffle wafers sandwiching a caramel filling.

PALING IN'T GROEN

Eel in green sauce (*anguilles en vert*in French) is another Flemish dish borne of the once bountiful Scheldt River. Freshwater eel is the main ingredient here, drowned in an herby stock-and-wine reduction flavored with chervil, sorrel, parsley, and tarragon. It should have just the right balance of earthy and citrus flavors. Even if you're not normally fond of eel, the freshwater variety has a more delicate texture and just falls apart at a touch.

Waffles

STOOFVLEES

Stoofvlees (*carbonade Flamande* in French) is the Flemish take on beef bourguignon stew, replacing red wine with lashings of malty abbey-brewed beers and a dash of cider vinegar, yielding a dark, fruity gravy smothering tender slow-cooked beef. In Brussels, you can find it made with sharp-tasting local lambic beers, though that's a step too far for some taste buds. Horse meat and pork (in the Netherlands) variations are also found.

FILET AMERICAIN

There's very little that's American about this dish. Created in Brussels's Au Vieux Saint-Martin restaurant in the 1920s, it is essentially a local take on steak tartare (raw minced beef or horse meat topped with an egg yolk). The Belgian version piles mayonnaise, mustard, and herbs onto fresh beef before grinding into a fine pinky paste. You'll find it commonly served with frites, or stuffed into baguettes at lunchtime.

FRITES

The secret to Belgian fries (*frites* in French; *friet* in Dutch) is the potato. The *bintje* variety is most commonly used here, cut thickly and double-fried in beef tallow for a golden, crunchy outer texture. Most frites stalls typically offer myriad sauces for a small fee.

SHRIMP CROQUETTES

Tiny North Sea gray shrimp are a delicacy here. They were traditionally harvested on horseback, with fishermen sitting atop their animals and dragging tightly woven nets through the shallow tide. This tradition has mostly died out, though it is still practiced on the coast in Oostduinkerke in summer. These shrimps are featured in a number of Belgian dishes, but the humble croquette is the most popular, and found on most *estaminet* menus.

Belgium's Best Beers

BRUSSELS BEER PROJECT
In the land of Belgian beers, it seems sacrilege to focus on a craft-brewer dabbling in lighter German-style wheat beers, lagers, and IPAs. But Belgium beer is a broad church, and in recent years this Brussels microbrewery and taproom has made a name for itself. Give its Grosse Bertha beer a try.

CANTILLON
Only around Brussels and the Zenne Valley are conditions right for spontaneous fermentation, the process by which the area's famous lambic beer is made. These days, Cantillon is the only lambic brewery left in the city. It's best known for its *gueuze* and *kriek* (cherry) beers.

WESTVLETEREN
When the Trappist brewers of St. Sixtus Abbey finally opened a website, it crashed within hours—such was the demand. Until then, the only way to buy its bottles, outside of a few bars, was to put in an order and drive to the abbey gates. Today their beers are a bit more widespread in Flanders.

3 FONTEINEN
The tiny village of Beersel, in the Zenne Valley, is home to another acclaimed lambic brewer. Try its blended 3 Fonteinen Oude Gueuze, which, like all its beers, is nonfiltrated, unpasteurized, and aged in the bottle. Its brasserie also serves a belly-busting Flemish-style dinner, which you can work off by walking to the nearby 15th-century castle.

CHIMAY
The Trappist monks of Notre-Dame de Scourmont are one of the more prolific abbey breweries, producing the blue-, red-, and white-labeled Chimay beers that are now ubiquitous across Belgium and Europe. The abbey is off-limits to the public, but you can find its beers on draft in most bars. It also makes rather excellent cheeses.

PAUWEL KWAK
So iconic is the Kwak glass—a kind of bell-bottomed test tube balanced in a wooden holder—that it became a popular souvenir item for light-fingered tourists. The Dulle Griet bar in Ghent even demands that you leave your shoe behind the bar as a deposit if you order one. The beer's not bad, either.

Chimay

SAISON DE PIPAIX
Saison beers are a staple of rural Wallonia and are typically lower strength and more like a pale ale in taste. For a classic example, try this beer by Brasserie à Vapeur, the last steam-powered brewery in Belgium. Its premises are also well worth a tour if you're in Pipaix.

BRUGSE ZOT
The ancient Halve Maan Brewery in Bruges set an unusual record a few years ago. Planning rules meant it couldn't expand its premises in town, so it built a record-breaking 2-mile pipeline beneath the medieval streets to pump its beers to a nearby bottling plant, while still brewing its iconic Brugse Zot within the city limits. It's worth sampling just knowing that.

GRUUT
Before there was beer made from hops, it was brewed from a medieval blend of herbs known as *gruut*.In Ghent, a local brewer has brought this technique back. The result is a lighter, more flowery beer; and while it's not widely found, its microbrewery-bar serves all five of its gruut brews on tap, as well as offering tours and tastings.

ORVAL
Belgium officially has six recognized Trappist breweries, though few are open to the public. Orval is no exception, but you can find this dry beer in most supermarkets and café-bars. It's well worth hunting down—even the chalice-like glass it's served in is rather special.

Best Castles in Belgium

OOIDONK CASTLE, DEURLE
A short drive from Ghent lies stately Ooidonk Castle. Rebuilt in the late 16th century, after locals revolted against Habsburg rule, it draws its influences from the Italian Renaissance as well as the Hispanic-Flemish style dominant at the time, with large, open windows, a step-gabled facade, and neo-Gothic flourishes.

BEERSEL CASTLE, FLEMISH BRABANT
Brussels's nearest medieval castle has been comparatively undeveloped compared with the rest of the buildings on this list. While it, too, has had multiple purposes, notably as a cotton mill in the 1800s, it appears pretty much as it must have done when it was rebuilt in the late 15th century as a moated, redbrick fortress, all turrets, murder holes, and medieval paranoia.

FREYR CASTLE, ARDENNES
This elegant riverside Renaissance castle has some of the most striking formal gardens in Belgium. But just as impressive is the interior. Its extravagance befits the historic status of a 20-generation-strong family home that once played host to France's Louis XIV.

GAASBEEK CASTLE, FLEMISH BRABANT
The castle interior is being renovated until 2023, and it isn't the first time. Its current neo-Renaissance exterior comes courtesy of a 19th-century marquise; before that, it was rebuilt across a 150-year period following its destruction by locals in the late 14th century.

BELOEIL CASTLE, WESTERN WALLONIA
Often cited as Belgium's answer to Versailles, Beloeil is every bit the French country palace estate, floating on a large moat in beautiful parkland. The site has been home to the princes de Lignes since the 14th century, and has all the trappings of historic wealth.

BOUILLON CASTLE, ARDENNES
You can really see a difference between Belgium's early medieval fortresses, protected by their geography and thick walls, and the more relaxed châteaux of later years. This 10th-century castle has been cunningly cut into the rock face above sleepy Bouillon.

Beersel Castle, Flemish Brabant

COUDENBERG, BRUSSELS
While the modern Palais Royale (a neoclassical fever dream redesigned at the whim of Leopold II) now stands atop modern-day Coudenberg Hill in Brussels, beneath it lies the excavated ruins of the original royal castle. This 11th-century building was destroyed during a great fire in 1731. Now, tours of the foundations and accompanying museum offer a fascinating glimpse of what was once the center of city life.

ANNEVOIE CASTLE, NAMUR
This 18th-century castle is as renowned for what surrounds it as the French-Italian-inspired building itself. The gardens here match any country estate in Europe, and are famed for their water features. Some 50 fountains, cascades, and waterfalls scatter the grounds, fed by a single canal. Most striking of all: each operates entirely by gravity.

GRAVENSTEEN CASTLE, GHENT
Ghent's "Castle of the Counts" has served as everything from a prison to a cotton mill. It has also had plenty of restoration work done. In the 19th century, in particular, it was changed to reflect that era's vision of what a castle should look like. However, despite its brooding fairy-tale vibe, its 12th-century bones can still be seen: above the entrance, a cross-shape opening indicates the count's role in the Crusades.

Best Museums in Belgium

HORTA MUSEUM, BRUSSELS

While Belgium didn't create the Art Nouveau movement, a Belgian journal did coin the phrase. The country also spawned the architect Victor Horta. Though born in Ghent, he made his mark mostly on Brussels, sculpting elegant town houses known for their light and natural curves.

PLANTIN-MORETUS MUSEUM, ANTWERP

Home to the oldest-surviving printing presses in the world, this museum lives inside the UNESCO-listed 16th-century home of Christopher Plantin, built when Antwerp was at the center of the printing world and he was its most successful figure. It tells the story of a revolution in books and communication, as information became available en masse for the first time.

MUSEUM OF WALLOON LIFE, LIÈGE

Set within a former Franciscan monastery, this inventive museum brilliantly unpicks local folklore and history, offering a tour of daily life in the region right up to the present day. It's a fascinating journey through customs, dialects, history, and marionettes (there's an entire theater celebrating Liège puppetry), cleverly interweaving them into one engaging visit.

IN FLANDERS FIELD MUSEUM, YPRES

Ypres's war museum recounts one of the bloodiest stalemates in human history. In 1915, Allied and German troops dug in outside Ypres, fighting a two-year battle of trench warfare that cost an estimated 500,000 lives. Battlefields scatter the area, but this museum offers perhaps the most moving overview of an unnerving period of history.

HERGÉ MUSEUM, LOUVAIN-LA-NEUVE
For a more in-depth look at the capital's most famous comic-book artist, head to Louvain-la-Neuve. The museum here is dedicated to Tintin creator George Remi (aka Hergé), and offers a fascinating look at a Belgian icon who yearned for more serious artistic approval, and the intrepid boy reporter who made him famous.

ROYAL MUSEUMS OF FINE ARTS, BRUSSELS
This is cheating, but given that four of these museums are connected, we're counting it as one. You could spend half the day in just the Magritte Museum alone, but then you'd be missing out on centuries of works in the Oldmasters, Fin-de-Siecle, and Modern museums across the road.

BASTOGNE WAR MUSEUM, BASTOGNE
In late 1944, The Battle of the Bulge marked one of the final turning points of World War II, as Hitler's Western Front collapsed and the Allied forces could march on Germany. It took place around Bastogne, on the Luxembourg border in Eastern Wallonia.

CHOCOLATE NATION, ANTWERP
Where else but Belgium would you find the world's largest chocolate museum? This audio-guide-led journey into the story of Belgian sweet stuff gives off Wonkaesque vibes, as groups explore each fanciful room at a time. It ends with demonstrations and the chance to gulp mouthfuls of melted chocolate like a demented toddler. You can even try "ruby chocolate," a naturally bright-pink version created in 2017 by a Belgian-Swiss company.

GARDEROBE MANNEKEN PIS, BRUSSELS
Not many people know that the Manneken Pis—the tiny, peeing statue that has become the symbol of Brussels—has a wardrobe. The tradition of donating outfits to it began when the French king, Louis XV, sought to placate citizens after his troops stole the original statue in 1747. Over the last century, in particular, it has become a diplomatic quirk, and a chunk of the bizarre 1,000-strong collection is displayed here in this tiny Brussels museum.

What to Watch and Read

FILM: *MAN BITES DOG*

The Belgian sense of humor—dry, dark, self-deprecating—is a richly debated topic. But nowhere is it so deliciously autopsied than in this pitch-black satire. Released in 1991, long before the mockumentary format wore itself out, a film crew follows charming serial killer Ben (Benoît Poelvoorde) through the suburbs of Namur, recording his murder spree and distaste for postmen with unnerving dispassion. Its stylized black-and-white style essays a stark, industrialized Belgium, and as the film crew becomes complicit in Ben's crime, so does the viewer. By the end, no one's hands are clean in this cult favorite.

FILM: *TWO DAYS, ONE NIGHT*

The Dardenne Brothers are icons of Belgian cinema. For years their movies have plowed a social realist furrow akin to that of the U.K. director Ken Loach. Their view of Belgium is unrelentingly stark, whether seen through the eyes of a teenager living in a caravan park with her alcoholic mother (*Rosetta*) or when a boy's neglect by his father condemns him to repeat the same mistakes (*The Kid with a Bike*). This later film, arguably their finest, features a mesmerizing Marillion Cotillard performance and is no less demanding, as it follows a young mother in a blue-collar town, near Liège, pleading with her colleagues to forsake a bonus so she can keep her job.

FILM: *IN BRUGES*

In Bruges isn't a Belgian film per se, but it is in spirit. Written and directed by the Irish playwright Martin McDonagh, and starring an international cast, it follows the exploits of two hitmen (Colin Farrell, Brendan Gleeson) as one suffers an existential crisis amid the fog-bound medieval cobbles of Bruges. The tourist town stands in as a form of chocolate-box purgatory as their anxieties play out. Yet its cult success saw the tourism board embrace this jet-black comedy, and, in truth, the city's Belfort and canals have never looked more magical. It may not be truly Belgian, but its humor is.

FILM: *BULLHEAD*

There seems to be something in the air in Belgium that lends itself to dark crime films; in this case, a 2011 "farm noir" written in the Limburgish-Dutch dialect common to parts of eastern Flanders. Its backbone is the true story of the murder of a government meat inspector investigating gangland cattle doping in 1995, but thereafter the story veers into its own territory, following a young, steroid-pumped farmer (a bullish Matthias Schoenaerts) with a traumatic secret, as he sinks in deeper with the local Mafia trade in illegal hormones.

PERFORMANCE: *JACQUES BREL LIVE* AT THE OLYMPIA

Not strictly a film but a series of legendary performances by the Belgian singer Jacque Brel recorded live in an old music hall in Paris. They were released as albums (1961 and '64) but you'll easily find their video recordings online. It's a perfect chance to acquaint yourself with a chanson whose songs skewered death and the hypocrisies of life as much as love. It was at his final performance at Olympia in 1966 that he announced he was quitting live music for good, going on to act in a number of films. Brel's work would influence the likes of Leonard Cohen and David Bowie, but outside of Belgium and France, where he is still revered, few know his name. They should.

PLAY: *PÉLLEAS AND MÉLISANDE* BY MAURICE MAETERLINCK

As the only Belgian to win the Nobel Prize for Literature, Ghent-born playwright Maeterlinck was feted as the breakout artist of Le Jeune Belgique (The Young Belgium) literary society. He was Flemish by birth but wrote primarily in French, becoming a leading member of the early-20th-century Symbolist movement. Indeed, Belgium was a fitting birthplace: he is an artist for whom language was everything yet so utterly insufficient to his needs. His most famous work remains *Pélleas and Mélisande*, a mythic tale of kings and young lovers that was later made into an opera by Claude Debussy.

COMIC BOOK: *ADVENTURES OF TINTIN: THE BLUE LOTUS* BY HERGÉ

It was the Belgian comic-book artist Georges Remi (aka Hergé) that formalized the drawing style of *ligne claire*. Taking inspiration from U.S. comics, particularly Winsor McCay's *Little Nemo*, its tenets were simple: strong lines, no hatching, and minimal contrast. It would go on to influence a generation of Belgian artists, spawning a style that inspired everything from *Blake and Mortimer* to *Where's Wally?* It's also what made his Tintin stories so special. By his fifth book, *The Blue Lotus* (1934), Hergé was in his artistic pomp, spawning some of the most enduring images in the series.

BOOK: *THE LION OF FLANDERS* BY HENDRIK CONSCIENCE

The 18th-century Flemish writer Hendrik Conscience was the pioneer of Dutch-language authors. His romanticist Flemish novels found popularity at a time when French dominated the discourse of the upper classes and literature. The subject of his most famous work, *The Lion of Flanders*, certainly played to his audience, set amid the 1302 "Battle of the Golden Spurs," when the Flemish guild cities rose up against the French aristocracy, defeating their army at Kortrijk. It captured the sentiment of the time (one which still pervades) and has become a founding text in national Flemish literature, not to mention a favorite of Flemish separatists.

BOOK: *THE DANCER AT THE GAI-MOULIN* BY GEORGES SIMENON

Belgium's most famous literary export, besides comic books, are the Inspector Maigret detective novels of George Simenon. Most of the novels were set in France, but this is one of the few where the French detective crosses the border, investigating the murder of a wealthy foreigner in Liège, the city in which Simenon grew up. It's rarely listed among the best in the series (for that, try *Pietr the Latvian*), but as an insight into the simmering chaos of post-World War I Belgium, it makes for a diverting read.

BOOK: *KING LEOPOLD'S GHOST* BY ADAM HOCHSCHILD

That this 1998 dissection of Belgium's colonization of the Congo region became a surprise best seller shows just how little is known of this part of history. Certainly, this is an often brutal and uncompromising book, as U.S. historian and journalist Hochschild strikes at the greed and violence that underpinned first the Belgium-backed Congo Free State (1885–1908), then later the Belgian Congo (1908–60), leading to the deaths of several million Congolese. The fact that this region is still living the trauma of that era is one of the world's great injustices. The book also spawned an excellent documentary film in 2006.

Belgium with Kids

Belgium is best known for its historical sites, which isn't always a huge lure for children. Yet there is plenty here to capture the imagination, especially when you sprinkle a little chocolate in the mix. From safari parks and underground caves to some of the most playful festivals in Europe, there's something to brighten every child's face.

SWEETEN THE DEAL

The word "museum" is poison to most children, but mention "chocolate" and smaller ears typically prick up. Belgium has its share of cocoa-fueled days out, with the two Choco-Story attractions (Bruges and Brussels) balancing their fustier history sections with demos and samples. But the real star is Antwerp's Wonka-esque Chocolate Nation. The installations are playfully grand, and at the end, you can pour as much melted chocolate down your gullet as you like. Bliss.

LAY SIEGE TO A MEDIEVAL CASTLE

Castles rarely fail to capture the imagination of little ones, and Belgium has some 3,000 of them. Ghent's Gravensteen, in particular, really looks the part. That its fairy-tale appearance comes courtesy of a 19th-century makeover is irrelevant to kids, who will love scrapping about the ramparts, mentally swashbuckling foes, and cooing at all the "murder holes," where boiling oil would be poured down on luckless invaders.

TAKE A RIDE

De Panne's Plopsaland, on the North Sea coast, is one of Belgium biggest amusement parks. There are lures for all sizes of thrill seeker, with the brand-new Ride to Happiness roller coaster topping speeds of 90 kph. A smaller version of the theme park, Plopsa Station Antwerp, also recently opened in the city's train station, offering a mini adrenaline fix.

LIVE THE HIGH LIFE

The Atomium—a giant atom-shape structure—was originally built for the Brussels World Fair in 1958. That it still stands is testament to the capital's embracing of the weird as much as the incredible views from its top sphere. Little ones will love the equally bizarre Mini Europe amusement park next door, as they tower over tiny monuments from around the world. Meanwhile, in Antwerp, hop on the giant Ferris wheel to gaze across the city, then descend to explore the neighboring zoo, famous for an Egyptian-temple enclosure that dates back to its original opening in 1856.

PARTY WITH BEARS AND CATS

Lots of Belgium's festivals have a magical, childlike quality. Ypres's Kattenstoet (Festival of Cats) parade is one of the more magical, as giant feline floats and puppets stomp the streets in May. Elsewhere, Brussels's biennial Flower Carpet (August) in the Grand Place is a wonderful sight, while the annual Waterloo reenactment (June) is filled with gun smoke and cavalry charges. Most magical of all is Andenne's Carnival of the Bears, which allegedly dates back to the story of a local nine-year-old boy fighting a bear that terrorized his grandmother. Now its streets fill with hundreds of furry ursine dancers and floats every March.

HEAD UNDERGROUND

The Ardennes is riddled with underground wonders. The Caves of Han, south of Rochefort, are among the most famous and are set within a safari park filled with bears, lynx, and other European wildlife royalty. Or for a more unusual underground adventure, head to a sewer tour of the historic subterranean canals of Antwerp, known as De Ruien. The smell is something else entirely, but kids will love dressing up in the overalls and stomping around this hidden world.

Chapter 2

TRAVEL SMART

Updated by
Tim Skelton

★ CAPITAL:
Brussels

POPULATION:
11,520,000

LANGUAGE:
Dutch (Flemish), French, German

$ CURRENCY:
Euro

COUNTRY CODE:
32

⚠ EMERGENCIES:
101 police; 100 fire and ambulance

DRIVING:
On the right

ELECTRICITY:
220v/50 cycles; plugs have two round prongs

TIME:
Six hours ahead of New York

WEB RESOURCES:
visit.brussels/en; www.visitflanders.com; walloniabelgiumtourism.co.uk

Know Before You Go

GET YOUR COVID-19 PAPERWORK SORTED

For as long as COVID-19 is with us, all travelers to Belgium, even if entering overland from a neighboring country, need to complete a Passenger Locator Form (PLF) online (*travel.info-coronavirus.be*), no more than 48 hours before arriving, providing a local address and other information; you'll be sent a QR code to present at passport control. The only exception to this is if you arrive overland and stay for less than 48 hours. Chances are you will also need proof of vaccination or recovery, and—if arriving by air—a negative PCR test before traveling. This information is prone to change, however, so always check the website of the U.S. Embassy in Brussels (*be.usembassy.gov*) for the latest advice and requirements.

PACK WISELY

The best advice for a trip to Belgium in any season is to pack light, be flexible, bring a waterproof jacket, and always have a sweater or jacket available. Belgians dress casually, so there is no need for formal attire unless you plan to visit an upper-echelon restaurant. Blue jeans are popular and are even sometimes worn to the office; sweat suits, however, are never seen outside fitness centers. For women, high heels may be nothing but trouble on the cobblestone streets of Brussels and Bruges. In your carry-on luggage, pack an extra pair of eyeglasses or contact lenses and enough of any medication you take to last a few days longer than the entire trip. Never pack prescription drugs or valuables in luggage to be checked.

NO NEED TO TIP 20%

Tipping is completely optional in Belgium, and more often than not is reserved for exceptional service. While Belgians do tip in cafés and restaurants, it is seldom a fixed amount, and no one will point out your error if you fail to meet an expected threshold. The most common practice is to top up the bill to a convenient round number, but leave no more than 10% extra. With electronic payments having become the norm, paying the exact amount stated on the bill is perfectly acceptable.

A NOT-SO-PRIVATE FUNCTION

Most restaurants, hotels, and all major attractions in Belgium have well-maintained modern restrooms, but that is not always the case in some older and more characterful bars and cafés. In a few (and by no means all) of these, there is a unisex restroom featuring a lockable cubicle, and an outer room containing a wash basin and next to that an open urinal. Women travelers should at least bear in mind that there is a possibility—albeit a small one—that on entering, they may encounter someone using the latter. He will no doubt ignore you, and you should pay him no heed, but it is perhaps better to be braced than surprised.

FLEMISH IS DUTCH REALLY

Belgium has three official languages: French, Dutch, and German. The capital region around Brussels is officially bilingual in French and Dutch. Wallonia in the south is French-speaking, except for a small pocket of German speakers near the border with Germany. Flanders in the north is officially Dutch-speaking, but people generally communicate in a local Dutch dialect known as Flemish (*Vlaams*). In practice, the differences between Flemish and "standard" Dutch are no more than those between American and British English (for example: garlic in Dutch is *knoflook*, while in Flemish it is *look*), and—as much as they sometimes like to pretend otherwise—Flemish Belgians and Dutch people from the Netherlands rarely have trouble understanding one another.

IT'S NOT ALL CHOCOLATES AND BEER

All the clichés you've heard are true: Belgium is one of the best places in the world to sip a great ale, to nibble on exquisitely tempered chocolate, or to chow down on a cream-smothered waffle, or a cone of twice-cooked French fries. But there are plenty of other local treats waiting to be discovered. Don't miss out on trying the moreish creamy stew *waterzooi*, originally from Ghent, or the Liège specialty *boulets* (succulent meatballs, now found across Wallonia), to name but two.

FINE DINING IS A NATIONAL SPORT

There is an old adage that "everyone eats well in Belgium," and people love to dine out. Great care is taken in the preparation of food, and much time is devoted to the enjoyment of consuming it. Even in midrange restaurants and cheaper Belgian cafés you are unlikely to experience a bad meal. No surprise then that after only London, Paris, and Barcelona, Brussels has the highest number of Michelin-starred restaurants in Europe, and on a per capita basis, Belgium boasts more stars than any other country besides Japan, Luxembourg, and Switzerland.

NEVER SAY BORING BELGIUM

Little old Belgium comes in for a lot of stick from its larger neighbors. It's unfairly known as "Boring Belgium" by the British, and is the butt of unkind jokes made by both the French and the Dutch, but scratch below the surface and you'll find a country full of cultural, culinary, and topographical charm. This is the land that gave the world the comic book adventurer Tintin, and the saxophone, and—despite their name—French fries are very much a Belgian creation. If you want to endear yourself to a local, learn the words to the popular cult 1998 song "Potverdekke, it's great to be a Belgian"—for the record, *potverdekke* is Flemish for "darn it."

GET TO GRIPS WITH CITY NAMES

It isn't just the language that people speak that changes from one part of Belgium to the next. If you're driving around, be prepared to see city names in French or Flemish, depending upon whether you are in the south or the north, respectively. You need to know that Antwerp is Antwerpen in Flemish and Anvers in French; Bruges is Brugge in Flemish and Bruges in French; Brussels is Bruxelles in French and Brussel in Flemish; Ghent is Gent in Flemish and Gand in French. Even more confusing, Liège and Luik are the same place, as are Louvain and Leuven, and Namur and Namen. Yet more difficult is Mons (French) and Bergen (Flemish), or Tournai (French) and Doornik (Flemish).

LEARN TO LOVE BRUSSELIZATION

"Brusselization" is a byword for indiscriminate urban development, and it stems from the 1960s and 1970s, when Brussels had few zoning regulations and lax planning laws. It meant new buildings were erected incongruously next to (and often on the site of) historical gems, with little thought given to fitting in, until the 1990s, when new laws prevented the demolition of buildings considered of architectural significance. Nevertheless, there is plenty to love about the random and unpredictable nature of the current Brussels skyline, and its higgledy-piggledy appearance gives the Belgian capital a special character all of its own.

Getting Here and Around

 Air

There are nonstop flights to Brussels from New York City, Newark, Chicago, and Washington, D.C. Flying time to Belgium is about seven hours from New York and 8½ hours from Chicago. Depending upon your routing and transit time, flights from Dallas last approximately 13 hours and flights from Los Angeles, approximately 16 hours.

AIRPORTS

The major international airport serving Belgium is Brussels Airport-Zaventem, 14 km (9 miles) northeast of Brussels. Belgium's national airline, Brussels Airlines, has routes to the United States, Africa, and all over Europe. Because of the country's size, there are no scheduled domestic flights within Belgium.

Ryanair uses the smaller Brussels South Charleroi Airport, 46 km (29 miles) south of Brussels, as a hub. Though farther out of the city, it's connected to Brussels by a regular bus service.

AIRPORT TRANSFERS

Trains run up to four times each hour from Brussels Airport to the city center, taking around 15 minutes. A one-way ticket costs from €9.20. Direct services also run from the airport to several other cities. Bus connections to the city leave from Level 0. These cost about the same, but take longer. Taxis cost around €45 to the city center.

Bus company **flibco.com** (*www.flibco.com*) operates every half hour between Brussels Midi Railway Station and Brussels South Charleroi Airport. The journey takes one hour and costs €14.70 one-way, €29.40 return. Rideshare app Uber can also be used to book cars to and from the airports.

Bicycle

Travel by bicycle is popular and easy in Belgium; bike paths border its scenic canals and seaside roads. Many towns provide special lanes parallel to main streets for bicycles, and bicycle racks are available to the public. Cycling in cities is less pleasant, as traffic is dense, bicycle paths are scarce, and drivers are less hospitable about sharing the road with cyclists.

You can rent bicycles at Belgium's seaside resorts and other major tourist destinations by the half day or day, with daily prices usually starting from around €12. If you are traveling in a group, consider another popular seaside rental option, a bicycle built for four or six pedalers.

Bus

Belgium has an extensive network of reasonably priced urban and intercity buses. STIB/MIVB (*www.stib-mivb.be*) covers services around Brussels and to other towns in the region. De Lijn (*www.delijn.be*) runs buses in Flanders, including Antwerp, Bruges, and Ghent, while TEC buses (*www.letec.be*) connect towns in Wallonia.

International bus travel is generally eclipsed by train service in terms of comfort and convenience, but some bus companies do offer connections between Brussels and nearby capitals. Eurolines (*www.eurolines.de*) and Flixbus (*www.flixbus.be*) have daily express services from Brussels and Antwerp to several international destinations, including Berlin, Frankfurt, and Paris.

Bus companies accept major credit cards and cash.

Car

Belgium is a small country and driving distances are not great. Most destinations are not more than two hours from Brussels. There are no tolls, but the major highways can get very congested, especially around Brussels and Antwerp. Driving within cities can be a nightmare if you're not used to Belgian roads. You may have to compete with trams, or taxi drivers with a death wish, for space, and city centers often have narrow roads with unfathomable one-way systems.

Belgium is covered by an extensive network of four-lane highways. Brussels is 204 km (122 miles) from Amsterdam on E19; 222 km (138 miles) from Düsseldorf on E40; 219 km (133 miles) from Luxembourg City on E411; and 308 km (185 miles) from Paris on E19.

From Calais, the fastest route to Ghent, Bruges, and Antwerp is along the coast; for Brussels either follow this route or head inland via Lille and Tournai; use the inland route for Mons, Namur, Liège, and Luxembourg.

CAR RENTALS

The major car rental firms have booths at the airports. This is convenient, but the airports charge rental companies a fee that is passed on to customers, so you may want to rent from the downtown locations of rental firms. Consider also whether you want to get off a transatlantic flight and into an unfamiliar car in an unfamiliar city.

Rental cars are European brands and range from economy, such as a Ford Fiesta, to luxury, such as a Mercedes. It is also possible to rent minivans. Rates in Belgium vary from company to company; daily rates for budget companies start at around €40 for an economy car including collision insurance. This may not include mileage, airport fee, and 21% V.A.T. tax. Weekly rates often include unlimited mileage. It is usually less expensive to reserve your car online before your departure.

You can drive your own car or rent one in Belgium with a valid driver's license from most English-speaking countries or from other European nations. You must also produce a national identity card or passport. If in doubt that your license will be recognized outside your home country, get hold of an international driving permit (IDP), available from AAA. These international permits, valid only in conjunction with your regular license, may save you a problem with local authorities.

You must be at least 21 years old to rent cars from most agencies. Some agencies require renters to be 25. There's usually a surcharge for adding a driver to your rental agreement. Before you pick up a car in one city and leave it in another, ask about drop-off charges or one-way service fees, which can be substantial. Also inquire about early-return policies; some rental agencies charge extra if you return the car before the time specified in your contract while others give you a refund for unused days. Most agencies note the tank's fuel level on your contract; to avoid a hefty refueling fee, return the car with the same tank level. If the tank was full, refill it just before you turn in the car. It's almost never a good deal to buy a tank of gas with the car when you rent it; the understanding is that you'll return it empty, but some fuel usually remains.

GASOLINE

Gasoline stations are plentiful throughout Belgium. Major credit cards are widely accepted. If you pay with cash and need a receipt, ask for a *reçu* (French) or *ontvangstbewijs* (Flemish). Unleaded gas and diesel fuel are available at all stations.Costs vary between €1.65 per

Getting Here and Around

liter for diesel fuel and €1.70 per liter for unleaded gas, but with global oil prices fluctuating wildly these may change. Drivers normally pump their own gas, but full service is available at a few stations. Unless you have a debit card from a Belgian bank, you must pay an attendant during open hours. On Sunday and late at night, drivers should look for a gas station on a major highway, which should be open and manned around the clock.

PARKING

With the narrow streets in many cities, on-street parking can be problematic, and often restricted to residents only. Every city center has at least one and usually several multistory parking lots. Some are pay-as-you-leave (pay at coin machines by the entry-exit); others are pay in advance and you display your ticket in your car window. Ticket machines usually accept both euro coins and debit and credit cards. Prices vary, but start from around €2 per hour.

ROAD CONDITIONS

A network of well-maintained, well-lit highways (*snelweg* in Flemish, *autoroute* in French) and other roads covers Belgium, making car travel convenient. There are no tolls. Under good conditions, you should be able to travel on highways at about 120 kph (75 mph). Directions to the major highways are indicated on blue signs that include the number of the highway and the direction in terms of destination city rather than "north," "south," "east," or "west." On the Brussels–Liège/Luik motorway, signs change language with alarming frequency as you crisscross the Wallonia–Flanders border. *Uitrit* is Flemish for exit; the French is *sortie*. Traffic can be heavy around the major cities, especially on the roads to southern Europe in July and August, when many Belgians begin their vacations, and on roads approaching the North Sea beaches on summer weekends. Summer road repair can also cause some traffic jams on highways and in town.

Rush hour traffic is worst from September until June. Peak rush hour traffic is 7 am–9:30 am and 4 pm–7:30 pm, weekdays. You are most likely to encounter traffic jams as you travel into cities in the morning, out of cities in the afternoon, and on ring roads around major cities in the morning and in the afternoon. The ring road around Antwerp is notoriously busy at all times.

City driving is often challenging. Beware of trams in some cities, and of slick cobblestone streets in rainy weather.

ROADSIDE EMERGENCIES

If you break down on the highway, look for emergency telephones located at regular intervals. The emergency telephones are connected to an emergency control room that can send a tow truck. It's also possible to take out emergency automobile insurance through a company such as Europ Assistance (*www.europ-assistance.be*) or Touring Secours (*touring.be*) that covers all of your expenses in case of a breakdown on the road.

RULES OF THE ROAD

Drive on the right in Belgium.

Be sure to observe speed limits. On highways in Belgium, the limit is 120 kph (75 mph), though the cruising speed is usually about 130 kph (about 80 mph). The speed limit on other rural roads is 90 kph (55 mph), and 50 kph (30 mph) in urban areas. Speed limits are enforced, sometimes with hidden cameras, and speeding penalties start from a hefty €53. If you're stopped by the police, fines are issued on the spot.

Drivers in Belgium can be impatient with slower drivers using the left lanes, which are considered strictly for passing. For safe highway driving, go with the flow, stay in the right-hand lane unless you want to pass, and make way for faster cars wanting to pass you. If you forget this rule of the road, drivers will remind you by flashing their high beams.

Fog can be a danger on highways in late fall and winter. In such cases, it's obligatory to use your fog lights. In cities and towns, approach pedestrian crossings with care. Stop signs are few and far between. Instead, white triangles are painted on the road of the driver who must yield. Unless stated otherwise, priority on minor roads is given to the driver coming from the right, and drivers in Belgium exercise that priority fervently.

Using a handheld mobile phone is illegal while driving, but you're allowed to drive while using a headset or earpiece.

Use of seat belts is compulsory in Belgium, both in front and rear seats, and there are fines for disobeying. Turning right on a red light is not permitted. Your car must carry a red warning triangle in case of breakdown. All cars rented in Belgium will already have these.

Drinking and driving is prohibited. Breathalyzer controls are routine on highways on weekend nights, and common throughout Belgium over holiday weekends, Christmas, and New Year's Eve. Drunk drivers are fined at least €125 and their cars are confiscated until the following day.

Illegally parked cars are ticketed, and the fines start from €58. If you park in a tow-away zone, you risk having your car towed, paying a fee of at least €100, and receiving a traffic ticket.

 Ride-Sharing

Uber is growing in popularity as a way to get around the larger cities in Belgium, and from Brussels Airport into town, as their cars are often more available and less expensive than taxis. The company is not popular with local taxi companies, however, and often faces legal challenges. As a result, services are occasionally suspended by court orders.

 Taxi

Taxis are a safe and reliable way of getting around all larger Belgian towns and cities, but are less popular for getting between towns. You can phone for a cab, or you can pick one up from taxi ranks outside train stations and at busy locations throughout city centers. Fares vary between cities, but typically start from around €2.50, plus €2 per km traveled.

 Train

The easiest mode of transportation within Belgium is train travel. Belgian National Railways (SNCB/NMBS) maintains an extensive network of prompt and frequent services. Intercity trains have rapid connections between the major towns and cities, while local and regional trains also stop at all smaller towns and villages in between. The exception is in the southeast of Belgium, particularly in the Ardennes. Tourist hubs such as La Roche-en-Ardenne are connected to the nearest rail stations only by infrequent buses. If you plan to do a lot of exploring in this region, renting a car can save you a lot of time and effort.

National train services are extensive and frequent. For example, four to five trains an hour link Antwerp with Brussels;

Getting Here and Around

the trip takes about 45 minutes. There are several train connections every hour between the Brussels Airport and Brussels, from early morning until late evening.

An expanding network of high-speed trains puts Brussels within commuting distance of many European cities. Eurostar trains, which leave from Brussels's Gare du Midi, take 2 hours, 20 minutes to get to London's St Pancras International station. One-way fares start from €49.50, if you book in advance and waive the right to make changes to your itinerary.

Thalys high-speed trains to Paris, Bordeaux, Avignon, Marseille, Liège, Cologne, Aachen, Amsterdam, Rotterdam, and The Hague also leave from the Gare du Midi. Standard one-way tickets from Brussels to Paris cost €35 in economy and €115 in first class if you book in advance. The trip lasts 1 hour, 20 minutes. Seat reservations are required for both Eurostar and Thalys trains. Thalys trains also run to Amsterdam and Cologne, taking around two hours. A cheaper, but slower, hourly train travels between Brussels and Amsterdam, via Antwerp. Reservations are not required for this.

To save money, look into rail passes. If you're under 26 years old, a Youth Multi pass allows you 10 one-way second-class train trips to any destination in Belgium for €55. The tickets are valid for one year. If you're between 26 and 65, you can buy a Standard Multi pass, which is identical to a Youth Multi, but costs €86. People over 65 should ask for a senior ticket (*seniorenbiljet* in Flemish, *billet seniors* in French), which entitles you to second-class round-trip travel anywhere in Belgium for only €7.20. You'll have to provide proof of age for this, and the tickets are not valid weekdays before 9 am.

Belgium is among the 33 countries in which non-European citizens or residents can use Eurail Passes, which provide unlimited first- or second-class rail travel, in all of the participating countries, for the duration of the pass. If you plan to rack up the miles, get a standard pass. These are available for 15 days ($605/$455 in first/second class), 22 days ($708/$531), one month ($917/$687), two months ($1,001/$750), and three months ($1,233/$926). If your plans call for only limited train travel, other available passes offer a limited number of travel days, in a limited number of adjoining countries, during a specified time period. Whichever pass you choose, remember that you must purchase your pass before you leave for Europe.

European citizens and residents can buy Interrail Passes that offer similar benefits to Eurail Passes, but are more expensive.

Major Belgian train stations have an information office for information about fares and schedules. All train stations post complete listings, by time, of arrivals and departures, including the track number. To avoid crowds, don't travel by train to the Belgian coast on Saturday morning or return from there on Sunday afternoon in the summer. Belgium's national holiday, July 21, also draws train travelers from Brussels to the seaside and the Ardennes.

Train tickets bought in Belgium can be paid for using currency or a major credit card. Reservations are obligatory on the Eurostar train to London and on the Thalys train to Paris. Reservations are not required (or indeed possible) for domestic trains.

Essentials

Dining

Belgium's better restaurants are on a par with the most renowned in the world. Prices are similar to those in France and the United Kingdom. The Belgian emphasis on high-quality food filters down to more casual options as well, from main-square cafés to the street vendors you'll find in towns large and small.

Restaurants and hotel pension packages serve hot three-course meals including a starter or soup, a main course, and dessert. A set-price, three-course menu for lunch (*déjeuner* in French, *lunch* in Flemish) is offered in many restaurants. Dinner (*dîner* in French, *diner* in Flemish) menus are very similar to lunch menus. Diners aren't commonly given a choice of vegetables or salad.

Larger hotels serve buffet breakfast (*petit déjeuner* in French, *ontbijt* in Flemish) with cooked American fare. Smaller hotels and bed-and-breakfasts serve bread, rolls, butter, jam, and cheese with juice and coffee or tea and occasionally a hard-boiled egg.

You can also order a quick sandwich lunch or a light one-course meal at cafés, pubs, cafeterias, and snack bars.

Most of Belgium's restaurants show a marked French influence on their menus. But there are also many specialties that are distinctively Belgian. Steamed North Sea mussels is what pops into most people's minds when they think of Belgian cuisine; they're served throughout the country. A long-standing Flemish dish, now popping up on menus throughout the country, is waterzooi, a creamy stew made with chicken, rabbit, or fish. *Carbonnade* or *stoverij*, a beef stew cooked in beer, also shows up in all regions. *Stoemp* is a filling mixture of mashed potatoes and vegetables. Eel is another Flemish specialty; the firm white flesh is often smoked or served in a cream-based sauce, and most notably as *paling in 't groen* (Flemish) or *anguilles au vert* (French), with a green herb sauce. Belgian endive (*chicons* in French, *witloof* in Flemish) is usually cooked with ham, braised, and topped with a cheese gratin. A popular first course is tomato filled with tiny gray shrimp (*crevettes grises* in French, *grijze garnaaltjes* in Flemish), fresh from the North Sea. During fall hunting season, restaurants and inns in the countryside turn out special game dishes with *sanglier* or *everzwijn* (wild boar) and *faisan* or *fazant* (pheasant). Belgium also produces several noteworthy cheeses; some of the best are handmade in monasteries, such as Maredsous.

Complete your meal with *frites* or *frieten* (French fries), which Belgians proudly claim to have been invented not in France but in Belgium. The secret to Belgian fries is that they are fried twice—usually in animal fat, so they don't always meet vegetarian standards. Throughout Belgium, roadside French-fry stands (*friterie* in French or *frituur* in Flemish) offer servings of French fries with a selection of condiments.

Another favorite snack is the famous Belgian waffle (*gaufres* in French, *wafels* in Flemish), which you can buy at waffle stands in cities. Waffles here are a dessert, not a breakfast food. There is a distinct difference between the waffles sold at waffle stands, often called *gaufres liègeoises* after Liège, their city of origin, and those that are sold in cafés and tea salons. The former are usually very sweet and more substantial, while the latter are lighter and fluffier, and topped with powdered sugar and a dollop of whipped cream. Other popular sweets include macaroons, *speculoos* (ginger cookies),

Essentials

and fruit tarts. It's a point of pride that classic Belgian dessert recipes haven't changed for centuries.

DISCOUNTS AND DEALS

Many upscale restaurants offer great lunch deals with special menus at cut-rate prices designed to give customers a true taste of the place. At high-end restaurants ask for tap water to avoid paying high rates for bottled water.

PAYING

Major credit cards are accepted in most restaurants. Visa and MasterCard are the most widely accepted credit cards. Smaller establishments often don't accept American Express or especially Diners Club, because of high commission charges, and some pubs and cafés are cash only.

Tipping 15% of the cost of a meal is not common practice in Belgium. Nonetheless, it is customary to round off the total, adding a small amount for good service.

RESERVATIONS AND DRESS

Always make a reservation at an upscale restaurant when you can. Some are booked weeks in advance.

As unfair as it seems, the way you look can influence how you're treated—and where you're seated. Generally speaking, jeans and a button-down shirt will suffice at most Belgian restaurants, but some pricier places require jackets, although few insist on ties. In reviews, we mention dress only where men are required to wear a jacket or a jacket and tie. If you have doubts, call the restaurant and ask.

MEALS AND MEALTIMES

Breakfast is served in hotels from about 7 to 10. Most restaurants are open for lunch and dinner only—in general, lunch is served in restaurants noon–3, and dinner 6–9. Many pubs and cafés serve meals all day, and snacks may even be available until midnight. Cafés and snack bars are sometimes open in the morning and serve coffee, tea, juice, and rolls, but don't serve a full American-style breakfast.

SMOKING

Smoking is banned in all restaurants and bars.

Health and Safety

Belgium is relatively disease-free and you are unlikely to encounter problems. If you do, the Belgian health service is regarded by many as the best in the world, so you'll be in safe hands. Nevertheless, COVID-19 has disrupted travel since March 2020, and travelers should expect sporadic ongoing issues. Always travel with a mask in case it's required, and keep up-to-date on the most recent testing and vaccination guidelines for Belgium.

Pharmacies (*pharmacie* in French, *apotheek* in Flemish) are clearly identified by a green cross displayed over the storefront.

The crime rate in Belgium is quite low, but basic common sense is always advisable to avoid problems. In crowded intersections and dark alleys, never flaunt your cash or expensive jewelry. Avoid deserted streets late at night. Be especially wary of pickpockets in busy areas and in and around major train stations, where thieves are on the lookout for vulnerable newly arrived tourists. When going out at night, stick to well-lit areas, and take a taxi if going somewhere unfamiliar.

Women can travel, check in at hotels, and relax at cafés and restaurants with virtually the same ease as men. Women traveling alone should nonetheless avoid lingering around neighborhoods near train stations, as these neighborhoods are traditionally where prostitutes operate. If you carry a purse, choose one with a zipper and a thick strap that you can drape across your body; adjust the length so that the purse sits in front of you at or above hip level.

Immunizations

All visitors to Belgium arriving by air must have a valid proof of COVID-19 vaccination and/or a booster, or proof of recent recovery from the disease; while the need and frequency of boosters is still being discussed in the medical community, it's important to verify the most recent requirements with your physician before you travel.

Lodging

Belgium offers a range of options, from the major international hotel chains and small, modern local hotels to family-run restored inns and historic houses. Hotels in Belgium are rated by the Benelux Hotel Classification System, an independent agency that inspects properties in Belgium, the Netherlands, and Luxembourg. The organization's star system is the accepted norm for these countries; one star indicates the most basic hotel and five stars indicates the most luxurious. Star rankings are posted at hotel entrances or at check-in desks. Stars are based on detailed criteria—mainly facilities and amenities, such as private baths, specific items of furniture in guest rooms, and so on. Rooms in one-star hotels are likely not to have a telephone or television, and two-star hotels may not have air-conditioning, or elevators. Four- and five-star hotels usually have conference facilities and offer amenities such as pools, tennis courts, saunas, dry-cleaning service, and room service. Three-, four-, and five-star hotels are usually equipped with hair dryers and coffeemakers. Single rooms in one- to three-star hotels often have a shower (*douche* in French and Flemish) rather than a bathtub (*bain* in French, *bad* or *ligbad* in Flemish).

Taking meals at a hotel's restaurant sometimes provides you with a discount. Some restaurants, especially country inns, require that guests take half board (*demi-pension* in French, *half-pension* in Flemish), at least lunch or dinner, at the hotel. Full pension (*pension complet* in French, *volledig pension* in Flemish) entitles guests to both lunch and dinner. Guests taking either half or full board also receive breakfast.

If you're planning a longer trip and want a home base that's roomy enough for a family and comes with cooking facilities, consider a furnished rental. These can save you money, especially if you're traveling with a group. Apartment and villa rentals and *gîtes* (farmhouse rentals) are easy to find in popular vacation areas, such as the Belgian coast and the Ardennes countryside. You can also rent vacation villas within Belgium's vacation parks. These self-contained parks, in rural or seaside settings, consist of residences and facilities such as swimming pools, hiking and bicycling trails, restaurants, and activities for children. There is often a one-week minimum, although it's possible to rent for shorter periods during the winter months.

Traditional bed-and-breakfast accommodations (*chambres d'hôtes* in French or *gastenkamers* in Flemish) are less common in Belgium than in the United Kingdom or the United States; the ones you do find are usually in rural or residential areas. As in many other countries, however, Airbnb has become very popular in Belgium. Here you'll find houses and apartments in both urban and rural areas, as well as properties that are some way off the beaten track, often with a more intimate feel and lower prices than more traditional places.

FACILITIES

You can assume that all rooms have private baths, phones, TVs, and air-conditioning, unless otherwise indicated. Breakfast is noted as "free breakfast" when it is included in *all* rates; otherwise, "no meals" means that no additional meals are included in the basic rates, even if they are offered at the lodging's restaurant.

PARKING

Hotel parking fees vary enormously across Belgium. Parking at a countryside hotel may be free, while the better places in central Brussels or Antwerp may charge in excess of €25 per night. Independent garages are often cheaper, and also easier to access in cities with narrow medieval streets such as Bruges. Street parking can be both hard to come by and expensive in larger urban areas, but easy to find and free in smaller towns and villages.

PRICES

Prices in metropolitan areas are significantly higher than those in outlying towns and the countryside. Most hotels that cater to business travelers will grant substantial weekend rebates. These discounted rates are often available during the week as well as in July and August, when business travelers are thin on the ground. Moreover, you can often qualify for a "corporate rate" when hotel occupancy is low. The moral is, always ask what's the best rate a hotel can offer before you book.

RESERVATIONS

Always reserve your hotel in advance. Rooms fill up quickly at the Belgian coast and in the Ardennes in July and August, during the period around Easter, and on May 1. Throughout the year conventions can fill up business hotels in Brussels, and hotels in Bruges are also busy year-round.

$ Money

Costs in Brussels are roughly on a par with those in London and New York; Antwerp and other major tourist centers are nearly as dear. Less-traveled areas are significantly less expensive. All taxes and service charges (tips) are included in hotel and restaurant bills and taxi fares. Gasoline prices are steep, but highways are toll-free.

Prices throughout this guide are given for adults. Substantially reduced fees are almost always available for children, students, and senior citizens.

ATMs (*distributeur automatique* in French, *geldautomaat* in Flemish) are in banks throughout Belgium, either inside the bank itself or on the facade of the bank building. They are accessible 24 hours a day, seven days per week.

Major credit cards are accepted in most hotels, gas stations, and restaurants in Belgium. Smaller establishments, shops, and supermarkets often accept Visa cards only. It's a good idea to inform your credit-card company before you travel, especially if you don't travel internationally very often. Otherwise, the credit-card company might put a hold on your card owing to unusual activity—not a good thing halfway through your trip.

Currency exchange booths are widely available throughout the large cities in

Belgium, at major train stations, and at major tourist destinations. There is a surcharge for each transaction, regardless of the amount exchanged—even if a currency-exchange booth has a sign promising "no commission," rest assured that there will be some kind of huge, hidden fee. As for rates, you're almost always better off getting foreign currency at an ATM or exchanging money at a bank.

Passport and Visa

Non-EU citizens entering Belgium require a current passport that is valid for at least three months beyond their expected period of stay. U.S., Canadian, and British citizens do not need a Schengen Visa before entering Belgium, provided they are traveling for no more than 90 days for tourism and business purposes. As from late 2022, however, U.S., Canadian, and post-Brexit British citizens do need to supplement their passports with an electronic ETIAS (European Travel Information and Authorization System) visa waiver. These can be used throughout the EU, and are valid for three years, or until your passport expires—whichever is the sooner.

Taxes

Airport taxes and passenger service charges levied in Belgian airports are always included in the total fare charged at the time of your ticket purchase. All hotels in Belgium charge a 6% Value-Added Tax (*TVA* in French, *BTW* in Flemish), included in the room rate; in Brussels, there is also a 9% city tax. In Belgium, V.A.T. ranges from 6% on food and clothing to 33% on luxury goods. Restaurants are in between; 21% is included in quoted prices.

To get a V.A.T. refund you need to reside outside the European Union and to have spent more than €125 in the same shop on the same day. Provided that you personally carry the goods out of the country within 30 days, you may claim a refund. When making a purchase, ask for a V.A.T. refund form and find out whether the merchant gives refunds—not all stores do, nor are they required to. Have the form stamped like any customs form by customs officials when you leave the country or, if you're visiting several European Union countries, when you leave the EU. After you're through passport control, take the form to a refund-service counter for an on-the-spot refund (which is usually the quickest and easiest option), or mail it to the address on the form (or the envelope with it) after you arrive home. You receive the total refund stated on the form, but the processing time can be long, especially if you request a credit card adjustment.

Global Blue is a Europe-wide service with around 300,000 affiliated stores and refund counters at all major airports and border crossings. Its refund form, called a Tax Free Form, is the most common across the European continent. The service issues refunds in the form of cash, check, or credit-card adjustment.

Tipping

In Belgium, a tip (*service compris* or *service inclusief*) may be included in restaurant and hotel bills; if it is, you'll see a clear indication on the bill. If service is not included, people often round up a bit when paying (adding 10% maximum), but it isn't offensive to pay the exact amount. Taxi drivers also appreciate a rounding up of the bill, but again, paying the exact amount is perfectly acceptable. Railway porters expect €1 per item. For

Essentials

bellhops and doormen at both hotels and nightspots, a few euro is adequate. Bartenders are tipped only for notably good service; again, rounding off is sufficient.

 U.S. Embassy/Consulate

The U.S. embassy in Belgium is located in central Brussels, a short walk from the royal palace. This is the place to go to replace a lost passport, or to seek advice if you need medical or legal assistance. The embassy is open to the public Monday to Thursday from 8 am to noon and from 2 to 4 pm, and on Friday from 8 am to noon, but it closes for all Belgian and American holidays. For emergencies during off hours, call (02) 811–4000.

There are no U.S. consulates in other cities.

 Visitor Information

Like many things in Belgium, the promotion of tourism is managed on a regional basis. Visit Brussels handles matters in the area around the capital; Visit Flanders covers the Flemish-speaking provinces; and Visit Wallonia is responsible for the French-speaking half of the country. All three organizations operate a string of tourist information offices in almost all of the places you are likely to visit.

 When to Go

Low Season: November, and January to Easter are the quietest times of year for visiting Belgium. The weather is often cold and wet, but one advantage is that queues at major attractions will be shorter.

Shoulder Season: The best times to visit the country are in the late spring—when the northern European days are long and the summer crowds have not yet filled the beaches, the highways, or the museums—and in early fall.

High Season: The busiest times to visit are during July and August, and also around Easter, and the Christmas/New Year period. Because Belgians take vacations in July and August, these months are not ideal for visiting the coast or the Ardennes, but summer is a very good time to be in cities like Brussels, Antwerp, or Liège, when you may be able to get a break on hotel prices; on the other hand, this is also vacation time for many restaurants.

WEATHER

Climate change has meant that the always unpredictable Belgian weather patterns have become even more unstable in recent decades.

The stereotype of overcast Belgian skies is not unfounded, and early spring and fall do get quite a bit of rain, but the weather can change dramatically in the space of a few hours.

Winters can be cold, but extreme snow events and long periods of freezing weather are becoming increasingly rare. You are more likely to encounter prolonged drizzle than blizzards, except at higher elevations in the Ardennes.

Summers vary from one year to the next. Some are cool and wet, with daytime highs struggling to peak beyond 70°F, while others may entail long periods of clear skies, and heat waves in excess of 95°F.

The key advice for any visitor to Northern Europe is to be prepared for all eventualities.

Contacts

Air

AIRLINES Brussels Airlines. *02/723–2362 in Belgium, 800/401–1801 in U.S.* *www.brusselsairlines.com.* **Ryanair.** *www.ryanair.com.* **United.** *800/864–8331 in U.S., 02/200–8868 in Belgium* *www.united.com.*

AIRPORTS Brussels Airport. *Leopoldlaan, Zaventem, Brussels* *www.brusselsairport.be.*

AIRPORT TRANSFERS Flibco.com. *flibco.com.* **Taxi Hendriks.** *02/752–9800* *www.hendriks.be.* **Unitax.** *Brussels* *02/725–2525* *www.unitax.be.* **Airport Driver.** *Brussels* *0488/093–651* *airport-driver.be.*

Bicycle

BICYCLE RENTALS Rent a road bike. *www.rent-a-road-bike.com.*

Bus

BUS COMPANIES TEC. *Charleroi* *081/322–711* *www.letec.be.* **De Lijn.** *Antwerp* *070/220–200* *www.delijn.be.* **STIB/MIVB.** *Brussels* *070/232–000* *www.stib.be.*

Car

CAR RENTALS Avis. *Brussels* *02/720–0944* *www.avis.be.* **Enterprise - Rent-a-car.** *012/390–959* *www.enterpriserentacar.be.* **Europcar.** *Brussels* *02/721–0592* *www.europcar.be.* **Hertz.** *Brussels* *02/720–6044* *www.hertz.be.* **Sixt.** *Brussels* *070/225–800* *www.sixt.be.*

Ride-Sharing

Uber *www.uber.com.*

Taxi

CONTACTS Taxi Antwerpen. *Antwerp* *0474/390–766* *www.taxibedrijfantwerpen.be.* **Taxis Verts.** *Brussels* *02/349–4949* *www.taxisverts.be.*

Train

RAIL COMPANIES SNCB/NMBS. *Brussels* *02/528–2828* *www.belgiantrain.be.*

RAIL PASSES Eurail. *www.eurail.com.*

Lodging

APARTMENT AND HOUSE RENTALS Airbnb. *www.airbnb.com.* **Gîtes et Chambres d'hôtes de Wallonie.** *Liège* *081/311–800* *gitesdewallonie.be/en.*

Taxes

V.A.T. REFUNDS Global Blue. *www.globalblue.com.*

U.S. Embassy/ Consulate

CONTACT U.S. Embassy in Belgium. *Blvd. du Régent 27, Upper Town* *02/811–4000* *be.usembassy.gov.*

Visitor Information

REGIONAL TOURIST OFFICES Visit Flanders. *Grasmarkt 61, Lower Town* *02/504–0300* *www.visitflanders.com.* **Visit Wallonia.** *Av. Comte de Smet de Nayer 14, Namur* *081/844–100* *walloniabelgiumtourism.co.uk.* **Visit Brussels.** *2–4 rue Royale, Brussels* *02/513–8940* *visit.brussels.*

Great Itineraries

Highlights of Belgium

Distances in Belgium aren't huge, so you could base yourself in one or two places and make day trips to other towns. The larger cities are easily reachable by train, but to get to grips with the Ardennes regions you'll need your own vehicle.

DAY 1: BRUSSELS

Start a walking tour of Brussels at the magnificent Grand Place, taking time to admire its soaring Gothic Hôtel de Ville. Once you've drunk your fill, swing past the Galeries Royales Saint-Hubert, one of Europe's oldest shopping arcades. Stop for lunch in one of the grand cafés around the Bourse, then head past the notorious Mannekin Pis statue of the urinating boy. Spend the afternoon in one or more museums, perhaps the enchanting Musical Instruments Museum, in a beautiful Art Nouveau mansion, or—if Surrealism is more your thing—the Musée Magritte. Dine in one of the many fine eateries on swish place du Grand Sablon.

DAY 2: BRUSSELS TO ANTWERP

Leave Brussels in the morning by heading north to Antwerp. In the old town, admire the 14th-century Onze-Lieve-Vrouwekathedraal, with its gravity-defying 404-foot tower. Nearby, Antwerp's main square, Grote Markt, is barely less grand. Stop for lunch, then see ancient printing presses at the Plantin Moretus Museum. Next, head north to the up-and-coming Het Eilandje district of former docklands. The area's centerpiece is the Museum aan de Stroom (MAS), with exhibits on local Flemish folklore and pre-Columbian art. Return to the Old Town in the evening to enjoy dinner in one of the district's many restaurants located in atmospheric centuries-old buildings, and perhaps take in a show at the opera house.

DAY 3: ANTWERP TO GHENT

More manageable in size than Brussels or Antwerp, and less of a tourist magnet than Bruges, Ghent is "Flanders in a nutshell" with its wonderful mix of Flemish architecture, culture, and cuisine. Start a tour at the Museum of Fine Arts Ghent, showcasing Flemish Primitives. For a bird's-eye view of the city, take the elevator to the top of the 300-foot Belfort, a belfry tower built in 1314. Back at ground level, dip into the Sint-Baafskathedraal to see the cathedral's masterpiece, the Jan van Eyck painted Ghent Altarpiece, often known as the *Adoration of the Mystic Lamb.* Then step even further back into history by visiting the moated Gravensteen (Castle of the Counts). Dine in a waterside restaurant along the Graslei, but before you sit down to eat, first cross the Leie River to fully appreciate the architectural grandeur of the buildings' stepped gable facades from over the water.

DAY 4: GHENT TO BRUGES

Leave Ghent and make the short hop down to the almost impossibly pretty city of Bruges. Hop on a boat for a cruise of the city's "reien" (canals), then earn your lunch by heading to the Markt square and climbing the 366 steps of the Belfort bell tower for panoramic views. Have lunch on the square below, or on the equally lovely Burg square, then marvel at Michelangelo's *Madonna and Child,* which you'll find in the Onze-Lieve-Vrouwekerk. Opposite the church, explore Sint-Janshospitaal Museum, one of Europe's oldest hospitals that first treated patients in the 12th century, and was still in use until 1977. Around the corner, get a feel for Bruges history by touring the Gruuthusemuseum, housed in a 15th-century merchant's house. Dine on one of the streets leading off from the north of the Markt, then round off the evening in one of the area's vaulted cellar bars, such as 't Poatersgat.

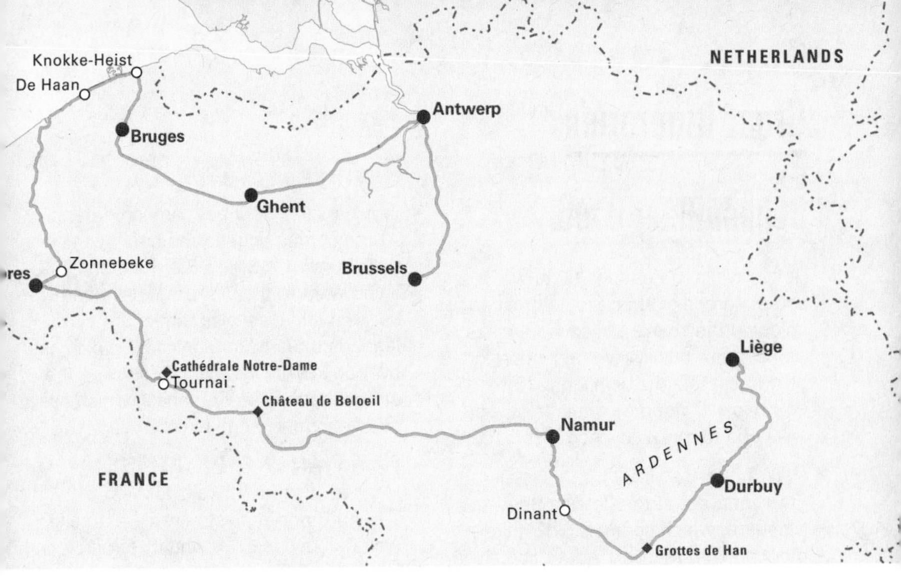

DAY 5: BRUGES TO YPRES

In the morning, make a beeline for the coast, visiting either the sprawling resort of Knokke-Heist, or the quieter and more genteel De Haan, depending on mood. Take in the sea air and admire the miles of sandy beach, perhaps riding the coastal tram for a short way before enjoying a seafood lunch in one of the countless eateries behind the beach. In the afternoon, head inland to the battlefields of World War I. Your first stop should be in Zonnebeke, at the Memorial Museum Passchendaele 1917. Close by, pay your respects at Tyne Cot—the final resting place of 12,000 British and Commonwealth troops, and the largest military cemetery in the region. Continue on to Ypres, and visit the affecting In Flanders Fields Museum in the magnificent Lakenhallen, a building that had to be rebuilt from rubble following World War 1. There are plenty of places for dinner around the town's Grote Markt, but time your meal carefully to ensure you are at the Menenpoort to witness the moving Last Post ceremony held daily at 8 pm.

DAY 6: YPRES TO NAMUR

Leave Flanders and head southeast into Wallonia, stopping first in Tournai. Don't miss the colossal 12th-century Cathédrale Notre-Dame. Continue east and call in at the lovely Chateau de Beloeil, set in 62 acres of gardens and referred to as the "Versailles of Belgium." In the afternoon head into Namur, the capital of Wallonia. From the old city center, ride the cable car across the river and up to the Citadelle de Namur for lovely city views. End your day with dinner in Namur's picturesque old town.

DAY 7: NAMUR TO DURBUY AND LIÈGE

Begin your last day by following the Meuse River south to Dinant, another town dominated by a cliff-top citadelle. Here, too, you can ride a cable car to the top if you don't fancy scaling the 400 steps. Leave Dinant and continue south into the Ardennes to visit architecture of a natural kind at the Grottes de Han limestone cave system near Rochefort, which you explore both on foot and by boat. From Han, head northeast to the tiny but lovely village of Durbuy, a picture-perfect spot in the shadow of a stunning fold of rock. You could end your tour by spending the night here in Durbuy, or—if you crave more nightlife—continue on to Liège to dine in its old town.

Great Itineraries

Belgian Beer Route

Belgium has more than 250 breweries and hundreds of specialist beer cafés, so doing the scene justice would take months, but this is our suggestion for how to sample the highlights. Note: to visit many of the breweries below you will need to make advance reservations.

DAY 1: BRUSSELS

Start your tour at the Belgian Beer Museum, which contains old equipment and interactive displays about the brewing process. Head from there to the Musée de la Gueuze—aka the Cantillon brewery—which has produced lambic and specialty beers through spontaneous fermentation since 1900. If it's a weekend, head to Midi station and take the short train ride to Lot, where you can visit another famous lambic name, Drie Fonteinen (*3fonteinen.be*) and its "Lambik-O-Droom." You can work off the beer sampled there by walking a mile or so to Beersel's 15th-century castle. Near the castle is Oud Beersel, another lambic maker, which you can visit on Saturday. Head back into Brussels from Beersel station then visit some of the city's most characterful bars, including Moeder Lambic Fontainas, or Á La Mort Subite with its tatty wooden tables and an early-20th-century atmosphere.

DAY 2: BRUSSELS TO ANTWERP

Leave Brussels and head north, stopping first in Mechelen at Brouwerij Het Anker, known for its flavorful Gouden Carolus brews, and home to one of Belgium's few whisky distilleries. Then continue to Antwerp, where you can visit Brouwerij De Koninck—makers of Bolleke, the city's "national drink"—and enjoy an interactive self-guided tour. In Antwerp's rejuvenated docklands area, Het Eilandje, you'll find the taproom of newer arrival Antwerpse Brouw Compagnie (*seef.be*), which makes Seef beer among others. At the cutting edge of the beer scene in the old town is Billie's Bier Kafétaria, but if you want to try an ale that has been cellared for years, visit the scruffy but legendary Bierhuis Kulminator, which has over 500 beers in stock. Or soak up the atmosphere at Oud Arsenaal, which has an interior unchanged in 100 years.

DAY 3: ANTWERP TO LIÈGE

Head east from Antwerp to Westmalle. The Abdij der Trappisten van Westmalle was founded in 1794, and its famous Dubbel and Tripel beers have been made here since 1836, and are considered the first (and still the best) of their kind. You cannot visit the abbey, but at nearby Café Trappisten (*trappisten.be*), you can order the house specialty "half-half," a blend of the brown and blond beers. Continue east to Achel, where Achelse Kluis (*www.achelsekluis.org*) is another abbey brewery with a café. From Achel, it is a short hop south to Bocholt, home to family brewers Martens since 1758. In the center of town is their Bocholter Brouwerijmuseum (*www.bocholterbrouwerijmuseum.be*). Once you've learned all there is to know, continue south into Wallonia and stay the night in Liège, ending the evening at Brasserie {C}, a brewery at the foot of the city's famous Montage de Bueren stairway.

DAY 4: LIÈGE TO ROCHEFORT

From Liège, take the E25 south through the Ardennes to Houffalize, close to the Luxembourg border, and visit Brasserie d'Achouffe, makers of La Chouffe among other beers. Head south again to the Abbaye d'Orval and you will experience something altogether more traditional. Another globally famous Trappist name, the brewery is sadly off-limits to outsiders, but you can visit the abbey grounds and try the deliciously dry beer at nearby cafés. From Orval, head to Rochefort to

spend the night in this quiet village. If you want, you can detour a short distance north to pay your respects outside the Abbaye Notre-Dame de Saint-Remy, where the famous Trappist Rochefort beers originate, but the monks here are even more private than those at Orval, so no visits are possible.

DAY 5: ROCHEFORT TO WATOU

Leaving Rochefort next morning, head west past Dinant and visit L'Abbaye de Maredsous, where you can tour the abbey and enjoy the house beers. Travel southwest to Chimay and the Abbaye Notre Dame de Scourmont. Although this abbey is also off-limits, the monks here have embraced the modern world, and a few minutes' walk away in the Espace Chimay (*chimay.com*), you can enjoy the Chimay Experience interactive tour and sample beers and cheeses in the café. On leaving Chimay, make your way northwest, to the village of Watou. Sign up for a tour at Brouwerij Sint Bernardus *(www.sintbernardus.be),* where visits end in the rooftop brasserie, with views across the hop fields. Stay the night here at the brewery, or opt for more lively Ypres. If you do stay, dine at 't Hommelhof (*www.hommelhof.be*), a pioneer in the world of beer and food pairing.

DAY 6: WATOU TO BRUGES

In the morning, head to Sint-Sixtus Trappist abbey in Westvleteren, home to some of Belgium's most revered beers. The abbey is closed to visitors, but the café in De Vrede across the street is a must-visit for any beer lover. From here, travel north and spend the day in Bruges. Take a tour at Halve Maan, go on a self-guided audio tour of the Brougogne des Flandres brewery, and have an interactive lesson at the Bruges Beer Experience. Imbibe in Bruges's historic bars, such as De Garre, and be awed by the choices at 't Brugs Beertje, one of the world's great beer pubs.

DAY 7: BRUGES TO GHENT

On the last morning make for Roeselare, which is home to Brouwerij Rodenbach *(be.rodenbach.be),* creators of superb Flemish Red ales. Join the tour to see the oak vats where the beers gain their sour cherry edge. Head east from there to Oudenaarde, and visit both Brouwerij Liefmans (*www.liefmans.com*), which dates back to 1679 and is known for its fruit beers, and Brouwerij Roman (*www.roman.be*), which has been in the Roman family for 12 generations. Finish in Ghent at beer bars like Dulle Griet and Waterhuis aan de Bierkant.

Great Itineraries

The Best of Brussels

Truly getting to know all the sights and museums of Brussels would require weeks, but three days is enough to give you a flavor of Belgium's charismatic capital.

BRUSSELS IN 3 DAYS

DAY 1

Any visit to Brussels should start on the lovely Grand Place, one of Europe's grandest medieval plazas. Once you've drunk your fill of the architectural wonders, wander the narrow, cobbled lanes surrounding the square and visit the graceful, arcaded Galeries St-Hubert, an elegant 19th-century shopping gallery. Head down rue de l'Etuve to see the Manneken Pis, the famous statue of the little boy urinating. Walk to the place du Grand Sablon to window-shop at its many fine antiques stores and galleries. If it's a weekend, enjoy the outdoor antiques market. Have lunch in one of the cafés lining the perimeter, and don't forget to buy chocolates at one of the top chocolatiers on and around the square. Then, for a cultural hit, head to the Musée Fin-de-Siècle and the Musée Oldmasters, and drop into their neighbor, the smaller but unmissable Musée Magritte. End with dinner on the fashionable rue Antoine Dansaert or have a drink in one of Grand Place's many cafés.

DAY 2

Start your second day at the Parc de Bruxelles, a formal urban park that originated as a game park. Check out the elegant place Royale across the street and then head to the Musée des Instruments de Musique, which houses one of Europe's finest collections of musical instruments. Hop a tram to avenue Louise in Ixelles for a little shopping, and perhaps lunch along place du Chatelain. After lunch, visit architect Victor Horta's own home, now the Musée Horta, on rue Américaine. If you crave more art and architecture, go to the Musée David-et-Alice-Van-Buuren. On the other hand, if you crave lighter entertainment, head toward the Gare du Midi and visit the Musée Bruxellois de la Gueuze in the Cantillon Brewery, to see how lambic beer is brewed the old-fashioned way, using wild yeast from the surrounding air. For dinner head to place Ste-Catherine for a feast of Belgian fish and seafood specialties. Later, check out the many cafés and bars that crowd the narrow streets around the Bourse.

DAY 3

Take the metro to Schuman and take a walk past the cluster of EU buildings on your way through Parc Cinquantenaire to the Autoworld museum, which houses a fantastic collection of vintage cars. Catch a tram from there to Tervuren and visit the Koninklijk Museum voor Midden Afrika, a legacy of Belgium's dubious role in the Congo, including not only objects and memorabilia from explorers that showcase African cultural creativity, but also exhibitions that recognize Europe's largely immoral colonial past. Relax in the surrounding park before heading back into town for another fine dinner.

Another option for your third day would be to visit some of the famous sights and towns on the border of Brussels. First on the list should be Waterloo, the battlefield that changed the course of European history, where you can explore the Musée Wellington, the Butte de Lion, and the Champ de Bataille field. Next, head for Gaasbeek, where you'll find the Gaasbeek Château and scenery straight out of a Bruegel painting.

On the Calendar

January/February

Carnival. Celebrated in (usually) late February with great gusto, the pre-Lent festivities at Binche—with its extravagantly costumed *gilles*—and at Tournai and Charleroi—each of which has its own style and verve—are especially great. Mardi Gras (Shrove Tuesday) and the preceding Sunday are the high points. *www.visitflanders.com*

Brugs Bierfestival. Try some of the more than 500 beers on offer at the weekend-long Bruges Beer Festival. *www.brugsbierfestival.be*

March/April

Cavalcade de Jemappes. This colorful traditional costumed procession is held in Mons on Easter Monday. *walloniabelgiumtourism.co.uk*

Floralia Brussels. Throughout the month of April, the 35-acre park and greenhouses of Groot-Bijgaarden castle, on the outskirts of Brussels, explode into color as more than 1 million spring bulbs burst into exuberant life. The stars are the 400 varieties of tulip, but daffodils and hyacinths are also out in abundance. *www.floralia-brussels.be*

Zythos Bierfestival (ZBF). The largest annual beer festival in Belgium brings 100 brewers and thousands of thirsty visitors to the Brabanthal in Leuven across one weekend each April. *www.zbf.be*

Erfgoeddag. On Flanders Heritage Day, which—despite its name—takes place across a whole weekend in April, buildings of architectural or historical interest across Flanders that are not normally accessible to the public throw open their doors. *www.visitflanders.com*

May/June

The Royal Greenhouses of Laeken. Every spring, usually from mid-May, these royal greenhouses, with superb flower and plant arrangements, are open to the public for a three-week period. *www.brussels.be/greenhouses-laeken*

Kunstenfestivaldesarts. Throughout May, Brussels hosts this international celebration of contemporary drama, dance, and music. *www.kfda.be*

De Heilig Bloedprocessie. On Ascension Day, the Procession of the Holy Blood in Bruges is one of the oldest and most elaborate religious and historical processions in Europe. *www.bloedprocessie-brugge.be*

Ducasse de Mons. Also known as the Doudou, the Ducasse, held in Mons on the first weekend following Whitsunday, is a fantastic citywide festival including a procession of the relics of the town's founding saint, and an enactment of St. George's battle with the dragon. *www.visitmons.co.uk/agenda/the-doudou*

Brussels International Film Festival. The glitterati of the international film world descend on the Belgian capital for a celebration of moviemaking in late June, with events and premieres held across the city. *briff.be/en*

Masters Expo. Fashionistas, artists, and designers all head to Antwerp in June for this presentation of the work of graduates from the Royal Academy of Fine Arts, bringing together people from the worlds of fashion, graphic design, jewelry design, painting, and sculpture. *www.antwerpmasters.be*

On the Calendar

July/August

Ommegang. The Ommegang takes on Brussels's Grand Place on the first Thursday each July. It's a sumptuous and stately pageant featuring over 2,000 players, who reenact a procession that honored Emperor Charles V in 1549. *www.ommegang.be*

Rock Werchter. Belgium's biggest rock festival is a multiday outdoor event in early July that pulls in major acts like Pearl Jam and The Killers. *www.rockwerchter.be*

Gentse Feesten. A 10-day celebration of indulgence in mid-July, this was originally intended to curb summer drinking by workers in Ghent. However, it seems to have had the opposite effect, and includes music making, entertainment, and assorted happenings in the streets of the city, and a world-class dance music festival that lasts until the wee hours. *gentsefeesten.stad.gent*

National Day. Belgium's National Day is celebrated with events nationwide on July 21. In Brussels, a military march is followed by a festival in the Parc de Bruxelles and spectacular fireworks. *visit.brussels/en*

Tomorrowland. Taking place across several weekends outside the little town of Boom, near Antwerp, this is Belgium's premier electronic dance music festival. *www.tomorrowland.com*

Hapje-Tapje. On the first Sunday in August, around 35 restaurants set up street stalls in central Leuven for a celebration of food, while a parallel beer festival takes place on nearby Oude Markt. The highlight is a competition between local bartenders, who race each other around the cobbled streets carrying trays full of beer glasses. *www.visitflanders.com*

Fête Médiévale de Bouillon. For two days each August, the castle in Bouillon plays host to a medieval fair, featuring displays of falconry, archery, sword fighting, and much more. *walloniabelgiumtourism.co.uk*

La Régate Internationale de Baignoires. In mid-August, Dinant hosts an international bathtub regatta, featuring an array of crazy custom-made tubs, most of which manage to stay afloat on the Meuse River. *walloniabelgiumtourism.co.uk*

MA Festival. The Musica Antiqua Festival in Bruges is an international celebration of early music, with concerts performed in various historical venues across the city. *mafestival.be*

F1 Belgian Grand Prix. At the spectacular Spa-Francorchamps circuit in the Ardennes, Belgium's contribution to the Formula 1 circus is always one of the highlights of the global motor-racing year. Unpredictable weather conditions mean the race is usually event-filled. *www.spagrandprix.com*

September/October

Nuit Blanche. Brussels stays up for this early October night's dream, during which musical and cultural events go on until 6 am. *nuitblanche.brussels*

Film Fest Ghent. Ghent's international film festival is the most important film festival in Belgium. It screens the work of new Belgian talent as well as an array of top-drawer international directors. *www.filmfestival.be*

November/December

Winter Wonders. Held across Brussels throughout the month of December, this festival includes musical events, rides, and cultural attractions. The highlights are the annual Christmas Market and ice-skating rink, both found on place De Brouckère. *www.plaisirsdhiver.be/en*

Helpful Phrases in French

BASICS

Yes/no	wee/nohn	Oui/non
Please	seel voo play	S'il vous plaît
Thank you	mair- **see**	Merci
You're welcome	deh ree- **ehn**	De rien
Excuse me, sorry	pahr- **don**	Pardon
Good morning/ afternoon	bohn- **zhoor**	Bonjour
Good evening	bohn- **swahr**	Bonsoir
Good-bye	o ruh- **vwahr**	Au revoir
Mr. (Sir)	muh- **syuh**	Monsieur
Mrs. (Ma'am)	ma- **dam**	Madame
Miss	mad-mwa- **zel**	Mademoiselle
Pleased to meet you	ohn-shahn- **tay**	Enchanté(e)
How are you?	kuh-mahn-tahl-ay **voo**	Comment allez-vous?
Very well, thanks	tray bee-ehn, mair- **see**	Très bien, merci
And you?	ay voo?	Et vous?

NUMBERS

one	uhn	un
two	deuh	deux
three	twah	trois
four	**kaht**-ruh	quatre
five	sank	cinq
six	seess	six
seven	set	sept
eight	wheat	huit
nine	nuf	neuf
ten	deess	dix
eleven	ohnz	onze
twelve	dooz	douze
thirteen	trehz	treize
fourteen	kah- **torz**	quatorze
fifteen	kanz	quinze
sixteen	sez	seize
seventeen	deez- **set**	dix-sept
eighteen	deez- **wheat**	dix-huit
nineteen	deez- **nuf**	dix-neuf
twenty	vehn	vingt
twenty-one	vehnt-ay- **uhn**	vingt-et-un
thirty	trahnt	trente
forty	ka- **rahnt**	quarante
fifty	sang- **kahnt**	cinquante
sixty	swa- **sahnt**	soixante
seventy	swa-sahnt- **deess**	soixante-dix
eighty	kaht-ruh- **vehn**	quatre-vingts
ninety	kaht-ruh-vehn-**deess**	quatre-vingt-dix
one hundred	sahn	cent
one thousand	meel	mille

COLORS

black	nwahr	noir
blue	bleuh	bleu
brown	bruhn/mar- **rohn**	brun/marron
green	vair	vert
orange	o- **rahnj**	orange
pink	rose	rose
red	rouge	rouge
violet	vee-o- **let**	violette
white	blahnk	blanc
yellow	zhone	jaune

DAYS OF THE WEEK

Sunday	dee- **mahnsh**	dimanche
Monday	luhn- **dee**	lundi
Tuesday	mahr- **dee**	mardi
Wednesday	mair-kruh- **dee**	mercredi
Thursday	zhuh- **dee**	jeudi
Friday	vawn-druh- **dee**	vendredi
Saturday	sahm- **dee**	samedi

MONTHS

January	zhahn-vee- **ay**	janvier
February	feh-vree- **ay**	février
March	marce	mars
April	a- **vreel**	avril
May	meh	mai
June	zhwehn	juin
July	zhwee- **ay**	juillet
August	ah- **oo**	août
September	sep- **tahm**-bruh	septembre
October	awk- **to**-bruh	octobre
November	no- **vahm**-bruh	novembre
December	day- **sahm**-bruh	décembre

USEFUL PHRASES

Do you speak English?	par-lay **voo** ahn- **glay**	Parlez-vous anglais?
I don't speak ...	zhuh nuh parl pah ...	Je ne parle pas ...
French	frahn- **say**	français
I don't understand	zhuh nuh kohm-**prahn** pah	Je ne comprends pas
I understand	zhuh kohm- **prahn**	Je comprends
I don't know	zhuh nuh say **pah**	Je ne sais pas
I'm American/ British	zhuh sweez a-may-ree- **kehn** / ahn- **glay**	Je suis américain/ anglais
What's your name?	ko-mahn vooz a-pell-ay- **voo**	Comment vous appelez-vous?
My name is ...	zhuh ma- **pell** ...	Je m'appelle ...
What time is it?	kel air eh- **teel**	Quelle heure est-il?
How?	ko- **mahn**	Comment?
When?	kahn	Quand?
Yesterday	yair	Hier
Today	o-zhoor- **dwee**	Aujourd'hui

Tomorrow	duh- **mehn**	Demain
Tonight	suh **swahr**	Ce soir
What?	kwah	Quoi?
What is it?	kess-kuh- **say**	Qu'est-ce que c'est?
Why?	poor- **kwa**	Pourquoi?
Who?	kee	Qui?
Where is …	oo ay	Où est …
the train station?	la gar	la gare?
the subway station?	la sta- **syon** duh may- **tro**	la station de métro?
the bus stop?	la-ray duh booss	l'arrêt de bus?
the post office?	la post	la poste?
the bank?	la bahnk	la banque?
the … hotel?	lo- **tel**	l'hôtel …?
the store?	luh ma-ga- **zehn**	le magasin?
the cashier?	la **kess**	la caisse?
the … museum?	luh mew- **zay**	le musée …?
the hospital?	lo-pee- **tahl**	l'hôpital?
the elevator?	la-sahn- **seuhr**	l'ascenseur?
the telephone?	luh tay-lay- **phone**	le téléphone?
Where are the …	oo sohn lay	Où sont les …
restrooms?	twah- **let**	toilettes?
(men/women)	(**oh**-mm/ **fah**-mm)	(hommes/femmes)
Here/there	ee- **see** /la	Ici/là
Left/right	a goash/a draht	A gauche/à droite
Straight ahead	too drwah	Tout droit
Is it near/far?	say pray/lwehn	C'est près/loin?
I'd like …	zhuh voo- **dray**	Je voudrais …
a room	ewn **shahm**-bruh	une chambre
the key	la clay	la clé
a newspaper	uhn zhoor- **nahl**	un journal
a stamp	uhn **tam**-bruh	un timbre
I'd like to buy …	zhuh voo- **dray** **ahsh**-tay	Je voudrais acheter …
cigarettes	day see-ga- **ret**	des cigarettes
matches	days a-loo- **met**	des allumettes
soap	dew sah- **vohn**	du savon
city map	uhn plahn de **veel**	un plan de ville
road map	ewn cart roo-tee- **air**	une carte routière
magazine	ewn reh- **vu**	une revue
envelopes	dayz ahn-veh- **lope**	des enveloppes
writing paper	dew pa-pee- **ay** a **let**-ruh	du papier à lettres
postcard	ewn cart pos- **tal**	une carte postale
How much is it?	say comb-bee- **ehn**	C'est combien?
A little/a lot	uhn peuh/bo- **koo**	Un peu/beaucoup
More/less	plu/mwehn	Plus/moins
Enough/too (much)	a-say/tro	Assez/trop
I am ill/sick	zhuh swee ma- **lahd**	Je suis malade
Call a …	a-play uhn	Appelez un …
doctor	dohk- **tehr**	docteur
Help!	o suh- **koor**	Au secours!

Stop!	a-reh- **tay**	Arrêtez!
Fire!	o fuh	Au feu!
Caution!/Look out!	a-tahn-see- **ohn**	Attention!

DINING OUT

A bottle of …	ewn boo- **tay** duh	une bouteille de …
A cup of …	ewn tass duh	une tasse de …
A glass of …	uhn vair duh	un verre de …
Bill/check	la-dee-see- **ohn**	l'addition
Bread	dew panh	du pain
Breakfast	luh puh- **tee** day-zhuh- **nay**	le petit-déjeuner
Butter	dew burr	du beurre
Cheers!	ah **vo**-truh sahn- **tay**	A votre santé!
Cocktail/aperitif	uhn ah-pay-ree- **teef**	un apéritif
Dinner	luh dee- **nay**	le dîner
Dish of the day	luh plah dew **zhoor**	le plat du jour
Enjoy!	bohn a-pay- **tee**	Bon appétit!
Fixed-price menu	luh may- **new**	le menu
Fork	ewn four- **shet**	une fourchette
I am diabetic	zhuh swee dee-ah-bay- **teek**	Je suis diabétique
I am vegetarian	zhuh swee vay-zhay-ta-ree- **en**	Je suis végétarien(ne)
I cannot eat …	zhuh nuh puh pah mahn- **jay** deh	Je ne peux pas manger de …
I'd like to order	zhuh voo- **dray** ko-mahn- **day**	Je voudrais commander
Is service/the tip included?	ess kuh luh sair- **veess** ay comb- **pree**	Est-ce que le service est compris?
It's good/bad	say bohn/mo- **vay**	C'est bon/mauvais
It's hot/cold	say sho/frwah	C'est chaud/froid
Knife	uhn koo- **toe**	un couteau
Lunch	luh day-zhuh- **nay**	le déjeuner
Menu	la cart	la carte
Napkin	ewn sair-vee- **et**	une serviette
Pepper	dew **pwah**-vruh	du poivre
Plate	ewn a-see- **et**	une assiette
Please give me …	doe-nay- **mwah**	Donnez-moi …
Salt	dew sell	du sel
Spoon	ewn kwee- **air**	une cuillère
Sugar	dew **sook**-ruh	du sucre
Waiter!/Waitress!	muh- **syuh** / mad-mwa- **zel**	Monsieur!/ Mademoiselle!
Wine list	la cart day vehn	la carte des vins

Helpful Phrases in Flemish

BASICS

Hello	Hallo	Hah-loh
Yes/no	Ja/Nee	Jah/Nay
Please	Alstublieft	**Ehls**-stew-bleeft
Thank you	Dank u wel	**Donk**-ee-vell
You're welcome	Graag gedaan	**Chraach** che-**daahn**
I'm sorry (apology - formal)	Het spijt me	Het **spayt** muh
Sorry (Excuse me - formal)	Pardon	Par-**don**
(I'm) sorry (informal)	Sorry	Sorry
Good morning	Goedemorgen	Choe-de **mohr**-chen
Good day	Goede dag	Choe-de **dach**
Good evening	Goedenavond	Choe-den **ah**-font
Goodbye	Tot ziens	**Taht** zeens
Mr. (Sir)	Meneer	**Muh**-near
Mrs.	Mevrouw	**Muh**-vrouw
Miss	Mevrouw	**Muh**-vrouw
Pleased to meet you	Prettig kennis met u te maken	**Preh**-tuch **ken**-nis met ooh tuh **mah**-kehn
How are you?	Hoe gaat het met je?	**Hoo** chaat het met **juh?**

NUMBERS

one-half	een helft	uhn **hellft**
one	een	ayn
two	twee	tway
three	drie	dree
four	vier	fihr
five	vijf	fayf
six	zes	zehs
seven	zeven	**zay**-vuh
eight	acht	uhcht
nine	negen	**nay**-chen
ten	tien	teen
eleven	elf	elf
twelve	twaalf	twaahlf
thirteen	dertien	**dehr**-teen
fourteen	veertien	**fihr**-teen
fifteen	vijftien	**fayf**-teen
sixteen	zestien	**zehs**-teen
seventeen	zeventien	**zay**-vuhn-teen
eighteen	achttien	**uh**cht-teen
nineteen	negentien	**nay**-chen-teen
twenty	twintig	twi**n**-tich
twenty-one	eenentwintig	**ayn**-ehn-**twin**-tich
thirty	dertig	**dehr**-tich
forty	viertig	**fihr**-tich
fifty	vijftig	**fayf**-tich
sixty	zestig	**zehs**-tich
seventy	zeventig	**zay**-vuhn-tich
eighty	tachtig	**tuh**cht-tich
ninety	negentig	**nay**-chen-tich
one hundred	honderd	**hohn**-dirt
one thousand	duizend	**day**-zint
one million	miljoen	mill-**yoon**

COLORS

black	zwart	zwahrt
blue	blauw	bliauw
brown	bruin	brauin
green	groen	chroon
orange	oranje	oh-**run**-yuh
red	rood	roaht
white	wit	vit
yellow	geel	cheal

DAYS OF THE WEEK

Sunday	zondag	**zohn**-duch
Monday	maandag	**mahn**-duch
Tuesday	dinsdag	**dinns**-duch
Wednesday	woensdag	**woohns**-duch
Thursday	donderdag	**daun**-der-duch
Friday	vrijdag	**fray**-duch
Saturday	zaterdag	**zah**-tur-duch

MONTHS

January	januari	yah-noo-**ari**
February	februari	fay-brew-**ari**
March	maart	mahrt
April	april	ahpr-**ill**
May	mei	may
June	juni	**yoo**-knee
July	juli	**yoo**-lee
August	augustus	auw-**chuss**-tuss
September	september	sehp-**tem**-ber
October	oktober	ock-**to**-ber
November	november	no-**fem**-ber
December	december	day-**sem**-ber

USEFUL WORDS AND PHRASES

Do you speak English?	Spreekt u Engels?	Spraykt euw **Ehn**guhls?
I don't speak Flemish	Ik spreek geen Vlaams	Ick sprayk chein Vlahms
I don't understand.	Ik begrijp het niet.	Ick buh-chr**ayp** heht neat
I don't know.	Ik weet het niet	Ick **fate** heht neat
I understand.	Ik begrijp het.	Ick buh-chr**ayp** heht
I'm American.	ik ben Amerikaans.	Ick ben Ahmeh-ree-**kahns**
I'm British.	Ik ben Brits.	Ick ben **Brits**
What's your name.	Hoe heet je?	Who **hate** yuh?
My name is ...	Mijn naam is…	Main **nahm** ihs ...?

What time is it?	Hoe laat is het?	Who **laht** ihs heht?
How?	Hoe?	Who?
When?	Wanneer?	**Vahn**-near?
Yesterday	Gisteren	**Chihs**-tuh-rihn
Today	Vandaag	Fun-**dahch**
Tomorrow	Morgen	**Mohr**-chihn
This morning	Vanmorgen	Fun-**mohr**-chihn
This afternoon	Vanmiddag	Fun-**mie**-duch
Tonight	Vanavond	Fun-**ah**-font
What?	Wat?	Vaht?
What is it?	Wat is het?	Vaht **ihs** heht?
Why?	Waarom?	Vah-**rohm**?
Who?	Wie?	Vieh?
Where is ...	Waar is…	**Vahr ihs**?
... the train station?	... het treinstation?	…heht **trayn**-stah-shone?
... the subway station?	... het metrostation?	…heht **may**-troh-stah-shone?
... the bus stop?	... de bushalte?	…duh **buhs**-hull-tuh?
... the airport?	... het vliegveld?	…heht **fleech**-felt?
... the post office?	... het postkantoor?	…heht **pohst**-can-tour?
... the bank?	... de bank?	…duh **bunk**?
... the hotel?	... het hotel?	…heht ho-**tel**?
... the museum?	... het museum?	…heht mu-**se**-um?
... the hospital?	... het ziekenhuis?	…heht **zee**-cun-heuiws?
... the elevator?	... de lift?	…duh lift?
Where are the restrooms?	Waar zijn de toiletten?	Waahr zane duh toi-**let**-ten?
Here/there	Hier/daar	Hiehr/dahr
Left/right	Links/rechts	Links/reh-chts
Is it near/far?	Is het dichtbij / ver weg?	Ihs heht deecht-**bay**
I'd like ...	Ik wil graag ...	Ick vill chraahch…
... a room	... een kamer	…ayn **kah**-muhr
... the key	... de sleutel	…duh s**lay**-tuhl
... a newspaper	…een krant	…ayn crunt
... a stamp	…een postzegel	…ayn **pawst**-zeh-chehl
I'd like to buy ...	Ik wil …. kopen	Ick vill ayn … **co**-pin
... a city map	…een stadsplan	… ayn **stuts**-plan
... a road map	…een wegenkaart	… ayn vey-**guhn**-cart
... a magaine	…een tijdschrijft	… ayn **tayt**-schrifft
... envelopes	…enveloppen	…ahn-vuh-**lop**-puh
... writing paper	…briefpapier	…**brief**-puh-pier
... a postcard	…een postkaart	… ayn **posst**-cart
... a ticket	…een ticket	… ayn **tic**-ket
How much is it?	Hoeveel is het?	Who-**fehl** is heht?
It's expensive/ cheap	Het is goedkoop/ duur	Heht ihs choot-**cope/**deuwr

A little/a lot	Weinig/veel	**Vay**-nihch/**Veal**
More/less	Meer/minder	May-r/minn-dehr
Enough/too (much)	Genoeg/te veel	Chuh-**nooch**/Tuh **veal**
I am ill/sick	Ik ben ziek	Ick ben **zeeck**
Call a doctor	Bel een dokter	Bell ayn **dock**-turr
Help!	Help!	Hehlp!
Stop!	Stop!	Stawp!

DINING OUT

A bottle of ...	Een fles …	Ayn **flehs** …
A cup of ...	Een kop …	Ayn **cawp** …
A glass of ...	Een glas …	Ayn **chlahss** …
Beer	Bier	Beer
Bill/check	Rekening	**Rayck**-eh-ning
Bread	Brood	Brohwt
Breakfast	Ontbijt	**Awnt**-bite
Butter	Boter	**Bow**-turr
Cocktail/aperatif	Cocktail/Aperitif	Cocktail/Aperitif
Coffee	Koffie	**Kohf**-fee
Dinner	Avondeten	**Ah**-fawnt-aytin
Fixed-price menu	Vaste prijs menu	**Fahst**-uh pryce me-**nu**
Fork	Vork	Foark
I am a vegetarian/I don't eat meat	Ik ben vegetariër / ik eet geen vlees	Ick ben veh-che-**tah**-rear/ick ayte **chayn** flays
I cannot eat ...	Ik kan geen … eten	Ick cun **chayn** … **ay**-ten
I'd like to order (some)...	Ik wil (wat) …. bestellen	Ick vill (vaht) … beh-**stehl**-lehn
Is service included?	Is service inbegrepen?	Ihs ser-**viss inn**-beh-chray-peh?
I'm hungry/thirsty	Ik heb honger/dorst	Ick hehp **hong**-uh/ **doarst**
It's good/bad	Het is goed/slecht	Heht is **choot/ slehcht**
It's hot/cold	Het is warm/koud	Heht is **wahr**im/ **cowt**
Knife	Mes	Mes
Lunch	Lunch	Lihnch
Menu	Menu	Menu
Napkin	Servet	Sir-**feht**
Pepper	Peper	**Pay**-purr
Plate	Bord	Boart
Please give me …	Mag ik een …	**Mahch** ick ayn …
Salt	Zout	Zowt
Spoon	Lepel	**Lay**-pill
Tea	Thee	Tay
Water	Water	**Vah**-tehr
Wine	Wijn	Vain

Chapter 3

BRUSSELS

Updated by
Gareth Clark

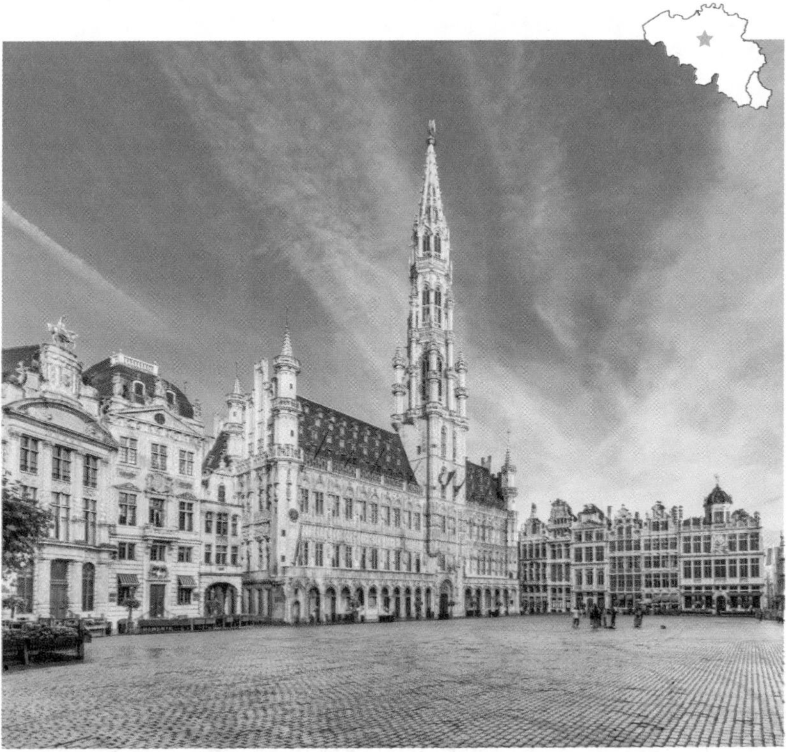

Sights	Restaurants	Hotels	Shopping	Nightlife
★★★★★	★★★★★	★★★★☆	★★★★★	★★★★☆

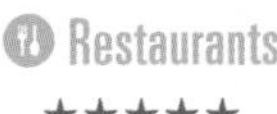

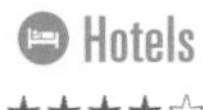

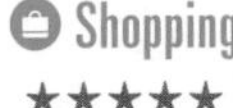

WELCOME TO BRUSSELS

TOP REASONS TO GO

★ **Bask in the Grand Place.** Brussels is home to, arguably, Europe's most beautiful square. As night falls and its gilded details shimmer under the lights, grab a warm waffle and just look around you in awe.

★ **Find your comic-book muse.** The city celebrates its comic-book heroes right. Around its streets are endless murals to discover, and its museum dedicated to the ninth art offers great insight into an art form dear to Belgium.

★ **See Art Nouveau wonders.** At the turn of the century, "starchitect" Victor Horta transformed the city while honing his vision of Art Nouveau. Witness his first steps in Schaerbeek and explore his legacy in Ixelles and Saint-Gilles.

★ **Treat yourself.** Beer, chocolate, and frites—Brussels is famous for all three. Wander a lambic brewery, pick out pralines from a local chocolatier, and ponder which of the 30 or so sauces in which to dip your frites.

1 Lower Town. The heart of the city. The Grand Place is one of the great squares of Europe, a gilded Flemish Baroque masterpiece around which the city's increasingly pedestrianized center flows. From here, historic streets whose names evoke the old marketplace this used to be, spider out, taking in the city's Manneken Pis, centuries-old flea markets, comic-book murals, and curious museums.

2 Upper Town. Ascend the steps of the Mont des Arts, not far from the Grand Place, and you'll discover where the city's nobles once presided over their fellow townsfolk. This regal quarter is home to the royal palace and park, and lines of stately mansions. It's also the cultural heartbeat of the city, with a number of museums and the impressive BOZAR arts center to discover.

3 Cinquantenaire and Schuman. The home of the European Union is a city of glass and steel. It's not pretty, but its history is fascinating and a chance to see how postwar Europe rebuilt itself. Just beyond is the great park of Cinquantenaire, easily the most beautiful in the city, and where King Leopold II built a grand arch to mark Belgium's 50th anniversary.

4 Ixelles and Saint-Gilles. Plush Ixelles and hip, slowly gentrifying Saint-Gilles are home to some of the city's best boutiques and most interesting bars and restaurants. The latter was also the home of inspirational

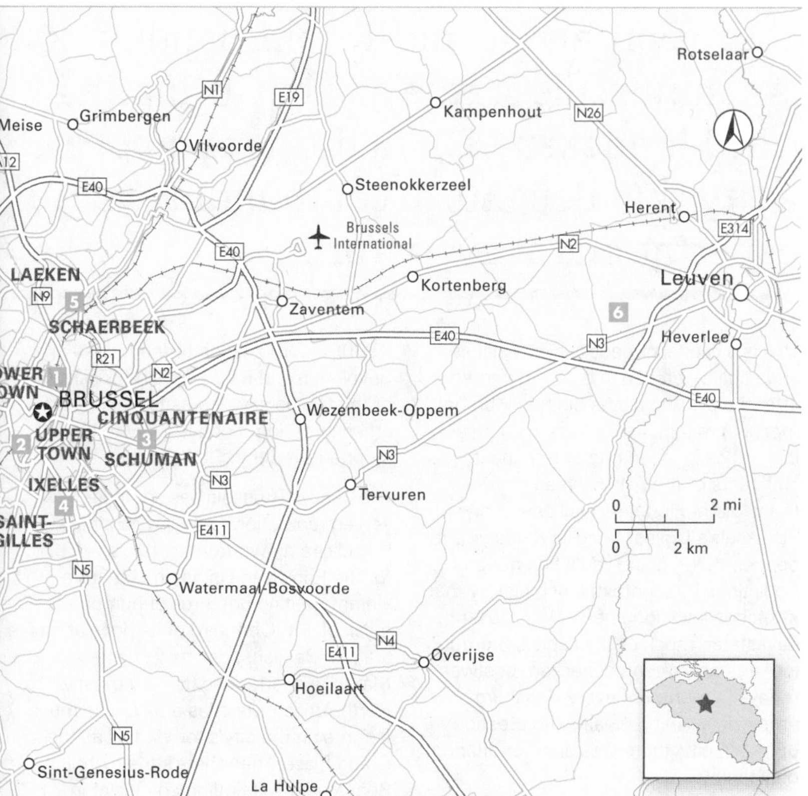

architect Victor Horta, who rebuilt the city in his own image. Examples of his work scatter the area and are readily spotted on walking tours.

5 **Laeken and Schaerbeek.** Laeken is where the royal family currently lives, and you can even visit their greenhouses in spring. It's also the site of another icon of the city: the Atomium, an enormous folly built for the World's Fair that still stands the test of time. On the other hand, Schaerbeek is far humbler but has great dining and a long rail history—its train museum is a real gem.

6 **Side Trips from Brussels.** Swaddling the capital is the small province of Flemish Brabant. Here, its bustling university capital (Leuven) gives way to the scenic countryside of the Zenne Valley and Pajottenland, filled with castles (Gaasbeek) and lambic breweries (Beersel). In Tervuren, a museum confronts Belgium's colonial past, while Meise is home to a beautiful botanic garden.

Brussels is the bilingual capital with a sense of humor. Its streets are signed in French and Flemish, to *everyone's* confusion, and its most iconic landmark is a minuscule statue of a boy urinating (the Manneken Pis)—a fitting symbol for a city that delights in confounding your expectations at every turn.

This is a capital of neoclassical palaces and squares etched in gold, yet named after the swamp it was built on ("bruoc," meaning marsh; "sella" meaning dwelling). It has inspired one of the finest architects of the Art Nouveau movement, Victor Horta, as well as a series of "Brussels's Ugliest Buildings" blogs. Dig deeper, though, and you'll find not contradictions but context: a rich history that stretches back long before World War II devastated much of the capital, prompting rampant, often unchecked, postwar redevelopment. For every Habsburg emperor lavishing wealth and prestige upon the city, there was another offering only the sword.

Some of the worst of this came in 1695 when Louis XIV's French army bombarded the city for days, demolishing the Grand Place entirely. It is symptomatic of its people's resilience that it was rebuilt in just five years. Brussels has been reset like this time and again, and with each rebuild, it lost a little something but gained so much more: history.

The 18th century saw Austrian rule prop up the capital, heralding the arrival of elegant mansion houses and grand neoclassical squares like place des Martyrs. Then, after Belgium's independence (1830), a combination of the Industrial Revolution and King Leopold II's pillaging of the Congo saw fantastic wealth and artistic freedom flood the city until war stopped everything in its tracks.

These days Brussels has an undeserved reputation for being "boring"—a lazy cliché drawn from its role as HQ for the European Union. In fact, it's a vibrant melting pot, droll of humor and quick of wit. One-third of its population are non-Belgians, and its Congolese Matonge quarter and its now mostly North African Marolles area are as much fixtures on the city's tourist trail as the Grand Place. Then there's the nightlife. Beer lovers will find no complaint in Brussels's myriad city-center bars, while its restaurants serve up more than just frites.

Even if you need a rest from the bars and the museums, it's well-placed to explore the surrounding province of Flemish Brabant, where little lies more than 30 minutes' drive from the capital. Here, among the peaceful rolling hills and castles of the Zenne Valley, or the palatial grounds of Tervuren, or the friendly streets of Leuven, one of the oldest university cities in Europe, you'll find a different kind of peace. But you'll soon be drawn back.

Sure, Brussels can be contrary, but therein lies its appeal. The city's mish-mash of ideas and landscapes seems a little slapdash at first glance, but from it comes urgency. It has some of Europe's most beautiful buildings, but you often have to walk past its ugliest to find them. And in doing so, it's hard not to fall in love with it all.

MAJOR REGIONS

Belgium is divided into three autonomous regions: Dutch-speaking Flanders, French-speaking Wallonia, and **Brussels**, the capital city between the two that is both French and Dutch in language, attitude, and signage. Swaddling the metropolitan city is **Flemish Brabant**, the smallest province in Flanders and perfect for day trips from the capital. Southwest of Brussels, you'll find the farmland, forests, and rolling hills of the Zenne Valley and Pajottenland, both famous for their castles (**Gaasbeek, Beersel**) and the lambic beers brewed there. The capital of this province is the bustling university town of **Leuven**, which is just a 30-minute train ride east of Brussels, past **Tervuren** and its 19th-century expo building, which was commissioned by King Leopold II to brag of his exploits in the Congo but is now a museum on Belgium's colonial era. North of Brussels lies **Meise**, the pretty home of the National Botanic Garden.

Planning

Getting Here and Around

AIR

Flying into Brussels is many people's first sight of Belgium. However, its major airport hubs are quite far from the city center. Most land at Brussels Airport-Zaventem International, 14 km (9 miles) northeast of the city; the rest arrive at Brussels South Charleroi Airport, which caters to low-budget inter-European and North African flights and is around 60 km (37 miles) south of town.

CONTACTS Brussels Airport. ✉ *Leopoldlaan, Zaventem* ☎ *070/232–000* 🌐 *www.brusselsairport.be*. **Brussels South Charleroi Airport.** ✉ *Rue des Frères Wright 8, Charleroi* ☎ *09/020–2490* 🌐 *www.charleroi-airport.com*.

AIRPORT TRANSFERS

Trains run up to six times an hour from Brussels Airport to the city center, taking around 20 minutes. A one-way train ticket costs €9.20. Alternatively, De Lijn (Nos. 272, 471) and STIB buses (No. 12) to the center leave from Level 0. These cost from €2.40 but take around 50 minutes; tickets can be bought from Go machines on the platform. Taxis cost around €45 to the center of Brussels.

A shuttle bus operated by FlibCo runs every half hour between Brussels-Midi Railway Station and Brussels South Charleroi Airport for €14.70, taking 55 minutes. Alternatively, a local bus system connects the airport to Charleroi Sud railway station, which has rail connections to Brussels taking one hour (€9.70).

CONTACTS Flibco. ☎ *070/211–210* 🌐 *www.flibco.com/en*.

BICYCLES AND E-SCOOTERS

Like many cities, Brussels and its suburbs have been invaded by scooter and bike-share schemes; just download the appropriate app to unlock the ride. The city center is quite small, and it's a quick and easy way to get around. Lime and Dott are the two most widespread e-scooter operators, costing €1 to unlock and then a further €0.17 and €0.22 per minute, respectively. The city bike scheme is Villo (*www.villo.be*), for which a €1.65 day ticket gives you the first 30 minutes of each ride for free.

BUS

When traveling intercity, European bus company FlixBus operates services between Brussels, Bruges, Hasselt,

Liège, and Antwerp from €4 one-way, but the train is always nearly twice as fast. FlixBus stops are at Midi/Zuid and Nord/Noord railway stations depending on your destination. Both Eurolines and FlixBus run services from Brussels to European cities outside Belgium, including Amsterdam, Cologne, London, Paris, and Luxembourg.

CONTACTS Eurolines. ☎ *69971/944-836* 🌐 *www.eurolines.de.* **Flixbus.** ☎ *30300/137–300* 🌐 *global.flixbus.com.*

CAR

Driving within Brussels can be an unnerving experience. Belgians weren't required to have driver's licenses until 1979, and those who are learning now are allowed to practice without chaperones for a limited period. Add to the difficulties trams and priority signs, which seem to change at every intersection, and you have a 3D ever-changing puzzle. It also gets very busy around peak hours. If you can, it's easier and far faster to take public transport in the city, as most roads are limited to a 30-kph speed limit.

PUBLIC TRANSPORT

Brussels has an extensive network of reasonably priced bus, tram, and metro services operated by STIB/MIVB; De Lijn run buses from the capital to the surrounding province of Flemish Brabant. Bus, tram, and metro rides can be paid for using a prepaid MoBIB card, which can be bought at stations, kiosks, and ticket machines for €5. A single fare is €2.40 for STIB/MIVB services; a discounted 10 journeys can be bought for €15.

Most areas of the city can be reached on Lines 1, 2, and 6 of the metro system. De Brouckère is the main stop for the city center, but note that each station has both a French and Dutch name; for example, Arts Loi is also Kunst Wet. STIB/MIVB tickets are valid for its services only and tickets can no longer be bought on board buses and trams. If taking a De Lijn bus service, you will need to buy a ticket (€2.50) from De Lijn Go terminal or online in advance.

CONTACTS STIB/MIVB. ☎ *070/23–20–00* 🌐 *www.stib.be.* **De Lijn.** ☎ *070/22–02–00* 🌐 *www.delijn.be/en.*

TAXIS AND RIDESHARE

You can catch a taxi at cab stands around town, indicated with yellow signs. All officially registered taxis have black bodywork and a mango-yellow checkered strip. The price starts at around €2.40 during the day and €4.20 at night, then goes up €1.80 per km within the city limits; €2.70 per km outside the city. Alternatively, despite repeated attempts to have it banned, Uber still operates here. Do check beforehand, though, as this situation seems to change quite regularly.

CONTACTS Taxi Verts. ☎ *02/349–4949* 🌐 *taxisverts.be/en.*

TRAIN

Brussels has three main railway stations, each with names in both French and Dutch: Bruxelles-Midi/Brussel Zuid in Saint-Gilles, Bruxelles-Central/Brussel Centraal in Lower Town, and Bruxelles-Nord/Brussel Noord in Schaerbeek.

An expanding network of high-speed trains puts Brussels within commuting distance of many European cities, with Eurostar connections to Paris, London, and Amsterdam, and Thalys trains adding Cologne to that trio. Most of these services leave from the Midi/Zuid station, which is well linked by metro services.

The easiest mode of transportation within Belgium is also by rail. Belgian National Railways (SNCB/NMBS) maintains an extensive network of prompt and frequent services. Intercity (IC) trains have rapid connections between the major towns and cities, while local and regional trains stop at smaller towns in between.

CONTACTS NMBS/SNCB. ☎ *02/528–2828* 🌐 *www.belgiantrain.be/en.* **Eurostar.**

✉ *Brussels* ☎ *02/400–6731* 🌐 *www.eurostar.com/be-en.* **Thalys.** ☎ *070/667–788* 🌐 *www.thalys.com/be/en.*

Hotels

Hotels in the capital range greatly in style, but most are geared toward business travelers. That's the oddity of Brussels: hotel prices actually drop on the weekends because their trade is primarily in businesspeople and politicos arriving during the week. Come Friday and Saturday night, most have departed, making the capital an affordable weekend getaway for many. As such, its regular clientele means service is usually a cut above most cities in Belgium (unlike restaurants, which are infamously brusque in the capital). Breakfast is typically included in the price and tipping is not expected. Those stays closer to the center are uniformly more expensive, but you'll find a good choice of hotels.

Prices below are for high season; hotels tend to be cheaper on weekends.

Hotel reviews have been shortened. For full information, visit Fodors.com.

What It Costs in Euros

$	$$	$$$	$$$$
FOR TWO PEOPLE			
under €100	€100–€150	€151–€220	Over €220

Nightlife

Brussels isn't best known for its late-night dance scene, and what few clubs there are tend to be scattered across the city, not in one area. Most music venues have also been driven out of the center in recent years, with nightlife here tending to revolve more around bars, which exist on every street and seemingly compete to have an ever-wider selection of beers. You'll find some of the best drinking dens in Europe here, slinging thousands of different Belgian beers, including the local lambic brews which are only made in Brussels and the surrounding area of Flemish Brabant. Accompanying these are a number of fine cocktail bars, specialist pubs that serve only *jenever* (Dutch gin), and a growing batch of natural wine bars, with a dozen cropping up in the last decade alone.

Performing Arts

The heart of the city's cultural arts world is the BOZAR (a corruption of "Beaux-arts") in Parc, a venue that hosts theater, concerts, and a series of art galleries. Nearby is also the Royal Parc Theatre, which is the center for theater performances in the capital. Elsewhere, you'll find the Brussels Philharmonic more regularly at its home at Studio 4 in Flagey. Alternatively, the Cirque Royal (where the city's circus used to be) on rue de l'Enseignement hosts an array of comics, theater, dance, and musicals. For bands and pop shows, Botanique (in a rusting old botanical garden), Flagey, Beursschouwburg, and Ancienne Belgique are the main venues, with Palais 12 at the Heysel Expo hosting the larger shows.

MAJOR EVENTS

Brussels Summer Festival. Big annual pop and rock music festival at place des Palais in August. 🌐 *bsf.be*

Brussels Jazz Festival. This celebration of jazz usually takes place in Flagey in January. 🌐 *www.flagey.be*

Kunstenfestivaldesarts. Theater, performance, dance, film, and visual arts performances spanning the city in May. 🌐 *kfda.be*

Classissimo! Yearly classical music series at the Royal Parc Theatre over the summer. 🌐 *www.classissimo.brussels*

TICKETS

Ticketmaster Belgium and Fnac are usually the best place to get tickets for the bigger gigs. Alternatively, Agenda Brussels is operated by the tourism board and sells tickets for a number of city concerts, events, and tours.

CONTACTS Ticketmaster Belgium. 🌐 *www.ticketmaster.be*. **Agenda Brussels.** 🌐 *agenda.brussels*. **FNAC.** ✉ *Brussels* 🌐 *www.fnactickets.be*.

Restaurants

Prices are per person for a main course at dinner, or if dinner is not served, at lunch.

Restaurant reviews have been shortened. For full information, visit Fodors.com.

What It Costs in Euros			
$	**$$**	**$$$**	**$$$$**
AT DINNER			
under €12	€12–€22	€23–€30	over €30

Brussels has an array of fine places to eat, ranging from Michelin-starred blowouts to tiny frites stalls that inspire such loyalty among locals that there is nothing guaranteed to start an argument faster than declaring your favorite. In between are a wealth of *estaminets* (café-bars) that sling classic Belgian staples, such as *boulettes* (meatballs), sole meunière, *carbonnade/stoofvlees* (beer stews), *paling in't groen* (eel in green sauce), gray-shrimp croquettes, and *americain* (a local take on steak tartare). Many also have fine beer selections and even use local lambic brews in their cooking. The more expensive restaurants typically offer a good deal at lunchtimes, where prix-fixe deals provide a taste of the chef's skills at half the usual price. Midweek can see spaces fill up fast though, so it's best to book.

Shopping

Shopping is everywhere here, and the main commercial artery of **rue Neuve** is home to the biggest collection of high-street brands. Also, drop by the **Galeries Royales Saint-Hubert**, near the Grand Place, if only to gaze at this beautiful mid-18th-century shopping arcade. For those with richer tastes, **rue Antoine Dansaert** is host to the city's best-known indie fashion boutiques, while the boulevards of **Waterloo** and **Louise** are where the bulk of the big fashion brands have made their stand. Everywhere are endless niches, with **rue au Buerre** ("street of butter") home to a wonderful cluster of chocolate shops, a number of small indie boutiques just next to Louise in the **Châtelain** area, while the **Marolles** is home to a regular flea market with antiques and vintage shops littering the **rue Haute** that leads up to it.

Tours

Architecture, beer, and chocolate make up the bulk of most city tours.

THEME TOURS

Arau

SPECIAL-INTEREST TOURS | A number of interesting tours that look at the city in different ways. Perhaps the most interesting is the Art Nouveau walk, which peers into the capital's turn-of-the-century houses. Walks are held intermittently; private tours can be booked any time. ☎ *02/219–3345* 🌐 *www.arau.org*.

Groovy Brussels

SPECIAL-INTEREST TOURS | Choose between tours strolling the chocolate shops of the city or more general cycling trips that blast through the big sights in 3½ hours. ☎ *0484/898–936* 🌐 *www.groovybrussels.com* 🎫 *From €35*.

Legends of Brussels

SPECIAL-INTEREST TOURS | Both historic walking tours (albeit with a chocolate tasting) and beer-tasting tours are available. Groups meet at the Grand Place. ☎ *0472/487–970* 🌐 *www.legendsofbrussels.com* 🎫 *From €20.*

Visitor Information

CONTACTS Brussels Tourist Information. ✉ *Grand Place, Lower Town* ☎ *02/513–8940* 🌐 *visit.brussels/en* Ⓜ *Metro: De Brouckère.*

When to Go

High season is quite nebulous here. There's never really a huge influx of visitors, though summer (July and August) certainly sees more people on the terraces and streets. The sheer amount of business travelers means there's a constant churn year-round, and it's more on the weekends that you notice the drop-off. Having said that, the shoulder months (April, September, and October) are certainly far from busy, and while winter might see much of the city turned into one giant market, Brussels doesn't have the chocolate-box allure of, say, Bruges or Ghent.

A cloudy day in Brussels certainly has more than 50 shades of gray. In winter, the clouds seem to press in all around but it never drops too low in terms of temperature, with an average of around 44°F at this time. Summer tops 70°F and sees locals spilling onto the bar terraces and parks en masse and makes this very social city seem perpetually good-humored.

Discounts and Deals

The Brussels Card give you free entry to 49 museums and discounts at various attractions for up to one (€29), two (€37), and three (€45) days, as well as the option of adding free public transport (from €8 extra; except airport transfers) and unlimited access to the "hop on, hop off" tourist buses (from €18 extra).

Lower Town

The center of Brussels is divided into the bustling Lower Town and the aristocratic Upper Town, which sits atop the Mont des Arts. By the 14th century, the former had become a thriving marketplace, still evident in the street names that spider out from the center. Here you'll find the likes of rue du Marché au Fromage, where the cheese makers set out their stalls, and you can imagine the feathers flying on rue du Marché aux Poulets (chicken-market street).

By the 15th century, what was once a covered market began its slow transformation into one of the world's most beguiling squares. Since then, the Grand Place has witnessed Protestant martyrs burned by the Inquisition, weathered almost complete destruction by the French army in 1695, and seen the German flag hoisted atop its Town Hall in 1914. Yet it is still the heartbeat of the city, and most visitors end up passing through it time and again, or cracking open a beer while watching the evening light show glint off its elegant gilded facades.

Sights

★ **Centre Belge de la Bande Dessinée** (*Comics Art Museum*)
ART MUSEUM | **FAMILY** | It fell to the land of Tintin to create the world's first museum dedicated to the ninth art—comic strips. While comics have often struggled for artistic recognition, they have been taken seriously in Belgium for decades. In the Belgian Comic Strip Center, they are wedded to another strongly Belgian art form: Art Nouveau. Based in an elegant 1903 Victor Horta–designed building, the museum is long on the history of the genre, if a little short on kid-friendly

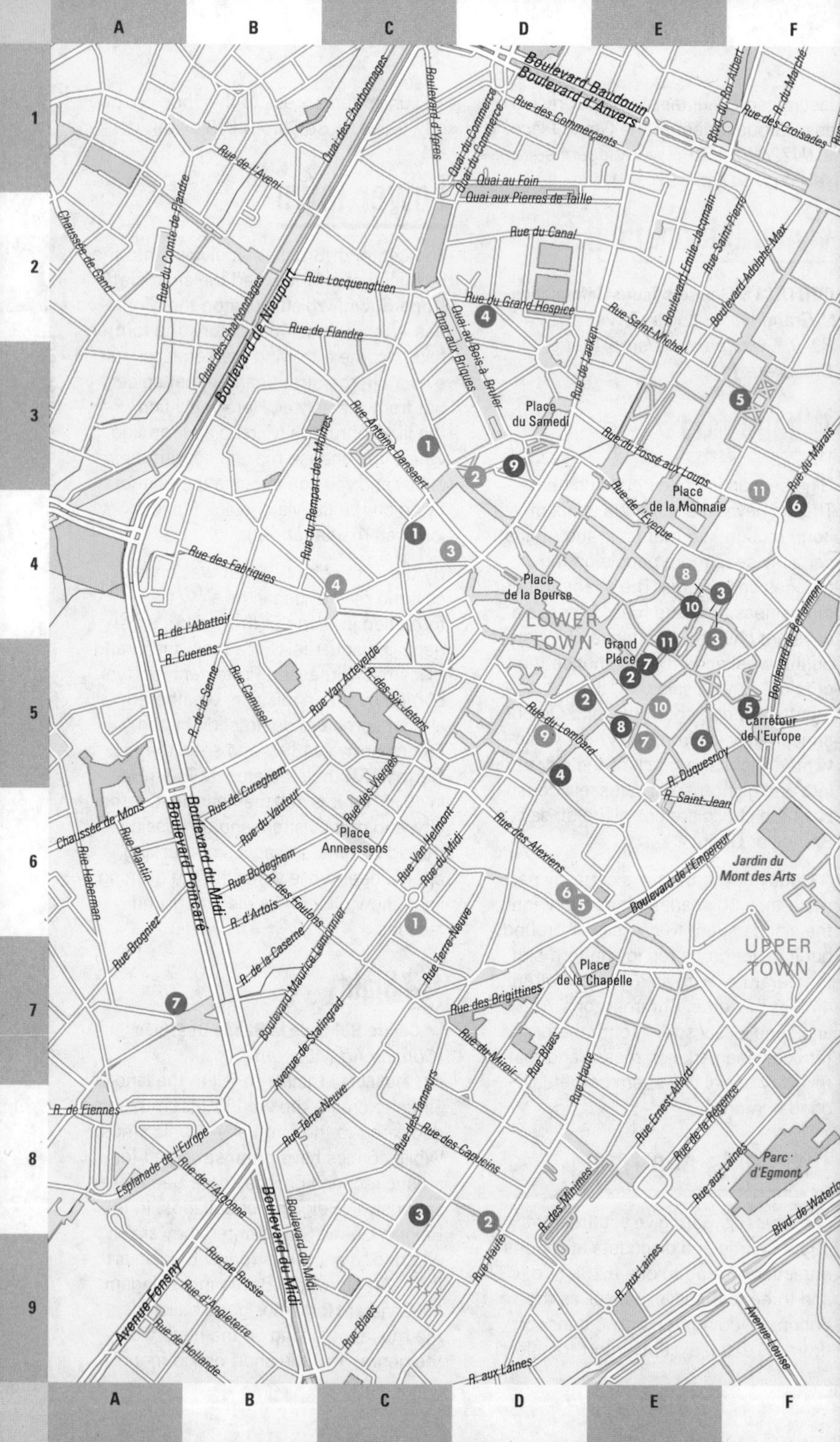

A
B
C
D
E
F
1
2
3
4
5
6
7
8
9
Boulevard Baudouin
Boulevard d'Anvers
Rue des Commerçants
Blvd. du Roi Albert
R. du Marché
Rue des Croisades
Quai des Charbonnages
Boulevard d'Ypres
Quai du Commerce
Quai au Foin
Quai aux Pierres de Taille
Rue de l'Aveni
Chaussée de Gand
Rue du Comte de Flandre
Rue du Canal
Rue Locquenghien
Rue du Grand Hospice
Quai aux Briques
Quai au Bois-à-Brûler
Rue de Flandre
Boulevard de Nieuport
Rue Saint-Michel
Boulevard Emile-Jacqmain
Rue Saint-Pierre
Boulevard Adolphe-Max
Rue de Laeken
Place du Samedi
Rue Antoine-Dansaert
Rue du Rempart des Moines
Rue du Fossé aux Loups
Rue de l'Évêque
Place de la Monnaie
Rue du Marais
Rue des Fabriques
Place de la Bourse
LOWER TOWN
Grand Place
Boulevard de Berlaimont
R. de l'Abattoir
R. Guerens
Rue Van Artevelde
R. des Six Jetons
R. de la Senne
Rue Camusel
Rue du Lombard
Carrefour de l'Europe
R. Duquesnoy
R. Saint-Jean
Rue de Cureghem
Rue du Vautour
Rue des Vierges
Chaussée de Mons
Rue Plantin
Rue Haberman
Boulevard du Midi
Boulevard Poincaré
Place Anneessens
Rue Van Helmont
Rue du Midi
Rue des Alexiens
Boulevard de l'Empereur
Jardin du Mont des Arts
Rue Bodeghem
R. des Foulons
R. d'Artois
Rue Brogniez
R. de la Caserne
Boulevard Maurice Lemonnier
Rue Terre-Neuve
UPPER TOWN
Place de la Chapelle
Rue des Brigittines
Avenue de Stalingrad
Rue du Miroir
Rue Blaes
Rue Haute
R. de Fiennes
Rue des Tanneurs
Rue Ernest-Allard
Rue de la Régence
Esplanade de l'Europe
Rue de l'Argonne
Rue des Capucins
Rue aux Laines
Parc d'Egmont
R. des Minimes
Blvd. de Waterloo
Avenue Fonsny
Rue de Russie
Rue d'Angleterre
Rue de Hollande
R. aux Laines
Avenue Louise

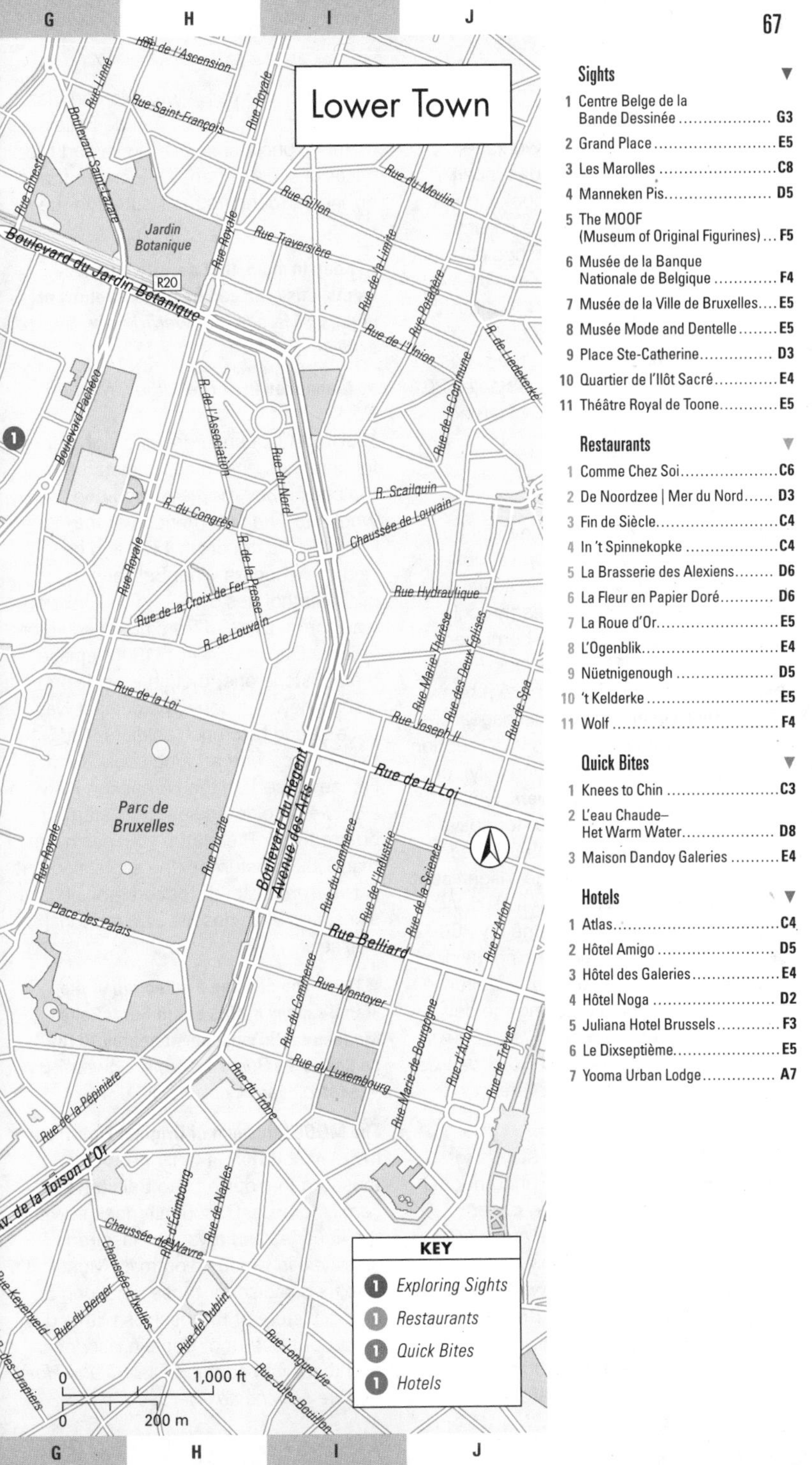

Sights

1. Centre Belge de la Bande Dessinée G3
2. Grand Place E5
3. Les Marolles C8
4. Manneken Pis.......................... D5
5. The MOOF (Museum of Original Figurines) ... F5
6. Musée de la Banque Nationale de Belgique F4
7. Musée de la Ville de Bruxelles.... E5
8. Musée Mode and Dentelle........ E5
9. Place Ste-Catherine............... D3
10. Quartier de l'Illôt Sacré............ E4
11. Théâtre Royal de Toone............ E5

Restaurants

1. Comme Chez Soi.................... C6
2. De Noordzee | Mer du Nord...... D3
3. Fin de Siècle......................... C4
4. In 't Spinnekopke C4
5. La Brasserie des Alexiens........ D6
6. La Fleur en Papier Doré........... D6
7. La Roue d'Or.......................... E5
8. L'Ogenblik............................. E4
9. Nüetnigenough D5
10. 't Kelderke E5
11. Wolf F4

Quick Bites

1. Knees to Chin C3
2. L'eau Chaude– Het Warm Water.................. D8
3. Maison Dandoy Galeries E4

Hotels

1. Atlas...................................... C4
2. Hôtel Amigo D5
3. Hôtel des Galeries................... E4
4. Hôtel Noga D2
5. Juliana Hotel Brussels............ F3
6. Le Dixseptième....................... E5
7. Yooma Urban Lodge............... A7

interaction. In addition to Tintin, the collection includes more than 400 original plates and 25,000 cartoon works. A library and brasserie are added incentives, but best of all is the bookshop, which sells a comprehensive collection of graphic novels and comic books, albeit largely in French or Dutch. Keep an eye out for the **comic-strip murals** that dot the city; walking maps showing the location of each one can be found at the tourist information office. ✉ *Rue des Sables 20, Lower Town* ☎ *02/219–1980* 🌐 *www.comicscenter.net* 🎫 *€10* Ⓜ *Metro: Gare Centrale.*

★ Grand Place

PLAZA/SQUARE | **FAMILY** | This jewelry box of a square is arguably Europe's most ornate and theatrical. It's also a vital part of the city—everyone passes through at some point. At night, the burnished facades of the guild houses look especially dramatic. Try to make it here for the **Ommegang**, a historical pageant re-creating Emperor Charles V's reception in the city in 1549 (in June and July), or for the famed **Carpet of Flowers,** which fills the square with color for four days in mid-August on even-numbered years. Dominating the square is the magnificent Gothic-era **Hôtel de Ville** (Town Hall). Work began on it in 1402, and it's nearly 300 years older than the surrounding guild houses. The belfry is topped by a bronze statue of St. Michael crushing the devil beneath his feet. ✉ *Grand Place, Lower Town* 🌐 *agenda.brussels* 🎫 *Hôtel de Ville tour: €8* Ⓜ *Metro: De Brouckère.*

★ Les Marolles

MARKET | If the Grand Place stands for old money, the Marolles neighborhood stands for old—and current—poverty. Times are changing, but the area still has some raffish charm. This was once home to the poor workers who produced the luxury goods for which Brussels was famous. As that industry faded, immigrants, mostly from North Africa and Turkey, made homes here. The hugely popular daily Vieux Marché (flea market) at the place du Jeu de Balle sells clothing, bric-a-brac, plain junk, and the occasional gem. Trendy shops are found on the surrounding rue Haute and rue Blaes.

⚠ **Keep in mind, that despite improvements, this area can be pretty sketchy at night.** ✉ *Marolles, Lower Town* Ⓜ *Metro: Louise.*

★ Manneken Pis (*The Little Urinating Boy*)

PUBLIC ART | Despite drawing sightseers for centuries, the minuscule statue of the peeing boy may leave you underwhelmed. The first mention of the Manneken dates from 1377, and he's said to symbolize what Belgians think of the authorities. The "original" version was commissioned from noted sculptor Jerome Duquesnoy in 1619 to replace the old stone one, though what is on display now is a copy. The original was once seized by French soldiers, and to quell local unrest, King Louis XV of France presented the Manneken Pis with a gold-embroidered suit, thus starting a bizarre trend. The statue now has more than 1,000 costumes (the safe-sex outfit is truly remarkable!) for ceremonial occasions, and even has his own personal dresser.

■ **TIP→ You can see a selection of the statue's many outfits at the GardeRobe Manneken Pis museum at nearby 19 rue du Chêne.** ✉ *Rue du Chêne, Lower Town* Ⓜ *Metro: Gare Centrale.*

The MOOF (Museum of Original Figurines)

OTHER ATTRACTION | **FAMILY** | Another museum that delves into Belgium's comic-book past, though it does so via the figurines and toys they inspired, displayed in various dioramas. Mostly, it's a selfie-paradise for those who long to have a picture of themselves with a giant Smurf or a cutout of Captain Haddock. And that's no bad thing. ✉ *Galerie Horta, Rue Marché-aux-Herbes 116, Lower*

Immerse yourself in the world of Tintin and the Smurfs at the Comics Arts Museum, which boasts 25,000 cartoon works.

Town ☎ *02/207–7992* 🌐 *www.moofmuseum.be* 🎫 *€12* ⏲ *Closed Mon.–Thurs. Jan.–Mar.; Apr.–June and Sept.–Dec.* Ⓜ *Metro: Gare Centrale.*

Musée de la Banque Nationale de Belgique (*Museum of the National Bank of Belgium*)
HISTORY MUSEUM | The irony of a museum about the means of payment being free to visit is lost on no one. It also doesn't stop this being one of the surprise joys of the Brussels museum scene. Exhibits unravel different concepts of money throughout history, from Mesopotamian clay tablets to why you need a moko drum to buy a house on the Indonesian island of Alor. ✉ *Rue Montagne aux Herbes, Lower Town* ☎ *02/221–2206* 🌐 *www.nbbmuseum.be* 🎫 *Free* ⏲ *Closed weekends* Ⓜ *Metro: Sainte-Catherine.*

Musée de la Ville de Bruxelles (*Brussels City Museum*)
HISTORY MUSEUM | **FAMILY** | No ruler ever lived in the 16th-century Maison du Roi (House of the King); instead, it housed Charles V's administrative offices, built on the site of Brussels's old covered marketplace. Then, in the 19th century, it was given a neo-Gothic makeover—all brooding spires and arches. Today, it houses the City Museum, which boasts some fine tapestries and paintings, notably the *Marriage Procession* by Pieter Bruegel the Elder. You can also see the "original" (1619 version) Mannekin Pis and an impressive 15th-century weather vane that used to top the town hall. ✉ *Maison du Roi, Grand Place, Lower Town* ☎ *02/279–4350* 🌐 *www.brusselscitymuseum.brussels* 🎫 *€8* ⏲ *Closed Mon.* Ⓜ *Metro: De Brouckère.*

Musée Mode and Dentelle (*Museum of Fashion and Lace*)
OTHER MUSEUM | The costume and lace museum pays tribute to Brussels' textile-making past. Housed in four 17th-century houses and a warehouse, the museum is something of a 17th- to 18th-century fashion show, with accessories, embroidery, and clothes on display, many featuring the delicate lace

No trip to Brussels is complete without seeing the Manneken Pis statue, said to symbolize what Belgians think of the authorities.

for which the city once became famous. ✉ *Rue de la Violette 12, Lower Town* ☏ *02/213–4450* 🌐 *www.fashionandlace-museum.brussels* 🎟 *€8* ⏲ *Closed Mon.* Ⓜ *Metro: De Brouckère.*

Place Ste-Catherine

PLAZA/SQUARE | If you find the Grand Place overrun by tourists, come to this square/market, a favorite among locals, who come to shop for necessities and banter with fishmongers (Thursday–Saturday 7–5; Wednesday organic market 7:30–3). At night, the square often has a mobile bar, while the fishmonger serves great seafood (see Restaurants). In the evening the action moves to the old **Vismet** (fish market), which branches off from the Eglise de Ste-Catherine. A canal used to run through here; it's now reduced to a couple of elongated ponds, but both sides are lined with seafood restaurants, some excellent, many of them overpriced. In good weather, there's waterside dining. ✉ *Pl. Ste-Catherine, Lower Town* Ⓜ *Metro: Ste-Catherine.*

Quartier de l'Ilôt Sacré (*small sacred island neighborhood*)

NEIGHBORHOOD | Many streets in central Brussels were widened as part of the preparations for the 1958 World's Fair, but the narrow rue des Bouchers and even narrower Petite rue des Bouchers escaped being demolished after locals complained. The area was given special protection in 1959. As long as you watch out for pickpockets, it's all good-natured fun in one of the livelier areas of the center, where restaurants and cafés stand cheek by jowl, their tables spilling out onto the sidewalks. They often make strenuous efforts to pull you in with huge displays of seafood and game, though the effort they put into the food itself is not as impressive. Stick to the traditionally reliable Aux Armes de Bruxelles (rue des Bouchers 13) and you won't go wrong. ✉ *Rue des Bouchers, Brussels* 🌐 *www.ilotsacre.be* Ⓜ *Metro: Gare Centrale.*

★ Théâtre Royal de Toone
PERFORMANCE VENUE | This marionette theater troupe has been going for eight generations, performing plays in the old Brusseleir dialect with hefty doses of local humor and innuendo. It's suitable for kids, though, and even if your French isn't up to scratch, there's fun to be had just looking around. Plays last two hours (including intermission) and are held on Thursday, Friday, and Saturday (twice). These range from "puppet" *Hamlet* and *Faust* to *The Passion*, with tickets sold just before each show. Alternatively, many people come just for the quirky downstairs bar, Toone (Tuesday–Sunday, noon–midnight), which is locally famous in its own right and is scattered with marionettes and memorabilia. ✉ *Impasse Ste-Pétronille, 66 rue du Marché aux Herbes, Lower Town* ☎ *02/513–5486* 🌐 *www.toone.be* 🎫 *€12* Ⓜ *Metro: De Brouckère.*

Restaurants

★ Comme Chez Soi
$$$$ | **FRENCH** | With superb cuisine, excellent wines, and attentive service, this two-star Michelin restaurant remains a regal choice, with an interior (and prices) to match. Lionel Rigolet, who took over the reins as chef from his father-in-law Pierre Wynants in 2006, is a ceaselessly inventive character with one foot in tradition, dishing up elegant racks of veal dashed with sweetbreads or cockerel breasts crowned with crayfish. **Known for:** an excellent, and often surprising, wine list; very busy—book before you step on the plane, let alone through the door; sumptuous cooking from a genuine star of the Belgian dining scene. $ *Average main: €53* ✉ *Pl. Rouppe 23, Lower Town* ☎ *02/512–2921* 🌐 *www.commechezsoi.be* ⏲ *Closed Sun.–Tues.* 👔 *Jacket and tie* Ⓜ *Metro: Anneessens.*

★ De Noordzee | Mer du Nord
$$ | **SEAFOOD** | What was once just a friendly fishmongers has evolved into one of the city's best, and most unexpected, street-food stops. It's set on place Ste-Catherine, which has been revitalized as the home of all things seafood, and visitors queue up at the counter outside, place an order, then grab it from the window when called. **Known for:** heavenly shrimp croquettes; the freshest seafood in Brussels; bargain prices. $ *Average main: €14* ✉ *Pl. Ste-Catherine 50, Lower Town* ☎ *02/513–1192* 🌐 *noordzeemer-dunord.be* ⏲ *Closed Mon.* Ⓜ *Metro: Ste-Catherine.*

Fin de Siècle
$$ | **BELGIAN** | Despite its minimal signage, Fin de Siècle holds to that peculiarly obstinate breed of restaurant that flourishes despite itself. Its brown interior, big communal tables, and hearty cooking—stews smothered in beer-infused gravy, sausages atop heaving mountains of *stoempe* mash, and the odd North African influence—has ensured a healthy popularity and lively spirit. **Known for:** generous portions; old-fashioned Flemish cooking in a traditional brown café; a great draft beer selection. $ *Average main: €17* ✉ *Rue des Chartreux 9, Lower Town* ☎ *02/732–7434* 🌐 *www.findesiecle.be* Ⓜ *Tram: Bourse.*

★ In 't Spinnekopke
$$ | **BELGIAN** | True Flemish cooking flourishes in this reliable old favorite. The low ceilings and benches around the walls remain from its days as a coaching inn during the 18th century, and little has changed since—including the menu. **Known for:** Belgium-size portions; incredible selection of Belgian gueuze (fruity and bitter) beers; great, old-fashioned Flemish cooking, with stews aplenty. $ *Average main: €20* ✉ *Pl. du Jardin aux Fleurs 1, Lower Town* ☎ *02/512–9205* 🌐 *spinnekopke.be* ⏲ *Closed Sun. and Mon.* Ⓜ *Metro: De Brouckere.*

La Brasserie des Alexiens
$$ | **BELGIAN** | A new restaurant that elevates the more traditional brasserie fare, proving there is a life beyond

carbonnades and meatballs (though they do a highly passable version of both). Chef Alex Cardoso, who made his name with the equally impressive Caves des Alex in Ixelles, embraces the kind of dishes that La Roue d'Or made its name on: here you'll find ox tongue in Madeira sauce and veal kidney in mustard sauce alongside the usual stewy Belgian hits. **Known for:** good-value dining; a chance to taste more old-school Belgian dishes; a pretty space—all red brick, green walls, and oak floors. *Average main: €20 ✉ Rue des Alexiens 63, Laeken ☎ 02/387–4769 🌐 www.brasseriedesalexiens.be ⏲ Closed Sun. and Mon. No lunch Sat. Ⓜ Bus: 52.*

La Fleur en Papier Doré

$$ | **BELGIAN** | From Magritte to Hergé, this convent-turned-estaminet was once a regular meeting point for Brussels's art elite—photos and doodles (traded for booze) are found everywhere. It went out of business in 2006, only to be rescued by the community regulars that adore it, and little has changed. **Known for:** menu packed with hearty Flemish fare; local icon with a colorful history (literally) writ large across its walls; excellent range of beers. *Average main: €18 ✉ Rue des Alexiens 53, Lower Town ☎ 02/511–1659 🌐 www.goudblommekeinpapier.be ⏲ Closed Sun. and Mon. Ⓜ Tram: 3, 4.*

La Roue d'Or

$$$ | **BELGIAN** | Bright orange and yellow murals pay humorous homage to the Surrealist René Magritte in this well-known Art Nouveau brasserie. Below these, brass plaques record the names of respected customers and famous diners gone by. **Known for:** bizarre decor inspired by the city's Surrealist artists; a cultured escape from the crowds of the Grand Place; reliably good food in an old-fashioned Belgian brasserie. *Average main: €24 ✉ Rue des Chapeliers 26, Lower Town ☎ 02/514–2554 ⏲ Closed Tues. Ⓜ Metro: Gare Centrale.*

L'Ogenblik

$$$ | **FRENCH** | This split-level restaurant, on a side alley off the Galeries Royales Saint-Hubert, has all the trappings of an old-time bistro: green-shaded lamps over marble-top tables, a forest's worth of dark wood paneling, and laid-back waiters. There's nothing casual about the French-style cuisine, however: grilled sweetbreads with baked courgettes, mille-feuille of crayfish and salmon with a puree of langoustines, and saddle of lamb with spring vegetables and potato gratin. **Known for:** it fills up fast, so book early; good for seafood; traditional-style bistro dishes, just a short walk from the city center. *Average main: €30 ✉ Galerie des Princes 1, Lower Town ☎ 02/511–6151 🌐 www.ogenblik.be ⏲ Closed Sun. and Mon. Ⓜ Metro: De Brouckère.*

★ Nüetnigenough

$$ | **BELGIAN** | This tiny, modest, well-executed Flemish restaurant with a superb beer menu was quite the hit when it opened. The brasserie is named after the Dutch phrase for those who "can't get enough," and the city voted with its feet. **Known for:** it's still got that hip factor; beer-drenched stews to die for; a fine selection of lambic and local brews, with some rare finds. *Average main: €14 ✉ Rue du Lombard 25, Lower Town 🌐 www.nuetnigenough.be ⏲ No lunch weekdays Ⓜ Tram: 4.*

't Kelderke

$$ | **BELGIAN** | **FAMILY** | Head down into this 17th-century vaulted cellar restaurant (watch out for the low door frame) for traditional Belgian cuisine served at plain wooden tables. Mussels are the house specialty, but the *stoemp et saucisses* (mashed potatoes and sausages) are equally tasty. **Known for:** its rather touristy vibe, but don't be put off; its atmospheric underground setting in the center of town; a solid entry for sampling some Belgian classics. *Average main: €19 ✉ Grand Place 15, Lower Town*

☎ 02/513–7344 🌐 *restaurant-het-kelderke.be/en* Ⓜ *Metro: De Brouckère.*

Wolf

$$ | **FAST FOOD** | Choice is the appeal here. Set in a 1940s bank building famed for its bronze doors, this dizzying food court brings together some of the better street food joints and former pop-ups in the city, ranging from the excellent Syrian restaurant My Tannour (all flatbreads, falafel, and veggies), to the healthy bowls of Hygge, and the Vietnamese-style noodle soups of Hanoi Station. **Known for:** there's so much to choose from—pick a starter, main, and dessert at different places; it's a great way to sample some of the city's restaurants in one place; the atmosphere is always pretty lively. $ *Average main: €14* ✉ *Rue du Fossé aux Loups 50, Lower Town* 🌐 *www.wolf.brussels* Ⓜ *Metro: De Brouckère.*

Coffee and Quick Bites

Knees to Chin

$ | **VIETNAMESE** | Spring rolls are the specialty at this über-popular fast-food café beloved by local office workers, though the fillings are hardly traditional: meat loaf, crispy bacon and avocado, caramelized tofu. There are a few locations in the city now (the original opened in Saint-Gilles), but this is the perfect snack stop for shoppers on rue Antoine Dansaert. **Known for:** it's a nice cheap snack; the coco-egg omelet wrap is heaven-sent; nice baos and rice bowls. $ *Average main: €10* ✉ *Rue de Flandre 28, Lower Town* ☎ *02/503–1831* 🌐 *www.kneestochin.com* ⏲ *Closed Sun.* Ⓜ *Metro: Ste–Catherine.*

L'eau Chaude - Het Warm Water

$ | **VEGETARIAN** | Located just above the place de Jeu de Balle in the heart of the Marolles area, this café is a local institution—legend has it that residents would come to fill their buckets full of hot water in times of need, hence the name. In 2014, its closure was imminent, but locals stepped in and reopened it as a social cooperative with an organic canteen dishing up hearty lunches and a dish of the day (11–4). **Known for:** sustainable produce sourced locally; a genuine local spirit, and some fierce political debate (on the right night); organic vegetarian cooking. $ *Average main: €10* ✉ *Rue des Renards 25, Lower Town* ☎ *02/213–9159* ▭ *No credit cards* ⏲ *Closed Mon.* Ⓜ *Metro: Porte de Hal.*

Maison Dandoy Galeries

$ | **CAFÉ** | It's a little touristy, but worth it if you've got a sweet tooth. Set within the beautiful old Galeries Royales Saint-Hubert, this rather distinguished tearoom is a fine spot to indulge in waffles and this famous old brand's speculoos cookies. **Known for:** those waffles are worth the wait; iconic Belgian speculoos treats and afternoon tea; the shopping center is a beautiful spot to rest up. $ *Average main: €8* ✉ *Les Galeries Royales Saint-Hubert, Lower Town* ☎ *02/669–5212* 🌐 *maisondandoy.com* Ⓜ *Metro: De Brouckère.*

Hotels

Atlas

$ | **HOTEL** | This hotel offers unpretentious comfort in a pleasant 18th-century building and a convenient base in Ste-Catherine, an area blessed with myriad fashionable boutiques, no end of interesting places to eat, and not a lot of accommodation. **Pros:** rooms are a good size; cheap for where it is; convenient location and on-site parking (€17). **Cons:** breakfasts offer little choice; a little worn in parts; no-frills rooms and standard decor throughout. $ *Rooms from: €99* ✉ *Rue du Vieux Marché aux Grains 30, Lower Town* ☎ *02/502–6006* 🌐 *www.atlas-hotel.be* *88 rooms* 🍽 *Free Breakfast* Ⓜ *Metro: Ste-Catherine.*

★ **Hôtel Amigo**

$$$$ | **HOTEL** | Location, charm, and history are Amigo's stock in trade—the

15th-century site was once a prison, and it's said Belgium's then Spanish occupiers mistook the word "vrunt" (prison) for "vriend" (friend), hence the name. **Pros:** a block from the Grand Place; polished service and faultless concierge; historical charm—the old 17th-century flagstones are still in place. **Cons:** private parking is extortionate (€40); nearby streets can be noisy; it's not cheap; in fact, it's eye-wateringly expensive. *Rooms from: €294* *Rue d'Amigo 1–3, Lower Town* *02/547–4747* *www.roccofortehotels.com* *154 rooms* *No Meals* *Metro: De Brouckère.*

★ Hôtel des Galeries

$$$ | **HOTEL** | This four-floor, stylish boutique stay in the center, opening onto rue des Bouchers, ticks just about every box you could want for a city stay. **Pros:** there are impressive duplex suites on the top floor; you couldn't be more central unless you pitched a tent in the Grand Place; the hotel restaurant is a star in its own right. **Cons:** it's in a noisy location; there's no parking here; breakfast is extra, though worth it. *Rooms from: €152* *Rue des Bouchers 38, Lower Town* *02/213–7470* *www.hoteldesgaleries.be* *23 rooms* *No Meals* *Metro: De Brouckère.*

Hôtel Noga

$$ | **HOTEL** | Opened in 1958, the well-maintained Noga is packed with sepia-tinted old nautical mementos, which include black-and-white photographs of the period and even a sailing-theme bar. **Pros:** superhelpful staff; it's been well maintained despite its age; basic breakfast is supercheap (from €5) and tasty. **Cons:** parking is a pricey €18 per night; it's quite expensive for the facilities on offer; bathrooms lack tubs. *Rooms from: €130* *Rue du Béguinage 38, Lower Town* *02/218–6763* *www.nogahotel.com* *19 rooms* *Free Breakfast* *Metro: Ste-Catherine.*

★ Juliana Hotel Brussels

$$$$ | **HOTEL** | The newest big boutique stay in the center sits on place des Martyrs, which holds a monument to the 445 patriots who died in the brief but successful 1830 war of independence. **Pros:** everything oozes class, from the service to the design; noon checkouts are always a plus; check out the afternoon tea (2–5) in the bar for a dash of civilized fun. **Cons:** parking is pricey; hard to pick fault, but all that luxury does get a bit much; it's just darn expensive. *Rooms from: €279* *Pl. des Martyrs 1–4, Lower Town* *02/214–0800* *www.juliana-brussels.com* *43 rooms* *Free Breakfast* *Metro: De Brouckère.*

Le Dixseptième

$$$ | **HOTEL** | This stylishly restored, 17th-century building lies between the Grand Place and the Gare Centrale. **Pros:** great, central location; romantic setting; gorgeous rooms. **Cons:** walls can be a bit thin; the "budget" room is pretty poky; no on-site parking. *Rooms from: €164* *Rue de la Madeleine 25, Lower Town* *02/517–1717* *www.ledixseptieme.be* *37 rooms* *Free Breakfast* *Metro: De Brouckère.*

Yooma Urban Lodge

$$ | **HOTEL** | **FAMILY** | This artsy hotel has taken the city's comic-book heritage to heart. **Pros:** ideally located if you've got to travel; its peppy and fun; you get a lot for the price—it's ideal for families. **Cons:** the bold decor is not to everyone's taste; the immediate area isn't the prettiest—around Midi is particularly scuzzy; it's a bit of a walk to the center. *Rooms from: €119* *Sq. de l'aviation 23–27, Lower Town* *02/520–6565* *yooma-brussels.com* *60 rooms* *Free Breakfast* *Tram: 3, 4.*

Nightlife

BARS AND PUBS

Au Soleil

BARS | A slightly scruffy interior (complete with resident cat) belies what is essentially a delightful old-school café-bar with a terrace on the street outside. It's popular with locals, who fill the tables outside in the evening. Just grab a beer and a croque monsieur and watch the world go by. ✉ *Rue du Marché-au-Charbon 86, Lower Town* ☎ *02/512–3430* Ⓜ *Tram: 3, 4.*

★ Bonnefooi

CAFÉS | This small, two-floor bar manages to be both laid-back and achingly hip with good beer and cocktails, a vintage Photomatique machine, chandeliers, free live jazz and electronica, and DJs on most nights. ✉ *Rue des Pierres 8, Lower Town* 🌐 *bonnefooi.be* Ⓜ *Metro: De Brouckère.*

Café des Halles

DANCE CLUBS | Set within a late 19th-century brick-and-iron covered market, Halles St-Géry was originally built to house the old meat market. The building itself was abandoned by traders in the 1970s though, and it lay derelict until the turn of the millennium, when it was renovated into an exhibition space (upper floor) and a bustling café-bar with a fine line in leather sofas and cocktails. Down in the vaulted cellar, you'll also find Club des Halles, which dishes up oodles of classic house music on weekends. Bring 50 cents for the toilet, though. ✉ *Pl. Saint Géry 1, Lower Town* ☎ *02/503–3325* 🌐 *www.cafedeshalles.be* Ⓜ *Tram: 3, 4.*

Cafe Roskum

BARS | This cozy café-bar has a good lineup of free jazz (mostly) concerts on Sunday night at 8 pm. At any other time though, it's typical of most Belgian bars in the city: noisy, friendly, and pretty lively, with a good selection of beers. ✉ *Rue de Flandre 9, Lower Town* ☎ *02/503–5154* 🌐 *www.cafe-roskam.be* Ⓜ *Metro: Ste-Catherine.*

Groupil Le Fol

COCKTAIL LOUNGES | Groupil Le Fol skirts a fine line between curiosity shop and bar, complete with jukebox, comfy old sofas, and no beer for once. The drinks menu consists of an array of fruit wines and punches, while its owner usually sprawls spiderlike in a corner cubbyhole watching TV. If the conversation ever drags, there's always something weird to look at. ✉ *Rue de la Violette 22, Lower Town* ☎ *02/511–1396* 🌐 *www.goupillefol.com* Ⓜ *Tram: 3, 4.*

La Porte Noir

BARS | A popular option, this lively, dimly lighted cellar bar is all brick, benches, and radio-friendly rock music. It does a good line in beers and (more unusually for Brussels) whiskies, though there's a certain *Logan's Run* vibe to the joint, and anyone over 30 might want to look elsewhere. ✉ *Rue des Alexiens 67, Lower Town* ☎ *02/511–7837* 🌐 *www.laporte-noire.be/en* Ⓜ *Metro: Bruxelles-Chapelle.*

Madame Moustache

LIVE MUSIC | Rather out of place in the otherwise refined Ste-Catherine area, this buzzing, vaudeville-theme after-hours bar/club is trashy, fun, and does good cocktails and theme nights. It's not a secret, though, so be prepared to queue after midnight—and bring change for the bathroom. ✉ *Quai au Bois a Bruler 5–7, Lower Town* ☎ *0489/739–912* 🌐 *www.madamemoustache.be* Ⓜ *Metro: Ste–Catherine.*

Monk

BARS | A favorite with the artsy crowd and lovers of a quiet afternoon with a board game, this former schoolhouse is now a bar that draws crowds late into the night with live music, a central location, and good beers. Its spaghetti isn't bad, either. ✉ *Rue Ste-Catherine 42, Lower Town* ☎ *02/511–7511* 🌐 *www.monk.be* Ⓜ *Metro: Ste-Catherine.*

Know Your Lambic Beers

Lambic beers, notable for their sour taste and unique brewing process, are the quintessential Brussels brews. Once there were some 300 lambic brewers here and in the surrounding Zenne Valley. Now the capital has just a single dedicated brewery, and only a handful scatter its outskirts amid the rolling countryside of Flemish Brabant. These unique beers are created through a process of spontaneous fermentation (begun by natural yeast molecules in the air, versus artificial cultures), which is unique to this area, thanks to its marshy climate. It is also the basis of many popular local beers, such as *gueuze* (an effervescent blend of lambics), cherry-flavored *kriek*, and raspberry-flavored *framboise*. In the capital, you can still visit **Cantillon Brewery** (*www.cantillon.be*) on rue Gheude 56, west of the center. It has produced lambic and specialty beers here since 1900, and also doubles as the Musée Bruxellois de la Gueuze. Tours (in English) reveal its aging containers and bottling machinery, and finish with a tasting. This is perhaps the most revealing part. Many commercially brewed lambics bear scant resemblance to the real thing and their somewhat vinegary notes than be a shock to some. It's certainly an acquired taste. Otherwise, head to Beersel in Flemish Brabant where the newly resurrected **Oud Beersel** and the well-established **Brouwerij 3 Fonteinen** (*see Beersel entries*) offer their own fascinating peek behind the lambic curtain on tours and visits.

BEER BARS

À La Mort Subite

BARS | A Brussels institution named after a card game called "Sudden Death," A la Mort Subite is practically unchanged since its 1920s heyday; and with its distinctive high ceilings, wooden tables, and mirrored walls, it remains a favorite of beer lovers from all over the world. It still brews its own traditional Brussels beers (lambik, gueuze, and faro). These sour, potent drafts may be an acquired taste, but, like singer Jacques Brel, who came here often, you'll find it hard to resist their (and the staff's) gruff charm. ✉ *Rue Montagne aux Herbes Potagères 7, Lower Town* ☎ *02/513–1318* 🌐 *www.alamort-subite.com* Ⓜ *Metro: De Brouckère.*

Brussels Beer Project

BREWPUBS | You might have thought that U.S.-style craft beer would go down like a lead balloon in the notoriously old-fashioned world of Belgian beer, but that's rather the point of this iconoclastic project. BBP's 24-tap taproom has quickly become an essential stop for any hop lovers in the city and was the first step to world domination—they're now even in Paris and Tokyo. A new taproom also recently opened in Ixelles on rue de Bailli. ✉ *Rue Antoine Dansaert 188, Lower Town* ☎ *2/502–2856* 🌐 *www.beerproject.be/en* Ⓜ *Metro: Ste. Catherine.*

Delirium Cafe

BARS | Yes, it's horrifically touristy, but the beer selection at the city's most popular bar now tops 3,000 brews, and that deserves sampling, even if most are only available at the tiny bar downstairs. Over the years it's expanded to more than three floors, with a taproom and the quieter "Hoppy Loft" offering respite from the barrel tables, tourists, and clutter on the first floor. Floris Bar, which is owned by the same people and specializes in absinthe, tequila, and a Dutch-style gin known as jenever, sits across the alleyway, and offshoot Little Delirium lies a short walk away at 9 rue du Marche aux Fromages. ✉ *Impasse de la Fidelite 4A, Lower Town* ☎ *02/514–4434* 🌐 *www.delirium.be* Ⓜ *Metro: De Brouckère.*

JAZZ CLUBS

L'Archiduc

LIVE MUSIC | The Art Deco design of L'Archiduc attracts a thirtyish, fashionable crowd, which is hardly surprising given the upmarket shopping area in which it resides. Add to the mix live jazz on weekends and fine cocktails, and it makes for one of the more polished entries in the city's bar scene. ✉ *Rue Antoine Dansaert 6, Lower Town* ☎ *02/512–0652* 🌐 *www.archiduc.net* Ⓜ *Metro: Ste-Catherine.*

The Music Village

LIVE MUSIC | The cozy, dimly lit Music Village hosts a plethora of international jazz musicians, with nightly concerts usually starting around 8:30 pm. You don't need a ticket, but it's usually best to make a reservation (pay on-site). ✉ *Rue des Pierres 50, Lower Town* ☎ *02/513–1345* 🌐 *www.themusicvillage.com* Ⓜ *Tram: 3, 4.*

LBGT

The rainbow-flag-draped area just behind the town hall is the base for a small enclave of LGBT bars catering to all stripes in the St. Jacques neighborhood. This runs the streets of rue du Marche au Charbon and rue des Pierres, where the fun continues long into the small hours. Pride Festival usually happens in May, but the weeks running up to it are a cavalcade of events and parties spread across the city's bars and cultural institutions.

Chez Maman

CABARET | Maman herself presides over this disco with a drag show (in French) every Friday and Saturday. ✉ *Rue des Grands Carmes 7, Lower Town* ☎ *02/310–7185* 🌐 *www.chezmaman.be* Ⓜ *Tram: 3, 4.*

Performing Arts

Ancienne Belgique

CONCERTS | City-center concert hall for mostly rock and pop acts. Tickets can be bought online or at the venue. ✉ *Bd. Anspach 110, Lower Town* 🌐 *www.abconcerts.be* Ⓜ *Metro: De Brouckère.*

Beursschouwburg

ARTS CENTERS | Located in a former brewery, this local music institution is one of the city's biggest pop and rock venues. It also hosts exhibitions, film screenings, and talks, and has a history of putting free summer concerts and gigs held on its rooftop in June. Buy tickets online or at the ticket office. ✉ *Rue Auguste Ortsstraat 20–28, Lower Town* ☎ *02/550–0350 ticket office* 🌐 *www.beursschouwburg.be* Ⓜ *Metro: De Brouckère.*

Shopping

The Lower Town is packed with avant-garde boutiques, predominantly clustered around **rue Antoine Dansaert,** which is the flagship street of Brussels's fashionable quarter and extends south past St-Géry and Ste-Catherine. Also head to the trendy **place du Nouveau Marché aux Grains,** near the Bourse, which has a number of boutiques carrying fashions by young designers and interior design and art shops.

Just north of the Grand Place lies the **Galeries Royales Saint-Hubert,** a rather stately shopping arcade lined with upscale brands selling men's and women's clothing, books, and objets d'art. It is as remarkable for its building as for the shops it contains and worth a look even if you're keeping the purse strings tight. And leading off the Grand Place is **rue au Buerre** (Butter Street), where you find all the big-name chocolate shops lined up beside each other.

Most city markets include traders with specialized, artisanal products and are worth a look. Head to **place Ste-Catherine** for a small but popular organic market held on Wednesday (7:30–3). **Place du Jeu de Balle** is also home to a famous flea market (*see Les Marolles entry*), which rarely has anything of value for sale but has been running since the 19th century and is something of an icon.

CHOCOLATE SHOPS

BS40

CHOCOLATE | Also known as Jitsk, this chocolaterie on rue au Buerre, which is packed with chocolate shops, is home to arguably the best macarons—soft yet flavorsome—in the city, ranging in flavor from passion fruit to crème brûlée. ✉ *Rue au Beurre 40, Lower Town* ☎ *02/502–1414* 🌐 *www.jitsk.com* Ⓜ *Metro: De Brouckère.*

Chocolaterie Mary

CHOCOLATE | A chocolatier to the royal family. The original owner, Mary Delluc, founded her shop in 1919 on rue Royale, where you'll still find a branch today along with others dotting the city. The pralines are the specialty here, and worth the indulgent prices when wrapped in their trademark elegant presentation boxes—a work of art in themselves. ✉ *Lombardstraat 28B, Lower Town* ☎ *02/512–3400* 🌐 *www.mary.be* Ⓜ *Metro: Central Station.*

Planète Chocolat

CHOCOLATE | As well as selling delicious handmade chocolates, this store also does demonstrations in French and English (€7) and runs lessons (€100) for those who want to learn how to make their own treats. ✉ *Rue du Lombard 24, Lower Town* ☎ *02/511–0755* 🌐 *www.planetechocolat.com/en* Ⓜ *Metro: Gare Centrale.*

CLOTHING

Ganterie Italienne

HATS & GLOVES | Brussels used to be famous for its gloves, and the old tanneries on the rue des Tanneurs once produced the finest of leather. This glove maker has been operating in the city since 1890, and its shop in Galeries Royales Saint-Hubert has been run by three generations. A real institution. ✉ *Galeries Royales Saint-Hubert, Galerie de la Reine 3, Lower Town* ☎ *02/512–7538* 🌐 *ganterie.com* Ⓜ *Metro: De Brouckère.*

Hunting and Collecting

WOMEN'S CLOTHING | This vast space dedicated to cutting-edge design in clothing, footwear, furniture, and accessories includes an art exhibition area in the basement. Its look is rarely the same and its provocative pieces cost a pretty penny. ✉ *Rue des Chartreux 17, Lower Town* ☎ *02/512–7477* 🌐 *www.huntingandcollecting.com* Ⓜ *Metro: Ste-Catherine.*

Icon

MIXED CLOTHING | Wild avant-garde fashions and timeless pieces—Dansaert's beloved store is appropriately named and rarely disappoints those willing to adopt a bold new look thanks to a choice of up-and-coming Belgian brands. ✉ *Pl. du Nouveau Marché aux Grains 5, Lower Town* ☎ *02/502–7151* 🌐 *www.icon-shop.be* Ⓜ *Metro: Ste-Catherine.*

Monsel

HATS & GLOVES | Something of an old stager, this traditional umbrella shop and milliners has a wide choice of caps and hats. It has also been going for generations (since 1847) and was one of the original shops in the Galeries Royales St-Hubert. ✉ *Galerie du Roi 5, Lower Town* ☎ *02/511–4133* 🌐 *www.monsel.be* Ⓜ *Metro: De Brouckère.*

Stijl

MIXED CLOTHING | Often credited with kickstarting the boutique rush on rue Antoine Dansaert, Stijl has been knocking around since the 1980s yet still retains its couture chops, championing a wide range of Belgian avant-garde designers for women. It also has a men's branch on place du Nouveau Marche aux Grains. ✉ *Rue Antoine Dansaert 74, Lower Town* ☎ *02/512–0313* 🌐 *www.stijl.be* Ⓜ *Metro: Ste-Catherine.*

COLLECTIBLES

Jeu de Bulles

ANTIQUES & COLLECTIBLES | Jeu de Bulles is a cult gem, home to some rare first-edition comic books, toys, and original prints from *Tintin, Blake and Mortimer, Lucky Luke,* and other Belgian icons inspired by the early *Spirou* comics. ✉ *Pl. du Jeu de Balle 79, Lower Town* ☎ *0475/697–538* 🌐 *www.jeudebulles.be* Ⓜ *Tram: 3, 4.*

SHOPPING CENTERS

Galeries Royales Saint-Hubert

SHOPPING CENTER | One of the oldest shopping malls in Europe, this elegant neo-Renaissance gallery first opened in 1847, and its towering columns and iron-and-glass roof make it worth a visit any time. ✉ *Rue du Marché aux Herbes 90, Brussels* 🌐 *www.grsh.be/en* Ⓜ *Metro: De Brouckère.*

Upper Town

It was under the rule of the Austrian Habsburgs (1705–95), and then later the French (1795–1815), that Brussels's commercial and urban development blossomed. With its newfound wealth, showy neoclassical facades and grand squares began sprouting in Upper Town, the spine of which is made up of rue Royal and rue de la Regence. Its sense of privilege was nothing new though, as this area had been the royal seat and administrative heart of the city since the Middle Ages. But, finally, it had a setting to match the sense of superiority.

The next century saw more of the same. When Belgium won independence in 1830 and money from King Leopold II's ravaging of the Congo started pouring in, a development boom ensued. Today, much of what was built during these two eras is still visible while strolling the antiques shops of the Sablon, the high-end boutiques of boulevard de Waterloo, or listening to a band in the Parc de Bruxelles (aka Royal Park). Finish your exploration in the museum district, where the relics of the old palace still dwell beneath the cobbles at Coudenberg and the orchestras of the BOZAR play long into the evening.

Sights

Cathédrale St-Michel et Ste-Gudula (*Cathedral of St. Michael and St. Gudula*)

CHURCH | All royal weddings take place in this fine cathedral, with its twin Gothic towers and stained-glass windows. One namesake, St-Michel, is recognized as the patron saint of Brussels, typically pictured slaying a dragon (Satan) but mention Ste-Gudule and most people will draw a blank. Very little is known about this daughter of a 7th-century Carolingian nobleman, but her relics have been preserved here for the past 1,000 years. Construction of the cathedral began in 1226 and continued through the 15th century; chapels were added in the 16th and 17th centuries. ✉ *Pl. Sainte-Gudule, Upper Town* ☎ *02/229–2490* 🎫 *Crypt: €3; archaeological site: €1* 🕑 *Treasury closed Sun., Mon., and Fri.* ✍ *Booking required for tours* Ⓜ *Metro: Gare Centrale.*

★ **Coudenberg/Musée BELvue**

CASTLE/PALACE | Under the place Royale lie the remains of the palace of Charles V. Known as Coudenberg, it was first constructed in the 11th century and upgraded over hundreds of years in line with the power and prestige of Brussels's successive rulers. However, it was destroyed by a great fire in 1731 and was never rebuilt. Parts of it, and one or two of the streets that surrounded the original building, have since been excavated. Access is through the Musée BELvue, which is worth seeing in its own right and unpicks Belgium's history of democracy and its royal family. ✉ *Pl. des Palais 7, Upper Town* ☎ *02/500–4554* 🌐 *www.coudenberg.com* 🎫 *€18 combo ticket* 🕑 *Coudenberg closed Mon.* Ⓜ *Metro: Gare Central.*

The Coudenberg palace, dating from the 11th century, is now an archaeological site complete with underground tunnels.

★ Musée des Instruments de Musique (MIM)

OTHER MUSEUM | **FAMILY** | This four-story building is almost as impressive as the museum it houses. Built in 1899, architect Paul Saintenoy didn't hold back. Its elaborate facade twists its glass and iron into a symphony of Art Nouveau. Inside, it's no less fascinating. If you've ever wanted to know what a gamelan or Tibetan temple bell sounds like, here's your chance. In addition to seeing more than 2,000 instruments, you can listen to most of them via headphones. Head to the rooftop café for fantastic views of the city; also look out for MIM's regular lunchtime concerts—some are even free. ✉ *Rue Montagne de la Cour 2, Upper Town* ☎ *02/545–0130* 🌐 *www.mim.be* 🎫 *€15* 🕓 *Closed Mon.* ✍ *Tickets for concerts can't be booked* Ⓜ *Metro: Gare Centrale.*

★ Musée Fin-de-Siècle

ARTS CENTER | The collection focuses on an era (1868–1914) when European art stopped gazing all moist-eyed at history and instead turned its attention to the world around it. The museum charts this changing of the guard, beginning with the rebellion against academic tradition and the dominant themes of Romanticism that gave rise to the birth of Realism, through to the freer style of the Impressionists, and all the way up to World War I. Belgian painters featured include Guillaume Vogel and the powerful imagery of Symbolist Léon Spillaert, who runs the gamut from Impressionist-style beaches to brooding self-portraits and Gothic-infused horror. Elsewhere, work by masters such as Paul Gauguin, Auguste Rodin, and Emile Galle place the collection and the art scene of the period at the center of a burgeoning international movement. A powerful reminder of a time when Brussels was one of the great creative capitals. ✉ *Rue de la Régence 3, Upper Town* ☎ *02/508–3211* 🌐 *www.fine-arts-museum.be* 🎫 *€10, combo ticket €15 (includes entry to Magritte and Oldmasters museums)* 🕓 *Closed Mon.* Ⓜ *Metro: Gare Centrale.*

Musée Juif de Belgique (*Jewish Museum of Belgium*)
HISTORY MUSEUM | This museum traces the history of the Jewish faith and the fate of its followers in Belgium. The extensive collection includes religious objects dating from the 16th century, including documents, religious items, and books. In addition, it has hosted some truly excellent temporary exhibitions, ranging from the Jewish influence on superheroes to the work of prominent Jewish artists. ✉ *Rue des Minimes 21, Upper Town* ☎ *02/512–1963* 🌐 *www.mjb-jmb.org* 🎟 *€12* ⏲ *Closed Mon.* Ⓜ *Bus: 95.*

★ **Musée Magritte**
ART MUSEUM | After years of sharing display space in the neighboring museum complex on rue de la Régence, Surrealist genius René Magritte (1898–1967) finally got his own, much-deserved space. The collection starts on level three, tracing Magritte's life and work chronologically. The artist's mother committed suicide when he was 13; certainly, her profession as a milliner is difficult to separate from his later obsession with hats. The museum expands key moments through letters, sculptures, films, and, of course, some 200 paintings, including the haunting *The Domain of Arnheim*. ✉ *Entrance at pl. Royale 1; buy tickets at rue de la Régence 3, Upper Town* ☎ *02/508–3211* 🌐 *www.musee-magritte-museum.be* 🎟 *€10, combo ticket €15 (includes entry to Oldmasters and Fin-de-Siècle museums)* ⏲ *Closed Mon.* Ⓜ *Metro: Gare Centrale.*

Musée Oldmasters
ART MUSEUM | The Oldmasters Museum pays special attention to the so-called Flemish Primitives of the 15th century, who revolutionized the art of painting with oil. The Spanish and the Austrians pilfered some of the finest works, but there's plenty left to savor, including works by Memling, Petrus Christus, Rogier van der Weyden, and Hieronymus Bosch. The collection of pieces by Pieter Bruegel the Elder is particularly eye-catching; it includes *The Fall of Icarus*, in which the figure of the mythological hero disappearing in the sea is but one detail of a scene where people continue to go about their business. There are English-language brochures and guided tours available. ✉ *Rue de la Régence 3, Upper Town* ☎ *02/508–3211* 🌐 *www.fine-arts-museum.be* 🎟 *€10, combo ticket €15 (includes entry to Magritte and Fin-de-Siècle museums)* ⏲ *Closed Mon.* Ⓜ *Metro: Gare Centrale.*

★ **Palais Royale**
CASTLE/PALACE | The Belgium Royal Family lives in the Château de Laeken these days, and it's become a tradition to open up their inner-city residence to visitors during summer. The building was erected on the site of the former Palace of the Dukes of Brabant (aka Coudenburg), which burned down in 1731—you can still tour its underground excavation next door. Work on the existing palace was begun in 1820 but redesigned in a more garish neoclassical style in the early 19th century by Leopold II. Today, it holds a remarkable collection of tapestries, art, and antiques from all over the world. ✉ *Rue Brederode 16, Laeken* ☎ *02/551–2020* 🌐 *www.monarchie.be* 🎟 *Free* ⏲ *Closed Oct.–June* Ⓜ *Metro: Gare Centrale.*

Place du Grand Sablon
PLAZA/SQUARE | Once nothing more than a sandy hill, "Sand Square" is now an elegant place, surrounded by numerous restaurants, cafés, and antiques shops, some in intriguing alleys and arcades. For a little tranquillity, pop into the beautiful **Église Notre Dame du Sablon** at the eastern end of the square, a flamboyant Gothic church founded in 1304. It's one of Brussels's most beautiful churches, and at night its stained-glass windows are illuminated from within to magical effect. Opposite the Grand Sablon, you'll find the pretty garden **place du Petit**

A
B
C
D
E
F
1
2
3
4
5
6
7
8
9
Rue des Commerçants
Rue des Croisades
R. du Marché
Quai du Commerce
Quai au Foin
Quai aux Pierres de Taille
Place Charles Rogier
Rue Gineste
Rue du Canal
Rue du Comte de Flandre
Boulevard de Nieuport
Quai des Charbonnages
Rue Locquenghien
Rue du Grand Hospice
Boulevard Emile Jacqmain
Rue Saint-Pierre
Boulevard Adolphe Max
Rue de Flandre
Quai au Bois à Brûler
Quai aux Briques
Rue Saint-Michel
Rue de Laeken
Place du Samedi
Rue Antoine Dansaert
Rue du Rempart des Moines
Rue du Fossé aux Loups
Rue du Marais
Rue de l'Evêque
Place de la Monnaie
Rue des Fabriques
Place de la Bourse
R. de l'Abattoir
R. Cuerens
Rue Van Artevelde
Parc de la Cathédrale Saints-Michel-et-Gudule
Boulevard de Berlaimont
Grand Place
R. de la Senne
Rue Camusel
Rue du Lombard
LOWER TOWN
Carrefour de l'Europe
R. Duquesnoy
R. Saint-Jean
Rue de Cureghem
Boulevard du Midi
Boulevard Poincaré
Rue du Vautour
Place Anneessens
Rue Van Helmont
Rue du Midi
Rue des Alexiens
Boulevard de l'Empereur
Jardin du Mont des Arts
Rue Royale
Rue Bodeghem
Rue d'Artois
Rue Broghiez
R. de la Caserne
Boulevard Maurice Lemonnier
Rue Terre-Neuve
de la Paille
Ruysbroeck
Place de la Chapelle
UPPER TOWN
Avenue de Stalingrad
Rue du Miroir
Rue Blaes
Rue Haute
R. des Minimes
Rue Ernest Allard
Rue de la Régence
Rue de Fiennes
Rue des Tanneurs
Rue des Capucins
Parc d'Egmont
Esplanade de l'Europe
Rue aux Laines
Av. de la Toison d'Or
Rue de la Rasière
Rue Keyenveld
Avenue Fonsny
Rue de Russie
R. des Drapiers
Rue d'Angleterre
R. aux Laines
Avenue Louise
Rue de Hollande
R. aux Laines
1
2
3
4
5
6
7
9
10

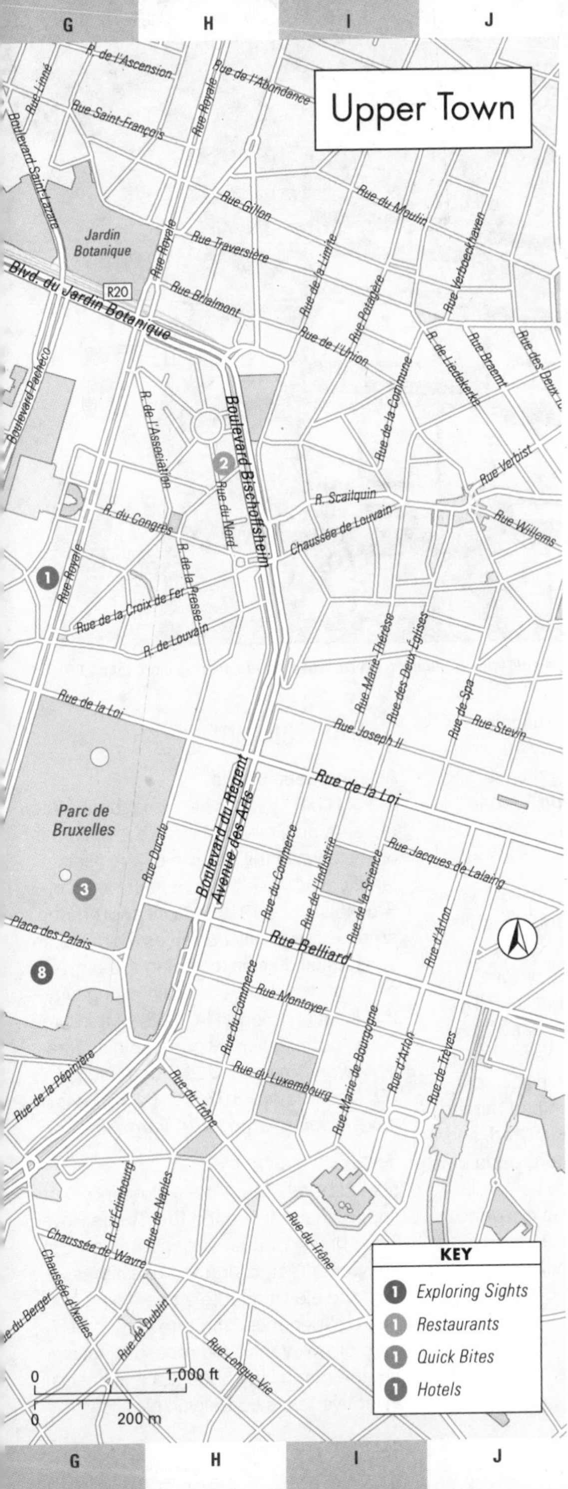

Upper Town

Sights

1 Cathédrale St-Michel et Ste-Gudula F4
2 Coudenberg/Musée BELvue F6
3 Musée des Instruments de Musique (MIM) F6
4 Musée Fin-de-Siècle F7
5 Musée Juif de Belgique E7
6 Musée Magritte F6
7 Musée Oldmasters F6
8 Palais Royale G6
9 Place du Grand Sablon E7
10 Place Royale F6

Restaurants

1 Au Vieux Saint Martin E7
2 Gus H3
3 Liu Lin D7
4 Lola E7
5 Wine Bar des Marolles D8

Quick Bites

1 Jat' Café F7
2 Wittamer E7
3 Woodpecker G6

Hotels

1 Motel One G4
2 NH Collection Brussels Grand Sablon E7
3 9Hôtel Sablon E6

KEY

1 *Exploring Sights*
1 *Restaurants*
1 *Quick Bites*
1 *Hotels*

0 — 1,000 ft
0 — 200 m

The Musée des Instruments de Musique, with its stunning Art Nouveau facade, houses more than 2,000 musical instruments.

Sablon. It's surrounded by a magnificent wrought-iron fence, topped by 48 small bronze statues representing the city's guilds. ✉ *Pl. du Grand Sablon, Upper Town* Ⓜ *Bus: 33.*

Place Royale

CITY PARK | There's a strong dash of Vienna in this white, symmetrical square, built in the neoclassical style by Brussels's then Austrian overlords. Elegantly proportioned, it is the centerpiece of the Upper Town, which became the center of power during the 18th century. Place Royale was built on the ruins of the palace of the Dukes of Brabant, which had burned down. The site has been excavated, and it is possible to see the underground digs of Coudenberg and the main hall, Aula Magna, where Charles V was crowned Holy Roman Emperor in 1519, and where, 37 years later, he abdicated to retire to a monastery. ✉ *Pl. Royale, Upper Town* Ⓜ *Metro: Parc.*

Restaurants

Au Vieux Saint Martin

$$ | **BELGIAN** | Even when neighboring restaurants on Grand Sablon are empty, this one is always full. It's run by the Niels family, who have been restaurateurs in Brussels since 1915, and its short menu emphasizes local specialties; portions are substantial. **Known for:** being the birthplace of the "filet Americain"; longevity—this location opened in 1968; nothing too fancy, but exquisitely good Belgian fare. Ⓢ *Average main: €20* ✉ *Grand Sablon 38, Upper Town* ☎ *02/512–6476* 🌐 *www.auvieuxsaintmartin.be* Ⓜ *Tram: 95.*

★ **Gus**

$$$ | **BELGIAN** | There are a cluster of bars and restaurants around the Cirque Royal. This "brassonomie" experiment is a cut above the rest, taking the usual brasserie fare and elevating it to a fine-dining bistro experience, and throwing in its own brewery for good measure. **Known for:** the menu isn't huge but it is special; inventive takes on Belgian classics;

the seasonal beers are pretty good. *$ Average main: €26 Rue des Cultes 36, Upper Town 02/265–7961 www.gus-brussels.be Closed weekends. No dinner Mon.–Wed. Tram: 2, 6.*

Liu Lin

$$ | **TAIWANESE** | The definition of on-trend Brussels dining. It's not flashy, it's not too expensive, but this Taiwanese-inspired, plant-based street food restaurant, run by a pair of sisters, has certainly captured a mood. **Known for:** the noodle soups are perfect for a winter's day; plant-based vegan dining with good flavors; there's no alcohol—you grab cans of pop from the fridge. *$ Average main: €15 Rue Haute 20, Upper Town 02/455–0830 liulin.be Closed Mon. and Tues. Tram: 92, 93.*

Lola

$$$ | **FRENCH** | In and among the pricey antiques and jewelry shops of the Sablon, you'll find a fair amount of stylish dining. Among these establishments comfortably snuggles Lola, an undeniably charming brasserie of black-leather booths and a bar counter for those grabbing a quick lunch. **Known for:** the wine list is pretty darn good; a bright and breezy lunch or dinner; there's a small terrace to sit outside and watch folks go by. *$ Average main: €28 Pl. du Grand Sablon 33, Upper Town 02/514–2460.*

Wine Bar des Marolles

$$$ | **FRENCH** | Despite its name, this is not really a wine bar (though they run a roof terrace in summer where you can go for a drink) and it's just on the edge of the Marolles. Owners Vincent Thomaes and Joël Vandenhoudt relocated to rue Haute from Sablon in 2013, back when this was a popular bar. **Known for:** the wine selection is always interesting and the sommelier knows his stuff; the rooftop is nice in summer; old-school French dining with a dash of elegance. *$ Average main: €28 Rue Haute 198, Upper Town 0496/820–105 www.winebarsablon.be Tram: 92, 93.*

Coffee and Quick Bites

Jat' Café

$$ | **CAFÉ** | A large, hip coffee shop with art and design books strewn around its cozy lounging area. There are bagels, salads, and the juices are particularly good. **Known for:** good juices; there's brunch on weekends; people-watching spot. *$ Average main: €12 Rue de Namur 28, Upper Town 02/503–0332 www.jat.cool Metro: Parc.*

Wittamer

$$ | **CAFÉ** | One of the grandes dames of Brussels's many excellent pastry shops has an attractive tearoom and terrace on the Sablon, which also serves breakfast and light lunches. The profiteroles and crème fraîche truffles are particularly tempting. **Known for:** the chocolates make good souvenirs; you come for the desserts—the rest is just the icing on the cake (so to speak); a great coffee spot to watch life on the square go by. *$ Average main: €12 Pl. du Grand Sablon 12, Upper Town 02/512–3742 wittamer.com Bus: 95.*

Woodpecker

$ | **CAFÉ** | **FAMILY** | Woodpecker cafés are strewn across the city, including a few kiosks (like this). But it's the setting that wins the day here. **Known for:** it's open every day; it's all about the location—shady trees on a hot summer's day; the coffee is decent enough. *$ Average main: €8 Parc de Bruxelles, Upper Town event.woodpeckerbxl.com Metro: Parc.*

Hotels

★ Motel One

$$ | **HOUSE** | **FAMILY** | There aren't too many options for stays in this thin sliver of the city, between Mont des Arts and the Sablon, particularly toward Cirque Royale, but this stylish offering is the exception, and a good one given it's a low-budget chain. **Pros:** great location within easier

walking of the royal museums and palace; service is professional and it's a good-value option for families; breakfast isn't included but it's pretty cheap (€11.50). **Cons:** it's not in the prettiest spot in the city; facilities are pared back given its budget ethos; rooms aren't huge but are comfortable. *Rooms from: €108 Rue Royale 120, Upper Town 02/209–6110 www.motel-one.com 490 rooms No Meals Metro: Parc.*

NH Collection Brussels Grand Sablon

$$$ | HOTEL | As part of Sablon's lineup of antiques shops, cafés, and chocolatiers, this hotel offers discreet luxury behind an elegant white facade. **Pros:** great breakfasts and digital newspapers to read; lovely older building; shady courtyard. **Cons:** the gym is rather sparsely fitted; you're a steep walk back from the center; front rooms can be noisy. *Rooms from: €191 Rue Bodenbroeck 2–4, Upper Town 02/518–1100 www.nh-hotels.be 193 rooms Free Breakfast Metro: Louise.*

9Hôtel Sablon

$$ | HOTEL | Squirreled away down a small lane off Grand Sablon square, this is a more modern boutique stay than the usual grandes dames you'll find in this area. **Pros:** you're well placed for exploring the Sablon; nice private terrace next to the lobby; the pool is a stunner (and you can buy costumes in the lobby). **Cons:** there's a pretty steep walk from the center; no pets allowed; breakfasts are a pricey €23 per person. *Rooms from: €131 Rue de la Paille 2, Upper Town 02/880–0701 www.9-hotel-sablon-brussels.be 34 rooms No Meals Bus: 95.*

Nightlife

There's not a ton of action going on in this part of town in the evening. There are a few bars around Sablon, but the bulk of the nightlife here revolves around the Cirque Royal, with pre- and posttheater drinks and the workers from the nearby offices spilling into the bars and restaurants.

Bier Circus

BARS | One of the best beer pubs in the city is Bier Circus, out by the Cirque Royale, which has a huge list of obscure, small-batch Belgian beers, including some excellent organic brews. Part of the bar has now also become a shop, with some 250 bottles to choose from. *Rue de l'Enseignement 57, Upper Town 02/218–0034 www.bier-circus.be Metro: Gare Centrale.*

L'Apéroterie

BARS | A specialist food shop that doubles as a fine apéro bar as the sun sets. Locals spill onto the pavement terrace, where a good choice of small tapas bites, cocktails, and lesser-seen wines keeps out the cold in winter. *Rue du Congrès 24, Upper Town 0475/512–384 laperoterie.business.site Metro: Parc.*

Performing Arts

★ BOZAR: Centre for Fine Arts

FILM | This is the city's principal venue for classical music concerts and dance theater. Originally the first multipurpose arts complex in Europe, it was designed by acclaimed Belgian architect Victor Horta and was first opened in 1928. The Henry Le Boeuf concert hall has world-class acoustics. The complex also houses a theater and an art gallery, which plays host to some excellent traveling exhibitions. *Rue Ravenstein 23, Upper Town 02/507–8200 tickets www.bozar.be Metro: Parc.*

Cirque Royale

ARTS CENTERS | A major concert hall that has pop acts, theater, comedy, ballet, and just about anything else you can imagine. The building dates from 1878, and for years it was home to the capital's permanent circus—its basement stalls were able to accommodate 110 horses. Tickets can usually be bought at Ticketmaster or

The Palais Royale, one of the Belgium royal family's official residences, opens its doors to visitors in the summer.

FNAC. ✉ *Rue de l'Enseignement 81, Lower Town* 🌐 *www.cirqueroyalbruxelles.be* Ⓜ *Tram: Parc.*

Shopping

The Sablon, in particular, is known for its antiques, jewelry, and vintage shops, which wrap the rather plush square in a high-priced sheen of distressed furniture totally at odds with the more rough-and-ready antiques market that descends on the place on the weekends. Again, you won't find too many bargains, but it's still a great market to just putter about. Boulevard de Waterloo, which skirts the Ixelles area, is one of the main shopping thoroughfares and where you'll find mostly high-end-couture, from Gucci to Prada. This is a moneyed area, and it shows.

CHOCOLATE SHOPS

Laurent Gerbaud

CHOCOLATE | A wonderful café and chocolate shop perfect for resting your feet between museums. Sit down with a hot chocolate and a cake, or sample one of its confections. It's a bit unusual by Belgian chocolatier standards, as the quirky creations here are not only low sugar but have no alcohol or additives. Fillings include everything from curry masala and olive ganache to more conventional offerings, while chocolate-making workshops are run every Saturday (11:30–1; booking essential). ✉ *Rue Ravenstein 2d, Upper Town* ☎ *02/511–1602* 🌐 *www.chocolats-gerbaud.be* Ⓜ *Tram: 92, 93.*

Pierre Marcolini

CHOCOLATE | Marcolini's talents have long since outgrown his flagship chocolate shop in Sablon. He has stores stretching all the way to Japan these days, but his chocolate is still traceable back to a single origin. Other branches are found in Louise and Galeries Royales Saint-Hubert. ✉ *Rue des Minimes 1, Upper Town* ☎ *02/514–1206* 🌐 *eu.marcolini.com/en* Ⓜ *Bus: 95.*

CLOTHING

Kure

WOMEN'S CLOTHING | Boulevard de Waterloo's Kure is a firm fixture on the fashionista front, with a mix of French, Belgian, and Scandinavian designers all touting everyday wear with a dash of flair. ✉ *Bd. de Waterloo 13A, Upper Town* ☎ *02/414–2177* 🌐 *kurebrussels.com* Ⓜ *Metro: Porte de Namur.*

STREET MARKETS

Sablon Antique Market

MARKET | Each weekend morning, a lively antiques market (Saturday 9–5, Sunday 9–3) takes over the upper end of the square. It isn't for bargain hunters, though. It's been running since the 1960s, and sellers drive a pretty hard bargain. ✉ *Pl. du Grand Sablon, Upper Town* Ⓜ *Tram: 92, 93.*

Cinquantenaire and Schuman

Technically a part of Upper Town, this area is often known as the European Union (EU) quarter. The EU project brought jobs and investment to the city, but in the process, entire blocks were razed to make room for unbendingly modern steel-and-glass buildings. Its behemoth constructions won't win any prizes for architecture, but you will find relics of the older neighborhoods as you wander—not to mention some of the city's finest frites.

Sights

Autoworld

OTHER MUSEUM | **FAMILY** | A vast collection of vintage automobiles sits in what was originally planned (in the early 1900s) to be a grand exhibition hall. As time rolled on, hosting such fairs proved impractical due to how built-up the area became. These days, the hall makes the perfect showcase, its curved steel-and-glass roof giving the impression of a huge Art Deco garage. Exhibits range from Model T Fords to '50s Americana vehicles. ✉ *Parc du Cinquantenaire, Cinquantenaire* ☎ *02/736–4165* 🌐 *www.autoworld.be* 🎫 *€15* Ⓜ *Metro: Merode.*

European Union Quarter

GOVERNMENT BUILDING | The European Union was born in the embers of World War II, as an antidote to the nationalism that had swept Europe and caused such chaos. Its parliament shifts monthly between Strasbourg (France) and Brussels, where it occupies the Paul-Henri Spaak building (rue Wiertz 43). Hour-long audio-guide tours of Parliament and the Hemicycle, the debating chamber where plenary sessions are held, are available on weekdays (book online). The nearby **Parliamentarium** visitor center is more accessible and attempts to break down just how the EU works. ✉ *Paul-Henri Spaak Bldg., rue Wiertz 60, Upper Town* 🌐 *europarl.europa.eu/visiting* 🎫 *Free* Ⓜ *Metro: Schuman.*

La Maison Cauchie (*Cauchie House*)

HISTORIC HOME | Art Nouveau architect Paul Cauchie built this house for himself in 1905, using the facade as a virtual shop window for his *sgraffito* expertise. Sgraffito work begins with a light-color base layer; a darker color is added on top, and then, while the paint is still wet, etched with a design that allows the lighter color underneath to show through. Here, Cauchie covered the front with graceful, curving images of women playing lyres. The home's interior, only open to the public on guided tours on Saturday (and the first Sunday of the month), is a wonderful example of the Art Nouveau aesthetic. ✉ *Rue de Francs 5, Schuman* ☎ *02/733–8684* 🌐 *cauchie.be* 🎫 *€10 (include guided tour)* 🕒 *Closed Sun.–Fri.* ✍ *Booking required* Ⓜ *Metro: Merode.*

Maison de l'Histoire Européenne (*House of European History*)
HISTORY MUSEUM | FAMILY | Set within Parc Léopold, this modern museum tackles the political upheavals that shaped Europe. It's essentially a conscience in museum form, lest anyone forget the mistakes of the past, with permanent exhibitions charting the rise of industrialization, the authoritarianism and wars of the early 1900s that saw Europe's crumbling empires and global ambitions stretched to breaking point, and how a fragmented continent slowly drew itself back together. ✉ *Parc Léopold, rue Belliard 135, Schuman* ☎ *02/283–1220* 🌐 *www.historia-europa.ep.eu* 🎫 *Free* Ⓜ *Metro: Maelbeek.*

Musée Art et Histoire (*Art and History Museum*)
HISTORY MUSEUM | For a chronologically and culturally wide-ranging glimpse into the past, the Cinquantenaire Palace building is home to a number of antiquities and ethnographic treasures accumulated over the years. The Egyptian, Grecian, and Byzantine sections are particularly noteworthy and there's a strong focus on home turf, with significant displays on Belgian archaeology and the immense and intricate tapestries for which Brussels was once famous. ✉ *Parc du Cinquantenaire 10, Upper Town* ☎ *02/741–7331* 🌐 *www.artandhistory.museum* 🎫 *€10* ⏲ *Closed Mon.* Ⓜ *Metro: Schuman, Merode.*

Musée des Sciences Naturelles (*Museum of Natural Science*)
SCIENCE MUSEUM | FAMILY | The highlights here are the skeletons of some of the 30 iguanodons found in 1878 in the coal mines of Bernissart, which are believed to be about 120 million years old. It also has a fine collection of stones and minerals numbering in the tens of thousands. But the impressive Gallery of Humankind is worth the trip alone and charts the evolution of the human race to the present day. ✉ *Rue Vautier 29, Upper Town* ☎ *02/627–4211* 🌐 *www.naturalsciences.be* 🎫 *From €13* ⏲ *Closed Mon.* Ⓜ *Metro: Maelbeek.*

Musée du Tram (*Tram Museum*)
OTHER MUSEUM | While its opening hours are somewhere mercurial, it's worth timing a visit right to ride one of the museum's vintage trams, which date from the 1935 World's Fair. Most visits include a 40-minute ride, though on Sunday between April and September, you can do the four-hour tram tour. The journey, accompanied by a commentary on the city, includes a stop for lunch at Schaerbeek's station, where you'll also find the Train Museum. Alternatively, the Tram Museum has around 90 examples of old horse-drawn carriages, trams, and buses from the late 19th century onward to peruse. ✉ *Av. de Tervueren 364b, Cinquantenaire* ☎ *02/515–3108* 🌐 *tram-museum.brussels* 🎫 *€20 tram ride; €9 museum* ⏲ *Closed weekdays; days vary Oct.–Mar.* ✍ *Reservations required* Ⓜ *Tram: 8, 39.*

★ **Musée Royal de l'Armée et d'Histoire Militaire** (*Royal Museum of the Armed Force and Military History*)
HISTORY MUSEUM | FAMILY | The history of Belgium is one of invasion, and Cinquantenaire Park itself has even played its role. In the dying days of World War II, it was the scene of skirmishes between the Belgian resistance and the German army. Exhibits include uniforms, weaponry, and even Leopold I's camp bed, with items dating from the Middles Ages up until the wars of the 20th century, though English translation can be sporadic. More compelling are the later sections, when suddenly you find yourself (without warning) in a vast hangar of some 50 fighter planes, gliders, cargo craft, and tanks that appear out of nowhere, or reading about the first Belgian expedition in the Antarctic. ✉ *Parc du Cinquantenaire* ☎ *02/737–7811* 🌐 *www.klm-mra.be* 🎫 *€11* ⏲ *Closed Mon.* Ⓜ *Metro: Merode.*

Cinquantenaire and Schuman
A
B
C
D
E
F
1
2
3
4
5
6
7
8
9
R. des Confédérés
Rue de Pavie
Rue des Éburons
Rue Van Campenhout
Rue Jenneval
Rue Bordiau
Rue du Noyer
Square Ambiorix
Avenue Palmerston
Square Marguerite
Rue des Patriotes
Parc Juliette Herman
Rue Stevin
Rue Charles Martel
Rue du Taciturne
Rue Archimède
Avenue Michel-Ange
Rue Le Corrège
Rue Véronèse
Rue Le Titien
Avenue de Cortenbergh
R. Léonard de Vinci
Rue de Spa
Rue Joseph II
Rue de la Loi
Rue Franklin
Rue du Commerce
Rue de l'Industrie
Rue de la Science
Rue Jacques de Lalaing
Avenue de la Renaissance
Rue d'Arlon
Rue Belliard
Rue de Pascale
Avenue de la Joyeuse Entrée
Rue Montoyer
Rue Marie de Bourgogne
Rue de Trèves
Parc du Cinquantenaire
Parc Léopold
Avenue des Nerviens
Rue Froissart
R. de la Tourelle
Avenue d'Auderghem
Rue du Cornet
Rue Général Leman
Chaussée Saint-Pierre
Rue Louis Hap
Rue Baron Lambert
Rue du Trône
Rue Goffart
Rue de l'Étang
Rue de l'Orient
Rue Fétis
Rue Champ du Roi
Rue du Viaduc
Rue Sans Souci
Rue du Sceptre
Rue du Brochet
Chaussée de Wavre
Rue Van Aa
Rue Gray
Rue de Theux
Rue Général Capiaumont
Ave. Jules-Malou
Rue de Chambéry
Avenue de la Chasse
Rue Maes
Rue Wéry
Rue du Vivier
Rue Philippe Baucq
Rue Marie-Henriette
Rue Maria Malibran
Rue Jean Van Volsem
Avenue Victor Jacobs
Avenue des Casernes
R. Alphonse Hottat
R. Alfred Giron
Rue Jean Paquot
Rue Borrens
Avenue Hergé
Avenue de la Couronne
Avenue Nouvelle
R. Beckers
Rue de Haerne
Rue Beckers
KEY
Exploring Sights
Restaurants
Quick Bites
Hotels

Sights

1 Autoworld G4
2 European Union Quarter B4
3 La Maison Cauchie G5
4 Maison de l'Histoire Européenne C4
5 Musée Art et Histoire F4
6 Musée des Sciences Naturelles C5
7 Musée du Tram J5
8 Musée Royal de l'Armée et d'Histoire Militaire G3
9 Parc du Cinquantenaire F3
10 Parc Léopold C5

Restaurants

1 Berlaymont Café Brasserie D2
2 Maison Antoine D5
3 Nona H4
4 Origine D5
5 Schievelavabo C5

Quick Bites

1 Leopold Café Presse J5
2 Sowl E3

Hotels

1 Aloft Brussels Schuman D4
2 B&B A Côté du Cinquantenaire F5
3 Martin's Brussels EU D2

★ **Parc du Cinquantenaire**

CITY PARK | FAMILY | The most picturesque park in the city is a joy in summer when its shaded grassy lawns and paths fill with joggers, picnickers, dance troupes, and even climbers practicing on its walls. It is home to a number of museums as well as the capital's take on the Arc de Triomphe: the Arcade du Cinquantenaire. Pay special attention to the park's northwest corner where you'll find the **Great Mosque**. This was originally built as an Arabic-style folly for a national exhibition in 1880 but was gifted to King Faisal ibn Abd al-Aziz of Saudi Arabia to use as a place of worship in 1967, and has remained a mosque ever since. ✉ *Parc du Cinquantenaire, Cinquantenaire* Ⓜ *Metro: Merode.*

Parc Léopold

CITY PARK | This tranquil park, just next to the EU Quarter, has a strange history of failures. First, it was a poorly maintained 19th-century pleasure garden, then home a zoo in which most of the animals died (its two entrance pavilions date from this era). By the 1930s, thankfully, it found its purpose and became an important scientific library and institute, around which a pair of museums were later added. It's largely peaceful except at lunchtime, when seemingly every corner is invaded by local schoolkids. ✉ *Parc Léopold, Schuman* Ⓜ *Metro: Maelbeek.*

Restaurants

Berlaymont Café Brasserie

$$ | BELGIAN | Moules (mussels) and steaks, along with a small handful of the usual standbys, set the pace at this much-adored brasserie. Breakfast, lunch, dinner, drinks—it's pretty much all things to the large contingent of expats who have made this a popular local spot. **Known for:** simple, quick, crowd-pleasing brasserie food; there's a terrace outside for the warmer weather; its pubby interior shows sport on some evenings. $ *Average main: €21* ✉ *Rue Archimède 6, Cinquantenaire* ☎ *02/720–6630* Ⓜ *Metro: Merode.*

★ **Maison Antoine**

$ | BELGIAN | FAMILY | The Maison Antoine frites stand sells the best fries in the capital, say some people, accompanied by a dizzying range of condiments; try either local fave "Bicky" or the indulgent vol-au-vent sauce. **Known for:** picky management (be sure to clean up after yourself); excellent fries; condiment heaven. $ *Average main: €4* ✉ *Pl. Jourdan 1, Schuman* ☎ *02/230–5456* 🌐 *www.maisonantoine.be* Ⓜ *Metro: Maelbeek.*

Nona

$ | PIZZA | FAMILY | This organic Neapolitan-style pizzeria has a couple of branches now: two (one pizzeria, one pasta joint) in St-Catherine and another opposite the eastern entrance to Cinquantenaire. In summer, it's not unusual to see locals queuing for a takeaway to sit and eat their wood-fired pizzas on the grass of the park, and it's not a bad option. **Known for:** the takeaway option is always tempting; reliable local pizza that rarely disappoints; a good selection of local craft beers. $ *Average main: €11* ✉ *Av. de Tervueren 5, Cinquantenaire* 🌐 *www.nonalife.com* Ⓜ *Metro: Merode.*

★ **Origine**

$$$$ | FRENCH | A short walk from place Jourdan reveals this elegant, modern French restaurant, its pared-down, neat decor broken up with colorful prints of animals and the bustle of the open kitchen. The choice of food is equally sparse but to the point: four-course set menus deliver with imagination and no little amount of skill, letting you mix and match from your pick of cold, warm, hot, and sweet dishes on the blackboard. **Known for:** good value for money; original cooking that's delightfully presented; helpful staff and a decent selection of wines by the glass. $ *Average main: €46* ✉ *Rue Général Leman 36, Schuman* ☎ *02/256–6893* 🌐 *origine-restaurant.*

Just behind a peaceful park lies the massive Parliament building, part of the European Union Quarter.

be ⏲ *Closed Sun. and Mon.* Ⓜ *Metro: Maelbeek.*

Schievelavabo

$$ | **BELGIAN** | **FAMILY** | This sturdy Belgian chain nestles on the pedestrianized Chaussée de Wavre, just opposite place Jourdan, where you'll find slightly better dining options than around the square. It's as reliable as its gravy-soaked meats are tasty, dishing up the classics (meatballs, beery beef stews, ham and mustard sauce) amid walls plastered with old advertising posters from the '50s and '60s. **Known for:** it's really good value; a reliable chain with few surprises but much to savor; it's one of the better options off place Jourdan. $ *Average main: €15* ✉ *Chau. de Wavre 344, Schuman* ☎ *02/280–0083* 🌐 *www.schievelavabo.com* Ⓜ *Metro: Maelbeek.*

Coffee and Quick Bites

★ Leopold Café Presse

$ | **CAFÉ** | This cozy café is the epitome of Brussels decor: bicycles hang from the ceiling, there are Tintin statues everywhere, and shelves overflow with books. It's sculpted chaos and part of a chain of cafés that is slowly taking over the city. **Known for:** around the desk is a bookshop with plenty of guides (some in English) and comics; it's just a lovely, warm, charming space; the choice of cakes is particularly good. $ *Average main: €8* ✉ *Av. de Tervueren 107, Cinquantenaire* ☎ *02/736–2298* 🌐 *leopoldcafepresse.com* Ⓜ *Metro: Montgomery.*

Sowl

$ | **CAFÉ** | This popular spot among health-conscious office workers lets you fill your bowl with healthy veggies, grains, meats, and berries (or just take one of the standard blends). Everything is tasty, good for you, and the word "superfood" crops up endlessly. **Known for:** it's a good way to get a load of fresh inside you; it's perfect for vegans and those with food allergies; the breakfast bowls are good if you're on the go. $ *Average main: €10* ✉ *Rue de la Loi 238, Schuman*

☎ *02/792–5779* 🌐 *sowl.be* Ⓜ *Metro: Schuman.*

Aloft Brussels Schuman
$$$ | HOTEL | FAMILY | A business hotel that wants to be just that little bit cooler than the rest—granted its design is a little industrial in places, but this slick offering has large, loftlike rooms, a fun bar area, a fitness center, and a small café area clearly geared to tempt those whose business meetings ran over. **Pros:** it's pet-friendly; despite the business vibe, it's a good place to hole up for families; you're surrounded by restaurants nearby. **Cons:** its slightly garish design isn't for everyone; you're a long walk or short metro ride from the center; you're close to a busy main road. $ *Rooms from: €164* ✉ *Pl. Jean Rey, Schuman* ☎ *02/800–0888* 🌐 *www.marriott.com* *102 rooms* *Free Breakfast* Ⓜ *Metro: Schuman.*

★ **B&B A Côté du Cinquantenaire**
$$ | B&B/INN | FAMILY | This little B&B was a shell when owner Laurent took it on but rebuilt the workshop at the end of the garden and turned it into two rooms, installed a glass corridor leading to them, and huge patio doors in the breakfast room. **Pros:** there's a (rare) single bedroom for those traveling alone; light, modern, cleverly designed B&B; the interior garden is a great spot for breakfast. **Cons:** it's a B&B, so there aren't many facilities; it's not super cheap, except on off-season days; you're a metro ride from the center. $ *Rooms from: €122* ✉ *Rue du Cornet 139, Cinquantenaire* ☎ *0475/581–508* 🌐 *www.cotecinquantenaire.be* *5 rooms* *Free Breakfast* Ⓜ *Metro: Merode.*

Martin's Brussels EU
$$$ | HOTEL | This suave boutique chain is aimed plumb at the politicos and businessfolk who swarm this area during the week. **Pros:** pleasant garden to explore on sunnier days; it's a stylish, sensible hotel with large rooms; small gym and sauna on the top floor. **Cons:** you're a walk or metro ride from the action; there's no parking, so you'll have to find a place on the street; despite the price, there's no pool. $ *Rooms from: €193* ✉ *Bd. Charlemagne 80, Cinquantenaire* ☎ *02/230–8555* 🌐 *www.martinshotels.com* *100 rooms* *Free Breakfast* Ⓜ *Metro: Schuman.*

This is more of an area for white-collar workers to let their hair down. Around place Jourdan you'll find lots of bars, all roughly the same, but they mostly serve one purpose: to allow those with a greasy cone of frites in hand to sit and have a beer.

Deja Vu
WINE BARS | A friendly neighborhood wine bar near the eastern entrance to Cinquantenaire. There's a good choice of organic wines, decent cocktails, and a smattering of beers. ✉ *Av. des Celtes 42–44, Cinquantenaire* ☎ *02/346–9678* Ⓜ *Metro: Merode.*

Nabu
WINE BARS | Wrapped in the streets off the eastern exit of Cinquantenaire is this cheerful neighborhood natural-wine bar (from the people behind Tarzan in Ixelles) with a good choice of tapas. Its redbrick interior and friendly vibe make it a charming spot. ✉ *Av. Albert-Elisabeth 35, Cinquantenaire* ☎ *02/479–6887* Ⓜ *Metro: Merode.*

The Wild Geese
PUBS | There's, unsurprisingly, a proliferation of Irish bars around the EU area. This is certainly one of the better lit and more modern. It's also a friendly spot to watch sports or even grab some posh fish-and-chips. Needless to say, it is packed to the gills with expats. ✉ *Av. Livingstone 24, Schuman* ☎ *02/588–6803* Ⓜ *Metro: Schuman.*

Ixelles and Saint-Gilles

Lying just south of the city center, Ixelles and Saint-Gilles are like a city within a city. These two communes are a mass of hidden courtyards, Art Nouveau town houses, old-school beer bars, boutiques, and shopping streets. You won't find as many sights, but what it has above all else is life.

Sights

Musée Constantin Meunier (*Constantin Meunier Museum*)
ART MUSEUM | Nineteenth-century painter and sculptor Constantin Meunier (1831–1905) made his mark capturing the hardships of Belgian workers in a distinctive, realistic style. Examples of his work are displayed in his former house and studio. ✉ *Rue de l'Abbaye, Ixelles* ☎ *02/648–4449* 🌐 *www.fine-arts-museum.be* 🎫 *Free* 🕑 *Closed Mon.; only open to groups on weekends.*

★ **Musée Horta** (*Horta Museum*)
OTHER MUSEUM | The house where Victor Horta (1861–1947), one of the major forces in Art Nouveau design, lived and worked until 1919 is the best place to see how he thought. Inspired by the direction of the turn-of-the-20th-century British Arts and Crafts movement, he amplified its designs into an entire architectural scheme, shaping iron and steel into fluid, organic curves. Horta had a hand in every aspect of his design, from the door hinges to the wall treatments. ✉ *Rue Américaine 25, Saint-Gilles* ☎ *02/543–0490* 🌐 *www.hortamuseum.be* 🎫 *€12* 🕑 *Closed Mon.* ✍ *Reservations required* Ⓜ *Tram: 81.*

Musée Wiertz (*Wiertz Museum*)
ART MUSEUM | This workshop-museum began life in 1850 when the painter, sculptor, and writer Antoine Wiertz (1806–65) agreed to leave his collection to the Belgian government before his death. All the more surprising given he was a somewhat controversial figure, drawn to create huge canvases of often shocking subjects, from a naked woman staring down a skeleton, to gruesome accounts of Greek history, and the truly macabre *Premature Burial,* where a hand is seen clawing its way out of a coffin. ✉ *Rue Vautier 62, Ixelles* ☎ *02/648–1718* 🌐 *www.fine-arts-museum.be* 🎫 *Free* 🕑 *Closed Sat.–Mon.* Ⓜ *Metro: Maelbeek.*

Porte de Hal (*Halle Gate*)
HISTORIC SIGHT | Built in 1381, this gate is a unique remnant of Brussels's city walls, which tend to reappear in unusual places. (For example, if you continue down nearby rue Haute, you'll spy a huge chunk of wall next to the bowling alley at the crossroads with boulevard de l'Empereur.) In 1847, this gate became one of the first museums in Europe, though it lost its collections to the Cinquantenaire complex in the 1870s. It now has a permanent exhibition on medieval Brussels, and if you climb its 169 steps to the roof, a crenelated walkway affords sweeping views of the neighborhood. ✉ *150 bd. du Midi, Saint-Gilles* ☎ *02/534–1518* 🌐 *www.kmkg-mrah.be* 🎫 *€10* 🕑 *Closed Fri.* Ⓜ *Tram: 4.*

Restaurants

Au Vieux Bruxelles
$$ | **BELGIAN** | Matonge's St. Boniface area is a great spot to grab some food, and this Brussels institution (open since 1882) is as lively as any and a favorite among locals. The cuisine is decidedly Belgian, with *anguilles au vert* (freshwater eels in a green sauce) and hearty Flemish carbonnades on the menu, best accompanied by a draft beer. **Known for:** old-school hospitality; a vast array (even for Brussels) of mussels dishes; cozy interior and people-watching terrace. $ *Average main: €17* ✉ *Rue St-Boniface 35, Ixelles* ☎ *02/503–3111* 🌐 *www.auvieuxbruxelles.com* 💳 *No credit cards* Ⓜ *Metro: Porte de Namur.*

Ixelles and Saint-Gilles
UPPER TOWN
Boulevard du Midi
Boulevard du Midi
Rue de Russie
R. d'Angleterre
Rue Émile Feron
Rue Blaes
Rue de la Rasière
Rue des Capucins
Rue Haute
Rue du Miroir
Rue Blaes
Rue Haute
R. des Minimes
Rue Ernest Allard
Rue de la Régence
Rue aux Laines
R. aux Laines
R. aux Laines
Boulevard de Waterloo
Av. de la Toison d'Or
Avenue de la Toison d'Or
R. des Drapiers
Rue Keyenveld
Rue du Berger
Rue de la Pépinière
Avenue Louise
R. Dejoncker
Rue Jean Stas
R20
Rue Jourdan
R. d'Écosse
Rue de Suisse
Rue Berckmans
Rue de la Source
Rue de l'Hôtel des Monnaies
Rue de la Victoire
Rue Jourdan
Chaussée de Forest
R. de l'Église Saint-Gilles
Rue d'Ardenne
R. Vanderschrick
Rue Dethy
R. Théodore Verhaegen
Rue du Fort
Chaussée de Waterloo
Rue du Métal
Rue de la Croix de Pierre
Rue de Bordeaux
Rue Saint-Bernard
Chaussée de Charleroi
Rue Veydt
R. Blanche
Rue de Livourne
R. de Florence
Avenue Louise
Rue de la Concorde
Rue du Président
Rue Jean d'Ardenne
Rue Souveraine
Rue Faider
R. Paul Émile Janson
Rue Defacqz
Rue Simonis
Rue du Bailli
Rue de l'Hôtel des Monnaies
R. de Roumanie
Rue de la Victoire
Rue de Parme
Rue d'Irlande
Rue d'Espagne
Avenue du Parc
Avenue du Parc
Rue Jean Robie
Rue Saint-Bernard
Rue Maurice Wilmotte
Rue Moris
Chaussée de Waterloo
Rue d'Albanie
Rue de Lombardie
Avenue des Villas
Rue de Savoie
Rue Antoine Bréart
Avenue Ducpétiaux
R. Henri Wafelaerts
Rue Africaine
Rue du Tabellion
Rue du Page
Rue Américaine
Rue de l'Aqueduc
Chaussée de Waterloo
Rue du Mail
R. du Prévôt
Rue de Tenbosch
Rue de la Réforme
Chaussée d'Alsemberg
Avenue de la Jonction
Avenue Brugmann
Avenue Albert
Rue Berkendael
Rue Darwin
Rue Franz Merjay
Avenue Louis Lepoutre
R. Mignot Delstanche
Rue Alphonse Renard
R. Camille Lemonnier
Rue Jean-Baptiste Colyns
KEY
Exploring Sights
Restaurants
Quick Bites
Hotels

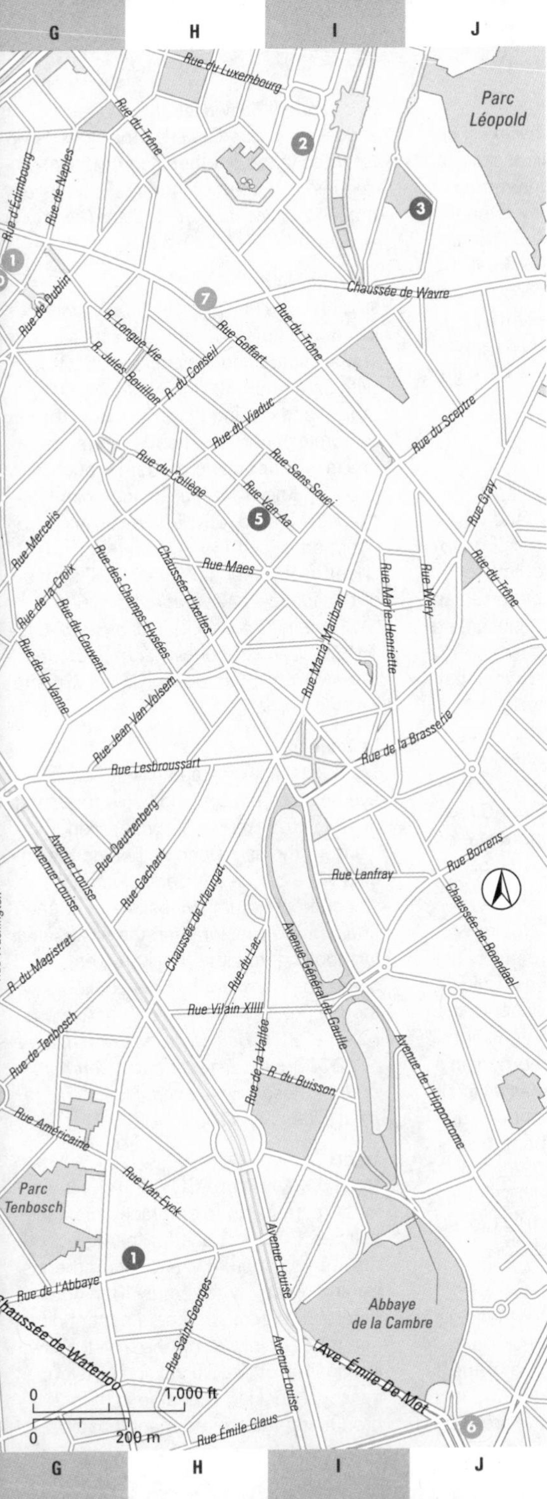

Sights

1 Musée Constantin Meunier H8
2 Musée Horta E6
3 Musée Wiertz J2
4 Porte de Hal B3

Restaurants

1 Au Vieux Bruxelles G2
2 Ballekes D6
3 Café des Spores A7
4 Colonel E3
5 Friterie de la Barrière A6
6 La Truffe Noire J9
7 Le Tournant H2
8 Le 203 .... B6
9 Le Waterloo C6
10 Yamato G2

Quick Bites

1 Hinterland D6
2 Karsmakers Coffee House I1
3 Mamy Louise E3
4 Wild Lab C7

Hotels

1 Harmon House E4
2 Made in Louise E5
3 Manos Premier E5
4 The Scott Hotel D4
5 Steigenberger Wiltcher's E3
6 Vintage Hotel E3

Ballekes

$$ | **BELGIAN** | Meatballs (or *ballekes*) are Belgium's current fast-food obsession. This restaurant chain is everywhere now but began here in Saint-Gilles, even if it's looking its age these days. **Known for:** nice selection of craft ales for a local chain; Belgian comfort food—the way your maman would make it; quick service. *Average main: €14 ✉ 174 Chau. de Charleroi, Saint-Gilles 🌐 www.ballekes.be Ⓜ Tram: 92.*

★ Café des Spores

$$$ | **FRENCH** | Finally, the mushroom-theme restaurant of your dreams ... well, someone's dreams. And while diners might discover that it isn't quite as eccentric as they'd expect (mushrooms feature in all dishes but often as side ingredients), it is nonetheless quite out there, particularly the desserts: try the cakey *flan diplomate* and wood-ear fungus! **Known for:** the desserts are something special; wonderfully imaginative slow-food menu; wide selection of natural wines. *Average main: €29 ✉ Chau. d'Alsemberg 103, Saint-Gilles ☎ 02/534–1303 🌐 cafedesspores.be/en ⏲ Closed Sun. and Mon. Ⓜ Bus: 52.*

Colonel

$$$ | **STEAKHOUSE** | Even in Belgium, where meat tends to feature pretty high on the agenda of most menus, Colonel is something different. It's all about the steak here—marbled, aged, and kept on display like a treasured memory in a cabinet by the bar counter. **Known for:** its oddly transfixing meat counter; beautifully aged (pricey) French beef; great service. *Average main: €28 ✉ Rue Jean Stas 24, Saint-Gilles ☎ 02/538–5736 🌐 www.colonelbrussels.com ⏲ Closed Sun. and Mon. Ⓜ Metro: Louise.*

Friterie de la Barrière

$ | **FAST FOOD** | It divides opinion (as this hotly debated topic often does), but this is an outside shout for one of the best frites kiosks in the city. Locals who know tout it as such, and who are we to disagree? **Known for:** the choices of sauces is as good as any other; best stop for frites in the southerly communes; queues, and plenty of them. *Average main: €3 ✉ Av. du Parc 5, Saint-Gilles Ⓜ Bus: 52.*

La Truffe Noire

$$$$ | **ITALIAN** | Luigi Ciciriello's Michelin-starred "Black Truffle" attracts a sophisticated and well-heeled clientele with its modern design, well-spaced tables, and cuisine that often requires bottomless pockets. Its menu draws on classic Italian and modern French cooking. **Known for:** quality ingredients; truffles—grated, drizzled (in oil), juiced, chopped, sliced—with everything; its cheerful, if rather self-conscious, sense of decadence. *Average main: €40 ✉ Bd. de la Cambre 12, Ixelles ☎ 02/640–4422 🌐 www.truffenoire.com ⏲ Closed Sun. No lunch Sat. or Mon. Jacket and tie Ⓜ Tram: 3, 7.*

Le Tournant

$$$$ | **BISTRO** | A restaurant with a firm eye on seasonal cooking, slow food, and organic produce. No surprise, then, that it's from the same people behind the Titulus wine bar (*see Nightlife*), and that its selection of natural wines is among the finest in any restaurant in the city. **Known for:** cooking that lets the ingredients speak for themselves; slow-cooked slow food; a great wine selection. *Average main: €38 ✉ Chau. de Wavre 168, Ixelles ☎ 02/502–6165 🌐 restaurantletournant.com ⏲ Closed weekends. No lunch Mon., Tues., and Thurs.*

Le 203

$$$$ | **BISTRO** | While COVID-19 forced a lot of restaurants to embrace reservation policies, 203 has gone for the first-come, first-served approach, and recommends turning up at 7 (we'd argue 10 minutes beforehand) to guarantee a spot at dinner. It's certainly worth the effort. **Known for:** queues of people waiting outside; seasonal cooking with an eye of local producers; the limited menu ensures

The 14th-century Porte de Hal gate is an ancient remnant of Brussels' old city walls.

each dish really pops. [$] *Average main: €37* ✉ *Chau. de Waterloo 203, Saint-Gilles* ☎ *02/539–2643* 🌐 *www.le203.com* ⏲ *Closed Sun. and Mon. No lunch Sat.* [M] *Bus: 52.*

Le Waterloo

$$ | **BELGIAN** | **FAMILY** | A really solid and reliable Belgian brasserie that rarely lets you down. One thing you are guaranteed: all food will be slathered in creamy, beery, or mustardy sauces and frites will fall from the air like raindrops on the battlefield this restaurant is named after. **Known for:** all the Belgian favorites; simple brasserie cooking done right; a nice selection of local beers (and on draft). [$] *Average main: €15* ✉ *Chau. de Waterloo 217, Saint-Gilles* ☎ *02/539–2804* 🌐 *lewaterloo.be/en* ⏲ *Closed Mon. and Tues.* [M] *Bus: 52.*

★ **Yamato**

$$ | **RAMEN** | There's plenty of debate as to Brussels's best ramen. This cozy little joint on rue St. Boniface is undoubtedly in with a claim. **Known for:** great value; one of the best ramens in the capital—especially the katsu; the countertop dining and scents are a joy. [$] *Average main: €13* ✉ *Rue Francart 11, Ixelles* ☎ *02/511–0200* [M] *Metro: Porte de Namur.*

Coffee and Quick Bites

Hinterland

$ | **CAFÉ** | With its all-day brunch ricocheting between healthier options (acai and Buddha bowls) and more indulgent offerings, including a guacamole, bacon, and cheddar toast, this is a good spot to bag a late-morning or early-afternoon pick-me-up (until 3 weekdays; 3:30 on weekends). **Known for:** it's avocado paradise, with most things slathered in the green stuff; there are good breakfast options; there are gluten-free and vegan options. [$] *Average main: €11* ✉ *Charleroise Steenweg 179, Saint-Gilles* ☎ *02/537–9747* 🌐 *hntrlnd.be* ⏲ *Closed Wed.* [M] *Tram: 92.*

Karsmakers Coffee House

$ | **CAFÉ** | A bustling little coffee shop that's usually packed with gossiping, bitching politicos—which is always entertaining to overhear—because it just edges the European district. The bagels are fresh and rightfully celebrated, while the coffee is first-rate. **Known for:** everyone loves the bagels here; there's a small patio in the back for warmer days; a good selection of cakes and treats. *Average main: €8 ✉ Rue de Trèves 20, Ixelles ☎ 02/502–0226 ⊕ www.karsmakers.be ⏲ Closed weekends* Ⓜ *Bus: 38, 95.*

Mamy Louise

$$ | **FRENCH** | This branch of a local minichain is one of several good-quality lunch spots on the pedestrianized rue Jean Stas, just off avenue Louise. With a vaguely beach-house decor and outdoor tables in warm weather, the restaurant's equally breezy menu includes Belgian staples like *boudin noir* (blood sausage) as well as quiches and salads; the latter are huge. **Known for:** light, hip layout; great quality cakes and sweet stuff; stylish food and upmarket nibbles. *Average main: €12 ✉ Rue Jean Stas 12, Ixelles ☎ 02/534–2502 ⊕ www.mamylouise.be ⏲ Closed Sun.* Ⓜ *Metro: Louise.*

Wild Lab

$$ | **CAFÉ** | Power food, in all its acai glory. Wild Lab is the kind of place you get chia jam on your chocolate-banana pancakes or can find a "Goodness Bowl" brimming with lentils, roasted parsnip, and za'atar. **Known for:** where else can you get your "superfood latte"; lots of vegan and gluten-free options; organic teas and fresh juices aplenty. *Average main: €13 ✉ Rue Antoine Bréart 44a, Saint-Gilles ☎ 0492/540–062 ⊕ www.thewildlab.be ⏲ Closed Mon.* Ⓜ *Tram: 81.*

Hotels

Harmon House

$$ | **HOTEL** | Having opened in 2017, this is one of the newer kids on the block (and by block we mean the street of big hotels that is Chausée de Charleroi) but this is certainly one of the better-value stays. **Pros:** a great spa to relax in and mighty breakfasts; the suites tend to come with balconies; you're in a great location for shopping. **Cons:** as with all the others on this street, it can be a bit noisy outside; it doesn't have a restaurant, though the area is well stocked; there's no hotel parking. *Rooms from: €147 ✉ Chau. de Charleroi 50, Ixelles ☎ 02/899–3334 ⊕ harmon.house ⇆ 27 rooms ⑩ Free Breakfast* Ⓜ *Metro: Louise.*

★ Made in Louise

$$ | **HOTEL** | A charmingly renovated 18th-century building is the setting for this exquisite, family-run boutique hotel, found deep in the fashionable Louise neighborhood. **Pros:** ideally located for cramming in some shopping; large, bright rooms in a quiet residential area off the main streets; you can get local restaurants to deliver food to the desk and pick it up. **Cons:** there are lots of stairs; residential setting might be too quiet for some; it's a 10-minute walk to the Louise subway. *Rooms from: €104 ✉ Rue Veydt 40, Ixelles ☎ 02/537–4033 ⊕ www.madeinlouise.com ⇆ 48 rooms ⑩ No Meals* Ⓜ *Tram: 92.*

Manos Premier

$$ | **HOTEL** | This upscale hotel has expansive terraces, a rose-filled garden populated by waterfowl and songbirds, and a good restaurant, Kolya. **Pros:** good spa facilities plus a small fitness center; it's a handsome hotel that oozes grande-dame style; there's a lovely garden to lounge about in. **Cons:** some noise from passing traffic; its classical interior might be old hat to some; pets are welcome but only for a fee. *Rooms from: €143 ✉ Chau. de Charleroi 100–106, Saint-Gilles ☎ 02/537–9682 ⊕ www.manospremier.com ⇆ 62 rooms ⑩ Free Breakfast* Ⓜ *Metro: Louise.*

The Scott Hotel

$ | HOTEL | Until quite recently this was the Pantone Hotel, and as garish as its name implies. **Pros:** it's been recently refurbished to a high standard; it's a quiet, cheap stay not far from the edge of Ixelles; the price is good for what you get. **Cons:** there's no hotel parking, though there's space across the road; there are few facilities beyond the bar and breakfast room; you'll need to walk a bit to find some action. *Rooms from: €95 Pl. Loix 1, Saint-Gilles 02/541–4898 www.thescotthotel.be 75 rooms Free Breakfast Tram: 92.*

Steigenberger Wiltcher's

$$$ | HOTEL | After years in the wilderness, a titanic makeover has turned this back into one of Brussels's plushest stays. **Pros:** nice cocktail bar; well placed for the shopping streets of Ixelles; large outdoor terrace. **Cons:** it can be rather businesslike; the views aren't the greatest; rooms over the street can be a little noisy. *Rooms from: €200 Av. Louise 71, Ixelles 02/542–4242 www.steigenberger.com 267 rooms Free Breakfast Metro: Louise.*

Vintage Hotel

$$ | HOTEL | This hotel is vintage by virtue of having a fair amount of clutter adorning its spaces—think a CHiPs-style motorcycle on a balcony and old silver food truck in the yard. **Pros:** pick the one room with a balcony (and sit on its motorbike); it's a nice secluded spot with little noise to bother you; the fourth and fifth floors have a/c. **Cons:** the room decor can be an acquired taste; no hotel parking; there are few facilities, though the bar is lively. *Rooms from: €100 Rue Dejoncker 45, Saint-Gilles 02/533–9980 vintagehotel.be 37 rooms Free Breakfast Tram: 92, 93.*

Nightlife

BARS

Café Belga

BARS | Set in an ocean-liner-like Art Deco building, this is a favorite among Brussels's beautiful people. It's the kind of place you'd spot a local TV star sipping a cocktail or mint tea at the zinc bar or outside gazing at the swans on the Ixelles ponds. DJs play until late; it's also a popular brunch spot for hungover locals on Sunday. *Pl. Eugène Flagey 18, Ixelles 02/544–0100 belgacafe.com Tram: 8.*

Cafe Maison de Peuples

BARS | The hipster-dense Parvis de Saint-Gilles area is stuffed with great bars, but this popular joint is among the more pristine. It does a great brunch, and late-night DJs often go on until late on weekends. It's named after a demolished Victor Horta–designed building, the loss of which is often used as one of the worst examples of Brussels's gentrification. *Parvis de Saint-Gilles 39, Saint-Gilles 02/850–0908 www.cafemdp.com Tram: 3, 4.*

Chez Moeder Lambic

BREWPUBS | The first bar of the Moeder Lambic brewery opened in the 1980s. It's an icon on the Brussels beer scene, and alongside its own brews, it claims to stock 300 Belgian beers and quite a few foreign ones. Soak up the old-school vibe and pore over a fine collection of comic books while you sip. It has a second branch on place Fontainas in the center. *Rue de Savoie 68, Saint-Gilles 02/544–1699 www.moederlambic.com Tram: 3, 4.*

Dynamo (Bar de Soif)

BARS | This likable craft beer bar usually has at least 15 draft beers on tap and an ace in its pocket. The selection is huge, the staff are friendly and knowledgeable, but you can also order Japanese food from the rather fine restaurant across the street (Tokidori). A definite winner.

✉ *Chau. d'Alsemberg 130, Saint-Gilles* ☎ *02/539–1567* Ⓜ *Tram: 3, 4.*

Jane's

BARS | Jane's has the air of a chill after-party, with guests from the city's art world occasionally invited to soundtrack the evening by their genial host (the bar's own Jane Haesen, a veteran of the city's party scene). A good selection of natural wines, cocktails, and beers make the evening swim. ✉ *Chau. de Waterloo 393, Ixelles* ☎ *02/851–1039* Ⓜ *Tram: 92.*

★ The Modern Alchemist

COCKTAIL LOUNGES | A fantastically hip, cozy, stylish brick-walled cocktail bar where the quality is never less than high and the drinks deceptively potent. A huge selection of rums and whiskeys also adorn the menu, but you can't go wrong with the slightly sour "Last Shot"—you can even order a bottle of it to take away. ✉ *Av. Adolphe Demeur 55, Saint-Gilles* 🌐 *www.themodernalchemist.bar* Ⓜ *Tram: 3, 4.*

Tarzan

WINE BARS | Another to add to the growing number of natural wine bars in the capital. Together with Titulus, this bar and neighboring shop stock some 400 references from France, Italy, Spain, Georgia, and what owner Matthieu Vellut calls "punk wines"—those you're not even sure are a wine! The bar also runs tasting nights and courses. ✉ *Rue Washington 59, Ixelles* ☎ *02/538–6580* Ⓜ *Tram: 93.*

Titulus

WINE BARS | The first of what is now a flood of natural wine bars in the capital. This cozy, chic shop-cum-bar in the Matonge area even has its own label, made on the owners' vineyard in France's Loire Valley, where they all grew up. With bottles from €17, it's good value (natural wine usually has a high markup), and staff will cheerfully talk newbies through the selection of some 400 references. ✉ *Chau. de Wavre 167A, Ixelles* ☎ *02/512–9830* 🌐 *www.titulus.be* Ⓜ *Bus: 38, 95.*

JAZZ CLUBS

Sounds

LIVE MUSIC | Sounds has been dishing up contemporary jazz along with decent Italian food since 1986, and it shows no signs of losing its rhythm. ✉ *Rue de la Tulipe 28, Ixelles* ☎ *02/3115–2975* 🌐 *www.sounds.brussels* Ⓜ *Bus: 71.*

 Shopping

Ixelles is where you go to spend. Its streets are filled with stylish boutiques, big-brand couture, and all those little places in between. The second-busiest shopping street in Brussels, **Chaussée d'Ixelles**, runs right through it. This spans the whole gamut of capital consumerism, from high-street brands to an African-centric shopping center. More fine-tuned are the avenues of **Toison d'Or** and **Louise**, which runs for 3 km (2 miles) all the way to the Bois de Cambre. However, the first stretch of the latter is given over to pure couture, and you'd better bring your wallet. More niche, slightly more boutique finds are sourced around **rue du Bailli** and the **Châtelain** quarter, where you can usually find a wine bar to rest up in after burning through your credit card.

CHOCOLATE SHOPS

Elizabeth Chocolaterie

CHOCOLATE | A window packed with artisanal marshmallow cakes and meringues tempts visitors into this boutique sweet and chocolate shop, which also conjures traditional Flemish biscuits and heavenly truffles. There are also a pair of branches on rue de Buerre, next to the Grand Place. ✉ *Av. Louise 49, Ixelles* ☎ *02/269–8078* 🌐 *elisabeth.be* Ⓜ *Metro: Louise.*

CLOTHING

Mellow Concept Store

WOMEN'S CLOTHING | Stylish concept store and fashion boutique offering clothes, accessories, and a few small furniture

The Chocolatey History of Brussels

Many years ago, visitors to Brussels, stepping out of the Midi train station, would be greeted by the sight of the Côte D'Or chocolate factory. The plumes of smoke rising from its stacks would scent the air with a seductive aroma of freshly made chocolate. Though the factory closed in the late 1970s, you won't lack for reminders of one of the country's signature industries. With nearly 500 large- and small-scale chocolatiers vying for a place at the top, Belgian chocolate is a prodigious and cutthroat business. The domestic market alone is formidable; Belgium has one of the world's highest chocolate consumption rates, at an average of more than 15.8 pounds per person per year.

The country's reputation for high quality rests on choice raw materials and meticulous production practices—not to mention a history of pillaging the Congo. Chocolate making here really took off in the 1880s, after King Leopold II took his first brutal steps in Central Africa. These days companies go after the rare criollo cocoa beans and the trinitario variety (a cross between criollo and the hardier, less subtle forastero cocoa), both of which have complex, nonbitter flavors. The bean roasting and crushing is done with exceptional precision. The best producers conch their chocolate—a refining process of mixing the chocolate with extra cocoa butter or other additions—for days rather than a few hours, as standard manufacturers do. Extended conching creates a smooth, even texture and reduces acid levels, enhancing the chocolate taste.

You can get a full rundown on the production process at the Choco-Story (*choco-story-brussels.be*) on rue de l'Etuve 41. Of course, you should also indulge in a little self-education at some of the local chocolate shops as well, who often run workshops, demonstrations, and lessons. Check out the Brussels shopping listings to find out which ones.

Brussels's (and indeed Belgium's) chief contribution to the history of chocolate making came in 1912, when Belgian chocolatier Jean Neuhaus created the first pralines, bite-size chocolates filled with a mixture of nuts and sugar. This was created at the Neuhaus Boutique in what was then Galerie de la Reine, which later became part of Brussels's Galeries Royales Saint-Hubert, which still stands today. These treats were billed as "individual masterpieces," handcrafted delicacies that proved an excellent way for chocolatiers to distinguish themselves.

Neuhaus's "couverture" chocolate formed a shell that could hold all kinds of fillings: caramels, creams, flavored ganaches, and more. Combining visual elegance with exquisite taste, the praline continues to undergo reinvention generation after generation. Classic examples such as *gianduja* (hazelnut) share display cases with newcomers flavored with ginger, tea, or herbs. Many chocolatiers make seasonal or special-event pralines and increasingly emphasize the single origins of their cocoa beans. But it arguably all started with one Brussels store.

pieces from selected designers. ✉ *Parv. de la Trinité 3, Ixelles* ☎ *02/538–2629* 🌐 *mellowconcept.com* Ⓜ *Tram: 92.*

Mook's

WOMEN'S CLOTHING | Long established on the Châtelain scene, Mook's has a slick range of women's clothes and accessories. It also has a sister store, Chouke (rue du Bailli 25) that skews a bit younger and focuses on Parisian brands. ✉ *Rue du Bailli 72, Ixelles* ☎ *02/649–4494* Ⓜ *Tram: 93.*

Performing Arts

Flagey

ARTS CENTERS | Large performing arts and cinema center, and the home of the Brussels Philharmonic, who perform regularly in Studio 4. ✉ *Pl. Sainte-Croix, Ixelles* ☎ *02/641–1020 ticket office* 🌐 *www.flagey.be* Ⓜ *Tram: 81.*

Laeken and Schaerbeek

North of the center are two very different sides to Brussels. Beyond the river is Laeken, the second (and preferred) residence of Belgium's royal family. It's mostly a grand concoction of parkland and palaces, with the unusual addition of an avenue of Asian-style pagodas built by King Leopold II in the early 1900s.

On the flip side, the communes of Schaerbeek and its tiny neighbor St-Josse-ten-Noode are largely residential and home to some of the poorer areas. Things get seedy in the streets around Gare du Nord, which is best avoided at night, yet Schaerbeek, in particular, is filled with Art Nouveau mansions and one of the finest parks in the city.

Sights

★ **Atomium**

OTHER ATTRACTION | **FAMILY** | Like a giant, shiny child's toy rising up out of a forest, the Atomium was created in 1958 as part of the World's Fair of Brussels. It's shaped like an atom, with an elevator taking you up the central axis where walkways link to the protruding spheres by escalators. One sphere contains a permanent exhibition about the building's history; the others are set aside for temporary displays on design and architecture. Audio guides in English are available and there are great views from the top sphere, known as the Panorama. ✉ *Av. de l'Atomium, Laeken* ☎ *02/475–4775* 🌐 *www.atomium.be* 🎫 *€16; includes visit to ADAM* Ⓜ *Heisel.*

Charlier Museum

HISTORIC HOME | This museum was originally an artist's home. Sculptor Guillaume Charlier and his friend Henri Van Cutsem were avid art collectors and asked Victor Horta to convert two houses into one to contain their treasures. It's an eclectic mix, with piles of decorative objects from the 18th to 20th centuries, an impressive collection of Belgian art, and Charlier's own realistic works vying for attention. ✉ *Av. des Arts 16, St-Josse-ten-Noode, Schaerbeek* ☎ *02/217–8161* 🌐 *www.charliermuseum.be* 🎫 *€5* ⏲ *Closed weekends* ✍ *Reservation required* Ⓜ *Metro: Arts-Loi.*

Greenhouses of Laeken

GARDEN | Laeken is where you'll find the Royal Greenhouses, a glorious mid-19th-century mesh of steel and glass set within the grounds of the summer palace, where the Belgian royal family spends most of their time. It's only open to visitors for three weeks every spring (between April and May), but it's worth catching. The height of its winter garden, designed by Alphonse Balat, made it possible to plant palm trees for the first time in Belgium; the originals still stand here. ✉ *Av. du Parc Royal, Laeken* ☎ *02/551–2020* 🌐 *www.monarchie.be* 🎫 *Free* ⏲ *Closed June–Mar.* Ⓜ *Tram: 3.*

The Atomium, one of Brussels' most iconic structures, was created in 1958 as part of the World's Fair.

Maison Autrique (*Autrique House*)
HISTORIC HOME | The first house designed in Brussels by the architect Victor Horta (he'd done others in Ghent by this time) was built in 1893 for a friend, Eugene Autrique. It was to have "not a single luxury," and became the first manor house built by Horta, marking his early explorations in Art Nouveau. At the time, Schaerbeek was mostly agrarian, best known for the small, sour cherries used to brew kriek beers—a state almost unimaginable given its current urban sprawl. Having undergone extensive renovation to return it to its original state, the house is now a museum on Horta's early days, and holds the odd exhibition. ✉ *Chau. de Haecht 266, Schaerbeek* ☎ *02/215–6600* 🌐 *www.autrique.be* 🎫 *€7* 🕒 *Closed Mon. and Tues.* ✍ *Reservations required* Ⓜ *Tram: 3.*

Mini-Europe
AMUSEMENT PARK/CARNIVAL | FAMILY | Just a short stroll from the Atomium lies this kids' favorite, which is essentially a park full of scale models of important European monuments. The 350 monuments range from the Eiffel Tower to a model of Santiago de Compostela Cathedral that was said to have taken 24,000 hours to build. It's a slightly kitsch selfie wonderland. ✉ *Bruparck, Laeken* ☎ *02/478–0550* 🌐 *www.minieurope.com* 🎫 *€17* 🕒 *Closed Jan.–Mar.* Ⓜ *Metro: Heisel.*

Musée d'Art Spontané (*Spontaneous Art Museum*)
ART MUSEUM | Art from the fringes. Set in an old print house, this museum turns its lens on outsider, naive, and folk art in particular, though you'll find more traditional pieces as well among its rotating collection, ✉ *Rue de la Constitution 27, Schaerbeek* ☎ *02/426–8404* 🌐 *musee-art-spontane.be* 🎫 *€4* 🕒 *Closed Sun. and Mon.* Ⓜ *Tram: 92.*

Musée Schaerbeekois de la Bière (*Schaerbeek Museum of Beer*)
BREWERY | As much a love letter to Belgian beer culture as a museum. It was started by one person donating 300 (empty) bottles of Belgian beer,

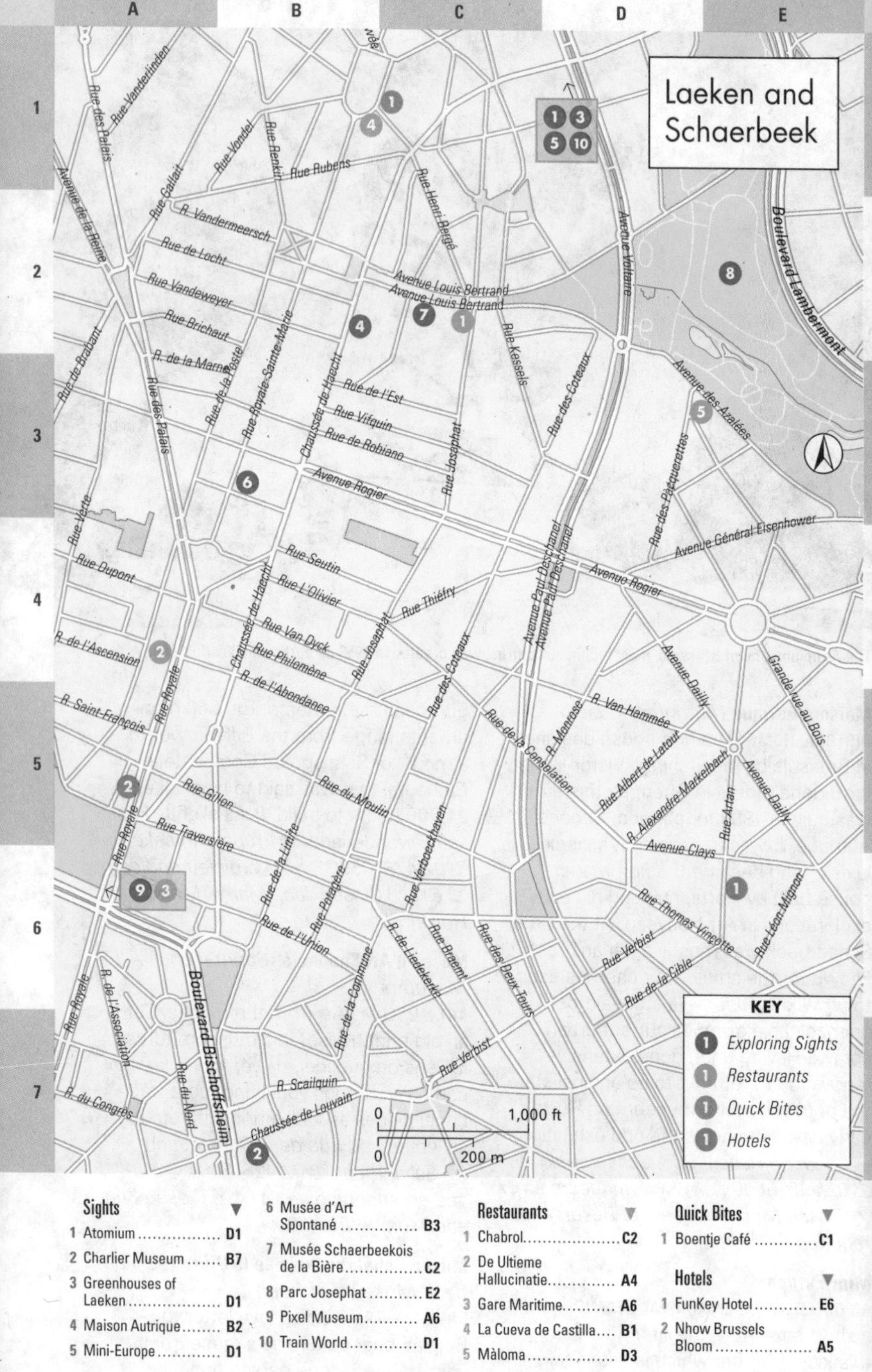

Sights

1 Atomium D1
2 Charlier Museum B7
3 Greenhouses of Laeken D1
4 Maison Autrique B2
5 Mini-Europe D1
6 Musée d'Art Spontané B3
7 Musée Schaerbeekois de la Bière C2
8 Parc Josephat E2
9 Pixel Museum A6
10 Train World D1

Restaurants

1 Chabrol C2
2 De Ultieme Hallucinatie A4
3 Gare Maritime A6
4 La Cueva de Castilla B1
5 Màloma D3

Quick Bites

1 Boentje Café C1

Hotels

1 FunKey Hotel E6
2 Nhow Brussels Bloom A5

then volunteers sought out all kinds of brewing paraphernalia. Now it has over 2,500 bottles and some 5,000-plus glasses, as well as endless signs, logos, bits of brewing equipment, and relics of breweries long since departed. It's only open two days a week (Wednesday and Saturday), and tickets include a tasting of Schaerbeekoise and Eizelskop beers. ✉ *Av. Louis Bertrand 33–35, Schaerbeek* ☎ *0470/814–300* 🌐 *museedelabiere-schaerbeekois.be* 🎫 *€5* ⏲ *Closed Sun.–Tues., Thurs., and Fri.* Ⓜ *Bus: 65, 66.*

Parc Josephat (*Jospehat Park*)
CITY PARK | **FAMILY** | One of the prettiest stretches of parkland in Brussels made all the more welcome for being deep among the residential mélange of Schaerbeek. Its archways of cherry blossoms are particularly enchanting in spring. In summer there are free concerts and Glacier Cocozza, across the road, draws a queue all the way down the road for its ice creams. The park is best known for its Cherry Festival (last Sunday in June) when locals gather to compete in a highly competitive cherry-pit-spitting contest. ✉ *Av. Ambassadeur van Vollenhoven, Schaerbeek* Ⓜ *Bus: 65, 66.*

Pixel Museum
OTHER MUSEUM | **FAMILY** | Set in the Tour & Taxis building on the riverfront, the city's first computer-game museum only opened in 2020. Its collection charts the history of gaming from 1972, the launch of the Odyssey by Magnavox, to the present day, and elicits great waves of nostalgia among those who lived through this era. ✉ *Tour & Taxis, rue Picard 3, Laeken* 🌐 *pixel-museum.brussels* 🎫 *€12* ⏲ *Closed Mon. and Tues.* Ⓜ *1000.*

Train World
HISTORY MUSEUM | **FAMILY** | In 1835, Belgium established the first steam passenger railway on mainland Europe—it connected Brussels and Mechelen—and it was one of the first to establish a national railway network. Train World pays full homage to this illustrious railway history. Located in the hangars of Belgium's oldest functioning station, Schaerbeek, it contains 20 full-size locomotives, many of which you can clamber aboard and explore. ✉ *Pl. Princesse Elisabeth 5, Schaerbeek* ☎ *02/224–7588* 🌐 *www.trainworld.be* 🎫 *€14* ⏲ *Closed Mon.* Ⓜ *Metro: Bruxelles Nord.*

 Restaurants

While St-Josse-ten-Noode is largely a mass of takeaways and Laeken is more of a day trip, Schaerbeek has a growing array of innovative new bars and restaurants. Many are homegrown neighborhood joints with a firm focus on sustainability, local produce, or even DIY producers themselves. Most are centered on the upmarket place Colignon, though you'll find a growing number on avenue Louis Bertrand and around Parc Josephat. What was once a residential black hole is becoming a hip little enclave.

★ **Chabrol**
$$ | **EUROPEAN** | Another example of a restaurant making the most of its appeal: charming Art Nouveau decoration, recycled tables, and a sustainable ethos. A pair of sisters are behind this admirable neighborhood eatery, where menus are short but sweet and limited by what is fresh and local that season (and day). **Known for:** a charming escape from the busy world; friendly staff and chill atmosphere; well-prepared, fresh cooking. Ⓢ *Average main: €21* ✉ *Av. Louis Bertrand 57–61, Schaerbeek* ☎ *02/463–1304* 🌐 *www.chabrol-restaurant.be* ⏲ *Closed Sun. and Mon.* Ⓜ *Bus: 65, 66.*

De Ultieme Hallucinatie
$$ | **BELGIAN** | This beautiful mid-18th-century town house was redone in the Art Nouveau style in 1904, adding an elegant bow window and balcony. It's been a brasserie since the early '80s, but remained empty for years after the previous owners went bankrupt. **Known**

Hop a tram to Schaerbeek to visit Maison Autrique, the first house in Brussels designed by architect Victor Horta.

for: they have the odd jazz night; solid Belgian cooking; the setting is a work of pure early-19th-century elegance. *Average main: €17* *Rue Royale 316, Saint-Josse-ten-Noode* *02/889–0316* *www.ultiemehallucinatie.be* *Closed Mon. and Tues.* *Tram: 92.*

★ Gare Maritime

$$ | **FAST FOOD** | **FAMILY** | The city isn't short of good street food markets, not since Wolf opened in the center, but out in Laeken, where the options are not nearly as interesting, this new addition was a godsend when it opened in the Tour & Taxis center in 2021. The choice here is a mix of slightly more upmarket and downright crowd-pleasing, ranging from the frites of "140" (the perfect temperature for cooking fries) to the Ayurvedic veggies of Xgreen. **Known for:** regular music nights; Carne's Mauro Colagreco is a veteran of the three-Michelin-starred Mirazur in France; Just Graze has a load of local cheeses to try. *Average main: €14* *Rue Picard 7, Laeken* *Closed weekends* *Metro: Ribaucourt.*

La Cueva de Castilla

$$$ | **SPANISH** | Paella is the prime reason to come here. It dominates the menu and holds to the old-school Valencian style, with rabbit and snails added to the usual chicken, pork, and fruits of the sea. **Known for:** some of the best paella in Belgium; a friendly neighborhood restaurant that does what it does well; a good spot on the hip place Colignon. *Average main: €26* *Pl. Colignon 8, Schaerbeek* *02/241–8180* *www.cuevadecastilla.be* *Closed Sun.*

★ Màloma

$$$$ | **EUROPEAN** | Hidden away in the streets just to the south of Parc Josephat, opposite the wine bar Ethylo, the local buzz is strong about this charming restaurant. The "market menu" is adapted in case of intolerances and geared around local producers. **Known for:** its focus on malolactic fermentation puts it in an interesting niche; the market menu is a pleasing journey; smart, friendly staff keen to help. *Average main: €70* *Rue Josse Impens 3, Schaerbeek*

02/732–5816 comptoir-maloma.squarespace.com Closed Sun. and Mon. Bus: 65.

 Coffee and Quick Bites

★ Boentje Café

$ | **CAFÉ** | Just a brilliant café run by a pair of owners who really care about what they do. Their aim is to be zero-waste, whether that means repurposing used coffee grounds to grow mushrooms, composting everything that's left over, or handing out reusable containers. **Known for:** great options for vegans and those with allergies; ethical, guilt-free lunching at its finest; the all-day (until 2:30) breakfast menu is pretty tasty. *Average main: €8 Pl. Colignon 18, Schaerbeek 02/672–0837 www.boentjecafe.com Bus: 65, 66.*

 Hotels

★ FunKey Hotel

$ | **HOTEL** | **FAMILY** | A great little budget stay, though buried among the residential weeds. **Pros:** there's free parking and you're in a pretty quiet area of town; lots of things to do and great value; breakfast is simple but amiable. **Cons:** there are no TVs in rooms (this may be a good thing); tea/coffee-making equipment is downstairs; you're a good walk from anywhere really. *Rooms from: €79 Rue Artan 116, Schaerbeek 02/733–2353 funkeyhotel.com 39 rooms Free Breakfast Bus: 29.*

Nhow Brussels Bloom

$$ | **HOTEL** | What was the BLOOM! hotel has been rebranded to create the kind of hotel name that looks like someone just fell on a keyboard. **Pros:** good transport links; it's just a 10-minute walk to Schaerbeek center or Upper Town; breakfast is served until noon, so late sleepers are well taken care of. **Cons:** traffic and gigs at neighboring Botanique can be noisy; parking is €27 a day; not one of the city's prettiest areas—you're quite close to Gare du Nord. *Rooms from: €124 Rue Royale 250, Laeken 02/588–0062 www.nh-hotels.com 305 rooms No Meals Metro: Botanique.*

 Nightlife

Achille

WINE BARS | An intriguing neighborhood wine bar that does a roaring trade in crowd-pleasing sharing plates, from shiitake arancini to frites drizzled in Parmesan and truffle. It's mostly good-quality French wines, though you can just as easily bag a beer or kombucha. *Pl. Colignon 14, Schaerbeek 0470/832–172 achillebar.be Tram: 92.*

Brasserie & Bar de la Mule

BREWPUBS | A brand-new local brewery and tap house set in a former stables. This used to be where they kept the mules that pulled Schaerbeek's trams until the first electric line was installed in 1894. Now tables have been strewn across the old stable yard, and its friendly, mulleted owner pours out glasses of his own brewed German-style wheat beers, along with the odd saison and lager. *Rue Rubens 95, Schaerbeek www.facebook.com/brasseriedelamule Tram: 92.*

Ethylo

COCKTAIL LOUNGES | An excellent and discreet neighborhood cocktail bar buried among the houses a street back from Parc Josephat. It's surprisingly good given its location and dishes up drinks with no little amount of flair. *Rue Josse Impens 2, Schaerbeek 02/307–3731 www.facebook.com/ethylococktailbar Bus: 65, 66.*

Le Berbator Bierotheque

BARS | A great little local beer bar with an excellent selection of bottled and draft (usually around 20) brews, all typically from the smaller breweries that don't

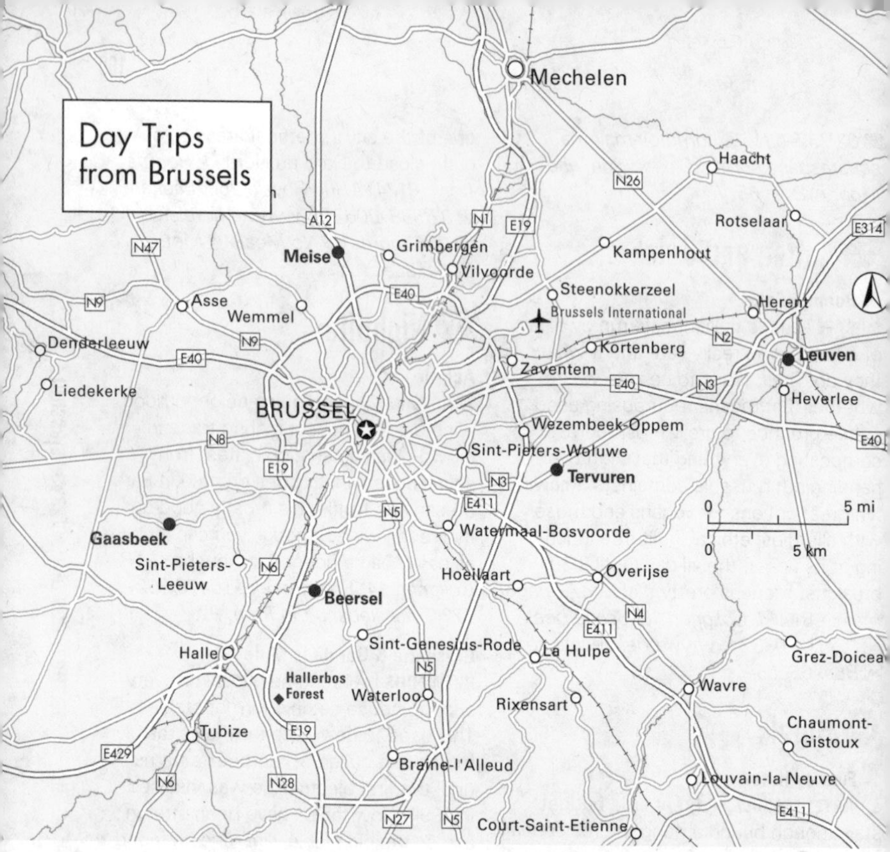

Day Trips from Brussels

Mechelen
Haacht
N26
Rotselaar
E314
A12
N1
E19
N47
Meise
Grimbergen
Vilvoorde
Kampenhout
Steenokkerzeel
Brussels International
Herent
N9
Asse
Wemmel
E40
N9
N2
Kortenberg
Leuven
Denderleeuw
E40
Zaventem
E40
N3
Heverlee
Liedekerke
BRUSSEL
Wezembeek-Oppem
E40
N8
Sint-Pieters-Woluwe
E19
Tervuren
N3
E411
0
5 mi
N5
Watermaal-Bosvoorde
0
5 km
Gaasbeek
Sint-Pieters-Leeuw
N6
Hoeilaart
Overijse
Beersel
N4
E411
Sint-Genesius-Rode
Halle
La Hulpe
Grez-Doiceau
N5
Hallerbos Forest
Waterloo
Wavre
Rixensart
Chaumont-Gistoux
Tubize
E19
E429
Braine-l'Alleud
N6
N28
Louvain-la-Neuve
E411
N27
N5
Court-Saint-Etienne

find their way onto most bar menus. ✉ *Av. Louis Bertrand 23, Schaerbeek* ☎ *0470/832–172* Ⓜ *Bus: 65, 66.*

Performing Arts

Botanique

ARTS CENTERS | Located in a former botanical garden, this is one of the larger live venues for independent and alt-music, championing local up-and-coming bands as well as the occasional visiting big name. It also has a good reputation for eye-catching art exhibitions. Tickets can be bought from the box office. ✉ *Rue Royale 236, Schaerbeek* ☎ *02/218–3732 box office* 🌐 *botanique.be* *Prices vary* ⏲ *Exhibitions closed Mon.–Thurs.*

Day Trips from Brussels

Wrapping the outskirts of metropolitan Brussels is Flemish Brabant, the smallest of the provinces of Flanders. Much of the area is forest and farmland, particularly the Pajottenland and the Zenne Valley to the south. This is where the bulk of Belgium's lambic beers are brewed and relics of the castles of the Dukes of Brabant still loom. To the east are the royal park of Tervuren and the northerly fringes of the vast Forêt de Soigne (Sonian Forest), whose wild trails cut deep into the lower region. Further on lies Leuven, the provincial capital and one of the oldest university towns in Europe, with a feisty history to boot. Or head north to Meise where the national botanic garden offers a scenic retreat. All are within 30 minutes' drive of Brussels.

Leuven

28 km (17 miles) from Brussels.

Leuven ("Louvain" in French) is an old university town—one of the oldest on the continent. Its Catholic university, founded in 1425, was one of Europe's great seats of learning during the late Middle Ages and continues to hold sway over a city where some 60,000 students register every year.

These days, the capital of Flemish Brabant is a friendly, lively town but its history is one of war and division. The city was pillaged and burned by the Germans in 1914 and bombed again in 1944. Then, in the 1960s, a different kind of explosion went off—a cultural one. Flemish Nationalism found a cause in a university where many classes were still taught in French, despite being in a Dutch-speaking region. Riots between students overspilled into other cities, causing the "Leuven Crisis" in 1968. The solution was to divide the student population, with a new French-speaking university created in the purpose-built town of Louvain-la-Neuve in Walloon Brabant. Leuven continued as before—a university town of lively nights and quiet mornings.

GETTING HERE AND AROUND

Leuven is easily reached from Brussels. It's only 30 km (18½ miles) away, with around four or five trains an hour going from Centraal and Midi stations (€5.50), taking around 30 minutes. If driving, it takes a similar amount of time if you follow the E40 east. You can even cycle there (around 90 minutes), with bike lanes most of the way, though the journey is not particularly attractive. Once there, the city is easily walkable, though parts of it are spread out; it would take a good 25 minutes to walk from the station to the beguinage. Luckily, there is a good network of internal buses if you're not up for the walk.

VISITOR INFORMATION

Leuven Tourist Information. ✉ *Naamsestraat 3, Leuven* ☎ *016/203–020* 🌐 *www.visitleuven.be.*

Sights

Groot Begijnhof (*Great Beguinage*)
HISTORIC DISTRICT | Beguinages were where unmarried women could dedicate themselves to God without taking the orders of a nun (poverty, chastity). This is one of the larger examples in the country, home to some 700 beguines at its peak. Its foundation dates back to 1232, but most of its 72 redbrick houses were built in the 17th century. The last beguine left here in the 1980s; by then, it had already been bought by the university, who set about restoring its houses. ✉ *Groot Begijnhof, Leuven* 🎫 *Free.*

Grote Markt (*Town Square*)
PLAZA/SQUARE | At the bustling center of the city is the triangular wedge of the Grote Markt, home to the magnificent St. Peter's Church and Town Hall. On one side are the old guild houses, now café-bars. Gaze up to the tips of their gabled roofs and you'll spy elaborate decorations, from dancing girls to sailing ships, that lend a clue to their former masters. On the other side is the Tafelrond, formerly a theater that was destroyed in 1817. This was rebuilt in the Gothic style as a bank; now it's a very expensive (€400 a night) boutique stay. ✉ *Grote Markt, Leuven.*

M Leuven
ART MUSEUM | An art gallery that focuses on Leuven and Flemish Brabant artists from the Middle Ages until the 19th century. Its permanent collection includes the work of sculptor Jef Lambreaux, whose mildly erotic *Temple of Human Passions* caused such a scandal when it opened in Brussels in 1886, and George Minne, a leading figure from the Latem School of Impressionists who set up their base in the villages south of Ghent.

Temporary exhibitions ranging from the Old Masters to more contemporary art mix things up a bit. ✉ *Leopold Vanderkelenstraat 2, Leuven* ☎ *016/272–929* 🌐 *www.mleuven.be* 🎫 *€12* ⏲ *Closed Wed.*

★ **Sint-Pieterskerk** (*St. Peter's Church*)
CHURCH | This magnificent Gothic church was originally built in AD 986, though the current version dates to the 15th century. It has survived countless wars, most notably in 1914 when fire collapsed its roof, and then again in 1944 when the northern transept was bombed. Inside, the church is filled with art of the late medieval era. Among the finest pieces is the 15th-century *Last Supper* triptych by Leuven-based Flemish Primitive artist Dirk Bouts, still hanging in its original place in the chapel. ✉ *Grote Markt 1, Leuven* ☎ *016/272–959 tour* 🌐 *www.diericbouts.be* 🎫 *€12 HoloLens tour; €5 tablet tour* ⏲ *Closed Wed. Oct.–Mar.*

★ **Stadhuis** (*Town Hall*)
GOVERNMENT BUILDING | There is no grander Town Hall in Belgium than Leuven's 15th-century folly. Built to dazzle, the profits from its cloth trade were sunk into letting everyone know just how wealthy its merchants were. Some 235 individually carved stone figures decorate the outside, cut into small alcoves and giving the building a strange texture from afar. These figures were added after 1850, and each tells a different folk tale, bible parable, or story of the city; you'll also find grotesques of local nobles and dignitaries. ✉ *Grote Markt, Leuven* ☎ *016/203–020* 🌐 *www.visitleuven.be/en/town-hall* 🎫 *€4 guided tour; €2 booklet.*

Stella Artois Brewery
BREWERY | Few realize "Stella," the pilsner of choice among European soccer fans, is even Belgian, but it traces its Leuven roots back to 1726. These days, it's part of the massive AB InBev company, which owns everything from Budweiser to Leffe. As you'd expect, the brewery is highly automated, making for an interesting gear change to the usual small brewers most beer tours frequent. Two-hour tours and tastings for individuals are held on Saturday from 3 pm (in English), with online booking in advance advised if you want to get a slot. ✉ *Aarschotsesteenweg 20, Leuven* 🌐 *www.breweryvisits.com* 🎫 *€12* ✍ *Booking required* Ⓜ *Bus: 600.*

★ **Universiteitsbibliotheek** (*University Library*)
HISTORIC SIGHT | The original Flemish-Renaissance library was set up in the old Cloth Hall on Naamsestraat in 1636. But after the university was disbanded during the French Revolutionary Wars, its collection was ushered away to Paris. Though destroyed in 1940 by British-German artillery fire, postwar it was rebuilt to the same design and today, visitors can climb the 300 steps to the top of the tower where a carillon of 63 bells, weighing 35 tons, rings out across the square. ✉ *Monseigneur Ladeuzeplein 21, Leuven* 🎫 *€7 tower and audio guide* ✍ *Reservations required.*

Restaurants

Baracca
$$$ | ITALIAN | The novelty of this Italian pizza and food-sharing restaurant is proving pretty enduring. Set on the busy food street of Tiensestraat, this is one of few restaurants here not part of the usual Belgian chains (Wasbar, Balls & Glory, Bavet, etc.). **Known for:** the cocktails are also spot on; playful dishes that always surprise; good pizza. $ *Average main: €25* ✉ *Tiensestraat 34, Leuven* 🌐 *www.baracca.be.*

Dewerf
$ | EUROPEAN | This cheap, satisfying neighborhood café-restaurant never fails to please. Slightly removed from the center, on Hogeschoolplein, it's as much a lunch spot as a restaurant, but its cheap pastas and salads make for a

Leuven's Town Hall, built in the 15th century from cloth trade profits, is one of Belgium's most dazzling buildings.

good, filling meal on the go. **Known for:** it's also a fine spot for a postdinner beer; it's cheap (very cheap) and satisfying; the atmosphere is always young and bouncy. *Average main: €11 Hogeschoolplein 5, Leuven 016/237–314 www.dew-erf-leuven.be Closed weekends.*

Domus

$$ | **BELGIAN** | This sprawling brewpub-restaurant is pretty much the city's old standby for when you've run out of ideas. It's particularly good for families, it's always packed, the menu is littered with Flemish favorites (carbonnade, meatballs, vol-au-vent), and the service is impossibly quick no matter how full it is. **Known for:** the "Belgian dinner plate"; it's a cheap, popular spot for families; it's worth it to try the beer, which is pretty good. *Average main: €18 Tiensestraat 8, Leuven 016/201–449 domusleuven.be Closed Mon.*

't Kiekekot

$$ | **EUROPEAN** | **FAMILY** | In a city of students, it's no surprise that something so simple as a "chicken and bread" restaurant would take off. But it is also a thing of beauty. **Known for:** the staff are friendly and the drinks choice is good; tasty, and cheap—just a few euros for a half chicken; it's the perfect quick pick-up meal when shopping. *Average main: €14 Mechelsestraat 46, Leuven 016/657–508 www.restobartkiekekot.be Closed Sun. and Mon.*

Zarza

$$$$ | **FRENCH** | Leuven has a good reputation for its dining, with a couple of Michelin stars knocking about its streets. This isn't one of them, but it's not far off. **Known for:** the set menus (especially lunch) are good value; the choice is small but dishes are intricately prepared and full of whimsy; service is impeccable. *Average main: €38 Bondgenotenlaan 92, Leuven 016/205–005 www.zarza.be/en Closed Sun. and Wed. No lunch Thurs.*

Coffee and Quick Bites

Koffie Onan

$ | **CAFÉ** | This beloved local favorite lingers on a busy street of cafés behind the Oude Markt. Its small terraces and ethical approach are popular lures, with most of its coffee beans directly sourced from the farmers. **Known for:** good hot chocolates with a choice of interesting flavors; the pick of coffees and teas is the best in town; a cheerful terrace to watch the world go by. *Average main: €6 Parijsstraat 28, Leuven onan.be.*

Lettuce

$$ | **CAFÉ** | Salads packed with flavor, great hunks of quiches, and homemade lemonades are what keeps locals healthy at this popular lunch spot. **Known for:** there's a good selection of vegetarian options; a seat at the window lets you watch the urban flow hustle past; the salads mix together interesting combinations of veg, fruit, and meat. *Average main: €13 Tiensestraat 6, Leuven 0468/310–600 lettuce-leuven.be Closed Sun.*

Quetzal Chocolate Bar

$ | **CAFÉ** | All desserts, all of the time. This chocolate-theme café might be part of a chain, but it's captured the imagination of locals in part due to the sheer abundance of melted chocolate, particularly the fountainlike fondue. **Known for:** the fruit smoothies are good if you're sick of chocolate; everyone comes for the chocolate fountain; the chocolate milks come in myriad flavors. *Average main: €8 Alfons Smetsplein 3, Leuven 016/825–988 www.quetzal.be.*

Hotels

While this section is about day trips, it's worth spending a night in Leuven. It's a city that comes alive in the evening and has a good array of bars and restaurants, not to mention interesting hotels.

De Pastorij

$$ | **HOTEL** | **FAMILY** | This family-run hotel is, in truth, more like a grand B&B: owner Carmen still rents the building, which used to be a rectory, from the church (Sint-Michelskerk) across the road. **Pros:** you're only a five-minute walk from the center, but it's so much quieter here; rooms not facing the pretty garden get views of the magnificent church; owner Carmen is a charming, friendly host. **Cons:** the church bells can be noisy; there are only six rooms, so it fills up fast; despite renovation, some rooms do look their age. *Rooms from: €132 Sint-Michielsstraat 5, Leuven 016/822–109 www.depastorij.com 6 rooms Free Breakfast.*

★ **Martin's Klooster**

$$$ | **HOTEL** | Arguably the city's most complete stay is the attractive Martin's Klooster, which (as its name suggests) used to be a 15th-century Augustinian monastery and hospice. **Pros:** the interior garden makes it feel you're not even in town; it's a beautiful hotel with a long history; a quiet night's sleep in an often noisy city. **Cons:** parking is €25 per night; because of its conversion, there arent many facilities for the price you pay; breakfasts are a pretty pricey €22. *Rooms from: €151 O.L. Vrouwstraat 18, Leuven 016/213–141 www.martinshotels.com 103 rooms No Meals.*

Nightlife

The pretty cobbles of the Oude Market are wrapped by 18th-century buildings, all now converted into almost identical bars, their offers of 2-for-1 shots emblazoned in posters tacked to the old brickwork above. This is the heart of student nightlife and a pretty messy night out if you're so inclined. It's often described as "the longest bar in Europe," as most just hop from one terrace to another. Away from here, however, you'll find a much more laid-back night out if you stick around for the evening.

Café Commerce

BARS | A charming bar set on the corner of Ladeuzeplein. Old wooden floors, high ceilings, and a stash of board games you can play while having a beer make it a laid-back escape. There's also always a pot of soup on the go if you're hungry. ✉ *Herbert Hooverplein 16, Leuven* ☎ *016/225–578* 🌐 *www.cafecommerce.be.*

De Metafoor

BARS | On Parijsstraat, this aging but very cozy bar heaves with both young and old. It's unpretentious, has a really good choice of local beers, and there's just nothing else to it—no elaborate effort to make it more than it is. That in itself makes it special. Plus you can bring your own food. ✉ *Parijsstraat 34, Leuven* ☎ *0496/254–465.*

Shopping

The main shopping streets here are **Bondgenotenlaan** and **Diestsestraat**, which run parallel, and the eastern end of **Brusselsestraat.** Each is filled with chain stores, well-known clothing brands, and a few independent fashion retailers. For something more niche, head to the busy little cobbled enclave of **Mechelstraat,** which is packed with indie food shops and small fashion and interiors stores. You'll also find a fair number of fashionable clothing shops on **Parijstraat**, behind the Oude Markt. Note that stores open 1 to 6 on the first Sunday of the month, but are normally closed on Sunday.

FOOD SHOPS

Bittersweet

CHOCOLATE | An inspired local chocolaterie whose flavors range from out-there breakfast (yogurt, praline, and maple syrup) and robotski (a little robot-shape chocolate filled with ginger) chocolates to the rather heavenly gin and cardamom. ✉ *Bondgenotenlaan 108, Leuven* ☎ *0495/800–888* 🌐 *www.bittersweet.be.*

Elsen Kaasambacht

FOOD | This excellent cheese shop specializes in raw milk, small-scale, and traditional cheeses from Belgium and France. The €12 platters are a great way to taste something new, such a raw blue cheese from Ghent's Het Hinkelspel or a creamy berbizou from Bergerie de Lisbelle in Rendeux. On most days you can see the queues stretching down Mechelsestraat. ✉ *Mechelsestraat 36, Leuven* ☎ *016/221–310* 🌐 *www.elsenkaasambacht.be.*

STREET MARKETS

Artisanal Market

MARKET | The Saturday market sees stalls filled with antiques, secondhand goods, food, flowers, and plants scatter the streets of Brusselsestraat, Parijsstraat, Pensstraat, Mathieu de Layensplein, and Mechelsestraat between 9 am and 6 pm. ✉ *Mechelsestraat, Leuven.*

Flower Market

MARKET | Thursdays (1–6) on Brusselsestraat erupt in stalls brimming over with floral delights and bouquets. ✉ *Brusselsestraat, Leuven.*

Tervuren

12 km (7½ miles) from Brussels.

When you say Tervuren, locals tend not to think of the small town of that name, which is made up primarily of wealthy expats (there are no less than two British schools here), but the old royal park that sits on its fringes. This was once home to the Dukes of Brabant, who built a mighty castle here in the 12th century at the confluence of the Voer and Maalbeek rivers, using its vast forests as a hunting ground. But the park's modern history is far more relevant—and infinitely darker.

The Dukes' castle was destroyed in 1782, and by the mid-1800s, a royal vacation home had been built on the grounds. This was later used by King Leopold II's sister, Charlotte (briefly empress of Mexico), whose mental state after her husband's death at the hands of a firing squad, led to her confinement. But under her watch, it burned down in 1879, after which Leopold built the grand "Colonial Palace" on its remains for his 1897 Exposition celebrating his success in the Congo Free State.

From then on, Tervuren's history has been tied to Belgium's brutal rule in the Congo, and the museum that now occupies the old Colonial Palace is a must-see, if only to learn more about this period. The park is also beautiful in its own right, with an arboretum of some 700 species, and also sits on the northeasternmost edge of the Forêt de Soignes, which continues for miles into Flemish and Walloon Brabant. There are few better spots for walking or cycling than the 170 km (105 miles) of trails that thread the Soigne's oak and beech forests.

GETTING HERE AND AROUND

The quickest way to reach Tervuren is via the No. 44 tram (€2.40), which leaves from the roundabout outside Montgomery (Line 1) metro station, just up from Cinquantenaire Park. It takes 19 minutes and drops you off next to Tervuren Park.

Sights

★ **Musée Royal de l'Afrique Centrale** (*Royal Museum for Central Africa*)

HISTORY MUSEUM | Any visit to Brussels should include a visit here, if only to understand Belgium's difficult relationship with its own past. While much of its collection is invaluable from a scholarly point of view, it came at an incalculable cost, rooted in Leopold II's brutal colonial rule. Even the building itself, built for Leopold II's 1897 Exposition trumpeting his violent success in the Congo Free State (1885–1908), commemorated the names of those Belgians who died there, etched into its very walls; nothing on the 10 million Congolese estimated to have died under Belgian rule. It reopened in 2018 with less emphasis on explorers and stuffed wildlife (though there is still some). The new version focuses more on Congolese voices and accurately reflecting the horrific consequences of Belgium's colonial rule (1908–62) of a country 76 times its own size. ✉ *Leuvensesteenweg 13, Tervuren* ☎ *01/769–5211* 🌐 *www.africamuseum.be* 🎫 *€12* ⏲ *Closed Mon.*

Park van Tervuren (*Tervuren Park*)

CITY PARK | **FAMILY** | Tervuren Park, once the hunting grounds of the Dukes of Brabant, was the venue for King Leopold II's 1897 Exposition. His aim was to showcase the wealth and "culture" he was tearing out of the then Congo Free State. International condemnation eventually forced him to even make it a colony. In preparation, he built the Koloniënpaleis (Colonial Palace), which now hosts the Royal Museum for Central Africa; and created gardens in the French style. The exposition itself was considered a success, though is now thought to be a stain on Belgian history. It contained a human zoo of Congolese, several of whom died in the crossing to Europe. But the park is more than this dark corner of history—its 205 hectares span a pair of valleys, and for those walking or cycling the trails here, it's the gateway to the northeasternmost reaches of the Forêt de Soigne, a vast forest of boundless trails. ✉ *Leuvensesteenweg 13, Tervuren* 🎫 *Free.*

Restaurants

Capriccio

$$ | **ITALIAN** | A much-revered Italian restaurant that has been remodeled in recent years to be more of a meal out. There's a nice garden terrace, the wine selection is proficient, and the cooking is never less than spot on. **Known for:** you're a stone's throw from the park; decent-value pasta dishes; friendly and helpful staff. 💲 *Average main: €20*

✉ *Kerkstraat 15, Tervuren* ☎ *02/767–3526* 🌐 *www.capriccio1989.be* 🕒 *Closed Sun. and Mon.*

La Couscoussière

$$ | AFRICAN | FAMILY | This Tunisian restaurant is newer to the Tervuren scene but has quickly established a loyal following among locals. The blackboard menu is never huge, but that's no bad thing; it just means they do a few things well, and that's better than most manage. **Known for:** you'll find a new appreciation for Tunisian wine; a charming little setting that feels quite intimate; the tagines are beloved. $ *Average main: €17* ✉ *Chau. de Bruxelles 56, Tervuren* ☎ *0487/276–032* 🌐 *lacouscoussieretervuren.be* 🕒 *Closed Sun.*

Beersel

10 km (6 miles) from Brussels.

Nestled among the pressed green fields of the Zenne Valley, Beersel is a serene slice of rural Flanders. Even without an abbey to its name, it's long had a reputation among beer lovers, for whom its old lambic breweries are unique. This is one of only a few places in Belgium where you can make this kind of beer due to environmental conditions. There are even lambic walking and cycling trails you can pick up, as you (presumably) wobble from one site to the next. But the real lure here is Beersel's beautiful castle. It remains one of the most elegant examples of medieval pragmatism you'll find in Belgium, hovering above the water with its towers hunched like the shoulders of a soldier expecting the worst. It makes for a delightful day's excursion, especially combined with a few local beers afterward.

GETTING HERE AND AROUND

The train from Bruxelles-Central to Braine-Le-Comte stops in Lot (€6.20), which is only a 20-minute, 2-km (1-mile) walk from Beersel Castle. Or you could get bus No. 154 to Beersel from Lot. Alternatively, the train from Brussels's Merode metro station (Line 1) to Halle stops in Beersel. It takes around 20 minutes and costs €5.80.

Sights

Hallerbos Forest

FOREST | FAMILY | About 8 km (5 miles) south of Beersel, you'll encounter the wilderness area of Hallerbos. It's known locally as "the blue forest" for good reason: come mid-April and early May, the ground underneath becomes a dazzling carpet of blue-violet flowers, as bluebells cover every inch. It's a small window of opportunity, though it's a pleasant spot to wander at any time of year. To get there, take the train from Beersel to Halle, then either hire a bike at the station (*www.blue-bike.be*) and cycle or take the No. 155 bus. ✉ *Hallerbos, 4 km (2½ miles) southeast of Halle, Beersel* 🎫 *Free.*

★ **Kasteel van Beersel**

CASTLE/PALACE | Beersel Castle floats on the waters of its moat like some medieval bath toy. It's a wonderful sight, and one of the country's best-preserved châteaux. It was built around 1420, though fell foul of the 1489 rebellion against the rule of the Holy Roman Emperor Maximilian I and was subsequently rebuilt. Its moat, drawbridge, and battlements couldn't be more medieval in appearance if they tried. It's been undergoing renovations since the early 2000s and now visitors can explore freely. ✉ *Lotsestraat 65, Beersel* ☎ *02/359–1636* 🎫 *€4* 🕒 *Closed Mon. and Dec.–Feb.*

Oud Beersel Brewery

BREWERY | Founded in 1882, this is one of the last remaining original lambic breweries in Belgium. Lambic beers require a special kind of brewing that uses spontaneous fermentation. This relies on certain a kind of microflora found in only a few areas: the Pajottenland region, the Zenne Valley, and Brussels. Whether you have acquired the taste (and it is an acquired taste) for the gueuze and kriek beers it produces, it's still a fascinating process. This brewery sadly closed in 2002, when its iconic tiled Beerhuis (bar) became a flower shop. A few years later, however, it was bought by new owners and reopened, with its old bar starting up again in 2022. Tours of the brewery are organized on Saturday, lasting 45 minutes plus a tasting session. ✉ *Laarheidestraat 230, Beersel* ☎ *02/680–7954* 🌐 *oudbeersel.com* 🎫 *€10* ✍ *Booking required.*

Restaurants

Restaurant 3 Fonteinen

$$$ | BELGIAN | Some brewery restaurants tend to be slightly chaotic affairs, relying on their draft brews to pick up where the food falls short. Not so this dining offshoot from the local 3 Fonteinen lambic brewery. **Known for:** the mussels are heaven; a cut above the usual brewery eatery; the selection of lambic beers is naturally excellent. $ *Average main: €23* ✉ *Herman Teirlinckplein 3, Beersel* ☎ *02/331–0652* 🌐 *www.3fonteinenrestaurant.com* 🕒 *Closed Tues.–Thurs.*

Gaasbeek

14 km (8½ miles) from Brussels.

Visiting Gaasbeek is like stepping inside one of the more rural paintings of 16th-century Flemish artist Pieter Bruegel the Elder—only minus the toiling peasants. The reason is that this is the heart of Pajottenland, a region featured frequently in his works, many of which were painted here. The area has certainly lost none of its impact in the intervening centuries, if only because the one main landmark of Gaasbeek is still here: the castle. This magnificent building is undergoing renovation at present, but you can still enjoy its park and gardens, then hop to the nearby town of Lennik for a dash of fine dining.

GETTING HERE AND AROUND

Bus No. 142 (€2) goes direct from Bruxelles-Midi station to Gaasbeek and takes around 45 minutes. Alternatively, to save time, you can take metro Line 5 to Erasmus and pick up the same bus there.

Sights

★ Kasteel van Gaasbeek

CASTLE/PALACE | Originally built in 1240, Gaasbeek has had numerous makeovers, though its current Romantic look hails from its last remodeling by the Marchioness Arconati Visconti in the 19th century. She refurbished the castle as a museum to stash her vast art collection before gifting it all to the state in 1921. From its terrace is a fine panoramic view of Pajottenland. You'll have to wait until April 2023 to see it, as the interior of the castle is undergoing a major restoration. That said, the grounds are a fair consolation and the park remains open to visitors and picnickers year-round. The gardens only open in summer. Look out especially for the early Baroque walled French garden, which has a staircase affording fine views of the castle ✉ *Gaasbeek* ☎ *02/531–0130* 🌐 *www.kasteelvangaasbeek.be* 🎫 *€5 park and gardens* 🕒 *Gardens closed Oct.–Apr.*

Restaurants

August

$$$$ | BISTRO | A couple of miles west of Gaasbeek is the rather bijou little town of Lennik, home to a fair number of high-priced dining options. One of the finer is August, a wine shop-cum-restaurant that oozes class and is set in an 18th-century wine merchant's premises. **Known for:** it's a gorgeous old building; the wine selection is backed by good knowledge; the cooking is pretty exciting with well-balanced set menus. $ *Average main: €49* ✉ *Alfred Algoetstraat 2b, Lennik, Gaasbeek* ☎ *02/532–4220*

A highlight of any visit to the village of Gaasbeek is its magnificent castle, originally built in 1240.

www.augustwijnbar.be Closed Mon. and Tues. No lunch Wed. and Sat.

Restaurant Molensteen

$$$ | **BELGIAN** | Only a 10-minute walk from the castle, in the village of Gaasbeek, is this pleasant country restaurant with a pretty courtyard. Its building dates back to the late 18th century, and it has been a brewery, a tavern, and a farm in its day. **Known for:** reliable dining in an old-world country setting; a friendly local welcome; it's one of few good options within easy walking distance of the castle. *Average main: €27 Donkerstraat 20, Gaasbeek 02/532–0297 molensteen.be Closed Tues.–Thurs.*

Meise

10 km (6 miles) from Brussels.

The history of Meise is inseparable from that of the Château de Bouchout. The castle itself dates back to the 12th century, when the Knights of Bouchout roamed these lands, though little but its square tower remains from that era. It was partially destroyed during the French Revolution but subsequently rebuilt in neo-Gothic style, and in the late 1800s it became the home of King Leopold I's widowed sister, Empress Charlotte of Mexico. She and her Austrian-born husband, Maximillian I, had spent a brief time as the head of the Second Mexican Empire, created on the dubious advice of France's Napoléon III, who wanted a pro-French monarchy in Mexico following the French-Spanish-British invasion of 1861. Sadly for them, Maximillian's three-year reign came abruptly crashing down with the withdrawal of the French, whereupon he met a swift end at the barrel of a Republican firing squad. The princess never recovered and spent her final decades in confinement in the castle. In 1939, its grounds finally became home to the Botanical Garden.

GETTING HERE AND AROUND

Meise has no train station. A pair of buses (Nos. 250, 251) run direct from Gare du Bruxelles-Nord railway station in

Brussels. It takes 35 minutes and costs €2. From Meise, you can pick up bus No. 821 to Grimbergen, which is around 3 km (2 miles) away; it takes around 10 minutes.

Sights

★ **Plantentuin Meise** (*Meise Botanical Garden*)

GARDEN | **FAMILY** | Belgium's national botanic garden is a sprawling site that takes up most of the southern fringes of Meise. It wraps the old estate of Kasteel van Bouchou, which, despite being utterly destroyed during the French Revolution, was later rebuilt and now houses a museum all about the grounds. Beyond its moat lies an English-style garden filled with exotic plants from around the world, but the pièce de résistance here is the Plant Palace, the largest greenhouse in Belgium and one of the biggest in Europe. It is a vast biome of 35 hothouses filled with huge water-lily pads and tropical wonders. Other sights, such as the much smaller, mid-19th-century Balat Greenhouse, which was originally intended for a zoo, are just as fascinating for those interested. In addition, you'll find medieval, medicinal, and rose gardens, rhododendron woods, trails, art, an apiary, and some 18,000 plant species. Visit any time, though spring is naturally the most colorful season. ✉ *Nieuwelaan 38, Meise* ☎ *02/260–0970* 🌐 *www.plantentuinmeise.be* 🎫 *€9.*

Sint-Servaasbasiliek Grimbergen (*Basilica of Saint Servatius*)

CHURCH | Not far from Meise, the neighboring town of Grimbergen is as famous for its abbey as the beer that (as of 2021) is once again brewed on its grounds. Sadly, like most abbeys in Belgium, visitors aren't welcome, though the Basilica of Saint Servatius is open to the public. It was even one of the few buildings to be spared by the wrath of the French Revolutionary army. The abbey has been destroyed and rebuilt three times in its history: first by the Lords of Grimbergen in 1142, then by Protestants in 1566, and last by the French in 1798. Only the church and rectory survived the last of these, a magnificent Baroque structure with a carillon of 48 bells. ✉ *Kerkplein 1, Grimbergen* ✥ *2½ km (1½ miles) east of Meise* ☎ *02/272–4077 abbey* 🌐 *www.abdijgrimbergen.be* 🎫 *Free.*

Restaurants

Auberge Napoleon

$$$$ | **FRENCH** | This elegant dining spot has a charming terrace surrounded by a grassy lawn and trees. The menu is grandiose but not afraid of the more interesting rural delights of French cooking, from saddle of hare to fillet of fawn via a number of interesting pheasant dishes. Just as exciting is its new food-sharing menu, as it tries to capture the post-garden walk-in crowd, where baked sweetbreads, caviar, and Duroc pork belly offer a more classically French take on the format. **Known for:** refined cooking in a gorgeous garden setting; the sharing plates are really different than the usual fare; the wine selection is mostly French and excellent. 💲 *Average main: €35* ✉ *Bouchoutlaan 1, Meise* ☎ *02/269–3078* 🌐 *www.aubergenapoleon.be* 🕒 *Closed Sun. and Mon. No dinner Tues. and Wed. No lunch Sat.*

Het Fenikshof

$$ | **BELGIAN** | While tours of the Grimbergen Abbey brewery aren't possible, you can taste the fruits of its labor at its brasserie in town, which is slightly more upmarket than you'd imagine. A pretty terrace overlooks the abbey, while the food served is unrepentantly Flemish: beery stews, gray-shrimp croquettes, Ostend-style fish stew. **Known for:** it's open every day; frites, meat, and delicious, delicious beer; the terrace is a nice spot in summer. 💲 *Average main: €19* ✉ *Abdijstraat 20, Grimbergen* ☎ *02/306–3956* 🌐 *www.grimbergen.com/fenikshof.*

Chapter 4

ANTWERP AND THE NORTHEAST

4

Updated by
Tim Skelton

Sights ★★★★★ Restaurants ★★★★★ Hotels ★★★★★ Shopping ★★★★☆ Nightlife ★★★★☆

WELCOME TO ANTWERP AND THE NORTHEAST

TOP REASONS TO GO

★ **Shop 'til you drop.** Antwerp is a sophisticated shopper's paradise, with a center crammed with trendy stores and designer boutiques, but you may need fresh air when you glimpse some of the price tags.

★ **Diamonds are forever.** Shiny rocks are not just a girl's best friend in Europe's largest center of diamond trading.

★ **No struggling artist.** Van Gogh may have had to barter his paintings in exchange for meals, but it's clear from a visit to Peter Paul Rubens's home that the Flemish master had no such problems earning a crust.

★ **Seafood lover's heaven.** From a steaming bowl of mussels to turbot sautéed in butter, Antwerp's restaurants take full advantage of the city's port lands and abundance of fresh fish.

★ **Under-the-radar charms.** Mechelen, a short hop from Antwerp, offers medieval splendors that almost rival those of its larger neighbor, but without the swathes of tourists.

1 **Antwerp.** Belgium's second city is a paradise for foodies, fashionistas, culture vultures, and night owls. The central old town is home to grand architecture and atmospheric cafés in equal measure, while to the north, Het Eilandje—the former docklands—have been reborn as a culture and nightlife district. The station area is a major shopping hub, while the prosperous southern districts are the place to find fashionable restaurants and art museums.

2 **Mechelen.** Antwerp's southern neighbor is smaller and more manageable, but its Sint-Romboutskathedraal is as impressive as any church in Belgium.

3 **Lier.** This little town is a quiet escape from Antwerp, and home to the 15th-century Zimmertoren and its colorful astronomical clock.

4 **Limburg Province.** Rural Limburg is peppered with towns with wildly differing stories: wealthy **Hasselt** owes its success to the distilling of jenever, while little **Tongeren** can claim Roman origins.

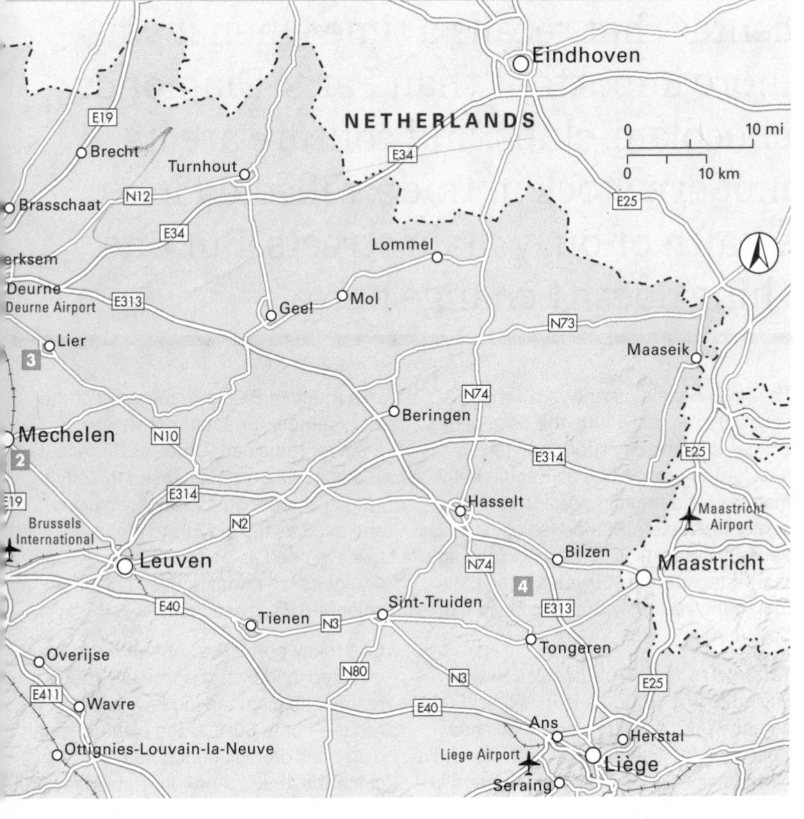
Eindhoven
NETHERLANDS
E19
Brecht
Turnhout
Brasschaat
N12
E34
E34
erksem
Deurne
Deurne Airport
E313
Geel
Mol
Lommel
0
10 mi
0
10 km
E25
N73
Maaseik
Lier
3
N74
Beringen
Mechelen
N10
2
E314
E25
E314
Hasselt
E19
Maastricht Airport
N2
Brussels International
Leuven
Bilzen
Maastricht
N74
4
E40
Sint-Truiden
E313
Tienen
N3
Tongeren
Overijse
N80
N3
E25
E411
Wavre
E40
Ans
Herstal
Ottignies-Louvain-la-Neuve
Liege Airport
Liège
Seraing

Antwerp is Belgium's capital of cool. It's a city styled by fashion icons, 16th-century painters, and a medieval center that recalls a time when it was more important than Paris. Diamonds, chocolate, clubs, and couture are its modern stock in trade, reflected in a wealth of busy main streets. But one thing doesn't change here.

The River Scheldt is Antwerp's meal ticket. By the mid-1400s the decline of Bruges saw the city's fortunes take a turn for the prosperous as it took on the mantle of the most important trading center in Western Europe, shipping silver, pepper, and textiles. It was a golden age that lasted around 100 years until it fell foul of the zealously Catholic Philip II of Spain.

Yet even as Antwerp's population was halved to just 42,000 and its skilled Protestant workers ejected under this new Spanish rule, it soon recovered. Nor did it halt the city's artistic growth. Painters like Rubens, Van Dyck, and Jordaens made it one of Europe's leading cultural centers well into the 17th century.

The end of the Dutch-Spanish War (1648) saw the good times grind to a halt. The Scheldt closed, and it wouldn't be until the arrival of Napoléon to the city in 1803 that it reclaimed its river. By the time the German army marched into Antwerp in 1914, it had grown into the third-largest port in the world.

Like much of Belgium, the wars of the 20th century devastated Antwerp. But the river remained. Timeless. In recent years, it has even witnessed the city's industrial roots be thoroughly plucked and dyed as the old Eilandje port area has swapped cargo for museums. Even one of its old pump houses has been colonized as a restaurant.

Like many port cities, Antwerp retains an outsized influence in some unexpected realms. Its diamond industry is world-famous—some 80% of the planet's rough diamonds are still traded here—and since the 1980s, Antwerp-trained fashion designers have become renowned for their experimental styles, as seen in the many boutiques that lie off the Meir and make this the country's shopping capital.

Often, Belgium's cities seem hamstrung by their past. In Antwerp, you'll find the opposite. It has kept its beautiful historic center of towering Gothic churches and cathedrals, yet it's also where Belgium's bright young things come to party. It might not always be pretty, but this mix of old and new makes it one of the country's most underrated destinations.

Planning

Getting Here and Around

AIR

These days, just a few airlines service Antwerp's Flanders International Airport. Tui flies to Alicante, Split, Malaga, Innsbruck, Florence, and others, but services are mostly aimed at Belgian holidaymakers. A better alternative for most international visitors is Brussels Airport (Zaventem), which serves many more airlines and has convenient transportation connections to Antwerp.

BIKE

Antwerp has one of the best (and cheapest) city bike schemes in Belgium. Bike lanes and stations are everywhere (even out in the suburbs), meaning you're never lumbered with having to go too far out of your way to find a cycle station, and it really opens up the city. The bikes are sturdy, comfortable, and even have gears. Sign up online (*www.velo-antwerpen.be/en*) and buy a pass; it's €5 for a day, €11 for a week, and free for the first 30 minutes. You will be given a code to unlock the bikes at each station. Do be careful cycling on the roads, though, as the wheels can get caught in the tram lines.

BUS

Low-cost intercity coach company FlixBus connects Antwerp to Ghent, Bruges, Brussels, and beyond; its central bus stop is found on Koningin Astridplein. Train connections are usually faster, however.

De Lijn operates bus services in every city in Flanders, and it's an easy system to use. In Antwerp, most lines begin outside Centraal Station, and all stops are clearly marked with a yellow pole. Tickets cost €2 and are good for one hour; a €7.50 day pass allows for unlimited travel for one day. Buses run frequently, roughly 6 am–midnight, with limited night buses on Friday and Saturday leaving from Antwerp South (1:25 and 3:30 am) and Rooseveltplaats (1:45 and 3:30 am).

CONTACTS De Lijn. ✉ *Antwerp* ☎ *070/22–02–00* 🌐 *www.delijn.be/en.*

CAR

Antwerp is surrounded by a ring road from which expressways shoot off like spokes in a wheel. The city is 48 km (29 miles) north of Brussels on the E19, 60 km (36 miles) northeast of Ghent on the E17, and 119 km (71 miles) northwest of Liège on the A313.

A car isn't necessary—and is more often than not a burden—when exploring Antwerp's central area. The city's streets may not be quite as busy as those in Brussels, but they're crowded enough to make driving difficult. Avoid rush hours, generally 6:30–9:30 am and 4–7 pm, and keep a sharp eye out for one-way streets, aggressive drivers, and trams. Remember that drivers have priority from the right. Street parking is rare, but there are several central parking lots, including some near Grote Markt and Groenplaats. Most city center hotels also charge steep fees for parking (around €20 per night).

If you still plan to drive into central Antwerp, be aware that is a Low Emission Zone (LEZ), and higher-polluting cars are not welcome—check the website to see if your vehicle qualifies.

Like Antwerp, Mechelen, Lier, Hasselt, and Tongeren are all on Belgium's extensive rail network, and easily reachable by public transport.

PUBLIC TRANSPORT

Antwerp operates what's called a "pre-metro" public transit system (known locally as "the metro"), which translates as a tram network that runs partly underground for some of its more central routes. It isn't the fastest public transport in the world, but given the size of the city, it doesn't need to be. It is, however, extensive and reliable. The most useful line for visitors (No. 9) links Centraal Station (metro: Diamant) with the left bank, which is the other side of the river (Linkeroever), via the Groenplaats (for the cathedral and Grote Markt). It is operated by De Lijn; tickets are the same price as for the bus and can be used across both networks (see Bus Travel for details). The metro system is open 6:30 am–midnight (1 am on Friday and Saturday). Stations are marked by large arrows indicating the entrances.

TAXI

There are taxi stands marked with a "taxi" sign at every principal point in the city center, such as Groenplaats and in front of Centraal Station, but it's often easier to call for one. All taxis are metered, starting with a base rate of €2.95 plus €1.80 per km. The rates are higher at night (10 pm–6 am).

TRAIN

NMBS/SNCB, the national railway, connects Antwerp with all other major Belgian cities. There are four to five trains an hour between Antwerp and Brussels (also stopping in Mechelen), and six trains every hour make the 15-minute trip between Antwerp and Lier. There are hourly trains from Antwerp to Hasselt and Tongeren. Among other routes, high-speed Thalys trains run several times a day between Antwerp and Paris, and between Antwerp, Rotterdam, and Amsterdam. Slower trains also run hourly between Antwerp and the Dutch cities of Breda, Rotterdam, and Amsterdam.

CONTACTS NMBS/SNCB. ☎ *02/528–2828* 🌐 *www.belgiantrain.be.*

Hotels

Antwerp's hotels with the most character are generally found in the Oude Stad and its adjacent neighborhoods. There are several intimate boutique hotels, but as these can fill up far in advance, be sure to make reservations as early as possible. Some hotels have set prices throughout the year but many of those that target business customers offer advantageous weekend rates. All hotels include taxes in their room rates.

The city's tourism bureau, Visit Antwerpen, keeps track of the best places and can make reservations for you. For a list of recommended bed-and-breakfast accommodations, see *www.bb-antwerp.be.*

Restaurants

Antwerp cuisine understandably focuses on fish, presented with few frills in even the finest restaurants, often poached or steamed, and reasonably priced. From the chilled whelks and periwinkles (marine snails) picked out of their shells with pins, to piles of tender little *grijze garnalen* (small shrimp), to the steamy white flesh of the mammoth *tarbot* (turbot), the scent of salt air is never far from your table. The ubiquitous *mosselen* (mussels) and *paling* (eels), showcased in midpriced restaurants throughout the city center, provide a heavier, heartier version of local fish cuisine. Bought live from wholesalers, the seafood is irreproachably fresh.

Antwerp has a high number of restaurants for a city its size. Many of the traditional places, both formal and casual, are clustered in Oude Stad. There are plenty of tourist-focused restaurants on the Grote Markt, but if you look along the smaller streets around the square you'll find some excellent local favorites. Het Zuid, meanwhile, is known for trendier cafés and restaurants. Peak dining hours are generally from noon until 3 and from 7 to 10. Since the dining scene is quite busy, it's best to make reservations.

HOTEL AND RESTAURANT PRICES

Hotel prices in the reviews are the lowest cost of a standard double room in high season. Restaurant prices in the reviews are the average cost of a main course at dinner, or if dinner is not served, at lunch.

What It Costs in Euros

$	$$	$$$	$$$$
RESTAURANTS			
under €12	€12–€22	€23–€30	over €30
HOTELS			
under €100	€100–€150	€151–€220	over €220

Safety

For a city of its size, Antwerp has no major safety issues to be concerned about. Be alert for pickpockets in crowded areas, especially after dark. The city is generally open and welcoming, and even solo women travelers should experience no problems. Nevertheless, basic commonsense precautions are always advisable, no matter where in the world you are.

Tours

Antwerp by Bike

BICYCLE TOURS | Antwerp by Bike offers two-hour guided bike tours of all the city's main sights. Customized tours can be arranged on request. Tours depart from the company's office beside the Steen fortress. If you prefer to explore on your own, the company also rents bikes (€8 for two hours, €12.50 all day). ✉ *Steenplein 1, Oude Stad* ☎ *0497/185–345* 🌐 *www.antwerpbybike.be* 🎫 *From €25.*

Flandria

BOAT TOURS | Flandria operates 90- and 180-minute boat trips (€15/€19) on the River Scheldt, departing from the Kattendijkdok-Oostkaai dock in Het Eilandje. These run from March to October. Both tours have English-speaking guides. ✉ *Kattendijkdok-Oostkaai 22, Het Eilandje* ☎ *0472/214–096* 🌐 *flandria.nu* 🎫 *From €15* Ⓜ *Tram 24.*

Touristram

OTHER TOURS | Touristram operates 45-minute tram tours with audio commentary in the Oude Stad and old harbor area. Tickets are sold on the tram, and tours leave on the hour—there's even a pub crawl option. Departure is from Groenplaats. ✉ *Groenplaats, Oude Stad* ☎ *0497/113–974* 🌐 *www.touristram.be* 🎫 *€8.*

Walking in Antwerp

WALKING TOURS | Walking in Antwerp organizes guided walking tours with English-speaking guides. Various options and tour lengths are offered, but the most popular is the two-hour Highlights of Antwerp tour, which departs from Handschoenmarkt 3. ✉ *Steenplein 7, Oude Stad* ☎ *0497/185–345* 🌐 *www.walkinginantwerp.be* 🎫 *From €15.*

Visitor Information

CONTACTS Visit Antwerpen. ✉ *Steenplein 1, Oude Stad* ☎ *03/232–0103* 🌐 *www.visitantwerpen.be.*

Oude Stad and Het Eilandje

The Oude Stad is where visitors and locals alike go to find a taste of old Antwerp. The narrow, winding streets—many of them restricted to pedestrian traffic—are wonderful for strolling, the Gothic squares are full of charm, and the museums and churches are the pride of the city. The mooring site for cruise ships and charter-boat tours has given the Steenplein, the area between the terminal and the Steen fortress, a new burst of energy.

In sharp contrast, Het Eilandje (The Little Island) is Antwerp's old docklands neighborhood. Run-down and neglected for many years, the area has been spruced up and largely redeveloped. It now features a yacht harbor, several key museums, and an ever-increasing number of former warehouses transformed into chic bars and restaurants.

Sights

★ De Ruien (Underground Antwerp)

TUNNEL | What seems like a million miles from the Rubens paintings and shops of the Meir is actually just a few meters below street level. Beneath Antwerp lie 8 km (5 miles) of sewers, streams, and tunnels that date from the 16th century. In 1885 they disappeared from view when the city brought in covered drains, but their story continued. During WWI and WWII, these tunnels became a way to smuggle goods into the city and people out. Suit up (special protective suits are supplied) and wander old vaults, canals, bridges, and medieval fortifications on guided tours (day and night), with boats for the deeper sections; or simply explore by yourself with a tablet and map. Rats and some rather big spiders also make these tunnels their home, so the squeamish should beware. Tours will also be called off in the event of heavy rain—this makes parts of the tunnels unnavigable. ✉ *Ruihuis, Suikerrui 21, Oude Stad* ☎ *03/344–0755* 🌐 *ruien.be/en* 🎫 *From €19* ⏲ *Closed Mon.* Ⓜ *Tram 3, 4, 5, 9.*

DIVA

OTHER MUSEUM | The city's diamond trading and smithing past gets a gloriously theatrical presentation in this interactive museum. Visitors are guided through six rooms by their audio "butler" Jerome, gawking at some rampant abuses of wealth, from a diamond-encrusted gold tennis racket to a king's ransom of jewels, silverware, and chinoiserie. Ensconced in all this glitz, however, is a serious history lesson in how a city was built on its ability to turn rough stones into polished jewels, as well as the fads that accompanied the industry, such as the "Egyptmania," fanned by Napoléon's campaigns in the late 18th century, or Japan's opening up to the West in the mid-1800s, enabling its aesthetic to influence everything from Art Nouveau to a sudden bourgeois craze for kimonos. ✉ *Suikerrui 17, Oude Stad* ☎ *03/360–5253* 🌐 *www.divaantwerp.be/en* 🎫 *€12* ⏲ *Closed Wed.* Ⓜ *Tram: 11, 24.*

Grote Markt

PLAZA/SQUARE | The heart of the Oude Stad is dominated by a huge fountain splashing water onto the paving stones. St. George is perched on top of a 16th-century guild house at Grote Markt 5 about to fight a dragon. The lopsided square is lined on two sides by guild houses and on the third by the Renaissance Stadhuis. Antwerp's town hall was built in the 1560s during the city's Golden Age, when Paris and Antwerp were the only European cities with more than 100,000 inhabitants. In its facade, the fanciful fretwork of the late-Gothic style has given way to the discipline and order of the Renaissance. ✉ *Grote Markt, Oude Stad.*

The Museum aan de Stroom, housed in a striking red sandstone-and-glass building, tells the history of Antwerp.

Havenhuis

NOTABLE BUILDING | One relatively recent addition to the dynamic Antwerp skyline is the Port House, home of Antwerp's Port Authority. Located at the northern end of Het Eilandje, the shiny diamond-shape lozenge on stilts actually rests on top of a beautifully restored old fire station. It was designed by renowned architect Dame Zaha Hadid, and completed shortly before her death in 2016. You can only visit the neo-futurist construction by arranging a group tour (Tuesday, Thursday, and the first Saturday of each month only), which costs a hefty €150 per group, but its stunning exterior appearance has made it a noteworthy showstopper even if you don't go in. ✉ *Zaha Hadidplein 1, Het Eilandje* 🌐 *experienceantwerp.be* ⏲ *Closed Wed. and Fri.–Mon., except 1st Sat. of month.*

Het Steen

OTHER MUSEUM | The Steen is more than 1,000 years old. A 9th-century waterfront fortress, it was built to protect the western frontier of the Holy Roman Empire. It was partially rebuilt 700 years later by Emperor Charles V. You can distinguish the darker, medieval masonry extending midway up the walls from the lighter upper level of 16th-century work. The only survivor of the original waterfront, the Steen was used as a prison for centuries. Today it houses Antwerp's visitor information center, as well as **The Antwerp Story**, a permanent exhibition that serves as a good introduction for anyone new to the city. Through a series of rooms, interactive multimedia displays give you an overview of Antwerp's people, industry, monuments, and its museums. You can also head up to the roof terrace for a panoramic view. ✉ *Steenplein 1, Oude Stad* ☎ *03/232–0103* 🌐 *www.visitantwerpen.be* 🎫 *€7* Ⓜ *Tram: 4, 11.*

Mode Museum (MoMu)

OTHER MUSEUM | To get up to speed on the latest clothing designers, head to MoMu for a fashion crash course. Inside the early-20th-century building you'll find comprehensive exhibits, some highlighting the avant-garde work of contemporary

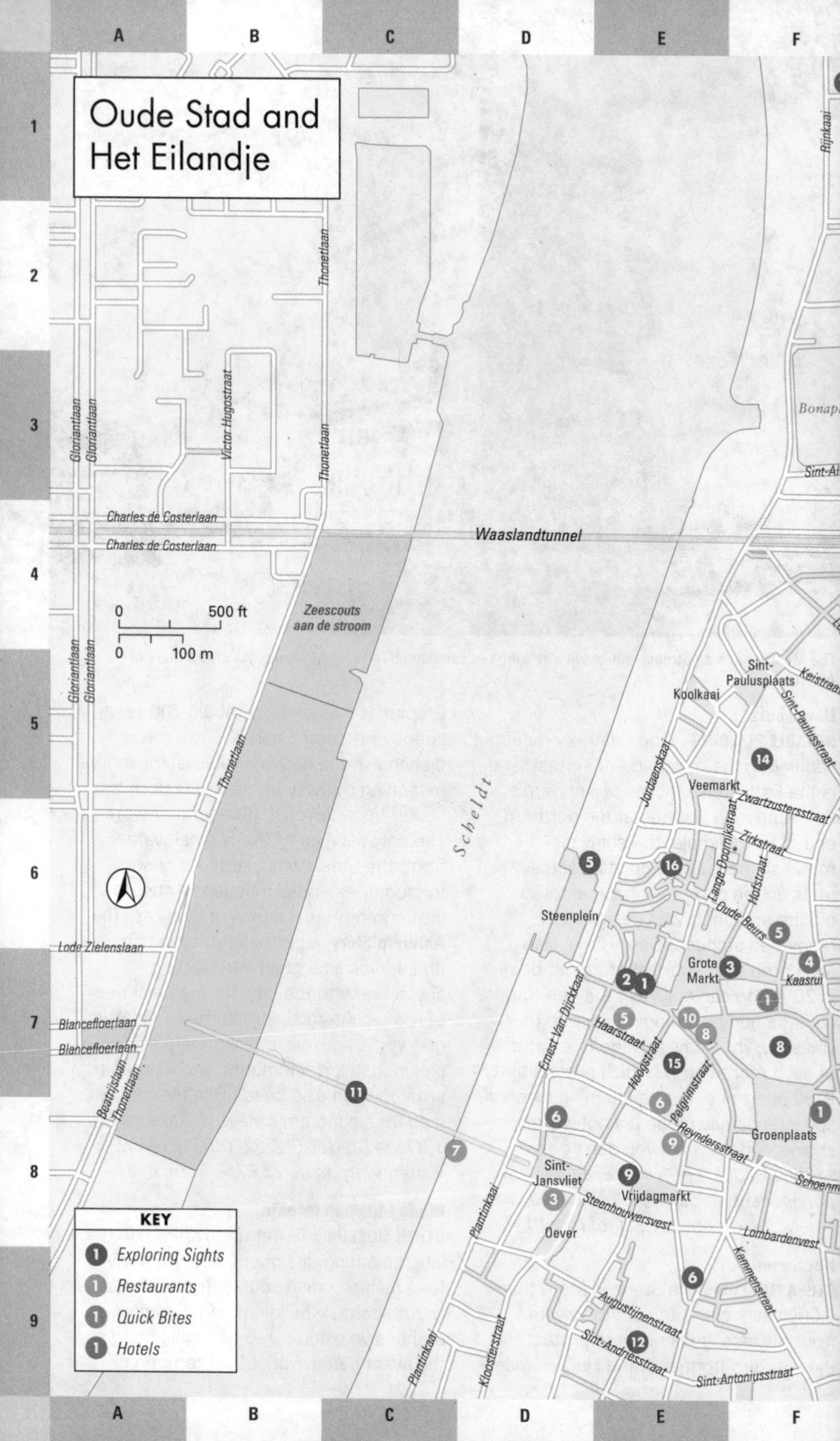

Oude Stad and Het Eilandje
A
B
C
D
E
F
1
2
3
4
5
6
7
8
9
Rijnkaai
Thonetlaan
Victor Hugostraat
Gloriantlaan
Bonapa
Sint-Al
Charles de Costerlaan
Waaslandtunnel
Zeescouts aan de stroom
0
500 ft
100 m
Sint-Paulusplaats
Keistraat
Sint-Paulusstraat
Koolkaai
Jordaenskaai
Veemarkt
Zwartzustersstraat
Zirkstraat
Lange Doornikstraat
Hofstraat
Scheldt
Steenplein
Oude Beurs
Grote Markt
Kaasrui
Lode Zielenslaan
Ernest Van Dijckkaai
Haarstraat
Hoogstraat
Pelgrimstraat
Blancefloerlaan
Beatrijslaan
Reyndersstraat
Groenplaats
Schoenm
Sint-Jansvliet
Vrijdagmarkt
Steenhouwersvest
Lombardenvest
Oever
Plantinkaai
Kammenstraat
Augustijnenstraat
Sint-Andriesstraat
Kloosterstraat
Sint-Antoniusstraat
KEY
Exploring Sights
Restaurants
Quick Bites
Hotels

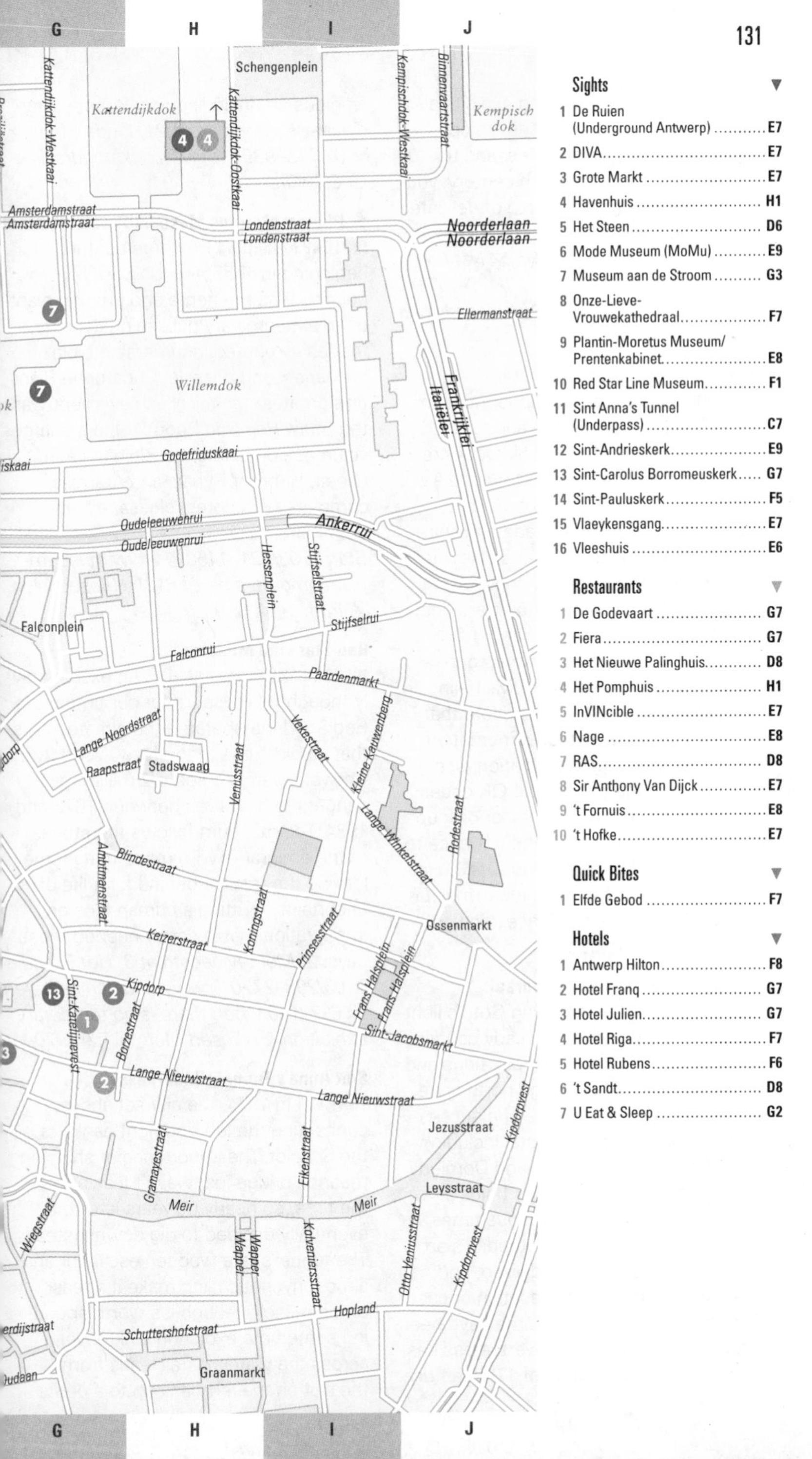

Sights

1 De Ruien (Underground Antwerp) E7
2 DIVA E7
3 Grote Markt E7
4 Havenhuis H1
5 Het Steen D6
6 Mode Museum (MoMu) E9
7 Museum aan de Stroom G3
8 Onze-Lieve-Vrouwekathedraal F7
9 Plantin-Moretus Museum/Prentenkabinet ... E8
10 Red Star Line Museum F1
11 Sint Anna's Tunnel (Underpass) C7
12 Sint-Andrieskerk E9
13 Sint-Carolus Borromeuskerk G7
14 Sint-Pauluskerk F5
15 Vlaeykensgang E7
16 Vleeshuis E6

Restaurants

1 De Godevaart G7
2 Fiera G7
3 Het Nieuwe Palinghuis D8
4 Het Pomphuis H1
5 InVINcible E7
6 Nage E8
7 RAS D8
8 Sir Anthony Van Dijck E7
9 't Fornuis E8
10 't Hofke E7

Quick Bites

1 Elfde Gebod F7

Hotels

1 Antwerp Hilton F8
2 Hotel Franq G7
3 Hotel Julien G7
4 Hotel Riga F7
5 Hotel Rubens F6
6 't Sandt D8
7 U Eat & Sleep G2

Flemish designers. Rotating exhibits also make the most of the museum's collections of clothing, accessories, and textiles dating back to the 18th century; you can ponder the workmanship of delicate antique lace alongside deconstructed blouses from the late 1990s. ✉ *Nationalestraat 28, Oude Stad* ☎ *03/470–2770* 🌐 *www.momu.be* 🎫 *€12* ⏲ *Closed Mon.* Ⓜ *Tram: 4.*

★ Museum aan de Stroom (*MAS*)

OTHER MUSEUM | This ambitious museum, in a striking red sandstone and glass building next to Antwerp's old dock area, aims to place Antwerp's history into a world context. Five floors of exhibits explore themes such as trade and shipping, men and gods, here and elsewhere, and prestige and symbols, showcasing everything from pre-Columbian artifacts to gas masks from World War II. It's all capped off with a panoramic rooftop view (free to visit) and a Michelin three-star restaurant, 't Zilte. Note that most of the museum's documentation is not in English; for a translation, use your smartphone to read the QR codes placed next to many exhibits, or pick up an information booklet at the entrance to each room. ✉ *Hanzestedenplaats 1, Het Eilandje* ☎ *03/338–4400* 🌐 *www.mas.be* 🎫 *€12 (€10 if no temporary exhibition)* ⏲ *Closed Mon.* Ⓜ *Tram: 7.*

★ Onze-Lieve-Vrouwekathedraal

CHURCH | A miracle of soaring Gothic lightness, the Cathedral of Our Lady contains some of Rubens's greatest paintings and is topped by a 404-foot-high north spire. The monument is the work of a succession of remarkable architects, including Peter Appelmans, Herman and Domien de Waghemakere. The tower holds a 49-bell carillon played at various times throughout the year. The cathedral's art treasures were twice vandalized, and many were either sold at auction or carried off to Paris—though some have been returned. The cathedral nevertheless has an outstanding collection of 17th-century religious art, including four Rubens altarpieces. ✉ *Groenplaats 21, Oude Stad* ☎ *03/213–9951* 🌐 *www.dekathedraal.be* 🎫 *€8* Ⓜ *Tram: 3, 4, 5, 9.*

★ Plantin-Moretus Museum/Prentenkabinet

HISTORY MUSEUM | For three centuries, beginning in 1555, this UNESCO-listed building was the home and printing plant of an extraordinary publishing dynasty; the family printed innumerable bibles, breviaries, and missals. Christophe Plantin's greatest technical achievement was the *Biblia Regia* (in Room 16), eight large volumes containing the Bible in Latin, Greek, Hebrew, Syriac, and Aramaic, complete with notes, glossaries, and grammars. ✉ *Vrijdagmarkt 22–23, Oude Stad* ☎ *03/221–1450* 🌐 *www.museum-plantinmoretus.be* 🎫 *€12* ⏲ *Closed Mon.* Ⓜ *Tram: 3, 4, 5, 9.*

Red Star Line Museum

HISTORY MUSEUM | **FAMILY** | An exceptionally thoughtful museum for our times, the Red Star Line operated the old steamers that would cross to the New World from Antwerp, carrying some 2 million passengers to new lives between 1873 and 1934. The museum follows the stories of the emigrants who made that journey, leaving the familiar behind for a life of uncertainty, putting a human face on immigration that is sorely needed these days. ✉ *Montevideostraat 3, Het Eilandje* ☎ *03/298–2770* 🌐 *www.redstarline.be/en* 🎫 *€12 (€10 when there is no temporary exhibition)* ⏲ *Closed Mon.* Ⓜ *Tram: 70.*

Sint Anna's Tunnel (Underpass)

TUNNEL | In 1874, the city set about connecting the left and right banks of the Scheldt. The importance of shipping meant a bridge just wasn't feasible at the time, so nearly 60 years later they eventually decided to dig down instead. The tunnel's rare wooden escalator and almost hypnotic tiling make it a reason to enter in itself, though it's worth spending some time exploring Linkroever, across the water. A trail leads from the exit on the left bank up to a petite

The Onze-Lieve-Vrouwekathedraal's 404-foot-high tower holds a 49-bell carillon played at various times throughout the year.

stretch of beach known as Sint-Annastrand that looks out over the Scheldt—a bizarre splash of nature amid the docks. ✉ *Sint-Annatunnel, Oude Stad* 🎫 *Free.*

Sint-Andrieskerk (*St. Andrew's Church*)
CHURCH | This late-Gothic church dedicated to St. Andrew dates from 1514 but reflects substantial Baroque influences from its extension during the 18th century. The church is notable for the magnificence of its Baroque high altar, stained-glass windows, and columns. Its most striking feature is the pulpit depicting Peter and his brother Andrew, created by Jan-Baptist Van Hoof and Jan-Frans Van Geel in 1821. The church is closed to visitors during services. ✉ *Sint-Andriesstraat 7, Oude Stad* ☎ *03/232–0384* 🌐 *www.sint-andrieskerk.be* 🎫 *Free* Ⓜ *Tram: 4.*

Sint-Carolus Borromeuskerk
CHURCH | Like so much of Antwerp, the Jesuit St. Charles Borromeo Church bears the imprint of Rubens. The front and tower are generally attributed to him, and his hand can certainly be seen in the clustered cherubim above the entrance. The church's facade suggests a richly decorated high altar, inviting the observer inside. The interior was once magnificent, but most of Rubens's frescoes were destroyed by fire, and other works were carted off to Vienna when the Austrians banned the Jesuits in the 18th century. The square is one of the most attractive in Antwerp, flanked by the harmonious Renaissance buildings of the Jesuit convent, now occupied by the City Library. ✉ *Hendrik Conscienceplein 12, Oude Stad* ☎ *03/231–3751* 🎫 *Free* 🕓 *Closed Sun. (unless attending services)* Ⓜ *Tram: 10, 11.*

Sint-Pauluskerk (*St. Paul's Church*)
CHURCH | The late-Gothic St. Paul's Church, built 1530–71, is a repository of more than 50 outstanding paintings, including a series known as the 15 mysteries of the Rosary by Antwerp's finest painters of the time. There are three by Rubens, including a visceral depiction of Jesus's flagellation, as well as early works by Jordaens and Van Dyck. The church is further enriched by more than

Wander amid ancient printing presses at the Plantin-Moretus Museum, the former home of the Plantin family of publishers.

200 17th- and 18th-century sculptures, including the 10 Baroque confessionals attributed to Peeter Verbruggen the Elder. A Baroque altar completed in 1639 towers over the more somber Gothic nave. Sint-Pauluskerk was restored in 1968 after damage from a major fire. ✉ *Veemarkt 14, Oude Stad* ☎ *03/232–3267* 🌐 *www.sintpaulusantwerpen.be* 🎫 *Free* ⏲ *Closed weekdays Nov.–Mar.* Ⓜ *Tram: 7.*

Vlaeykensgang

STREET | This quiet cobblestone lane in the center of Antwerp seems untouched by time. The mood and style of the 16th century are perfectly preserved here. There is no better time to linger than on a Monday night when the carillon concert is pealing from the cathedral. The alley ends in Pelgrimsstraat, where there is a great view of the cathedral spire. ✉ *Vlaeykensgang, Oude Stad* 🎫 *Free* Ⓜ *Tram: 4.*

Vleeshuis

OTHER MUSEUM | The Gothic butcher's guild is Antwerp's oldest remaining public building and was once the only place in the city where meat could be sold. Over the centuries it has morphed from a guild hall into a refined music museum, focusing on 600 years of the musical life of the city. ✉ *Vleeshouwersstraat 38, Oude Stad* ☎ *03/292–6101* 🌐 *www.museumvleeshuis.be* 🎫 *€8* ⏲ *Closed Mon.–Wed.* Ⓜ *Tram: 7.*

Restaurants

De Godevaart

$$$$ | **BELGIAN** | Tradition gets a modern infusion here, where a resolutely old-school atmosphere is enlivened by a smattering of contemporary art, while the kitchen turns out seasonal classic dishes presented with an artist's eye for flair. From fillet of lamb surrounded by a forest of green and wild garlic, to a deliciously gamey pigeon en croute, the choices are seasonal and big on flavor. **Known for:** good-value lunch menu; imaginatively presented dishes; fresh, seasonal cooking in a sumptuous setting. Ⓢ *Average main: €42* ✉ *Sint-Katelijnevest*

Lange Wapper

There are myriad 16th-century legends surrounding Lange Wapper, the water devil, but all agree he lived near water. That's why a bronze statue of this famous demon trickster, built by Albert Poels, was placed by the Scheldt river in front of the Steen Castle, now home to The Antwerp Story. Lange Wapper could change his size—he could make himself as small as a baby or as large as a giant. As a formidable giant, he would stand with a foot planted on either side of the canal and frighten drunks during the night. Many men who stayed too long at the bars used Lange Wapper's antics as an excuse for lateness. Virile and cheeky, he garnered the reputation of a fertility god—it's claimed that young women who visit the statue after marriage go on to bear many children. Himself a philanderer, he used every ploy possible to get close to women. One story tells how he turned himself into a newborn baby and waited on a public bench. A woman who had just given birth pitied the foundling and proceeded to breast-feed him, only to receive the fright of her life when he transformed into a grown man!

23, Oude Stad ☎ 03/291–9799 🌐 www.degodevaart.be ⏲ Closed Mon. and Tues. Ⓜ Tram: 11, 12.

Fiera

$$$$ | CONTEMPORARY | For those who fancy dining in epic surrounds, this restaurant occupies a former trading hall of the neo-Gothic stock exchange building, which dates from 1872. In contrast to the historic setting, the pan-global dishes are ultramodern works of art on a plate—prepared in the open kitchen on one side of the hall, their names derive from their geographical inspiration: a riff on a ceviche, for example, might be called "Lima," while a pasta-based dish might be titled "Florence." **Known for:** located in a stupendously grand neo-Gothic hall; check out the churchlike vaulted ceiling, 80 feet above your head; contemporary fine dining taking inspiration from around the world. Ⓢ *Average main: €36 ✉ Lange Nieuwstraat 14, Oude Stad ☎ 03/369–2332 🌐 fiera.be ⏲ Closed Mon.*

Het Nieuwe Palinghuis

$$$$ | SEAFOOD | Aptly named, The New Eelhouse specializes in various preparations of sweet-fleshed eel, along with grilled turbot, sole, scallops, and myriad other crustaceans, including lobster and mussels (in season). Fittingly for an Antwerp landmark, the restaurant has dark wood and a comfortable, deep-rooted air. **Known for:** high prices but good quality; remarkably fresh seafood; redbrick walls bedecked in old pics. Ⓢ *Average main: €37 ✉ St-Jansvliet 14, Oude Stad ☎ 03/231–7445 🌐 www.hetnieuwepalinghuis.be ⏲ Closed Mon., Tues., and Fri. Ⓜ Tram: 3, 4.*

Het Pomphuis

$$$$ | CONTEMPORARY | The name translates to the Pump House, and in its heyday it drained the neighboring dry dock to allow for ship maintenance. It still looks the part; a vast interior boasts an impressive 23-foot pit with iron parapets and round Art Nouveau–style windows with their original metal rods. **Known for:** an incredible setting in an old industrial pump house; classic bistro food with an international twist; good if pricey (€34) set lunch menu. Ⓢ *Average main: €33 ✉ Siberiastraat Z/N, Het Eilandje ☎ 03/770–8625 🌐 www.hetpomphuis.be ⏲ Closed Mon. No lunch Sat. Ⓜ Tram: 24.*

To take a stroll along the charming cobbled lane called Vlaeykensgang is to step back to the 16th century.

InVINcible

$$$ | **FRENCH** | Located in a house on a narrow side street just seconds' walk from the Grote Markt, this small French-style bistro has one of the better wine lists in the city, paired expertly with some old Gallic standards; try the homemade pâté or bone-marrow appetizers. To get a sense of the scene, and what's cooking, grab a seat at the bar overlooking the exhibition kitchen. **Known for:** some of the most imaginative cooking in the city; watching your food being cooked and chatting with the chefs; an excellent wine selection with some more affordable options. *Average main: €25* *Haarstraat 7, Oude Stad* *03/231–3207* *www.invincible.be* *Closed weekends* *Tram: 4, 11.*

Nage

$$$ | **CONTEMPORARY** | Simplicity is the buzzword—both in the contemporary Belgian cooking, and in the decor—in this elegant but cozy parquet-floored bistro with minimal decorations on the walls to distract you from the food. Lunch is à la carte, but the three- to five-course prix-fixe dinner menus are also pared down and kept simple, with no more than two or sometimes three choices per course—but simplicity doesn't prevent each dish being a masterpiece. **Known for:** the fish and seafood dishes are particular stars; simple dishes with few ingredients so that each one can stand out; naturally fermented wines to accompany the meal. *Average main: €28* *Reyndersstraat 17, Oude Stad* *0456/322–072* *www.restaurantnage.be* *Closed Tues. and Wed. No lunch weekends.*

RAS

$$$ | **EUROPEAN** | Perched atop a huge glass-and-black-metal construction designed by avant-garde architect bOb (his spelling) Van Reeth, this cozy riverside restaurant—with bistro-style food as modern as the surroundings—resembles a docked cruise ship. You're virtually assured a good view, since large windows stretch around the building—boat traffic bustles on the Schedlt River to one side and, on the other, there's a

fine view of the cathedral and the Oude Stad. **Known for:** pretty decent wine list; set high up above the Schedlt River with 360-degree panoramic views; all-day service on weekends. *Average main: €28 Ernest Van Dijckkaai 37, Oude Stad 03/234–1275 www.ras.today Tram: 3, 5, 9, 15.*

Sir Anthony Van Dijck

$$$ | **FRENCH** | This fine-dining restaurant has long been a fixture on Antwerp's dining scene, dishing up exquisite cooking in the interior courtyard of its elegant dining room since 1975. Longtime chef and local legend Marc Paesbrugghe, who once gave away his two Michelin stars because he was tired of the red tape, has long-since hung up his apron, but the torch has been passed on in the kitchen with no drop in standards, and a prix-fixe menu that delicately picks its way through a host of big flavors. **Known for:** consistent quality for more than 40 years; excellent fine dining in a rather stately setting; a great value lunch deal that doesn't skimp on culinary imagination. *Average main: €29 Vlaeykensgang, Oude Koornmarkt 16, Oude Stad 03/231–6170 www.siranthonyvandijck.be Closed Sun. and Mon. Tram: 4.*

★ 't Fornuis

$$$$ | **FRENCH** | Burrowed deep in the heart of old Antwerp, there is something likeably stubborn about the defiantly traditional t' Fornuis, a place where stock Flemish surroundings with heavy oak chairs and beamed ceilings are the setting for some of the best (and priciest) food in the city. Charismatic Michelin-starred chef-owner Johan Segers likes to change his French-accented menu regularly; however, roasted sweetbreads with a wild-truffle sauce are a permanent fixture and worth trying. **Known for:** gregarious owner who's always willing to chat; likeable old-world setting; high-priced French cooking that more than lives up to the bill. *Average main: €37 Reyndersstraat 24, Oude Stad 03/233–6270 Closed weekends and 1 month in summer Tram: 3, 4, 5, 9, 15.*

't Hofke

$$ | **BELGIAN** | It's worth visiting here for the location alone, in the Vlaeykensgang (the oldest alley in the city), where time seems to have stood still. The cozy dining room has the look and feel of a private home. **Known for:** Flemish classics; its venerable setting, in the oldest neighborhood in Antwerp; good lunch options. *Average main: €21 Vlaeykensgang, Oude Koornmarkt 16, Oude Stad 03/233–8606 www.thofke.com Tram: 4.*

Coffee and Quick Bites

Elfde Gebod

$ | **BELGIAN** | With a name that means 11th Commandment, and an interior crammed with more than 600 plaster saints and angels salvaged from old churches, this atmospheric café enjoys a prime location, tucked into a tiny street between the Grote Markt and the cathedral. The food and drink are straightforward but hearty, with a lunchtime menu that revolves around club sandwiches and croques (pricier full meals are served in the evenings), and you can sit on the terrace in the shadow of the cathedral. **Known for:** efficient service, despite the crowds; unique interior packed with religious iconography; very popular at peak times. *Average main: €11 Torfbrug 10, Oude Stad 03/288–5733 elfdegebod.com Tram 11.*

Hotels

Antwerp Hilton

$$ | **HOTEL** | This five-story complex incorporates the fin-de-siècle facade of what was once the Grand Bazar department store. **Pros:** centrally located with an entrance in the Groenplaats metro station; grandly opulent without breaking

the bank; large rooms. **Cons:** service can feel a bit aloof; breakfast is expensive; part of a chain. *Rooms from: €135 ✉ Groenplaats 32, Oude Stad ☎ 03/204–1212 🌐 www.hilton.com 210 rooms No Meals Ⓜ Tram: 3, 4, 5, 9.*

Hotel Franq

$$$ | **HOTEL** | Opened in 2017, Hotel Franq's Belgian-French restaurant gained its first Michelin star just a year later, and if that doesn't hint at what you're getting, then the first glimpse of its elegant, stately lobby will. **Pros:** low-season prices are pretty reasonable for what you get; it's only a short walk to the city center; the restaurant is a delight and must be tried. **Cons:** high-season prices befit its elegance; the gym is rather dark and small; parking is pricey for Antwerp. *Rooms from: €180 ✉ Kipdorp 10, Oude Stad ☎ 03/555–3180 🌐 www.hotelfranq.com 39 rooms No Meals Ⓜ Tram: 11, 24.*

★ **Hotel Julien**

$$$ | **HOTEL** | Informality is the trademark of this stylish, elegant hotel housed in two renovated 16th-century houses that spill over into a quiet patio. **Pros:** great rooftop terrace and spa; friendly staff; historic building. **Cons:** the street outside can be pretty noisy; not all rooms have air-conditioning; no private parking. *Rooms from: €185 ✉ Korte Nieuwstraat 24, Oude Stad ☎ 03/229–0600 🌐 www.hotel-julien.com 21 rooms No Meals Ⓜ Tram: 11, 24.*

Hotel Riga

$$$ | **HOTEL** | The reception and bar of Hotel Riga are located in what used to be the old Riga suitcase shop, hence the rather vintage sign that still hangs above its door—but don't be confused, because this stylish new boutique spreads across three buildings. **Pros:** hip new hotel with friendly staff and restaurant; great views from the top-floor rooms; quiet location just a stroll from the city center. **Cons:** not very cheap for what you get; there aren't many rooms, so it fills up fast; no parking. *Rooms from: €189 ✉ Korte Koepoortstraat 4, Oude Stad ☎ 03/369–4422 🌐 www.hotelriga.be 12 rooms No Meals Ⓜ Tram: 11, 24.*

Hotel Rubens

$$ | **HOTEL** | Located directly behind the Grote Markt, a complete renovation has seen this tucked-away gem gain a new lease on life. **Pros:** quiet courtyard garden; friendly staff; free breakfast. **Cons:** rooms are rather businesslike; the walls are a little thin; parking space limited. *Rooms from: €139 ✉ Oude Beurs 29, Oude Stad ☎ 03/222–4848 🌐 www.hotelrubensantwerp.be 36 rooms Free Breakfast Ⓜ Tram: 11, 24.*

't Sandt

$$$ | **HOTEL** | A 17th-century neo-Rococo mansion that has served as a customs house, soap factory, and fruit importer, this is one of Antwerp's more endearing retreats. **Pros:** quiet Italian-style courtyard garden; great location; free breakfast. **Cons:** sound insulation in rooms not great if you have noisy neighbors; difficult to access by car; limited parking spaces, though it is a closed garage. *Rooms from: €196 ✉ Zand 13–19, Oude Stad ☎ 03/232–9390 🌐 www.hotel-sandt.be 29 rooms Free Breakfast Ⓜ Tram: 3, 4, 9, 15.*

U Eat & Sleep

$$$ | **HOTEL** | The Het Eilandje "port area" has changed a lot over the last decade—gone is the slightly seedy edge it used to exude, replaced by an increasing number of stylish new haunts including this design boutique hotel. **Pros:** it's located in one of the best settings in the city; good views over the docks; the restaurant is definitely worth your time. **Cons:** smaller rooms lack much natural light; handy for the MAS museum, but away from other sights; the smallest rooms can be overly cozy. *Rooms from: €205 ✉ Nassaustraat 42, Het Eilandje ☎ 03/201–9070 🌐 www.u-eatsleep.be 15 rooms No Meals Ⓜ Tram: 7.*

The National Beer of Antwerp

Belgium's kinship to brewing figures high in the country's culture and regional differences give way to local flavors. Antwerp's most famous brewery is De Koninck (The King), and its favorite beer is that brewery's flagship offering: a delightfully dry and malty amber pale ale, intended to be drunk in a special glass goblet known as a *bolleke* (literally, a "little bowl"). The beer itself was originally, and for more than a century, named De Koninck, but throughout that time everyone in the city always insisted on ordering it by asking for a "bolleke." In the end, the brewery gave up fighting popular opinion, and in 2019 the beer was officially relabeled as Bolleke, in honor of the glass. Now, no one can go wrong—until someone rechristens the glass, maybe.

Nightlife

There are 2,500 taverns in Antwerp—one for every 200 inhabitants—and the city is the club-going capital of Belgium, which means that the centers of nightlife are abuzz until the wee hours of the morning. The **Grote Markt** area attracts many tourists as well as locals with a range of traditional Belgian alehouses and some small discos, especially in the narrow, winding streets around the cathedral.

BARS

Bierhuis Kulminator

PUBS | This is often cited as one of the world's great beer bars. When open (it closes on Sunday and seemingly shuts its doors on a whim), Kulminator's grouch of an owner pours some 600 brews, with many hailing from little-known or long-since-defunct breweries. Its interior is best described as "old clutter," and as long as you don't expect a warm welcome, you'll leave happy. ✉ *Vleminckveld 32, Oude Stad* ☎ *03/232–4538* 🌐 *www.facebook.com/Kulminator.friends* Ⓜ *Tram: 4, 7.*

★ Billie's Bier Kafétaria

PUBS | A hefty tome of a menu details the brewery, style, and country of a worldly range of craft ales and Belgian favorites. There are up to 11 beers on draft and around 150 bottled, but if you're at a loss, just ask—the staff are extremely knowledgeable. Grab a board game and settle down for the day, or head upstairs for some excellent Flemish home cooking. It's closed on Tuesday. ✉ *Kammenstraat 12, Oude Stad* ☎ *03/226–3183* 🌐 *www.billiesbier.be* Ⓜ *Tram: 3, 4, 5.*

Cocktails at Nine

COCKTAIL LOUNGES | This modish cocktail bar—all stone floors and leather sofas—lies in a 200-year-old building in the shadow of the Cathedral of Our Lady. Drinks are made with fanciful infusions, homemade bitters, and great skill—though with prices starting at €15, it isn't cheap. When the seats and terrace are full, drinkers are turned away, so get here early. ✉ *Lijnwaadmarkt 9, Oude Stad* ☎ *03/707–1007* 🌐 *www.cocktailsatnine.be* Ⓜ *Tram: 11, 24.*

Den Engel

BARS | Facing the main square's fountain, Den Engel draws an eclectic and friendly clientele. It's a great place for people-watching and something of a step back in time; chances are that it hasn't changed much since it opened in 1903. ✉ *Grote Markt 3, Oude Stad* ☎ *03/233–1252* 🌐 *www.cafedenengel.be/1Home/home.html* Ⓜ *Tram: 3, 5, 9, 15.*

Pelgrom

BARS | The atmospheric Pelgrom is in the vaulted brick cellars of a 16th-century tavern, and it stocks more than 100 different beers. ✉ *Pelgrimstraat 15, Oude Stad* ☎ *03/234–0809* 🌐 *www.pelgrom.be* Ⓜ *Tram: 3, 4, 5.*

CLUBS AND JAZZ BARS

Cargo Club

DANCE CLUBS | Formerly known as Red & Blue, the biggest gay disco in Benelux has changed its name in recent years and expanded its offerings. Relentless house is still the music du jour on its industrial-style dance floor, though, as the party continues until 7 am. Its famous men-only Saturdays are now slightly more ad hoc. ✉ *Lange Schipperskapelstraat 11–13, Het Eilandje* ☎ *03/213–0555* 🌐 *www.cargoclub.be* Ⓜ *Tram: 7.*

De Muze

LIVE MUSIC | De Muze has train-station decor and good jazz sounds daily. Check their website for the latest schedule of performers. ✉ *Melkmarkt 15, Oude Stad* 🌐 *jazzcafedemuze.be* Ⓜ *Tram: 11.*

Performing Arts

Check the *Bulletin,* a weekly English-language news magazine, for details on arts events in Antwerp. You can pick up a copy at bookstores and newsstands.

Theater 't Eilandje

BALLET | The city's major ballet company is the Koninklijk Ballet van Vlaanderen (Royal Ballet of Flanders), whose productions tour regularly across Belgium and appear regularly in this theater. ✉ *Kattendijkdok Westkaai 16, Het Eilandje* ☎ *03/234–3438* 🌐 *www.operaballet.be/en* Ⓜ *Tram: 70.*

Shopping

Much of Antwerp's reputation for edgy chic comes from its clothing designers; dedicated followers of fashion consider the city in a league with Milan and Paris, and Antwerp-based couturiers regularly appear in the international glossies. Credit for this development goes to the so-called Antwerp Six (students of Linda Loppa from the class of 1981 at Antwerp's Fashion Academy) and in equal measure to the new wave of talent that has more recently stormed the catwalks. Many have shops based in Antwerp's fashion epicenter, located around Nationalestraat, which runs from the edge of Oude Stad and into Sint-Andries, and also in the Het Zuid area.

The nearby Schuttershofstraat and Kammenstraat are also fizzing with new spots. Another pedestrian area for general shopping is **Hoogstraat,** between Grote Markt and Sint-Jansvliet, with its appendix, **Grote Pieter Potstraat.** Here you find good secondhand bookshops and all kinds of bric-a-brac. Also, **Kloosterstraat,** above Het Zuid, in the Sint-Andries area, is dotted with all manner of antiques and art shops, and is perfect for discovering something a little bit different.

Bear in mind that pretty much everything grinds to a halt on most Sundays, but unlike the rest of Belgium, on the first Sunday of the month, retailers' shops doors are miraculously flung open and customers are welcomed inside. In January and July, these special shopping days signal the start of the sales.

CLOTHING

Ganterie A. Boon

HATS & GLOVES | For a fascinating glimpse of how shopping used to be, stop by Ganterie A. Boon, which stocks old-fashioned leather gloves that appeal to grandparents and young Antwerp fashionistas. The shop was opened in 1929 and still has the original fittings inside. The retro window display looks like it hasn't been updated since the 1950s. ✉ *Lombardenvest 2, Oude Stad* ☎ *03/232–3387* 🌐 *glovesboon.be.*

Het Modepaleis: Dries Van Norton
WOMEN'S CLOTHING | One of the iconic Antwerp Six that turned this city into the couture haven it became, Dries Van Noten collections for men and women can be found in the splendid Modepaleis, a five-story Belle Époque building that he bought in 1989. ✉ *Nationalestraat 16, Oude Stad* ☎ *03/470–2510* 🌐 *www.driesvannoten.be.*

Louis
WOMEN'S CLOTHING | Opened in 1986 to sell clothes by the Antwerp Six, this stalwart of the Antwerp fashion scene is now run by Marjan Eggers, who, as well as stocking it with established names like Ann Demeulemeester, also has one eye on the future, inviting final-year fashion students to exhibit in its window. ✉ *Lombardenstraat 2, Oude Stad* ☎ *03/232–9872* 🌐 *www.louisantwerp.be.*

STREET MARKETS

Though you can shop for antiques on Kloosterstraat throughout the week, there's a special antiques market on **Lijnwaadmarkt** (Saturday 9–5), north of the cathedral. The **Rubensmarkt** (Rubens Market, mid-August annually) is held on the Grote Markt, with vendors in 17th-century costumes hawking everything under the sun. Public auction sales of furniture and other secondhand goods are held at **Vrijdagmarkt** (Friday 9–1). Fashion fans should check out the chic **Markt Van Morgen** (Market for Tomorrow; Sunday noon–6), off Kloosterstraat; this is where burgeoning designers and jewelry makers pay their dues.

Meir, Diamond Quarter, and Centraal Station

Here you'll find two of Antwerp's icons: the shopping street that runs to the old city and the Diamantwijk (Diamond Quarter), the world center of the international diamond trade. Both tell the story of modern Antwerp.

Sights

Antwerp Zoo
ZOO | FAMILY | Antwerp's zoo houses its residents in style. Giraffes, ostriches, and African antelopes inhabit an Egyptian temple and a thriving Congolese okapi family grazes around a Moorish temple. In part, this reflects the public's taste when the zoo was created 170 years ago. Today, animals are allowed maximum space, and much research is devoted to endangered species. The zoo also has sea lions, an aquarium, and a house for nocturnal animals. ✉ *Koningin Astridplein 26, Centraal Station* ☎ *070/233–354* 🌐 *www.zooantwerpen.be* 🎫 *€31* Ⓜ *Tram: 2, 3, 11, 24.*

Begijnhof
HISTORIC DISTRICT | This beguinage—a community of women who dedicated themselves to religious duties without taking any vows—dates from the 13th century, but by the 1960s there was only one beguine left. Redbrick buildings surrounding a courtyard garden give a sense of tranquility as you stroll the roughly cobbled walk. The building is a little difficult to find, but your efforts will be rewarded with serene surroundings and charming houses, which you can only view from the outside. ✉ *Oude Begijnhof, off Wijngaardstraat, Meir* ☎ *03/232–0103,* 🎫 *Free* Ⓜ *Bus: 1, 13, 17.*

Centraal Station
TRAIN/TRAIN STATION | The neo-Baroque railway terminal was built at the turn of the 20th century during the reign of Leopold II of Belgium, a monarch not given to understatement. The magnificent exterior and splendid, vaulted ticket-office hall and staircases call out for hissing steam engines, peremptory conductors, scurrying porters, and languid ladies wrapped in boas. Today most departures and arrivals are humble commuter trains,

Antwerp's Brilliant Industry

Knowing that 80% of rough diamonds pass through Antwerp and 50% are sold in the city, it's hard to imagine that India dominated the diamond trade from the 4th century BC to the 18th century. In the 13th century, Venice was a shipping point for Indian goods (including diamonds) to the West. Strategic cities in Northern Europe maintained trading routes with Venice during the Middle Ages, and eventually diamond traders made their way to Bruges. In fact, it was Lodewijck van Bercken, a Bruges resident, who invented the technique of polishing diamonds with diamonds. The silting up of Bruges's harbor meant the gradual relocation of the diamond industry to Antwerp in the 15th century, and Antwerp's liberal and welcoming atmosphere encouraged immigrants to settle here.

Today, Antwerp's diamond sector maintains its unique multicultural atmosphere. Indians, Jews, Belgians, Australians, Russians, Lebanese, Africans, and Japanese contribute to the hub of activity found here. The heavily guarded Diamond Square Mile is the headquarters of 1,500 firms, four diamond exchanges, 350 workshops, specialized diamond banks, security and transport firms, brokers, consultants, and diamond schools, employing some 30,000 people.

The bourse is the meeting point for buyers, sellers, and brokers. Individuals must become members and adhere to strict rules. Transactions are conducted in a traditional and informal way. There are no written contracts. A handshake and the phrase *Mazal U'Brach* (may the deal bring you luck) closes a deal. Trade disputes are handled in-house, where two members are commissioned each week to solve conflicts.

The HRD is the customs office for all diamonds moving in and out of Belgium. Each day, the council checks 1,000 diamonds with strict anonymity and objectivity, confirming their authenticity based on the characteristics of each stone using the 4Cs (carat, color, clarity, cut).

The global trade in diamonds has come under a great deal of scrutiny in recent years, particularly in the wake of the Hollywood movie *Blood Diamond*, which drew attention to so-called conflict diamonds. Dealers in Antwerp are understandably keen to distance themselves from this tarnished image, and the strict checks carried out by the HRD are there to ensure that all gems passing through the city are ethically correct.

but the station still inspires. Two underground levels, added to accommodate high-speed trains, has turned the track areas into an impressively vast open space. ✉ *Koningin Astridplein 27, Centraal Station* ☎ *02/528–2828* Ⓜ *Tram: 2, 3, 6, 8, 9, 11, 12, 15, 24.*

★ Chocolate Nation

OTHER ATTRACTION | FAMILY | Taking its cue more from Willy Wonka than any museum, this carnivalesque look at the humble cocoa bean is one of the city's biggest crowd-pleasers. Relentlessly inventive and whimsical, room after room boasts Heath Robinson–esque contraptions that make the history of

Antwerp's Centraal Station is a neo-Baroque masterpiece built at the turn of the 20th century.

chocolate making and its production a story worth telling. It's as theatrical as it is informative, using projections, stage-craft, and workshops to draw you in. Audio guides are pointed at information points along the way, and some rooms are time-locked so you can't leave until your group is done, but there's often a handful of chocolates on hand to quiet the impatient. The finale is a tasting room where you're free to try 10 different kinds of melted chocolate. ✉ *Koningin Astridplein 7, Centraal Station* ☏ *03/207–0808* 🌐 *www.chocolatenation.be* 🎫 *€19* Ⓜ *Tram: 2, 3, 5.*

Diamond Quarter

BUSINESS DISTRICT | Some 85% of the world's uncut diamonds pass through Antwerp, and the diamond trade has its own quarter, where the skills of cutting and polishing the gems have been handed down for generations by a tightly knit community. Twenty-five million carats are cut and traded here every year, more than anywhere else in the world. The district occupies a few nondescript city blocks west of Centraal Station. A large part of the community is Jewish, so you'll see shop signs in Hebrew and Hasidic men with traditional dark clothing and side curls, though many of the business-es are now Indian-owned. Below the elevated railway tracks, a long row of stalls and shops gleams with jewelry and gems. Diamond cutting began in Bruges but moved to Antwerp in the late 15th century, and the industry now employs some 8,000 workers. Many shops close for the Saturday sabbath. ✉ *Bounded by DeKeyserlei, Pelikaanstraat, Lange Herentalsestraat, and Lange Kievitstraat, Diamond Quarter* Ⓜ *Tram: 2, 6, 9, 15.*

Maagdenhuis (*Maidens' House*)

HISTORY MUSEUM | The chapel and entrance gateway of the Maagdenhuis (Maidens' House), a foundling hospital for girls of the poor, was constructed from 1564 to 1568 and closed in 1882, when more modern institutions became avail-able. A museum houses a collection of clothes, workbooks, and needlework, as well as paintings and statuary. ✉ *Lange*

Meir, Diamond Quarter, and Centraal Station
Willemdok
Godefriduskaai
Oudeleeuwenrui
Oudeleeuwenrui
Ankerrui
Waaslandtunnel
Hessenplein
Stijfselstraat
Stijfselrui
Leguit
Falconplein
Falconrui
Paardenmarkt
Sint-Paulusplaats
Keistraat
Sint-Paulusstraat
Koolkaai
Lange Noordstraat
Vekestraat
Kleine Kauwenberg
Klapdorp
Raapstraat
Stadswaag
Venusstraat
Jordaenskaai
Veemarkt
Zwartzustersstraat
Minderbroedersrui
Lange Winkelstraat
Zirkstraat
Ambtmanstraat
Blindestraat
Lange Doornikstraat
Hofstraat
Oude Beurs
Koningstraat
Prinsesstraat
Steenplein
Keizerstraat
Frans Halsplein
Frans Halsplein
Grote Markt
Kaasrui
Kipdorp
Sint-Katelijnevest
Ernest Van Dijckkaai
Haarstraat
Hoogstraat
Borzestraat
Sint-Jacobsmar
Lange Nieuwstraat
Lange Nieuwstraat
Pelgrimstraat
Groenplaats
Reyndersstraat
Gramayestraat
Eikenstraat
Sint-Jansvliet
Schoenmarkt
Meir
Meir
Vrijdagmarkt
Steenhouwersvest
Wiegstraat
Otto Veniusstraat
Oever
Lombardenvest
Wapper
Wapper
Kolveniersstraat
Kammenstraat
Jodenstraat
Hopland
Augustijnenstraat
Everdijstraat
Schuttershofstraat
Langegang
Sint-Andriesstraat
Graanmarkt
Meirstraat
Lange Riddersstraat
Sint-Antoniusstraat
Oudaan
Pompstraat
Happaertstraat
Arenbergstraat
Nationalestraat
Schoytestraat
Theaterplein
Tabakvest
Vleminckveld
Leopoldstraat
Oudevaartplaats
Oudevaartplaats
Lange Vlierstraat
Aalmoezenierstraat
Plantentuin
Prekersstraat
Mechelseplein
Frankrijklei
Frankrijklei
Begijnenstraat
Tabakvest
Leopoldplaats
Rubenslei
Kapucinessenstraat
Louizastraat
0
500 ft
0
100 m
KEY
Exploring Sights
Restaurants
Quick Bites
Hotels
A B C D E F
1 2 3 4 5 6 7 8 9

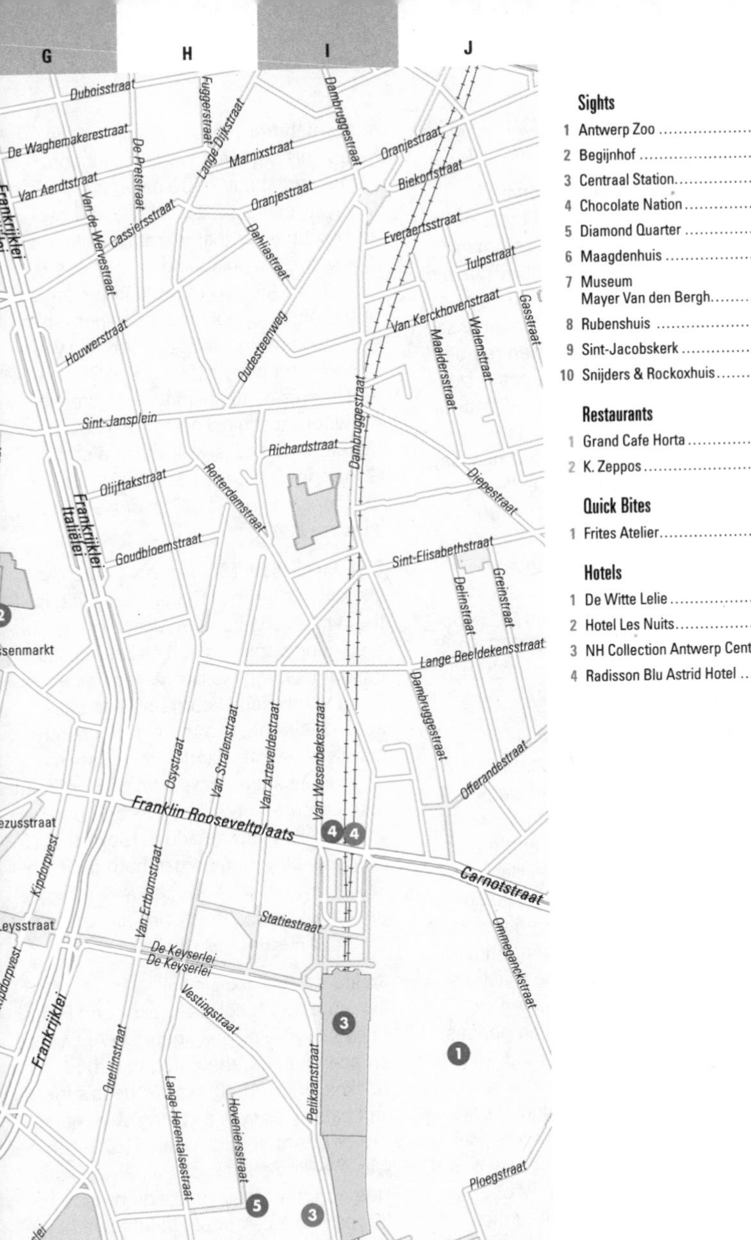

Sights

1 Antwerp Zoo J7
2 Begijnhof G4
3 Centraal Station........................ I7
4 Chocolate Nation........................ I5
5 Diamond Quarter H8
6 Maagdenhuis D8
7 Museum Mayer Van den Bergh........................ D7
8 Rubenshuis E7
9 Sint-Jacobskerk F5
10 Snijders & Rockoxhuis........................ D4

Restaurants

1 Grand Cafe Horta E7
2 K. Zeppos C8

Quick Bites

1 Frites Atelier........................ C7

Hotels

1 De Witte Lelie D4
2 Hotel Les Nuits........................ D7
3 NH Collection Antwerp Centre........................ I8
4 Radisson Blu Astrid Hotel I5

Gasthuisstraat 33, Meir ☎ *03/435–9910* 🌐 *maagdenhuis.be* 🎫 *€8* Ⓜ *Tram: 4, 7.*

★ **Museum Mayer Van den Bergh**

ART MUSEUM | Pieter Bruegel the Elder's arguably greatest and most enigmatic painting, *Dulle Griet*, is the showpiece of the 4,000 works that passionate art connoisseur Mayer Van den Bergh amassed in the 19th century. It has been restored to its full, hellish glory and is the prize of a collection that also includes Bruegel's witty, miniature illustrations in the *Twelve Proverbs*, based on popular Flemish sayings, and such treasures as a life-sized polychrome statue from about 1300 of St. John resting his head on Christ's chest. There's an English-language pamphlet included with admission that reviews part of the collection. ✉ *Lange Gasthuisstraat 19, Meir* ☎ *03/338–8188* 🌐 *www.mayervandenbergh.be* 🎫 *€10* 🕓 *Closed Mon.* Ⓜ *Tram: 4, 7.*

★ **Rubenshuis** (*Rubens House*)

HISTORIC HOME | A fabulous picture of Rubens as painter and patrician is presented here at his own house, where the elaborate portico and temple, designed by Rubens in Italian Baroque style, were the only things still standing three centuries after the house was built. Most of what's here is a reconstruction (completed in 1946) from the master's own design. It represents Rubens at the pinnacle of his fame, when he was appointed court painter to Archduke Albrecht and, with his wife, was sent on a diplomatic mission to Madrid, where he also painted some 40 portraits. He conducted delicate peace negotiations in London on behalf of Philip IV of Spain, and while in London he painted the ceiling of the Whitehall Banqueting Hall and was knighted by Charles I of Great Britain. The most evocative room in Rubens House is the huge studio, where drawings by Rubens and his pupils, as well as old prints, help to re-create the original atmosphere. In Rubens's day, visitors could view completed paintings and watch from the mezzanine while he and his students worked. Rubens completed about 2,500 paintings, nearly all characterized by the energy and exuberance that were his hallmark. A few of his works hang in the house, including a touching sketch in the studio of the Annunciation and a self-portrait in the dining room. Unfortunately, his young widow promptly sold off some 300 pieces after his death in 1640. A re-creation of Rubens's original garden exists within the grounds and is well worth a stroll. ✉ *Wapper 9–11, Meir* ☎ *03/201–1555* 🌐 *rubenshuis.be* 🎫 *€12* 🕓 *Closed Mon.* Ⓜ *Tram: 3, 4, 5.*

Sint-Jacobskerk (*St. Jacob's Church*)

CHURCH | Peter Paul Rubens is buried in the white sandstone St. Jacob's Church. A painting depicting him as St. George posed between his two wives, Isabella Brant and Helena Fourment, hangs above his tomb. The three-aisle church blends late-Gothic and Baroque styles. The tombs are a who's who of prominent 17th-century Antwerp families. A notable visitor (Wolfgang Amadeus Mozart) allegedly played the organ here during his 1727 stay in the city. ✉ *Lange Nieuwstraat 73, Meir* 🌐 *www.sintjacobantwerpen.be* 🎫 *Free* Ⓜ *Tram 10, 11.*

Snijders & Rockoxhuis

ART MUSEUM | Nicolaas Rockox and Frans Snijders were pivotal figures in Antwerp's art scene during the Baroque period. Rockox (1560–1640) was Rubens's friend and patron, as well as being seven-time mayor of Antwerp; Snijders (1579–1657) was a skilled painter of animals and still lifes. Together they lived side by side for 20 years in a pair of beautiful town houses on Keizerstraat, which have now been turned into one museum. It was here that humanist and art collector Rockox built an enviable art collection, and on display are two of Rubens's works: one is *Madonna en Kind* (*Madonna and Child*), a delicate portrait of Rubens's first wife, Isabella, and their son, Nicolaas, and the

Rubinshuis, the former home of renowned Flemish artist Peter Paul Rubens, is now a museum dedicated to his life and work.

other is a sketch for the *Kruisiging* (*Crucifixion*). The collection also includes works by Van Dyck, Joachim Patinier, Jordaens, Pieter Bruegel (including his infamous *Proverbs*), and, of course, Snijders himself, whose work features prominently. The paintings are shown in the context of a pair of upper-class Baroque homes, furnished in the style of the period. Handheld tablets give you information on each painting. ✉ *Keizerstraat 10–12, Meir* ☎ *03/201–9250* 🌐 *www.rockoxhuis.be* 🎫 *€10* 🕒 *Closed Mon.* Ⓜ *Tram: 7, 11, 24.*

Restaurants

Grand Cafe Horta

$$$ | **CONTEMPORARY** | **FAMILY** | The iron framework of the 19th-century Maison du Peuple, a building designed by famed Art Nouveau architect Victor Horta, supports this brasserie. It siphons a hip crowd from trendy Hopland Street and keeps a sunny feel with large mustard-yellow industrial beams and windows all around. **Known for:** some fine lunch options; a bright and airy spot to rest your feet and grab a bite while shopping; a wonderful setting within a fabulous Victor Horta–designed building. $ *Average main: €28* ✉ *Hopland 2, Meir* ☎ *03/203–5660* 🌐 *www.grandcafehorta.be* 🕒 *No dinner Sun.* Ⓜ *Tram: 4, 7, 8, 10.*

K. Zeppos

$$ | **BELGIAN** | This busy café-bar is found deep in the hipster spawning grounds of Mechelseplein, and while the menu is limited to a half dozen Flemish and French crowd-pleasers (beef carbonnade/ *stoofvlees*, vol-au-vent, and the like) and burgers, it executes them extremely well—and at a good price. High, ornate ceilings, a long bar, and closely packed tables help perpetuate the communal vibe that carries most evenings along. **Known for:** good prices for the quality of food; hip atmosphere and communal dining tables; classic Flemish favorites. $ *Average main: €17* ✉ *Vleminckveld 78, Meir* ☎ *03/231–1789* 🌐 *cafezeppos.be* Ⓜ *Tram: 4, 7.*

Coffee and Quick Bites

Frites Atelier

$ | **BELGIAN** | Brussels may be the city best known for its frites, but that hasn't stopped this high-end Dutch friture from muscling in. Created by three-star Michelin chef Sergio Herman, its Antwerp branch was the first in Belgium (now in Ghent and Brussels), and its elaborate sauces, from "deep truffle" to seasonal specials like "olive and Catalan cream," make it something special. **Known for:** quick service and tasty results; frites are the focus, but the burgers and croquettes are also great; the sauces are pretty special, too. *Average main: €8 Korte Gasthuisstraat 32, Meir www.fritesatelier.com Tram: 4.*

Hotels

★ De Witte Lelie

$$$$ | **HOTEL** | Three step-gabled 17th-century houses have been combined to create Antwerp's most exclusive hotel. **Pros:** complimentary minibars; large rooms; friendly, attentive service. **Cons:** its rates make it something of an indulgence; breakfast not included in room rate; some rooms have no elevator access. *Rooms from: €266 Keizerstraat 16–18, Meir 03/226–1966 www.dewittelelie.be 10 rooms No Meals Tram: 10, 11.*

Hotel Les Nuits

$$ | **HOTEL** | These modern surroundings come with convenience to Antwerp's main shopping streets. **Pros:** room service from hotel restaurant; quiet location; air-conditioning. **Cons:** no on-site parking (though public parking nearby); no minibars; no real lobby. *Rooms from: €149 Lange Gasthuisstraat 12, Meir 03/225–0204 www.hotellesnuits.be 22 rooms No Meals Tram: 4, 7.*

NH Collection Antwerp Centre

$$ | **HOTEL** | In the middle of the diamond district, and across the street from Antwerp Centraal railway station, this modern chain hotel is perfectly located for a quick getaway, or if you are in the mood for a bit of jewelry window-shopping. **Pros:** quiet at night, especially the back rooms; super-big bath towels; handily located opposite Centraal Station. **Cons:** street outside is not the prettiest; a 15-minute walk from the Old Town; hotel bar area is a bit cold and impersonal. *Rooms from: €134 Pelikaanstraat 84, Centraal Station 03/446–0330 www.nh-hotels.com 186 rooms No Meals.*

Radisson Blu Astrid Hotel

$$ | **HOTEL** | Directly across from Antwerp's Centraal Station and a stone's throw from the National Express stop, convenience is the key at this newly refurbished old-stager, which now has a pair of new restaurants, its own Starbucks, and a rather minimalist look. **Pros:** free Wi-Fi in rooms; near train station; 24-hour fitness center. **Cons:** the square outside is pretty noisy; somewhat generic feel; bit of a walk to cathedral and Grote Markt. *Rooms from: €150 Koningin Astridplein 7B, Centraal Station 03/203–1234 www.radissonhotels.com 253 rooms Free Breakfast Tram: 2, 3, 5, 11, 24.*

Nightlife

BARS

Beerlover's Bar

BARS | Sometimes the name says it all. Just a five-minute walk from Centraal Station, the selection here runs the gamut of craft ale and Belgian favorites, with a dozen draft brews on tap. Its minimalist interior is more cocktail joint that your typical "brown café," but friendly, knowledgeable staff make exploring a bottle list 150-strong a delight. *Rotterdamstraat 105, Centraal Station 0497/472–620 www.beerlovers.be Tram: 12.*

Korsakov

BARS | Taking its name from a neurological disorder linked to alcohol abuse, this quirky, artsy café-bar has cultivated a loyal following among the in-crowd of hipster-drenched Mechelseplein. There's live music some nights. ✉ *Sint Jorispoort 1, Meir* 🌐 *korsakov.beer* Ⓜ *Tram: 4, 7.*

Oud Arsenaal

PUBS | This typical "brown café" (old-style bar, all dark wood and nicotine-stained walls) has been operating since 1929—and little has changed. It's been in the same family for three generations and serves up a good selection of beers (particularly some unusual *gueuze* and *kriek* beers) at a decent price—much to the delight of its dedicated locals. ✉ *Maria Pijpelincxstraat 4, Meir* ☎ *03/232–9754* 🌐 *www.dorstvlegel.be* Ⓜ *Tram: 3, 5, 9.*

CLUBS

Ampère

DANCE CLUBS | Belgium's first "ecological" venue lies under the train tracks. As well as club nights, it also runs lectures, vinyl fairs, and workshops, but most come for the music. Nights run the spectrum from deep house to future jazz every Friday and Saturday, so check out the website for upcoming events. ✉ *Simonsstraat 21, Centraal Station* 🌐 *ampere-antwerp.com* Ⓜ *Tram: 2, 6, 9.*

Performing Arts

Check the *Bulletin* (*www.thebulletin.be*), an English-language news and listings source, for details on arts events and shows in Antwerp.

Opera Antwerpen

OPERA | Opera Vlaanderen was voted the world's best opera company in 2019, and the chance to see them, as well as their sister ballet company, perform at this regular venue, a five-minute walk from Centraal Station, is not to be missed. ✉ *Frankrijklei 1, Centraal Station* ☎ *03/202–1020* 🌐 *www.operaballet.be.*

Shopping

The elegant **Meir,** together with its extension to the east, **De Keyserlei,** and at the opposite end, **Huidevettersstraat,** serves up high-street standbys and long-established names. The latter marks the edge of the **Wilde Zee,** a five-street-wide shopping area of boutiques and pop-ups. Shopping galleries branch off from all three streets: **Century Center** and **Antwerp Tower** from De Keyserlei, **Meir Square** from Meir, and **Nieuwe Gaanderij** from Huidevettersstraat. The area in and around the glamorous **Horta Complex,** on Hopland, the street parallel to the Meir between Centraal Station and the Oude Stad, is also a popular shopping hub.

CLOTHING

★ Graanmarkt 13

WOMEN'S CLOTHING | Tucked just off a lovely square in a 19th-century town house, Graanmarkt 13 offers a nicely edited selection of women's clothes, including pieces by local designers Bernadette and Sofie D'Hoore, plus unique ceramics, pottery, and jewelry. Its first floor has something of a shoe fetish, stocking the likes of Mansur Gavriel, K Jacques, and Aeyde; it's also worth a postshopping stop for lunch or dinner at its namesake restaurant downstairs. ✉ *Graanmarkt 13, Meir* ☎ *03/337–7991* 🌐 *www.graanmarkt13.be.*

Stadsfeestzaal

MALL | Built in 1908 as an exhibitions and events space, the Stadsfeestzaal was gutted by a major fire in 2000. Now fully restored, it houses a lively shopping mall across 40 shops. Clothing stores include Urban Outfitters, Green Ice, and COS. Even if you're not in the mood for retail therapy, it's worth dropping by just to marvel at the spectacular neoclassical architecture. ✉ *Meir 78, Meir* ☎ *03/202–3100* 🌐 *stadsfeestzaal.com.*

DIAMONDS

The heart of the city's diamond industry is in and around Appelmansstraat, near the Centraal Station. Here merchants from the world over have dealt in diamonds for 500 years.

■ TIP→ If you buy a loose stone and plan to set it, be sure to choose a reputable establishment for the work, so that your diamond is not switched for an inferior one.

Antwerp World Diamond Centre

JEWELRY & WATCHES | For advice on buying diamonds at the retail level (and details of the essential four Cs: carat, color, clarity, and cut) you can contact the Antwerp World Diamond Centre Association, which operates under the umbrella of the Antwerp Diamond High Council. Information on its members and a suggested route for exploring the area are included on the website. ✉ *Hoveniersstraat 22, Centraal Station* ☎ *03/222–0511* 🌐 *www.awdc.be* ⏲ *Closed weekends.*

FOOD SHOPS

Bakkerij Goossens

FOOD | Founded in 1884, Bakkerij Goossens is a popular old favorite with locals. Try their classic *roggeverdommeke*—a rye bread stuffed with raisins. ✉ *Korte Gasthuisstraat 31, Meir* ☎ *03/226–0791.*

The Chocolate Line

CHOCOLATE | For chocolate filled with unusual flavors like Japanese wasabi, Coca-Cola, or crisp fried onion, head to this self-proclaimed "shock-o-latier." Although you'll undoubtedly have to queue for your chocolates, you should use the time to admire your surroundings: the gilded ceilings and crystal chandelier of the opulent Paleis op de Meir (Palace on the Meir). ✉ *Paleis op de Meir, Meir 50, Meir* ☎ *03/206–2030* 🌐 *www.thechocolateline.be.*

DelRey

CHOCOLATE | This stylish family-run chocolatier and pâtissier has been going since 1949, and remains one of the finest in the city. Its "Chocolate Lounge," next door, also makes for an excellent lunch spot—and needless to say, the desserts are flooring. ✉ *Appelmansstraat 5, Centraal Station* ☎ *03/470–2861* 🌐 *www.delrey.be.*

Kaas Vervloet

FOOD | Kaas Vervloet is the best address for regional, award-winning cheeses and other culinary delicacies. Try the Achelse Blauwe. ✉ *Wiegstraat 28, Meir* ☎ *03/233–3729* 🌐 *www.kaasvervloet.be.*

Philip's Biscuits

FOOD | If you're after an edible souvenir from Antwerp, head for the old-fashioned biscuit and cake store Philip's Biscuits. *Speculaas* (spiced cookies), macaroons (coconut cookies), and *peperkoek* (gingerbread) are best and can be ordered in attractive tins—a good gift alternative to chocolate. There is also a second branch at Oude Kornmarkt 8. ✉ *Korte Gasthuisstraat 39, De Wilde See* ☎ *03/231–2660* 🌐 *www.philipsbiscuits.be.*

STREET MARKETS

On **Theaterplein** (a block south from Rubenshuis on Wapper), there is a general weekend market (Saturday 8–4, Sunday 8–1) selling flowers and exotic goods, with plenty of hot food on offer. Many locals still refer to the Sunday edition as *Vogelenmarkt* (bird market), in spite of the fact that the sale of live animals at street markets is now banned.

South of the Center

Head south of the center and you'll find relics of Antwerp's past, the city's best dining, and a resurgent bohemian vibe that has transformed its old suburbs. Hugging the banks of the Schedlt lies Het Zuid, a 19th-century residential district of wide boulevards and elegant squares that has been polished into a bustling arts hub. Amid its excellent photography and modern art centers (the fine arts museum finally reopened in 2022 after more than a decade of renovation work)

Sights

1 De Koninck Brewery F3
2 Fotomuseum (FOMU)..... A1
3 Koninklijk Museum voor Schone Kunsten (KMSKA) B1
4 Museum of Modern Art (MuHKA)................... A1
5 Zurenborg H2

Restaurants

1 Dôme....................... H2
2 Fiskebar.................... C1
3 The Jane................... G3

Quick Bites

1 Murni Zuid................ B1

Hotels

1 August G3
2 Boulevard Leopold F2
3 Budget Boetiek Hotel Rubenshof................. B2
4 Hotel Pilar B1

After a tour of the brew hall, sample some world-famous Belgium beer at De Koninck Brewery.

are achingly hip bars, indie galleries, and restaurants well worth the trip.

Sights

★ De Koninck Brewery

BREWERY | The De Koninck Brewery is almost as old as the city of Antwerp itself and still resides on the site of the inn from which it was converted back in 1833. Back then, De Plaisante Hof (or The Merry Garden) lay in plain view of Antwerp's notorious hanging fields; today its view of King Albert Park is mercifully less shocking. Visitors can now take ambling tours inside the brew hall that include a wealth of interactive video screens and gizmos, as well as a couple of beers to taste. The brewery has also expanded to include a number of local artisanal food and drink producers and a meat-heavy gourmet restaurant, The Butcher's Son, that already boasts a Michelin star. Classes range from beer cookery to sessions on how to pair beers and cheese (or chocolate). ✉ *Mechelsesteenweg 291, South of the Center* ☎ *03/866–9690* 🌐 *www.dekoninck.be* 🎫 *€12* 🕒 *Closed Mon.* Ⓜ *Tram: 2, 6, 7, 15.*

Fotomuseum (FOMU)

ART MUSEUM | The city's home of contemporary photography is a four-story, in-your-face epic, with each floor dedicated to a different theme or artist. Past exhibitions have featured Henri Cartier-Bresson, William Klein, and Man Ray, with two or three exhibitions every four months. The building is also home to the art house movie theater, Cinema Lumière (*www.lumiere-antwerpen.be*). ✉ *Waalsekaai 47, South of the Center* ☎ *03/242–9300* 🌐 *fotomuseum.be* 🎫 *€10* 🕒 *Closed Mon.* Ⓜ *Tram: 4, 8.*

★ Koninklijk Museum voor Schone Kunsten (KMSKA)

ART MUSEUM | Finally reopened in 2022 after more than a decade of extensive restoration work, the Royal Museum of Fine Arts collection is studded with masterworks from Bruegel to Ensor, and is a must for any student of Flemish art. Paintings recovered from the French after the fall of Napoléon form the nucleus of a collection of 2,500 artworks. There are rooms devoted to both Peter Paul Rubens and to Anthony van Dyck, and other focused almost entirely on Jacob Jordaens and Bruegel. The collection of Flemish Primitives includes works by Van Eyck, Memling, Roger van der Weyden, Joachim Patinir, and Quinten Metsys. On the ground floor, there's a representative survey of Belgian art of the past 150 years—Emile Claus, Rik Wouters, Permeke, Magritte, Delvaux, and especially James Ensor. ✉ *Leopold de Waelplaats 2, South of the Center* ☎ *03/224–9550* 🌐 *kmska.be* ⏲ *Closed Mon.* Ⓜ *Tram: 8.*

Museum of Modern Art (MuHKA)

ART MUSEUM | In one of Belgium's most important contemporary art venues, you'll find paintings, installations, video art, and experimental architecture from a range of international artists. Among its collection are works by Antwerp-born Flemish polymath Jan Fabre, whose often bizarre sculptures and installations have established him as a leading figure in the Belgian art world. The museum, which also contains an art house cinema and library, is housed in a renovated grain silo. There's also a rooftop café. ✉ *Leuvenstraat 32, South of the Center* ☎ *03/260–9999* 🌐 *www.muhka.be* 🎟 *€12* ⏲ *Closed Mon.* Ⓜ *Tram: 4.*

Zurenborg

NEIGHBORHOOD | Southeast of the city center, past Centraal Station, lies the most beautiful neighborhood in Antwerp: Zurenborg. It was one of few parts of the modern city that was actually planned—and not simply a result of industrial necessity—when it was transformed in the early 20th century with street after street of Belle Époque, neoclassical, and Art Nouveau town houses. The highlight is Cogels-Osylei, a street famed for its elaborate Art Nouveau "flower" houses, all named after different flora. Its urban palaces once housed the city's bourgeoisie, while the larger Dageraadplaats was designed for the middle classes but remains no less ambitious and has long since been adopted by Antwerp's "bobo" set, with plenty of hip bars and cafés nearby. Historical walking tours are a good way to explore the area and are easily booked at the tourist information. ✉ *Just north of Berchem Station, Cogels-Osylei and Dageraadplaats, South of the Center* Ⓜ *Tram: 11.*

Restaurants

Dôme

$$$$ | FRENCH | Architecture and food aficionados will appreciate both the food and somber decor in this splendid Art Nouveau building in the upscale Zurenborg neighborhood—this former teahouse, sewing school, and police office maintains its original floor mosaic, and the whitewashed walls and dome-shape roof parallel its haute cuisine. Michelin-starred head chef Frédéric Chabbert learned his trade working in Hong Kong, and brings touches of his international experiences into the classic-inspired dishes of his French homeland. **Known for:** an easy-to miss sign by the door; excellent wine list; glorious Art Nouveau setting. 💲 *Average main: €40* ✉ *Grote Hondstraat 2, South of the Center* ☎ *03/239–9003* 🌐 *www.domeantwerp.be* ⏲ *Closed Sun. and Mon.* Ⓜ *Tram: 9.*

★ **Fiskebar**

$$$ | SEAFOOD | This hip Scandinavian-style fish joint is the place to try seasonal, organic, and sustainable seafood—arguably the best in the city—served simply as a *fruits de mer* platter, grilled with hand-cut fries on the side, or as an always-excellent bouillabaisse. If the weather cooperates, opt for a seat on their spacious terrace instead of the rather cramped dining room, all the better for prime Het Zuid people-watching—it's always packed, but walk-ins can grab a high stool if you arrive early and forgot to book. **Known for:** a bouillabaisse to remember; some of the best seafood in Antwerp; great atmosphere in a perennially popular (though tiny) restaurant. $ *Average main: €25* ✉ *Marnixplaats 11, South of the Center* ☎ *03/257–1357* 🌐 *www.fiskebar.be* Ⓜ *Tram: 4.*

★ The Jane

$$$$ | EUROPEAN | Having held two Michelin stars since 2017, this shooting star on the Belgian gastronomy scene is located in the chapel of a former military hospital, albeit an open kitchen has replaced the altar and stained glass takes its inspiration from the tattoo parlor. The wine list is vast and the average dining experience usually runs past three hours thanks to its 10-course (€215) tasting menu, which is heavily slanted toward fish and seafood. **Known for:** fabulous setting in a former chapel; lengthy tasting menus with international inspiration; a fantastic wine list with well-thought-out pairing options. $ *Average main: €50* ✉ *Paradeplein 1, South of the Center* ☎ *03/808–4465* 🌐 *www.thejaneantwerp.com* ⏲ *Closed Mon.–Wed.* Ⓜ *Tram: 4.*

 Coffee and Quick Bites

Murni Zuid

$ | INTERNATIONAL | Directly opposite the KMSKA fine arts museum, this place is open from early until late and will satisfy your needs whether you're after breakfast pancakes or a chicken burger dinner. The pan-global menu, with dishes inspired from every continent, leans toward—but is far from exclusively—plant-based and healthy. **Known for:** plentiful options for both vegans and vegetarians; "build-your-own" avocado toasts with various toppings; healthy, fresh produce. $ *Average main: €8* ✉ *Leopold de Waelplaats 10, South of the Center* ☎ *03/246–6067* 🌐 *www.murni.be* ⏲ *Closed Wed. and Thurs.*

★ August

$$$ | HOTEL | Set within the complex of a former military hospital, this stylish design hotel has been ingeniously built into an old Augustinian convent, its lounge and bar area occupying the beautiful old chapel. **Pros:** it's a few minutes' walk from Berchem Railway Station; the chapel-bar is a beautiful space to relax; who doesn't love a swimming pond?. **Cons:** rooms can feel a little sparse; there's not much else to do in the area; it's a long walk from the center. $ *Rooms from: €175* ✉ *Jules Bordetstraat 5, South of the Center* ☎ *03/500–8080* 🌐 *www.august-antwerp.com* *44 rooms* *No Meals* Ⓜ *Tram: 4.*

★ Boulevard Leopold

$$ | B&B/INN | Located deep in the Jewish quarter, not far from Stadspark, this grand 19th-century house has been run by the friendly Willems family as a boutique-style B&B since 2010. **Pros:** friendly owners; stylish, vintage accommodation; great breakfasts. **Cons:** it's quite pricey for a B&B; only five rooms, so it fills up fast; it's a bit of a walk to the center. $ *Rooms from: €130* ✉ *Belgelei 135, South of the Center* ☎ *0486/675–838* 🌐 *www.boulevard-leopold.be* *5 rooms* *Free Breakfast* Ⓜ *Tram: 2, 4, 6.*

Budget Boetiek Hotel Rubenshof

$ | HOTEL | Once a cardinal's residence, this hotel shows remnants of its former glory with a mixture of turn-of-the-20th-century styles. **Pros:** friendly and helpful staff; good value for money; historic building. **Cons:** no elevator; some rooms share bathrooms; furnishings showing their age. $ *Rooms from: €75* ✉ *Amerikalei 115–117, South of the Center* ☎ *03/237–0789* 🌐 *hotel-rubenshof.hotels-antwerpen.net* *22 rooms* *No Meals* Ⓜ *Tram: 4, 12, 24.*

Hotel Pilar

$$$ | HOTEL | Yet another stylish address in the Het Zuid area, Hotel Pilar has the feel of an establishment where every last detail has been agonized over. **Pros:** it's a short walk to a number of nearby galleries and museums; well located for Antwerp's trendiest area; the in-house restaurant is a good spot for lunch. **Cons:** some rooms in need of a little TLC; it's not very centrally located; there's no hotel parking. *Rooms from: €165* *Leopold de Waelplaats 34, South of the Center* *03/292–6510* *www.hotelpilar.be* *17 rooms* *No Meals* *Tram: 4.*

Nightlife

BARS AND JAZZ CLUBS

Cafe Hopper

LIVE MUSIC | Café Hopper is open daily as a bar, but also presents jazz performances every Monday at 9 pm in a rather formal environment. Check their website for other performance times. *Leopold De Waelstraat 2, South of the Center* *03/248–4933* *www.cafehopper.be* *Tram: 4.*

Chatleroi

BARS | In über-trendy Het Zuid, it can be hard to find a traditional "brown café" bar. Chatleroi is the lone survivor, sticking out like a slightly down-at-heels sore thumb, and all the better for it. Old posters, cat paintings, mismatched furniture, and the odd jazz band set the scene for a no-nonsense bar that has survived the area's gentrification and kept its charm. *Graaf van Hoornestraat 2, South of the Center* *0486/600–459* *Tram: 4.*

Het Roze Huis and Café Den Draak

BARS | Het Roze Huis (*www.hetrozehuis.be*) is Antwerp's gay and lesbian community house, with a straight-friendly café-bar, Den Draak ("The Dragon"), on the ground floor; evenings downstairs tend to run into the small hours on most nights. *Draakplaats 1, South of the Center* *03/290–5304* *www.dendraak.be* *Tram: 11.*

Ta-Nnin

WINE BARS | Global street food paired with fine wines is the name of the game at this cozy wine bar with an urban vibe. *Volkstraat 50, South of the Center* *0470/104–483* *tannin.be* *Tram 4.*

Shopping

CLOTHING

Ann Demeulemeester

WOMEN'S CLOTHING | Ann Demeulemeester belongs to that golden generation that set the city's couture apart from the rest. She sells her clothes in an elegant corner store across the street from the Royal Museum of fine Arts (KMSKA). *Leopold de Waelplaats 3, South of the Center* *03/216–0133* *www.anndemeulemeester.be* *Tram: 4.*

Mechelen

24 km (15 miles) south from Antwerp, 26 km (17 miles) north from Brussels.

Mechelen (Malines in French), handily placed midway between Brussels and Antwerp, is a small, peaceful gem that has preserved its medieval and Renaissance past but that, unlike Bruges, is never overrun with tourists. As the residence of the Roman Catholic Primate of Belgium, it's an important ecclesiastical center. It's also a center of vegetable production: the town and its environs are known for *witloof*, the Belgian delicacy known elsewhere as chicory or endive, and asparagus, whose stalks reach their height of perfection in May.

GETTING HERE AND AROUND

Mechelen is situated almost exactly between Brussels and Antwerp. By car it is easy to reach from both cities via the E19 highway. Five or six trains every hour connect Mechelen with both Antwerp and Brussels, the fastest services taking around 20 minutes.

VISITOR INFORMATION

CONTACTS Visit Mechelen. *Vleeshouwersstraat 6, Mechelen* *015/297–654* *visit.mechelen.be.*

Sights

Brouwerij Het Anker

BREWERY | The first document referring to the brewery dates from 1369, making it one of the oldest breweries in Belgium. Touring this small, intimate brewery, the birthplace of Mechelen's pride and joy, the dark, sweet Gouden Carolus (Golden Charles) beer, you can witness every stage of the beer-making process. Tours and tastings in English lasting 1 hour 30 minutes must be arranged in advance, but leave at least once a day (except Monday), more often on weekends. It is also possible to tour Het Anker's own De Molenberg distillery, either separately or in combination with a brewery tour. The distillery is at another location 8 km (5 miles) away, but the ticket price includes transfers. The brasserie next to the brewery is open daily, and serves the entire range of Gouden Carolus beers and several beer-seasoned dishes at affordable prices. There is also a hotel in the brewery complex (see below), so devoted beer fans can spend the night. ✉ *Guido Gezellelaan 49, Mechelen* ☎ *015/287–141* 🌐 *www.hetanker.be* 🎫 *Individual brewery or distillery tours €11; combi tours €22* ⏲ *Closed Mon.*

Brusselpoort

MONUMENT | Dating from the 13th century, the imposing stone Brussels Gate is all that remains of the medieval walls that once kept Mechelen safe. Today, it stands in the middle of the busy ring road around the center, and is no longer open to the public, but in its day it was the highest and most impressive of 12 gates that controlled people's passage in and out of the city. ✉ *Hoogstraat 83, Mechelen* 🌐 *visit.mechelen.be.*

Grote Markt

PLAZA/SQUARE | Barely a notch down in splendor from Antwerp's Grote Markt, or the magnificent Grand Place in Brussels, Mechelen's main square deserves its billing among Belgium's finest plazas. Looming over the western end is the soaring stone tower of St-Romboutskathedraal, while at the opposite end, parts of the **Stadhuis** (City Hall) date back to the 14th century. The north and south sides are lined with bars and restaurants, with bustling terraces that bring the area to life in summer. ✉ *Grote Markt, Mechelen* 🎫 *Free.*

Kazerne Dossin

HISTORY MUSEUM | This former Belgian army barracks was used as a holding center and deportation camp by occupying Nazi forces during World War II. Of the more than 25,000 Jewish people who were processed and deported from here, very few made it back to Belgium. Today the buildings house a moving Holocaust memorial dedicated to those people, as well as a documentation center, and a museum explaining Jewish life in Belgium before and during the war. ✉ *Goswin de Stassartstraat 153, Mechelen* ☎ *015/290–660* 🌐 *kazernedossin.eu* 🎫 *€10* ⏲ *Closed Wed.*

Museum Hof van Busleyden

ART MUSEUM | This museum, in a flamboyant 16th-century Renaissance palace, has an extensive collection of artworks and period bric-a-brac that illustrate life during the height of the Burgundian Netherlands in the 15th and 16th centuries. One particularly noteworthy treasure is a gorgeously illustrated choir book that once belonged to Margaret of Austria. ✉ *Frederik de Merodestraat 65, Mechelen* ☎ *015/294–030* 🌐 *www.hofvanbusleyden.be* 🎫 *€12* ⏲ *Closed Mon. and Tues.*

★ **Sint-Romboutskathedraal**

CHURCH | Begun in the 13th century, but only completed in the 1520s, this cathedral represents a magnificent achievement by three generations of the Keldermans family of architects, who were active in cathedral building throughout Flanders. The beautifully proportioned tower, 318 feet high, was intended to be the tallest in the world, but the builders ran out of money before they could reach

One of the most notable buildings in the town of Mechelen is the massive Sint-Romboutskathedraal.

their goal. Inside are two remarkable 40-ton carillons of 49 bells each. Carillon playing was virtually invented in Mechelen (the Russian word for carillon means "sound of Mechelen"). The best place to listen to the bells is in the Minderbroedersgang. Chief among the art treasures is Van Dyck's *Christus an het Kruis* (Crucifixion) in the south transept. The remains of the cathedral's namesake, Sint-Rombout (St. Rumbold), are hidden in the high altar. Climb to the top of the tower and you'll be rewarded with an exhilarating 360-degree panoramic view of the city and the surrounding region—space at the top is limited, however, so advance reservation is recommended. ✉ *Onder-den-Toren, Mechelen* ☎ *015/294–032* 🌐 *visit.mechelen.be* 🎟 *Cathedral: free; tower: €8.*

Restaurants

De Fortuyne

$$$ | BELGIAN | Along a quiet street just off the Grote Markt, this chic restaurant creates a relaxing vibe with its rustic, bare brick interior walls, and a secluded rear terrace. The modern Belgian cuisine is served as a four-course set menu that changes every two months—each course consists of two separate dishes that are designed for sharing. **Known for:** high tea on Saturday; beer pairings with each dish; good wine list. 💲 *Average main: €28* ✉ *Befferstraat 20, Mechelen* ☎ *0483/389–966* 🌐 *defortuyne.be* ⏲ *Closed Sun. and Mon. No lunch Tues.–Fri.*

De Witten Vos

$$$ | BELGIAN | Commanding a prime spot on the main square, the White Fox serves good portions of pan-European food at fair prices, with a menu that juggles Italian pasta, Belgian and French favorites, and—in the fall season—a range of game dishes. Choose a spot on the front terrace for fine views of the cathedral and the city hall, or simply for people-watching. **Known for:** excellent seafood; food served all day; friendly service. 💲 *Average main: €23* ✉ *Grote*

Markt 30, Mechelen ☎ 015/206–369 ⊕ dewittenvos.be.

Hotels

Hotel Brouwerij Het Anker

$$ | HOTEL | Spending the night in a brewery doesn't have to be the exclusive preserve of devoted beer fans—anyone is welcome to enjoy this hotel's quiet but central location, and its spacious, comfortably appointed modern rooms. **Pros:** comfortable beds; free breakfast; a short walk from the Grote Markt. **Cons:** lack of elevator limits access to some rooms; parking limited and costs extra; reception not staffed at night. *$ Rooms from: €109 ✉ Guido Gezellelaan 49, Mechelen ☎ 015/287–141 ⊕ www.hetanker.be 22 rooms 🍴 Free Breakfast.*

Nightlife

Den Stillen Genieter

PUBS | This long-running pub is a beer lover's paradise that stocks around 500 Belgian ales. *✉ Korenmarkt 21, Mechelen ☎ 0473/297–597 ⊕ www.denstillengenieter.be.*

Lier

17 km (11 miles) southeast from Mechelen, 45 km (28 miles) northeast from Brussels.

The small town of Lier may seem a sleepy riverside settlement, but it has long attracted poets and painters and has even known its moment of glory. It was here in 1496 that Philip the Handsome of Burgundy married Joanna the Mad of Aragon and Castile, daughter of King Ferdinand and Queen Isabella of Spain. From that union sprang Emperor Charles V and his brother and successor as Holy Roman Emperor, the equally remarkable Ferdinand I of Austria.

GETTING HERE AND AROUND

Lier is a short drive from Antwerp on the N10. From Brussels, take the E19/N14 via Mechelen. As many as seven trains an hour make the trip from Antwerp in around 15 minutes.

VISITOR INFORMATION

CONTACTS Visit Lier. *✉ Grote Markt 58 ☎ 03/800–0555 ⊕ www.visitlier.be.*

Sights

Begijnhof

STREET | Lier's Begijnhof differs from most other beguinages in that its small houses line narrow streets rather than being grouped around a common. A Renaissance portico stands at the entrance, and on it is a statue of St. Begge, who gave his name to this congregation and who probably derived his own from the fact that he was *un begue* (a stammerer). Beguines were members of ascetic or philanthropic communities of women, not under vows, founded in the Netherlands in the 13th century. *✉ Begijnhofstraat Free.*

Sint-Gummaruskerk

CHURCH | The church where Philip and Joanna were wed is a product of the De Waghemakere–Keldermans architectural partnership that worked so well in building the cathedral in Antwerp. The interior is notable for its stained-glass windows from the 15th and 16th centuries—those in the choir were the gift of Maximilian of Austria (father of Philip the Handsome), who visited in 1516 and is depicted in one of the windows, along with his wife, Mary of Burgundy. *✉ Kardinaal Mercierplein 8 ⊕ www.sintgummaruskerktelier.be Free ⊙ Closed Nov.–Mar.; Apr.–Oct. closed weekdays.*

Zimmertoren

CLOCK | This 14th-century tower was renamed for Louis Zimmer, who designed its astronomical clock with 11 faces in 1930. His studio, where 57 dials show the movements of the moon, the tides, the zodiac, and other cosmic phenomena, is inside the tower. ✉ *Zimmerplein 18* ☎ *03/491–1395* 🌐 *zimmertoren.be* 🎫 *€5* ⏲ *Closed Mon.*

Restaurants

Nethe & Drinke

$$ | INTERNATIONAL | In fine weather the front terrace of this lively café-restaurant has a to-die-for view of the Zimmertoren, while the bright, modern interior has high ceilings and a mezzanine above to create a sense of space. The extensive international menu of pasta, salads, and steaks in generous portions also finds room for a few Belgian classics, including oven-baked witloof (Belgian endive) in a creamy sauce. **Known for:** mussels in season; lunchtime croques and pancakes; food served all day. 💲 *Average main: €19* ✉ *Zimmerplein 3* ☎ *03/326–1912* 🌐 *www.nethe-drinke.be.*

Limburg Province

The easternmost province of Dutch-speaking Flanders, Limburg is a largely flat expanse of farmland and heath, but is also a region with a proud industrial past. In the mid-20th century there were seven operating coal mines in the area employing over 40,000 people, although the last of these closed in 1992. At the heart of the province, the prosperous city of **Hasselt** owes part of its wealth to the distilling of jenever, while to the south, the smaller town of **Tongeren** can trace its history back to Roman days and before.

Hasselt

67 km (42 miles) southeast from Lier, 77 km (48 miles) southeast from Antwerp, 82 km (51 miles) east from Brussels.

The principal town of Limburg province has busy shopping streets, innovative museums, and a cathedral with the de rigueur carillon. In mid-October, it hosts an annual weekend festival for its signature drink, jenever. In the late 1990s, the ring road around the old town center, which followed the line of the medieval city walls, was revamped; now called the "Groen Boulevard" (Green Boulevard), it's lined with trees and has a wide pedestrian walkway. This, plus a handful of pedestrian-only blocks, makes Hasselt particularly easy to navigate.

GETTING HERE AND AROUND

Hasselt is a straight drive, almost as the crow flies, from Antwerp on the A13/E313 motorway (which continues to Liège); from Brussels, take the E40/A2 via Leuven to Exit 26, then the E313 for the last few miles. There are hourly direct trains from Antwerp's Centraal Station to Hasselt (1 hour, 33 minutes), and two hourly services from Brussels, the fastest of which takes 50 minutes.

VISITOR INFORMATION

CONTACTS Toerisme Hasselt. ✉ *Maastrichterstraat 59, Hasselt* ☎ *011/239–540* 🌐 *www.visithasselt.be.*

Sights

★ **Abdijsite Herkenrode**

RELIGIOUS BUILDING | Around 5 km (3 miles) northwest from central Hasselt, the vast Herkenrode Abbey complex was founded more than 800 years ago as the first Cistercian monastery in Benelux. Over the centuries it became a site of pilgrimage, and it experienced periods of great conflict and prosperity, until the monastic order was abolished following the French Revolution. After years of neglect, the Flemish government bought 250 acres of the site and began a lengthy restoration project, partly financed by the sale of Herkenrode abbey beers—not brewed here, but available in the on-site shop and café. Inside, an audio-guided "Experience Center" recounts the site's turbulent past in a series of galleries.

Behind the abbey, a meticulously planted Herb and Inspiration Garden covers 5 acres and contains 500 different species—divided by hedges into a series of peaceful small spaces, some with water features. Elsewhere, accessible without an entry ticket, do not miss "The Quiet View," a permanent artwork by the artist Hans op de Beeck—it's a stunning monochrome landscape diorama that makes ingenious use of mirrors to create a sense of infinite space. ✉ *Herkenrode-abdij 4, Hasselt* ☎ *011/239–670* 🌐 *www.abdijsiteherkenrode.be* 🎫 *Experience Center: €5; Herb and Inspiration Garden: €4* ⏲ *Closed Mon. Sept.–June; gardens closed Nov.–Mar.*

Japanse Tuin

GARDEN | Just east from the city center, the delightful 6-acre Japanese Garden is the largest of its kind in Europe. As you'd expect, everything is serenely ordered and precise, with a maze of paths surrounded by lush greenery, streams, waterfalls, koi carp ponds, and delicate pavilions. It was designed by the Japanese architect Takayuki Inoue and built when the Japanese city of Itami became twinned with Hasselt in 1985. At quiet times, the silence is only broken by the sound of trickling water, and the occasional chiming of a Peace Bell, which was installed in 2016. ✉ *Gouverneur Verwilghensingel 15, Hasselt* ☎ *011/239–666* 🌐 *www.visithasselt.be* 🎫 *€6* ⏲ *Closed Nov.–Mar.; Apr.–Oct. closed Mon.*

Jenevermuseum

OTHER MUSEUM | Perpetuating Hasselt's slightly raffish distinction of having had jenever as its major industry, the museum occupies a building that was a commercial distillery from 1803 until 1971, and the original equipment is still in use and on display. On a tour of the installations, you'll learn about the production process, while other exhibits include glassware and advertising posters. In the paneled tasting room you can sample jenever of various ages, flavors, and proofs from two dozen Belgian distilleries—your entry ticket includes one free drink. ✉ *Witte Nonnenstraat 19, Hasselt* ☎ *011/239–860* 🌐 *www.jenevermuseum.be* 🎫 *€7* ⏲ *Closed Mon.*

Openluchtmuseum Bokrijk

HISTORY MUSEUM | A 10-minute train ride, or drive, northeast from Hasselt, this huge open-air museum features around 150 mostly agricultural buildings, in different architectural styles, that were brought here stone by stone from all over Flanders, and rebuilt in a series of regional clusters across a largely wooded site. Many of the buildings date back to the 17th century, and they are furnished and decorated with thousands of pieces of period furniture, farm equipment, and general bric-a-brac. There are themed events here throughout the year, including Sunday walks even during the winter shutdown when the museum buildings are closed. Bring walking shoes: the whole site covers a whopping 2 square miles. ✉ *Bokrijklaan 1, Hasselt* ☎ *011/265–300* 🌐 *www.bokrijk.be* 🎫 *€15* ⏲ *Closed Oct.–Mar.*

Restaurants

De Windmolen

$$ | **BELGIAN** | In an old yellow-painted brick farmhouse just east of the center, the leafy front terrace and rustic interior both provide a charming setting for enjoying this small restaurant's generously portioned and innovative takes on Belgian and European classics. The beer list is short but outstanding, as is the wine list—unsurprising as the same family also runs the wine store next door. **Known for:** simple but authentic Flemish food; period furnishings; friendly service. 💲 *Average main: €18* ✉ *Casterstraat 46, Hasselt* ☎ *0474/273–712* 🌐 *www.wijnhandellucbollen.be/de-windmolen* ⏲ *Closed Tues.–Thurs.*

Herkenrode Abbey, in the town of Hasselt, was founded 800 years ago as the first Cistercian monastery in Benelux.

Hotels

Holiday Inn Express Hasselt
$ | **HOTEL** | Ideally situated on Hasselt's inner ring road, just a few minutes' walk from the central restaurants and shops, this welcoming hotel's spacious, modern rooms offer a comfort level that more than compensates for the slightly anonymous corporate styling. **Pros:** free breakfast; friendly staff; centrally located. **Cons:** part of a chain so lacking character; no free parking; bathrooms are quite small. *$ Rooms from: €95 ✉ Thonissenlaan 37, Hasselt ☎ 011/379–300 🌐 www.ihg.com ⇨ 89 rooms 🍽 Free Breakfast.*

Tongeren

20 km (12 miles) southeast from Hasselt, 87 km (54 miles) east of Brussels.

Tongeren started life as a Roman army encampment. It is one of Belgium's two oldest cities (along with Tournai) and is visibly proud of the fact. This is where Ambiorix scored a famous but short-lived victory over Julius Caesar's legions in 54 BCE. (There's a statue of the strapping warrior in the Grote Markt square.) The Roman city was considerably larger than the present one; over the centuries, it was repeatedly sacked and burned. By the end of the 13th century, the city had retreated within its present limits and enjoyed the occasionally burdensome protection of the prince-bishops of Liège. The Moerenpoort gate and sections of the ramparts remain from that period.

GETTING HERE AND AROUND

Hourly trains from Liège Guillemins take 35 minutes to reach Tongeren. Two trains run each hour from Brussels, taking one hour 30 minutes, and passing through Hasselt en route. The journey time from Hasselt is 25 minutes.

VISITOR INFORMATION

CONTACTS Toerisme Tongeren. ✉ *Via Julianus 2, Tongeren ☎ 012/800–070 🌐 www.toerismetongeren.be.*

Gallo-Romeins Museum

HISTORY MUSEUM | FAMILY | The Gallo-Roman museum traces the region's human history, and features a host of local archaeological finds, not just from Roman days but all the way back, via the Celts, to the original Neanderthal settlers. To get the kids inspired, ask for the special child-oriented audio guide, which features stories told by the archaeologist "Bob the Digger." ✉ *Kielenstraat 15, Tongeren* ☎ *012/670–330* 🌐 *www.galloromeinsmuseum.be* 🎫 *€8* ⏲ *Closed Mon.*

★ Onze-Lieve-Vrouwebasiliek

CHURCH | The elaborate Basilica of Our Lady is one of the most beautiful medieval monuments in the world. The original church was built on Roman foundations in the 4th century and was the first stone cathedral north of the Alps. A siege in 1213 destroyed everything but the 12th-century Romanesque cloister; soon afterward construction of the present-day Basilica of Our Lady began, a project that would take three centuries to complete. The central nave, up to the pulpit, the choir, and the south transept, dates from 1240. The candlesticks and lectern, from 1372, are the work of Jehan de Dinant, one of a number of outstanding metalworkers who flourished in the Meuse valley at that time. The basilica has excellent acoustics and is often used for symphony concerts. ✉ *Stadhuisplein, Tongeren* 🌐 *www.tongeren.be* 🎫 *Free.*

Teseum

RELIGIOUS BUILDING | Located in the Chapter House and cloisters of the adjacent church, the Teseum is the treasury of the Onze-Lieve-Vrouwebasiliek, and it contains arguably the the richest collection of religious art in the country. Highlights including a 6th-century ivory diptych of St. Paul, a Merovingian gold buckle from the same century, and a truly magnificent head of Christ sculpted in wood in the 11th century. ✉ *Museumkwartier 2, Tongeren* ☎ *012/800–228* 🌐 *teseum.be* 🎫 *€6* ⏲ *Closed Mon.*

Intermezzo

$$ | ITALIAN | This modern café-restaurant with a prime spot on the main square serves pan-European dishes, but with a notable Italian slant that also spills over into the wine list. The long, narrow design of the sleek interior feels a little like dining in a train carriage, but grab a spot on the terrace and you can contemplate the strapping features of Celtic warrior Ambiorix as you eat. **Known for:** all-day service; friendly service; generous portions. 💲 *Average main: €20* ✉ *Grote Markt 13, Tongeren* ☎ *012/741–574* 🌐 *www.intermezzo-tongeren.be.*

Boutique Hotel Caelus VII

$ | HOTEL | Ideally situated a stone's throw from the basilica and the main square, this elegant boutique hotel in a central mansion has spacious, elegantly furnished rooms spread over several floors. **Pros:** friendly personal service; excellent location; quiet at night. **Cons:** elevator only for luggage; small size means rooms sell out fast; parking costs extra. 💲 *Rooms from: €90* ✉ *Kloosterstraat 7, Tongeren* ☎ *012/697–777* 🌐 *www.caelus.be* 🛏 *7 rooms* 🍽 *No Meals.*

Chapter 5

GHENT AND THE LEIE

Updated by
Gareth Clark

Sights	Restaurants	Hotels	Shopping	Nightlife
★★★★★	★★★★☆	★★★☆☆	★★☆☆☆	★★★☆☆

WELCOME TO GHENT AND THE LEIE

TOP REASONS TO GO

★ **Spy medieval wonders.** The area flourished in the late Middle Ages, sprouting magnificent castles, belfries, town halls, churches, and cathedrals in myriad Gothic styles that can still be seen today.

★ **See incredible art.** The Ghent Altarpiece is one of the most famous artworks in Europe, while the villages of the Leiestreek recall a brief time when this was Belgium's artistic center.

★ **Enjoy the great beer.** The beer bars and breweries of the area, especially in Ghent, are some of the most famous in Belgium. It's a great opportunity to expand your knowledge.

★ **Hit the water.** Whether you paddle or take a cruise, the rivers Leie and Scheldt offer a unique way to explore the area, as you drift these historic waterways.

★ **Pedal wild countryside.** The Vlaamse Ardennen, in particular, is famed among cyclists, with large chunks of the annual Tour of Flanders held here. Follow in their tire tracks and head out into the country.

1 **Ghent.** The medieval streets of Ghent are wonderfully preserved, but this is no musty museum; it's a vibrant university town with a glowing reputation for its food, beer, and atmosphere, where Gothic wonders and history just so happen to lurk around every corner.

2 **Leiestreek Villages.** Found just a few miles south of Ghent, the pretty artists' villages of Sint-Martens-Latem and Deurle are a joy to explore, while Deinze's Kasteel Ooidonk is among the finest castles in Belgium.

3 **Dendermonde.** Famed for its Bayard Steed festival, which only happens every 10 years, this pretty town on the River Dender has a beautiful beguinage to explore, and its heritage railway is a joy.

4 **Vlaamse Ardennen.** The countryside here—famed for its sunken roads, bergs (hills), and cobbles—is among the prettiest in Belgium. Walkers and cyclists regard it as hallowed ground and flock to its small towns, such as **Oudenaarde** and **Geraardsbergen**, in droves. The former is best known as the finale of the annual Tour of Flanders cycling race, while the latter is home to the "original" Manneken Pis statue, which predates the one in Brussels by centuries.

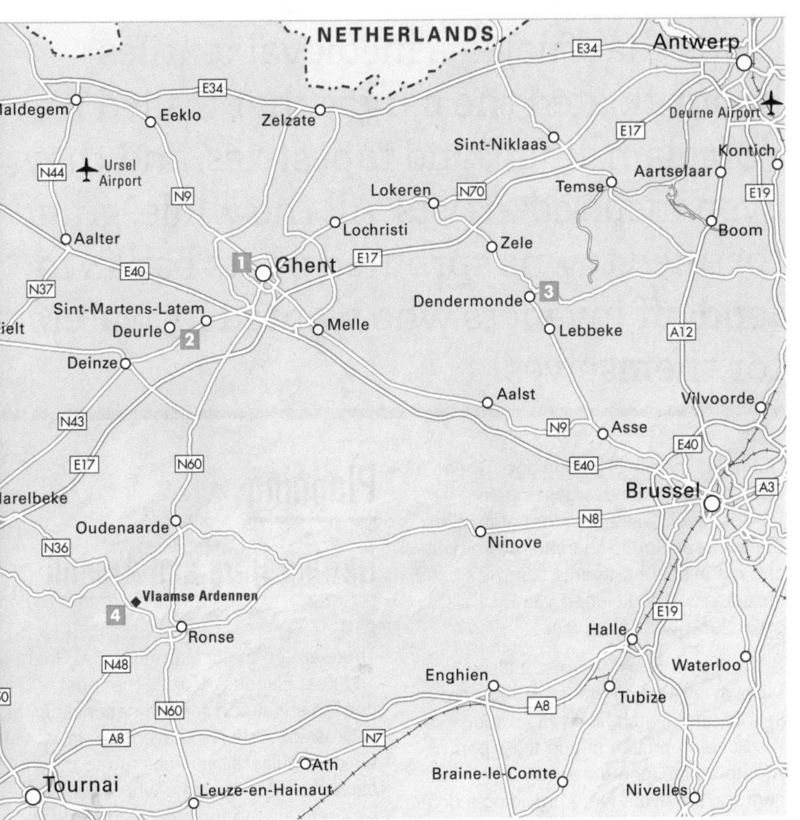

5 Kortrijk. War might have destroyed much of its medieval past, but this city is still home to perhaps the finest surviving beguinage in Belgium, not to mention prestigious Flemish history. Learn about the Battle of the Golden Spurs in a new interactive exhibition.

The rivers Leie and Scheldt have shaped the fortunes of this part of Flanders for generations. They irrigated the crops that fueled a medieval textiles boom, floated the barges that traded its porcelain, linen, and tapestries, and they even inspired artists. All the while, grand fortified towns sprouted on its banks to fend off invaders who wanted its waters for themselves.

During its medieval golden age, Ghent became the second-largest city in Europe, such was the extent of its cloth trade. Great Gothic churches were built and magnificent artworks commissioned, including Jan and Hubert van Eyck's oft-stolen Ghent Altarpiece.

But just as the water gives, it also takes away. During the fall of Antwerp in 1585, the Dutch finally blockaded the Scheldt, pushing trade to its port of Amsterdam. Upon the arrival of the 20th century, the rivers were providing a different kind of muse. In the villages south of Ghent and in the Vlaamse Ardennen, artists' colonies were quickly sprouting as a new generation of Belgian Impressionist and Expressionist painters rose to fame, inspired by the countryside and its riverbanks.

In the south of Flanders, where the Scheldt picks its way through the unusually hilly terrain of the Vlaamse Ardennen, there was never much wealth. Today, it's best known for its role as the finale of the Tour of Flanders cycling race.

Planning

Getting Here and Around

AIR

There are no major airports in the Ghent and East Flanders region. The most convenient airport for international flights is Brussels Airport in Zaventem, from which regular rail services run to the capital's major stations, where you can pick up trains to the area. Kortrijk does have an airport—the ambitiously named Flanders International—but that is largely for charter flights and shipping.

BUS

While rail is easier for traveling between the larger towns, in areas such as the Leiestreek villages and the Vlaamse Ardennen in particular, the local (De Lijn) bus services are more useful. There is no direct train between Oudenaarde and Geraardsbergen but buses (No.16/17) run on the hour. The same goes for Sint-Martens-Latem and Deurle, which have no railway stations but can be reached by buses from Ghent and Deinze (No. 77). Tickets can be purchased from contactless machines at bus stops (though these are few and far between), or simply buy a MOBiB card (€5) from any De Lijn office and top it up online with trips.

CONTACTS De Lijn. ☎ *070/22–02–00* 🌐 *www.delijn.be/en.*

CAR

To reach Ghent from Brussels by car, take the E40 motorway before turning off onto the B401 (signed Gent-Centrum); it should take around 50 minutes. From there, the N43 takes you through the Leiestreek villages and down to Kortrijk, though a faster, more direct route is the E17. The cobbled country roads found in the Vlaamse Ardennen can be pretty rough, but national roads also connect each town. Dendermonde is reached via the N47/9 from Brussels, which connects with the E19.

TRAIN

The area is well-connected by rail. The Belgian national railway (SNCB/NMBS) has four services an hour running between Ghent and Brussels's Gare de Midi/Brussel Zuid and Central/Centraal stations. The InterCity (IC) usually takes about 30 minutes and costs from €9.20 one-way for a second-class ticket. A special "weekend ticket" (from €10.40 return) is valid for use between 7 pm on Friday until Sunday night. Regular trains link Ghent's Sint-Pieters Station and Kortrijk (€7.10) via Deinze. Kortrijk is similarly well-connected to Brussels (€13.10), with two services an hour running via Oudenaarde. Geraardsbergen can only be reached on this line if you change at Zottegem. Last, the same rail line connects Ghent and Kortrijk to Dendermonde, which also has regular trains to Brussels (€6.30)..

CONTACTS NMBS/SNCB. ☎ *02/528–2828* 🌐 *www.belgiantrain.be.*

Hotels

The area's accommodation varies from town to town. In Ghent, you'll find the most diversity, with sleek, modern boutique stays alongside the usual B&Bs, hotels, and budget sleeps. Here, especially, you'll find a number of historic stays, adapted from aristocratic mansions, old public buildings, and town houses. These rarely have many facilities but are often more atmospheric. Kortrijk, which was heavily bombed in World War II has fewer such stays, and its hotels tend to be more modern and businesslike. In the Leiestreek villages and Vlaamse Ardennen towns, you're limited to B&Bs, small hotels, and inns. The latter area caters especially well to cyclists, due to its popularity with riders, and often has specialist facilities for bikes. It pays to book far in advance here because choice is limited and they fill up fast, particularly in summer. Accommodation typically includes a hearty Belgian breakfast: bread, cereal, cold cuts, cheese, yogurt, eggs, and fruit.

Restaurants

In Ghent, high-class establishments stand next to modest brasseries where you can enjoy just a drink or a snack. The city is particularly famed for its cooking, not just because it is the home of *Gentze waterzooi,* a popular creamy stew made with either chicken or fish, but because recent years have seen a number of famous Belgian chefs come out of the city. It has a reputation for adventurous pop-up joints that often go on to become staples of the dining scene.

Outside of the city, the villages of the Leiestreek have become a haven for foodies seeking refined, mostly French, country cooking, where game and hare feature high on menus. Kortrijk and Dendermonde are less well known for their restaurants, though you'll find plenty of interesting spots hidden around the Vlaamse Ardennen, where cycling cafés are especially popular.

Although many serve food all day long, it's safer to respect regular lunch and dinner hours, which are noon to 2 and 6 to 9. A service charge and V.A.T. are always included in the tab. Although tipping is not unknown, you don't need to leave a tip unless you receive exceptional service. Rounding up the bill is sufficient.

BREWERIES

The area is particularly well respected for its beer. Around Ghent you'll find some of the finest beer bars in Belgium, but just as interesting are the inventive brewpubs that are now popping up here, churning out everything from medieval herb brews to fusions blending abbey-style beer with modern craft ales. A few also offer tours and tastings. Farther south, you'll encounter the more classic brands, made by breweries that date back more than a century. Here, dark beers are particularly common, with brewers such as Omer and Liefmans not just popular locally but found in bars across the country. Brewery tours here are a good way to increase your knowledge.

HOTEL AND RESTAURANT PRICES

Hotel prices in the reviews are the lowest cost of a standard double room in high season. Restaurant prices in the reviews are the average cost of a main course at dinner, or if dinner is not served, at lunch.

What It Costs in Euros

$	$$	$$$	$$$$
RESTAURANTS			
under €12	€12–€22	€23–€30	over €30
HOTELS			
under €100	€100–€150	€151–€220	over €220

Tours

BOAT TOURS

The Leie and Scheldt meet in Ghent, making boat tours along the rivers a great way to explore the area and see other towns.

Booot

BOAT TOURS | A company that rents motorized sloops for up to eight hours. No sailing license is required, so you can explore the rivers all day by yourself, or hire a captain for the day. Boats can fit up to 12 people, depending on which you choose, and can be arranged from Ghent (main office), Sint-Martens-Latem, or Deinze. ✉ *Coupure Links 9a, Ghent* ☏ *0476/571–818* 🌐 *booot.be* 🎫 *From €80.*

Cruise 4 Two

BOAT TOURS | Bag day tours along the rivers Leie and Scheldt in a yacht. Most itineraries set out from Ghent but drift south as far as the Leiestreek villages, Kortrijk, and Oudenaarde. Theme cruises include walking and dining; there is also an overnight option. ✉ *Snepkaai 42, Ghent* ☏ *0475/496–338* 🌐 *www.cruise4two.be* 🎫 *From €375.*

CYCLING TOURS

The region's great passion is cycling, and every year the Tour of Flanders race culminates in the Vlaamse Ardennen where the hilly cobbles make for a tough challenge. Elsewhere, it's pretty flat, especially among the Leiestreek villages outside Ghent.

Bergs and Cobbles

BICYCLE TOURS | Multiday cycling trips operate across Flanders but focus especially on the Vlaamse Ardennen region, whose "bergs" (hills) and cobbles are from where the company takes its name. ✉ *Ghent* ☏ *0499/396–720* 🌐 *www.bergscobbles.com* 🎫 *From €425.*

Visitor Information

CONTACTS Visit Gent. ✉ *Sint-Veerleplein 5, Ghent* ☎ *09/266–5660* 🌐 *visit.gent.be.* **Toerisme Oost-Vlaanderen.** ✉ *Woodrow Wilsonplein 2, Ghent* ☎ *09/267–7070* 🌐 *www.routen.be.* **Toerisme Kortrijk.** ✉ *Begijnhofpark, Kortrijk* ☎ *056/277–840* 🌐 *www.toerismekortrijk.be.*

Ghent

60 km (37 miles) from Brussels.

Like its near neighbor Bruges, Ghent (spelled "Gent" in Dutch; "Gand" in French) was once one of the richest and largest towns in Western Europe. A medieval metropolis raised on the banks of the Scheldt and the Leie, it was famed throughout the continent for textiles trade. By the end of the 15th century, Ghent's cloth trade had begun to wane.

Unlike Bruges, Ghent was not saved by tourism but the Industrial Revolution. A visit to Manchester, England, by one enterprising Flemish entrepreneur led to him stealing plans for an early-model "mule jenny" (a machine for spinning cotton). A few years later the city was churning out cloth faster than ever.

For all its palpable history, Ghent still feels like a real city today. Bikes and trams course its cobblestone arteries, and its culinary and graffiti scenes are among the ripest in Belgium. It has also carved a niche for itself as the unofficial capital of beer, especially around the Patershol area. Those in the know say that it has a better concentration of excellent bars and microbreweries than anywhere else in the country.

DISCOUNTS AND DEALS

To make the most of Ghent's sights, get hold of a CityCard Gent, which gives free entrance to many of the city's sights and museums and can be used both on transport and to hire a bike. Valid for either 48 (€38) or 72 (€44) hours, cards are available from the tourist office and participating venues.

GETTING HERE AND AROUND

BICYCLE

Cycling is the best way to get around Ghent. The city-bike rental scheme is easy to use, with several pick-up locations, including the train station and city center. Rental starts from €12 for a day, but it's free with a CityCard. Bike lanes are everywhere but be careful of the tram lines, as it's easy to get your wheels stuck.

CONTACTS De Fietsambassade. ✉ *Voskenslaan 27, Ghent* ☎ *09/266–7700* 🌐 *fietsambassade.gent.be.*

CAR

To reach Ghent from Brussels by car, take the E40 motorway before turning off onto the B401 (signed Gent-Centrum); it should take around 50 minutes.

TRAIN AND TRAM

By rail, take a Belgian Railways (SNCB) train from Brussels's Gare de Midi/Brussel Zuid or Central/Centraal stations; there are up to four an hour. The InterCity usually takes about 30 minutes and costs from €9.20 one-way for a second-class ticket. Gent St-Pieters station is a little distance from the city center, so hop on a tram or take a taxi when you arrive. Tram 1 (Flanders Expo to Evergem) leaves from *perron* (platform) 2 and heads toward the center. Get off at Korenmarkt. Tickets can be bought from contactless vending machines and cost €2.50 for an hour's travel across all forms of public transport. MoBIB cards can also be bought (€5) and loaded with trips to use across trams and buses.

TOURS

BOAT TOURS

Ghent is built at the meeting point of two rivers, the Leie and the Scheldt, meaning trips on the water are a great way to see first-hand how the city rose to such historic importance during its medieval and

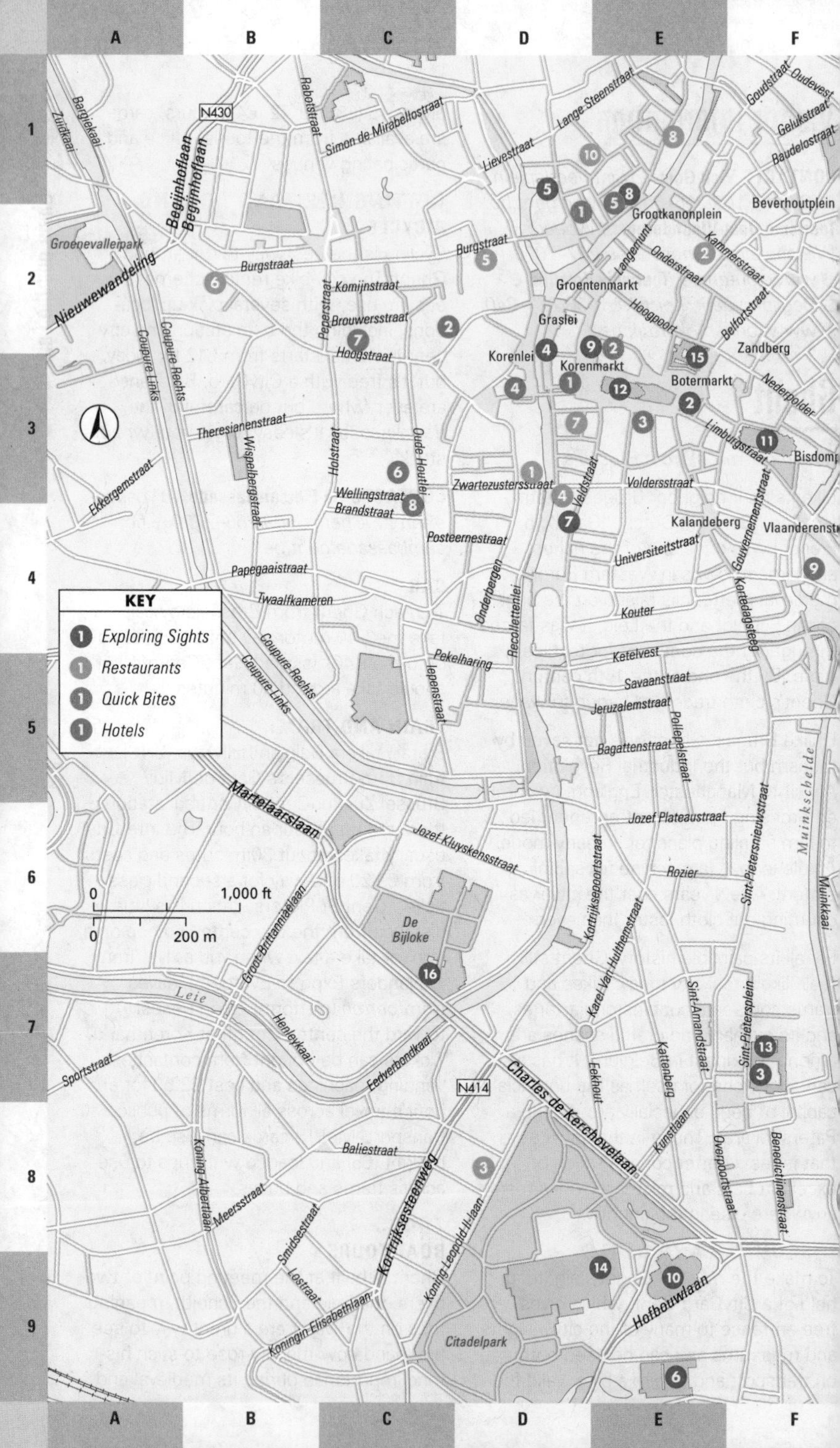

A
B
C
D
E
F
1
2
3
4
5
6
7
8
9
KEY
Exploring Sights
Restaurants
Quick Bites
Hotels
0
1,000 ft
0
200 m
N430
N414
Bargiekaai
Zuidkaai
Begijnhoflaan
Groenevalleipark
Nieuwewandeling
Burgstraat
Rabotstraat
Simon de Mirabellostraat
Lievestraat
Lange Steenstraat
Goudstraat
Oudevest
Gelukstraat
Baudelostraat
Beverhoutplein
Grootkanonplein
Kammerstraat
Onderstraat
Langemunt
Groentenmarkt
Hoogpoort
Belfortstraat
Zandberg
Graslei
Korenlei
Korenmarkt
Botermarkt
Nederpolder
Limburgstraat
Bisdom
Komijnstraat
Peperstraat
Brouwersstraat
Hoogstraat
Coupure Links
Coupure Rechts
Theresianenstraat
Wispelbergstraat
Holstraat
Oude Houtlei
Ekkergemstraat
Wellingstraat
Brandstraat
Zwartezusterstraat
Veldstraat
Voldersstraat
Kalandeberg
Vlaanderenstraat
Posteernestraat
Universiteitstraat
Gouvernementstraat
Papegaaistraat
Twaalfkameren
Onderbergen
Kortedagsteeg
Kouter
Recollettenlei
Pekelharing
Iepenstraat
Ketelvest
Savaanstraat
Jeruzalemstraat
Pollepelstraat
Bagattenstraat
Muinkschelde
Martelaarslaan
Jozef Plateaustraat
Jozef Kluyskensstraat
Rozier
Kortrijksepoortstraat
Sint-Pietersnieuwstraat
Muinkkaai
Groot-Brittanniëlaan
De Bijloke
Karel-Van Hulthemstraat
Leie
Henleykaai
Sint-Amandstraat
Sint-Pietersplein
Sportstraat
Fedverbondkaai
Charles de Kerchovelaan
Eekhout
Kattenberg
Kunstlaan
Overpoortstraat
Benedictijnenstraat
Baliestraat
Koning Albertlaan
Kortrijksesteenweg
Meersstraat
Smidsestraat
Koning Leopold-II-laan
Lostraat
Koningin Elisabethlaan
Hofbouwlaan
Citadelpark

Ghent

Sights

1 Begijnhof H5
2 Belfort van Gent E3
3 De Wereld van Kina (The World of Kina) F7
4 Graslei D2
5 Gravensteen (Castle of the Counts) D1
6 GUM – Ghent University Museum E9
7 Huis Arnold Vander Haeghen D4
8 Huis van Alijn E1
9 Korenmarkt D2
10 MSK – Museum of Fine Arts Ghent E9
11 Sint-Baafs Kathedraal F3
12 Sint-Niklaaskerk E3
13 Sint-Pietersabdij F7
14 SMAK - Municipal Museum of Contemporary Art E9
15 Stadhuis E3
16 STAM - Ghent City Museum C7

Restaurants

1 Balls and Glory D3
2 Brasserie Keizershof E2
3 Jan van dèn Bon D8
4 Le Botaniste D3
5 Mémé Gusta D2
6 Oak B2
7 Pakhuis D3
8 Prince E1
9 Publiek G1
10 Roots E1

Quick Bites

1 Boon D2
2 Mokabon E2
3 Soup'r E3

Hotels

1 1898 The Post D3
2 Erasmus C2
3 Ganda Rooms and Suites F2
4 Hostel Uppelink D3
5 Hotel Harmony E2
6 Monasterium PoortAckere C3
7 Pillows Grand Hotel Reylof C2
8 The Vanhaegen B&B C3
9 YALO F4

19th-century heydays. Numerous companies run 50-minute trips, all costing €8.50 and leaving from landing stages clustered at the north end of Graslei and by the Groentenmarkt. But there are multiple ways to explore the river.

Kajaks Korenlei

BOAT TOURS | This kayak-rental service operates out of The Hostel Uppelink, on the corner of St-Michael's Bridge, and rents kayaks for up to three hours for €23. ✉ *Hostel Uppelink, Sint-Michielsplein 2, Ghent* ☎ *09/279–4477* 🌐 *www.kajakskorenlei.be.*

Water Tramway

BOAT TOURS | The hop-on, hop-off Water Tramway visits a half-dozen areas along the Leie, with commentary along the way. It also has self-guided walking tours at each historic stop. Trips cost €15 but are free with a CityCard. ☎ *09/330–2249* 🌐 *www.hoponhopoff.be.*

BEER WALKS

Ghentish Medieval Beer Walk

SPECIAL-INTEREST TOURS | This three-hour walk (stumble?) guides people through the backstreets of Ghent, taking in the city's brewing past. It's not your typical boozy beer crawl but a chance to unravel the curious story of medieval Ghent and its "hop vs herb" beer divide. Tours start at the Gruut brewpub, and there's no limit on participants. Tour includes five tastings. ✉ *Stadsbrouwerij Gruut, Rembert Dodoensdreef 1, Ghent* ✉ *ariel83@zeelandnet.nl* 🎫 *€45 per person.*

Begijnhof

HISTORIC HOME | There are three beguinages ("begijnhof" in Dutch) in Ghent, built centuries ago to house women (beguines) who lived lives of prayer and devoted themselves to charitable works but did not take religious vows. It sounds like something from another age, but the last beguine to live in Ghent only died in 2013. The best surviving example is **Our Lady ter Hoyen**, founded in 1235 by Countess Joanna of Constantinople. This is the smallest of the three and is protected by a wall and portal. The surrounding homes were built in the 17th and 18th centuries and are still organized in a medieval style, each holding a statue of a saint. Today, you can walk quietly through the main building and peek into the stone chapel—the houses are off-limits, with the larger ones leased for residential use. The smaller houses have become artists' workshops. Although entry is free, a gate closes to keep out nonresidents 10 pm–6:30 am.

■ TIP→ **The city's second beguinage, the UNESCO-listed Groot Begijnhof, is found on Van Arenbergstraat, west of the city center. At its peak, some 600 beguines lived there. The city's third and final beguinage is on Begijnhofdries, but its walls have long since come down.** ✉ *Lange Violettestraat 77–273* 🎫 *Free* Ⓜ *Bus: 2.*

★ **Belfort van Gent** (*Ghent Belfry*)

NOTABLE BUILDING | This 300-foot belfry tower symbolizes the power of the city guilds and was constructed in 1314 to serve as Ghent's watchtower. (The current stone spire was added in 1913.) Inside the Belfort, documents listing the privileges of the city (known as its *secreets*) were once kept behind triple-locked doors and guarded by lookouts, who toured the battlements hourly to prove they weren't sleeping. When danger approached, bells were rung—until Charles V had them removed. The view from the tower is one of the city's highlights. ✉ *Sint-Baafsplein* ☎ *09/233–3954* 🌐 *www.belfortgent.be* 🎫 *€8; guided tour €3 (daily 3:30 pm; entrance not included)* Ⓜ *Tram: 1.*

De Wereld van Kina (The World of Kina)

GARDEN | **FAMILY** | This kid-friendly natural-history museum exhibits cover geology, the evolution of life, human biology and reproduction, and a diorama room of indigenous birds. There is also a garden site a short bus ride

Begijnhofs are complexes where women could devote themselves to charitable works without taking religious vows.

from Sint-Pietersplein (No. 5; get off at Tolhuislaan) with more than 1,000 plant species, a bee colony, and live tarantulas. ✉ *Sint-Pietersplein 14* ☎ *09/323–6250* 🌐 *www.dewereldvankina.be* 🎫 *€6* ⏲ *Closed Sat.* Ⓜ *Tram: 1.*

★ Graslei

HISTORIC HOME | This magnificent row of guild houses in the original port area is best seen from across the River Leie on the **Korenlei** (Corn Quay). The guild house of the **Metselaars** (Masons) is a copy of a house from 1527. The **Eerste Korenmetershuis** (the first Grain Measurers' House), representing the grain weigher's guild, is next. The oldest house of the group, the brooding, Romanesque **Koornstapelhuis** (Granary), was built in the 12th century and served its original purpose for 600 years. It stands side by side with the narrow Renaissance **Tolhuis** (Toll House), where taxes were levied on grain shipments. No. 11 is the **Tweede Korenmetershuis** (Grain Measurers' House), a late-Baroque building from 1698. The **Vrije Schippers** (Free Bargemen), at No. 14, is a late-Gothic building from 1531, when the guild dominated inland shipping. ✉ *Graslei* Ⓜ *Tram: 1.*

★ Gravensteen (Castle of the Counts)

CASTLE/PALACE | **FAMILY** | Surrounded by a moat, the Castle of the Counts of Flanders resembles an enormous battleship steaming down the sedate Lieve Canal. From its windswept battlements there's a splendid view over the rooftops of old Ghent. Today's brooding castle has little in common with the original fortress, which was built to discourage marauding Norsemen. Its purpose, too, changed from protection to oppression as the conflict deepened between feudal lords and unruly townspeople. At various times the castle has also been used as a mint, a prison, and a cotton mill. ✉ *Sint-Veerleplein* ☎ *09/243–9730* 🌐 *gravensteen.stad.gent/en* 🎫 *€12* Ⓜ *Tram: 1.*

GUM – Ghent University Museum

SCIENCE MUSEUM | **FAMILY** | What do you do when you have a scientific collection so sprawling and disparate that there's no coherent way to display it? This new

Did You Know?

This magnificent row of guild houses on the Graslei along the banks of the River Leie is one of the prettiest spots in Ghent and a magnet for tourists. Centuries ago, these houses were used to weigh, store, and levy taxes on essential goods like grain. The 12th-century Koornstapelhuis is the street's oldest building.

museum offers an ingenious solution: simply look into *how* such things are investigated. Sections touch upon "classification," "doubt," "measurement," and other scientific conundrums, explored via formaldehyde-preserved animals, fossils, zoetropes, ancient sites, and even sex surveys. ✉ *Karel Lodewijk Ledeganckstraat 35* ☎ *09/264–4930* 🌐 *www.gum.gent* 🎫 *€8* ⏲ *Closed Wed.* Ⓜ *Tram: 1.*

Huis Arnold Vander Haeghen (*House of Arnold Vander Haeghen*)
HISTORY MUSEUM | The home of Arnold Vander Haegen, the city's 18th-century former governor, and the recently opened aristocratic residence of the d'Hane Steenhuyse family can be seen in one visit. The Nobel Prize–winning playwright and poet Maurice Maeterlinck (1862–1949) kept a library at the former, which still contains his personal objects, letters, and documents. The latter home is simply a charming glimpse at the *ancien régime*, as the era is brought to life by historical clips and tales of etiquette. ✉ *Veldstraat 82* ☎ *09/233–7788 tickets* 🌐 *www.uitbureau.be* 🎫 *Free; €6 guided tours* ⏲ *Closed Mon.–Thurs.* Ⓜ *Tram: 2.*

★ **Huis van Alijn** (*House of Alijn*)
CASTLE/PALACE | **FAMILY** | The museum itself comprises several settings, with its interior largely devoted to everyday 20th-century household items lovingly preserved. The courtyard features 18 medieval almshouses surrounding a garden, reconstructed to offer an idea of life here 100 years ago. The visitors' route takes you from the houses to the chapel and out through the crypt. Children are often drawn to the giant pageant figures, board games, and frequent shows in the beamed-and-brick puppet theater, where the star is "Pierke," the traditional Gent puppet. Tickets to shows can be bought at Uitbureau. ✉ *Kraanlei 65* ☎ *09/235–3800, 09/233–7788 Uitbureau (show tickets)* 🌐 *www.huisvanalijn.be* 🎫 *Museum €8* ⏲ *Closed Wed.* Ⓜ *Tram: 1.*

Korenmarkt
PLAZA/SQUARE | The city's main square is fringed with gabled buildings, cafés, and shops; it's also the site of one of the city's busiest tram stops. Adjoining the square, along Korte Munt, is the Groentenmarkt, the former vegetable market and site of the city's pillory, where criminals were put in the stocks and exposed to public abuse, back in the Middle Ages. ✉ *Next to St. Niklaaskerk, Ghent.*

★ **MSK – Museum of Fine Arts Ghent** (*Museum voor Schone Kunsten Gent*)
ART MUSEUM | This is one of Belgium's finer art museums, and its temporary exhibitions are usually exceptional. Built in 1902 at the edge of Citadelpark, the neoclassical Museum of Fine Arts (or Museum voor Schone Kunsten) has holdings that span the Middle Ages to the early 20th century, including works by Rubens, Géricault, Corot, Ensor, and Magritte. Its collection of Flemish Primitive painters is particularly noteworthy, with two paintings by Hieronymus Bosch: *Saint Jerome* and *Christ Carrying the Cross*. It also has a fine collection of sculpture and French painting. When panels from the Ghent Altarpiece go for restoration, they are done here, with visitors able to see the restorers at work. ✉ *Fernand Scribedreef 1* ☎ *09/323–6700* 🌐 *www.mskgent.be* 🎫 *€8* ⏲ *Closed Mon.* Ⓜ *Tram: 1.*

★ **Sint-Baafs Kathedraal** (*St. Bavo's Cathedral*)
CHURCH | Construction on the cathedral of St. Bavo (or Sint-Baaf) began in the 12th century but it wasn't finished for hundreds of years. Consequently, you can spy every flavor of medieval Gothic in its stonework, from the more austere early sculpting to the fine Brabantine style that swept the Low Countries in the 15th and 16th centuries. Inside is breathtaking but, for the past five centuries, most visitors come here for one thing: to see the famous Ghent Altarpiece, one of the

While known as the home of the famous Ghent Altarpiece, Sint-Baafs Kathedraal also features incredible Gothic stonework.

most influential paintings of the Middle Ages.

The altarpiece, a series of 12 panels, was created by the brothers Jan and Hubert van Eyck and has long lived in infamy. It has been the victim of several thefts, and after one of its lower panels was stolen in 1934, it was never recovered (a replica stands in its place), giving rise to numerous conspiracy theories and inspiring Albert Camus's novel *The Fall.* Ongoing restoration of the altarpiece since 2012 has seen what remains gradually returned to its original condition, with visitors able to see the restoration work up close at the Museum of Fine Arts. The rest now sits in a newly built visitor center, with augmented-reality tours offering an in-depth look at the history of this iconic artwork.

Elsewhere, the cathedral has many works of art. Its ornate pulpit, made of white Italian marble and black Danish oak, was carved in the 18th century by the sculptor Laurent Delvaux. A Rubens masterpiece, *Saint Bavo's Entry into the Monastery,* also hangs in one of the chapels. Other treasures include a baroque-style organ built in 1623 and a crypt crammed with tapestries, church paraphernalia, and 15th- and 16th-century frescoes. ✉ *Sint-Baafsplein* ☎ *09/397–1500* 🌐 *www.sintbaafskathedraal.be* 🎫 *Cathedral free; Altarpiece visit €13; AR tours €16* 🕑 *Closed during mass* Ⓜ *Tram: 1.*

Sint-Niklaaskerk (*St. Nicholas's Church*)
CHURCH | Perhaps Belgium's best example of Scheldt-Gothic, St. Nicholas's Church was built in the 11th century in Romanesque style, destroyed a century later after two disastrous fires, and later rebuilt by prosperous merchants. During the French Revolution, the church was used as a stable, and its treasures were ransacked. The tower, one of the many soaring landmarks of this city's famed skyline, dates from about 1300 and was the first belfry in Ghent. ✉ *Cataloniestraat, Ghent* ☎ *09/234–2869* 🌐 *www.kerkeninvlaanderen.be* 🎫 *Free* Ⓜ *Tram: 1.*

Sint-Pietersabdij (*St. Peter's Abbey*)
RELIGIOUS BUILDING | There has been an abbey on this site since the 7th century, and during the Middle Ages this was one of the richest and most important in Flanders. Most of the Baroque buildings you see today were built in the 17th century, however, and now house the St. Peter's Abbey Arts Center. You can walk around the abbey, the ruined gardens, and the cellars, where there is an exhibition about the monks, or watch the "movie guide" (€4), which explores the building's checkered history. There are also changing exhibitions upstairs ranging from painting to photography. ✉ *Sint-Pietersplein 9* ☏ *09/266–8500* 🌐 *historischehuizen.stad.gent/en/st-peters-abbey* 🎟 *Free entry to ground floor; exhibition prices vary* ⏲ *Closed Mon.* Ⓜ *Tram: 1.*

SMAK - Municipal Museum of Contemporary Art (*SMAK - Stedelijk Museum voor Actuele Kunst*)
ART MUSEUM | Located in a former flower show hall, this edgy, contemporary art gallery couldn't be farther removed from its dainty origins. Known for housing the odd daring exhibition, together with a permanent collection that includes the likes of Warhol, Christo, and Hockney, it does what good contemporary art does best: it challenges the viewer to leave their preconceptions at the door. ✉ *Jan Hoetplein 1* ✣ *Inside Citadelpark* ☏ *09/323–6001* 🌐 *www.smak.be* 🎟 *€15* ⏲ *Closed Mon.* Ⓜ *Tram: 1.*

Stadhuis
GOVERNMENT BUILDING | The Town Hall is an early example of what excessive taxes can do for a city. In 1516, Antwerp's Domien de Waghemakere and Mechelen's Rombout Keldermans, two prominent architects, were called in to build a town hall that would put all others to shame. However, before the building could be completed, Emperor Charles V imposed new taxes that drained the city's resources. The architecture thus reflects the changing fortunes of the city: the side built in 1518–60 and facing Hoogpoort is in flamboyant Gothic style; when work resumed in 1580, during the short-lived Protestant Republic, the Botermarkt side was completed in a stricter and more economical Renaissance style. ✉ *Botermarkt 1* ☏ *09/233–0772 tour reservations* 🌐 *gentsegidsen.be* 🎟 *€8 (booked online) town hall and city walking tour* Ⓜ *Tram: 1.*

STAM - Ghent City Museum
HISTORY MUSEUM | Explore the history of Ghent through nine rooms, all documenting significant moments in the formation of the city. Each room addresses a different era, from the time human beings first settled in the area some 70,000 years ago, to the city's medieval-era clashes with the Dukes of Burgundy, right up to its modern industrial heritage. The tour winds its way through a 14th-century abbey, a 17th-century monastery, and the modern museum, and there is also a giant map room that allows you to see how the city has expanded over the years. ✉ *Godshuizenlaan 2* ☏ *09/267–1400* 🌐 *www.stamgent.be* 🎟 *€10* ⏲ *Closed Wed.* Ⓜ *Tram: 1, 2.*

Restaurants

Ghent has long held a place in the hearts of Belgian gourmands, in part due to the enduring popularity of Gentse waterzooi—a classic Flemish dish of chicken or fish covered in thin strips of leek, carrot, and onion, all swamped in a delicious creamy broth. However, these days the city is causing a very modern stir in the food world thanks to a group of young childhood friends, now chefs, dubbed the "Flemish foodies." Their emergence has turned this old industrial port into something of a culinary destination—the Patershol area is particularly blessed. But away from the glare of Michelin stars, there's still plenty of good-value traditional food to be found here.

Balls and Glory

$$ | **BELGIAN** | This now ubiquitous "fast food" meatball joint has found plenty of love across Belgium but it all started here in Ghent in 2012 with a simple pop-up. The idea is simple: pick from a choice of large meatballs (as well as a veggie option), served with either *stoempe* (Belgian-style mash and vegetables) or salad. **Known for:** free jugs of water—a rarity in the parched restaurants of Belgium; darn fine meatballs; bowls of free fruit on tables. *Average main: €18 Jakobijnenstraat 6 0486/678–776 ballsnglory.be Closed Sun. Tram: 1.*

Brasserie Keizershof

$$ | **BELGIAN** | **FAMILY** | Here, you'll find the kind of food typical of a Flemish table, with plenty of steaks and classic stews accompanied by less local dishes, just in case, with an array of pastas. Staff are friendly and will happily translate the Dutch menu, but bring an appetite because portions are huge. **Known for:** a pretty good beer selection; hearty Flemish food and a friendly face; good for large groups. *Average main: €20 Vrijdagmarkt 47 09/223–4446 keizershof.net Closed Mon. Tram: 1.*

Jan van den Bon

$$$$ | **BELGIAN** | This distinguished restaurant is a local favorite for French and classic Belgian dishes, particularly seafood and seasonal specialties. Its tasting menus are on the steep side, but the service is uniformly excellent and the presentation borders on the inspired. **Known for:** good service; Gallic gastronomy with no little flair—and a fine garden; an elegant setting in a traditional old town house. *Average main: €75 Koning Leopold II Laan 43 09/221–9085 www.janvandenbon.be Closed Sun. and Mon. No lunch Sat. Jacket and tie Tram: 1, 2.*

Le Botaniste

$$ | **INTERNATIONAL** | Organic, plant-based vegan food and natural wines are the specialty of this canteen with the air of an apothecary. It couldn't be more on trend if it tried—and it has, hard! **Known for:** ethical eats in a fast-food setting; healthy, organic fast food that tastes great; an interesting selection of natural wines. *Average main: €15 Hoornstraat 13 09/233–4535 www.lebotaniste.be Closed Sun. Tram: 1.*

Mémé Gusta

$$ | **BELGIAN** | Whoever Grandma (Mémé) Gusta was, she didn't tolerate a 28-inch waist. Portions veer on the gigantic here, while the cooking is firmly traditional. **Known for:** a friendly atmosphere and service; rustic, traditional cooking and a decent choice of beers; gigantic portions of meat and frites. *Average main: €22 Burgstraat 19 09/398–2393 www.meme-gusta.be Closed Sun. and Mon. No lunch Wed. Tram: 1, 4.*

★ **Oak**

$$$$ | **INTERNATIONAL** | A fair contender for the best meal in Ghent, Oak more than deserves the Michelin star it bagged in 2018. Chef Marcelo Ballardin worked previously in the lauded Vrijmoed before setting up on his own, and demand is high: with just 24 seats, it's wise to book far in advance. **Known for:** a good-value lunch menu; exquisitely prepared food in an intimate setting; simple food with massive flavors. *Average main: €114 Hoogstraat 167 09/353–9050 www.oakgent.be Closed Sat.–Mon. Tram: 1, 2.*

Pakhuis

$$$ | **CONTEMPORARY** | At peak times, this enormously popular brasserie in an old warehouse off the Korenmarkt crackles with energy. A giant Greek statue makes an incongruous counterpoint to the marble-top tables, parquet floors, and long oak bar, but there's no denying its craft. **Known for:** great seafood—especially the year-round oyster bar; a remarkable warehouse setting that recalls the city's shipping past; fresh ingredients. *Average*

main: €25 ✉ Schuurkenstraat 4 ☎ 09/223–5555 🌐 www.pakhuis.be ⏲ Closed Sun. and 2 wks in July Ⓜ Tram: 1.

Prince

$$ | INTERNATIONAL | The owners of this food-sharing joint on bustling Oudburg have managed to make its interior look like an enchanted forest—all green walls, fake branches, and pale-pink flowers lit with clever lighting. The theatrics don't end with the decor, either, as each dish on the four- or six-course tasting menu pit-stops in another culinary realm. **Known for:** good cocktails; the interior is pretty adorable; its sharing plates are packed with flavor. $ *Average main: €16 ✉ Oudburg 58 ☎ 09/278–3413 🌐 www.prince-gent.com ⏲ Closed Sun. Ⓜ Tram: 1.*

★ Publiek

$$$ | BISTRO | Dishes at this Michelin-starred bistro from established Ghent chef Olly Ceulenaere are intricately prepared with a depth of flavor that belies their often simple ingredients. A small, ever-changing set menu invariably delivers. **Known for:** great value considering the quality of the cooking; exquisitely prepared bistro food; boundless culinary creativity. $ *Average main: €25 ✉ Ham 39 ☎ 09/330–0486 🌐 www.publiekgent.be ⏲ Closed Sun. and Mon. Ⓜ Bus: 3, 8, 39.*

Roots

$$$$ | BELGIAN | This charming restaurant is located amid the cobbled alleys of Patershol, an area that has transformed from an early-20th-century slum into one of the hippest locations in the city. Inside, Roots is all rather minimalist: just bare wood, stark tiles, and an open kitchen to stare at. **Known for:** creative cooking with good local produce; the walled terrace garden is a grand spot on a warm evening; it's great to watch the open kitchen at work. $ *Average main: €65 ✉ Vrouwebroersstraat 5, Ghent ☎ 09/310–6773 🌐 www.rootsgent.be ⏲ Closed weekends. No dinner Wed. Ⓜ Tram: 1, 4.*

Coffee and Quick Bites

Boon

$$ | CAFÉ | This health-conscious café majors in vegetarian and vegan treats, largely in the form of plate-sized salads, quiches, and soups. It's a charming location, having been sculpted out of an old ice-cream parlor; the Art Deco moldings lend it a distinguished air and there's a quiet courtyard at the rear. **Known for:** healthy eating in a nice café setting; the veggie-dumpling soups are particularly good; great coffees. $ *Average main: €13 ✉ Geldmunt 6, Ghent ☎ 0477/770–181 🌐 www.boon.gent ⏲ Closed Sun. Ⓜ Tram: 1, 4.*

Mokabon

$ | CAFÉ | Just off the Korenmarkt, the scent of fresh coffee beans is enough to draw you to this charming backstreet roastery complete with a café, neighboring take-away stall, and decent waffles. **Known for:** it's the city's most reliable hit of caffeine; a great choice of roasted blends; it's a good place to sit with a book. $ *Average main: €8 ✉ Donkersteeg 35 ☎ 09/225–7195 🌐 www.mokabon.be ⏲ Closed Sun. Ⓜ Tram: 1.*

Soup'r

$ | CAFÉ | One of the endearing eccentricities of Ghent is its number of soup-theme cafés. There are four in the center alone: all cheap, satisfying, and popular with students. **Known for:** it's a popular spot for locals; it's just good, cheap food; the choice of soups changes regularly. $ *Average main: €9 ✉ Sint-Niklaasstraat 9 🌐 www.facebook.com/SOUPR-177261612333422 ⏲ Closed Sun. and Mon. Ⓜ Tram: 1.*

Hotels

Accommodation in Ghent is often sleek and modern, and there are several stylish hotels in historic buildings. However, these generally target weekend and short-term guests.

★ 1898 The Post

$$$ | **HOTEL** | This stately boutique hotel, on the quayside of the Graslei, set hearts aflutter when it opened in 2018. **Pros:** it's a fascinating piece of local history; the city-center location means you're never far from the action; the Cobbler is one of the better cocktail bars in the city. **Cons:** it's a bit of a labyrinth inside; the noise from the bars in the center does drift up; there's no pool, gym, spa, or restaurant. *$ Rooms from: €179 ✉ Graslei 16 ☎ 09/277–0960 🌐 1898thepost.com 38 rooms 🍽 Free Breakfast Ⓜ Tram: 1.*

Erasmus

$$ | **HOTEL** | From the flagstone and wood-beam library-lounge to the stone mantels in the individually decorated bedrooms, every inch of this noble 16th-century town house has been scrubbed, polished, and decked with period ornaments. **Pros:** it's got a long history; a huge amount of charm; professional staff. **Cons:** older rooms can be a little on the dark side; feels a bit worn in places; lacks some modern conveniences. *$ Rooms from: €120 ✉ Poel 25 ☎ 09/224–2195 🌐 www.erasmushotel.be ⏲ Closed mid-Dec.–mid-Jan. 12 rooms 🍽 Free Breakfast Ⓜ Bus: 5.*

Ganda Rooms and Suites

$$ | **HOTEL** | Genial owners Annik and Kristof have turned this elegant 1756-built town house into a delightful stay. **Pros:** an abundance of free cake for all; it's got a tasteful and a stylish look; grand breakfasts in the pretty kitchen or dining room. **Cons:** there are stairs but no elevator; some rooms can get a bit chilly in winter; it's a 10-minute walk to the center. *$ Rooms from: €134 ✉ Houtbriel 18 ☎ 09/330–2022 🌐 gandaroomsandsuites.be 8 rooms 🍽 No Meals Ⓜ Bus: 3.*

Hostel Uppelink

$ | **HOTEL** | Lying on the banks of the Leie, Hostel Uppelink is cheap, cozy, and surprisingly storied. **Pros:** easy meeting point for walking and kayak tours; cheap accommodation in the city center; you get to stay in a piece of history. **Cons:** most private rooms have bunk beds; it can be a little noisy in this part of town; private rooms are on the small side. *$ Rooms from: €25 ✉ Sint-Michielsplein 21, Ghent ☎ 09/279–4477 🌐 www.hosteluppelink.com 12 rooms 🍽 No Meals Ⓜ Tram: 1.*

Hotel Harmony

$$ | **HOTEL** | It's always a surprise just how much is packed into this unassuming boutique stay in the Patershol area. **Pros:** good value for all the facilities; breakfast comes with views of the canal; one of few outdoor hotel pools in the city. **Cons:** parking in the covered garage costs €25; the gym is tiny; it can be a little dark inside. *$ Rooms from: €138 ✉ Kraanlei 37 ☎ 09/324–2680 🌐 hotel-harmony.be 40 rooms 🍽 Free Breakfast Ⓜ Tram: 1, 4.*

Monasterium PoortAckere

$ | **HOTEL** | A complex comprising a former abbey, convent, and beguinage is now a serene place to stay in a central neighborhood, though an ongoing expansion is doubling its capacity. **Pros:** bargain-priced rooms; unique historical setting; breakfasts are outstanding. **Cons:** older rooms are a little worn; continuing renovation means noise; a lot of stairs to climb (though there are two elevators). *$ Rooms from: €54 ✉ Oude Houtlei 56 ☎ 09/269–2210 🌐 www.monasterium.be 64 rooms 🍽 No Meals Ⓜ Tram: 2.*

Pillows Grand Hotel Reylof

$$$ | **HOTEL** | This converted 18th-century town house hotel is one of the more distinguished addresses in town, with a luxurious spa that occupies the former stables and the pervading sense that you've just stepped onto a particularly meticulous film set. **Pros:** surprisingly good value and a free minibar; excellent spa with hammam, pool, and sauna; staff are pitch-perfect. **Cons:** there's little in the way of a budget option; it's lost its over-the-top charm; more than a 10-minute walk to the center (in Ghent, that's a lot).

$ *Rooms from: €165* ✉ *Hoogstraat 36* ☎ *09/235–4070* 🌐 *www.pillowshotels.com* 🛏 *157 rooms* 🍽 *Free Breakfast* Ⓜ *Tram: 1, 2.*

★ The Vanhaegen B&B

$$$ | B&B/INN | A truly unique B&B crafted by a pair of interior designers and antiques dealers, Jan and Marc, with a reverence for the past that borders on the zealous. **Pros:** the owners are friendly; breakfast overlooks the incredible garden; for sheer historic grandeur it is unmatched. **Cons:** clumsier guests will live in fear of knocking over the antiques; rooms in the old house have been restored not modernized; there is a house dog, so those with allergies beware. $ *Rooms from: €215* ✉ *Oude Houtlei 110* ☎ *09/265–0765* 🌐 *www.theverhaegen.com* 🛏 *8 rooms* 🍽 *Free Breakfast* Ⓜ *Tram: 2.*

YALO

$$$ | HOTEL | For those unaware, "Yalo" is a local slang term for "Wow." Ghent's new urban boutique hotel certainly gives off a need to impress. What else could have prompted them to build its "disco toilets"—yes, they're public bathrooms with a big button on the wall that turns off all the lights, strobes flashing colors (epileptics beware!), and blares out deafening dance music. **Pros:** there's a chef's table in the restaurant; it's opening the city's first rooftop bar; there is underground parking on Vlaanderenstraat. **Cons:** the sheer number of meeting rooms make it very business-y; there's no pool; it is almost annoyingly hip. $ *Rooms from: €153* ✉ *Brabantdam 33* ☎ *09/395–9200* 🌐 *www.yalohotel.com* 🛏 *92 rooms* 🍽 *Free Breakfast* Ⓜ *Tram: 2.*

Nightlife

Ghent's large student population ensures a busier, more varied nightlife than you'll find in the likes of near-neighbor Bruges. Locals have also come up with a very Belgian compromise to avoid tensions between residents and partying students. In an idea akin to horror film *The Purge,* the worst of the student revelry is contained within one hedonistic street, Overpoort, containing 30-plus bars and myriad kebab shops. The result is that the center's bars aren't overrun by beer-fueled teens and are left mostly to locals and tourists. And what a bar scene it is. Ghent's beer and brewpubs, in particular, are some of the finest in Belgium.

Should you still desire to find your rhythm away from the sticky mayhem of Overpoort, the area around Oude Beestenmarkt and Vlasmarkt, near Portus Ganda, is a good spot for clubs, albeit of the cheesier variety, while you'll find a surprising number of jazz bars in the center. There is also a thriving LGBTQIA+ community, with several gay bars, and gay and lesbian organizations offering help and assistance.

BARS

Brouwbar

BREWPUBS | A microbrewery that leans more to the U.S. craft ale style than its native Belgian, though the odd *saison* does appear. This plucky bar typically has eight beers on tap at any one point. A home-brewers mentality means it's constantly changing beers but you'll always find an IPA or New England–style brew to slake your thirst. ✉ *Oudburg 70a–72a* ☎ *0485/406–319* 🌐 *www.brouwbar.be* Ⓜ *Tram: 1.*

De Dulle Griet

BARS | In this quintessential Ghent pub, there are more than 500 kinds of beer, but the specialty is the 1.2-liter *Kwak* (a blond 8.5% beer), complete with traditional hourglass-shape glass and stand—ask for a "Max." If you brave this beer, though, you must leave one of your shoes as a deposit when you order. The pub is open most days noon–1 am, apart from Sunday evening when it closes early, and Monday when it doesn't open until 4:30 pm. ✉ *Vrijdagmarkt 50*

☎ *09/224–2455* 🌐 *www.dullegriet.be* Ⓜ *Tram: 1.*

Dok Brewing Co.

BREWPUBS | It's a bit of a distance from the center of town, but well worth the excursion. This microbrewery and taproom is the largest and most experimental in Ghent, with 30 beers on tap. Set in the old Dok Noord complex, around 10 to 15 are brewed on-site, and are only ever made once. The choice is almost overwhelming. Hour-long brewery tours and tastings (€18) can be booked in advance, and the building also has independent street-food stalls inside, with BBQ joint RØK particularly recommended. ✉ *Dok-Noord 4B, Dok Noord* 🌐 *www.dokbrewingcompany.be* Ⓜ *Tram: 4.*

★ Gruut

BREWPUBS | Brewer Annick de Splenter's prolific brewpub has lost none of its ability to surprise. Based in an old galley, relics of the building's former life remain, with various cow statues proliferating the bar. Gruut's beers are made to a medieval recipe, using herbs, not hops; the result is a more subtle, lighter-tasting brew than the usual Belgian offering. Tours of the brewery (€20) can be arranged; you can even add a boat trip to your visit. If you have the time, spare some for its "beeralchemy" sessions (€22) and the chance to brew your own herb beer to take home; it's easily done in an afternoon and the session includes a brief tour and tastings. ✉ *Rembert Dodoensdreef 1* ☎ *09/269–0269* 🌐 *www.gruut.be* Ⓜ *Bus: 3, 5.*

Het Waterhuis Aan De Bierkant

BARS | Back in the plague-ridden early 1500s, this fine estaminet was the city's main source of clean drinking water. As the years went by, it morphed from water house to brothel to barbershop, and finally an inn. Today, it remains one of the city's iconic "brown bars." Come here for the selection; with several beers on tap, including a few of their own house brews and hundreds of bottled beers, it's pretty much perfection. Its small waterside terrace fills up quickly in fine weather though. ✉ *Groentenmarkt 9* ☎ *09/225–0680* Ⓜ *Tram: 1.*

★ Jiggers

COCKTAIL LOUNGES | This superb cocktail bar re-creates a 1920s speakeasy vibe. The drinks are uniformly excellent, with homemade bitters and infusions decorating an ever-changing menu that has something of a gastronomy vibe, while the outdoor, waterside terrace is cozily hidden. While so many of Ghent's cocktail bars err on the tacky side, Jiggers is an oasis of cool, though at around €15 a drink, it doesn't come cheap. ✉ *Oudberg 16, Ghent* ☎ *09/335–7025* 🌐 *www.jiggers.be* Ⓜ *Tram: 1.*

't Dreupelkot

BARS | To taste a potent Flemish and Dutch specialty, head to 't Dreupelkot (sister bar to Het Waterhuis Aan De Bierkant), which produces its own jenever—a liquor similar in flavor to, and said to be the precursor of, gin. Here, it's all homemade and comes in a multitude of flavors, including vanilla, chocolate, and even cactus. The owner is also a character of the eccentric variety. A "barometer" behind the bar indicates his mood at any given time—it rarely points to "happy." ✉ *Groentenmarkt 12* ☎ *09/224–2120* Ⓜ *Tram: 1.*

Trollekelder

BARS | Yet another beer specialist, although one located in a 15th-century cellar and with an atmosphere a tad livelier than its more laid-back rivals. The crowd is a bit younger, too. ✉ *17 Bij Sint-Jacobs* ☎ *0477/409–237* 🌐 *www.trollekelder.be* Ⓜ *Tram: 1.*

LBGT

Casa Rosa / A-Pluss

BARS | This LGBT center has information on gay and lesbian bars, events, and organizations, and also offers help and advice (website in Dutch). On the ground floor, the A-Pluss bar and café has a fine selection of gins, a new street terrace, and live music on weekends. ✉ *Kammerstraat 22* ☎ *09/269–2812* 🌐 *www.casarosa.be* Ⓜ *Tram: 1.*

MUSIC CLUBS

Missy Sippy

LIVE MUSIC | A little slice of New Orleans on the Leie. Missy Sippy may lie square in the historic center, in the shadow of the Sint-Niklaaskerk, yet still feels like a back-alley discovery, dishing up thumping blues and roots bands alongside a decent selections of Belgian brews and bourbons. ✉ *Klein Turkije 16, Ghent* ☎ *0484/925–684* 🌐 *www.missy-sippy.be* Ⓜ *Tram: 1.*

Muziekcafé Charlatan

LIVE MUSIC | There are concerts as well as dance nights at Charlatan. Music starts up at 10, and entry to most events is free. The lineup includes alt-rock, electro, and lots of DJ nights. ✉ *Vlasmarkt 6* ☎ *09/224–2457* 🌐 *www.charlatan.be* Ⓜ *Tram: 1.*

Performing Arts

Check English-language magazine *The Bulletin* (*www.thebulletin.be*) to find schedules of the latest art shows and cultural events.

De Handelsbeurs

CONCERTS | This concert hall hosts all kinds of music events, including jazz, folk, world, and classical. The ticket office is on Sint Baafsplein 17 and it's open weekdays 10–6 and on Saturday 2–6. The on-site box office does, however, open an hour before each performance for those looking for a last-minute way in. ✉ *Kouter 29* ☎ *09/265–9160 office, 09/265–9165 tickets* 🌐 *www.handelsbeurs.be* Ⓜ *Tram: 1.*

Opera Ballet Vlaanderen

BALLET | The old opera house is a beautiful venue, having opened in 1840. A packed program sees the royal ballet and opera company split its time between performances here and in Antwerp. The box office is open Tuesday–Saturday 11–6. ✉ *Schouwburgstraat 3* ☎ *070/220–202 tickets* 🌐 *operaballet.be* Ⓜ *Tram: 1.*

Vooruit

ARTS CENTERS | Located in the former Socialist Party building, Voorhuit is the biggest arts venue in town. It serves up everything from dance, rock, pop, classical, and jazz to lectures, talks, and the performing arts. The cafeteria has also become a popular meeting area for students and the local arts scene. The box office is open Tuesday–Friday 2–6, and one hour before the beginning of a performance. ✉ *Sint-Pietersnieuwstraat 23* ☎ *09/267–2828 tickets* 🌐 *www.vooruit.be* Ⓜ *Tram: 1.*

Shopping

Langemunt and Veldstraat are the major shopping streets. Smart fashion boutiques cluster along Voldersstraat, while Brabantdam and Vlaanderenstraat serve up a couture blizzard of designer stores. From there it's a short walk to Het Zuid and the streetwear of the SoGo area (Sint-Pietersnieuwstraat, Walpoortstraat, and Kortedagsteeg). Alternatively, plenty of vintage, antiques, and secondhand shopping is to be found in Oudberg and the area around Sint-Jacobskirk, on Serpentstraat, Baudelostraat, and Ottgracht.

But for something a little different, there is an increasing number of artisan food shops worth exploring in Ghent, from the Gruut Brewery to some local gems that have been perfecting their recipes for hundreds of years. These scatter the city but are well worth finding.

FOOD SHOPS

Temmerman

FOOD | Part of a family business since 1904, Temmerman eschews Belgium's chocolate obsession for locally made artisanal candy and gingerbread. The family is also credited with inventing what is now the famous Ghent *cuberdons*

Ghent noses); raspberry-flavored ,weets, the insides of which stretch out ike cooked mozzarella when pulled apart. ✉ *Kranlei 79* ☎ *09/279–5901* Ⓜ *Tram: 1.*

ierenteyn-Verlent

OOD | You'll find this revered and ,trong-tasting mustard served all over the :ity, but you can only buy it here, along vith a dazzling array of spices, pickles, ıoneys, and teas. This family-run shop ıas been in Ghent since 1790, and no ›reservatives are used in their products. ✉ *Groentenmarkt 3* ☎ *09/225–8336* ⊕ *www.tierenteyn-verlent.be* Ⓜ *Tram: 1.*

'uzu

:HOCOLATE | Created by archaeolo- ıist-turned-chocolatier Nicolas Vanaise, 'uzu reflects its owner's obsession with ıll things Japanese. Hence, even in the and of chocolate, it stands out for its ,trange combinations of ingredients and ,tark minimalist interior. The selection is :onstantly changing, but flavors such as vasabi, sake, and Cuban tobacco have ›een featured in the past. ✉ *Walpoort- 'traat 11a* ☎ *0473/965–733* Ⓜ *Tram: 2.*

IARKETS

lower Market

1ARKET | A daily flower market is held ›n the Kouter, although it's best to visit ›n Sunday morning (7 am–1 pm), when he full market kicks in and there's often brass band playing (April–September). ✉ *Kouter* Ⓜ *Tram: 1.*

ousbergmarkt

1ARKET | A covered market that has ›xpanded to include a collective of ›akers, organic grocers, and a rather ıne canteen called De Bergen, which ›ses the produce of its neighbors. But he star remains the cheese makers lét Hinkelspel, which was started 30 ears ago by a group of students who vere experimenting in making organic heeses with raw cow's and goat's milk. hey are one of only a handful of cheese nakers in Belgium to make blue cheese, nd the Pas de Bleu comes highly recommended. ✉ *De Lousbergmarkt, F. Lousbergstaai 33* ☎ *09/224–2096* ⊕ *www.hethinkelspel.be* Ⓜ *Tram: 2.*

The City of Flowers

Every five years, the city of Ghent is awash with color as it hosts the *Gentse Floraliën*. This huge botanical exhibition is what earned Ghent its "City of Flowers" nickname. The first event was held in 1809 and filled an exhibition space of just 500 square feet; since then it has grown beyond recognition, giving the region's gardeners a chance to place their wares in an international shop window. Today's Floraliën attracts hundreds of thousands of visitors from around the world. Visit *floralien.be* to find out about the next event.

Vrijdagmarkt

MARKET | The largest market in town is the attractive and historic Vrijdagmarkt, held Friday 7:30–1 and (as a smaller version) Saturday 11–6:30. This huge square is where leaders have rallied the people of Ghent from the Middle Ages to the present day. It is dominated by a turret that was part of the tanner's guild house, and the statue in the middle is of Jacob van Artevelde, who led a rebellion starting here in 1338, defending the neutrality of the city and Flanders during the Hundred Years' War. These days, you're more likely to march off with a supply of *Gentse mokken* (syrup-soaked biscuits) or the famously strong Ghent mustard than in anger. ✉ *Vrijdagmarkt* Ⓜ *Tram: 1.*

VINTAGE AND ANTIQUES

Fallen Angels & Gallery

ANTIQUES & COLLECTIBLES | Named after a clutch of abandoned angel statuettes found by Isabelle Steel when she opened the shop in 1980, this remains a treasure trove of vintage and eccentric ephemera, including dolls, tin boxes, and religious items. Her daughter, Ganesha, runs the Fallen Angels Gallery next door, which is filled with posters of old Belgian advertisements and movie posters. ✉ *Jan Breydelstraat 29–31* ☎ *09/223–9415* 🌐 *the-fallen-angels.com* Ⓜ *Tram: 1.*

Leiestreek Villages

Barely a few miles southwest of Ghent, the River Leie (Lys) snakes gently into the countryside, as the rough edges of the city dissolve into quiet meadows, pretty polders, medieval villages, rustic restaurants, and mansions of every size, hue, and heft. As late as the early 20th century, this was mostly farming land; then the arrival of a colony of nature-loving Belgian artists changed it forever. Now, villages like **Sint-Martens-Latem** and **Deurle**, which were at the center of that artistic community, fill with expensive galleries and art museums. It has become a wealthy area and a popular weekend getaway for Ghentians, for whom the riverside paths, country trails, golf course, and the presence of one of Belgium's finest castles make for excellent walking and cycling all the way down to **Deinze**.

Sint-Martens-Latem

7 km (4 miles) from Ghent.

Sint-Martins-Latem is a village that boasts more galleries than food shops. The reason for this lies in the early 20th century and the arrival of the first Latem School, a colony of Symbolist and Impressionist landscape painters, poets, and sculptors. They settled here, seeking inspiration in rural life, trailing collectors and the more adventurous fringes of the bourgeoisie in their wake. A second, Expressionist Latem School followed in 1905, and over the decades others arrived as much for the scene as the scenery.

These days, the village is a popular weekend getaway from Ghent, with artistry found not just in the bijou galleries and museums, but the rather distinguished dining scene that has grown around them. With wealth comes the finer things, and the village outskirts are scattered with country restaurants and a sprawling golf course, around which avenues of mansions and stately farm conversions cluster like an episode of *Grand Designs* gone wildly off-budget.

Back in town, you'll find the old medieval center cloistered around the Dorp, where the church leans handsomely over the Leie. To its south, the shopping street of Latemstraat is awash in boutiques and galleries, as the village's true boho colors are revealed. But its real lure remains unchanged from a century ago: the beautiful countryside and walks on its doorstep.

GETTING HERE AND AROUND

Driving is the quickest way to get around the Leiestreek, though there is little parking in the villages. Alternatively, the train between Ghent and Kortrijk doesn't stop at Sint-Martens-Latem, but it does visit nearby De Pinte, only 4 km (2½ miles) away. From there it's an hour's walk, or you can take the No. 35/36 bus. Buses from Ghent via Sint-Martens-Latem also link Deinze (No. 77) and the villages of Deurle and Sint-Martens-Leerne (No. 34) which is a 20-minute walk from Kasteel van Ooidonk. But the best way to get around here is by bicycle. Rent a city bike at Ghent's Sint-Pieters Station and cycle the 8 km (5 miles) to Sint-Martens-Latem. The route is flat and follows cycle lanes out of the city and into the polders Once in the country, all the villages are easily pedaled, and if you make it to Deinze, you can take your bike on the train (for an extra €4 fee) back to Ghent.

Sights

Gevert-Minne Museum
ART MUSEUM | The painter, poet, writer, and composer Edgar Gevart married the daughter of George Minne, one of the central figures of the first Latem School of artists, in 1916. They built their home soon after, a charming mix of Gothic and traditional cottage styles. When he died, his wife, Marie, opened his studio to the public, showing not just her husband's work but that of her father. Today, its collection on display is much broader, ranging from Xavier de Cock's early paintings to the arrival of the prewar Expressionists. Its "sheep stable" also holds temporary exhibitions. Note: visiting hours can be a little eccentric here, with doors only opening between 2 and 5 pm. ✉ *Edgard Gevaertdreef, Sint-Martens-Latem, Sint-Martins-Latem* ☎ *09/220–7183* 🎟 *Free* 🕒 *Closed Mon. and Tues.*

Sint-Martinuskerk (*St. Martin's Church*)
CHURCH | This whitewashed church on the banks of the Leie likely dates back to the 11th century. Built using limestone from Tournai, shipped via the rivers Scheldt and Leie, it was heavily renovated in 1900, creating its current neo-Gothic hall. In the graveyard, you'll find the resting places of many of the artists who made the village their home, including Albijn van den Abeele and George Minne, whose grave lies beneath a bronze cast of a mother cradling her child. Inside are a number of impressive works, including a large panel by Gustave van de Woestyne. Behind the church, you'll also spy a much-admired 17th-century farmhouse linked to the old abbey, which has been featured in many classic paintings. Stroll the waterside for one of the more peaceful, scenic stretches of the river. ✉ *Dorp 1, Sint-Martins-Latem* ☎ *09/282–3288* 🎟 *Free.*

Restaurants

★ **D'Oude Schuur**
$$$$ | **FRENCH** | The reputation of D'Oude Schuur often sees Ghentians make a weekend of their visit just to indulge here. As its name (The Old Barn) suggests, it was once part of a farm, though there's little rustic about its neat, spare interior. **Known for:** a fantastic wine cellar of French classics; its country setting, out in the leafy suburbs of the village; some accomplished cooking. $ *Average main: €38* ✉ *Baarle-Frankrijkstraat 1, Sint-Martins-Latem* ☎ *09/282–3365* 🌐 *www.oudeschuur.be* 🕒 *Closed Wed. and Thurs.*

L'Homard Bizarre
$$$$ | **BRASSERIE** | As its name (The Weird Lobster) suggests, lobster is the specialty here, prepared every which way on special menus that recur on Thursday and Sunday. Otherwise, go for the more local fare. **Known for:** a pretty garden terrace at the back; knowing its way around a lobster; country cooking elevated to fine dining. $ *Average main: €35* ✉ *Kortrijksesteenweg 259, Sint-Martins-Latem* ☎ *09/281–2922* 🌐 *homard-bizarre.be* 🕒 *Closed Mon.–Wed.*

Hotels

Auberge du Pêcheur
$ | **HOTEL** | This riverside inn, in one of the area's prettiest settings, lies on a calm bend of the Leie and boasts a fine brasserie with a terrace that lingers on the water's edge, its grassy lawns scattered with colorful modern art. **Pros:** great views if you get the right room; a great location on the water, not far from the villages; it has one of the better wine cellars in the area. **Cons:** the road out front is the main thoroughfare to Ghent—and noisy; there is something of a "corporate retreat" vibe here; room decor is rather basic. $ *Rooms from: €93* ✉ *Pontstraat 41, Sint-Martins-Latem* ☎ *09/282–3144* 🌐 *www.auberge-du-pecheur.be* *32 rooms* *Free Breakfast.*

The charming village of Sint-Martins-Latem is a popular weekend getaway from Ghent.

★ Torenhof

$$ | HOTEL | This sturdy country house was built by the artist Albert Servaes, who used it as both a home and studio between 1917 and the end of World War II. **Pros:** free parking for visitors; it's an important relic of the area's artistic history; well located for some of the better restaurants. **Cons:** there aren't many facilities at present; you need a car, or at least a bike, to get there; its interior can be a little dark. *Rooms from: €100* ✉ *Baarle-Frankrijkstraat 10, Sint-Martins-Latem* ☎ *09/282–3320* 🌐 *torenhof.be* *13 rooms* *Free Breakfast.*

Shopping

The Boutique Gallery

ART GALLERIES | This chic modern-art gallery, opposite the church, is hard to miss. Works by a number of Belgian and South African artists (it has another branch in Cape Town) scatter its exterior, including sculptures by Marieke Prinsloo-Rowe, whose playful bronze "swimmers" can also be seen peering out from a nearby bar. Other artists sold in the past include Guy du Toit, Samuel Allerton, and Olivier Pauwels. ✉ *Dorp 6, Sint-Martins-Latem* ☎ *0470/030–502* 🌐 *theboutiquegallery.com.*

Gallerie Oscar de Vos

ART GALLERIES | An art dealer with a particular interest in the works of the Latem Schools of the early 20th century and their Flemish predecessors. While this gallery (which only opens on weekends) is primarily a seller to private collectors, it also runs regular exhibitions, featuring artists such as Emile Claus, Constant Permeke, Gustave De Smet, and Albert Servaes. ✉ *Latemstraat 20, Sint-Martins-Latem* ☎ *09/281–1170* 🌐 *www.oscardevos.be.*

Deurle

2½ km (1½ miles) from Sint-Martins-Latem.

The village center of Deurle is barely more than a cobbled street lined with

The Art of the Leie

The arrival of the original Latem School of artists to Sint-Martens-Latem in 1899 sparked a gradual change in the life of the villages of the Leiestreek that is still seen today. The group, cloistered around the Symbolist sculptor **George Minne** and his troubled painter friend **Valerius De Saedeleer**, formed an artists' colony. It would become the prototype for much of what followed, as generations of bohemians, socialites, and collectors ebbed into the largely pastoral region. But they also weren't the first.

Minne had been drawn to the Leie Valley by another acquaintance, the artist and writer **Albijn van den Abeele**. He was raised in Sint-Martens-Latem and was the man who perhaps did the most to realize the dream of a "painter's village," having also convinced Belgium's **De Cock** brothers to find their muse in the fields around Deurle decades earlier.

Even more influentially, the painter **Emile Claus** had moved to the nearby village of Astene in 1881. He was arguably the first star here, having championed Belgium's Luminist (a late-Impressionist style) movement, drawing on the fields and laborers of the area for his inspiration. His fame attracted not only other artists but the fringes of Brussels's bourgeoisie.

The original Latem School drew greatly on the influence of Claus and, before him, the Flemish Masters of the 16th century. But at the center of their philosophy was the idea of nature as religion, a kind of mysticism. The early Latemse artists sought a purity in the countryside that they believed they couldn't find elsewhere, in life or art. The result was an altogether dreamier vision of the same fields and farm workers that Claus and the De Cocks had also lingered upon.

Later came the Second Latem School in 1905, heralded by the arrival of **Constant Permeke**, **Frits van den Berghe**, and **Gust De Smet**, who would go on to found the Flemish Expressionist movement, rooted in the countryside of the Leiestreek. Despite the antipathy between the two schools, the techniques of the latter, ironically, drew on a member of the original Latemse group, **Albert Servaes**, who gradually moved away from the mysticism of the Symbolists as he grew more religious.

Others "schools" and artists followed, but none quite captured the fire of those early pioneers. Yet the area changed with them, and what was once a hard-living farming community became a middle-class suburb of Ghent, filled with charm, galleries, golf, and all the accoutrements of modern life; ironically, the very things the first painters here sought to escape.

a friendly inn, a church, and a few artsy shops. Yet its charm and influence goes much further. Some of the most respected Belgian painters of the early 20th century lived here, with a number of their houses now preserved as monuments. Art is everywhere: in boutique shops, galleries, and even a modern art museum. Yet what originally drew the artists remains untouched: a sense of peace. Deurle is surrounded by lush walks and shaded lanes soundtracked only by the rustle of leaves overhead.

GETTING HERE AND AROUND

It's only a few miles meander from the village of Sint-Martens-Latem to Deurle, with the pretty, forested paths north of the N43 making for a pleasant stroll. Alternatively, the No. 34 bus connects the two villages.

Sights

★ Museum Dhondt-Dhaenens

ART MUSEUM | The museum is named after its two founders, Jules and Irma Dhondt-Dhaenens, whose private collection of modern art is exhibited piecemeal throughout the year. Temporary exhibitions fill the rest of the schedule, typically leaning towards more challenging works. It offers a fascinating counterbalance to the fiercely antimodern Latem Schools, for which the region became famous. ✉ *Museumlaan 14, Deurle* ☎ *09/330–1730* 🌐 *museumdd.be* 🎫 *€9* 🕒 *Closed Mon. and Tues.*

Museum Gust De Smet

ART MUSEUM | Before his death in 1943, this was the home and studio of the artist Gust De Smet, one of the later stars of the Flemish Expressionists who found their way to the villages of the Leie in the early 1900s. On the bottom floor, his home is kept as it was; upstairs, his work hangs in situ, charting the various stages of artistic development. There is even a Gust De Smet "wandelroute" (walking trail), which starts at the house and offers a pleasant stroll around Deurle and its sights. ✉ *Gustaaf de Smetlaan 1, Deurle* ☎ *09/245–8280* 🎫 *Free* 🕒 *Closed Mon.–Thurs.*

Restaurants

Brasserie Vinois

$$$ | **BRASSERIE** | Hidden away among the museum streets of Deurle, this brasserie is best known for its "grandma cooking." Expect veal kidneys lashed with sharp Ghentish Tierenteyn mustard, a hearty stoofvlees of stewed pork cheeks with a side of rough-cut apple sauce, and beef from the Basque Country. **Known for:** a covered terrace that escapes the rather echoey interior; its quiet location; an interesting sharing-plates menu. $ *Average main: €24* ✉ *Philippe de Denterghemlaan 31, Deurle* ☎ *09/282–7018* 🌐 *www.brasserie-vinois.com* 🕒 *Closed Sun. and Mon.*

Deboeveries

$$$$ | **BELGIAN** | North Sea sole is the specialty here, fried and served with frites or grilled with a side of dijonnaise. It might not sound like the most sophisticated of dishes, but it is cherished among locals. **Known for:** the quality of its sole; great service; a "luxury" afternoon menu that changes with the seasons. $ *Average main: €32* ✉ *Lijnstraat 2, Deurle* ☎ *09/282–3391* 🌐 *deboeveries.be* 🕒 *Closed Wed. and Thurs. No dinner Tues. and Fri.*

D'Ouwe Hoeve

$$$ | **BRASSERIE** | **FAMILY** | An old favorite among locals. Its village-center location, spilling onto the cobbles beneath the church, sets a convivial scene. **Known for:** a good standard of cooking; charming village location; the terrace makes for a pleasant escape in warm weather. $ *Average main: €24* ✉ *Dorpsstraat 48, Deurle* ☎ *09/282–3252* 🌐 *www.douwehoeve.be.*

Hotels

Boldershof

$ | **B&B/INN** | Sat across from the 19th-century church of Sint-Aldergondis, on the cobbles of Duerle's tiny main street, its five bedrooms have a rustic gentility and make a fine base for those exploring the trails and museums of the area. **Pros:** free parking and a likeable restaurant; an ideal setting in the center of the village; kindly staff and good service. **Cons:** standard rooms share a toilet; there are few facilities bar the basics; it can be too quiet for some. $ *Rooms from: €79*

Dorpsstraat 37, Deurle *09/282–7545* *www.boldershof.com* *5 rooms* *Free Breakfast.*

Shopping

Vhite Interiors 49

IOUSEWARES | A chic gallery-cum-interi-rs shop on the village Dorpsstraat run y an Italian-Belgian husband and wife, nna and Mike. It has a second shop n Oostend. *Dorpsstraat 49, Deurle* *0479/401–282* *www.whiteinteri-rs49.be.*

Deinze

7½ km (5 miles) from Deurle.

he city of Deinze doesn't have the post-ard appeal of the villages surrounding it. f you follow the river south into the city, ou'll see the point at which the pretty neadows, private jetties, and long strips f garden give way to the first scuffs f old industry. The town does have a ather illustrious past when it comes to ycling, though. The 1926 Tour de France hampion Lucien Buysse hailed from Deinze, and in recent years it has been he default home of the Team Sky racing eam (now Ineos Grenadiers). But for nost visitors, its rail links simply make t a good jumping-off point for nearby Kasteel Ooidonk, a 16th-century Renais-sance beauty of a castle, originally built o defend the river upstream of Ghent. he 6-km (4-mile) path to get there runs longside the Leie and is a delightful oute to walk or cycle, especially if you top at the old *sashuis* (canal lock house), vhich is now a rather pleasant café.

GETTING HERE AND AROUND

Deinze is connected to Deurle and Sint-Martens-Latem via the No. 77 bus. It is lso well linked by rail, with hourly trains onnecting Antwerp via Ghent, and more ocal services running in between. At Deinze station, you'll also find a Blue Bike ick-up point. This cycling scheme is free here for the first 24 hours of use, thanks to an intervention by the city, though bikes must be returned to the stand from which they were taken and there is a membership fee (€12).

CONTACTS Blue Bike. *Brielstraat 2, Deinze* *www.blue-bike.be.*

Sights

★ **Kasteel Ooidonk** (*Ooidonk Castle*)

CASTLE/PALACE | Of the 3,000 or so castles found in Belgium, Ooidonk still numbers among the most eye-catching. It stands on the site of a 13th-century fortress that was destroyed when Ghent rose up against the Habsburg ruler Maximilian I. It was, again, razed during the social upheavals of the 1500s, before its trans-formation into a residential estate by the wealthy Antwerp merchant Martin della Faille. In doing so, its Hispanic-French architecture broke away from the "murder holes" and pragmatism of the early Middle Ages, adding Renaissance flourishes like its "onion" towers. It has been in the family of owners Count and Countess t'Kint de Roodenbeke since 1864, and they still live in residence. For part of the year, the castle interior can be visited on guided tours (April–Octo-ber), revealing magnificent tapestries, antiques, and artworks; the rest of the time you can only visit the park and gardens, though these are sufficiently grand to make the trek worthwhile. The best way to reach the castle is to walk, or cycle, the 6 km (4-mile) riverside trail from Deinze. *Ooidonkdreef 9, Deinze* *09/282–2638* *www-ooidonk-be* *€12 castle visit; €3 park and gardens* *Castle entry closed Nov.–Mar.*

Museum van Deinze en de Leiestreek (MUDEL)

ART MUSEUM | The star of this museum is its collection of regional artworks from the late 19th and early 20th centuries, including two masterpieces: Emile Claus's *Beets Harvest* (1890), which fills

Taking pride of place in Deinze is Ooidonk Castle, a 16th-century Renaissance beauty.

an entire wall of the gallery, and Gustave Van de Woestyne's *The Wilful Blind and the Lame Who Wants to Teach a Child How to Walk*. It's probably the most rounded collection in the area, with works by the De Cocks, Servaes, De Smet, Raveel, and others scattering the walls. The second floor is given over to the city's industrial history and its heroes, such as 1926 Tour de France winner Lucien Buysse, but with little in the way of English translation. ✉ *Lucien Matthyslaan 3/5, Deinze* ☎ *09/381–9670* 🌐 *www.mudel.be* 🎫 *€6* 🕐 *Closed Mon.*

Restaurants

Grand Café Het Koetshuis Ooidonk

$$$ | **BELGIAN** | The setting is everything here. The beautiful terrace, on the doorstep of Ooidonk Castle, makes for a delightful retreat for the walkers, cyclists, and day-trippers that make up the clientele. **Known for:** brasserie-style comfort food in a countryside setting; it's a great spot for when you're visiting the castle; there are plenty of walking trails nearby to work off the food. $ *Average main: €24* ✉ *Ooidonkdreef 28, Deinze* ☎ *09/282–7313* 🌐 *www.hetkoetshuisooidonk.be* 🕐 *Closed Wed. and Thurs.*

Coffee and Quick Bites

'T Oud Sashuis

$ | **CAFÉ** | An enticing café-bar with a long history and, many say, the best setting on the Leie. It lies next to the old *sas* (a drawbridge over the lock), and this was where the bridge controller once lived. **Known for:** a welcome rest stop while walking the Leie; house-brewed beers; a blissful setting by the water's edge. $ *Average main: €8* ✉ *Hellestraat 20, Deinze* ☎ *0476/810–114.*

Dendermonde

53 km (33 miles) from Deinze.

When Belgians think of Dendermonde, their thoughts drift to the legend of the Bayard Steed, a saga that dates back o the Middle Ages. It has long since seeped into local culture, helped by a colorful, UNESCO-listed pageant of giant floats that has marauded through the streets here every decade for five centuries. It is known as the Ros Beiaardommegang and draws thousands to a city largely unused to visitors despite its beautiful beguinage and captivating abbey.

The legend goes that the Lord of Dendermonde had four sons with the sister of King Charlemagne. Each was presented a horse, only for the strongest son, Reinout, to kill his with a single blow. As punishment (or perhaps reward), he was given a fearsome beast that no other man could master: the bayard horse. He soon tamed it, but a quarrel with Charlemagne's son led to the king demanding the horse be destroyed. Fearing for his family, Reinout attempted to weigh it down and drown it in the river, only for the powerful animal to break his bonds and swim to him out of loyalty. But when Reinout turned his back, the brokenhearted beast finally let itself be drowned.

Owing to COVID, the tradition of hosting the festival every 10 years was broken recently, with the last one pushed to May 2022. Those lucky enough to see it will witness giant horse floats carried through town and fireworks lighting up the night sky. At any time, however, you can pick up a Bayard walking map from the tourist office and follow its traditional route. It will lead you through a likable, old, eccentric city that was mostly destroyed in World War I, only for it to be rebuilt in the 1920s, often in extravagant Flemish Renaissance style.

GETTING HERE AND AROUND

Dendermonde is well connected by rail to both Ghent (€5.50) and Brussels (€6.30), both journeys taking around 30 minutes. Once there, you can take bus No. 252 to reach the Baasrode Noord Station, from where the nearby steam train runs.

VISITOR INFORMATION

CONTACTS Dendermonde Tourism Office. ✉ *Stadhuis, Dendermonde* ☎ *052/213–956* 🌐 *www.toerismedendermonde.be.*

Sights

Bastion VIII

GARDEN | This small nature reserve on the western edge of town takes its name from the 11 bulwarks that used to reinforce the city defenses. This was where the eighth once stood, though only parts of the wall still survive here, with bats having taken up residence in the old gunpowder bunker. It makes for a pleasant stroll or picnic spot and is filled with beehives. ✉ *Begijnhoflaan 45, Dendermonde* ☎ *053/210–874* 🎫 *Free.*

Brusselse Forten

TRAIL | Up until the end of the 1800s, like most towns in Brussels, Dendermonde was still wrapped by ramparts and wide canals, a hangover from its days as an important position on the banks of the Scheldt and Dender. Their remains still scatter this pretty park alongside the water's edge, southwest of the center, where you'll find plenty of locals peacefully fishing. ✉ *Brusselse Forten, Dendermonde* 🎫 *Free.*

★ Sint-Alexius Begijnhof and Museum

HISTORIC SIGHT | The begijnhofs ("beguinages" in French) were home to religious-minded women who wanted a life of devotion to God without having to take the Orders (of fidelity and poverty) that nuns were beholden to. This UNESCO-listed begijnhof was originally formed in 1288, and in its 17th-century heyday was home to some 200 beguines. The last beguine here died in 1975, but you'll find an interesting **museum** spread across a pair of houses that covers the life of the beguines and local folklore. ✉ *Begijnhof 11–24–25, Dendermonde* ☎ *052/213–018 museum* 🎫 *Free* ⏲ *Museum closed Mon.*

Sint-Pieters en Paulus Abbey (*Abbey of Sts. Peter and Paul*)

CHURCH | This Benedictine abbey is just one of those remarkable sights you find in small Flemish cities like Dendermonde. The building is breathtaking, a vast rose redbrick, gabled facade in the Flemish neo-Renaissance style, interrupted only by the Gothic twin towers of the church. The interior may only be visited once a year, on Whit Monday (2–6 pm). You can, however, buy its tripel-style beer, which is made externally by Brewery de Block, at the Liturgisch Kunstapostolaat on Dijkstraat any time. ✉ *Vlasmarkt 23, Dendermonde* ☎ *052/338–780* 🌐 *www.abdijdendermonde.be* 🎫 *Free.*

Stadhuis and Belfort (*Town Hall and Belfry*)

HISTORIC SIGHT | Overlooking the Grotemarkt stands the Stadhuis (town hall) and belfry. It was built originally as a cloth hall in the 14th century. However, like the rest of the town, it was destroyed in World War I, the belfry having collapsed onto the market square below. Only the outer walls and a few paintings survived. It was restored in the 1920s, when a new 49-bell carillon was bought for the belfry, which has recently also opened to visitors. ✉ *Grotemarkt, Dendermonde* ☎ *052/213–956* 🌐 *www.toerismedendermonde.be* 🎫 *Free* 🕓 *Closed Mon.*

★ **Steamtrain Dendermonde–Puurs** (*Dendermonde Steam Train*)

TRAIN/TRAIN STATION | **FAMILY** | These charming heritage trains (both steam and diesel) only run in the summer, between July and September. The oldest (Cockerill 2643) dates back to 1907, though the steamers mostly come from the early 20th century. Its journey from Baasrode-Noord, a few miles east of Dendermonde, to the small village of Puurs takes you through countryside wrapped by the Scheldt. There is room for bicycles, so if you only want to travel one-way and cycle the 17 km (10½ miles) back alongside the river to Dendermonde, you can. For €200, you can even be the "stoker" of the train for a day and ride upfront. ✉ *Baasrode-Noord Station, Dendermonde* ☎ *052/330–223* 🌐 *www.stoomtrein.be* 🎫 *€9 return* 🕓 *Closed Oct.–June* Ⓜ *Bus: 245 or 252.*

Vleeshuis Museum

HISTORY MUSEUM | The city museum is set within the old butcher's hall, built in the mid-15th century. Over the years, this building has filled just about every function a city requires: cloth hall, aldermen's house, prison, guild hall, theater, guardroom. The current museum was installed in the early 1900s and begins its exhibits in prehistory, working its way up to the end of the ancien régime and France's collapse into revolution in the late 1700s. It's an enjoyable grab bag of history, with a 28,000-year-old mammoth skeleton among its most engaging exhibits. ✉ *Grote Markt 32, Dendermonde* ☎ *052/213–018* 🎫 *Free* 🕓 *Closed Mon.*

Restaurants

Bar Proef

$$ | **BRASSERIE** | Sometimes you're just in the mood for a solid bar-brasserie meal, and this well-loved spot on the corner of the Vlasmarkt is as good an option as any in the city. Inside, its publike interior has been decked out in hip but cozy sofas and long tables. **Known for:** the choice of drinks is vast; a nice spot to sit outside in the sun; the menu is as comfortable as an old sweater. 💲 *Average main: €22* ✉ *Vlasmarkt 45, Dendermonde* ☎ *052/526–244* 🌐 *barproef.be* 🕓 *Closed Tues. and Wed.*

Fleems

$$$$ | **BISTRO** | The hot new restaurant in town comes fresh from the success of its former pop-up (Heems) and has now settled on Brusselsestraat. It's a small, intimate joint with a great secluded terrace at the rear. **Known for:** a likeable terrace at the rear will be nice in summer; beer pairing is a brilliant alternative o the usual wine; talented chefs using heir full imagination. $ *Average main: €58* ✉ *Brusselsestraat 72, Dendermonde* ☎ *0468/248–509* 🌐 *fleems.be* 🕒 *Closed Mon.*

Kokarde

$$$ | **FRENCH** | Expect beautifully prepared dishes served in an elegant mansion house on the Grotemarkt. Everything about Kokarde screams good taste, especially the menu where dishes of cod and *ceps* (wild mushrooms) in truffle butter mingle with scallops and pork cheek. **Known for:** immaculate cooking in a well-placed restaurant; well-mannered, professional service; there's a nice terrace. $ *Average main: €24* ✉ *Grote Markt 9–10, Dendermonde* ☎ *052/520–580* 🌐 *www.kokarde.be* 🕒 *Closed Mon.*

Mirage

$$$ | **FRENCH** | Uncluttered dishes of classic French-Belgian favorites are the stock in trade of this elegant local restaurant. Their specialty is lobster (there's even a dedicated lobster tasting menu), but you'll find a wealth of interesting flavors here, from a dish of local pheasant, chestnut, and pear to wallet-busting Belgian caviar. **Known for:** it even has a homemade house gin; a great spot for a refined lunch or dinner; friendly staff and a quiet terrace. $ *Average main: €28* ✉ *Brusselsestraat 99, Dendermonde* ☎ *052/554–826* 🌐 *mirage-ma.be* 🕒 *Closed Tues. and Wed.*

Coffee and Quick Bites

Happy Days Cafe

$ | **CAFÉ** | This lovely family-run café is nestled in the corner of the Vlasmarkt. There's a good choice of teas, coffees, and great hunks of homemade cakes to tide you over. **Known for:** nice little terrace off the main street; good choice (and portion size) of cakes; well-made coffees. $ *Average main: €6* ✉ *Vlasmarkt 33/7, Dendermonde* ☎ *052/577–977* 🌐 *www.happydaysonline.be* 🕒 *Closed Sun. and Mon.*

Hotels

Cosy Cottage

$ | **B&B/INN** | **FAMILY** | If you don't mind staying a few miles outside town, this beautiful cottage with large private garden and pond makes for a compelling setting in the Flanders countryside, right on the banks of the Scheldt. **Pros:** the rural setting is just delightful; you can see the Scheldt from some bedrooms; there are oak beams in the suite. **Cons:** there isn't much to see nearby; the apartment requires a minimum two-night stay; you're around 6½ km (4 miles) from town. $ *Rooms from: €95* ✉ *Eegene 38, Dendermonde* ☎ *052/428–443* 🌐 *www.cosycottage.be* *3 rooms* *Free Breakfast.*

Dendernachten

$ | **B&B/INN** | There aren't many places to stay in Dendermonde, which makes this B&B on the banks of the Dender something of a precious rarity. **Pros:** you're pretty central for everything in town; there's a communal kitchen if you want to cook; everything is well-kept and clean. **Cons:** Dendermonde is more a day trip; parking is free but public; it's a B&B, so there aren't many facilities. $ *Rooms from: €95* ✉ *Franz Courtensstraat 15, Dendermonde* ☎ *0478/961–405* 🌐 *www.dendernachten.be* *3 rooms* *Free Breakfast.*

Nightlife

BARS

Den Ouden Tinnen Pot

BARS | An old local favorite. Its small terrace overlooks the Stadhuis, and inside it's just a nice, cozy pub, with a TV pumping out soccer in the evenings. It also has a choice of hundreds of different gins and jenevers. ✉ *Kerkstraat 9, Dendermonde.*

Steca

BARS | Another solid bar overlooking the Grotemarkt and with a rather slick interior. It opens early, closes late, and drinks are accompanied by a small sharing plate of popcorn, olives, and chips. Its selection of whiskies and local beers is also pretty good. ✉ *Grotemarkt 26, Dendermonde* ☎ *0495/310–099.*

Zeta

BARS | A charming little bar on the main street into town with a good choice of local beers, cocktails, and mostly South African wines. It also does a small (€17) lunch menu, which changes daily. Bar snacks are ambitious (think cod ceviche and pizza with figs) and there's a great terrace at the back. ✉ *Brusselsestraat 66, Dendermonde* ☎ *052/303–217* 🌐 *zeta-bar.be.*

MUSIC CLUBS

Honky Tonk Jazz Club

LIVE MUSIC | A local institution, this jazz club has been operating since 1962, with regular concerts in its vaulted basement of blues, roots, and jazz music. Everyone from Chuck Berry and Curtis Mayfield to Jerry Lee Lewis has played here, and inside you'll find a small museum about its history. ✉ *Leopoldlaan 12A, Dendermonde* ☎ *0475/699–416* 🌐 *www.honkytonk.be.*

Shopping

Dendermonde is not a great shopping city, but it is one of Belgium's oldest market towns and hosts a number of weekly markets. You'll also find a range of branded and local stores around Oude Vest, Vlasmarkt, and Brusselsestraat.

Flower Market

MARKET | The most colorful of all the city's markets is found on a Sunday morning as florists descend on Gedempte Dender (Kasteelstraat). ✉ *Kasteelstraat, Dendermonde.*

Weekly Market

MARKET | Every Monday between 8 am and 1 pm, the traffic-free center of the city plays host to around 150 stalls at one of the largest regular markets in Belgium. ✉ *Oude Vest, Dendermonde.*

Vlaamse Ardennen

The **Vlaamse Ardennen** (Flemish Ardennes) has little to do with its namesake, which lies around 100 km (62 miles) to the southeast. Roughly bound by the rivers Leie, Scheldt, Dender, and the southern border with Wallonia, it sits apart from the rest of Flanders—in every respect. It isn't wealthy, nor does it have a grand history. Yet for a hit of unfiltered, wild countryside, there's little else here to match it. Some fine medieval relics can also be found in its towns, including the "original" Manneken Pis (a whole other story).

GETTING HERE AND AROUND

The Vlaamse Ardennen is linked via its four main towns. Both Oudenaarde (€9.70) and Zottegem (€7.50) are on the Brussels-Kortrijk rail line. Trains take around 50 minutes and 35 minutes, respectively, from the capital. At Zottegem, you can change for a local train to Geraardsbergen (€3.10), while Oudenaarde connects Ronse (€2.90); both take an extra 15 minutes.

To travel anywhere else in the area, you'll need to either drive, take a bus, or just cycle. The region has a good network of local buses, though the rides are pretty bumpy in places. Cobbled roads may be pretty, but they aren't kind on your bottom. The same goes for driving. Outside of the national roads (N8, N42, N48, and N60) that link the big towns, it is quite slow going, but all the better to take in the scenery.

Oudenaarde

30 km (18 miles) from Kortrijk.

Like many Flemish river towns, Oudenaarde began life in the 11th century as a fortress built by the Count of Flanders to guard the Scheldt. It set the tone for the centuries that followed.

Frequently besieged during the late medieval period, the city was the site of two major battles. The first was in 1452, when Ghent, rebelling against the high taxes of their Burgundian rulers, laid siege to the city for over a year. The second saw one of the greatest defeats in French history when, in 1708, Louis XIV overreached himself in the War of Spanish Succession; some 6,000 soldiers died in just one day as Anglo-Dutch-Austrian forces seized the city, before retaking Bruges and Ghent from the French.

Yet the fighting did little to halt Oudenaarde's progress. By the 1500s it was in its pomp, having built a glowing reputation for its silversmithing and tapestry weaving. The town hall, a stately wonder in Brabantine Gothic, is testimony to its success and now holds an excellent museum on these crafts. But the good times were fleeting. Tapestries were made here as late as the 18th century, but the Reformation saw many of its weavers flee as the town sided with the Protestants. French competition and changing tastes eventually saw off the industry entirely as Oudenaarde fell from the spotlight by the early 1700s.

These days, the town is best known as the finishing point for the annual Tour of Flanders cycle race (known as "De Ronde"), a role it has held since 2012. The infamous Koppenberg, a thigh-sappingly steep cobbled street, marks the final ascent into town, and those interested should visit the cycling museum or pedal some of its famous Tour routes, which are a great way to see the area. But, unless you're an avid Tour fan, avoid visiting in early April when tens of thousands arrive to greet those crossing the finish line.

GETTING HERE AND AROUND

Oudenaarde is on the Kortrijk-Brussels SNCB rail line, with connections every hour from Kortrijk railway station (€5.90; 20 minutes). Trains also connect to Ghent (€6.70) and take just 30 minutes. The railway station is only a short five-minute walk from the city center.

The only direct transport link to nearby Geraardsbergen is via the Nos. 16/17 buses, which go from opposite the railway station. If driving, Oudenaarde can be reached via the N60 and N8 from Ghent and Kortrijk, respectively.

TOURS

Centrum de Ronde van Vlaanderen

BICYCLE TOURS | **FAMILY** | Based in the same building as the Tour of Flanders Museum, this center rents bikes, sells cycling maps and equipment, and offers guided tours of the surrounding Vlaamse Ardennen. It's a one-stop shop for anyone with Lycra in their veins. The **Peloton Cafe** is also a popular meet-up spot for cyclists of all stripes. ✉ *Markt 43, Oudenaarde* ☎ *055/339–933* 🌐 *crvv.be.*

 Sights

Liefmans Brewery

BREWERY | Lying just north of town, this brewery has an enviable heritage. Liefmans has been going since 1679, and its dark beers are a staple of local bars. Outside of Oudenaarde, it's perhaps best known for its commercial fruit beers. Visits must be booked online, but make sure you get a peek at the magnificent Baudelot hall no matter what. Several beers are made here, including the dark Oud Bruin, the Goudenband, and the very sweet Kriek (cherry) and Frambozen (raspberry) beers. ✉ *Aalststraat 200, Oudenaarde* ☎ *038/609–400* 🌐 *www.liefmans.com* 🎟 *€12* ⏲ *Closed Sun.* ✍ *Visit must be booked online.*

MOU – Museum Oudenaarde and the Flemish Ardennes

HISTORY MUSEUM | Oudenaarde's town hall is a dazzling expression of just how wealthy the city was by the 16th century. Even today it takes the breath away, and once prompted the novelist Victor Hugo to declare: "There is not a single detail [of it] that is not worth looking at." The main building is adjoined by the city's UNESCO-listed Brabantine-Gothic belfry, etched in elaborate hunting scenes and flocks of angels. Within, you'll find tourist information and the city museum (MOU), the centerpiece of which is a collection of tapestries hanging in the adjoining 14th-century cloth hall. These were Oudenaarde's golden ticket. By the 1500s, the fame of its artisans had spread across Europe and their work fetched high prices. Audio tours circumvent the Dutch info plaques, elaborating the secrets stitched within the hangings and what made them so prized. Less successful is the rather disparate silver collection, though some fine examples of curiosity cabinets and the strange objects coveted by the wealthy make it worth your perusal. ✉ *Markt 1, Oudenaarde* ☎ *055/317–251* 🌐 *www.mou-oudenaarde.be* 🎫 *€10* 🕒 *Closed Mon.*

Onze-Lieve-Vrouwekerk van Pamele
(*Church of Our Lady of Pamele*)

CHURCH | Built on the banks of the river from blue Tournai stone, the 13th-century Church of Our Lady of Pamele is a fine example of the Scheldt Gothic style. It lies across the river from the center in what was a separate town until the 1950s. To the rear of the church, you can see the tombs of the Lords of Oudenaarde, though these have been badly damaged. Entrance is only on weekends, but even if you can't venture inside, it's worth visiting as part of a stroll along the historic riverfront. To the north lies the stately **Huis de Lailing**, a 15th-century mansion that used to hold the town's tapestry collection until it was moved to the MOU. Further south is the rose-colored **Maagdendale Abbey**, founded in 1233 and now a school for the arts. ✉ *Pamelekerkplein, Oudenaarde* 🎫 *Free* 🕒 *Closed weekdays.*

PAM – Provincial Archeological Museum

MUSEUM VILLAGE | **FAMILY** | Based in the adjoining village of Ename (a 10-minute bus ride from the center), this interactive museum narrates the last 1,000 years of history in the region. Its sites sprawl a village that once stood on the border between medieval France and Germany. Visits include the open-air museum of the archaeological park, where you'll find the first stone inklings of a Benedictine abbey and the foundations of the old city that once stood here. ✉ *Ename Heritage Centre, Lijnwaadmarkt 20, Oudenaarde* ☎ *055/309–040* 🌐 *www.pam-ov.be* 🎫 *€7* 🕒 *Closed Mon.* Ⓜ *Bus: 41.*

★ **Tour of Flanders Museum**

HISTORY MUSEUM | Cycling is everything in this part of Flanders. It's here that the famous Tour of Flanders (known as "De Ronde") culminates, and the city even has its own museum dedicated to the race. Regardless of whether you get shivers at the sight Eddie Mercx's racing glove or care little about the sport, it draws you in nicely. Audio guides explain what you're seeing; there's even a virtual cycling machine to give you a taste of the Tour. It's not just about the race, either, and gives an interesting overview of the Flemish Ardennes, whose hills, history, and isolation made it the perfect playground for the Tour organizers. At the ticket desk, you can also organize bike hire and cycling tours of the area. ✉ *Centrum Ronde van Vlaanderen, Markt 43, Oudenaarde* ☎ *055/339–933* 🌐 *crvv.be* 🎫 *€12.*

Restaurants

La Pomme D'or

$$$ | **BRASSERIE** | This historic building, opposite the town hall, makes for a winning impression. It has also recently ıken on new owners, who understand ıe beauty in classic Flemish cooking hink: *americain*, eel in green sauce, and ɔ on) alongside some simple sharing lates. **Known for:** great views over the quare; there are few better locations; a efined brasserie menu worth exploring. *Average main: €27* ✉ *Markt 62, Oudenaarde* ☎ *055/311–900* 🌐 *www.pommedor.be* 🕓 *Closed Tues. and Wed.*

largaretha's

$$$ | BELGIAN | You enter Margaretha's ırough one of the oldest buildings still tanding in Oudenaarde, a Romanesque atrician tower built in the 12th centuy. It has a rich past: this was once an mshouse, then a school, and it takes its ame from Margarita de Palma, Charles 's illegitimate daughter who went on ɔ rule the Netherlands and was said to ave lived here at one point. **Known for:** cultured menu with plenty of delights; ne service is top rate; a historic setting ɔr a fine meal. *Average main: €32* ✉ *Markt 40, Oudenaarde* ☎ *055/311–001* 🌐 *www.margarethas.com* 🕓 *Closed Tues. and Wed.*

Coffee and Quick Bites

OEF Oudenaarde

$ | CAFÉ | Perched over the road from ne river, this waterfront café-restaurant s a popular brunch spot, dishing up varm soups, casseroles, and plenty of reakfast treats, from *shakshouka* to almon brioche. Even its coffees are on he indulgent side: latte with honey and *stroopwaffel*, anyone? **Known for:** nice views over the river and across to the ıistorical buildings; a good lunch spot vith some hearty eating; friendly staff. *Average main: €16* ✉ *Tussenbruggen 20, Oudenaarde* ☎ *055/603–952* 🌐 *www-boef-oudenaarde-be* 🕓 *Closed Sun. and Mon.*

Hotels

★ Jezuietenplein 21

$$ | B&B/INN | This 18th-century manor house makes charming use of its setting, with an elegantly finished interior and delightful terrace and garden. **Pros:** a regal stay in beautifully converted old mansion house; useful central location not far from the main square; outside space and terrace area perfect for summer evenings. **Cons:** it's one of the pricier stays in town; the design can err on the minimalist side; there aren't many rooms, so it fills up fast. *Rooms from: €121* ✉ *Jezuïetenplein 21, Oudenaarde* ☎ *055/603–779* 🌐 *j21.be* *6 rooms* *No Meals.*

Leopold Hotel

$$ | HOTEL | A tidy, elegant boutique stay in the center of the city. **Pros:** bar terrace to while away the evening; friendly, helpful staff; easy location in the city center. **Cons:** quiet efficiency is rarely a sexy quality; there aren't many facilities—just the basics; it can be noisy outside. *Rooms from: €111* ✉ *De Ham 14, Oudenaarde* ☎ *055/699–965* 🌐 *gb.leopoldhoteloudenaarde.com* *66 rooms* *Free Breakfast.*

Nightlife

De Carillon

BARS | Look for the "Special Oudenaardes" sign out front. This is one of the oldest bars in the city and also among the more unusual. The building's gabled exterior comprises two 17th-century brick houses that were once part of a much larger terrace. That they survived at all, having weathered various wars, is miraculous. Inside, it's a typical Belgian brown bar, with an excellent beer selection and a lively atmosphere. In summer, the terrace fills up fast. ✉ *Markt 49, Oudenaarde* ☎ *055/311–409* 🌐 *www.decarillon.be.*

Wijnbar Markt 30
WINE BARS | Perched on the eastern edge of the town square, this decidedly bijou escape has the look and air of a modern gentleman's club, while the terrace outside gazes over to the stately town hall. A decent wine and tapas menu accompanies some fine people-watching. ✉ *Markt 30, Oudenaarde* ☎ *0479/746–381* 🌐 *markt30.be.*

Geraardsbergen

24 km (15 miles) from Oudenaarde.

Found deep in the Vlaamse Ardennen, Geraardsbergen is a hilly town that delights in its eccentricities. It even claims to have the oldest Manneken Pis, a statue famously associated with Brussels. A replica stands outside the town hall, but inside you'll see the original, dating from 1459. There is a rivalry between the two cities as to whose is older, though this version predates the capital's surviving statue by nearly 200 years.

The city is also home to one of the most famous, and punishing, sections of the Tour of Flanders cycle race. The Muur, or "Wall," is a 3,526-foot climb up the energy-sapping Oudenburg Hill. There was outrage when it was banished from the tour in 2012, only to be reinstated five years later. Those attempting it now would do well to grab one of the city's iconic *mattentaarts* first, which adorn every bakery window. This sweet pastry wraps a dry, eggy, curd-cheese filling, and it is something of a mouthful. You'll need to cycle the Muur just to burn off the calories.

It's worth arriving in early spring when the UNESCO-listed festival of Krakelingen and Tonnekensbrand marks the end of winter. This features a feast and a thousand-strong parade, which climbs to the chapel on Oudenberg Hill where 10,000 *krakelingen* (Dutch-style pretzels) are hurled into the crowd. At night, locals return to the hill to light a wooden barrel (*tonnekensbrand*), then march back down, lit by fiery torches, to symbolize spring's rebirth.

GETTING HERE AND AROUND

Geraardsbergen is only connected by train via Zottegem (€3.10), which is on the Kortryk-Brussels line. Buses connect the city to the rest of the region, with regular direct services (No. 16/17) running to Oudenaarde. If driving, the town is reached via the N42; this connects with the N8, which runs between Brussels, Oudenaarde, and Kortrijk.

VISITOR INFORMATION

The information office on the market square is a great spot to pick up walking and cycling tour maps of the area. These are free, and there are around three different routes for each, including a 42-km (26-mile) pedal through the Vlaamse Ardennen. It's a great way to explore the region and visit some of the famous cycling cafés that are found here. Bikes can be rented from most hotels and B&Bs.

CONTACTS Tourist Information. ✉ *Infokantoor Visit Geraardsbergen, Markt, Geraardsbergen* ☎ *054/437–289.*

Sights

Grote Markt (*Town Square*)
HISTORIC SIGHT | The dominant building on the market square is the Stadhuis (Town Hall), a fairy-tale-like medieval aldermen house. Its turrets once ran to street level but various sieges and fires have taken their toll. It has been frequently redesigned, but gained its current neo-Gothic facade in 1891. The architect drew inspiration from a 17th-century engraving of the building and sought to give it back its medieval charm, sapped by endless renovations. Beside it you'll find a pair of replica fountains: the Mannekin Pis and the Marbol, the original of which dates back to 1392. ✉ *Markt 51, Geraardsbergen.*

lanneken Pis

IONUMENT | Everyone knows the Maneken Pis. It's Brussels's famous peeing herub, or is it? The modern version tanding in the capital is actually a replica f a statue made by Jérôme Duquesnoy ı 1619 to replace the original 15th-centuy fountain (then known as "Petit Julian") ıade in 1450. Around the same time, ı 1452, Geraardsbergen was in the rocess of being destroyed by Ghentish orces. In rebuilding the city, they ordered new *lattoenen mannekin* ("man in rass") from the Brussels fountain maser Jan Van Der Schelden. By 1459, the eeing putto (cherub) was in place, and vhile a replica now stands in the square, he original can still be seen in a new isitor center beside the town hall. So, vhile Brussels's statue was made first, it s long since gone, and Geraardsbergen's s the older surviving example. If you rrive on the first Sunday of June, it gets ven more curious, with the traditional throwing" of a golden Manneken Pis rom the steps of the Town Hall. And t gets stranger still: inside the visitor enter, you can also see a selection of 00 special outfits gifted to the statue. ☒ *Infokantoor Visit Geraardsbergen, Markt, Geraardsbergen* ☎ *054/437–289* 🌐 *www.visitgeraardsbergen.be* 🎫 *Free.*

Muur van Geraardsbergen (*Wall of Geraardsbergen*)

RAIL | A popular local joke goes that here are only three famous walls: Berlin's, China's, and Geraardsbergen's. The Muur (or "Wall") is a cobbled street hat runs up Vesten, Oudenbergstraat, nd Kapelmuur, culminating at a pretty eo-Baroque chapel on the summit of Oudenberg Hill. It is here where the nnual Karakelingen and Tonnekensbrand rocessions center each year in spring. The actual hill is only 360 feet high, but he steep cobbles are infamous among yclists, and it is a regular section in the Tour of Flanders. The walk up is less than a mile, but it isn't too punishing. It takes around 25 minutes from the river and is worth it for the views. ☒ *Kapelmuur, Geraardsbergen* 🎫 *Free.*

Sint-Batholomeuskerk (*St Bartholemew's Church*)

CHURCH | Much of the current church building was built in the 15th and 16th centuries. By the mid-1700s, though, it had received a Baroque makeover, with its impressive pulpit one of few surviving items from that era. Come the 19th century, the church acquired its current neo-Gothic interior and spectacular murals. Most prized of all are the relics of St. Bartholemew, which were moved here in 1515. Since then, a procession has taken place on the Sunday around his saint's day (August 24), where the relics are carried from the church and paraded around the city, followed by a folk festival on the main square. ☒ *Markt 51, Geraardsbergen* ☎ *054/437–289* 🎫 *Free.*

Restaurants

Bistro Andre

$$$ | BISTRO | This charming redbrick eatery on the corner of Collegestraat rings all the right bells. There is nothing too adventurous here; French and Flemish crowd-pleasers are the order of the day, from cordon bleu and stoofvlees to fillet of *Mechelse koekoek* (a local breed of chicken from Mechelen). **Known for:** gigantic portions; classic Belgian cooking; a friendly local welcome. $ *Average main: €24* ☒ *Wijngaardstraat 38, Geraardsbergen* ☎ *054/415–083* 🌐 *www.bistroandre.be* 🕒 *Closed Tues. and Wed.*

★ **T'Grof Zout**

$$$$ | EUROPEAN | A seasoned performer. This classy restaurant, run by owners Marniek and Christine, has been dishing up imaginative takes on classic bistro dishes since 1999. **Known for:** modern takes on classic dishes; a quiet little oasis within the town; good cooking and a friendly welcome. $ *Average main: €45* ☒ *Gasthuisstraat 20, Geraardsbergen* ☎ *054/423–546* 🌐 *www.grofzout.be*

⏲ *Closed Mon. and Tues. No dinner Sun. No lunch Sat.*

Coffee and Quick Bites

Bakkerij De Vesten

$ | **DESSERTS** | You'll find an absolute sea of bakeries selling mattentaarts, the iconic local curd pastry that errs decidedly on the sweet and dry side. Everyone has their favorite bakery, though the more mean-spirited might argue there's little difference in quality. **Known for:** the finest mattentaarts in town; there's a nice selection of other cakes; friendly staff. [$] *Average main: €2* ✉ *Vesten 92, Geraardsbergen* ☏ *054/412–313* 🌐 *www.bakkerijdevesten.be* ⏲ *Closed Mon. and Tues.*

Bar Gidon

$$ | **CAFÉ** | This café-bar on the market square is popular among cyclists, as any glance at its walls—festooned in photos, jerseys, and memorabilia from the Tour of Flanders—will tell you. Owned by a former professional rider, Frederik Penne, it's a good spot to grab a coffee, a beer, or a few ideas for places to pedal in the area. **Known for:** a noisy spot to watch any cycling race; good beer selection; great atmosphere and decor. [$] *Average main: €8* ✉ *Markt 11, Geraardsbergen* ☏ *047/591–602.*

Hotels

Casa Dodo

$ | **B&B/INN** | This small B&B with just three guests rooms and a studio is instantly recognizable from the street thanks to its bright, colorful exterior; things are more subtly finished on the inside, while the studio comes with a small balcony and modern kitchen. **Pros:** bike hire (€10 per day) is available; well located and friendly; wine and gin tastings can be arranged. **Cons:** not many facilities; the town is pretty quiet at night; there's not a lot to do in the area. [$] *Rooms from: €80* ✉ *Nieuwstraat 12, Geraardsbergen* ☏ *0471/332–242* 🌐 *www.casadodo.be* *4 rooms* *Free Breakfast.*

★ **Hotel Grupello**

$$ | **HOTEL** | If you're walking up from the station into town, you can't miss Grupello. **Pros:** handy location between town and station; great brasserie with a good selection of local beers; an elegant Art Deco stay. **Cons:** there are few alternatives in town; there's a road outside; rooms over the brasserie can be noisier (try and get one facing the inner courtyard). [$] *Rooms from: €120* ✉ *Gustaaf Verhaeghelaan 17, Geraardsbergen* ☏ *054/416–007* *11 rooms* *Free Breakfast.*

Kortrijk

50 km (31 miles) from Geraardsbergen.

While Kortrijk (spelled "Courtrai" in French) lacks the medieval hustle of Bruges or Ghent, it does have Flemish history on its side. Just outside the city lies the site of the Battle of the Golden Spurs where, in 1302, townspeople from across Flanders banded together to defeat a troop of French knights sent by King Philip IV. There's no story guaranteed to raise more of a smile in Flanders.

The city's fortunes once revolved around the flax industry, grown and processed here to make linen and lace famed across Europe. However, postwar rebuilding and the economic fallout from Kortrijk's faltering trade saw the city flounder in the late 20th century. Only in recent decades has it picked itself up. The riverside area has also been transformed, there's fine dining, a historic brewery, magnificent churches, and a museum on flax that is far more entertaining than it has any right to be.

ETTING HERE AND AROUND

traveling by car, Kortrijk is reached via e E17 from Ghent. Regular train servic-s also link to Ghent via the Leiestreek illages, taking 30 minutes from St ieters Station. If traveling from Brussels, ains connect to Kortrijk via Oudenaarde just over one hour.

 Sights

Begijnhof van Kortrijk (*Kortrijk Beguinage*)

ISTORIC HOME | Kortrijk's 13th-century eguinage ("begijnhof" in Dutch) was ome to a religious group of women nown as "beguines" who weren't ound by the Orders of nuns. Although hey were cloistered away, many had to arn their stay in the community through eaching and handicrafts, and the story f the beguinage runs alongside that of e city. It was plundered by the French, long with the rest of Kortrijk, in the ftermath of the 1382 Battle of Westro-ebeke, and later repurposed as a field ospital when Europe descended into crimony at the end of the 18th century. t was even taken out of the hands of he beguines for a period, when inns and rothels moved in, much to the distaste f the Grand Mistress. By 2013, the final eguine in Belgium had died and an era nded. Only recently has the 35-year-long roject to restore the cluster of white-vashed town houses and chapel that nakes up the beguinage been complet-d, and it remains perhaps the finest xample of its kind in Belgium. Visits are ree; there is a new museum in the St. Anna room but this is largely in Dutch, o audio guides (€2) are well worth the mall outlay. *Begijnhofstraat 2, Kortrijk www.toerismekortrijk.be Free (€2 for audio guide).*

Buda Island

SLAND | Central to the recent revival of he city has been its renovation of the iverfront and Buda Island. This small coop of land, between two branching arms of the Leie, is typically reached by Broel Bridge, guarded at either end by 14th-century **twin towers** built to control traffic on the Leie. They were part of the original city fortifications, but can only be entered with a guide these days. On the banks on either side of the river runs a stepped pedestrian and terrace area. Just a few years ago this was a miserable car park; now, it is the most popular part of the city in summer, when a beach (May–September) is created and the bars open long into the evening. The island itself has been colonized by arts studios, and while there is little here for tourists, the vibe is rather hipper than it used to be. Wander its bridge and you will find the beautiful courtyard of the Hospital of Our Lady. Its monumental gate was erected in 1658, but it dates back to the early 13th century when it was built to provide a night's stay for vagrants outside the city gates. *Buda Island, Kortrijk Free.*

Grote Markt (*Town Square*)

GOVERNMENT BUILDING | The centerpiece of the city is the market square, in the middle of which stands its UNESCO-listed belfry. First mentioned in 1248, it was originally part of the old cloth hall that stood here but the surrounding buildings have long since been demolished. Statues of the folk figures of Manten and Kalle, a couple said to symbolize fidelity, strike the bell on the hour. But in 1382, the original Manten was stolen by the Burgundian armies of Philip the Bold and given to Dijon. Replacements were added over the years. Across from the belfry lies the magnificent Stadhuis (City Hall), built in the Gothic-Renaissance transition style in 1520. Visitors can enter for free in the summer between 2 and 5; at any other time, you can only see its richly decorated alderman's hall, council hall, and art collection with a guide. *Grotemarkt, Kortrijk (056)/277–840 tourism office Free City hall opens July and Aug.*

The Begijnhof van Kortrijk in the city of Kortrijk dates back to the 13th-century—a restoration project was recently completed.

Omer Vander Ghinste Brewery

BREWERY | Based in the small town of Bellegem, a few miles south of Kortrijk, this historic brewery is best known for its traditional blond beer, which is found in most Belgian bars. Do, however, seek out its "Vanderghinste Roodbruin" brew, a slightly sour dark lambic blend that replicates the original beer made in 1892 by founder Omer Vander Ghinste, which he sold around Bellegem in a horse and cart. Tours last two hours and finish with a tasting. ✉ *Brouwtorenstraat 5, Bellegem* ✣ *7 km (4½ miles) south of Kortrijk* ☎ *056/277–840* 🌐 *www.omervanderghinste.be* 🎟 *€12* ✍ *Booking in advance is required* Ⓜ *Bus: 12, 16.*

Onze-Lieve-Vrouwe Kerk (*Church of Our Lady*)

CHURCH | The 13th-century Church of Our Lady is arguably the grander of the two city center churches, though little remains of the original facade after the church was largely destroyed and rebuilt after the Battle of Westrozebeke in 1382. A 14th-century addition, in the form of the Count's Chapel, was built as a personal mausoleum for Count Lodewijk van Male; it, too, was heavily bombarded during World War II but has been well restored. A number of fine artworks hang here and in the church, including the *Erection of the Cross* by Flemish master Anthony Van Dyck. Famously, this is where the looted 500 gilded spurs, taken from the defeated French knights in the 1302 Battle of the Golden Spurs, were hung afterwards; these were likely later taken away by the French but were replaced in 1952 by replicas that still hang here. At the time of writing, a new augmented-reality exhibition was to be launched in the summer of 2022, where visitors can learn of the history of the battle while touring the church. Nearby, you'll also find the Artillery Tower, which was part of the original 14th-century fortifications. ✉ *Deken Zegerplein 1, Kortrijk* 🎟 *Free.*

'int-Maartenskerk (*St. Martin's Church*)
HURCH | Like many of the early medieval hurches, St. Martin's has been rebuilt nd renovated numerous times since it vas first constructed in the 12th century. mong its large collection of medieval rt, the crown jewels are the 16th-century altarpiece *Triptych of the Holy Spirit* y Kortrijk-born Bernard de Rijckere and magnificent 6.5-meter-high tabernacle ower with some fine reliefs. A free rochure explains many of the artworks. 'ou can also climb its 246-step tower for weeping views of the city; tickets for his are free but you'll need to scan the QR code at the gate to download them. *Jozef Vandaleplein, Kortrijk* *Free.*

★ **Texture Museum**
HISTORY MUSEUM | Flanders's damp conditions were perfect for growing flax, crop used to make food, oil, and fibers, particularly linen. It might seem an uninspiring subject, but the crop is so woven nto the history of Kortrijk that visits to Texture are surprisingly fascinating. The lax grown in the area had a lighter color, gaining the Leie the nickname the "Golden River." When processed in its waters, lax was even thought to gain unique properties, such was the quality of the inen produced. In reality, it was just generations of local knowledge that made ts cloth so fine. By the 15th century, Flanders was the epicenter of the linen ndustry, and Kortrijk its jewel, especially amed for its damask. The city's fortunes ebbed and flowed with the industry, taking a hit in the 19th century, as industrial cotton and linen flooded the market; post World War II, it would collapse entirely. The museum explores this journey, from the multitude of uses for the crop (even the U.S. dollar bill is made of 25% flax) to ts complicated history, with no shortage of style. *Noordstraat 28, Kortrijk* *056/277–470* *www.texturekortrijk.be* *€6* *Closed Mon.*

Restaurants

De 7 Zonden
$$ | ITALIAN | This place is well hidden from the street, as you enter what is seemingly a mall. But that quickly gives way to a whimsical open-air terrace and a rather cozily lit bar-restaurant. **Known for:** surprisingly excellent value, with most dishes less than €20; wonderfully discreet location; good Italian and Flemish comfort food. *Average main: €19* *Leiestraat 22, Kortrijk* *056/280–905* *www.d7z.be* *Closed weekends.*

★ **Rebelle**
$$$$ | EUROPEAN | The only downside to Rebelle is that it's not exactly convenient. It lies a few miles outside the city center, in the small village of Marke, but it's more than worth the effort to get there. **Known for:** friendly, knowledgeable service; creative cooking in a slick setting; its three-course menu is decent value at €45. *Average main: €45* *Rekkemsestraat 226, Kortrijk* *056/219–450* *restaurantrebelle.be* *Closed Sun. and Mon.*

Table d'Amis
$$$$ | FRENCH | When Table D'Amis closed in 2018, art historian-turned-chef Matthieu Beudaert handed in Kortrijk's only Michelin star and decided to go back to basics: gastronomic food at a decent price. It has recently reopened and is no less inspired, with dishes such as breaded veal sweetbreads smoked on a tobacco leaf hinting at the daring below the surface. **Known for:** a menu full of surprises; wonderfully creative cooking; informal fine dining. *Average main: €34* *Sint-Maartenskerkhof 8, Kortrijk* *0480/610–718* *www.tabledamis.be* *Closed Sun. and Mon. No lunch Tues.*

Va et Vient
$$$$ | EUROPEAN | Chef Matthias Speybrouck got his start working under mercurial Belgian chef Kobe Desramaults, and he learned well. His modern riverside

restaurant has a rather industrial vibe, but it fits the "rough and refined" ethos of the menu, where he digs deep into local produce to create some surprising combinations. **Known for:** nice terrace in summer; great setting along the Leie riverbank; decent-value set menus at €45. *$ Average main: €45 ✉ Handboogstraat 20, Kortrijk ☎ 056/204–517 🌐 vaetvient.be ⏲ Closed Sun. and Mon.*

Coffee and Quick Bites

De Trog

$$ | CAFÉ | A beautiful old mansion house is the home of this charming organic bakery and café. Its courtyard terrace is a pleasant spot on a sunny day, though the menu is typically geared towards cold weather: think heavy pastas and Flemish staples alongside a few salads. **Known for:** sweet treats like pain d'epice; the terrace is delightful; interesting daily specials. *$ Average main: €16 ✉ Plein 12, Kortrijk ☎ 056/202–018 🌐 detrog.be ⏲ Closed Sun. and Wed.*

Hotels

Hotel Damier

$$ | HOTEL | The location of this regal city-center stay, right across from the belfry, takes in some of the more cherished real estate in Kortrijk. **Pros:** it has a small number of free bikes to lend guests; an elegant city-center setting; the brasserie is well worth trying. **Cons:** parking isn't free; it lacks the facilities of a big hotel; the chiming of the belfry can be annoying. *$ Rooms from: €144 ✉ Grote Markt 41, Kortrijk ☎ 056/221–547 🌐 www.hoteldamier.be 🛏 65 rooms 🍴 Free Breakfast.*

★ **Hotel Messeyne**

$$ | HOTEL | Nestled amid the elegant town houses of Groeningestraat is arguably the most stylish retreat in town. **Pros:** free parking and a quiet location; free wellness center; sunny terrace on which to relax. **Cons:** the fitness room is quite small; the restaurant is quite pricey; no pool facilities. *$ Rooms from: €132 ✉ Groeningestraat 17, Kortrijk ☎ 056/212-166 🌐 www.hotelmesseyne.be 🛏 28 rooms 🍴 Free Breakfast.*

Parkhotel Kortrijk

$$ | HOTEL | FAMILY | This rather plush stay by the railway station has the air of a luxury business hotel. **Pros:** large car park beneath the hotel; nice pool and gym; infrared and salt saunas are always a plus. **Cons:** the breakfast bar is pretty cramped; it's a 10-minute walk to the city center; you can hear the soft rumble of trains in the nearby station. *$ Rooms from: €122 ✉ Stationsplein 2, Kortrijk ☎ 056/220–303 🌐 www.parkhotel.be 🛏 155 rooms 🍴 Free Breakfast.*

Nightlife

Ernest

WINE BARS | A cozy, candlelit wine bar in the center of the city, right on the Grote Markt. Inside, it's rather dinky but the terrace cheerfully spills onto the pavement outside. A good selection of French wines. *✉ Grote Markt 47, Kortrijk ☎ 0491/235–600 🌐 ernestkortrijk.be.*

'T Fonteintje

BARS | One of the oldest bars in Kortrijk sits on the banks of the Leie. The city has changed around it, and what was once a typical Belgian "brown bar" (its pale walls stained by years of tobacco smoke) in a run-down area is now one of the hipper locations on the riverfront for a beer. It has a nice terrace in summer. *✉ Handboogstraat 12, Kortrijk ☎ 056/449–160.*

Chapter 6

BRUGES AND THE COAST

Updated by
Tim Skelton

Sights
★★★★★

Restaurants
★★★★★

Hotels
★★★★★

Shopping
★★★☆☆

Nightlife
★★★☆☆

WELCOME TO BRUGES AND THE COAST

TOP REASONS TO GO

★ **Walk back in time.** Bruges's strict planning laws mean there are few new buildings to spoil the illusion that you've waltzed back to another age.

★ **Float on by.** The canals cutting though the center of Bruges are among the most beautiful anywhere. Take a boat trip and explore them at a pace that befits their grandeur.

★ **A land in miniature.** If you're looking to experience every Belgian cliché in one tidy package, Bruges is the place to find it: chocolate, lace, waffles, fries, beer, and Flemish stepped gables. All within steps of one another.

★ **Sand between your toes.** Belgium may only have 68 km (42 miles) of coastline, but what there is consists almost exclusively of sandy beach.

★ **Honor the fallen.** The fields of Flanders witnessed untold destruction in World War I, and Ypres's memorials serve as poignant reminders—the daily Last Post ceremony at Menin Gate is an unmissable experience.

1 **Bruges.** Belgium's best-preserved medieval city is awash with jaw-dropping architecture, stunning art and history museums, and award-winning restaurants.

2 **Damme.** This quaint little hamlet is a place where time seems to have stood still, and in summer it can be reached by boat from Bruges.

3 **Knokke-Heist.** Belgium's premier beach resort is a bustling place that is technically five towns in one.

4 **De Haan.** This quiet upmarket resort has a great beach and is filled with elegant villas from another age.

5 **Oostende.** Once a major seaport, this lively town has a thriving nightlife and long a stretch of golden beach.

6 **Koksijde.** Flanked by high dunes, this beach resort also boasts an important art gallery and the remains of a 12th-century abbey.

7 **Ypres.** Completely destroyed in World War I, this charming town has risen from the ashes, and is now home to several important memorials commemorating a dark time in European history.

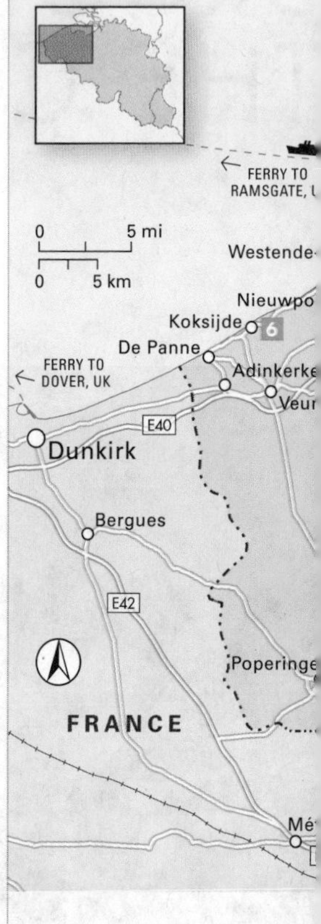

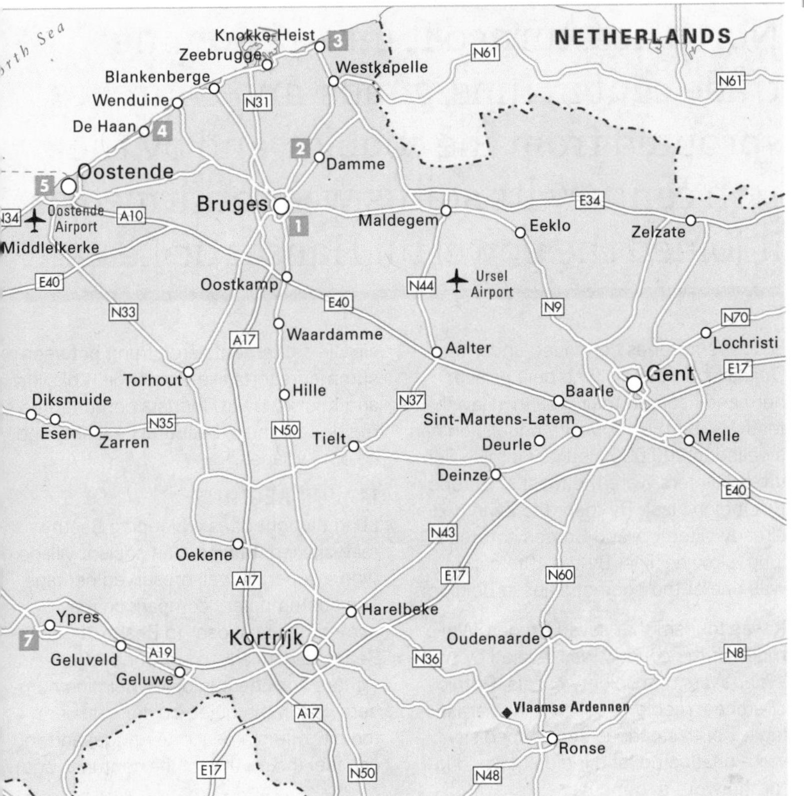
NETHERLANDS
Knokke-Heist
Zeebrugge
Blankenberge
Wenduine
De Haan
Westkapelle
Damme
Oostende
Oostende Airport
Middlelkerke
Bruges
Maldegem
Eeklo
Zelzate
Oostkamp
Ursel Airport
Waardamme
Aalter
Lochristi
Gent
Torhout
Diksmuide
Esen
Zarren
Hille
Baarle
Sint-Martens-Latem
Tielt
Deurle
Melle
Deinze
Oekene
Harelbeke
Ypres
Geluveld
Geluwe
Kortrijk
Oudenaarde
Vlaamse Ardennen
Ronse
N61
N31
E34
A10
E40
N44
N33
N9
N70
A17
E17
N37
N35
N50
N43
N60
A19
N36
N8
N48
1
2
3
4
5
7

In the late Middle Ages, Bruges was one of the richest cities in Europe. The River Zwin, a shallow inlet of the North Sea, turned it into a booming trade center. Inns, guilds, and churches sprouted from the cobbles, and by the 14th century its status was confirmed as it joined the powerful Hanseatic League.

Bruges's fortunes continued under the Dukes of Burgundy, who built palaces here and flaunted their wealth in lavish festivals. By the 1500s, its population had swelled to 200,000, and its Flemish Primitives painters were the toast of Europe. But it didn't last. By then, the Zwin had already silted up, and Bruges entered a long, slow decline. By the 19th century it was one of the poorest cities in Belgium.

It was tourism that saved Bruges. While much of the country was leveled by two World Wars, the spidery canals, Gothic churches, medieval cobbles, and artistic legacy of this curious egg-shaped city were unaffected, and it didn't take long for the word to get out.

In truth, though, little changes and little original is built. New shops and hotels open in old locations, and it's a city both liberated and constricted by its tourist appeal. To love Bruges, you need to accept it for what it is and just be grateful that it exists.

A few miles north of Bruges, the cold North Sea also wrote the history of Flanders's wealth and politics, linking its ports, protecting its people, and providing crucial natural resources. Today, the coast is irresistible to invaders of a more peaceful kind. Along the shoreline, simple settlements are strung between summer resorts like Oostende, Koksijde, and Knokke-Heist. Tourists come for the region's fresh air, beautiful beaches, and colorful villages.

MAJOR REGIONS

Long thought of as a Sleeping Beauty reawakened, **Bruges** is an ancient village with a superbly well-preserved heritage. The contemporary comparison may sometimes be closer to Beauty and the Beast, particularly in summer, when visitors flock here in overwhelming numbers, but in the quiet, colder seasons, the city offers a peaceful refuge, and you can feel the rhythm of life centuries ago.

To the north of Bruges, the **Belgian Coast** consists of an almost unbroken stretch of sand stretching all the way from the French to the Dutch border. Resort towns such as Knokke-Heist, De Haan, Oostende, and Koksijde are packed on summer days when the water warms.

Inland from the coast, brave little **Ypres** was the epicenter of several key battles in World War I. It had to be rebuilt from rubble following the Armistice in 1918, and the many memorials to those terrible events remain deeply moving more than a century later.

Planning

Getting Here and Around

AIR

Oostende-Brugge airport is in Oostende, 28 km (17 miles) west of Bruges, but almost all flights are designed to fly Belgian tourists to Mediterranean sunshine destinations. The vast majority of international visitors arriving by air will travel through Brussels Airport, some 105 km (65 miles) to the east. There are regular direct train services from the airport to Bruges, taking around 1 hour, 30 minutes.

BIKE

Considering the flat-as-a-pancake terrain, it's easy to travel on two wheels. You can rent bikes at rental shops or at the train station. Rates start from around €6 for a three-hour rental, €12 for a full day. At Bruges Bike Rental, e-bikes, tandems, and bikes with buggies to pull little ones are available. Rentals start at €4 for an hour.

CONTACTS Bruges Bike Rental. ✉ *Niklaas Desparsstraat 17* ☎ *050/616–108* 🌐 *www.brugesbikerental.be.*

BOAT

The canals (*reien*) in the center of Bruges make for lovely sightseeing, even if the city still can't seem to convince its cabal of boat operators to allow kayaking or canoeing in the canals. Independent motor launches depart from five jetties along the Dijver and Katelijnestraat and by the Vismarkt as soon as they are reasonably full (every 15 minutes or so) daily from March through November (10–6) and at other times, depending on the weather, at the boat operators' discretion. The trips last half an hour and cost €12.

In summer, the *Lamme Goedzak* plies the canal between Bruges and Damme, taking 35 minutes to complete the journey, and traveling four times daily in each direction. Tickets cost €10 one-way, €15 for a round-trip.

CONTACTS Boottochten Brugge. ✉ *Nieuwstraat 11* ☎ *05/033–293* 🌐 *www.boottochten-brugge.be.* **Lamme Goedzak.** ✉ *Damse Vaart Zuid 12, Damme* ☎ *0485/036–695* 🌐 *www.visitdamme.be/lammegoedzak.*

BUS

The De Lijn bus company provides bus and tram services throughout Flanders, including a network of lines that connect Bruges railway station with the old center every few minutes. Tickets costing €2 for one hour, multiride tickets (€16 for 10 journeys), and day passes (€7.50) can be bought online or loaded onto the company's App.

Along the coast there's a tram service all the way from Knokke to De Panne. The trams are modern, and it's a pleasant ride, but don't expect uninterrupted views of the sea; the tram tracks are often on the landward side of the dunes.

CONTACTS De Lijn. ☎ *070/22–02–00* 🌐 *www.delijn.be/en.*

CAR

Bruges is 5 km (3 miles) north of the E40 motorway, which links it to Brussels. It is 126 km (76 miles) from Le Shuttle terminus at Calais. Access for cars into Bruges's center is severely restricted. The historic streets are narrow and often one-way. There are huge parking lots at the railway station and near the exits from the ring road, plus underground parking at 't Zand.

The E40 continues west from Bruges en route to Oostende and Calais in France. Keep in mind that traffic on the E40 can be bumper-to-bumper on summer weekends. At such busy times, a better alternative is the N9; for Knokke, you branch off on N49. The coastal road, N34, is also very busy in summer, so allow ample time for driving between resorts.

To visit the battlefields from here, driving is definitely the best solution, because the various World War I sights are in different directions from Ypres. The easiest way to reach Ypres is via the A19 from Kortrijk, which peters out north of the city.

TAXI

Bruges has large taxi stands at the railway station and at the Markt. Taxis are metered and the rates are reasonable, but buses are plentiful and, at only €2, are always a much cheaper way of getting around.

TRAIN

The Belgian national railway, NMBS/SNCB, sends two trains each hour to Bruges from Brussels via Ghent (50 minutes), and three trains an hour from Oostende (15 minutes).

CONTACTS NMBS/SNCB. ☎ *02/528–2828* 🌐 *www.belgiantrain.be.*

Hotels

Bruges is a popular weekend escape, full as it is of romantic suites and secluded hideaways. You'll find old-fashioned accents at most hotels in the "City of Swans." The tourist office can help you make reservations for lodgings, in Bruges and in the surrounding countryside. You can make reservations through its website (*www.brugge.be*), which has an extensive list of hotels, and dozens of bed-and-breakfast entries; staying in the latter, often very picturesque, is an easy way to make contact with locals. Rates, which are sometimes higher than in regular hotels, usually include a hearty Belgian breakfast of bread, cereal, cold cuts, cheese, yogurt, eggs, and fruit.

If you'd like to stay in a coastal town in summer, be sure to make arrangements at least a few weeks in advance. Tax and service are included in all accommodation rates.

Restaurants

There are hundreds of restaurants in Bruges, ranging from taverns offering a quick snack to stylish establishments serving Flemish or international (mostly French) delicacies. Seafood is great here, as the coast is nearby; meals cooked with Belgian beer are a treat as well. While in the Markt, snack like a Belgian with mayonnaise-covered fries.

Unless you're going to a high-class restaurant, casual dress is always appropriate. You should make reservations, especially on weekends and holidays. Otherwise, your best strategy for getting a table is to come just as the restaurant opens or after the main rush. The busiest mealtimes tend to be from noon to 1:30 and 7 to 9. After 10 pm it can be hard to find restaurants that are still serving. Many restaurants serve meals outdoors, even in winter on heated terraces. A service charge and tax (V.A.T.) are always included in the tab, so you don't need to leave a tip, although most people round off upward.

HOTEL AND RESTAURANT PRICES

Hotel prices in the reviews are the lowest cost of a standard double room in high season. Restaurant prices in the reviews are the average cost of a main course at dinner, or if dinner is not served, at lunch.

What It Costs in Euros			
$	$$	$$$	$$$$
RESTAURANTS			
under €12	€12–€22	€23–€30	over €30
HOTELS			
under €100	€100–€150	€151–€220	over €220

Tours

Quasimodo Tours

BUS TOURS | Quasimodo runs full-day bus tours from Bruges to the World War I battlefields and several other out-of-town sights, which can be a good way to explore if you don't have your own transport. The company also runs tours to Damme, and to Kasteel van Loppem, an impressive 19th-century stately home around 6 km (4 miles) south of Bruges. ✉ *Veldmaarschalk Fochstraat 69* ☎ *050/370–470* 🌐 *www.quasimodo.be* 🎫 *Day tours from €79.*

Quasimundo Bike Tours

BICYCLE TOURS | "Bruges by bike" is the classic bumpy tour on offer here. It takes in the city sights (Markt, behijnhof, windmills) along with quite a few cobblestones. Rides (€33) depart daily at 10 am from their shop on Predikherenstraat (show up 10 minutes beforehand). Reservations are required. ✉ *Predikherenstraat 28* ☎ *050/330–775* 🌐 *www.quasimundo.com* 🎫 *From €33.*

Visitor Information

Bruges Tourist Information 't Zand. ✉ *'t Zand 34* ☎ *050/444–646* 🌐 *www.visitbruges.be.* **Bruges Tourist Information Markt.** ✉ *Markt 1* ☎ *050/444–646* 🌐 *www.visitbruges.be.*

Bruges

95 km (59 miles) northwest from Brussels.

Bruges often feels like a city immune to time. Strict bylaws ensure that its medieval center looks much as it did during its pomp. But while the presence of huge crowds of tourists during summer and on weekends can make it seem like one giant Gothic theme park, that doesn't diminish just what a unique place this is.

Sights

Arentshuis

ART MUSEUM | The upper floor of this 18th-century building is dedicated to the multitalented artist Frank Brangwyn (1867–1956), born in Bruges to British parents. His works include everything from book illustrations to a mural in New York City's Rockefeller Center, but he is perhaps best known for his World War I posters. He also influenced the reconstruction of many Bruges buildings in a pseudo-Gothic style, and many of his brooding drawings, etchings, and paintings of Bruges are on view here. On the ground floor, special exhibits on a variety of themes cycle through every few months. ✉ *Dijver 16* ☎ *050/448–711* 🌐 *www.museabrugge.be* 🎫 *€7* 🕒 *Closed Mon.* Ⓜ *Bus 1, 12.*

Brewery Bourgogne de Flandres

BREWERY | After almost 60 years away, the Bourgogne de Flandres brewery returned to Bruges in 2015, and added a new visitor center and tour. It's aimed squarely at families, with lots of diversions for kids while their parents get to quiz brewmasters and point their audio guides at various triggers, unraveling the mysteries of the brewing process. For example, did you know that Brussels's famous lambic beer can only be brewed in that region because of a wild yeast that grows in the air there, creating spontaneous fermentation? ✉ *Kartuizerinnenstraat 6* ☎ *050/335–426* 🌐 *www.bourgognedesflandres.be/en/brewery-visit/individual* 🎫 *€11* 🕒 *Closed Mon., Tues., and Thurs.* Ⓜ *Bus: 88, 91.*

Bruges Beer Experience

OTHER MUSEUM | Frites and chocolate already have their own museums in the city, so it was only a matter of time before the third comestible in Belgium's holy trinity received its due. It's atop the old post office building on Markt Square, and once you've scaled the *many* flights of stairs, you'll be handed a tablet to scan

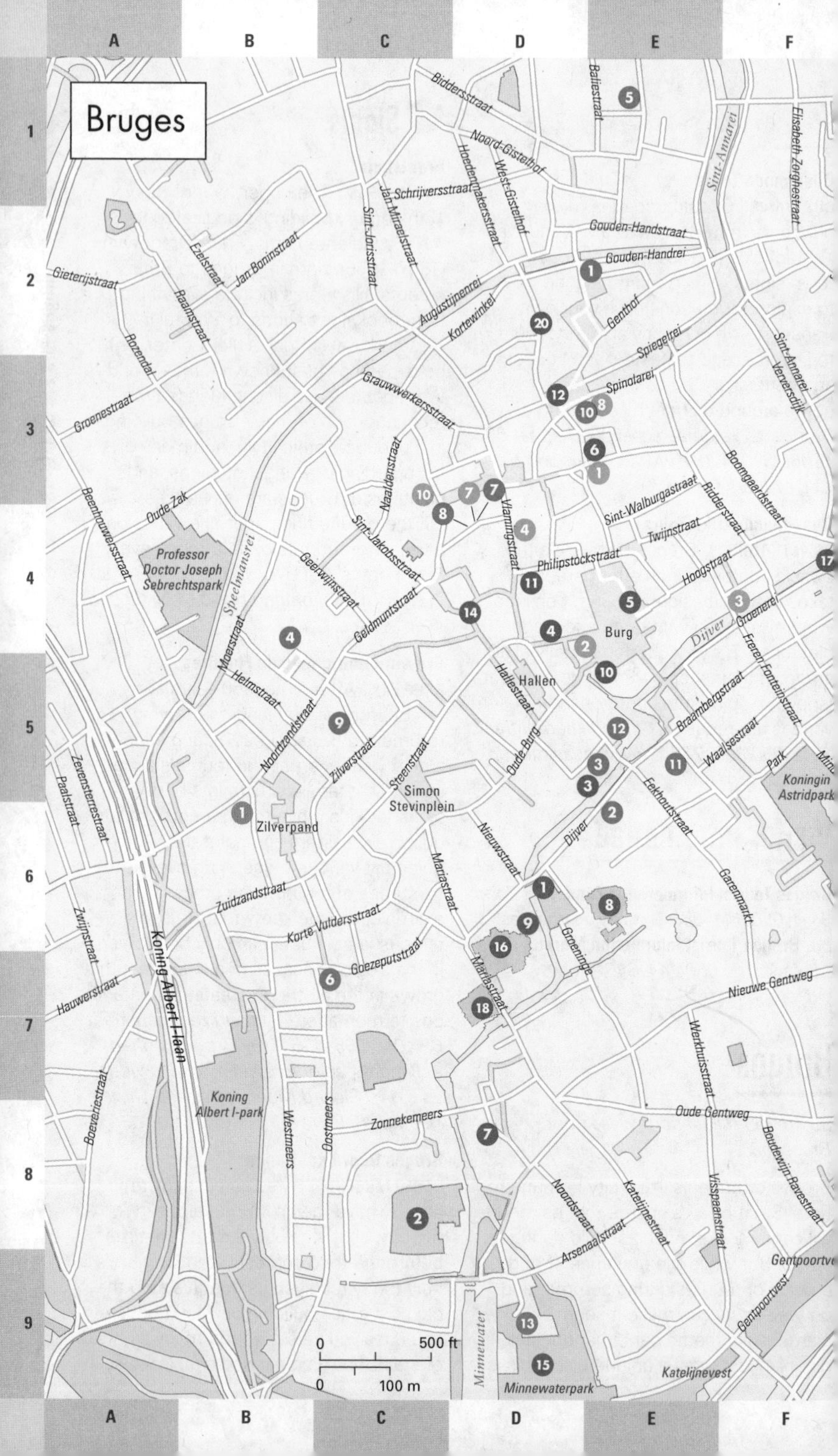
Bruges
A
B
C
D
E
F
1
2
3
4
5
6
7
8
9
Biddersstraat
Baliestraat
Noord-Gistelhof
Hoedenmakersstraat
West-Gistelhof
Schrijversstraat
Jan Miraelstraat
Sint-Jorisstraat
Sint-Annarei
Elisabeth Zorghestraat
Gouden-Handstraat
Gouden-Handrei
Ezelstraat
Jan Boninstraat
Gieterijstraat
Raamstraat
Rozendal
Augustijnenrei
Kortewinkel
Genthof
Spiegelrei
Spinolarei
Sint-Annarei
Verversdijk
Grauwwerkersstraat
Groenestraat
Naaldenstraat
Boomgaardstraat
Beenhouwersstraat
Oude Zak
Sint-Walburgastraat
Ridderstraat
Twijnstraat
Professor Doctor Joseph Sebrechtspark
Speelmansrei
Sint-Jakobsstraat
Vlamingstraat
Geerwijnstraat
Philipstockstraat
Hoogstraat
Geldmuntstraat
Dijver
Groenerei
Burg
Moerstraat
Helmstraat
Hallestraat
Hallen
Freren Fonteinstraat
Braambergstraat
Noordzandstraat
Zilverstraat
Steenstraat
Oude Burg
Waalsestraat
Park
Koningin Astridpark
Zevensterrestraat
Paalstraat
Simon Stevinplein
Zilverpand
Nieuwstraat
Eekhoutstraat
Dijver
Mariastraat
Garenmarkt
Zuidzandstraat
Zwijnstraat
Korte Vuldersstraat
Groeninge
Goezeputstraat
Koning Albert I-laan
Mariastraat
Hauwerstraat
Nieuwe Gentweg
Werkhuisstraat
Koning Albert I-park
Westmeers
Oostmeers
Zonnekemeers
Oude Gentweg
Boudewijn Ravestraat
Boeveriestraat
Noordstraat
Katelijnestraat
Visspaanstraat
Arsenaalstraat
Gentpoortvest
Minnewater
Minnewaterpark
Katelijnevest
0
500 ft
0
100 m

G H I

Sights

1 Arentshuis D6
2 Begijnhof C8
3 Brewery Bourgogne de Flandres.................. E5
4 Bruges Beer Experience D4
5 Burg E4
6 Choco-Story............. E3
7 De Halve Maan D8
8 Groeningemuseum E6
9 Gruuthusemuseum D6
10 Heilig Bloed Basiliek E5
11 Historium Brugge....... D4
12 Jan van Eyckplein D3
13 Kantcentrum G2
14 Markt.................... D4
15 Minnewater Park....... D9
16 Onze-Lieve-Vrouwekerk D6
17 Reien F4
18 Sint-Janshospitaal Museum D7
19 Sint-Janshuismolen and Koeleweimolen I1
20 Spanjaardstraat........ D2
21 Volkskundemuseum.... G2

Restaurants

1 Belgian Pigeon House E3
2 Breydel-De Coninc D4
3 Bruut F4
4 Curiosa.................. D4
5 Eetcafé Lion Belge H3
6 Je........................ H3
7 Le Mystique D4
8 Spinola.................. E3
9 Teasers by Rock-Fort... G4
10 Zwart Huis................ C3

Quick Bites

1 That's Toast.............. B6

Hotels

1 Bryghia.................. D2
2 De Tuilerieëen E6
3 Hotel de Orangerie E5
4 Hotel Dukes' Palace.... B4
5 Hotel Fevery E1
6 Hotel Goezeput........... C7
7 Hotel Heritage........... D4
8 Hotel Marcel D4
9 Hotel Sablon.............. C5
10 Martin's Relais E3
11 The Pand.................. E5
12 Relais Bourgondisch Cruyce E5
13 't Fraeyhuis D9

KEY

1 Exploring Sights
1 Restaurants
1 Quick Bites
1 Hotels

G H I

the displays' QR codes; these bring up information on the history of Belgian beer (in 10 languages). There is a particular focus on the medieval period, including Trappist and abbey brewing, and "gruut," herbal beers that were once common to the region. A beautifully illustrated kids' tour tells the parallel story of a trapped bear. At the end, visitors get to sample a trio of draft beers from a choice of 16 in the tasting room. ✉ *Breidelstraat 3* ☎ *050/699–229* 🌐 *mybeerexperience.com* 🎫 *€16 (€10 without tasting)* Ⓜ *Bus 3, 4, 14.*

★ Burg

PLAZA/SQUARE | A popular daytime meeting place and an enchanting, floodlit scene after dark, the Burg is flanked by striking civic buildings. Named for the fortress built by Baldwin of the Iron Arm, the Burg was also the former site of the 10th-century Carolingian Cathedral of St. Donaas, which was destroyed by French Republicans in 1799. The Burg is not all historic splendor, though—in sharp contrast to these buildings stands a modern construction by Japanese artist Toyo Ito, added in 2002. ✉ *Burg* Ⓜ *Bus: 1, 12.*

Choco-Story

OTHER MUSEUM | Choco-Story may deviate from the historical quaintness found everywhere else in Bruges, but it makes for a diverting bookend if you've been trawling the delightful chocolate shops in town. This collection traces the history of the cocoa bean, from its origins in the Americas to its popularity in Europe. There are also chocolate-making demonstrations and a chance to taste. It is certainly the best of a linked trio of disparately themed museums. ✉ *Wijzakstraat 2* ☎ *050/612–237* 🌐 *choco-story-brugge.be* 🎫 *€10* Ⓜ *Bus: 4, 6, 14.*

De Halve Maan

BREWERY | This working brewery may not be the only one in Bruges anymore, but it's still rather special. It produces the Bruges Zot and Straffe Hendrik brands that you'll see in many bars around town, and if you want to see the brewery in action, daily 45-minute tours include a glass of the house blond beer in its unfiltered form. You'll also find out how a 3-km (2-mile) length of pipeline was laid under the city's medieval streets to allow for enough beer to fill 12,000 bottles an hour to flow beneath the cobbles to a plant outside the city limits. True beer lovers can opt for the extended tour, which descends into the cellars for a more in-depth tasting session and hopped-up tales. ✉ *Walplein 26* ☎ *050/444–222* 🌐 *www.halvemaan.be* 🎫 *From €15* Ⓜ *Bus: 11, 12.*

★ Groeningemuseum

ART MUSEUM | The tremendous holdings of this gallery give you the makings for a crash course in the Flemish Primitives and their successors. Petrus Christus, Hugo van der Goes, Hieronymus Bosch, Rogier van der Weyden, Gerard David, Pieter Bruegel (both Elder and Younger), Pieter Pourbus—all the greats are represented. Here you can see Jan van Eyck's wonderfully realistic *Madonna with Canon Van der Paele*. There's also one of Hans Memling's greatest works, the *Moreel Triptych*. As if this weren't enough, the museum also encompasses a strong display of 15th- to 21st-century Dutch and Belgian works, sweeping through to Surrealist and modern art. The Groeninge is set back from the street in a pocket-size park behind a medieval gate. It isn't a huge museum; nonetheless, its riches warrant a full morning or afternoon. An audio guide is available in English. ✉ *Dijver 12* ☎ *050/448–743* 🌐 *www.museabrugge.be* 🎫 *€14* 🕒 *Closed Mon.* Ⓜ *Bus: 1, 4, 6, 11, 12, 14, 16.*

★ Gruuthusemuseum

HISTORY MUSEUM | Arguably the city's finest museum lies within a house built in the 15th century for the Gruuthuses, a powerful family who made their money on the exclusive right to sell "gruut," an herbal mixture used for flavoring beer. Louis, the patriarch behind its rise, was a

The Burg, Bruges' famous market square, is lined with medieval buildings, including the 14th-century Gothic Town Hall.

businessman, diplomat, patron, and a lover of culture. Of course, its history didn't end there, and it has stood throughout the ups and downs of one of the great medieval cities. The museum tells the story of Bruges through its most powerful family and their legacy of art and relics, but also through the museum's own collection of crafts—lace, amber, porcelain, jewels—that formed the backbone of the city's trade. ✉ *Dijver 17C* ☎ *050/448–743* 🌐 *www.museabrugge.be* 🎟 *From €14* 🕒 *Closed Mon.* Ⓜ *Bus: 1, 11.*

★ **Heilig Bloed Basiliek** (*Basilica of the Holy Blood*)

CHURCH | The Basilica of the Holy Blood manages to include both the austere and the ornate under one roof—not to mention one of Europe's most precious relics. The 12th-century Lower Chapel retains a stern, Romanesque character. Look for the poignant, 14th-century Pietà and the carved statue of Christ in the crypt. From this sober space, the elaborate, external late-Gothic De Steegheere staircase, with a reconstructed bluestone facade, leads to the stunningly lavish Upper Chapel, which was twice destroyed—by Protestant iconoclasts in the 16th century and by French Republicans in the 18th—but both times rebuilt. (Note that the Upper Chapel is closed to visitors during Eucharistic Mass on Friday and Sunday 10:45–12:15.) The original stained-glass windows were replaced in 1845, and then again after an explosion in 1967, when they were restored by the Bruges painter De Loddere. The basilica's namesake treasure is a vial thought to contain a few drops of the blood of Christ, brought from Jerusalem in 1149 by Derick of Alsace when he returned from the Second Crusade. It is exposed in the Upper Chapel every Friday 10:15–11, and every afternoon 2–3 (sometimes until 4): queue up to place your right hand on the vial and take a moment for quiet reflection. On Ascension Day, it becomes the centerpiece of the magnificent De Heilig Bloedprocessie (Procession of the Holy Blood), a major medieval-style pageant in which it is carried through the streets of Bruges. The small museum

Bruges is famous for its chocolate—see chocolate-making demonstrations (and try a sample) at the Choco-Story museum.

next to the basilica is the usual home of the basilica's namesake reliquary. ✉ *Burg 13* ☎ *050/336–792* 🌐 *www.holyblood.com* 🎫 *Church: free; treasury: €3* Ⓜ *Bus: 1, 12.*

Historium Brugge

HISTORY MUSEUM | FAMILY | Similar to the tablet-dominated Beer Museum around the corner, Historium Brugge uses technology (film and virtual reality) to depict the story of the city's golden age. Housed on the site of the old Waterhalle, a vast warehouse that was once at the heart of the trading hub that was medieval Bruges, the museum makes fine use of its impressive setting. However, whether you learn anything depends less on your tolerance for history and more on your ability to absorb tales of romance played out on virtual reality headsets. ✉ *Markt 1* ☎ *050/270–311* 🌐 *www.historium.be* 🎫 *€19 including VR experience; €15 without VR* Ⓜ *Bus: 3, 4, 14.*

Jan van Eyckplein

PLAZA/SQUARE | A colorful yet low-key square that lies at the center of Hanseatic Bruges, the Jan van Eyckplein is landmarked with a statue of the famed 15th-century painter. It includes the old **Tolhuis** (Customs House), built in 1477, where vehicles on their way to market had to stop while tolls were levied on goods brought from nearby ports. The **Poortersloge,** a late-Gothic building with a slender spire, was owned by the guild of porters and used as a meeting place for the burghers. It's occasionally open for contemporary art exhibitions. The bear occupying one niche represents the legendary creature speared by Baldwin of the Iron Arm that later became the symbol of the city. ✉ *Intersection of Academiestraat, Spiegelrei, and Spanjaardstraat, Jan van Eyckplein* Ⓜ *Bus: 4, 14.*

Kantcentrum

OTHER MUSEUM | The Lace Center maintains the quality and authenticity of the ancient Belgian craft of lace making. This foundation includes a lace museum in the Jerusalem almshouses in Balstraat, as well as a school where youngsters are taught the intricate art of the bobbins. The building is the former home of the Adornes family, and adjoins their mausoleum in the Jeruzalemkerk. ✉ *Balstraat 16* ☎ *050/330–072* 🌐 *www.kantcentrum.eu* 🎫 *€6; combi tocket with Volkskundemuseum €11* ⏲ *Closed Sun.* Ⓜ *Bus 4, 14.*

★ Markt

PLAZA/SQUARE | Used as a marketplace since AD 958, this square is still one of the liveliest places in Bruges. In the center stands a memorial to the city's medieval heroes, Jan Breydel and Pieter De Coninck, who led the commoners of Flanders to their short-lived victory over the aristocrats of France. On the east side of the Markt stand the provincial government house and the former post office, an excellent pastiche of Burgundian Gothic. Old guild houses line the west and north sides of the square, their step-gabled facades overlooking the cafés spilling out onto the sidewalk. These buildings aren't always as old as they seem, though—often they're 19th-century reconstructions. The medieval **Belfort** (Belfry) on the south side of the Markt, however, is the genuine article. The tower dates from the 13th century, its crowning octagonal lantern to the 15th century. Altogether, it rises to a height of 270 feet, commanding the city and the surrounding countryside with more presence than grace. The valuables of Bruges were once kept in the second-floor treasury; now the Belfort's riches are in its remarkable 47-bell carillon, which rings even truer thanks to the new bells it was given in 2010. Impressing Belgians with a carillon is no mean feat, as Belgium has some of the best in the world.) However, their playlist can be a little limited, and after listening to at least a half dozen renditions of "It's a Long, Long way to Tipperary," you might wish that they'd skimped on the quality a little. If you haven't walked enough, you can climb 366 winding steps to the clock mechanism, and from the carillon enjoy a gorgeous panoramic view. At the base of the belfry is a gallery containing a permanent collection of sketches and watercolors by (of all people) Salvador Dalí. Back in the square, you may be tempted by the horse-drawn carriages that congregate here; a half-hour ride for up to five people, with a short stop at the Begijnhof, costs €60 plus "something for the horse." ✉ *Markt* 🌐 *www.the-markt.com* 🎫 *Belfort €14; Salvador Dalí €10* Ⓜ *Bus: 1, 12.*

Minnewater Park

CITY PARK | In the south of Bruges you'll find Minnewater, a pleasant spot of greenery with a large rectangular lake at its center that's dotted with willow trees. So the legend goes: a Saxon warrior returned from fighting to discover his lover dead, so he built a dyke and covered her grave with a lake. Lovers who walk its scenic bridge are said to be blessed. The park lies southeast of the water, and at its far end is Powder Tower, a 12th-century defensive battlement named for the gunpowder it used to store. In summer, the park hosts a number of festivals, most notably the Cactus music festival in July.

■ TIP→ **Combine a visit here with a stop at the Begijnhof.** ✉ *Minnewater* Ⓜ *Bus: 11, 12.*

Onze-Lieve-Vrouwekerk *(Church of Our Lady)*

CHURCH | The towering spire of the plain Gothic Church of Our Lady, begun about 1220, rivals the Belfry as a symbol of Bruges. At 381 feet high, it is the second-tallest brick construction in the world. The art history highlight here is the *Madonna and Child* statue carved by Michelangelo, an early work. The choir museum contains many 13th- and 14th-century polychrome tombs, as well as two mausoleums: that of Mary of Burgundy, who died in 1482 at the age of 25 after a fall from her horse; and that of her father, Charles the Bold, killed in 1477 while laying siege to Nancy in France. Mary was as well loved in Bruges

Bruges and the Flemish Primitives

When Flanders became a Burgundian state in the 15th century, it sparked an era of unprecedented wealth and artistic creation. The famed Flemish Primitives style of painting evolved across the region at this time, representing a revolution in realism, portraiture, and perspective, bringing the era alive in astonishing detail. In Bruges, Hans Memling took portraiture in a new direction with his depiction of the Moreel family in their namesake triptych. You can see this work in the Groeningemuseum, one of the city's matchless art collections, and, in fact, most of Memling's best paintings are still in Bruges.

Another of the city's famous sons, Jan van Eyck, grew to become one of the most renowned and most successful of the Primitives artists. He was named court painter to Philip the Good, Duke of Burgundy, and two of his finest creations—*Madonna with Canon Joris van der Paele*, and *Portrait of Margareta van Eyck*—have also remained in Bruges and can both be seen in the Groeningemuseum.

as her husband, Maximilian of Austria, was loathed. ✉ *Dijver and Mariastraat* ☎ *050/448–711* 🌐 *www.museabrugge.be* 🎫 *Church free; museum €6* ⏲ *Closed Mon.* Ⓜ *Bus: 1, 12.*

★ Reien

BODY OF WATER | Bruges's narrow and meandering canals, or *reien*, with their old humpback stone bridges, give the city its character, opening up perspective and imposing their calm. The view from the **Meebrug** is especially picturesque. Farther along the Groenerei are the **Godshuizen De Pelikaan**, almshouses dating from the early 18th century. There are several such charitable buildings in the city, tiny houses built by the guilds for the poor, some still serving their original purpose. **Steenhouwersdijk** overlooks the brick rear gables that were part of the original county hall. The **Vismarkt** (Fish Market) has 19th-century buildings designed in classical style; fresh seafood from Zeebrugge is sold Tuesday–Saturday. Just beyond is the little **Huidenvettersplein** (Tanners' Square), with its 17th-century guild house. Next to it, from the **Rozenhoedkaai** canal, the view of the heart of the city includes the pinnacles of the town hall, basilica, and Belfry—the essence of Bruges.

For a swan's-eye view of the city, 30-minute canal cruises costing €12 are offered by five different companies. All five ply the same route and depart from jetties along the Dijver, between the Gruuthusemuseum and Vismarkt. ✉ *Bruges.*

★ Sint-Janshospitaal Museum

ART MUSEUM | Home to an impressive collection of Hans Memling paintings, this is one of the oldest surviving medieval hospitals in Europe. It was founded in the 12th century and remained in use until the 20th century. The highlights of the collection are the seven major works (and plenty of minor ones) by Hans Memling (1440–94) that are of breathtaking quality and rank among the greatest—and certainly the most spiritual—of the Flemish Primitives school. Memling was born in Germany, but spent the greater part of his life in Bruges. *Note: There are plans for the museum to close for an unspecified period in 2023 for necessary restoration work.* ✉ *Mariastraat 38* ☎ *050/448–743* 🌐 *www.museabrugge.be* 🎫 *€12* ⏲ *Closed Mon.* Ⓜ *Bus: 1, 11, 12.*

The ornate Upper Chapel of the Heilig Bloed Basiliek features spectacular stained-glass windows.

Sint-Janshuismolen and Koeleweimolen
WINDMILL | The outer ramparts of the medieval city of Bruges used to be dotted with windmills; now four remain along the ring road. The two most impressive are the St-Janshuismolen (1770) and close to it the Koeleweimolen (1765). Of these, only St-Janshuismolen can be visited, and it is still used to grind flour. The wooden steps leading up to it are quite steep and not for the fainthearted. ⊠ *Kruisvest 3* ☎ *050/448–743* 🎫 *€4* 🕐 *Closed Mon.–Thurs. and Oct.–Mar.* Ⓜ *Bus: 4.*

Spanjaardstraat (*Spaniard Street*)
STREET | The street leads up to the quay where goods from Spain were unloaded, near Jan van Eyckplein Square. The house at No. 9 was where St. Ignatius of Loyola stayed when he came to Flanders on holidays from his studies in Paris. Directly ahead are the three arches of the **Augustijnenbrug.** Dating from 1391, it's the oldest bridge in Bruges. On the other side of the canal, **Augustijnenrei** is one of the loveliest quays. ⊠ *Spanjaardstraat* Ⓜ *Bus: 4, 14, 43, 90.*

Volkskundemuseum
HISTORY MUSEUM | A row of 17th-century whitewashed almshouses originally built for retired shoemakers now holds an engaging Folklore Museum. Within each house is a reconstructed historic interior: a grocery shop, a living room, a tavern, a cobbler's workshop, a classroom, a pharmacy, and a kitchen. Another wing holds a tailor's shop and a collection of old advertising posters. You can end your tour at the suitably historic museum café, In de Zwarte Kat (the "Black Cat"). ⊠ *Balstraat 43* 🌐 *www.museabrugge.be* 🎫 *€7; combi ticket with Kantcentrum €11* 🕐 *Closed Mon.* Ⓜ *Bus 4, 14.*

Restaurants

There are plenty of gems to be uncovered among Bruges's dining options, including stately old-timers that dish up Flemish classics in buildings that date back to the Holy Roman Empire. It pays to wander the back alleys, away from the tourist traps of the main squares, to uncover quaint (and cramped) family-run restaurants and weathered old estaminets, where a little more care is taken and the service tends to be a bit friendlier.

Belgian Pigeon House

$$$ | **BELGIAN** | This fine bistro-style restaurant is a glorious celebration of the simpler things in life—the stars of the show are the less starry meats on offer: the rabbit stew and pigeon fillets justify their slightly inflated prices owing to the quality of the cooking, backed up by a decent wine menu. Space is at a premium, with most tables downstairs in the cozy bunker of a basement (lined with various pigeon knickknacks) and a terrace during summer. **Known for:** cozy upstairs bar—in case you just want a drink; pigeon dishes that surprise you; rustic Belgian cooking. *Average main: €24* ✉ *Sint-Jansplein 12* ☎ *050/661–690* 🌐 *belgianpigeonhouse.com* ⏲ *Closed Tues. and Wed. No lunch Mon. and Thurs.* Ⓜ *Bus: 4, 14.*

Breydel–De Coninc

$$$ | **BELGIAN** | In a plum spot along the route from the Markt to the Burg, this no-frills restaurant is well known among locals—the plain furnishings leave the focus on the fresh seafood for which the establishment is famed. Although eel and steak are available, the restaurant's biggest draw is mussels—there's nothing more basically, and deliciously, Belgian than a huge crock heaped high with shiny, blue-black shells. **Known for:** generous portions; some of the best seafood in Flanders; the lobster is not cheap, but worth it. *Average main: €28* ✉ *Breidelstraat 24* ☎ *050/339–746* 🌐 *restaurant-breydel.be* ⏲ *Closed Wed.* Ⓜ *Bus: 1, 11.*

Bruut

$$$$ | **CONTEMPORARY** | Set above a quiet canal, with white swans gliding below, this charming restaurant in a step-gabled town house is purely romantic—for the best views, request a window seat next to the water. And yet, while the surroundings drip with history, the food is anything but old-fashioned: cutting-edge head chef Bruno Timperman uses impeccably fresh seasonal ingredients to create beautifully presented plates of food that paint a spectacular picture, both for the eyes and for the palate. **Known for:** art on a plate; unusual ingredients including foraged herbs; always-changing prix-fixe menus. *Average main: €35* ✉ *Meestraat 9* ☎ *050/695–509* 🌐 *www.bistrobruut.be* ⏲ *Closed weekends* Ⓜ *Bus: 4, 14.*

Curiosa

$$ | **BELGIAN** | A Bruges institution for more than three decades, this cross-vaulted, medieval crypt has evolved over the years from a lively tavern with loud music at night, into a more genteel restaurant that provides a quiet spot for conversation over a meal and a glass of wine. The menu covers steaks, and Belgian classics such as *vispannetje* (fish stew), mussels, or rabbit, all at very reasonable prices. **Known for:** cozy cellar atmosphere; three-course set lunch menu is a steal; some of the best-value mussels in Bruges. *Average main: €21* ✉ *Vlamingstraat 22* ☎ *050/342–334* 🌐 *www.curiosa-brugge.com* Ⓜ *Bus: 4, 14.*

Eetcafé Lion Belge

$$ | **BELGIAN** | A 15-minute walk from the Markt, this informal Belgian café-restaurant attracts a roaring crowd—a legacy of being just a few doors up from one of the city's busier hostels. The menu changes regularly, although the food inevitably veers toward the comfort variety, with some excellent stews (like its simple but winning pot-au-feu) regularly cropping up. **Known for:** prices that suit every pocket; keeping it simple, to delicious effect; a great beer selection to go with the food. *Average main: €15* ✉ *Langestraat 123* ☎ *0496/210–244* 🌐 *www.lionbelge.eu* ⏲ *Closed Mon. and Tues.* Ⓜ *Bus: 6, 16.*

A Taste of the Sea

The backbone of Flanders food is the local produce that's served fresh and presented simply. Naturally, this is also seafood country, with fresh fish shipped in daily to Bruges; the coastal towns serve authentic North Sea delicacies at terrace restaurants whipped by sand and salt air. Flemings are particularly mad about *mosselen* (mussels)—try them steamed, curried, or bathed in a white-wine broth accented with celery, onions, and parsley. Main courses are inevitably accompanied by a mountain of *frieten* (French fries), fried twice, making them especially crisp and delicious, then dipped in a big dollop of accompanying mayo.

Paling (eels) are one of the region's specialties. The flesh is firm, fatty, and sweet, and served in long cross-sections with a removable backbone. *Paling in t'groen* is eel served in a green herb sauce, a heady mix of sorrel, tarragon, sage, mint, and parsley. Sole and turbot are also popular main courses, served broiled, poached with a light mousseline sauce, or grilled with a rich béarnaise or mustard sauce. Herring, on the other hand, is eaten *maatjes* (raw) in the spring.

When the Flemish aren't eating their fish straight or in a blanket of golden sauce, they consume it in the region's most famous dish, *waterzooi*, a thick seafood broth rich with cream and vegetables (which is served with chicken instead of fish in the Ghent version).

e

$$ | **FRENCH** | A 10-minute walk east f central Bruges, this cozy gastrobar erves up modern takes of classic French ishes, but with a twist. Instead of full nain courses, the food is delivered apas style: pick six savory treats of your hoice, and they will be served together n a self-styled *grand plateau* (a large vooden platter). **Known for:** good if short rench wine list; friendly service; a trip round France on one platter. *Average nain: €27 Langestraat 83 050/920–75 www.jerestaurant.be Closed un. and Mon. No lunch Bus: 6, 16.*

e Mystique

$$$ | **BELGIAN** | Attached to Hotel eritage, the elegant dining room at e Mystique dates from 1869, and its igh ceilings, chandeliers, and linen ablecloths create a refined atmosphere, erfect for quiet conversation. Here, hef Raoul de Koning creates a blend of modern French/Flemish cuisine using the freshest seasonal and local ingredients, served in fixed-price menus of three or four courses. **Known for:** elegant dining; pricey but worth it; mixing fresh, bold flavors to create some eye-catching dishes. *Average main: €38 Niklaas Desparsstraat 11 050/444–445 www.lemystique.be Closed Sun. No lunch Bus: 4, 14.*

Spinola

$$$ | **EUROPEAN** | This canal-house restaurant by the Jan van Eyck statue is a real charmer—from an intimate main dining room, an iron staircase leads to the upper tables; the open kitchen is in back. Here, chef-owners Sam and Vicky Storme cook up rich Burgundian cuisine: fresh game, goose liver, fabulous mussels, pigeon with truffles. **Known for:** well-honed menu of French classics; the city's smallest restaurant—book in advance; an adorable setting with a canal-side

terrace. $ *Average main: €30* ✉ *Spinola-rei 1* ☎ *050/341–785* 🌐 *www.spinola.be* ⏲ *Closed Sun. and Mon.* Ⓜ *Bus: 4, 14.*

★ Teasers by Rock-Fort

$$$ | FRENCH | Teasers is the ice cube down the back of Bruges's "traditional" dining scene; it's brash and modern, serving a relentlessly inventive menu of French-inspired sharing tapas dishes slanted heavily towards seafood. The growing Rock-Fort empire also encompasses the Glocal shop and take-home service next door, and—above that—the more upmarket Orange District restaurant, which serves fixed-price fine-dining menus. **Known for:** eye-catching cocktails; inventive, sumptuous flavors with a seafood bias; one of the better wine menus in the city. $ *Average main: €24* ✉ *Langestraat 15* ☎ *050/960–617* 🌐 *www.rock-fort.be* ⏲ *Closed weekends. No lunch Wed.* Ⓜ *Bus: 6, 16.*

Zwart Huis

$$$ | BELGIAN | This stylish, redbrick bar and restaurant lies above the old Cinema Liberty in a Gothic-style building that dates from 1482—all wooden beams, iron latticework, and stained glass. The fare is bistro-style comfort food at its finest: Flemish stews, bloody steaks, and the odd exotic meat (kangaroo). **Known for:** good wine selection to complement its meat-heavy menu; live music on Sunday; great atmosphere. $ *Average main: €25* ✉ *Kuipersstraat 23* ☎ *050/691–140* 🌐 *www.bistrozwarthuis.be* ⏲ *Closed Mon. and Tues.* Ⓜ *Bus: 5, 15.*

Coffee and Quick Bites

That's Toast

$ | EUROPEAN | There may be a clue in the name, but there's far more to life than basic ham and cheese croques at this lively and simple-but-hip café—the toast-based dishes here come lavishly spread with a list of ingredients ranging from smoked salmon and asparagus, to chicken korma, or sauerkraut with chipotle mayo. Reservations are not possible and it's a local hot spot, so get here early, or be prepared to queue. **Known for:** vegan- and veggie-friendly; all-day grilled breakfasts; very popular, don't be late. $ *Average main: €8* ✉ *Dweersstraat 4* ☎ *050/688–227* 🌐 *www.thatstoast.com* ⏲ *No dinner* Ⓜ *Bus: 1, 11.*

Hotels

Bruges is a popular weekend escape, full of romantic suites and secluded hideaways. You'll find old-fashioned accents at most hotels in the "City of Swans." The tourist office can help you make reservations for lodgings in Bruges and the surrounding countryside.

Bryghia

$ | HOTEL | What was once an Eastern European trade center makes for a handsome, 15th-century landmark building, with its Flemish Renaissance Revival–style facade. **Pros:** a building with a remarkable history; efficient service; removed from the noisy bustle of the city center. **Cons:** can't compete with some of Bruges's grander stays; the rooms can be a little basic; a fair walk from the main sights, though very quiet. $ *Rooms from €95* ✉ *Oosterlingenplein 4* ☎ *050/338–059* 🌐 *www.bryghiahotel.be* *21 rooms* *No Meals* Ⓜ *Bus: 4, 14.*

De Tuileriëen

$$$ | HOTEL | This 15th-century mansion is the epitome of Brugian elegance, and each salon is more extravagant than the next: the firelit bar with its cozy tartan wing chairs, the neo-Baroque breakfast salon topped by a coffered ceiling, and the parlor with tufted Victorian chairs and a blazing fireplace. **Pros:** well-equipped spa; some room rates are a bargain for what you get; turndown service includes chocolates. **Cons:** not very family-friendly (baby cots cost €25); parking is a mighty €30 per night; some front rooms are noisy. $ *Rooms from: €189* ✉ *Dijver 7* ☎ *050/343–691* 🌐 *www.hoteltuilerieen.com* 🛏 *45 rooms* 🍴 *No Meals* Ⓜ *Bus: 1, 11.*

★ Hotel de Orangerie

$$$ | **HOTEL** | Hotel de Orangerie, one of a swarm of boutique hotels that have colonized central Bruges, is family owned—and perhaps the most enchanting of its kind. **Pros:** heavenly afternoon teas; perfect location with picturesque views; wonderful old building. **Cons:** the entry-level "comfort" rooms are a little tight; parking costs are steep, even by Bruges's standards; canal-view rooms come at a hefty price. $ *Rooms from: €178* ✉ *Kartuizerinnestraat 10* ☎ *050/341–649* 🌐 *www.hotelorangerie.be* 🛏 *20 rooms* 🍴 *No Meals* Ⓜ *Bus: 1, 11.*

★ Hotel Dukes' Palace

$$$$ | **HOTEL** | Set in a 15th-century former residence of the Dukes of Burgundy, it lies off the main drag of one of the city's more upmarket shopping areas—and in terms of sheer grandeur, nothing in Bruges can compete with this. **Pros:** great spa with lots of facilities; fairy-tale-like setting; close to shopping streets. **Cons:** it's all a bit nouveau riche; nothing about this place is cheap; parking is expensive. $ *Rooms from: €229* ✉ *Prisenhof 8* ☎ *050/447–888* 🌐 *www.dukespalace.be* 🛏 *110 rooms* 🍴 *No Meals* Ⓜ *Bus: 2, 12.*

Hotel Fevery

$ | **B&B/INN** | **FAMILY** | This little hotel is part of a comfortable family home situated in a quiet corner of the city. **Pros:** good value; family-friendly atmosphere; owners know the best local attractions. **Cons:** breakfasts are simple affairs; its location lacks the bustle of the center, but it is quiet; basic rooms. $ *Rooms from: €79* ✉ *Collaert Mansionstraat 3* ☎ *050/331–269* 🌐 *www.hotelfevery.be* 🛏 *10 rooms* 🍴 *Free Breakfast* Ⓜ *Bus: 4, 14.*

Hotel Goezeput

$ | **HOTEL** | Housed in a fine whitewashed 19th-century building that was formerly a monastery, this simple hotel, centrally located between 't Zand and the Sint-Janshospitaal Museum, has few facilities beyond a breakfast room, but it does have charm in abundance. **Pros:** centrally located; friendly service; upper rooms have great views across central Bruges. **Cons:** no parking nearby; bathrooms are very small; no elevator. $ *Rooms from: €90* ✉ *Goezeputstraat 29* ☎ *050/342–694* 🌐 *www.hotelgoezeput.be* 🛏 *15 rooms* 🍴 *No Meals* Ⓜ *Bus 4, 14.*

Hotel Heritage

$$$ | **HOTEL** | Once a private mansion, this charming 19th-century building has been converted into a sumptuous hotel—even if renovation has robbed the exterior of much of the original patina. **Pros:** great location; helpful staff; grand building. **Cons:** valet parking is expensive; pretty pricey, even for Bruges; some rooms are quite small. $ *Rooms from: €218* ✉ *Niklaas Desparsstraat 11* ☎ *050/444–444* 🌐 *www.hotel-heritage.com* 🛏 *22 rooms* 🍴 *No Meals* Ⓜ *Bus: 2, 12.*

Hotel Marcel

$ | **HOTEL** | **FAMILY** | Run by a husband-and-wife team, this hotel's fresh, simple design stands in stark contrast to the antiques-heavy, more stately style of its rivals. **Pros:** friendly, helpful staff; stylish, modern hotel; great breakfast. **Cons:** few rooms have a/c; no elevators to the top floors; not as charming as other, more old-world hotels. $ *Rooms from: €85* ✉ *Niklaas Desparsstraat 7–9* ☎ *050/335–502* 🌐 *www.hotelmarcel.be* 🛏 *24 rooms* 🍴 *Free Breakfast* Ⓜ *Bus: 4, 14.*

Hotel Sablon

$$$ | **HOTEL** | Situated in what used to be the Grand Hotel du Sablon, a grande dame of an establishment whose decline was long and slow, the more simply named Sablon is an altogether different affair. **Pros:** down a peaceful alleyway, so

Did You Know?

Bruges' canals once served as the economic lifeblood of the city, moving textiles and other goods during its 15th-century Golden Age. During the 19th century, travelers visited and marveled at the city's charm, and still today, a cherished way of exploring Bruges is via boat along its many waterways.

totally quiet at night; bountiful breakfasts; centrally situated, close to the main shopping street. **Cons:** no on-site parking; it's not that easy to find at first; not many facilities (no gym, pool, or restaurant). *Rooms from: €161* *Kopstraat 10* *050/960–246* *www.hotelsablon.be* *43 rooms* *No Meals* *Bus: 4, 14.*

Martin's Relais

$ | **HOTEL** | Five grand merchants' houses in the elegant Hanseatic district combine the grace of another era with the polish of a modern, first-class property. **Pros:** pleasant bar; great 17th-century exteriors; eye-popping antiques. **Cons:** parking is a short walk away and costs €22 per night; could do with touching up in places; some rooms can be noisy. *Rooms from: €91* *Genthof 4a* *050/341–810* *www.martinshotels.com* *44 rooms* *No Meals* *Bus: 4, 14.*

★ The Pand

$$$ | **HOTEL** | Great care has been taken in the conversion of this 18th-century carriage house, and the result is a stylish, romantic hideaway shielded from the throngs of tourists but still just two minutes' walk from the center. **Pros:** a gorgeous old house; brilliant central location; tasty breakfast. **Cons:** rooms are typically pricey for Bruges; on-site parking is expensive; no wheelchair access. *Rooms from: €193* *Pandreitje 16* *050/340–666* *www.pandhotel.com* *26 rooms* *No Meals* *Bus: 4, 14.*

Relais Bourgondisch Cruyce

$$$ | **HOTEL** | Situated in one of the most romantic nooks in Bruges, this lovingly and stylishly restored historic pair of houses with half-timbered facades offers enchanting views over the reien. **Pros:** free breakfast if you book through the website; a fairy-tale setting with lovely decor throughout; suites get great canal views. **Cons:** not many facilities on-site; breakfast buffet is expensive if not included; limited parking (reserve in advance) is €25 per night. *Rooms from: €175* *Wollestraat 41–47* *050/337–926* *www.relaisbourgondischcruyce.be* *16 rooms* *Free Breakfast* *Bus: 1, 4.*

't Fraeyhuis

$$ | **HOTEL** | A gorgeous, gabled, yellow-hued 18th-century mansion, this is just the place to play lord of the manor, even if the rooms have been modernized and many of the period details have disappeared. **Pros:** the bar is a great escape; a beautiful location amid the city's best park; cozy fireplaces in the larger suites. **Cons:** some rooms are a little cramped; noise from the bar-restaurant can be a little loud; a bit far from the action. *Rooms from: €139* *Minnewater 11–15* *050/960–301* *www.fraeyhuis.be* *12 rooms* *No Meals* *Bus: 11, 12.*

Nightlife

Bruges is not the liveliest city at night, but there are a handful of good hangouts, including several bars that attract a younger crowd at 't Zand. Pubs, mostly catering to an under-thirty clientele, are clustered around the Eiermarkt, at the back of the Markt.

BARS

Brugs Beertje

PUBS | Arguably the most famous pub in town, Bruges's original specialist beer café is an iconic destination for hop lovers and stocks around 300 different brews. Expect to sample a few curiosities like the Wallonian Bush beer (one of the strongest in Belgium), the odd brew from the famed Sint-Sixtusabdij Westvleteren monastery, an excellent choice of lambic beers from Brussels's Cantillion, and a good selection from the local Halve Maan brewery. *Kemelstraat 5* *050/339–616* *www.brugsbeertje.be* *Bus: 1, 4, 14.*

Brugse Gin Club

BARS | With more than 350 gins—from your standard "mother's ruin" to Dutch-style jenever—served every way you can magine, this bar is the very definition ɔf a gin palace. It's a bit off the beaten track (hidden on a cobbled street near Koningen Astridpark), and a tad at odds with the rest of beer-swilling Bruges. But sometimes that's not a bad thing, with most of the gins also for sale in 5-cl or 10-cl pharmacy bottles, to take home. ☒ *Josef Suvéestraat 19* ☎ *0472/628–243* ⊕ *www.brugseginclub.be* Ⓜ *Bus: 4, 14.*

Cafe Rose Red
BARS | This busy café-bar might be attached to a hotel, but it remains a destination in itself—a wood-and-stone interior, copious (albeit fake) red roses for decor, knowledgeable staff, and a beer menu topping 150 that includes some rare Trappist finds, are all potent lures. ☒ *Cordoeaniersstraat 16–18* ☎ *050/339–051* ⊕ *www.rosered.be* Ⓜ *Bus: 2, 12.*

De Garre
PUBS | This old-school estaminet, lying down a narrow alleyway off Breidelstraat, is something of a local icon. Its 140-strong beer list is encyclopedic and well curated, and the 11% house tripel is so potent ("suitable for gourmets," it claims) that staff will only serve you a maximum of three. Classical music sets the scene for an older audience that many of the city bars don't cater to. ☒ *De Garre 1* ☎ *050/341–029* ⊕ *www.degarre.be.*

Joey's Cafe
PUBS | This "brown café" lies tucked away off the main shopping street, and has found a firm following among locals for its late-night blues and rock. It's cash-only, so leave your plastic at home, and the beer selection is superb. ☒ *Zilversteeg 4* ☎ *050/341–264* Ⓜ *Bus: 4, 14.*

Le Trappiste
PUBS | This lovely pub is in the cryptlike cellar of an 800-year-old building, the perfect setting for sampling some of its many hundreds of different Belgian and global ales. ☒ *Kuipersstraat 33* ☎ *0471/684–562* ⊕ *www.letrappistebrugge.com.*

't Poatersgat
PUBS | Part of the joy of this "hobbit hole"–esque pub lies in finding it; the hidden entrance (be prepared to duck) is basically the old service hatch, where goods would be delivered direct to the cellar. In this case, the bar is the cellar. Novelty aside, this is a good, old-fashioned pub, and its beer selection is among the best in the city. ☒ *Vlamingstraat 82* ☎ *0495/228–650* Ⓜ *Bus: 5, 15.*

2be
BARS | Tourists flock here en masse to see the beer wall, a glass case displaying one bottle for every brand of Belgian beer, but the real lure is the view from the terrace, overlooking the Djiver canal. A prolific selection of local brews also helps. There's a good beer shop, too. ☒ *Wollestraat 53* ☎ *050/611–222* ⊕ *www.2-be.biz* Ⓜ *Bus: 1, 4.*

Yesterday's World
PUBS | Timeless hospitality and great beers are the name of the game at this quaintly old-fashioned café—one that is part historical pub, and part antiques shop. ☒ *Wijngaardstraat 6* ☎ *0476/458–542* Ⓜ *Bus: 1, 11.*

CLUBS

Retsin's Lucifernum
LIVE MUSIC | Ring the bell and wait to be ushered past the old paintings, voodoo temple, and weird Gothic, slightly steampunk clutter (owner Don "Willy" Retsin considers it to be a museum of sorts, but then he also claims to be a vampire...) of this former Masonic lodge-turned-secret bar. The live music has a Latin vibe, though the occasional performance from its P.T. Barnum-esque owner is worth the wait. Havana-style rum punches dominate the drinks menu, but the real star is the decor: kitsch, unique and utterly memorable. ☒ *Twijnstraat 6–8* ☎ *0476/350–651* ⊕ *lucifernum.be* Ⓜ *Bus: 4, 14.*

WINE BARS

Blend

WINE BARS | In a city of beer bars, Blend is a tiny oasis. This new wine bar–wine shop was recently opened by two gentlemen who have both previously shared the title "Best Sommelier in Belgium," so the selection is excellent, with 30 wines by the glass and some 300 bottles to peruse, with a big emphasis on Italian grapes. ✉ *Kuipersstraat 6–8* ☎ *0497/172–085* 🌐 *www.blendwijnhandel.be* Ⓜ *Bus: 4, 14.*

Performing Arts

The monthly *Agenda Brugge,* available in English, gives details of all events in the city; you can get a copy at the tourist office. Listings for events and movie screenings are also published in the local Flemish newspaper *Exit,* available at bookstores and in the public library. Movies (except those aimed at small kids) are invariably screened in their original language with Flemish subtitles, and there are plenty of English-language films on the local screens.

Concertgebouw Brugge

THEATER | What has long been the center of the city's cultural scene, putting on music, dance, and theater shows throughout the year, has now added another string to its bow: guided tours (from €12). It offers the chance to go behind the scenes, visiting the dressing rooms and the practice studio, and get a good grounding in the acoustics of architecture. ✉ *'t Zand 34* ☎ *050/476–999* 🌐 *www.concertgebouw.be* Ⓜ *Bus: 42.*

Shopping

Most shops in Bruges are open Monday–Saturday 9 or 10–6; some souvenir shops are also open on Sunday. Although there are a couple of tacky tourist stores, Bruges has many trendy boutiques and shops, especially along Nordzandstraat, as well as Steenstraat and Vlamingstraat, both of which branch off from the Markt. Ter Steeghere mall, which links the Burg with Wollestraat, deftly integrates a modern development into the historic center. The largest and most pleasant mall is the Zilverpand off Zilverstraat, where 30-odd shops cluster in Flemish gable houses around two courtyards fringed with sidewalk cafés.

FOOD SHOPS

The Chocolate Line

CHOCOLATE | For chocolate filled with unusual flavors like Japanese wasabi or crisp beetroot, head to this self-proclaimed "shock-o-latier," which first opened in Bruges. Try the chocolate lipstick or "chocolate shooter"—a bizarre device created to catapult a cocoa-herb mixture up your nostrils, essentially having you inhale it. The shop here also recently expanded to include a "from tree to bar" exhibition, letting you see the chocolate-making process from start to finish, by gazing over into the open kitchen. ✉ *Simon Stevinplein 19* ☎ *050/341–090* 🌐 *www.thechocolateline.be* Ⓜ *Bus: 4, 14.*

Chocolaterie Spegelaere

CHOCOLATE | Famed for its charming "chocolate grapes" (marzipan- or praline-filled chocolate balls wired to look like a bunch of grapes), Spegelaere is something of an institution. Despite this, few tourists make it out to the shop, which lies in the edge of the historic center, so grab yourself a "chocolate cobblestone" and congratulate yourself on finding a gem. ✉ *Ezelstraat 92* ☎ *050/336–052* 🌐 *www.sweetchocolatedreams.be* Ⓜ *Bus: 3, 13.*

Depla Chocolatier

CHOCOLATE | This old-timer has been in the historic center since the late 1950s and remains Bruges's oldest artisanal chocolatier to make its chocolate on the premises. It's especially famed for its chocolate swans, filled with a mix of praline and gruut (herbs more common in brewing beer), and lacy traditional *kletskoppen* biscuits. ✉ *Mariastraat 20*

3 050/347–412 🌐 www.poldepla.be
] Bus: 1, 4, 14.

EWELRY AND CRAFT SHOPS

inGin

EWELRY & WATCHES | Artisan jewelers 'icolaas and Natalie craft exquisite rings om their shop-workshop on Ezelstraat, 'hich has become something of a haven or handmade goods in Bruges. ✉ *Ezel-traat 27* ☎ *050/341–909* 🌐 *www.kingin.e* Ⓜ *Bus: 3, 13.*

laud Bekaert

THER SPECIALTY STORE | Since medieval mes, Bruges has been a center for alligraphy and letters—a tradition carried n in the studio-cum-shop of Maud Beka-rt, a talented local artist and calligrapher 'hose gifts, inscriptions, and letters ıake for a fine souvenir. ✉ *Sint-Claras-aat 40* ☎ *0475/269–558 weekdays only 1–noon* 🌐 *maudbekaert.be* Ⓜ *Bus: 4.*

Apostelientje

ABRICS | In the early 20th century, ere were some 47,000 lace makers Belgium, and 70% of them worked Bruges. The city has a proud history f lace making, and 't Apostelientje, 'hich was established some three ecades ago, sells intricate handmade eces and beautiful antique lace gems, ometimes even framed. ✉ *Balstraat 11* *050/337–860* 🌐 *www.apostelientje.be* *Bus: 6, 16.*

ARKETS

ıe Markt is the setting for the weekly **'oensdag Markt** (Wednesday Market), ith vegetables, fruit, flowers, specialty ıeeses, and hams. (Occasionally, if ere is a major event taking place on the larkt, the market moves to the Burg.) ruges's biggest market is the **Zaterdag arkt** (Saturday Market) on 't Zand, elling all kinds of cheeses, hams, and ooked meats, as well as some clothing ıd household items. The **Vismarkt** (Fish larket) is held, appropriately, on the Vis-arkt, daily except Sunday and Monday. l three markets are morning events, from 8 to approximately 1:30. On week-ends March 15–November 15 there's a **flea market** (Boottochten Markt) open throughout the day along the Dijver—although it's not very large.

Damme

7 km (4 miles) northeast from Bruges.

A quiet agricultural village with a population of about 10,000 Flemings, Damme lies in a peaceful polder landscape of waving fields and far horizons. Walking its streets today feels much as it would have centuries ago. If you take the miniature paddle steamer *Lamme Goedzak*, which travels along a canal lined with slender poplars, the town is a half hour from Bruges. You could even hike or bike the distance along a common canal path.

Damme owes its place in history to a tidal wave that ravaged the coast in 1134 and opened an inlet from the Zwin to the environs of Bruges. The little town grew up as a fishing village until a canal was dug to connect it to Bruges. The former settlement was soon a key port and snapped up exclusive rights to import such treasured commodities as Bordeaux wine and Swedish herring. The "Maritime Law of Damme" thus became the standard for Hanseatic merchants. Later, when the Zwin channel silted up, Damme's fortunes slowly declined; however, its Burgundian architecture remains well-preserved.

GETTING HERE AND AROUND

The road from Bruges to Damme follows the canal and is a short ride (by bike or car) through one of the most beautiful parts of *de platteland* (the flat country). From Bruges take R30 (the circular road around the city) and follow the Damse Vaart-Zuid. By public transport the journey is more of an issue—bus line 43 connects Brugge's train station and Markt with Damme in about 15 minutes, but buses only run twice each day. From

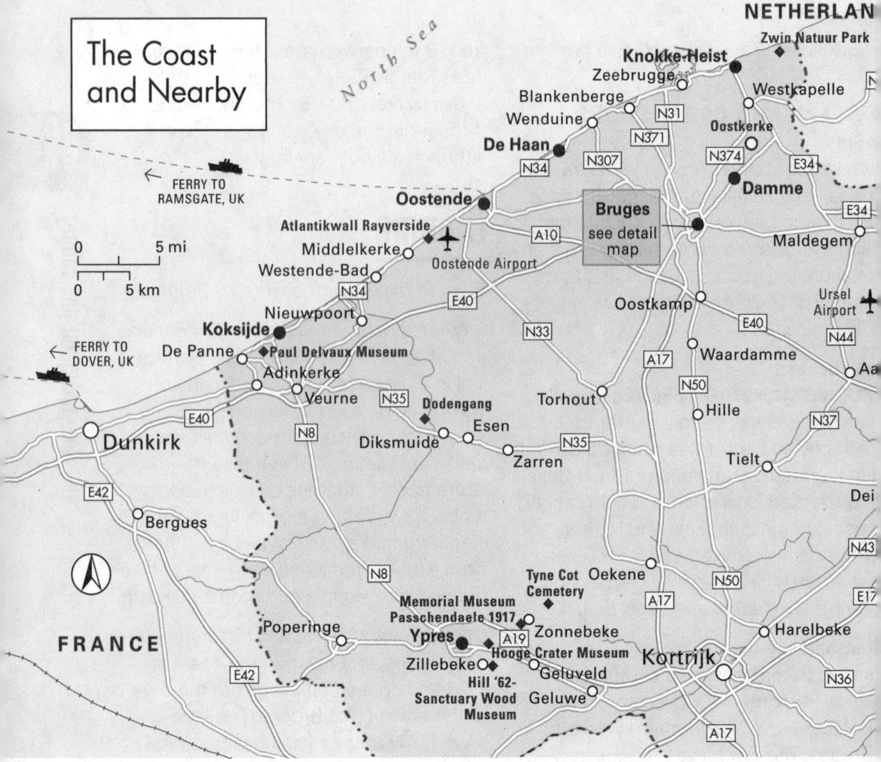

The Coast and Nearby

North Sea
NETHERLAN
Zwin Natuur Park
Knokke-Heist
Zeebrugge
Westkapelle
Blankenberge
N31
Wenduine
Oostkerke
N371
De Haan
N374
N307
N34
E34
Damme
FERRY TO RAMSGATE, UK
Oostende
Bruges see detail map
E34
Atlantikwall Rayverside
A10
Maldegem
0 5 mi
Middelkerke
0 5 km
Oostende Airport
Westende-Bad
N34
Ursel Airport
E40
Oostkamp
Nieuwpoort
E40
Koksijde
N33
N44
FERRY TO DOVER, UK
De Panne
Paul Delvaux Museum
Waardamme
Adinkerke
A17
Veurne
N35
Dodengang
Torhout
N50
E40
Hille
N37
Esen
N8
Dunkirk
Diksmuide
N35
Zarren
Tielt
E42
Dei
Bergues
N43
Tyne Cot Cemetery
Oekene
N8
N50
E17
Memorial Museum Passchendaele 1917
A17
Poperinge
Zonnebeke
Harelbeke
FRANCE
Ypres
A19
Hooge Crater Museum
Kortrijk
Zillebeke
Geluveld
E42
Hill '62- Sanctuary Wood Museum
Geluwe
N36
A17

April to mid-November, you can reach Damme in 35 minutes aboard the river barge *Lamme Goedzak* (*lammegoedzak-damme.com*), which sails four times daily in each direction. The Bruges jetty is 2 km (1 mile) northeast from the center at Noorweegse Kaai 31 (accessible from the Markt via bus line 4), and and a round-trip costs €15.

VISITOR INFORMATION

CONTACTS Visit Damme. ✉ *Jacob van Maerlantstraat 3, Damme* ☎ *050/288–610* 🌐 *www.visitdamme.be.*

Sights

Marktplein

PLAZA/SQUARE | Jacob van Maerlant's statue stands tall and poetic in the center of Damme's market square. On the facade of the Gothic Stadhuis (Town Hall) you can see Charles, the noble duke, pr senting the wedding ring to his fiancée Margaret, plus other stone effigies of Flemish counts set in niches between the high windows. The step-gabled buil ing's interior moldings and clock tower are especially outstanding. Note the Huyse de Grote Sterre, a 15th-century patrician's residence that was also hom to the Spanish military governor in the 17th century; it's now the tourist office and a literary museum. ✉ *Marktplein, Damme.*

Onze-Lieve-Vrouw-Hemelvaartkerk

CHURCH | On a clear day you can see as far as the Netherlands by climbing the 206 steps to the top of the tower of the Onze-Lieve-Vrouwekerk (*Church of Our Lady*), which was founded in 1225 and rises high above the surrounding farmland as a symbol of Damme's prou ast. Poet Jacob van Maerlant, who ved and worked in Damme during the te 13th century, is buried under the nain portal below the tower. Charles the old and Margaret of York were married ere. ✉ *Kerkstraat z/n, Damme* 🌐 *www. isitdamme.be* 🎫 *Church: free; tower: €3*) *Tower closed Oct.–Mar.*

ostkerke
OWN | Around 4 km (2½ miles) north om Damme, Oostkerke has to be ne of the cutest villages in Flanders. very house in the tiny hamlet is white-vashed, and at the center stands the nposing bulk of the Sint-Quintinuskerk, ounded around 1100. Also nearby is 19th-century mill and a 14th-century astle, albeit the former is in a poor state f repair, and the latter is now a private esidence and closed to visitors. If you're n need of refreshment, Eetcafé De notwilg (*www.deknotwilgoostkerke.be*; losed Tuesday and Wednesday) serves imple snacks and full meals. ✉ *Oostk-erke, Damme.*

Restaurants

e Lamme Goedzak
$$ | **BELGIAN** | Commanding a fabulous ocation right on the main square, this harming restaurant occupies a lovely vhite-painted old house, and boasts inte-ior furnishings, including a large chande-er and plentiful oak beams, that create n atmosphere of timelessness. The food ves up to the decor, with beautifully pre-ented French-Belgian dishes that are not fraid to bring in influences from Asia and lsewhere. **Known for:** secluded courtyard errace at the rear; good wine list; glori-ous historical decor. 💲 *Average main: €28* ✉ *Kerkstraat 13, Damme* ☎ *050/692–266* 🌐 *www.delammegoedzak.be* 🕒 *Closed Ved. and Thurs. No lunch Fri.*

a Bouffée
$$ | **BELGIAN** | This place close to the nain square is so unassuming from he outside that, were it not for the simple front terrace, you might think it was simply someone's home, but step through the front door and on the inside you'll find a welcoming and cozy modern bistro. The menu is not long, but usually features well-presented takes on Belgian classics such as *paling* (eel) and *vispan-netje* (fish stew). **Known for:** a quiet rear terrace; Belgian classics with a modern makeover; friendly service. 💲 *Average main: €25* ✉ *Kerkstraat 26, Damme* ☎ *050/680–588* 🌐 *www.bistrolabouffee. be* 🕒 *Closed Tues. and Wed.*

Knokke-Heist

11 km (7 miles) north from Damme, 17 km (10 miles) north of Bruges, 108 km (65 miles) northwest of Brussels.

Knokke-Heist is an area of dunes and sea, purple wildflowers and groomed golf courses, which actually encompasses five resorts. Heist, Albertstrand, and Duinbergen are sports- and family-oriented beaches, while to young Belgians of ample means, Knokke is the beach to show off designer fashions or a buff new beau. To the east, Het Zoute is a wealthy area of old-money villas. Along the Kustlaan, one block inland from the beach, you'll find branches of virtually every fashionable shop in Brussels. The Casino has an enormous 2,000-light Venetian-crystal chandelier in the foyer. Gaming, however, is for members only.

In the late 19th century, painters settled in this coastal pleasure zone, and today there are dozens of galleries with works by Belgian and international artists; the Casino displays treasured murals by René Magritte. The Albertplein, widely known as the Place M'as-tu-vu (Did-You-See-Me Square), is a gathering place for the chic-at-heart.

GETTING HERE AND AROUND

Hourly direct trains get you from Bruges to Knokke in around 20 minutes. Knokke-Heist is also connected to all the other coastal resorts by the coastal tram service (*www.dekusttram.be*), which is a fun way to get about and runs up to six times an hour at peak times.

VISITOR INFORMATION

CONTACTS Tourisme Knokke-Heist. ✉ *Zeedijk-Knokke 660, Knokke-Heist* ☎ *050/630–380* 🌐 *www.myknokke-heist.be.*

Sights

For Freedom Museum

HISTORY MUSEUM | Preaching a message of tolerance and freedom, this small museum 5 km (3 miles) southwest from central Knokke-Heist (bus No. 3 from the railway station will drop you close by) focuses on events during the Nazi occupation of 1940–44, and commemorates the Battle of the Scheldt, and the liberation of the region by Allied forces a few months after D-Day. A series of dioramas featuring original uniforms, weapons, and vehicles will immerse you in the period. ✉ *Ramskapellestraat 91–93, Knokke-Heist* ☎ *050/687–130* 🌐 *www.forfreedommuseum.be* 🎫 *€10* 🕓 *Closed weekdays mid-Nov.–Easter.*

★ Zwin Natuur Park

NATURE PRESERVE | Zwin is a remarkable 390-acre nature reserve and bird sanctuary reaching the Netherlands border, preserved thanks to the efforts of naturalist Count Léon Lippens in the early 20th century. The Zwin was once a busy estuary, connecting Bruges with the North Sea. In fact, in 1340 Edward III of England and his Flemish allies sailed here to conquer the French fleet, readying to attack England. But after silting up in the 16th century, the waterway has retreated into quiet marsh and tidal channels, encircled by dunes and dikes—the largest salt marsh in Belgium. Saltwater washes into the soil, making for some unusual flora and fauna. Visit in spring for the bird migrations and from mid-July for the flowers, especially the native *zwinneblomme*, or sea lavender. From the top of the dike there's a splendid view of the dunes and inlets. Storks nes in the aviary, which also holds thousand of aquatic birds and birds of prey, includ ing the red-beaked sheldrake, gray plove avocet, and sandpiper. If you get hungry The Shelter bistro is at the park entranc ✉ *Graaf Léon Lippensdreef 8, Knokke-Heist* ☎ *050/607–086* 🌐 *www.zwin.b* 🎫 *€12 (€10 if bought 24 hrs in advance)* 🕓 *Closed weekdays Jan. and Feb.*

Beaches

Knokke-Heist Beach

BEACH | FAMILY | Knokke-Heist's beach is officially split into four different areas (Heist, Duinbergen, Albertstrand, and Het Zoute), but to untrained observers they form one continuous 9-km (5½-mile stretch of sand, bordering the industrial port of Zeebrugge at one end, and the dunes of Het Zwin nature reserve and the Dutch resort of Cadzand at the othe The eastern half is more popular, with the bulk of the facilities concentrated around Albertstrand Beach, which is steps from central Knokke.If you're looking for solitude, head to the westerr end, although the views from there of Zeebrugge are somewhat less appealing **Amenities:** food and drink; lifeguards; parking (fee); showers; toilets; water sports. **Best for:** partiers; sunset; surfing swimming; walking; windsurfing. ✉ *Kust laan and Zeedijk-Knokke, Knokke-Heist.*

Restaurants

Alexandra

$$$ | SEAFOOD | This smart modern restaurant takes its inspiration primarily from the nearby North Sea, with fishy and sea food stars ranging from the familiar mussels, to rarer menu treats like skate wing or more indulgent lobster. The adjacent "Bar a Vina" wine bar (open evenings only), under the same ownership, offers tapas-style sharing dishes prepared in the same kitchen, but designed to be enjoyed in slightly less formal surrounds. **Known for:** great wine list; fine dining at a price that won't (quite) break the bank; excellent seafood. *Average main: €28* *Van Bunnenplein 17, Knokke-Heist* *050/606–344* *www.restaurantalexandra.be* *Closed Thurs. and Fri.*

Brasserie Rubens

$$$ | **BELGIAN** | **FAMILY** | The brasserie restaurant beside the coastal promenade in downtown Knokke has a slightly old-fashioned feel, but it serves reliably good, hearty portions of Belgian classics, and some excellent seafood to boot. The latter should come as no real surprise given the location: snag a table on the outside terrace in summer and you enjoy a sea view, and inhale the fresh salty air as you dine. **Known for:** an extensive wine list with more than 350 choices; friendly, efficient service; kitchen open all day long. *Average main: €25* *Zeedijk-Albertstrand 589, Knokke-Heist* *050/603–501* *rubens-knokke.be.*

Hotels

Hotel Adagio

$$ | **HOTEL** | **FAMILY** | This small family-run hotel is just a two-minute walk from the beach, and is even nearer to shops and restaurants, yet despite being close to the action it is on a quiet street, and never gets too noisy at night. **Pros:** close to beach and central restaurants; family-run means attentive service; free breakfast. **Cons:** on-site parking is expensive; parking elevator not suitable for large vehicles; hotel is one block back from the coast, so no sea views. *Rooms from: €130* *Van Bunnenlaan 12, Knokke-Heist* *050/624–844* *www.hoteladagio.be* *20 rooms* *Free Breakfast.*

La Réserve

$$$$ | **RESORT** | This vast five-star resort hotel, complete with a sixth-floor spa and swimming pool, and a man-made lake outside, has a country-club approach to pampering. **Pros:** most rooms have balconies and/or lake views; on-site spa is free for guests; a few minutes' walk from the beach. **Cons:** breakfast is an expensive extra; very pricey, although room price does include access to the spa; large size makes it a bit cold and impersonal, especially in public areas. *Rooms from: €385* *Elizabetlaan 160, Knokke-Heist* *050/610–606* *la-reserve.be* *110 rooms* *No Meals.*

De Haan

21 km (13 miles) southwest from Knokke-Heist, 18 km (11 miles) northwest from Bruges.

Often cited as one of the prettiest villages in Flanders, De Haan is an elegant upscale resort full of early-20th-century villas, and is surrounded by attractive expanses of dunes and woodland that make for pleasant hiking. Most of the roads around the village away from the beach area are green and tree-lined, and very much more akin to country lanes than to urban streets. Albert Einstein spent six months in De Haan during the spring and summer of 1933. The home where he stayed, Villa Savoyarde (*Shakespearelaan 5*), is not open to visitors, but there is a statue of the great man reclined on a park bench—you'll find it in a small park-let at the junction of Prinses Astridlaan and Normandiëlaan.

GETTING HERE AND AROUND

De Haan is a 25-minute drive northwest from Bruges along the N9 and N307. By public transport, take the trains that run four times each hour from Bruges to Oostende, then board the coastal tram (*www.dekusttram.be*)—the total journey time is around 45 minutes. De Haan is also connected to all the other resort towns by the coastal tram, which runs up to six times an hour in each direction at peak times.

VISITOR INFORMATION

CONTACTS Tourisme De Haan - Centrum. ✉ *Tramlijn-Oost z/n, De Haan* ☎ *059/242–135* 🌐 *www.visitdehaan.be.*

Beaches

De Haan Beach

BEACH | FAMILY | Despite its relatively diminutive size, De Haan lays claim to having Belgium's largest beach: an expanse of white sand stretching around 12 km (7½ miles) from end to end. This size means that even in high summer it never gets overly crowded. At the western end is the Belgian coast's only officially designated nudist beach. **Amenities:** food and drink; lifeguards; parking (free); toilets; water sports. **Best for:** nudists; sunset; swimming; walking; windsurfing. ✉ *Zeedijk, De Haan.*

Restaurants

Bistro Villa Julia

$$$ | BELGIAN | The food at this intimate bistro in a half-timbered villa is French-influenced modern European, but with a few nods to Flemish traditions thrown in to suit the old-fashioned surrounds, such as rabbit cooked "grandma's way" in Trappist beer. You can order most dishes as a starter or as a larger main, but if you want to try several at once, ask for the smaller "tapas" portions. **Known for:** friendly and attentive service; local oysters; small but well-chosen menu. $ *Average main: €24* ✉ *Van Eycklaan 2, De Haan* ☎ *059/449–342* 🌐 *villajulia.be* ⏲ *Closed Mon. and Tues.*

Hotels

Romantik Hotel Manoir Carpe Diem

$$$ | HOTEL | Occupying a lovely white-painted villa just a few blocks back from the beach, this genteel yet affordable hotel has a leafy garden at the front and a secluded outdoor swimming pool at the rear. **Pros:** free on-site parking; quiet yet central location; free breakfast. **Cons:** pool is outdoors, so dips are weath er-dependent; no sea views; minimum two-night stay at weekends. $ *Rooms from: €180* ✉ *Prins Karellaan 12, De Haa* ☎ *059/233–220* 🌐 *www.manoircarpediem.com* *17 rooms* *Free Breakfast.*

Oostende

12 km (8 miles) southwest from De Haan, 28 km (17 miles) west from Bruges.

A transportation and fishing center and an old-fashioned, slightly raffish resort, Oostende (pronounced *ohstender* in Flemish), otherwise known as Ostend in English, leads a double life. It's the largest and oldest town on the coast, with a history going back to the 10th century. Long a pirates' hideout, Oostende has hosted many a famous rogue and adventurer, and it was from here that Crusaders also set sail for the Holy Land. In the 17th century, when villagers backed the Protestant cause, Oostende withstood a Spanish siege for three years.

One of Europe's first railways was built between Oostende and Mechelen in 1838, resulting in regular mail packet services to Dover, England, beginning in 1846. A hundred years ago, the town was at its belle epoque height, with a boom of neoclassical buildings dripping with ornamentation. During World War II many of the buildings were bombed, and the glamour dimmed, but in recent years Oostende has regained much of its grandeur. Historic buildings have beer embellished, and there's been a revival o cultural activities.

GETTING HERE AND AROUND

The E40 highway from Brussels passes both Ghent and Bruges en route to Oostende and Calais in France. Keep in mind that traffic can be bumper-to-bumper on summer weekends. Hourly trains from Bruges get you there in 15 minutes; from

A golden glow descends over the harbor in the seaside town Oostende.

Brussels, it takes one hour 15 minutes. Oostende is connected to all the other coastal resort towns by the coastal tram service (*www.dekusttram.be*), which runs up to six times an hour in each direction at peak times.

VISITOR INFORMATION

CONTACTS Tourist office Oostende. ✉ *Monacoplein 2, Oostende* ☎ *059/701–199* 🌐 *www.visitoostende.be.*

 Sights

Atlantikwall Rayverside

MILITARY SIGHT | Just to the west of town among the dunes (bus lines 68 and 69 stop outside), this is one of the best preserved parts of the German "Atlantikwall" defensive line, built to repel Allied invasion during World War II. You are free to explore around 60 bunkers, observation posts, and gun emplacements, all connected by 2 km (1.3 miles) of open trenches and underground passages. On the same site is **Anno 1465**, a re-creation of a long-vanished medieval fishing settlement that once stood on this spot. ✉ *Nieuwpoortsesteenweg 636, Oostende* ☎ *059/702–285* 🌐 *www.raversyde.be* 🎫 *Atlantikwall: €6; Anno 1465: €5; combi ticket: €8* 🕒 *Closed Mon. and mid-Nov.–mid-Mar.*

James Ensorhuis

ART MUSEUM | The James Ensorhuis is an introduction to the strange and hallucinatory world of the painter James Ensor (1860–1949), who was recognized late in his life as one of the great artists of the early 20th century. Using violent colors to express his frequently macabre or satirical themes, he depicted a fantastic carnival world peopled by masks and skeletons. The displays in this house, which was his home and studio, include many of the objects found in his work, especially the masks, and copies of his major paintings. Beside the house are five interactive spaces that use audiovisual displays to bring Ensor's paintings to life. ✉ *Vlaanderenstraat 29, Oostende* ☎ *059/418–900* 🌐 *www.ensorstad.be* 🎫 *€12* 🕒 *Closed Mon.*

Mercator

NAUTICAL SIGHT | This handsome three-masted training ship of the Belgian merchant marine, which sailed from the 1930s to the 1960s, is now moored close to the city center, ready to sail if needed. Decks, fittings, and the spartan quarters have been kept intact, and there's a museum of mementos brought home from the ship's exotic voyages; during one they hauled back mysterious statues from Easter Island. ✉ *Mercatordok, Vindictivelaan 1, Oostende* ☎ *0494/514–335* 🌐 *www.zeilschipmercator.be* 🎫 *€5* 🕒 *Closed Mon.*

Mu.ZEE

ART MUSEUM | Oostende's modern art museum contains works by Belgian contemporary artists, from 1880 to the present day, and is well represented by Pierre Alechinsky, Roger Raveel, and Paul van Hoeydonck (whose statuette, *The Fallen Astronaut,* was deposited on the moon by the Apollo XV crew), among others. Ceramics, paintings, sculpture, and graphic art are all displayed. ✉ *Romestraat 11, Oostende* ☎ *059/508–118* 🌐 *www.muzee.be* 🎫 *€12* 🕒 *Closed Mon.*

Beaches

Groot Strand

BEACH | **FAMILY** | Oostende's long, sandy Large Beach is popular with sun-seeking families and sporty surfers alike. On the landward side, the elevated Albert I Promenade is lined with shops and tearooms that compete for attention with views of the sand and sea. **Amenities:** food and drink; lifeguards; parking (fee); showers; toilets; water sports. **Best for:** sunset; surfing; swimming; walking. ✉ *Albert I Promenade, Oostende.*

Klein Strand

BEACH | To the east of the Groot Strand, Klein Strand (Small Beach) occupies the area beside the breakwaters at the entrance to Oostende Harbor. It's less popular than its neighbor as swimming here is prohibited. instead, it is used for activities and events. **Amenities:** food and drink; parking (fee). **Best for:** sunset; walking. ✉ *Westelijke Streekdam, Oostende.*

Restaurants

Bistrot de la Mer

$$ | **BELGIAN** | Although the menu at this simple but cozy family-run place splits itself evenly between seafood and meat-based dishes, its location—directly across from the harbor where the fishing boats land their harvest—means you will seldom go wrong if you opt for the catch of the day. Scallop starters and lobster mains add extra sparkle for those in need of a little indulgence. **Known for:** friendly service; good beef and tuna carpaccio starters; excellent mussels. 💲 *Average main: €22* ✉ *Visserskaai 21, Oostende* ☎ *059/801–800* 🌐 *www.bistrot-de-la-mer.com* 🕒 *Closed Mon. and Tues.*

Lobster

$$$$ | **SEAFOOD** | Astute readers may spot the tiny hint in the restaurant's name about what to expect from this centrally located and long-standing seafood-obsessed institution, directly opposite the casino and Kursaal. The excellent *fruits de mer* platters and lobster mains certainly don't come cheap, but if you are looking for something more affordable that is still a mouthwatering treat, go for the three-course prix-fixe menu. **Known for:** three decades of good service; there's a clue in the name; great fruits de mer seafood platters. 💲 *Average main: €40* ✉ *Van Iseghemlaan 64, Oostende* ☎ *059/500–282* 🌐 *www.lobster.be* 🕒 *Closed Mon. and Tues.*

Hotels

C-Hotels Andromeda

$$ | **HOTEL** | Ideally located next door to the Kursaal, this centrally located modern hotel has public rooms in black and white and guest rooms in restful

colors. **Pros:** free breakfast; large indoor pool; close to beach. **Cons:** large hotel, so can feel a little impersonal; parking is expensive; rooms with sea view and balcony are more expensive. *$ Rooms from: €135 ✉ Kursaal-Westhelling 5, Oostende ☎ 059/806–611 🌐 www.c-hotels.be/andromeda 111 rooms 🍽 Free Breakfast.*

Thermae Palace Hotel
$$ | **HOTEL** | King Leopold II, who dabbled in architecture, helped to design this grand Art Deco beachfront building, which first opened in 1933 and was the only grande-dame hotel in Oostende to survive the pummeling of World War II. **Pros:** room rates drop outside the summer season; quiet spot away from bustling city; beachside location. **Cons:** no free parking, despite distance from center; rooms with a sea view are more expensive; a little way from the city center. *$ Rooms from: €150 ✉ Koningin Astridlaan 7, Oostende ☎ 059/806–644 🌐 www.thermaepalace.be 159 rooms 🍽 No Meals.*

Nightlife

Café Botteltje
BARS | Below the hotel of the same name, the "Little Bottle" has enjoyed a legendary status among Belgian beer lovers for more than three decades—a quick glance at the more than 300 choices on offer on the menu will soon tell you why. *✉ Louisastraat 19, Oostende ☎ 059/700–928 🌐 www.botteltje.be.*

Performing Arts

Kursaal
ARTS CENTERS | Concerts of all kinds, from classical to rock, pop, and jazz, draw crowds from far away to the 1,700-seat hall at the Kursaal. *✉ Kursaal-Westhelling 12, Oostende ☎ 059/295–050 🌐 www.kursaaloostende.be.*

Koksijde

27 km (17 miles) southwest from Oostende, 48 km (30 miles) west from Bruges.

Koksijde and Sint-Idesbald are small resorts, separated by a few kilometers, that offer more than beach life. Koksijde has the highest dune on the coast, the Hoge Blekker, 108 feet high.

GETTING HERE AND AROUND

Koksijde is just north of the E40 highway, which connects it with all the major cities of Flanders. By train, Koksijde is one hour from Bruges, including a change in Lichtervelde. The service runs hourly. Koksijde is connected to all the other resort towns by the coastal tram service (*www.dekusttram.be*), which runs up to six times an hour in each direction at peak times.

Sights

Abdijmuseum Ten Duinen
RELIGIOUS BUILDING | On the southern edge of Koksijde are the ruins of the Cistercian Duinenabdij (Abbey of the Dunes), founded in 1107 and destroyed by the iconoclasts in 1566. Traces of the original abbey, the cloisters, and columns from the refectory remain. An adjacent archaeological museum shows collections from the digs, as well as interesting examples of regional plants and animals.

A few minutes' walk east from the abbey, on Kerkplein, the strikingly modern architecture of the **Onze-Lieve-Vrouw ter Duinenkerk** (Our Lady of Sorrows of the Dunes Church), suggests both the dunes and the sea through bold colors, undulating forms, and stained glass. A crypt holds the remains of the first abbot of the abbey. *✉ A. Verbouwelaan 15, Koksijde ☎ 058/533–950 🌐 www.tenduinen.be €7 🕓 Closed Mon.*

Paul Delvaux Museum

ART MUSEUM | Art lovers will want to head for nearby Sint-Idesbald—effectively a western suburb of Koksijde—to discover the Paul Delvaux Museum in a reconverted Flemish farmhouse. It is dedicated to the painter, famous for his Surrealist mix of nudes, skeletons, and trains, who died in 1994 at the age of nearly 100. This collection has work from the various stages of Delvaux's career, including his later, somewhat eerie female nudes. ✉ *Paul Delvauxlaan 42, Koksijde* ☎ *058/521–229* 🌐 *www.delvauxmuseum.be* 🎫 *€10* ⏲ *Closed Mon.*

Beaches

Koksijde Beach

BEACH | FAMILY | Koksijde's stretch of the Belgian coast is another expanse of white sand, popular with families. There are orientation poles here at regular intervals, each with a different brightly colored figure on top, designed to be easily recognizable wayfinders for lost children. **Amenities:** food and drink; lifeguards; parking (fee); toilets; water sports. **Best for:** sunset; swimming; walking; windsurfing. ✉ *Zeedijk, Koksijde.*

Restaurants

De Huifkar

$$$ | SEAFOOD | If the "lobsters in buckets" artwork above the front door doesn't get you thinking, then the large tank of live specimens in the middle of the dining room will leave you in no doubt whatsoever as to where the gastronomic heart of this chic modern restaurant in the center of town lies. Most dishes follow the seasons, though fruits de mer seafood platters are a menu staple, and there are always several steak choices to keep the meat lovers happy. **Known for:** excellent quality for the price; game dishes served in fall season; attentive service. $ *Average main: €28* ✉ *Koninklijke Baan 142, Koksijde* ☎ *058/511–668* 🌐 *www.dehuifkar.be* ⏲ *Closed Wed. and Thurs. and mid-Jan.–mid-Feb.*

Ypres

36 km (23 miles) southeast from Koksijde, 71 km (44 miles) southwest from Bruges.

Known as the Ypres of World War I infamy, "Wipers" to the Tommies in the trenches, and Ieper (pronounced *eeper*) to the locals, this town was the Hiroshima of the Great War. Founded in the 10th century, Ypres's textile industry helped it expand into one of the region's major mercantile centers during the Middle Ages. Epidemics, sieges, repressions, and strife took their toll, and the cloth makers packed their bags in the 16th and 17th centuries. Ypres remained a quiet convent town, but was drawn into the crossfire of World War I three centuries later, in 1914, after neutral Belgium was forced into the Great War when the Germans invaded France from the north.

There were four major battles at Ypres; in the second (1915), the German army introduced a new weapon, poison gas, while the third (1917) was a particularly infamous disaster of roiling mud and horrifying casualties in which the Allies gained only a few kilometers. In the last battle in 1918, the Allies decisively broke through the German lines, finally securing the western front.

Completely destroyed in the war, modern Ypres is a painstaking reconstruction of major medieval buildings—the last were laid in the 1960s. The city proudly stands as homage to the spirit of the Flemings, and to the memory of the almost half a million soldiers who fell in the surrounding fields, on the front line that formed a "bulge" (in military terms, a salient) around the city of Ypres, and who now lie in more than 170 vast cemeteries spreading over the flat polder plains.

Hops and Glory

The land west of Ypres, particularly around the town of Poperinge, is Belgium's hop country, where most of the crops used in the country's prestigious brewing industry are produced. Perhaps inevitably, the same region is also home to several fine breweries, some of whose names give rise to reverential nods of recognition whenever they are mentioned.

Chief among them is **Westvleteren**, the beer brewed since 1839 by the Trappist monks of **Sint Sixtus abbey** (*sintsixtus.be*), in the village of Vleteren, 15 km (9 miles) northwest from Ypres. Considered by some enthusiasts to be the best beer in the world, it's neither mass-produced nor widely distributed, and isn't available in regular stores. Even stocks at the abbey shop are limited, and buying is deliberately made a complicated process, as the monks only produce enough beer to support themselves. Moreover, the abbey itself and the brewery are off-limits to outsiders.

An easier way to try their three beers—Blonde (5.8%), Eight (8%), and Twelve (10.8%)—is to visit the abbey's **Café In de Vrede** (*www.indevrede.be*). Somewhat ironically, the café is modern and consequently a rather soulless place, but you will no doubt be supping in the company of beer pilgrims from every continent.

Some 12 km (7½ miles) southwest from Vleteren, **Brouwerij Sint Bernardus** (*www.sintbernardus.be*) is altogether more welcoming from a visitor's perspective. The brewery was originally founded in 1946 to create commercial versions of the Westvleteren beers to cope with demand, but since the early 1990s it has been producing its own excellent Sint Bernardus range. You can book tours of the brewery, or sample a brew with a meal in their chic top-floor taproom, **Bar Bernard**, which has a rooftop terrace and panoramic views of the surrounding hop fields. Real devotees can even stay overnight in the brewery's own guesthouse next door.

Just a mile north from Sint Bernardus, the village of Watou is home to another great brewer, **Van Eecke** (*www.leroybreweries.be*), which produces the excellent Kapittel range of beers. But a bigger reason to come here is to dine at **'t Hommelhof** (*www.hommelhof.be*) . In business for three decades, this restaurant has long been a frontrunner in the world of beer cuisine, and its menu is packed with hearty Belgian dishes that are both cooked and paired with the finest ales.

Nowadays, the peaceful "plat pays," the flat countryside that haunted singer Jacques Brel's imagination, still carries the scars of that gruesome period—every year, farmers still dig up more than 200 tons of ammunition from the fields.

GETTING HERE AND AROUND

From Bruges, take the E403 highway toward Kortrijk, where you get on the A19; take Exit 4, and follow the N37 to the city center. Hourly direct trains from Ghent get you to Ypres (Ieper) in 1 hour and 10 minutes. There are hourly trains from Bruges as well, taking around the same time, but you have to change in Kortrijk.

There is little public transport around the area of the battlefields sights. To visit them properly and independently, you will either need your own vehicle, or a lot of patience.

VISITOR INFORMATION

CONTACTS Tourist Office Ieper. ✉ *Lakenhallen, Grote Markt 34, Ypres* ☎ *057/239–220* 🌐 *www.toerismeieper.be.*

Sights

Dodengang

MILITARY SIGHT | Twenty-five kilometers (16 miles) north of Ypres, close to Diksmuide—a town, which, like Ypres, was completely flattened during World War I—you can visit the so-called *Dodengang* (Trench of Death), a network of trenches on the banks of the IJzer river where Belgian troops faced and held off their German adversaries for four years. Make sure to dress warmly on a cold day, as the wind tends to add some extra drama by howling across the plain. The Dodengang is only a mile or so from the Museum aan de IJzer, making it easy to combine a visit to both. ✉ *Ijzerdijk 65, Diksmuide* ☎ *051/505–344* 🎫 *€5* ⏲ *Closed Mon., Wed., and Fri. and Nov.–Mar.*

Hill '62 - Sanctuary Wood Museum

MILITARY SIGHT | Head 5 km (3 miles) east from Ypres along the N8, then follow the signs via Canadalaan and Sanctuary Wood to Hill '62, an old-fashioned museum and dusty café. In addition to photographs, weapons, and assorted objects salvaged from the battlefield, the owner has preserved some of the original trenches on his land. They were part of a tunnel complex that stretched from the coast at Nieuwpoort to the French-Swiss border (at least 600 km [400 miles]). The ground is muddy even on sunny days, so you might need boots to inspect them. ✉ *Canadalaan 26, Ypres* ☎ *057/466–373* 🌐 *www.hill62trenches.be* 🎫 *€10* ⏲ *Closed Mon. and Dec. and Jan.*

Hooge Crater Museum

HISTORY MUSEUM | In Zillebeke, 6 km (4 miles) east from Ypres, this museum is installed in an old chapel. Items on display include bombs, grenades, rifles, and uniforms. More than 6,500 British soldiers lie in the cemetery across the street. ✉ *Meenseweg 467, Ypres* ☎ *057/468–446* 🌐 *www.hoogecrater.com* 🎫 *€7* ⏲ *Closed Mon. and Tues.*

★ In Flanders Fields Museum

HISTORY MUSEUM | The powerful interactive displays in the In Flanders Fields Museum preserve the terrors of trench warfare and the memory of those who died in nearby fields. The museum focuses on World War I, but expands to the universal theme of war. Computer screens, sound effects, scale models, and videos realistically portray the weapons, endless battles, and numerous casualties of the area's wars. Each visitor receives a "smart card" with details of a soldier or civilian and follows that person's fortunes throughout the war. The museum is housed on the second floor of the magnificent Lakenhallen (Cloth Hall) on the Grote Markt, a copy of the original 1304 building. If you climb the 264 steps in the square belfry, the view of turrets, towns, and fields seems endless. There are smart cards and other information in English. The museum also maintains casualty databases, which can be used by the public. ✉ *Grote Markt 34, Ypres* ☎ *058/239–220* 🌐 *www.inflandersfields.be* 🎫 *€10* ⏲ *Closed Mon. in mid-Nov.–Mar.*

★ Memorial Museum Passchendaele 1917

HISTORY MUSEUM | In Zonnebeke, 10 km (6 miles) east from Ypres (take the N37) this museum is, simply put, a must-see. It houses the largest public collection of World War I memorabilia in western Flanders. Weapons, uniforms, documents, and photographs re-create the tragedy of the Third Battle of Ypres. You can even smell the different types of poison gas that were used. The cellar holds a realistic reconstruction of a dugout, a subterranean camp that lodged soldiers during the war; it was, according to one of them, "one of the most disgusting places I ever lived in." ✉ *Berten Pilstraat 5A, Zonnebeke* ☎ *051/770–441* 🌐 *www.passchendaele.be* 🎫 *€11* 🕓 *Closed mid-Dec.–Jan.*

★ Menenpoort

MILITARY SIGHT | About 100 yards east of the Grote Markt, the Menenpoort is among the most moving of war memorials. It was built near the old Menin gate, along the route Allied soldiers took toward the front line. Troops on the "Menin road" endured brutal, insistent German artillery attacks; one section was dubbed "Hellfire Corner." After World War I, the British built the vast arch in memory of the 300,000 soldiers who perished in this corridor. The names of some 55,000 soldiers who died before August 15, 1917, and whose bodies were missing, are inscribed. Since 1928, every night at 8, traffic is stopped at the Menin gate as the **Last Post** is blown on silver bugles, gifts of the British Legion. The practice was interrupted during World War II, but it was resumed the night Polish troops liberated the town, September 6, 1944. Be sure to witness this truly breathtaking experience. ✉ *Menenstraat, Ypres* 🎫 *Free.*

Museum Aan de IJzer

MILITARY SIGHT | At the western edge of Diksmuide, some 23 km (15 miles) north from Ypres, and just a mile south from the Dodengang (above), the centerpiece of this memorial site is the **IJzertoren**, a 275-foot tower, rebuilt in 1965 to honor defenders and casualties from both world wars and to represent the Flemish struggle for autonomy. The giant letters on the monument beside the tower (AVV-VVK), mean "Everything for Flanders, Flanders for Christ." The 22-story tower houses a museum chronicling the two wars and the emancipation of Flanders using images, text, and sound. The top floor and the roof terrace provide a splendid view of the entire area. ✉ *IJzerdijk 49, Diksmuide* ☎ *051/500–286* 🌐 *www.museumaandeijzer.be* 🎫 *€8.*

Tyne Cot Cemetery

CEMETERY | Three kilometers (2 miles) north from the Memorial Museum Passchendaele 1917, the British cemetery Tyne Cot is—with almost 12,000 graves—the largest and best known of more than 170 military cemeteries in the area. In its awe-inspiring austerity, it evokes the agony of anonymous and unknown losses. A significant majority of the graves here are for unidentified casualties, and a curving wall lists the names of nearly 35,000 Commonwealth soldiers killed after August 1917 whose bodies and graves vanished in the turmoil of war. A large cross stands atop one of the German pillbox bunkers for which the site was named; British troops trying to gain the ridge dubbed it a cot, or cottage. ✉ *Vijfwegestraat 4, Passendale* ✣ *24 km (16 miles) north from Ypres* 🌐 *www.passchendaele.be* 🎫 *Free* 🕓 *Visitor center closed mid-Dec.–Jan.*

Restaurants

A L'Envers

$$$ | **BELGIAN** | A L'Envers is French for "inverted," and the name reflects this modern restaurant's simple but effective concept: to present dishes with edgy new flavor combinations, and old-school traditional fare, all on the same menu. The house specialties include beef carpaccio, and scampi cooked half a dozen ways, the latter served both as a starter and as a main, but it is on the three-course "surprise" menu that the chef really lets his imagination run wild. **Known for:** unusual but always delicious flavors; experimental cuisine; traditional classics like vispannetje (fish stew). *$ Average main: €25* ✉ *Patersstraat 2, Ypres* ☎ *0489/026–081* 🌐 *www.alenvers.be* 🕓 *Closed Tues. and Wed. No lunch Mon.–Sat.*

De Ruyffelaer

$$ | **BELGIAN** | Lace curtains in the front windows—and an interior that looks unchanged in a century, but which was probably carefully crafted to look that way—set the tone in this traditional restaurant serving hearty portions of no-frills Belgian classics, prepared in a style of which Grandma would have approved. Even French fries and side salads have no place here: all mains are served with cooked vegetables and creamy mashed potato—if you're looking for cutting-edge nouvelle cuisine you may be disappointed, but if you want a homey feast you won't go hungry. **Known for:** historic ambience; old-fashioned but heart-warmingly delicious comfort food; dishes cooked with beer. *Average main: €20 De Stuersstraat 11, Ypres 0499/415–198 www.deruyffelaer.be Closed Mon.–Thurs. No lunch Fri. and Sat.*

Hotels

Hotel New Regina

$$ | **HOTEL** | In a sturdy neo-Gothic brick building directly on the Grote Markt, this good-value hotel is steps from the In Flanders Fields museum and only a few minutes' walk from the Menenpoort. **Pros:** free breakfast; the location couldn't be more central; front rooms have a view of the Lakenhallen. **Cons:** reception is not staffed at night; front rooms can suffer from traffic noise; no on-site parking. *Rooms from: €118 Grote Markt 45, Ypres 059/690–090 www.newregina.be 28 rooms Free Breakfast.*

★ **Main Street Hotel**

$$$$ | **B&B/INN** | Occupying a lovely old brick town house a five-minute walk from the center, everything abut this quiet retreat is a luxurious indulgence. **Pros:** free parking on-site; quiet location in a residential suburb; great free breakfast spread with homemade bread. **Cons:** with such coddling you may forget to visit the sights; such luxury does not come cheap; a little away from the center. *Rooms from: €259 Rijselstraat 136, Ypres 057/469–633 mainstreet-hotel.be 6 rooms Free Breakfast.*

Chapter 7

WESTERN WALLONIA

7

Updated by
Gareth Clark

Sights ★★★★★ | Restaurants ★★★★☆ | Hotels ★★☆☆☆ | Shopping ★★★☆☆ | Nightlife ★★★☆☆

WELCOME TO WESTERN WALLONIA

TOP REASONS TO GO

★ **Discover incredible castles.** This part of Wallonia is bursting with fine châteaux, typically rebuilt in the 16th and 17th centuries in the fashionable French neoclassical style and wrapped by forested parklands.

★ **Explore mining country.** Hainaut Province was the country's industrial heartland from the early-19th century until the last mines closed in the 1980s. Many have now been converted into museums telling engrossing stories.

★ **It's a festival wonderland.** Belgium's most colorful folkloric festivals take place in Binche, Mons, Tournai, Ath, and Lessines.

★ **Beer, beer, and beer.** From the Trappists of Chimay to the country's only steam-powered brewery in Pipaix, the region is famous for its old-school brews.

★ **Finally facing your Waterloo.** The battlefield that saw Napoléon's final defeat brought to an end one of Europe's most torrid periods and makes for a thrilling day out.

1 Mons. This bustling, medieval university city is packed with museums, UNESCO-listed sights, and good food. And if you're there in June, the weeklong Ducasse is among Belgium's most riotous festivals.

2 Tournai. History abounds on every corner of this city, while its famed Cathédrale Notre-Dame de Tournai is still one of the grandest sights in the country.

3 Ath. Life here revolves around its annual August festival, when giants walk the streets. You'll also find good cycling trails and beautiful castles on its doorstep.

4 Lessines. This quiet, pious town is somewhat off the tourist beat, but its vast medieval hospital-cum-convent is one of Wallonia's most captivating sights.

5 Nivelles. A beautiful Romanesque church with a curious history lies at the heart of this pretty town in Walloon Brabant.

6 Waterloo. The site of Napoléon's final defeat in 1815 is still one of the most famous battles in European history and explored in fascinating tours of the area.

7 Louvain-la-Neuve. A university town with a wild past. It was only created in the 1970s after a crisis at Leuven University forced out its francophone students. But most come here for the Tintin museum.

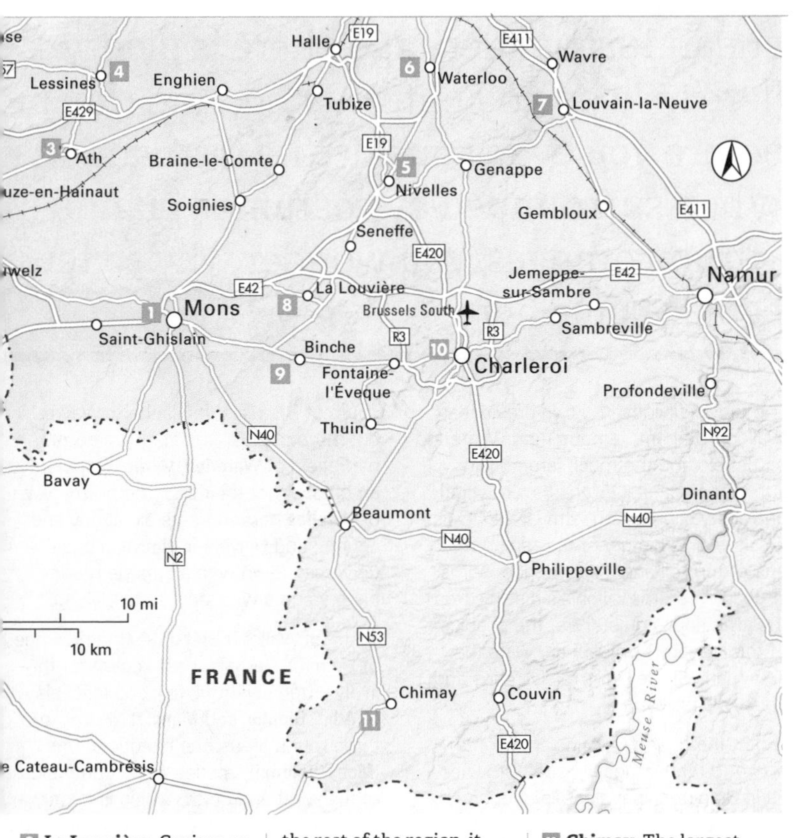

8 **La Louvière.** Cruises on the canals that changed the region's industrial fortunes are de rigueur, while the city's outskirts are filled with castles, old mines, and excellent museums.

9 **Binche.** Another town that lives for its carnival. Binche is famed for its parade of *gilles*, and unlike the rest of the region, it has also retained some of its medieval fortifications, which make for a fine walk.

10 **Charleroi.** Once voted the "Ugliest City in the World," Charleroi is no beauty, but it is gradually changing minds, and has some of the best museums in the country on its outskirts.

11 **Chimay.** The largest town in the Botte du Hainaut was made famous by its eponymous Trappist beer, which is still brewed in the nearby abbey. Its castle and beautiful countryside are just as compelling.

Western Wallonia might not have the Ardennes, but in its grab bag of medieval towns, battlefields, castles, breweries, and industrial heritage, there is plenty here to keep you entertained. And that's before you even consider its festivals. When surrounded by costumed giants hurling oranges, you wonder why so few people come here.

The region divides into two provinces: Walloon Brabant, famous for its Waterloo battlefield and the much larger Hainaut, whose capital, Mons, is a bustling university city packed with UNESCO-listed sites. The history of the region is one of turmoil and glory. France looms large in Western Wallonia's history, from the ambitious Louis XIV to the chaos of the French Revolutionary wars that saw many of the region's churches and abbey's destroyed.

Today, the region remains an enigma, home to the two least-visited provinces in Belgium. That alone is enough to pique the curiosity of most travelers. What you'll find is an area at peace with itself, where old mine workings narrate their tragic past in plush museums and beautiful castles throw open their doors. This is a land without need of a full stop; its story is still being written …

MAJOR REGIONS

In the northern reaches of Western Wallonia, cradling the rump of Brussels, is the province of **Walloon Brabant.** The region is mostly made up of small towns intermingled with a few castles and the large Soigne (Sonian) forest that dribbles south of Brussels. Its capital is Wavre, but more popular destinations are the battlefield of **Waterloo**, where Napoléon's ambitions met their end; the pretty town of **Nivelles**, famed for its old abbey and church; and **Louvain-la-Neuve**, a busy university town with a strange modern history and a wild story to tell.

South of Walloon Brabant is the province of Hainaut, perhaps best known for the lively, often eccentric folkloric festivals of **Ath, Binche,** and **Mons.** It divides into three rough areas: the historic towns (**Mons**, **Tournai**), castles, and countryside of the west and north, which is largely green and pretty; the old industrial center stretching east of Mons, across to **La Louvière** and **Charleroi**; and the Botte du Hainaut ("the boot"), a small, rustic southern corner of breweries and small medieval towns (**Chimay**), which has more in common with the Ardennes than the cities directly to its north.

Planning

Getting Here and Around

AIR

The name Brussels South Charleroi Airport has more to do with branding than geography. It certainly has little to do with Brussels as it sits around 45 miles away, in Wallonia, on the edge of the city of Charleroi. It is the country's second-busiest airport because this is where most European budget flights destined for "Brussels" land. It sees around 8 million passengers a year, and while most arrivals take a FlibCo shuttle bus straight to the capital (€14.70), it is more fittingly also the gateway to Wallonia. Combined train-and-bus tickets to and from the airport to any destination in the region can be bought from the NMBS/SNCB (*www.belgiantrain.be*) website or app, typically going via Charleroi Sud railway station.

CONTACTS Brussels South Charleroi Airport. ✉ *Rue des Frères Wright 8, Charleroi* ☎ *09/020–2490* 🌐 *www.brussels-charleroi-airport.com/en.*

BUS

If you don't have a car, you will be occasionally using a bus. Most towns are well linked by rail, but if you want to reach Chimay, down in the Botte du Hainaut, or some of the châteaux or attractions on the outskirts of the cities and towns, buses are the easiest way to do so. TEC operates the bus network in Wallonia, but it isn't always easy to work out how to get a ticket. Machines aren't plentiful and you can no longer buy tickets onboard. This means that you need to either get a MoBIB travel card (€5) and fill it up with TEC tickets at a machine or online, or download the TEC app (iOS/Android) and buy tickets that way. If using a MoBIB, note that tickets you buy online only appear on your card the following day, which often leaves you stuck. The app lets you use them immediately. Ticket prices for one trip vary between €2.10, €3, and €5 depending on the distance.

CONTACTS TEC. ☎ *065/388–811 Hainaut, 010/235–353 Walloon Brabant* 🌐 *www.letec.be.*

CAR

A car is the easiest way to get around Western Wallonia. Each city is well connected by motorways, with the E19 (Nivelles, La Louvière, Mons), E420 (Charleroi), E429 (Ath, Tournai), and E411 (Louvain-la-Neuve) the main arteries linking Brussels. Smaller locations, such as Lessines or Chimay, are certainly easier to reach by car, as are a number of the major sights. The old mining villages (now turned into wonderful museums) and the region's myriad châteaux all lie a few miles outside of the towns and cities, making bus travel often the only other way to reach them. Driving makes things easier, though bear in mind that most of the region's small hotels don't have their own parking. The usual big car-rental brands are all available, with many based at Brussels South Charleroi Airport.

CONTACTS Avis. ✉ *Airport Brussels South Charleroi, Gosselies* ☎ *071/351–998* 🌐 *www.avis.be.* **Europcar.** ✉ *Rue des Frères Wright 8, Charleroi* ☎ *071/890–400* 🌐 *www.europcar.be.*

TRAIN

Western Wallonia is well served by rail links. Only the villages of the "Botte du Hainaut," deep in the southern toe of the region, are cut adrift. Direct lines from the capital connect Tournai and Ath; Mons; Charleroi Sud, Nivelles, and Waterloo; or Louvain-la-Neuve, all in less than one hour, with most tickets costing between €6 and €9. A line running east to west also connects Tournai, Mons, Binche, La Louviere, and Charleroi, finishing in Liège. Lessines can only be reached by train via a connection at Ath. Remember that discount weekend tickets are half price if you get a return between Friday and Sunday evenings.

Buy tickets on the platform, online, or on the SNCB/NMBS app.

CONTACTS NMBS/SNCB. ☎ *02/528–2828* 🌐 *www.belgiantrain.be/en.*

Hotels

Western Wallonia is not blessed when it comes to hotels. It's not that those here aren't any good; it's just that there aren't many of them. Even in Mons, the capital of Hainaut Province, you won't find more than a handful, and even then, mostly spread around the outskirts of the historic center. It's partly a symptom of this region not being as well visited as other parts of Belgium, but also that most towns are less than an hour from Brussels, so can easily be seen on day trips from the capital. It's no surprise that Hainaut has the fewest overnight stays of any province in Belgium barring Walloon Brabant (Waterloo, Nivelles, Louvain-La-Neuve). Apart from Mons and Charleroi, which have a few large branded hotels, most city stays are small boutiques with few facilities. They're usually great value, but be warned that breakfast is rarely included in the price, so factor in an extra €10 to €15 per person if you want food. It's worth bearing in mind that the local *auberge de jeunesse* (youth hostel) is often a good, clean option if you're stuck for a room, and of a higher standard than you'll find in most European cities. In smaller towns, B&Bs may be the only option. Their owners invariably speak English, serve huge breakfasts, and cheerfully offer helpful tips.

Restaurants

The restaurants of the region tend to be a little more varied than elsewhere, if only because you don't typically see the usual Belgian chains (Bavet, Ballekes, Balls and Glory, Exki, etc.) that dominate most cities. As such, there is a wide choice of independent, mostly French-Belgian brasseries and bistros, usually serving an array of game, offal, and steaks slathered in creamy, often beery sauces. You'll also encounter a few regional specialties. In Mons, look for its *côte de porc à l'berdouille* (pork chop in mud), a chop drizzled in a tangy cream sauce flavored with mustard and pickles. Or in Tournai, there's *lapin a la Tournaisienne*, a dish of rabbit and stewed prunes that is traditionally eaten on the Monday following Epiphany. Nivelles has a cheese, chard, and parsley pie, known as a *tarte al djote,* and Charleroi even gets its own pork-and-veal meatball (*vitoulet*). Everywhere, you'll never not find the humble *mitraillette*, a frites (fries) sandwich that is a student favorite, usually stuffed with meat and slathered in sauce. It's mostly served in scruffy *fritures*, but Mons is the only city in Belgium with an entire restaurant dedicated to them.

HOTEL AND RESTAURANT PRICES

Hotel prices in the reviews are the lowest cost of a standard double room in high season. Restaurant prices in the reviews are the average cost of a main course at dinner, or if dinner is not served, at lunch.

What It Costs in Euros

	$	$$	$$$	$$$$
RESTAURANTS	under €12	€12–€22	€23–€30	over €30
HOTELS	under €100	€100–€150	€151–€220	over €220

Visitor Information

CONTACTS Visit Wallonia. 🌐 *walloniabelgiumtourism.co.uk.* **Wallonie Picard Tourism (WAPI).** ✉ *Quai Saint-Brice 35, Tournai* ☎ *069/789–816* 🌐 *www.visitwapi.be.*

The beautiful UNESCO-listed Belfry in Mons is one of the city's landmarks.

Mons

70 km (43½ miles) from Brussels.

Mons ("Bergen" in Dutch) is the ebullient, student-filled cobbled capital of Hainaut Province. As you ascend to its Grand Place, above which the 49-strong carillon of its belfry still rings true, you can't help but wonder: why don't more people come here? It's got great food, a famous festival, five UNESCO-listed sites, and some excellent museums. Yet it's still Wallonia's little secret.

GETTING HERE AND AROUND

Mons is the main railway hub for the region. Construction continues on its long-overdue station makeover, and for all that it looks like a rusty spaceship in the meantime, it continues to operate. Regular trains connect to Brussels from here in less than an hour (from €9.70) and run roughly every 30 minutes during the day. The Liège line, linking Tournai, La Louvière, and Charleroi, is particularly useful. Another train running north to Geraardsbergen (Flanders) connects Ath and Lessines.

Regional TEC buses run from opposite the railway station. These connect to the smaller destinations, such as Binche and sites like the Grand-Hornu and Spiennes's mines, which perhaps only have hourly connections via train or have no service at all. Be sure to have your tickets in advance, as these places tend not to have ticket machines and you can't buy them onboard.

By car, Mons is surrounded by a ring road that runs atop what was once its fortifications. The E42 connects the three big cities of the region, Tournai, Mons, and Charleroi, with the latter offering a turn-off onto the E19, the main artery into Brussels from the south.

VISITOR INFORMATION

CONTACTS Mons Tourist Information.
✉ *Grand Place 27, Mons* ☎ *065/335–580*
🌐 *www.visitmons.be.*

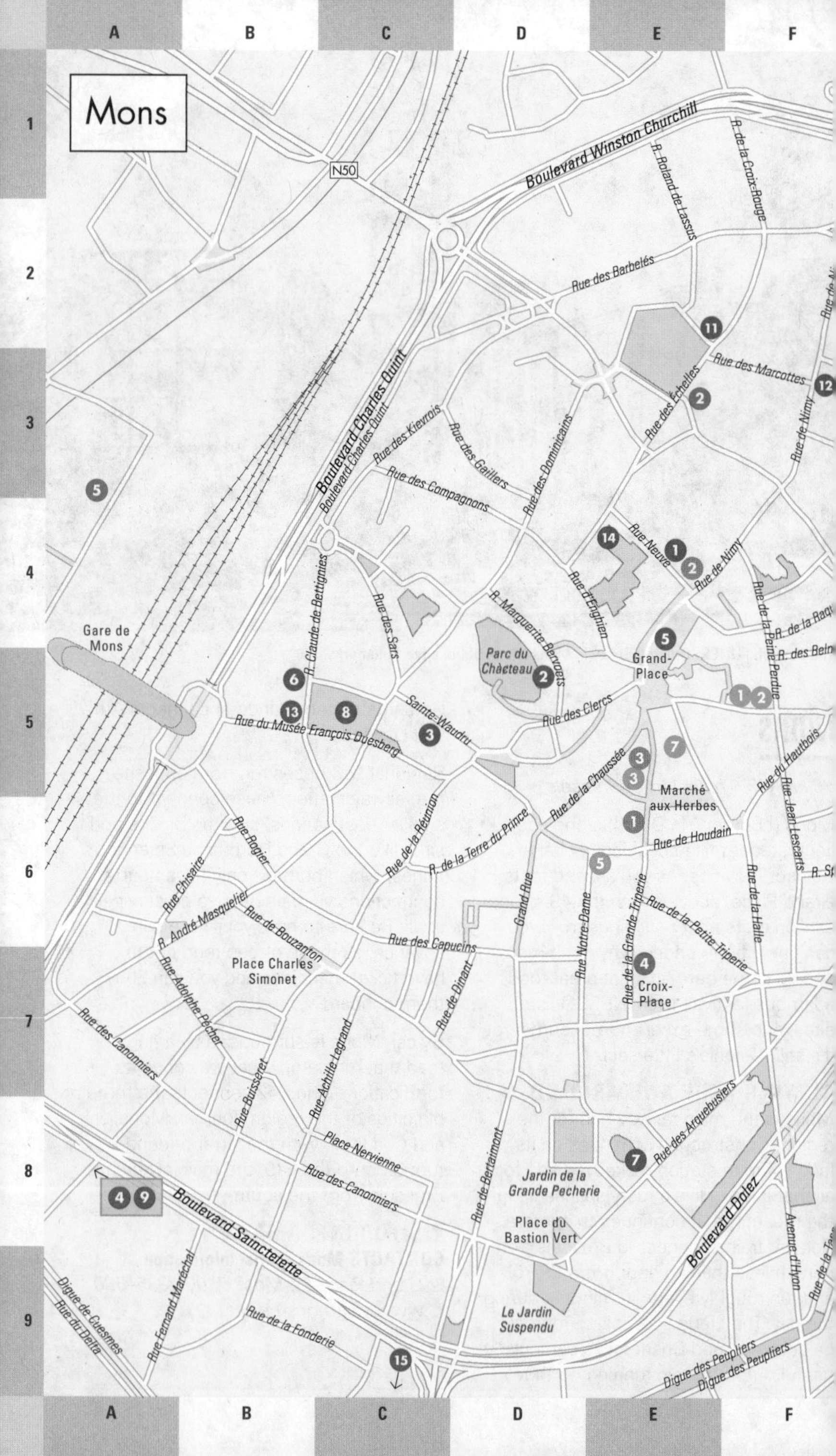

Mons
Boulevard Winston Churchill
N50
R. Roland-de-Lassus
R. de-la-Croix-Rouge
Rue des Barbelés
Rue des Marcottes
Rue des Echelles
Rue de Nimy
Boulevard Charles Quint
Rue des Kievrois
Rue des Gaillers
Rue des Dominicains
Rue des Compagnons
Rue Neuve
R. Claude-de-Bettignies
Rue des Sars
R. Marguerite Bervoets
Rue d'Enghien
Rue de la Petite Perdue
R. de la Raq
R. des Beln
Gare de Mons
Parc du Châteu
Grand-Place
Sainte-Waudru
Rue des Clercs
Rue du Musée François Duesberg
Rue de la Chaussée
Marché aux Herbes
Rue du Hautbois
Rue Jean Lescarts
Rue de la Réunion
R. de la Terre du Prince
Rue de Houdain
Rue Rogier
Rue Chisaire
R. André Masquelier
Rue de Bouzanton
Grand Rue
Rue Notre-Dame
Rue de la Grande Triperie
Rue de la Petite Triperie
Rue de la Halle
Rue des Capucins
Place Charles Simonet
Rue Adolphe Pecher
Rue de Dinant
Croix-Place
Rue des Canonniers
Rue Achille Legrand
Rue Buisseret
Rue des Arquebusiers
Place Nervienne
Rue des Canonniers
Rue de Bertaimont
Jardin de la Grande Pecherie
Boulevard Dolez
Avenue d'Hyon
Boulevard Sainctelette
Place du Bastion Vert
Rue Fernand Maréchal
Digue de Cuesmes
Rue du Delta
Rue de la Fonderie
Le Jardin Suspendu
Digue des Peupliers
Digue des Peupliers

Sights

1 Beaux-Arts Mons E4
2 Beffroi D5
3 Collégiale Sainte-Waudru de Mons C5
4 Grand-Hornu A8
5 Grand Place E4
6 L'Artothèque B5
7 Les Ancien Abattoirs E8
8 Lucie et les Papillons C5
9 Maison Van Gogh A8
10 Mons Memorial Museum G7
11 MUMONS E2
12 Mundaneum F3
13 Musée des Arts Décoratifs François Duesberg B5
14 Musée du Doudou E4
15 SILEX'S: Neolithic Flint Mines at Spiennes C9
16 St. Symphorien Military Cemetery J5

Restaurants

1 La Table du Boucher F5
2 La Vie Est Belle F5
3 L'Envers E5
4 Les Gribaumonts G5
5 Mitraillette E6
6 Rebelge J5
7 Twenty Buns E5

Quick Bites

1 Boule de Bleu E6
2 Green Witches E4
3 Mémé Tartine E5

Hotels

1 Hotel Lido G2
2 Hotel St. George E3
3 Hotel St. James I5
4 Martin's Dream Hotel E7
5 Van der Valk Hotel Mons A3

Sights

Beaux-Arts Mons (*Mons Fine Art Museum*)

ART MUSEUM | The city's premier art gallery is a blank slate: all white walls and glass. It was only built in 2015, when it opened with a retrospective on Van Gogh in the Borinage. Since then, temporary exhibitions tend to have only loose connections to the region and have ranged from the photography of Dave LaChapelle to the distorted paintings of Colombian artist Fernando Botero. ✉ *Rue Neuve 8, Mons* ☎ *065/405–325* 🌐 *www.bam.mons.be* *€9* ⏲ *Closed Tues.*

Beffroi (*Belfry*)

HISTORIC SIGHT | The city's UNESCO-listed belfry is a beauty. On this site previously stood a clock tower, which housed a "workers bell" from 1382 that chimed the hours of the working day and warned of attacks. But by 1661, this had collapsed and a new blue-stone belfry was built on its site. The architect drew inspiration from a trip to Renaissance Italy, hence the Baroque style as opposed to the Gothic towers scattering the rest of Wallonia. Its crown of onion domes is especially beautiful, and beneath it is a carillon 49 bells strong. ✉ *Parc du Château, Mons* ☎ *065/335–580* *€9* ⏲ *Closed Mon.*

★ **Collégiale Sainte-Waudru de Mons** (*Collegiate Church of Ste Waltrude*)

CHURCH | Ste. Waudru (Waltrude) is the patron saint of the city, and was known for her kindness to the poor. Her pageant is a key moment in the yearly Ducasse of Mons, where a lavish procession wheeling the Car d'Or, a gilded chariot carrying the reliquary of her remains, is pushed from the church into the town center and back. The rest of the year, the chariot and relics lie in this magnificent 15th-century Brabant-Gothic church, founded by the canonesses of Mons. Inside, it now has 29 chapels filled with artworks as well as a magnificent organ made in 1694. ✉ *Pl. du Chapitre, Mons* ☎ *065/844–694* 🌐 *wordpress-v2.waudru.be* *€4 for entry to treasury.*

★ **Grand-Hornu**

ART MUSEUM | Around 12 km (7½ miles) east of Mons, the Borinage yields one of its grandest visions. Many of the industrialists of the late-18th and 19th centuries built accommodation for their workers. These were typically squalid, pragmatic affairs, but the Grand-Hornu was different. It was the dream child of the French industrialist Henri de Gorge (1774–1832), who created a vast neoclassical hub for his workers in 1810. Its 450 homes were spacious, had hot water, and the facilities were plentiful. Workers had access to a school, clinic, dance hall, and library. In 1829, some 2,500 people lived here, but by 1954, the local mines had closed and the site was abandoned. It has since been restored and is now home to an acclaimed contemporary art museum, yet it's worth visiting just to see the grounds, encircled by redbrick arches like some industrial colosseum. This remains a curious anachronism, out of step with what was mostly a dehumanizing era for workers, and was designated a UNESCO World Heritage site in 2012. ✉ *Rue Sainte-Louise 82, Boussu* ✢ *10 km (6 miles) east of Mons* ☎ *065/613–881* 🌐 *www.cid-grand-hornu.be* *€10* ⏲ *Closed Mon.* Ⓜ *Bus: 7, 9.*

Grand Place

PLAZA/SQUARE | The heart of the city is a cobbled square wrapped in bar terraces and crowned by a grand **Hôtel de Ville** (town hall) dating back to the 15th century. This government building is Gothic in its soul, though the original alderman in charge of construction ran out of money before it was completed. It was only finished the following century, then modified again some 200 years later when a magnificent campanile was added, hence the abundance of architectural styles in its facade. ✉ *Grand Place, Mons.*

Artotheque
THER MUSEUM | In some ways, this is the ıuseum of museums. The Artotheque a former chapel that once belonged) Ursuline nuns; now it is home to the verflow collections of museums across e city. In essence, it's a would-be :orage facility that has been opened to ıe public, with a series of exhibitions uilt around items from an array of t and cultural institutions that would therwise just lie in a basement. It also elves into the art and science of muse-n work. It does have some eccentric pening hours, so plan your visit well. *Rue Claude de Bettignies 1, Mons 065/405–380 www.artotheque.ons.be €6 Closed Mon.–Wed.*

s Ancien Abattoirs (*The Ancient bbatoir*)
RT GALLERY | Mons is constantly evolv-g. Back in the Middle Ages, the river ouille ran through this part of the city, hich was known as the fisherman's uarter. By the mid-1800s, the then badly olluted river was diverted away from e city and sewers were installed. At e same time, a slaughterhouse was uilt here, designed in the Lombard style ith a roomy courtyard. Even the streets ok on their new theme, and nearby you an walk down Rue de la Grande Triperie treet of Large Tripe). The slaughter-ouse is long since gone, and in 2006 it as turned into an arts center for crafts nd textiles. This is home to a perma-ent gallery and another with temporary xhibitions. *Rue de la Trouille 17, Mons 065/846–467 www.abattoirs.mons.e Entry prices for temporary exhibi-ons vary Closed Mon.*

cie et les Papillions
JBLIC ART | This permanent sculpture on ace Roosevelt is the work of the 3D ıaging artist David Mesguish, whose aughter is the focus of a piece ruminat-g on childhood innocence. The mirrored urface offers stark contrast with the grand Collégiale Sainte-Waudru de Mons church building behind it. *Pl. Franklin Delano Roosevelt, Mons.*

Maison Van Gogh (*Van Gogh's House*)
HISTORIC HOME | Before he was a pen-niless painter, Dutchman Vincent van Gogh trained, like his father, in the clergy. By 1879, he was hired as an evangelist in the village of Wasmes. At the time, this was a tough working-class area. Van Gogh's poor rhetorical skills found little traction with locals. His contract wasn't renewed, and his worried parents advised him to find a profession better suited to his skills. Van Gogh instead doubled down: he cut off contact, and with financial assistance from his brother, Theo, managed to live in nearby Cuesmes and preach for free. His sketch-es from this time were formative, though a far cry from his later euphoric work. *Rue du Pavillon 3, Cuesmes 3 km (2 miles) south of Mons 065/335–580 www.maisonvangogh.mons.be €4 Closed Mon. Bus: 1, 2, or 6.*

★ **Mons Memorial Museum**
HISTORY MUSEUM | This superb museum, set in an old water pumping station, views the history of Mons through the lens of the many battles fought over the city. You can't miss the M4 Sherman tank parked outside, with the words "In the mood" scrawled across its hull. It commemorates the day Allied forces rolled into town in 1944, when Mons became the first Belgium city to be liberated from German occupation in World War II. Certainly, for the past 500 years, Europe has been very much "in the mood" to fight over Mons. The museum chronicles this in dramatic detail, though the most engaging displays come from the 20th-century conflicts, where weapons, uniforms, memorabilia, and even VR experiences (there is a thrilling 360-degree re-creation of liberation day) immerse you in one of the darkest times in European history.

The heart of Mons is the Grand Place, a cobbled square lined with medieval buildings including the stunnir 15th-century town hall.

✉ *Bd. Dolez 51, Mons* ☎ *065/405–320* 🌐 *en.monsmemorialmuseum.mons.be* 🎫 *€9* ⏲ *Closed Mon.*

MUMONS

HISTORY MUSEUM | Owned by the University of Mons, this is the newest museum to open in the city. Its exhibitions delve into the building's history as a former chapel (complete with visitable crypt) and prison. However, at the time of visiting, it was still a work in progress. English explanations are due to be added in 2022 along with the bulk of the university's collection. A further permanent exhibition on the city's Freemasons will also arrive in 2023. ✉ *Pl. du Parc 24, Mons* ☎ *065/372–215* 🌐 *mumons.be* 🎫 *€5* ⏲ *Closed Sat. and Tues.*

★ **Mundaneum**

HISTORY MUSEUM | This UNESCO-recognized endeavor tells a little-known story. At the dawn of the 20th century, a pair of human-rights lawyers, Paul Otlet and Henri La Fontaine (Belgium's only Nobel Peace Prize winner), had the idea for a paper database of all knowledge. They called it the Mundaneum. By 1972 it he 12 million bibliographic records (index cards). The building is now a fascinating museum. ✉ *Rue de Nimy 76, Mons* ☎ *065/315–343* 🌐 *www.mundaneum.or* 🎫 *€7* ⏲ *Closed Mon. and Tues.*

Musée des Arts Décoratifs François Duesberg (*Museum of Decorative Arts*)

ART MUSEUM | One of the true gems of the city is also one of the few private museums, its collection assembled across a span of 50 years by a Belgian lawyer, François Duesberg, and his late wife. It focuses on two eras of French design, spanning 1775 to 1825, and delves particularly into the art movemer known as "Empire," which grew in the early 19th century. It spawned some incredible objets d'art, which would hav been the envy of high society at the time. ✉ *Pl. Franklin Delano Roosevelt 1, Mons* ☎ *065/363–164* 🌐 *en.duesberg.mons.be* 🎫 *€5* ⏲ *Closed Mon. and Wec*

Musée du Doudou (*Festival Museum*)
HISTORY MUSEUM | If you're not lucky enough to be in the city at the time of the Ducasse du Mons (known locally as Doudou), its weeklong, largely drunken medieval festival, then this is the next best thing. The museum lends some cultural context to the battle of St. George and the dragon, which is retold and celebrated across Europe in myriad different ways, and fills in the details around the procession of Ste. Waudru. The building itself is just as interesting, having been built in the 17th century as a kind of pawnbroker-cum-bank, hence its sturdy, rather forbidding exterior. ✉ *Grand Place, Mons* ✣ *Behind Jardin du Mayeur* ☎ *065/405–318* 🌐 *www.museedudoudou.mons.be* 🎫 *€9* ⏲ *Closed Mon.*

SILEX'S: Neolithic Flint Mines at Spiennes
MINE | The flint mines that lie 6 km (4 miles) outside the city were once a valuable resource to early humankind, its rock capable of being chipped into spearheads, knives, and tools. According to UNESCO, this is the largest and earliest mine of its type in Europe. Visits today descend by ladder into the chalky stone underbelly of the mines, accompanied by an archaeologist guide. ✉ *Rue du Point du Jour 300, Spiennes* ✣ *5 km (3 miles) southeast of Mons* ☎ *065/846–812* 🌐 *www.silexs.mons.be* 🎫 *€6* ⏲ *Closed Mon. and Nov.–Mar.*

St. Symphorien Military Cemetery
CEMETERY | The 1914 Battle of Mons was a bloody affair, in which British forces (some 75,000) found themselves up against a German army twice that size. It was the first engagement of the two opposing forces in World War I, and saw the British swiftly retreat by evening. Four years later, the same pair would meet in reverse as the Germans were forced from the city on the day the armistice was signed. In between, in 1916, a German soldier looking for a plot of land to commemorate his fallen comrades met a local botanist who agreed to help him on the sole condition that the cemetery would respect all nationalities. Thus, 284 German and 229 Commonwealth soldiers are buried here, including the unfortunate Canadian private George Price, who was killed just two minutes before the 11 am armistice. It makes for a moving, contemplative stroll. ✉ *Rue Nestor Dehon 32, Mons* ✣ *5 km (3 miles) east of Mons* Ⓜ *Bus: 22.*

Restaurants

La Table du Boucher
$$$ | **BISTRO** | Meat is the order of the day here, rumored to be sourced from the same supplier as the celebrated French chef Joël Robuchon. Pounds of fresh, sweet cuts adorn the menu of this chic brasserie, whose specialty is beef, whether in the form of entrecôte, fillet, *boulettes* (meatballs), or tartare (raw). **Known for:** the beef comes from Holstein and Blackmore cattle; meat—this isn't friendly territory for vegetarians; a good selection of wines. $ *Average main: €30* ✉ *Rue d'Havré 49, Mons* ☎ *065/316–838* 🌐 *www.latableduboucher.be* ⏲ *Closed Tues.*

La Vie est Belle
$$ | **BELGIAN** | **FAMILY** | The rather scruffy exterior hides a budget jewel in Mons's dining scene. This is home-cooked Belgian food at its most grandmotherly, with huge portions of sauce-swamped meats ranging from meatballs and rabbit to great mounds of chateaubriand. **Known for:** staff are friendly and helpful; Belgian classics at low prices; it's a meat haven, and you'll never leave hungry. $ *Average main: €15* ✉ *Rue d'Havré 39, Mons* ☎ *065/565–845.*

★ **L'Envers**
$$ | **BRASSERIE** | A friendly local favorite with charming service and a Mons classic to devour. The menu is, on the whole, standard brasserie fare, but the addition of *porc a l'Berdouille*, a dish created in the 1960s that smothers a pork chop (in

this case pork fillet) in a white-wine-and-cream sauce flavored with pickled onions and gherkins, is a delight. **Known for:** there's a terrace on the charming rue de la Coupe in summer; great-value dishes and good cooking; excellent service by knowlegeable staff. *$ Average main: €18 ✉ Rue de la Coupe 20, Mons ☎ 065/354-510 🌐 www.lenversmons.be ⏲ Closed Sun. and Wed. Ⓜ 7000.*

★ Les Gribaumonts

$$$$ | BISTRO | A fine-dining classic that has been around for nearly 30 years. During that time, Lisa Calcus has shaped the taste buds of the city. **Known for:** the €28 (main and dessert) lunch menu is good value; inventive fine dining in a charming setting; excellent cheese selection and wine lists. *$ Average main: €31 ✉ Rue d'Havré 95, Mons ☎ 065/750–455 🌐 www.lesgribaumonts.be ⏲ Closed Sun. and Mon. No dinner Tues. and Wed. No lunch Sat.*

★ Mitraillette

$$ | BELGIAN | From the mind of Belgium *Top Chef* finalist Jean-Philippe Watteyne (aka Jean-Phi), this diner is an ode to the drunken sandwich. *Mitraillettes* are typically served at frites stalls: it's a half baguette stuffed with as many Belgian-style fries as it'll hold, and often smothered in sauces, sausage, and others things guaranteed to lessen your life span. **Known for:** it's the first restaurant of its kind in Belgium; the Belgian sandwich to end all sandwiches; a good selection of local Brasserie de Borinage beers. *$ Average main: €14 ✉ Rue des Fripiers 22b, Mons ☎ 065/875–787 🌐 mitraillette.land ⏲ Closed Mon., Tues., and Fri.*

Rebelge

$$$$ | BELGIAN | The fine-dining restaurant by acclaimed local chef Jean-Phi is as eclectic as his frites-sandwich joint (see Mitraillette). The menu is defiantly local, with a wide choice of regional beers often accompanying either a sharing-plate (around €15) or main-sized version of the same dishes. **Known for:** it's a bit far out, so you'll have at least a 15-minute walk from the center; inventive local cooking by a bonified "Top Chef"; an inspired selection of beers and wines. *$ Average main: €31 ✉ Av. Reine Astrid 31, Mons ☎ 0493/999–666 🌐 re-belge.be ⏲ Closed Sun.–Tues.*

Twenty Buns

$$ | AMERICAN | Just around the corner from the Marché-aux-Herbes bar street lies this haven to all things American and calorific. It's a busy caveat to the city's main student drinking area, but also a rather good burger and hot-dog joint. **Known for:** they do a fun brunch on the first Sunday of each month; tasty wings, ribs, and cornflake chicken round out the starters; try the brownie and Kinder Bueno milk shakes. *$ Average main: €14 ✉ Rue de la Clef 18, Mons ☎ 065/363–222 🌐 www.twentybuns.be ⏲ Closed Sun.–Tues.*

Coffee and Quick Bites

Boule de Bleu

$$ | CAFÉ | If you take your salads seriously, this is the place to go. Despite the countrified café setting, they're not cheap (€18.50!) but come exquisitely prepared, piled high with protein, and are always creative. **Known for:** homemade cakes that never disappoint; the internal terrace is a shady escape on a hot day; creative salads, filling tartiflettes, and loads of vegetarian options. *$ Average main: €19 ✉ Rue de la Coupe 46, Mons ☎ 065/845–819 🌐 www.bouledebleu.com ⏲ Closed Sun. and Mon.*

Green Witches

$ | CAFÉ | A really friendly café that's just a few steps from the Beaux-Arts. It's got a good choice of vegan and vegetarian sandwiches, croques, soups, and salads, and the juices are delicious. **Known for:** everything is organic; nice outside seating come summer; it opens early (9 am), so it's always good for breakfast. *$ Average main: €9 ✉ Rue Neuve 2, Mons*

Mons and the Dragon

Every June, Mons bursts at the seams with revelers during its annual weeklong festival, the Ducasse de Mons (known locally as the Doudou). Begun in the 14th century by grateful souls who survived a plague, the Ducasse is so exuberant (beer is consumed in large quantities) that the local church officials asked that it not be celebrated during the Easter religious observances. The festival is a hodgepodge of events. It's officially opened with the Descente, which presents the relics of St. Waudru to the burgomaster. These are paraded through town on an ornate, 2-ton 18th-century carriage, which is then pushed up a sloping street, a massive effort called the Montée du Car d'Or, to return to the saint's namesake church. Everyone helps with the final push, because if it doesn't make it to the top in one go, it's bad luck for the rest of the year.

The Combat de la Lumeçon, an enactment of the story of St. George and the dragon, is, for many, the main highlight of the festival. It's held on the Grand Place, where the dragon's tail is topped off with a horsehair switch that brings good luck to the reveler who grabs it. But first, you have to get past the dragon's guards. St. George then finishes off the beast as concerts, carillons, and fireworks keep the city buzzing for several days.

☎ 065/953–246 🌐 www.greenwitches.be ⏲ Closed Mon.

Mémé Tartine

$ | CAFÉ | Think soups, stuffed *spianatas* (Sardinian-style flatbreads), and tartines (open sandwiches) spilling over with smashed avocado and served on rustic wooden boards. It's friendly, filling, decent value, and there's a terrace for the sunnier days. **Known for:** the choice is pretty wide, and there's a good selection of teas; the portions are suitably large for a granny-themed café; it's on a nice street. *$ Average main: €8 ✉ Rue de la Coupe 16, Mons ☎ 0488/880–481 🌐 meme-tartine.business.site ⏲ Closed Sun. and Mon.*

Hotels

One of the great curiosities of Western Wallonia is its lack of accommodation. Even in the capital of Hainaut Province, you'll struggle to find hotels in the historic center. What little there are largely scatter the fringes, perched on busy roundabouts, though you'll find a few closer to the Grand Place. Note that breakfasts are rarely included in the price, which can push up the cost of what are some otherwise good-value stays.

Hotel Lido

$ | HOTEL | A 10-minute walk north of the center takes you Hotel Lido, one of the larger stays in the city. **Pros:** professional, friendly staff and access to free wellness facilities; big breakfasts (€16) that never fail to delight; easy access in and out of the city, and good value. **Cons:** parking is €10 per night extra; it's a bit of a walk to the center; it's not a pretty area, with lots of roads surrounding you. *$ Rooms from: €92 ✉ Rue des Arbalestriers 112, Mons ☎ 065/327–800 🌐 www.lido.be 108 rooms No Meals.*

Hotel St. George

$$ | HOTEL | This old mansion house has been divided into 15 self-catering (fridge, microwave, cooking plate) studio apartments, with rooms at the back opening onto terraces and garden views. **Pros:** a garden at the rear makes for a pleasant escape on warm days; a great location and perhaps the stay closest to the center; the old building is just beautiful, with a common room full of games. **Cons:** parking is €5 extra per day; rooms come with cooking plates rather than ovens; there's no reception, so staff aren't often on hand unless you call. $ *Rooms from: €105* ✉ *Pl. du Parc 32, Mons* ☎ *065/652–014* 🌐 *hotelsaintgeorges.be* 🛏 *15 studio apartments* 🍽 *No Meals.*

Hotel St. James

$ | HOTEL | Its location, on the big roundabout south of the city, isn't inspiring but this little, family-run town house has a few surprises. **Pros:** it's easily accessed if you're driving; it's a great value stay for the city; staff are charming and friendly. **Cons:** some of the older rooms in the house are wearing a little; breakfast costs an extra €15; the main house is next to a busy road, and parking costs €10 per night. $ *Rooms from: €85* ✉ *Pl. De Flandre 8, Mons* ☎ *065/724–824* 🌐 *hotel-st-james.visit-wallonia.com/en* 🛏 *12 rooms* 🍽 *No Meals.*

★ **Martin's Dream Hotel**

$$ | HOTEL | The nicest stay in town is (unusually for Mons) well-placed near the town center—this plush boutique is part of a small chain of unique stays. **Pros:** a perfect location, next to the center on a quiet street; the rooms in the old chapel are just beautiful; breakfasts are plentiful (and include plant-based milks—a rarity). **Cons:** breakfasts cost extra (€18); parking costs €15 per night; wellness facilities are not free and very pricey to use (€99 for two hours). $ *Rooms from: €115* ✉ *Rue de la Grande Triperie 17, Mons* ☎ *065/329–720* 🌐 *www.martinshotels.com* 🛏 *62 rooms* 🍽 *No Meals.*

Van der Valk Hotel Mons

$$ | HOTEL | The biggest hotel in the city is also, unsurprisingly, the best equipped. **Pros:** free parking, plus there are Tesla chargers; breakfasts are as good as you'd expect; abundant facilities. **Cons:** breakfast is not included in the price and can really push up the cost of a stay; spa use isn't free, nor is it cheap; the station is between you and the town center, meaning you've got a long walk. $ *Rooms from: €115* ✉ *Av. Mélina Mercouri 7, Mons* ✥ *Behind the railway station* ☎ *065/390–207* 🌐 *www.hotelmons.eu* 🛏 *145 rooms* 🍽 *Free Breakfast.*

Nightlife

Mons is a student city, and, as such, there are a fair amount of bars here—more so than normal for its size. In the **Grand Place,** terraces wrap the square as in most Belgian cities. Normally, these would be the worst of the tourist traps, but in Mons they tend to be some of the more reliable options. From here, **rue de la Clef** and **rue de Clerc** have a good selection of bars and livelier cocktail joints. But, for all-out chaos, the student pick is **Marché-aux-Herbes,** a small, noisy bar street connecting rue de la Clef and the finer restaurants and boutiques of ru[e] de la Coupe.

Golden Coach

BARS | This friendly bar, next to La Lorgnette, has a neat quirk: it does self-service beer. You fill up your glass from around 20 taps using a card that yo[u] get from the bar, and it means that you can do small tastings of a large selection of different draft beers because you're paying by volume. ✉ *Rue des Clercs 6, Mons.*

La Lorgnette

BARS | The hospitality of many of the bars around Mons (especially on the Marché-aux-Herbes) tends to be on the brusque side. Yet this two-floor local favorite—all redbrick walls and leather chairs—just off the Grand Place is among the most friendly in town. Its specialty is a "flaming beer," which is everything you'd imagine (and more) when you hear those words. ✉ *Rue des Clercs 2, Mons* ☎ *065/844–566.*

e Chinchin
ARS | This narrow vaulted cellar is the etting for a popular bar where the house chinchin" shots are legendary among ocals. A lively weekend spot. ✉ *Rue des Clercs 15, Mons* ☎ *065/842–915.*

e Modjo
OCKTAIL LOUNGES | A slick bar in the orthern corner of the Grand Place. The wall of colorful bottles makes clear what you're in for: well-made cocktails longside fine dishes of antipasti. ✉ *Rue de Nimy 1, Mons.*

euvres and Tannins
IANO BARS | A cute little bar-cum-shop on he charming rue de la Coupe with room or only a few tables inside. Organic nd natural wines, beers, and teas are he specialty here; the owner even uns a natural vineyard near Harmignies village. ✉ *Rue De La Coupe 41, Mons* ☎ *0476/969–666* 🌐 *www.levuresettannins.be.*

Performing Arts

Théâtre Royal de Mons
THEATER | This 19th-century neoclassical building on the Grand Place houses he city's main theater. Events include musicals, opera, comedy, theater, and egular appearances by the Royal Wallonia Chamber Orchestra. Tickets can be bought online or over the phone (via Ticketmaster), or at the Mons tourism office. ✉ *Grand Place 22, Mons* ☎ *070/660–601 tickets* 🌐 *theatreroyalmons.be.*

Shopping

If you're looking for high-street stores, **rue de la Chaussée** is the main thoroughfare, though it has a smattering of clothing boutiques the closer you get to the Grand Place. At its southern tip, it leads onto **Grand Rue**, which has a number of sports shops (think Footlocker, JD Sports) but quickly gives way to the usual supermarkets, pharmacies, and vape stores that fill most high streets. For more interesting boutiques, head to **rue de la Coupe**, filled with vintage stores, art shops, and booksellers. This also intersects with **rue des Fripiers**, which is particularly rich in bobo stores showcasing elaborate shawls and housewares.

MARKETS

Flower Market
MARKET | On Sunday from 8 am to 2 pm, you can find the flower market on place Léopold, right in front of the station. There are 20 amazing stalls to inspire you. ✉ *Pl. Léopold, Mons.*

Vieux-Marché
MARKET | Sunday is also when a large market takes over place Nervienne and place du Béguinage between 7 am and 2 pm. The former is mostly fruit, veg, and local produce stalls, but the latter has a bit of everything: books, records, collectibles, old furniture, military knickknacks. ✉ *Pl. Nervienne, Mons.*

Tournai

85 km (53 miles) from Mons.

The site on which modern Tournai ("Doornik" in Dutch) sits has been occupied for more than 2,000 years, beginning life as an Iron Age Celtic settlement on the banks of the Scheldt (Escaut) before Roman merchants laid more solid roots here. By the 5th century, it was the first capital of the early Frankish Empire and birthplace of future king Clovis I—now perhaps best known for the local frangipane cake named after him. This kingdom would later become France, and Tournai remained a French territory for much of the next millennium.

Tournai today is a modern city in little hurry, and one where the past is everywhere, not just in its grand belfry and historical buildings, but in what was lost: a center torn apart by German and Allied bombing in World War II and rebuilt in the 1950s and '60s. This is a city with a long memory, and September sees the return of the Grand Procession that has taken place every year since AD 1092, in remembrance of a plague that tore through the region in the 11th century. It's the city that never forgets.

GETTING HERE AND AROUND

Tournai is well connected by rail, with direct trains running every half hour to Brussels via Ath (€15.60) and taking around 70 minutes. Trains to Kortrijk (€7.50) are similarly regular but only take 30 minutes. The city also has links to the rest of Western Wallonia, with connections to Charleroi via Mons, Binche, and La Louvière.

Buses are only really useful for reaching the surrounding small towns and villages, and leave from opposite the station. The No. 95 connects Tournai to Pipaix. By car, it's around 90 km (55 miles) to Brussels via the E429 and E19. The latter road connects most of the major towns in Western Wallonia.

VISITOR INFORMATION

CONTACTS Visit Tournai Tourism Office. ✉ *Pl. Paul-Emile Janson 1, Tournai* ☎ *069/222–045* 🌐 *www.visittournai.be.*

Sights

Unlike the rest of Wallonia (and indeed, most of Belgium), Tournai mirrors French opening hours in its museums, meaning the majority are closed on Tuesday rather than Monday, so plan ahead. Most only cost a few euros to visit, making them wonderful value, though a Museum Pass for entry to a half-dozen museums can be bought from the tourism office for €12.

Beffroi (*Belfry*)
HISTORIC SIGHT | Wrought in magnificent blue stone, Tournai's UNESCO-listed belfry is the oldest surviving example in Belgium. It dates back to AD 1188, when the town was granted the charter of municipal liberties by King Philippe of France. Only in the 16th century did it gain a carillon (now 55 bells strong), as its purpose became more social. This was one of few buildings to escape the bombing of World War II; however, it has recently been closed for renovation. Visitors can still only climb to the first floor, though its upper floors should reopen after 2022. ✉ *Vieux Marché aux Poteries, Tournai* ☎ *069/222–045* ⏲ *Closed Mon.*

★ **Cathédrale Notre-Dame de Tournai** (*Notre Dame Cathedral*)
CHURCH | Without doubt, the crowning glory of Tournai is its magnificent cathedral, which soars over the center and remains one of the great sights of Belgium. Its existence dates back to the 5th century, though work on the current building began some 700 years later, first in the Romanesque style, then becoming more Gothic as construction progressed. Its exterior is breathtaking, etched in blue stone with a huge rose window (replaced in the 19th century). Parts are still being renovated now but visitors are free to wander most of the interior, including the *Tresor* (Treasury), which contains, among its relics, tapestries, and the vestment worn by 12th-century saint Thomas Becket, a former Archbishop of Canterbury. ✉ *Pl. de l'Evêché, Tournai* ☎ *069/843–469* 🌐 *www.cathedrale-tournai.be* 🎫 *Treasury entry: €3 (cash only).*

Ecopark Adventures
AMUSEMENT PARK/CARNIVAL | **FAMILY** | This forest adventure park has plenty of tree climbing, as well as two of the largest ziplines in Belgium, tree houses, escape rooms, geocaching sites, and a subterranean world to explore. Outdoor fun for kids. ✉ *Rue de l'Orient 1, Tournai* ☎ *0474/077–068* 🌐 *ecopark-adventures.com* 🎫 *€23* ⏲ *Closed Nov.–Mar.*

Grand Place (*Town Square*)
PLAZA/SQUARE | The grandiose main square (well…triangle) is wrapped by

Be sure to visit Tournai's Cathédrale Notre-Dame, famed for its huge stained-glass rose window.

elegant 17th-century guild houses, each still flying the flags of the old guilds. These now contain a stream of terraced cafés and bars. But in the early days of Tournai, this was a very different place. For a long time, it was a cemetery, and the **Église Saint-Quentin**, with its 12th-century nave, is thought to date from that era. It was only when work on the town belfry began in 1188 that this area become the heart of the newly crowned city. ✉ *Grand Place, Tournai.*

Historical Houses

HISTORIC HOME | North of the river are some fine examples of Gothic and gabled Romanesque houses that escaped the blanket bombing of the city center in the 1940s. Waking maps can be found in the tourism office, or just head to rue Barre Saint-Brice where you can admire prototypes of the Flemish *stenen* (stone) style of architecture and a 15th-century Gothic manor house. ✉ *Rue Barre Saint-Brice, Tournai.*

★ **Maison Tournaisienne: Musée de Folklore** (*Folklore Museum*)

HISTORY MUSEUM | An eclectic wonder of a museum spread over a pair of gabled 17th-century houses. Its rooms narrate a life gone by in Tournai. Some items seem almost inconsequential, but when added together they paint a fascinating picture, as subjects skip from death, printing (Tintin publisher Casterman was based in Tournai), porcelain, and hats, to dog wheels (yes, there's a canine-powered butter churner), football memorabilia, Belgium's first frites stall, and plenty more. ✉ *Réduit des Sions 36, Tournai* ☎ *069/224–069* 🌐 *mufim.tournai.be* 🎫 *€3* 🕑 *Closed Tues.; also Sun. Nov.–Mar.*

Musée de la Tapisserie (*Tapestry Museum*)

ART MUSEUM | Between the 15th and 18th centuries, Tournai was famed for its tapestries. This converted neoclassical mansion holds some fine examples of the craft in its small collection, and it is also a workshop where tapestries are made and restored. The only downside is the lack of any explanation in English. ✉ *Pl. Reine-Astrid 9, Tournai* ☎ *069/234–285* 🌐 *tamat.be* 🎟 *€5* ⏲ *Closed Tues.*

★ **Musée des Beaux-Arts** (*Fine Arts Museum*)

ART MUSEUM | Even the building is a work of art. Opened in 1928, this museum was designed by Victor Horta, doyen of the Art Nouveau movement, though war interrupted the original commission and by the time he returned to it, his tastes had shifted to a more sober Art Deco style. The airy interior features fine works by Tournai's own Rogier van der Weyden and Flemish greats Peter Paul Rubens and Pieter Breughel. A particularly eye-catching piece by the Mouscron-born Rémy Cogghe, of a bar brawl gone wrong, is wonderfully fraught with drama. The showpieces are mainly French or Dutch, including scribbles by Toulouse-Lautrec, a sketch by Van Gogh, and works by Claude Monet, Georges Seurat, and a pair of paintings by Edouard Manet—perhaps the real gems here. A lack of any explanation in English doesn't diminish this fine collection. ✉ *Rue de l'Enclos Saint-Martin 3, Tournai* ☎ *069/332–431* 🌐 *mba.tournai.be* 🎟 *€3* ⏲ *Closed Tues.; also closed Sun. Nov.–Mar.*

★ **Musée d'Histoire Militaire** (*Military History Museum*)

HISTORY MUSEUM | By the late Middle Ages, Tournai was a wealthy bishopric and a fine prize for any European superpower. It's no surprise that its history is one of constant siege and invasion, as it swapped French, British, Spanish, Austrian, and German rulers for much of the past 500 years. As such, this unassuming two-floor military museum is the finest source of history on the city, backed by weapons and uniforms from the ages. Strangely, the 18th and 19th centuries remain untranslated, but most exhibits are in English, and coverage of the wars of the 20th century are superb, particularly the German and Allied bombing campaigns that leveled the city in 1940, 1943, and 1944. Photography from that era shows just how much of Tournai has been rebuilt. ✉ *Rue Roc Saint-Nicaise 59–61, Tournai* ☎ *069/211–966* 🌐 *mhm.tournai.be* 🎟 *€3* ⏲ *Closed Tues.*

Musée d'Histoire Naturelle (*Natural History Museum*)

OTHER MUSEUM | FAMILY | You won't learn much here unless you speak French, but the addition of a large vivarium to this cramped hall of taxidermied animals (dating back to 1828) makes it a far more entertaining prospect. Very-much-alive spiders, scorpions, tortoises, and lizards can all be seen as part of an international breeding program for rare species. ✉ *L'Hôtel de Ville, rue Saint-Martin 52, Tournai* ☎ *069/332–343* 🌐 *mhn.tournai.be* 🎟 *€3* ⏲ *Closed Tues.; Sun.: Nov.–Mar.*

Pont des Trous (*Bridge of Holes*)

BRIDGE | The River Scheldt (known in French as the "Escaut") once gave Tournai a vital route to the sea, making it a thriving medieval trading hub. The Pont des Trous (Bridge of Holes) was built as a fortified bridge in the 13th century to defend this vital waterway, and remains one of only three examples of its kind left in the world. Having said that, it was largely destroyed in World War II, only to be swiftly rebuilt with a larger arch to allow for modern transport barges to pass. At the time of writing, it was being enlarged again, despite vociferous public outcry. It is a great spot to watch the barges drift on by. ✉ *Pont des Trous, Tournai.*

Tour Henry VIII (*Tower of Henry VIII*)

MONUMENT | A fascinating relic from the only time that England, driven by the ambitions of young Tudor king Henry VIII, invaded what is now Belgium. He captured two French cities before moving on to Tournai, which was seized in the Battle of Guinegate. Just a year later, Henry's advisor, Thomas Wolsey, would sue for peace, and England kept Tournai. This tower was built to house Henry's troops in 1515 and was part of a larger citadel. Under Henry's rule, the town maintained a representative in the English parliament, but locals never took to their new owners and it proved costly to maintain a town so far from Calais. In 1519, Tournai was sold back to the French for 600,000 gold crowns (a huge amount). ✉ *Pl. Verte, Tournai.*

Restaurants

Brasserie Le Beffroi
$$ | **BELGIAN** | Among the sprawl of terraced bars and restaurants encircling the Grand Place, this down-to-earth brasserie is among the finer options. Its menu is packed with hearty Belgian brasserie classics, including beer stews, local-style tartare, and meatballs. **Known for:** it's a good lunch spot, with a large selection of croques and salads; nice food, good value, and a decent selection of regional beers; sitting on the terrace affords the best view in town. *Average main: €16* ✉ *Grand Place 15, Tournai* ☎ *069/848–341* 🌐 *www.le-beffroi.be.*

★ **La Petite Madeleine**
$$$$ | **BISTRO** | Set in a pretty, stone-fronted town house, this elegant mainstay on the city's fine-dining scene rarely disappoints. A sunlit terrace garden offers a break from the dark, sensible interior, but the food is the joy here, concocted with wit and imagination. **Known for:** exquisitely prepared food and a good wine selection; pared-down menus bursting with ideas; pretty garden terrace. *Average main: €35* ✉ *Rue de la Madeleine 19, Tournai* ☎ *069/840–187* 🌐 *www.lapetitemadeleine.be* 🕓 *Closed Mon. and Tues. No dinner Sun. No lunch Wed. and Sat.*

L'Arche de Noé
$$ | **BRASSERIE** | The discreet redbrick basement setting makes this one of the cozier candlelit meals in town. The name (Noah's Ark) has little to do with the menu except you will find such oddities as kangaroo steaks, albeit not by the pair. **Known for:** a wide selection of French wines (and also teas); a great setting, perfect for an intimate meal for two; you won't find another kangaroo steak in Wallonia. *Average main: €21* ✉ *Rue des Campeaux 34, Tournai* ☎ *069/223–797* 🌐 *www.larchedenoe.be* 🕓 *Closed Wed. and Thurs.*

Le Jardin Majorelle
$$ | **MOROCCAN** | Named after the famous garden in Marrakech, the setting here—among a colorful walled courtyard—is as much the star as the food. It certainly makes it popular in summer, when climate and cuisine combine to offer a real taste of Morocco with a menu that spans a litany of cheap tagines, *pastilla* (meat-filled pies beneath sweetened pastry), and couscous dishes with spicy merguez sausages or grilled meats. **Known for:** good-value food that is never less than tasty; authentic Moroccan cooking; a gorgeous setting perfect for sunny weather. *Average main: €17* ✉ *Rue des Puits l'Eau 33, Tournai* ☎ *069/687–498* 🕓 *Closed Mon.*

Coffee and Quick Bites

L'Èpicerie
$$ | **CAFÉ** | A friendly lunch spot with a good menu of busy spiced-up salads and pastas. On Friday and Saturday, lunchtime servings later bleed into the evening. **Known for:** really good-value meals; colorful local café-restaurant with a good kids' menu; fresh produce and friendly staff. *Average main: €15* ✉ *Rue du Cygne 27, Tournai* ☎ *069/234–900* 🌐 *lepicerietournai.be* 🕓 *Closed Sun. and Mon.*

Hotels

There's little in the way of hotels when it comes to the town center. Even B&Bs are hard to come by. But don't be put off by the youth hostel, which has some of the best facilities in town.

Auberge de Jeunesse de Tournai

$ | **HOTEL** | With the sheer lack of hotels in town, the youth hostel is a good fallback—in fact, it's a solid option either way. **Pros:** the sustainable breakfasts are filling; each room has a private bathroom; there are lots of facilities and free computers to use. **Cons:** rooms are pretty sparse and (as you'd expect) hostel-like; even the double rooms come with bunk beds; even the doubles have just showers and no toilets. *Rooms from: €55 Rue Saint-Martin 64, Tournai 069/216–136 www.lesaubergesdejeunesse.be 21 rooms No Meals.*

Ferme Delgueule

$$ | **HOTEL** | This beautiful 17th-century whitewashed farmhouse with a gabled exterior lies just 4 km (2½ miles) from the center of town. **Pros:** the restaurant stays opens until 10:30 pm every night; you couldn't ask for a nicer setting; it's the perfect base for exploring the countryside. **Cons:** it's quite close to the motorway; meals at the restaurant aren't cheap; you're a fair way out of town, with not much in the way of facilities nearby. *Rooms from: €110 Rue du Mont St Aubert 12, Tournai 0470/103–110 www.fermedelgueule.com 12 rooms Free Breakfast.*

Hotel Cathedral

$ | **HOTEL** | This city-center hotel doesn't have the best of reputations, and in truth, it could do with a touch-up here and there—but that's the problem, as it's perfectly positioned, near the cathedral, and it's well priced for the location. **Pros:** there's lots of good restaurants and bars nearby; location, location, location; it's good value given the paucity of alternative stays. **Cons:** there aren't many facilities; the street noise from the square outside can be loud; it's an old hotel that could do with a face-lift. *Rooms from: €84 Pl. Saint-Pierre 2, Tournai 069/250–000 www.hotelcathedrale.be 51 rooms No Meals.*

★ **L'Hôtel Alcantara**

$$ | **HOTEL** | An inconspicuous red-brick exterior hides a stylish boutique stay decked out in pop art and garish photographs of stars gone by. **Pros:** its comfortable rooms are just a short stroll from the city center; free parking; guests can borrow bicycles for free. **Cons:** standard bathrooms come with bathtub showers only; the choice at breakfast can be a little limited; the town chuch bells are pretty persistent in the morning. *Rooms from: €119 Rue des Bouchers Saint-Jacques 2, Tournai 069/212–648 www.hotelalcantara.be 24 rooms Free Breakfast.*

Nightlife

As with most Belgian cities, a stream of bar-restaurants wrap the larger squares. The **Grand Place** is a good choice if you want to sit on a terrace and watch the world go by. The noisier option is **place St-Pierre**, which is more of a going-out spot filled with bars and takeaway shops. Alternatively, head along the southern banks of the **river**, east of Pont-Notre-Dame, where the evenings drag on until late.

Aux Amis Réunis

BARS | This elegant "brown café" dates from the early 20th century but has weathered well. The mirror-and-wood paneling, leather banquettes, and tiled floors speak to a bar that knows its place in the world, and you can spot the regulars a mile off. There's a good selection of local beers and decent food. *Rue Saint-Martin 89, Tournai 069/559–659.*

Corto Malté

BARS | This bar-restaurant does a fine line in rather eclectic tapas, but it's also just a great spot to hang out thanks to its charming terrace, which nestles under a pair of trees overlooking the river. Have a drink and watch the barges drift on by. *Quai Saint-Brice 18, Tournai 069/223–400.*

The Brewing Arts of Pipaix

A few miles to the east of Tournai lies Pipaix, a tiny town home to a grand brewing history. The first of its famous breweries is **Brasserie à Vapeur** (*www.vapeur.com*), which first began making beer in 1785 and remains the only steam-operated brewery still in existence in Belgium. Visitors can still feel the heat of its engines on the last Saturday of each month, when staff spend all day mixing wort in the mash tub as the steam-powered engines kick in. It is perhaps best known for its Vapeur Cochon beer, whose bare-breasted pig logo was censored when it was exported to the United States. The village's other famous brewer is **Dubuisson** (*www.dubuisson.com*), which is the oldest brewery in Wallonia, established by Joseph Leroy in 1769. More amazingly, it's always been owned by the same family, spanning eight generations. Technically, it dates even further back, as Leroy used to brew in the old castle of Ghyssegnies before he fell foul of the tax laws of the empress of Austria, who ordered the destruction of his equipment. These days, the brewery is best known for its Cuvée des Trolls and super-strong Bush (12% ABV) beers, which you can sample on draft in the Trolls and Bush bars in Pipaix and Ath. You can also visit the brewery on tours held every Saturday.

enoBar

/INE BARS | This stylish cavelike bar is a pin-off from neighboring restaurant Le ;reco and has a bountiful selection of ;reek wines, tapas, and cocktails. ✉ *Pl. le Lille 25–27, Tournai* ☎ *069/228–169 e Greco* 🌐 *www.legrecotournai.be/ enobar.*

Shopping

TREET MARKETS

lea Markets

ECOND-HAND | There are a number of flea narkets across the city, but the most egular is held in **Les Bastion** car park on ;unday (6–1) on the eastern edge of the ity. Less common are **Les Chiffonades** extiles markets, which run the length f the quayside and typically take place n two dates in May and August (check nline). Between May and September, ou can also find a **secondhand book air** on the Grand Place. ✉ *Commercial Center des Bastions, Tournai.*

Grand Flower Market

FLORIST | The origins of this yearly Good Friday flower market date back to 1825; now some 75 florists and nurseries descend on Rue Royale and the quays of Saint-Brice and Dumon each year. ✉ *Rue Royale, Tournai.*

Ath

29 km (18 miles) from Tournai.

Ath is a bustling little town that finds its fifth gear on the fourth Sunday of every August. This is when Belgium's original Géants (giants) parade takes place, as huge, oversize floats and giant costumed figures march the cobbled streets. It's part of a celebration that dates back more than five centuries, though it has long since swapped its religious function for sheer spectacle, as more and more figures of local legend were admitted to its parade.

At the festival's heart is the story of the biblical giant Goliath, who has his trousers ceremonially burned on Friday, gets married in a bizarre ceremony on Saturday, and fights his foe, David, on Sunday. All the while, locals indulge in munching on hunks of *masteilles* (almond tart), which is the traditional cake you see everywhere at this time. It's a magical festival, though in recent years anger has arisen at the continued inclusion of the traditional "*sauvage*" black-face character in its parades, prompting calls for the removal of its UNESCO status. On the town's side, the debate over this was ongoing at the time of writing.

You can learn about the festival any time at a museum dedicated to the géants, which is reopening in 2022 after renovation. Alternatively, Ath makes a fine base for exploring some of the beautiful neoclassical châteaux that scatter the fringes of town.

GETTING HERE AND AROUND

Ath is on the rail line linking Brussels (€8.70) and Tournai. Trains take around 40 minutes from the capital. Local buses connect Ath to the castle at Beloeil (No. 81 or E40), while the train to Mons stops in nearby Mevergnies-Attre, next to Château d'Attre. Driving is the best way to get around here, though, and Ath is well connected to both Mons and Lessines (N54) and Tournai and Brussels (E429).

Sights

Château d'Attre (*Attre Castle*)
CASTLE/PALACE | This pretty château lies 6 km (4 miles) southeast of Ath. It was built in 1752 by François-Philippe Franeau d'Hyon atop the ruins of an older castle and possesses all the neoclassical ambitions of that era, with a fleet of Rococo-style rooms. In the late 18th century, its grounds were popular with hunting parties, and the remains of an artificial "mound" (known as the Rocher) used for sighting deer survives. The surrounding parkland makes for a pleasant stroll. ✉ *Av. du Château 8, Attre* ☎ *068/454–460* 🌐 *www.attre.be* 🎫 *€8* 🕙 *Closed weekdays (July and Aug.); Mon.–Sat. (Apr.–June, Sept., and Oct.)* Ⓜ *Train: Mevergnies-Attre.*

★ **Château de Beloeil** (*Beloeil Castle*)
CASTLE/PALACE | Many call it "the Versailles of Belgium," and while the building and grounds of Beloeil perhaps aren't the match of France's famous palace, they are nonetheless defiantly grand. The site has belonged to the Princes de Ligne since the 14th century, and a castle has stood here all that time. It is a "castle" in name only, though. This is more a neoclassical French-style château, the kind that became common in the 17th and 18th centuries, as Belgium moved away from its medieval pragmatism. Fine collections of antiques, furniture, and a 20,000-strong library recall its long heritage, though a fire in 1900 sapped the interior of much of its impact. ✉ *Rue du Château 11, Beloeil* ☎ *069/689–426* 🌐 *www.chateaudebeloeil.com* 🎫 *€12 castle and gardens* 🕙 *Closed Oct.–Mar. and weekdays Apr.–June and Sept.* Ⓜ *Bus: 81.*

L'Espace Gallo-Romain (*Gallo-Romain Museum*)
HISTORY MUSEUM | **FAMILY** | In 1975, a 9-meter-long Celtic-type barge, a canoe, and a mass of pottery were discovered at the Gallo-Roman dig in Pommerœul. Dating back to the 2nd century, the now-restored barge is one of the oldest examples of its kind in existence and, together with the rest of the findings, forms the centerpiece of a museum that is more family-focused than history buffs might like. The third floor hosts temporary historical exhibitions (not always in English, so check beforehand). ✉ *Rue de Nazareth 2, Ath* ☎ *068/681–320* 🌐 *espacegalloromain.be* 🎫 *€6* 🕙 *Closed Mon.; weekends Oct.–Mar.*

Maison des Géants
HISTORY MUSEUM | Most visitors to Ath come just to see the famous Ducasse

Beloeil Castle in Ath, with its sumptuous interiors of chandeliers, tapestries, and antiques is known as "the Versailles of Belgium."

festival) on the fourth weekend of August. If you can't make it then, this museum is the next best thing. Set in an 18th-century mansion, it unravels just how, why, and who takes part, looking at similar festivals around the world and the story of David and Goliath (Gouyasse), whose battle crowns Sunday's events, after the "Giants Parade." The building was undergoing renovation at the time of writing but is due to reopen at the end of 2022 along with its new Brasserie des Légendes tavern and a newly revamped tourism office. ✉ *Rue de Pintamont 18, Ath* ☎ *068/681–300* 🌐 *maisondesgeants.be* 🎫 *€6* ⏲ *Closed Mon.*

Pairi Daiza

ZOO | FAMILY | Probably the biggest reason Belgians come to this part of Wallonia is to visit the huge safari park in the grounds of a former Cistercian abbey. Look out for its botanical garden and some 7,000 animals spread over 160 acres, with everything from fish pedicures and ice-skating to the largest Chinese-style garden in Europe to keep families entertained. ✉ *Domaine de Cambron, Brugelette* ☎ *068/250–850* 🌐 *www.pairidaiza.eu* 🎫 *€37* Ⓜ *Train: Cambron-Casteau.*

Tour Burbant (*Burbant Tower*)

HISTORIC SIGHT | Baudouin IV, Count of Hainaut, began construction of this Norman-style keep in 1166. Sandwiched between the two arms of the Dender, it was the perfect position to defend against his ambitious neighboring lord, the Count of Flanders. These days it overlooks a few utility buildings and an adjacent schoolyard—a less menacing threat! Inside are treasures of the age and a video on its history in the guard room, but interior visits are restricted to guided tours, which can be arranged via the tourism office (currently in Espace Gallo-Romain). ✉ *Rue du Gouvernement, Ath* ☎ *068/681–300 tourism office* 🌐 *www.ath.be* 🎫 *€3.*

Restaurants

L' Entre Guillemets

$$$$ | BISTRO | Although it has similar signage to the neighboring hotel, this fine bistro is wholly independent and a real bright spot on the dining scene. Attentive staff and a studious menu that services the best of Belgian bistro fare prove a worthy combination. **Known for:** try the bouchée à la reine starter; friendly, professional staff; seafood is the chef's specialty. *Average main: €32* *Esplanade 13, Ath* *068/333–400* *www.lentreguillemets.be* *Closed Tues. No dinner Sun. No lunch Wed. and Sat.*

★ **Quai No. 4**

$$$$ | FRENCH | A sumptuous interior—all swampy green wallpaper and gold felt chairs—sets the scene for a menu just as rich. Think lobster and sweetbreads with a dash of caviar. **Known for:** creative cooking using unusual flavor combinations; fine dining with an eye for the extravagant; its desserts. *Average main: €35* *Quai St-Jacques 4, Ath* *0476/018–315* *www.quai-n4.be* *Closed Tues. and Wed.*

Trolls & Bush

$$ | BELGIAN | A spin-off restaurant from the Dubuisson Brewery (the oldest in Wallonia) in Pipaix. As you'd expect, its Cuvée des Trolls and mighty 12% ABV Bush beers feature heavily on draft, but they're also worked into the brasserie-style menu, mingling with beef-stew carbonnades, meatballs, and even worked into a duck confit. **Known for:** myriad sauce-slathered meat dishes; the local beer selection is second to none; there's a nice terrace in summer. *Average main: €15* *Grand Place 6, Ath* *068/335–834* *www.trolls-bush.com.*

Coffee and Quick Bites

L'Athéière

$ | CAFÉ | A charming little tea shop just a few doors down from the Maison des Géants. There's a lovely walled garden at the back, and books and newspapers (in French) are casually laid out to read. **Known for:** a wide selection of around a dozen teas, which they also sell loose; a quiet escape from the world; the terrace at the back is just delightful. *Average main: €5* *Rue de Pintamont 34, Ath* *0478/290–389* *No credit cards* *Closed Sun. and Mon.*

Hotels

There aren't many places to stay in Ath; it's mostly just small B&Bs. So, if visiting for the Ducasse D'Ath, be aware that rooms get booked up months in advance, so be sure to arrange your stay early before what few places there are disappear.

B&B L'Hôte des Géants

$$ | B&B/INN | FAMILY | This four-room B&B, set in a renovated 18th-century town house, has plenty of charm. **Pros:** the rooms are pretty big; sitting in the garden is an understated pleasure; there's bike storage in the garage and a charger for e-bikes. **Cons:** there's no free parking nearby; it's a B&B, so there are few extra perks; it fills up fast due to the small number of rooms. *Rooms from: €100* *Grand Rue des Bouchers 16, Ath* *0485/957–890* *lhotedesgeants.be* *4 rooms* *Free Breakfast.*

★ **Hôtel Du Parc**

$ | HOTEL | FAMILY | When you're the only hotel in town, you'd be forgiven for letting things slip, but it's far from the case at this sweet little boutique stay near the quay. **Pros:** the suite has a Jacuzzi bath; nice terrace garden at the rear; all floors are accessible. **Cons:** breakfast costs an extra €10; no private parking—just park in the street; there aren't really many facilities. *Rooms from: €98* *Rue de Bouchain 4, Ath* *0485/211–952* *www.hotelduparcath.com* *21 rooms* *No Meals.*

Lessines

11 km (7 miles) from Ath.

It might surprise some to know that quiet, God-fearing Lessines was the birthplace of the Surrealist artist René Magritte, whose statue sits cheerily on a bench in the main square, hat upturned on his head. There's little else to mark his time here except a sign signaling his birthplace, next to the station. The town is better known for its religious sights.

The Good Friday Procession of the Penitents has been taking place for at least five centuries, as locals march the streets solemnly dressed in hooded robes and carrying crosses. It's a moving if slightly unnerving sight. Easier to catch is the spectacular medieval hospital-cum-convent, which has been superbly restored and offers an often terrifying glimpse of medicine in the late Middle Ages.

In mid-August, look out for the El Cayoteu festival, which sees a parade of "giants" march the streets of Lessines. The town found fame in the 19th century for its quarries, filled with porphyry, an impossibly hard red stone. The parade is in honor of the feast day of St. Roch, the patron saint of the "*cayoteu*" (stonemasons).

GETTING HERE AND AROUND

Lessines lies on the rail line connecting Quevy (Wallonia) and Geraardsbergen (Flanders), which runs through Mons and Ath. To get there from Brussels (€8.70), you will need to change at Ath; it takes 70 minutes. If traveling by car, the E429 connects the town with Brussels via the N57.

VISITOR INFORMATION

CONTACTS Lessines Tourist Information. ✉ *Grand Place 12, Lessines* ☎ *068/270–761* 🌐 *tourisme.lessines.be.*

Sights

Dendre Valley RAVel Cycling Route
TRAIL | The RAVeL network is made up of old rail lines and canal towpaths that have been turned into countryside cycling and walking routes. The first 33 km (20½ miles) stage of the W1 route technically starts in Flanders, but you can just as easily pick it up in Lessines before threading a scenic trail to Ath and following the Blaton-Ath Canal to Beloeil Castle. It's a beautiful route and a day trip that includes some of the best sights in the area. See the RAVel Wallonie website for maps and details. ✉ *Lessines* 🌐 *ravel.wallonie.be.*

Église Saint-Pierre (*St. Peter's Church*)
CHURCH | This site has held numerous iterations of religious buildings: first a primitive chapel, then an 11th-century Romanesque church, parts of which you can still see in the great nave and tower, before this was replaced at the end of the 12th century by its current Gothic facade. It was heavily bombed in World War II, and items rescued from the fires of 1940 by the congregation can still be seen in the lobby, along with an interesting exhibition on the church's history. ✉ *Parv. Saint-Pierre 13, Lessines* ☎ *068/552–890* *Free.*

★ **Hôpital Notre-Dame à la Rose** (*Our Lady of the Rose Hospital*)
HISTORIC SIGHT | This sprawling medieval hospital complex and convent was founded in the 13th century, making it one of the oldest of its kind in Europe. Over the years, it had numerous expansions, with a farm added in the 16th and 17th centuries, and until 1980 it served as an old people's home. It has since been restored, with audio tours available. An herb garden, a beautiful chapel, and some terrifying examples (and illustrations) of medical equipment paint a fascinating portrait of the time. ✉ *Pl. Alix de Rosoit, Lessines* ☎ *068/332–403*

www.notredamealarose.be €11 Closed Mon.

Restaurants

★ **La Tramasure**

$$$ | **BISTRO** | There's not a lot of choice for dining in Lessines, with a number of popular old restaurants having closed their doors over recent years. La Tramasure remains the jewel in the crown, dishing up inventive bistro fine dining that leans heavily on local produce. **Known for:** wonderful desserts that often throw in a suprise ingredient; great French cooking using seasonal ingredients; a peaceful setting slightly removed from the center. *Average main: €28 Porte d'Ogy 3, Lessines 068/335–082 www.letramasure.be Closed Mon.*

Hotels

★ **Maison Des Anges**

$$ | **B&B/INN** | **FAMILY** | A beautifully renovated old town house is the setting for this classical-looking B&B, which has undergone previous lives as both a restaurant and even a ballroom. **Pros:** breakfast is huge and the terrace is gorgeous; large rooms and king-size beds; it's right in the center of town, on the edge of the main square. **Cons:** there are few facilities; there are house cats, so those with allergies beware; it's a pricey for the area. *Rooms from: €119 Rue de Gramont 4, Lessines 068/280–904 maisondesanges.net 5 rooms Free Breakfast.*

Nivelles

54 km (33½ miles) from Lessines.

Located in Walloon Brabant, Nivelles was once the capital of what used to be the Roman Pais (Roman Land) region, named after the Romance dialect that used to be spoken here. This has long since disappeared, but the same can't be said for its spectacular 6th-century Collégiale Sainte-Gertrude church. For years, this was a powerful abbey, and after the death of its first abbess, who was later canonized, it became a site of veneration for those on the pilgrim trail from Northern Europe to Santiago de Compostela. Like most Wallonie towns, its old ramparts were dismantled in the 1800s, but you can still see the sole survivor of its nine towers on the western edge of the historic center. A fine relic of another age entirely.

GETTING HERE AND AROUND

Nivelles lies on the rail line connecting Brussels and Charleroi, with the capital (€5.90) just 30 minutes away by train. It also has a direct link to Waterloo. The E4 bus route connects it to Louvain-la-Neuve.

VISITOR INFORMATION

CONTACTS Nivelles Tourist Information. *Rue de Saintes 48, Nivelles 067/215–413 www.tourisme-nivelles.be.*

Sights

★ **Collégiale Sainte-Gertrude** (*Collegiate Church of St. Gertrude*)

CHURCH | This grand building dates back to the mid-7th century when an abbey was founded here by the ancestors of Frankish king Charlemagne. Its first abbess, Gertrude, was his great aunt and was famously gentle in her manner. The abbey was among the most important in Europe right up until its closure by the French Revolutionary army in 1798. It is a magnificent structure, with a rising western facade topping five stories and a giant nave, beneath which you can visit the archaeological excavation where Charlemagne's first wife, Himeltrude, is buried. *Pl. Lambert Schiffelers 1, Nivelles 067/212–069 www.collegiale.be Free; €6 guided tours.*

Musée Communal de Nivelles (*Nivelles Museum*)
HISTORY MUSEUM | This 18th-century mansion was constructed on the site of a former church as a refuge for liberated Christian prisoners. By the 1800s it had fallen into private hands and now holds the city's collection of paintings, sculptures, and furniture. ✉ *Rue de Bruxelles 27, Nivelles* ☎ *067/882–280* 🌐 *musee-nivelles.be* 🎫 *€2* ⏲ *Closed Sat.–Mon.*

Saint-James Quarter
HISTORIC DISTRICT | This historic part of town was once popular with those walking the pilgrim trail to Santiago de Compostella via the Netherlands or Germany trail. They would visit in order to venerate the relics of Ste. Gertrude at the church. It was later adopted by local brewers. Hostelries once lined the streets here, and you can still see the scallop shell (symbol of St. James) on various facades along rue du Coq and rue Bayard. More recently, the town has traced where the Brabant Way and Gallia Belgica Way used to meet up here, with maps to follow local sections of the trail found in the tourist office. Ivy-strewn stairs also lead out of the St. James area via rue du Wichet to the pretty **Dodaine Park**. ✉ *Rue du Coq, Nivelles.*

Restaurants

Dis Moi Ou?
$$$ | **FRENCH** | A well-loved local favorite in the capable hands of chef Nicolas Michiels. The menu is a study in classic French fare, with boneless entrecôte steaks smothered in rich sauces, braised duck breasts, and sweetbreads in a truffle-flavored *jus*. **Known for:** accomplished French cooking; quality wine and whiskey list; knowledgeable and professional staff. $ *Average main: €28* ✉ *Rue Sainte-Anne 5, Nivelles* ☎ *067/646–464* 🌐 *dis-moiou.be* ⏲ *Closed Sun. and Mon. No lunch Sat.*

Le Cigalon
$$$ | **FRENCH** | Another excellent French-theme establishment that sets its cap at Lyonnaise-style cooking, meaning plenty of rustic cuts and offal on the menu, from roasted bone marrow and veal kidneys to Lyon-style herring. If your tastes veer toward meatier, classic Gallic cooking, then this is your heaven. **Known for:** good value for what you get; well-priced wine list; French country cooking. $ *Average main: €24* ✉ *Rue de Bruxelles 32, Nivelles* ☎ *0475/531–737* 🌐 *www.restaurantlecigalon.be* ⏲ *Closed Wed.*

Hotels

Van Der Valk Nivelles Sud
$$ | **HOTEL** | There's no getting away from just how large this hotel is compared to little Nivelles (it's been been squirreled far from the historic center and out by the ring road) but what it lacks in small-town charm, it makes up for with modern facilities. **Pros:** the gym is surprisingly huge; the wellness center is free to use for guests; you can add parking to the list of freebies. **Cons:** it can't escape the business-hotel vibe; you're not in the center of town and really need a car to stay here; its location, beside a busy road, is useful but hardly appealing. $ *Rooms from: €104* ✉ *Chau. de Mons 22, Nivelles* ☎ *067/218–721* 🌐 *www.hotelnivellessud.be/en* *155 rooms* *Free Breakfast.*

Waterloo

15 km (9 miles) from Nivelles.

The battle of Waterloo, like the events of Stalingrad and Hiroshima, changed the course of history. The defeat of the French here in June 1815 ended Napoléon's attempt to dominate Europe, and for Belgium especially, it provided the impetus for independence as Catholic Flanders and Wallonia fell into Protestant Dutch hands.

The British army's officers were at a swanky Brussels ball on the night of June 16, 1815, when they were called to face Napoléon's men. After joining their rank-and-file troops in Waterloo, they garrisoned at Hougoumont Farm, which still exists today, and spent the night of June 17 being lashed by rain.

At midday on June 18, the French soldiers, led by their emperor, started their offensive at the farm. Heavy fighting raged all day and the bad weather came to the Brit's aid, hindering the heavy French artillery and deadening the impact of its cannonballs. The allies held their positions and, eventually, the French army were hemmed in by the last-minute arrival of the Prussians. In the early evening, Napoléon and his men retreated, escaping back to France. Later, he surrendered to the British and was exiled to the far-off island of Saint Helena, where he died, miserable and depressed, in 1821. The short (just nine hours) battle made a hero of the British Duke of Wellington, but there was a gruesomely heavy toll on both sides, with 13,000 deaths and a further 35,000 wounded.

What the French writer Victor Hugo once called the *morne plain* (dismal plain) is now a patch of open space beyond the edge of the prosperous suburbs of Waterloo, which lies about 3 km (2 miles) away. Millions of euros have been poured into making the old battle site more of an experience, with buildings restored to their 19th-century heyday and the opening of an underground exhibition space next to the Lion's Mound.

GETTING HERE AND AROUND

The town of Waterloo is well connected by rail links, with direct trains running to Gare de Waterloo from Brussels (€3.90) in around 20 minutes. If traveling from Western Wallonia, you will usually need to change at either Charleroi Sud or Nivelles. Once you've arrived, the battlefield (Memorial 1815) sites lies a couple of miles outside town. W25 and W27 buses run from outside the Église Saint-Joseph to the site, or you can walk—it takes just over one hour. Once there, free shuttle buses operate regularly from the Memorial to Hougoumont Farm, which is otherwise a 20-minute walk away.

TOURS

Les Guides 1815

SPECIAL-INTEREST TOURS | In Waterloo, these expert guides can be hired to take you around the battlefield on differently themed walking and cycling tours (€90–€110 per guide). Shorter guided visits to the museums, farms, and memorials cost from €70 per guide, excluding entry fees. Book online. 🌐 *www.guides1815-waterloo.com.*

Sights

Combination tickets for the Musée Wellington in Waterloo and all the Memorial 1815 sites (Museum, Panorama, Lion's Mound, Hougoumont Farm) at the battlefield in nearby Braine-l'Alleud can be purchased for €22.

Butte du Lion (*Lion's Mound*)

MONUMENT | The battlefield, now made up of rye fields, is best surveyed from atop the Butte du Lion (Lion's Mound), a grassy pyramid 226 steps high and crowned by a 28-ton cast-iron lion statue. It was created by the Dutch 10 years after the fighting had ended using ground from the actual battlefield. Surprisingly, it wasn't originally conceived as a memorial or victory statue, as most people assume, but was built to mark the spot William I was knocked off his horse by a musket ball during the battle. Admission is included in the Memorial 1815 ticket. ✉ *Rte. du Lion 1815, Braine-l'Alleud, Waterloo* ☎ *023/851–912* 🌐 *www.waterloo1815.be* 🎫 *€18.*

Hougoumont Farm

HISTORIC SIGHT | This was the site of the first attack by the French on the morning of the battle. Historians surmise this was initially a feint to draw out Wellington's

he man-made Lion's Mound memorial is one the most iconic sites at the Battle of Waterloo, where apoleon was defeated.

eserves, but the fighting continued all day as the French were drawn in. In he novel Les Miserables, Victor Hugo alks of the 300 French bodies disposed of in the farm's well, but nothing has ever been found there. ✉ *Chem. du Goumont, Braine-l'Alleud, Waterloo* ☎ *023/851–912* 🌐 *www.waterloo1815.be* 🎫 *€8; €18 combo ticket* ⊗ *Closed Mon., Tues., Thurs., and Fri. Apr.–June and Sept. and Oct.; weekdays Nov.–Mar.*

★ **Musée du Mémorial 1815**
(*1815 Memorial Museum*)
HISTORY MUSEUM | Opened in time for the 200th anniversary of the Battle of Waterloo, this underground museum and visitor center puts the day's events in context. It details the rise of Napoléon, the makeup of the two sides, and the important consequences of what happened afterwards for Europe. An audio guide takes you through everything before finishing with a 4D movie of the battle. ✉ *Rte. du Lion 1815, Braine-l'Alleud, Waterloo* ☎ *023/851–912* 🌐 *www.waterloo1815.be* 🎫 *€18.*

Musée Wellington (*Wellington Museum*)
HISTORY MUSEUM | This modest little museum in the town of Waterloo is housed within a former 18th-century coaching inn and was the site of the Duke of Wellington's headquarters on the 17th and 18th of June 1815. It was here that he penned his victory dispatch to the British government. Now it is filled with relics collected from the battle, as well as temporary exhibitions on other wars. ✉ *Chau. de Bruxelles 147, Waterloo* ☎ *023/572–860* 🌐 *www.museewellington.be* 🎫 *€5.*

The Panorama
ART MUSEUM | Before VR, this was the closest you got to an immersive experience. This huge circular painting of the battle was created by the artist Louis Dumoulin in 1912 and is 360 feet long, wrapping the circular gallery in which it's displayed. Sound effects (yelling, cannon fire) set the scene. ✉ *Memorial 1815, Rte. du Lion 1815, Braine-l'Alleud, Waterloo* ☎ *023/851–912* 🌐 *www.waterloo1815.be* 🎫 *€18.*

After Waterloo...

What is often lost in the constant focus on French emperor Napoléon's charisma and his last fevered 100-day march across Europe is what stopping him actually meant. The battle at Waterloo was closer than most realize, with the Duke of Wellington, leader of the British army, claiming at the time that it was "the nearest-run thing you ever saw in your life." But Waterloo didn't just stop one man; it brought to an end a 15-year period of near-constant warring in Europe along with Napoléon's dream of building a great continental empire. In short: it left a big hole to be filled.

Even today in France it is still a difficult subject. During the battle's 200th anniversary in 2015, the country even tried to block Belgium from minting a "Battle of Waterloo" euro coin. The recent anniversary of Napoléon's death in 2021 was just as difficult for French politicians, for whom trying to weigh praise for his achievements as a statesman (the Napoleonic Code is still the basis for much of French and Belgian law) while condemning his warmongering was, for many, an enjoyably tricky balancing act to watch.

For the British, Waterloo is still a source of slightly blinkered pride, hazily trotted out when Channel rivalries emerge, regardless of the fact that only a third of the army that fought at Waterloo was British. The rest was made up of Prussians, Dutch, and Belgians. But it's what the battle heralded for the Brits that makes it so relevant. It ushered in a new age of profitable expansion, as the spoils of war saw territorial possessions such as South Africa, Trinidad, and Sri Lanka slip into colonial British hands, and a chance to finally claim the world stage from France.

For the Dutch, it was a national triumph. That the Lion's Mound is actually a monument to the bravery of William I, who was shot with a musket ball and fell off his horse on that very spot, is lost on most visitors who see it. After the battle, he was appointed king of the Netherlands (including Belgium). For Catholic-leaning Flanders and Wallonia, who now fell under the rule of the Protestant Dutch, it would hasten the formation of modern-day Belgium, which gained independence just 15 years later in 1830.

Even at the time, the battle's significance was apparent. As they were clearing the dead from the fields, collectors bagged and sold souvenirs. And in the weeks that followed, many Britons crossed the Channel just to stare at the patch of land where it happened. By 1821, Napoléon had died alone in his drafty house on the far-flung island of St Helena.

Restaurants

L'Amusoir

$$ | STEAKHOUSE | FAMILY | Popular with resident Americans, this is an unpretentious steak house in an old white-walled building in the center of town. It serves mouthwatering filet mignon, prepared with a variety of sauces, and hearty Belgian traditional dishes. **Known for:** a nice selection of Belgian classics; good-value steaks; friendly service. $ *Average main: €20* ✉ *Chau. de Bruxelles 121, Waterloo* ☎ *023/548–233* 🌐 *www.lamusoir.be.*

★ **Little Paris**

$$ | **FRENCH** | Waterloo is a rather affluent ttle suburb populated by expats, and ıas gathered for itself something of a eputation for its restaurants. Leading the vay is this French fine-dining favorite, vhich delves into the more rural side of Lyonnaise cooking, with a menu eking impossibly delicate flavors from saddle of hare, grilled venison, and pig's rotters. **Known for:** good-value dishes; old-fashioned cuts and ingredients given a modern spin; reasonably priced wine ist to complement the fine menu. $ *Average main: €28* ✉ *Chau. de Bruxelles 39, Waterloo* ☎ *023/548–457* 🌐 *www.little-paris.be* ⊙ *Closed Sat.–Mon.*

Hotels

★ **Hotel Le Côté Vert**

$$ | **HOTEL** | **FAMILY** | This relaxed hotel s in the center of Waterloo town and surrounded by greenery. **Pros:** there's a small fitness gym and free parking; the n-house restaurant is a great option; ush garden setting to relax in. **Cons:** ooms are basic; there's not much to do in the town of Waterloo; it's one of he pricier options here. $ *Rooms from: €180* ✉ *Chau. de Bruxelles 200, Waterloo* ☎ *023/540–105* 🌐 *cotevert.be* *47 rooms* *Free Breakfast.*

Martin's Grand Hotel Waterloo

$$ | **HOTEL** | What began as a 19th-century sugar-processing factory, and later became a film studio, is now one of he plusher stays in town. **Pros:** the fitness room is open 24/7; the restaurant is pretty spectacular; it's near to he bus stop for Memorial 1815. **Cons:** a number of rooms overlook the main road; there aren't that many facilities for the price you pay; it's on the edge of town. $ *Rooms from: €160* ✉ *Chau. de Tervuren 198, Waterloo* ☎ *012/521–815* 🌐 *www.martinshotels.com* *73 rooms* *Free Breakfast.*

Louvain-la-Neuve

29 km (18 miles) from Waterloo.

Within Ottignies-Louvain-la-Neuve is a town within a town. Yet walking the rather nondescript new-build university "village" of Louvain-la-Neuve, it's hard to understand how fraught its past has been. Construction only began in the early 1970s, after a crisis at Flemish Brabant's Leuven University, one of the oldest educational institutions in Europe, saw Flemish and Walloon students bitterly divided along linguistic lines. It would go on to cause a national storm.

Despite its main campus being in Dutch-speaking Flanders, the majority of classes at Leuven's university were taught in French, a hangover from when this was the default language of the Belgian elite. The rise of a Flemish nationalist movement in the late 1960s drew matters to a head and civil unrest broke out. It sparked a crisis that even led to the country's prime minister resigning. Eventually, a very Belgian compromise was reached: the building of a new town and university 30 km (19 miles) to the south of Leuven ("Louvain" in French), in the suburbs of French-speaking Wallonia's Ottignies. They called it "New Leuven" (Louvain-la-Neuve) and it now welcomes some 20,000 students a year.

GETTING HERE AND AROUND

Louvain-la-Neuve and Ottignies stations are connected to Brussels by hour-long trains (€5.50) running every hour. Rail links to the rest of the region are more difficult, with most train routes requiring a change at Wavre or Brussels. Buses are the quickest way to reach other parts of Walloon Brabant, with Nivelles (No. E4) and Waterloo (No. 39) services running regularly. By road, the E411 takes you to Brussels via Wavre.

Sights

★ **Musée Hergé** (*Hergé Museum*)

ART MUSEUM | FAMILY | The only museum in Belgium dedicated solely to the works of cartoonist and Tintin creator George Remi (aka Hergé) is set within an ambitiously designed glass-and-concrete geometric cocoon. Its design is a fitting testimony to the foremost proponent of the *ligne claire* drawing style, its clear, stong lines reminiscent of those that dominated Hergé's work. The museum is certainly a must if you're a fan, and is packed with original sketches, documents, letters, and items that inspired his beloved creations. Part nostalgia, part forensic excavation of his career, it is nothing if not in-depth when narrating every step of his journey from jobbing artist to national icon. The on-site shop is, as you'd expect, filled with precious collectibles. ✉ *Rue du Labrador 26, Louvain-la-Neuve* ☎ *010/488–421* 🌐 *www.museeherge.com* 🎫 *€12* ⏲ *Closed Mon.*

Musée L (*L Museum*)

OTHER MUSEUM | The university museum's collection stands some 20,000 items strong, spanning just about any topic you care to mention, from Congolese statues to Picasso monographs. It's ordered around some slightly esoteric themes, but essentially this is just a neat way of delving into the stories surrounding the collection. Temporary exhibitions have covered everything from the history of photographing the human body to ancient religious practices. ✉ *Pl. des Sciences 3, Louvain-la-Neuve* ☎ *010/474–841* 🌐 *museel.be* 🎫 *€8* ⏲ *Closed Mon.*

Restaurants

Altérez-Vous

$$ | INTERNATIONAL | FAMILY | A conscientious nonprofit café-restaurant with a zeal for organic and local producers. Good cocktails and a selection of lesser-seen Wallonie beers add to a menu that is particularly good for nonmeat-eaters and those with food allergies. **Known for:** friendly staff and good value; ethical eating that's actually tasty; lots of options for vegetarians. [$] *Average main: €15* ✉ *Pl. des Brabançons 6A, Louvain-la-Neuve* ☎ *010/844–003* 🌐 *www.alterezvous.be* ⏲ *Closed Sun.*

L'Horizon

$$$$ | FRENCH | It's a 13-km (8-mile) drive out of town, but the area's most accomplished fine-dining spot is worth the hassle. It piles headfirst into French-style gastronomy, producing dishes as finely tuned as their flavors. **Known for:** great value, imaginative food; gastronomic cooking but good-size portions; a fine wine selection to choose from. [$] *Average main: €40* ✉ *Rue du moulin 50, Chaumont-Gistoux* ☎ *010/227–565* 🌐 *restaurantlhorizon.be* ⏲ *Closed Tues. and Wed.*

Hotels

★ **Martin's Louvain-La-Neuve**

$$ | HOTEL | Louvain-la-Neuve has traditionally been a bit of a desert when it comes to accommodation, so this recent addition to the Martin's chain was much needed when it opened in 2018, just a short stroll from the lake. **Pros:** there's a giant spa, gym, and pool; all the facilities you could want, and it's pet-friendly; the terraced wine bar is a nice spot to relax. **Cons:** access to the wellness facilities is €35 per day; standard rooms aren't that large; private parking (€22) is quite pricey. [$] *Rooms from: €121* ✉ *Rue de l'Hocaille 1, Louvain-la-Neuve* ☎ *010/772–020* 🌐 *www.martinshotels.com* *108 rooms* 🍽 *Free Breakfast.*

La Louvière

41 km (25½ miles) from Louvain-La-Neuve.

La Louvière is a city whose identity is closely tied with the industrial revolution that transformed the fortunes of this region from the 18th century onward. North of its center, a canal network was dug in the late 1800s that used a series of hydraulic locks to link up the Meuse and Scheldt rivers. It was a monumental feat of engineering, but it also thrust this small town into the heart of the region's burgeoning coal and steel industry.

All of a sudden, the mines on its doorstep were able to ship to the North Sea, France, and Germany with ease. Money flooded into the area, and you can see where it went in nearby sights such as the grand château of Seneffe and the grounds of Mariemont, once owned by the wealthiest industrialist in Belgium. In truth, the city is less appealing and more a handy base for visiting these relics, from cruising the canals to exploring the mines and worker's villages of Bois-du-Luc. Having said that, some interesting local art museums and a good choice of restaurants mean you're rarely short of an escape on a rainy day.

GETTING HERE AND AROUND

La Louvière-Sud railway station lies on the line connecting Tounai and Liège, with stops including Mons, Binche, and Charleroi. If traveling from Brussels, there are direct trains (€8.30) from La Louvière taking just one hour. If driving, the E19 to Brussels runs just past the city. Buses are only really needed if traveling to the museums and sights on the fringes of town. These gather outside the railway station or stop on the main street.

VISITOR INFORMATION

Bike hire is available from the tourism office, as are cycling maps around the area.

CONTACTS La Louvière Tourist Information. ✉ *Pl. Jules Mansart 21–22, La Louvière, La Louvière* ☎ *064/261–500* 🌐 *www.centrissime.be.*

Sights

Bois-du-Luc

MINE | Along with the Grand-Hornu (Mons) and Bois-du-Cazier (Charleroi), UNESCO-listed Bois-du-Luc was one of the oldest and largest mines in Wallonia. It had been operating for nearly three centuries by the time its machinery stopped turning in 1973. By then, an entire industrial village had been purpose-built around it for its workers, consisting of shops, a church, schools, even a library. Guided (or audio-guide) tours of the site explore how these communities grew and developed. ✉ *Rue Saint-Patrice 2b, Houdeng-Aimeries* ☎ *064/282–000* 🌐 *www.boisdulucmmdd.be* *€10 (includes audio guide); €12 for weekend guided tour* *Closed Mon.* *Bus: 30, 82.*

Canal du Center and Boat Lifts

BODY OF WATER | An interlocking system of canals connects what was once the industrial heartland of Wallonia with the rivers Scheldt and Meuse. This allowed the shipping of goods to and from France, Germany, and the North Sea. But its creation wasn't easy. A 223-foot drop meant that a series of locks and hydraulic boat lifts had to be created between 1888 and 1917, as a new canal was dug on the outskirts of La Louvière. Now UNESCO-listed, these stretch the waterways between Thieu and Houdeng-Goegnies, around 2 km (1 mile) from the city center (look for "Asc. 1, 2, 3, and 4"). But by the 1980s, barges had become too big for the old system, and a single boat lift, known as the **Ascenseur Funiculaire de Strépy-Thieu,** was built to accommodate modern vessels. It is the largest of its kind in the world, and tours of the engine room and workings let you see just what a giant it is. Cruises also set off from here to tour the canals and boat lifts in summer (the ticket office is at Strépy-Thieu reception). If you'd rather explore under your own steam, you can rent electric boats (no license required) to chug the canals or cycle or walk the old towpaths. ✉ *Rue Raymond Cordier 50, Thieu* ☎ *078/059–059* 🌐 *www.canalducentre.be* 🎫 *€13 cruise; €8 to visit Strépy-Thieu Boat Lift* ⏲ *Closed Oct.–Mar.* Ⓜ *Bus: 82.*

Centre de la Gravure et de l'Image Imprimée (*Center for Engravings and Printed Images*)

ART MUSEUM | This graphic-design and printed images museum has changing exhibitions throughout the year, and most are surprisingly engaging, such as its excellent dissection of tropes in Belgian railway posters over the decades. ✉ *Rue des Amours 10, La Louvière* ☎ *064/278–727* 🌐 *www.centredelagravure.be* 🎫 *€8* ⏲ *Closed Mon.*

Château de Seneffe (*Seneffe Castle*)

HISTORIC HOME | Around 10 km (6 miles) northeast of La Louvière, this neoclassical estate offers an elegant escape from the gray pragmatism of industrial Wallonia. Its construction dates back to the 1760s, when it was built as the home of a wealthy entrepreneur, Julian Depestre. Since then, it's had a checkered past, having been requisitioned during World War II by the Nazi military governor of Belgium, then left to ruin. It was later rescued by the state, and these days the grounds alone are worth a visit. ✉ *Rue Lucien Plasman 7–9, Seneffe* ☎ *064/556–913* 🌐 *chateaudeseneffe.be* 🎫 *€6* ⏲ *Closed Mon.* Ⓜ *Bus: 23/72.*

Keramis Center of Ceramics

ART GALLERY | This museum has been created within the site of the former Royal Boch factory, a 19th-century ceramics manufacturer later known as Villeroy & Boch. The museum has kept much of the old building intact, and you can even still see the old bottle kilns, the last standing in Belgium. It also hosts changing exhibitions exploring ceramics and earthenware, including deep dives into its private Boch collection. ✉ *Pl. des Fours-Bouteilles 1, La Louvière* ☎ *064/236–070* 🌐 *www.keramis.be* 🎫 *€* ⏲ *Closed Mon.*

MiLL

ART MUSEUM | Set in what used to be the old courthouse, this gallery contains a permanent collection of works by Idel Ianchelevici, a Jewish Romanian-born sculptor who acquired Belgian citizenship post–World War II. You can also see works from the city's collection, which includes pieces by René Magritte and Paul Leduc. ✉ *Pl. communale 21, La Louvière* ☎ *064/282–530* 🌐 *www.lemill.be* 🎫 *€5* ⏲ *Closed Mon.*

Musée Royal de Mariemont (*Mariemont Royal Museum*)

HISTORY MUSEUM | This estate once belonged to Marie of Hungary, though her castle was destroyed in 1794. In the 19th century, it fell into the hands of Raoul Warocqué, heir to a coal-mining fortune. He was also an avid collector of antiquities, having built up the world's largest collection of Tournai porcelain as well as Greco-Roman and Egyptian artifacts. Don't miss Rodin's statue of the Burghers of Calais, one of a few that were cast during the artist's lifetime. ✉ *Chau. de Mariemont 100, Morlanwelz* ☎ *064/273–741* 🌐 *www.musee-mariemont.be* 🎫 *€5* ⏲ *Closed Mon.* Ⓜ *Bus: 82.*

Restaurants

Blue Note

$$ | INTERNATIONAL | Good food, wine, and jazz music are the three building blocks here. The entrance is rather discreet and easily missed, but inside it has a simple elegance: all wooden benches and musical murals. **Known for:** a delightful choice of wines; good music to accompany your digestion; inventive cooking with interesting pairings of ingredients. $ *Average main: €22* ✉ *Rue Sylvain Guyaux 81, La Louvière* ☎ *0471/831–510* 🌐 *www.bluenoteproject.be* ⏲ *Closed Mon.–Wed.*

Céma Passion
$$$ | **FRENCH** | This is the home of the finest of dining in La Louvière. It's a bit of a walk—away from the center and into more of a residential area—but once you arrive, it's worth the hassle. **Known for:** the lunch menu is pure decadence; exquisite cooking and fine service; a great wine list accompanies the food. *Average main: €35 Av. Gambetta 63, La Louvière 064/663–826 cemapassion.com Closed Sun. and Mon. No dinner Tues.–Thurs. No lunch Sat.*

Les Brasseries Mansart
$$ | **BRASSERIE** | **FAMILY** | This is very much the city's go-to brasserie, and has been on the corner of place Jules Mansart since 1920. It has a classical feel, with red-leather banquettes and a jazzy chandelier, and is invariably busy at lunchtimes. **Known for:** a great people-watching spot; perfect for a lunchtime filler; a popular local favorite heavy on the meat. *Average main: €23 Pl. Jules Mansart , La Louvière 064/261–259 www.brasseriesmansart.be.*

Les Gourmands Disent
$$ | **BELGIAN** | **FAMILY** | A cozy little bistro squirreled away on the main road through town. There's some well-made, decently priced French and Belgian dining here, from ham roasted with *sirop de Liège* to a huge selection of mussels dishes, cooked with every sauce, cream, and beer you can imagine. **Known for:** a peaceful escape from the busy street; it's the go-to place for mussels in town; the flambéed bone-in rib eyes are well loved. *Average main: €25 Rue Sylvain Guyaux 8, La Louvière 064/284–095 www.lesgourmandsdisent.be Closed Mon. and Tues. No lunch Sat.*

Coffee and Quick Bites

Chez Gus
$ | **CAFÉ** | A tiny canteen-style café on the main road out of town. It does a fine line in soups, sandwiches, and cakes, and everything is homemade and devoid of pretension. **Known for:** cozy and delicious soups; homemade treats; a fine meat loaf sandwich. *Average main: €6 Rue Hamoir 21, La Louvière 0497/945–049 Closed Sun.–Tues.*

Il Passatore
$$ | **ITALIAN** | A cozy little Italian lunch spot with a specialty in *piadina* wraps, typically stuffed with cheese and cured ham. It has a good selection of drinks, too. **Known for:** great charcuterie; really nice homemade desserts, especially the tiramisu; run by a friendly family. *Average main: €15 Rue Albert I 32, La Louvière 064/849–698 Closed Sun.*

Hotels

Hotel Tristar
$ | **HOTEL** | It might look a little old-fashioned from the outside, but this is the most assured stay in the city. **Pros:** staff are friendly and really helpful; you're close to the center of the city; there's lots of places to eat nearby. **Cons:** parking in the garage is €5 per night; it's pretty basic with few facilities; can be noisy for the rooms overlooking the street. *Rooms from: €88 Pl. Maugrétout 5, La Louvière 064/236–260 www.hoteltristar.be 25 rooms Free Breakfast.*

Orange Hotel
$ | **HOTEL** | **FAMILY** | La Louvière isn't the prettiest of cities, so this stay on the outskirts is a good option if you've got a car. **Pros:** it's pet-friendly and good value; breakfasts (costs extra) are plentiful and good quality; the restaurant is a good option if you're not eating out. **Cons:** you'll need a car to get there; you're not in the center of the city; there aren't that many facilities. *Rooms from: €80 Chau. du Pont du Sart 238, La Louvière 064/773-300 www.orangehotel.be 84 rooms No Meals.*

Binche

8 km (5 miles) from La Louvière.

In its 16th-century heyday, Binche was a walled city with one of the finest palaces in Belgium. Sadly, the French quickly put paid to the latter, and the town's walls, like the rest of those in Wallonia, were mostly dismantled in the 18th century. Unlike other towns in the area, though, you can still find hunks of its old ramparts and towers punctuating the parks and fringes in eruptions of medieval stonework. A 2-km (1.2-mile) trail follows in their wake and makes for a fine walk. But those planning a visit to Binche are usually arriving for another matter entirely.

Binche Carnival (late February/March) is famed in Belgium as one of its most colorful folkloric festivals. Its gilles, wearing hats sprouting great feathery plumes and waxed masks, are a sight to behold, their painted-on mustaches and green spectacles creepily iconic. Some 1,000 of them—all locals—dance the streets hurling oranges and warding off evil with their sticks on Mardi Gras morning. They are later joined by harlequins, pierrots, and musicians, as they parade the streets. The festivities continue for the three days preceding Ash Wednesday, as empty paper beer cups mount in the square beneath the beautiful Gothic town hall. Drinking is a big part of the carnival, and bars heave with merrymakers. It's an unforgettable (albeit woozy) time to visit the city.

GETTING HERE AND AROUND

Binche is on the same railway line that runs through Tournai, Mons, La Louvière and Charleroi. Trains along this route

Hail to the Gilles

The Carnaval de Binche is said to have been sparked by a week of festivities held for the visit of Charles V in 1549. Today, the carnival is taken very seriously by the Binchois, requires around six months of planning, and adheres to strict rules of conduct, none of which preclude large amounts of alcohol. The festivities begin on the Sunday before Ash Wednesday, when hundreds of men turn out in costume, some as *mam'zelles* (in Belle Époque women's clothing), others as *pierrots* (clowns), and many as *gilles*. Only the most upstanding residents whose families have lived in Binche for generations can be gilles—the signature figures of the Carnaval. They're costumed somewhat eerily in identical waxed masks painted with green spectacles and large mustaches. Two days of music and partying later, at dawn on Mardi Gras, a solitary drummer marches to the home of the head gille to escort him out into the street. They dance to the home of the next gille, and so on, until there are perhaps 100 men doing a slow, shuffling two-step to the ancient tunes of the musicians who, like the gilles, gradually join the procession. They troop down to the hôtel de ville to be welcomed by the burgomaster, and reappear after lunch in their enormous ostrich-plumed hats to toss out oranges to the crowd before gathering in the Grand Place for music and dancing. The day ends with fireworks, but the gilles continue cavorting through the night. Traditionally, they drink nothing but champagne at each stop. The results can sometimes be a little messy.

ypically go every hour. There is also a lirect service to Brussels (€9.70), which akes around 75 minutes. Bus services round the area are more regular than ains but there is no TEC ticket machine n Binche, so you'll need to fill up a MoBIB card in advance or buy tickets nline, as you can't buy them onboard. If riving, Binche is connected to Charleroi nd Mons via the N90.

ISITOR INFORMATION

ONTACTS Binche Tourist Information. *Grand Place 5, Binche* ☎ *064/311–580* *www.binchetourisme.be.*

Sights

ncient Wall Ramparts

ISTORIC SIGHT | While most of Belgium's ities had their medieval walls torn down n the 18th and 19th centuries, giving vay to ring roads and expansions, Binche s a little different. Over 2 km (1 mile) of its perimeter wall still survives, along with some 30 towers. It dates back to the 12th century, when the city was founded by the Counts of Hainaut. It's a rare sight, and you can find walking maps at the tourism office that follow a tour of the ramparts, beginning at the Town Hall. It takes around two hours in total. On the last Sunday in May, you can also visit the Brocante des Remparts, a popular flea market beneath the city walls in the Marie de Hongrie Park. ✉ *Grand Place, Binche* *Free.*

Beffroi et l'Hôtel de Ville (*Belfry and Town Hall*)

HISTORIC SIGHT | The town hall has undergone as many face-lifts as an aging Hollywood star. Originally built in the 14th century, the same architect responsible for Binche Palace gave it a Renaissance-style makeover after the city's sacking by French troops in 1554—the coat of arms of Charles V and Marie of Hungary still adorn the building. By the 18th century it had acquired a new neoclassical facade; this remained until 1901 when its current Romanesque look took shape. Throughout this period, its towering, UNESCO-listed belfry has stood with aloof abandon and a carillon that partly dates back to the 16th century. ✉ *Grand Place, Binche.*

Binche Palace Ruins

RUINS | The Municipal Park is home to the remains of what was reputedly one of the finest castles in Belgium. A building first stood here in the 12th century, though by the time Marie of Hungary, a regent of the Spanish Netherlands, was gifted the land by Charles V, it had fallen into ruin. In 1545, she commissioned an architect, who took five years to rebuild it in the Renaissance style, at which point it was hailed as one of the great palaces of Europe. Yet he needn't have bothered. Barely a moment later, France's King Henri II had it burned to ground and its restoration ceased after Mary moved to Spain. Subsequent attempts were made to resurrect it, but by the early 1700s what was left was demolished. Only a few stray remnants survive in the park, which was built atop the remains and is still wrapped by the ramparts of the old city walls. ✉ *Municipal Park, Binche* *Free.*

Église Collégiale Saint-Ursmer (*Collegiate Church of St. Usmer*)

CHURCH | This church is a pleasing melange of eras and influences, with flashes of its original 12th-century Romanesque brickwork visible in the "three ages" tower, which was adapted all the way up to the 17th century. In 1408, the Lobbes chapter came to Binche with some holy relics and chalices that can be seen in the treasury. The church has been looking rather shabby in recent years, and at the time of writing it was undergoing a much-needed renovation. ✉ *Rue des Promenades, Binche* *Free.*

Musée international du Carnaval et du Masque (*Museum of International Carnivals and Masks*)

HISTORY MUSEUM | The city's carnival museum, set within a sprawling former Augustinian college opposite the church, offers colorful context for February's festivities and even captures their atmosphere a little. It goes into great detail on the carnival's history, costumes and preparation—planning begins six months in advance and, judging from the photo display, requires a few beers to kickstart—and it looks at similar carnivals from Wallonia and the rest of the world. The star attractions, however, are the private cinema, which shows nonstop films of the day's festivities, and the VR headsets that drop you right into the day's action. Downstairs, temporary exhibitions usually focus on masks from around the world. ✉ *Rue Saint-Moustier 10, Binche* ☎ *064/335–741* 🌐 *www.museebinche.be/en* *€8* ⏲ *Closed Mon.*

Restaurants

★ Brasserie La Binchoise

$$ | **BELGIAN** | If there is an obvious go-to restaurant in Binche for a good meal and a beer, it's this old-school brasserie-cum-brewpub at the foot of the city ramparts. Its beers have been brewed in Binche since the late 1800s using the same traditional methods. **Known for:** try some of the best brews in Wallonia; you can get a brewery tour that ends in dinner; interesting use of beer in their cooking. $ *Average main: €15* ✉ *Faubourg Saint-Paul 38, Binche* ☎ *064/433–335* ⏲ *Closed Mon. and Tues.*

Cul de Poule

$$$$ | **BELGIAN** | Colorful, eccentric, and utterly charming. This small bistro, about five minutes' walk from the center, is full of imagination. **Known for:** great cooking using local ingredients; the set menu is excellent value at €38; friendly, professional service. $ *Average main: €38* ✉ *Av. Wanderpepen 44, Binche*

☏ *064/650–973* 🌐 *www.culdepoule.be*
⏲ *Closed Mon.–Wed.*

Charleroi

22 km (13½ miles) from Binche.

No one would describe Charleroi as pretty. In fact, the opposite is normally the case. In 2008, it was voted the "ugliest city in the world" by readers of a Dutch newspaper. Yet it is changing for the better and there is plenty to see here, especially among its old industrial outskirts.

Charleroi was founded in 1666 by the Spanish. It takes its name from Charles II, whose reign here lasted barely a year before the French troops of King Louis XIV marched in. The new ruler ordered his engineer, Vauban, to redesign the city walls, and the fortress of Charleroi was, by all accounts, a fine sight. But by 1870, the old fortifications of the Upper Town had been torn down. Little remains but a few underground passageways, and its old center had rather gone to seed before recent works started. Indeed, the city has been getting a polish over the last couple of years and the Lower Town has been transformed with a huge new shopping area.

But the reason for Charleroi's reputation isn't the fall of its old fortifications. This was the industrial heartland of Belgium for well over a century, and while the mines finally closed in the 1980s, the city is still wracked by the ghosts of that era, not to mention the pointed, forested spoil heaps that give the surrounding landscape its almost alien quality. Migrant workers were shipped here by the thousand after World War II, and this was a poor area for a long time. Poverty rarely lends itself to art or beauty, yet there is plenty to be found in the stories of the workers of the Bois du Cazier mine (now a fine museum), the world-class photography gallery nearby, or the pretty Vallée de la Paix (Valley of Peace) to the south.

Charleroi is many people's first glimpse of Belgium, usually while landing. The majority of European low-cost airlines soar into its airport on the northern fringe of the city. Yet most people never set foot here, preferring to catch a bus to the capital instead. It's a shame. Sure, it's not pretty, but there is great art, fascinating history, and a UNESCO-listed belfry to admire. And who doesn't want to say they stayed in the "ugliest city in the world?"

GETTING HERE AND AROUND

AIR

The confusingly named Brussels South Charleroi Airport sits on the edge of the city. This is where the low-cost airlines destined for Brussels land, and the entry point to Belgium for many people. Most travelers get a shuttle bus straight to the capital (€14.50). Alternatively, a bus system connects it to Charleroi Sud railway station, which is how most enter the city. This offers rail connections to Brussels in one hour (€9.70) as well as routes to the rest of Western Wallonia.

CONTACTS Brussels South Charleroi Airport. ✉ *Rue des Frères Wright 8, Charleroi* ☏ *09/020–2490* 🌐 *www.brussels-charleroi-airport.com/en.*

TRAIN AND BUS

Outside Charleroi Sud railway station is the main stand for the local TEC bus services. It even has a ticket machine (a rarity), so you don't have to fiddle with a MoBIB card or buying tickets in advance. Tickets cost from €2.10 each, or €3 for a longer-distance Horizon ticket. This is where you can pick up buses to Bois du Cazier, Musée de la Photographie, Aulne Abbey (during summer), and Chimay.

CAR

If driving to or from Charleroi, the E420 connects it to the E19, which runs to Brussels and west to La Louvière, Mons, and on into France.

VISITOR INFORMATION

CONTACTS Charleroi Tourist Information. ✉ *Pl. Charles II 20, Charleroi* ☎ *071/861–414* 🌐 *www.charleroi-metropole.be.*

Sights

Note that major works are ongoing in Upper Town until 2023, with many of the streets being dug up and replaced north of place Charles II, which will also get a much-needed makeover. It means that walking the upper area can be a bit frustrating.

Abbaye d'Aulne (*Aulne Abbey*)

RUINS | The landscape gets much prettier as you slip southwest of the city toward an area known as the **Vallée de la Paix** (Valley of Peace). The main reason to go is for the ruins of Aulne Abbey, which lie just 10 km (6 miles) from Charleroi. Its history dates back to the 7th century. In In its heyday, it was run by Cistercian monks. By the mid-1800s the last monk had moved on and the site became a hospice before being left to ruin. But with the demise of the abbey, so too vanished its beer-making roots, until they were resurrected in 1950 by a local brewer who followed the old methods of the monks. These beers can be tried at the nearby **Brasserie de l'Abbaye d'Aulne**, which also does good food. ✉ *Rue Émile Vandervelde 291, Thuin* ☎ *071/554–928* 🌐 *abbayedaulne.be/en* 🎫 *€5 (cash only)* ⏲ *Closed Mon. and Tues. Seasonal closure Oct.–Mar.*

Airspace Indoor Skydiving

OTHER ATTRACTION | **FAMILY** | Where else would you find an indoor skydiving center but out near the airport? If you want to experience the joys of skydiving without the effort of ascending to 14,000 feet, this is a good option. Basic packages include two "flights" on the freefall simulator. ✉ *Brussels South Charleroi Airport, Rue Charles Lindbergh 26, Charleroi* ☎ *071/919–100* 🌐 *www.airspaceindoorskydive.be* 🎫 *€5* ⏲ *Closed Mon. and Tues.* Ⓜ *Bus: Airport Shuttle, 68.*

Art Nouveau Walk

HISTORIC DISTRICT | For a city famed for its ugliness, you can find some rather prett examples of turn-of-the-century architecture. These date back to when Charleroi first expanded, as the fortress walls wer torn down in 1870 and avenues were built atop the old ramparts. By the early 20th century, a thriving middle class arose from the smog and dirt of industry. They built pretty Art Nouveau mansions, mostly clustered northeast of the old town center, off avenue de Waterloo. You can pick up a map for free at the tourism office which offers a nice guide to the area. ✉ *Av. de Waterloo, Charler* 🎫 *Free.*

Beffroi et l'Hôtel de Ville (*Belfry and Tow Hall*)

HISTORIC SIGHT | Chareloi was never a great beauty, but all its money has gone into polishing the Lower Town, leaving its former heart looking a bit shabby. It's a shame because the buildings surrounding it are quite beautiful. The Art Deco **City Hall**, clad in blue and white stone, dates from 1936 and makes a fin impression. Adjacent is the UNESCO-lis ed, 70-meter-high (230-foot) **belfry**, whic offers fine views across to the river. ✉ *Rue du Beffroi, Charleroi* ☎ *071/861–414 guided tours* 🎫 *Free.*

★ **Bois du Cazier**

MINE | On the outskirts of Charleroi are the old mining villages that were the heartbeat of the region from the early 1800s until the 1960s. Around them, the pointy hills of the old spoil heaps, now overgrown with forest, rise into the distance, and in the town of Marcinelle, its old works have been preserved as a superb day out. The site has a few muse ums but most interesting are the outdo workings, where an audio guide leads you through a tragedy that saw hundrec

›se their lives. A memorial pays tribute › the 262 victims. ✉ *Rue du Cazier 80, ⁄larcinelle, Charleroi* ☎ *071/880–856* › *www.leboisducazier.be* 🎫 *€8* ⏲ *Closed ⁄lon.* Ⓜ *Bus: 1, 52.*

oucle Noire (GR412)

RAIL | This 26-km (16-mile) Grand andonnée walking route traces a path ırough the old mining villages east f the city. The "Black Loop," as it's nown, traverses canal towpaths, former ıilways, and the area's main slag, or poil, heaps—the excavated soil and ʼaste from the mines—which have een left to rewild since the last pits ʻosed here in the early 1980s. These, ı particular, afford fine views across ı area that, while not always pretty, is till dramatic. Maps with directions in nglish can be picked up at the tourism ıformation office. You can pick up the oute at Charleroi Sud station. ✉ *Gare e Charleroi Sud, Sq. des Martyrs 18, ʼharleroi* 🎫 *Free.*

PS22

RT GALLERY | One of the largest art ıuseums in Wallonia takes over a pair f buildings north of the center. The ld industrial hall exhibition space is articularly dramatic. Exhibitions change ›gularly and tend to focus on contem-orary Belgian artists. ✉ *Bd. Solvay 22, ʼharleroi* ☎ *071/272–971* 🌐 *www.bps22. e* 🎫 *€6* ⏲ *Closed Mon.*

glise Saint-Christophe de Charleroi (*Church of St. Christopher of Charleroi*)

HURCH | When the French took over harleroi in 1667, Louis XIV ordered ıe construction of a chapel, which ventually became the parish church. ıside, a star-covered dome is particu-rly elaborate, with guided group tours nly) able to climb up to its covered ʼalkways. But most eye-catching of all is ıe beautiful nave created in 1957, which ıkes up an entire wall of the church. his has been smothered in gold leaf and olor-glass mosaics depicting dramatic scenes including the sacrificial lamb, dragons, the Antichrist, and the Virgin Mary. There's nothing else quite like it in Belgium. ✉ *Pl. Charles II, Charleroi* ☎ *071/861–414 guided tours* 🎫 *Free.*

★ **Musée de la Photographie**

ART MUSEUM | The largest and most impressive photography museum in Belgium (and perhaps Europe) lies in the inauspicious fringes of Charleroi, in Mont-sur-Marchienne. It resides in a neo-Gothic former Carmelite convent, though a new wing was built to extend it farther. The permanent exhibition extends across some 800 photographs, tracing the history of photography in Belgium and beyond, while another section delves into optical illusions and tricks of the trade. Temporary exhibitions take up the rest of the space. Buses to Mont-sur-Marchienne go from outside Charleroi Sud. ✉ *Pl. des Essarts, Mont-sur-Marchi-enne, Charleroi* ☎ *071/435–810* 🌐 *www. museephoto.be* 🎫 *€7* ⏲ *Closed Mon.* Ⓜ *Bus: 70, 71.*

Musée des Beaux-Arts (*Museum of Fine Arts*)

ART MUSEUM | At this writing, the Muse-um of Fine Arts was in the process of moving from its old location in the Palais des Beaux-Arts and Town Hall to a tailor-made space in the renovat-ed, late-19th-century Defeld Barracks Stables, on boulevard Mayence. It is due to reopen by the end of 2022, though its collection remains the same. Expect to see 19th- and 20th-century art from the surrounding area, with a lot of works depicting the old mining communities of the Hainaut basin. Featured artists include François-Joseph Navez, Paul Delvaux, and a small collection of works by famous Belgian surrealist René Mag-ritte, who grew up on the outskirts of the city, in Chatelet. ✉ *Bd. Pierre Mayence, Charleroi* 🌐 *charleroi-museum.be.*

Restaurants

★ Chez Duche

$$ | **FRENCH** | The "secret" neighborhood restaurant that everyone knows about is no less likeable for it. It's a bit of a walk from the center of the Lower Town, but chef Christophe Duchêne (known as Duche) has put together a great-value menu of French and Belgian cooking. **Known for:** good-value cooking that never disappoints; everyone knows it but it still feels like a bit of a find; friendly staff who are always helpful. *Average main: €22 Av. de Waterloo 5, Charleroi 071/311–642 chezduche.be Closed Mon.*

La Bouche des Gouts

$$$ | **FRENCH** | Old brick walls, tiled floors, and wooden beams overhead set the mood for this discreet Upper Town French bistro with a menu heavy on the meat. Hefty steaks smothered in sauce, sauerkraut-laden choucroute royale, and Brabant guinea fowl dominate. **Known for:** hearty French cooking; some old-school classics; friendly service and owner. *Average main: €25 Rue Vauban 14, Charleroi 0496/294–294 www.labouchedesgouts.be Closed Mon.*

★ La Table de La Manufacture Urbaine

$$$$ | **BELGIAN** | Across the river from Charleroi Sud lies the finer-dining offshoot from La Manufacture Urbaine (LaMU), an excellent brewpub (try its CharlesRoy beers) on rue de Brabant that does solid brasserie food. The tone is markedly different here, so don't be expecting a cheery pub meal. **Known for:** great service and well-prepared dishes; the brewery produces fine local beers, which you can buy at the counter; a refined escape in a city of not too many high-end options. *Average main: €34 Pl. Emile Buisset 10, Charleroi 071/702–018 www.manufacture-urbaine.com/be/latable Closed Sun. and Mon.*

Meatball's Bar

$$ | **BELGIAN** | A wonderfully likeable little restaurant with a simple concept: meatballs. They come in veggie, chicken, beef, and Charleroi's *vitoulet* pork-and-veal style, all slathered in a choice of tomato, barbecue, coconut curry, and house sauces, with a host of frites on the side. **Known for:** a nice selection of local beers and cocktails; superfriendly staff; a small, manageable menu of tasty dishes. *Average main: €15 Rue de Marcinelle 8, Charleroi 071/368–437 www.meatballsbar.com Closed Sun. and Mon.*

Coffee and Quick Bites

Livre ou Verre

$ | **CAFÉ** | As much a secondhand book shop as it is a café, this literary escape in the Passage de la Bourse has a little bit of everything. Owner Blandine Grandchamps has laid on board games, travel reads, concerts, large comfy armchairs, and an abiding sense that you'd rather be nowhere else. **Known for:** the pastries and drinks are nice, too; eclectic interior with always something to look at; there's monthly exhibitions of graphic artists. *Average main: €5 Passage de la Bourse, Charleroi 078/259–027 livreouverre.be Closed Mon.*

Hotels

There aren't that many hotels in the city, at least not reputable ones. But, since 2017, a couple of new additions have been added, making it far easier, and comfier, to stay overnight here. But do avoid stays along the eastern riverfront, as this tends to be an unsavory area at night.

Auberge de Jeunesse

$ | **HOTEL** | **FAMILY** | Charleroi doesn't have a wide array of stays, and this simple but comfortable youth hostel only opened a few years ago, so it's still got that fresh sheen about it. **Pros:** rooms are quiet and there isn't much noise; it's supercheap for what you get; every room has USB sockets and lockers. **Cons:** like any hostel, if you get a noisy group then you can't do much about it; facilities are as basic as you'd expect; breakfasts are free but uninspiring. *$ Rooms from: €55 ✉ Rue du Bastion d'Egmont 3, Charleroi ☎ 071/158–128 🌐 www.lesaubergesdejeunesse.be ⇨ 43 rooms 🍽 Free Breakfast.*

Le Gites du Pays de Charleroi
$ | **B&B/INN** | This early-20th-century house has been transformed into three self-catering apartments, each tastefully converted with light wooden flooring and everything you need. **Pros:** apartments are roomy and it's pretty cheap; it's only a short walk to Charleroi Sud station; they're well equipped for short stays, with kitchens and cooking equipment. **Cons:** there's no lift to get to the upper floors; there is a deposit required; it's near one of the busier roads. *$ Rooms from: €80 ✉ Rue de Montigny 93, Charleroi ☎ 0485/374–791 🌐 www.gitesdupaysdecharleroi.com ⇨ 3 apartments 🍽 No Meals.*

★ **Novotel Charleroi Centre**
$$ | **HOTEL** | **FAMILY** | It might feel a bit businesslike, but the Novotel's location, gazing down over the bustling center of the new Lower Town square, is the very heart of the city. **Pros:** great fluffy pillows and a comfy mattress; good value and a generous checkout time (noon); big rooms come with USB plugs—a real rarity in Wallonia. **Cons:** parking costs €10 per night; still feels a bit like a business stay; no pool or wellness facilities. *$ Rooms from: €107 ✉ Pl. Verte 17, Charleroi ☎ 071/282–828 🌐 all.accor.com ⇨ 123 rooms 🍽 Free Breakfast.*

Relais de la Haute Sambre
$ | **HOTEL** | **FAMILY** | Around 16 km (10 miles) outside the city, in the small village of Lobbes, this countryside escape couldn't be more different to anything in Charleroi. **Pros:** you're surrounded by lush walking and cycling paths; a country escape far from the urban hustle; free car park for guests. **Cons:** you're pretty much a short drive or long walk from anywhere; there are only 15 rooms, so it fills up fast; breakfast is an extra €9 per person. *$ Rooms from: €84 ✉ Rue Fontaine Pépin 12, Lobbes ☎ 071/597–969 🌐 www.rhs.be ⇨ 15 rooms 🍽 No Meals.*

Nightlife

Chez ta Mère
BARS | A bistro-bar-cum-secondhand shop, which spills onto the pavement outside on warmer evenings. Great cocktails, an excellent choice of beers, and friendly staff make this an enduring local favorite. *✉ Pl. de la Digue 29, Charleroi ☎ 0489/288–597.*

Le Carolopolitan
COCKTAIL LOUNGES | A friendly and altogether unpretentious cocktail bar that eschews the usual preciousness for a fun night out. Drinks are uniformly well made and creative, with a few ambitious "beer cocktails" to round out the menu, which is both huge and surprisingly good value (around €8–€9 a cocktail). *✉ Rue de Marchienne 25, Charleroi ☎ 0485/637–679 🌐 carolopolitan.be.*

Shopping

In 2017, in a bid to revitalize the Lower Town, the city opened the **Rive Gauche** shopping mall on place Verte. It's huge, with around 90 shops, and even incorporates one of the more classical examples of architecture in the city, in the shape of the Passage de la Bourse. This is the city's central shopping area, filled with mostly well-known brands and a few indie shops. But, as happens when any mall opens, you can see the effect on the surrounding streets, especially those on the hill to Upper Town, where many are now boarded over.

Passage de la Bourse
SHOPPING CENTER | This pretty shopping gallery occupies what was originally a convent, which had been on this site since 1681. By the early 1800s, it was mooted as a future town hall but it never came to pass, and at the end of that century it took its current neoclassical shape, a glorious construction of steel and glass. In 2017, the building got a revamp as part of the large Rive Gauche shopping center, and is home to some of the more intriguing local shops, including a fabulously sprawling bookstore, called Grandchamps Etienne. ✉ *Passage de la Bourse, Charleroi.*

Chimay

48 km (30 miles) from Charleroi.

The boot-shape **Botte du Hainaut** region dribbles into the southeast corner of the province, wrapping the French border. It's rich in wooded valleys, villages, châteaux, and lakes, and couldn't be more different than the gray, industrial cities to its north. In truth, as you head south of Charleroi, you can't help but breathe a little deeper. This is great walking and hiking country, and the towns here are invariably small, untouristy, and blessed with little to do but wander their medieval churches or grab a beer on the square.

The biggest town here is Chimay, which isn't saying much. Time seems to have come to a standstill in its old streets, which is rather fitting for the birthplace of the famous 14th-century historian Jean Froissart, whose statue stands in the main square. Relics of its former glory are everywhere, including the old castle that still looms over the Eau Blanche and the narrow flights of stairs built to limit the march of oncoming armies. These days, its fortifications are more likely to be invaded by visitors, eager to see the current domain of the Princes of Chimay, or bag a round of minigolf within its grounds.

A few miles south of town, the Abbaye Notre-Dame de Scourmont is perhaps the biggest reason anyone has ever heard of Chimay. Here, its Trappist monks still preside over the making of the region's eponymous beer and cheeses, which adorn the menus of every bar and restaurant here.

GETTING HERE AND AROUND

The "Botte" is not well connected to the rest of the region. A car is the best way to get around here, following the N53 down from Charleroi, which is around 50 minutes' drive away. Otherwise, bus services are the only way to get to Chimay, which doesn't have its own rail connection. The No. 109a from Charleroi Sud railway station is the only direct service, with tickets available from the machine. The route takes 90 minutes and crosses three "zones," so you'll need to buy a pair of "Horizon" tickets (€3 each; one for the return journey as well). The No. 53 bus from Chimay then connects to Scourmont Abbey

VISITOR INFORMATION

CONTACTS Chimay Tourism Office. ✉ *Rue de Noailles 6, Chimay* ☎ *060/211–846* 🌐 *visitchimay.be.*

Sights

Abbaye Notre-Dame de la Paix (Chimay Abbey) (*Our Lady of Peace Abbey*)
RELIGIOUS BUILDING | Like their counterparts in Scourmont, the Trappistine nuns of Chimay live a life of solemn prayer. Visits can be arranged here, however, with guided tours within the grounds, cloister, and abbey church held every Thursday and Saturday at 2:30 pm. You'll need to book in advance, especially if you need an English guide, but it's a fascinating insight into a little-seen world. ✉ *Chau. de Trélon 1, Chimay* ☎ *0475/397–836, 060/211–164* 🎫 *Free (a donation is customary)* ✍ *Reservations are essential.*

Abbaye Notre-Dame de Scourmont (*Our Lady of Scourmont Abbey*)
RELIGIOUS BUILDING | Chimay is synonymous with the beer that shares its name. But the brewery that makes it is actually 9 km (5½ miles) south of the village. Here, the monks of the Scourmont Trappist monastery still supervise the production of some of the best cheese and beer in Belgium. They have been here since 1850, when the Princes of Chimay gifted them a space on the plateau. But it's no longer just a small operation. You can find Chimay beer in most of Europe, and even in China these days. Its Red (brown and fruity) and Blue (darker, more bitter) beers are ubiquitous. Yet at the same time, little has changed here. The monks still live a life of seclusion. The abbey is not open to the public, except for retreats, but you can visit the church and the gardens. You can also taste their wares at the nearby bar-restaurant **L'Espace Chimay** (at the Auberge de Poteaupré), less than half a mile away, where an exhibition (€6) explores the history and workings of the abbey brewery and ends with a tasting. ✉ *Rte. du Rond Point 294, Chimay* ☎ *060/210–511* 🌐 *chimay.com* 🎫 *Free* 🕒 *Espace Chimay: closed Mon.* Ⓜ *Bus: 59.*

★ **Château de Chimay** (*Chimay Castle*)
HISTORIC HOME | FAMILY | The traditional home of the Princes of Chimay is a 15th-century, Renaissance-style castle that looms over the lower town. The first defense to stand here was likely built towards the end of the 9th century when this was part of the Frankish Empire. But over the years it has been endlessly rebuilt, including when a fire tore through the building in 1935. Today, it is still occupied by Prince Philippe and his family, and guided tours sometimes bump into them. The real showpiece here is the theater, built in 1863 as a grand neoclassical space wreathed in palm-tree columns and gold- and white-stucco reliefs. It even plays host to monthly jazz and classical concerts (book online). You'll also find minigolf and escape rooms in the grounds. ✉ *Rue du Château 14, Chimay* ☎ *060/214–531* 🌐 *www.event.chateaudechimay.be* 🎫 *€10 tour; €5 minigolf; €40 escape room* ✍ *Booking ahead is advised if you want to have a tour.*

La Collégiale Saints-Pierre-et-Paul (*Collegiate Church of St. Peter and St. Paul*)
CHURCH | A church is likely to have stood here since the 10th century, though the oldest surviving part of the current building is the chancel, which dates from some 300 years later. Like many churches in the region, it is finished in a number of styles, as additions were made over the centuries. The nave is more in the late-Hainaut Gothic design, while the Germanic-looking bell tower was rebuilt in the 18th century with an onion dome and hosts a 26-bell carillon. Look out for the mausoleum of Charles de Croÿ, first prince of Chimay, which is adorned with an alabaster figure of the recumbent royal. ✉ *Rue Fromenteau, Chimay* ☎ *060/513–827* 🎫 *Free.*

Lake Virelles
NATURE PRESERVE | About 3 km (2 miles) north of the village lies the artificial lake of Virelles. It's developed into an important reserve, and each year welcomes the arrival of the only white storks in Wallonia. Its waters are wrapped in hides and nature trails, though early-morning canoe paddles with guides (€30) can yield the best sightings. These tours are run by **Aquascope**, who also offer guided walks and rent bicycles for exploring the area. ✉ *Lake Virelles, rue du Lac 42, Chimay* ☎ *060/211–363 Aquascope* 🌐 *www.aquascope.be* 🎫 *Free; tours start at €20.*

Restaurants

La Charlotte
$$ | **FRENCH** | This cozy hideaway on place Froissart has a great garden terrace to its rear, which offers a wonderfully discreet escape. The classics of French cooking fill chef Vincent Gilbert's small blackboard

menus, packed with foie gras, kidneys in beery sauces, and muscley-but-tender "spider" steaks. **Known for:** its pretty terrace when the weather is nice; well-prepared French cooking using the best of local ingredients; amenable service and staff. *Average main: €21 Pl. Froissart 8, Chimay 060/212–100 Closed Wed. and Thurs.*

★ La Malterie

$$$ | BELGIAN | Chef François Nicolas is not afraid of the more rustic cuts of meat. His daily market menus sway with the seasons and often feature the game, offal, and sweetbreads that are the building blocks of French country cooking, raised to star status. **Known for:** there is a shop on-site known for its local delicacies; cooking that embraces the best of the region's produce; a fine selection of wines. *Average main: €26 Pl. Léopold 7, Chimay 060/213–230 www.lamalteriechimay.be Closed Tues. and Wed.*

Le Grand Café

$$ | BELGIAN | This recently renovated café on the main square is pretty much the heart of the town. Every local comes here, usually in search of its famous burgers, overflowing with melted Chimay cheese. **Known for:** charming owner and service; its excellent burgers, which are also pretty huge; a nice selection of local delicacies and draft beers. *Average main: €15 Grand Place 18, Chimay 060/511–225 Closed Wed. and Thurs.*

Hotels

Le Petit Chapitre Chimay

$ | B&B/INN | FAMILY | This adorable B&B nestles in a quiet spot behind the church, in a house that dates to around 1850—at some point it was part of a convent for the Sisters of Our Lady, and many of the old fixtures have been kept, including the beautiful wooden banisters and oak flooring. **Pros:** the setting is superquiet with views of the church; friendly owners who can help you with anything; Brigitte makes fine porridge in the mornings. **Cons:** there is a house cat, so those with allergies beware; some rooms are a little worn, though still charming; it's a B&B, so no real facilities. *Rooms from: €85 Pl. du Chapitre 5, Chimay 060/211–042 lepetitchapitre.be 5 rooms Free Breakfast.*

Villa Adélaide Hôtel

$ | HOTEL | FAMILY | This is the only hotel in town, though, with only six rooms, it just scrapes into that category (less than six and you can still be considered a B&B). **Pros:** free parking and good restaurants nearby; charming old-world setting in a beautiful converted house; it's just an eight-minute walk to the village center. **Cons:** there's no staff permanently on-site, so it's more like a B&B; breakfast costs an extra €13; the grounds are nice but it is on a main road. *Rooms from: €95 Rue de Forges 10, Chimay 060/514–121 villa-adelaide.com 6 rooms No Meals.*

Nightlife

The Queen Mary

BARS | This British-style pub is the only game in town when it comes to finding a simple bar. Its friendly owner is an avid motorbike fan, as the decor suggests, and there's a good choice of beers (including Chimay, of course). Just about every local face in town will be in there at some point, and it even does karaoke nights if you're inclined to belt out a number. *Grand Rue 22, Chimay 060/212–381.*

Chapter 8

THE MEUSE AND THE ARDENNES

Updated by
Tim Skelton

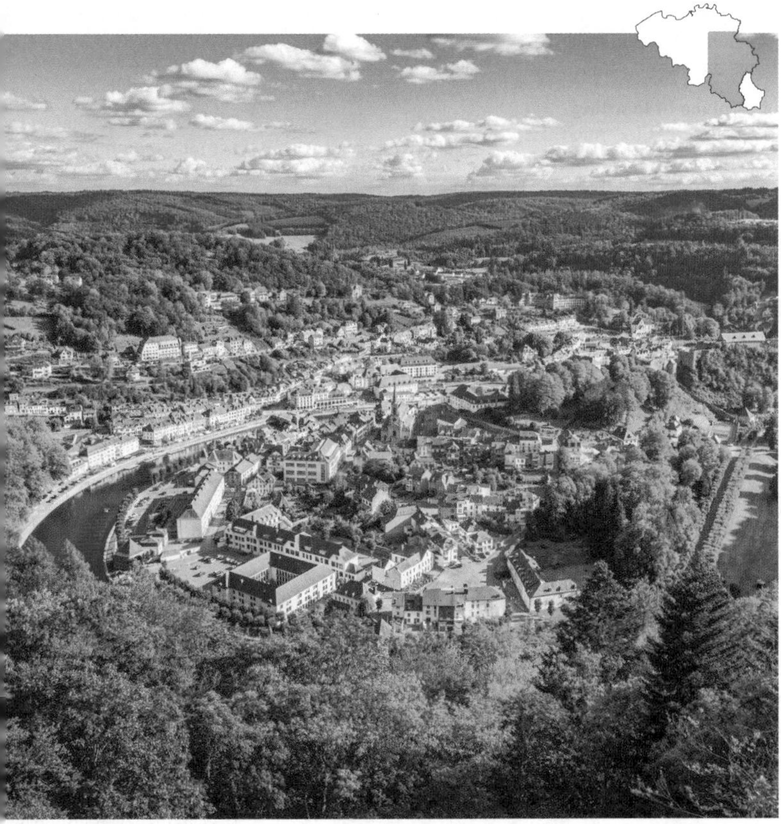

Sights	Restaurants	Hotels	Shopping	Nightlife
★★★★★	★★★★☆	★★★★☆	★★★★☆	★★★☆☆

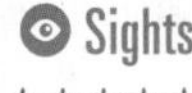

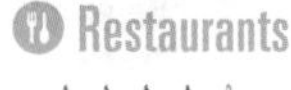

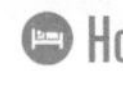

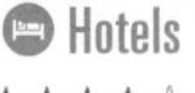

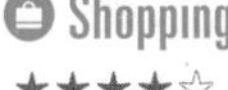

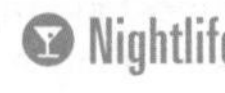

WELCOME TO THE MEUSE AND THE ARDENNES

TOP REASONS TO GO

★ **Back to nature.** Belgium's reputation for being flat and featureless is gloriously disproved in the Ardennes; even townscapes such as Namur and Liège are surrounded by thick greenery. Venture farther and you'll discover clandestine forest walkways and rugged trails.

★ **A place of learning.** Most towns offer much in the way of local history, from museums to battlegrounds, and provide insight into the region's sometimes turbulent history.

★ **Small town variety.** The Belgian countryside is densely populated and you'll be pleasantly surprised at the variety of small towns and villages. The area around Malmedy is especially rewarding.

★ **Keep active.** Set up camp in one of the local towns and spend a day or three hiking or biking in the hills and forests of the surrounding area.

★ **Step up a gear.** Held annually in late August, the Belgian Grand Prix at Francorchamps is one of the most internationally renowned race circuits.

This part of Belgium is marked by contrasts. The bigger cities of Namur and Liège mix a bit of cosmopolitan bustle with the historical appeal of ages-old European towns. In the countryside, major roads lead to tiny hamlets, and hills give way to deep river valleys. The region stretches over Wallonia's three eastern provinces, Namur, Liège, and, to the south, Belgian Luxembourg.

1 **Liège.** The region's largest city is a sprawling, cosmopolitan place, with a surprisingly compact medieval heart.

2 **Spa.** The original spa resort from which all others derive retains hints of its glory days.

3 **Huy.** This friendly riverside town is watched over by a rock-top fortress, reachable via cable car.

4 **Hautes Fagnes.** The wildest part of the Ardennes is a world of open fenland, great for hiking and wildlife spotting.

5 **Malmedy.** This small Ardennes town was deeply involved in the Battle of the Bulge, and is a handy base for visiting the Spa-Francorchamps Grand Prix.

6 **Stavelot.** Stavelot's old-world charm comes into its own during its annual spring Carnival.

7 **Namur.** The Wallonian regional capital is a small, manageable place, with a charming old town and a hill-top citadel.

8 **Dinant.** Spectacularly nestled in a narrow rocky gorge in the Meuse valley, this little town is also the birthplace of saxophone creator Adolphe Sax.

9 **Rochefort.** Rochefort is the jumping-off point for some of Belgium's greatest natural wonders, including the Grottes de Han cave system.

10 **Bastogne.** Ravaged by fighting during the winter of 1944–45, reminders of the Battle of the Bulge are all around this city.

11 **Durbuy.** With its sandstone buildings and cobbled streets, tiny Durbuy is the kind of picture-perfect village for which jigsaws were invented.

12 **La Roche-en-Ardenne.** This tourist center at the heart of the Ardennes is surrounded by countryside that's perfect for hiking and biking.

13 **Bouillon.** Close to the French border, on a narrow bend in the river, the Château de Bouillon is Belgium's largest medieval castle.

Aarschot
E314
Halen
Hasselt
Maasmechelen
Diepenbeek
Maastricht
Bilzen
NETHERLANDS
A44
E40
E313
E25
Sint-Truiden
Borgloon
Riemst
Tienen
Tongeren
Aachen
Visé
Kelmis
Waremme
E40
Ans
Hannut
Liege
Liège
Herve
E40
Eupen
Dison
Seraing
Fléron
Flémalle
Angleur
Verviers
E42
Amay
E42
N68
Meuse River
Huy
Hautes Fagnes
Spa
Namur
Andenne
E25
Malmedy
N66
Stavelot
E46
N97
N66
E42
Profondeville
Durbuy
N86
N68
Sankt Vith
N4
N89
Dinant
Marche-en-Famenne
N89
La Roche-en-Ardenne
Rochefort
Troisvierges
GERMANY
E25
N4
Clervaux
Bastogne
Wiltz
E421
N95
E411
Libramont-Chevigny
N4
E46
Diekirch
Ettelbruck
Neufchâteau
Bouillon
LUXEMBOURG
E411
E44
E421
Sedan
Arlon
0
10 mi
E25
Luxembourg
E44
0
10 km
LUXEMBOURG
Athus
Pétange
Remich
FRANCE
Differdange
Bettembourg
Schifflange
Esch-sur-Alzette
Mosel

To acquire the Wallonia habit, start by leaving the highway, stopping off in a town, or driving around the countryside—and arriving at your final destination a few hours, or a couple of days, late.

The Meuse comes rushing into Belgium from France, foaming through narrow ravines. In Dinant it is joined by the Lesse and flows, serene and beautiful, toward Namur, Wallonia's capital city. At Namur comes the confluence with the Sambre, tainted from its exposure to the steel manufacturing plants of Charleroi. Here, the river becomes broad and powerful, and gradually the pleasure craft are replaced by an endless procession of tugboats and barges. It passes through Liège, the region's largest city, then up through Holland, where, under a different name, the Maas, it reaches the sea.

MAJOR REGIONS

Liège, the area of Wallonia most influenced by the French, is a good jumping-off point for exploration of the Ardennes, a largely wooded region that stretches into the Grand Duchy of Luxembourg to the south.

Namur stands at the confluence of the Meuse and the Sambre rivers, and these strategic waterways neatly divide it into three distinct sections: the partly pedestrian historic center on the banks of the Sambre; the spur of the Citadelle; and the residential Jambes neighborhood, across the Meuse.

Surrounding the major cities, the **Ardennes** is a world of deep river valley, forested hills, and small towns and villages that have developed their own character and charm thanks to their isolation from each other until relatively recently.

Planning

Getting Here and Around

AIR

Liège Airport, 8 km (5 miles) west of that city, is almost exclusively used by cargo carriers, with only a few summer charter flights aimed at local vacationers. Almost all international air travelers will arrive via Brussels Airport, 89 km (55 miles) west of Liège and 64 km (40 miles) northwest of Namur.

BUS

From train stations in Liège, Verviers, Eupen, Trois-Ponts, and Namur there are bus services to other cities in the Ardennes, but buses depart infrequently, and connecting usually involves long waits. The national bus company TEC (Transports En Commun) serves the Ardennes region. In the major cities, TEC buses also provide local service.

In Liège, buses serve the downtown area, along the main boulevards, from the Coeur Historique to the train station. The main bus stations are on place St-Lambert, rue Léopold, place de la République Française, and at the Guillemins train station. Tickets can be urchased on the bus, in TEC kiosks, or stations. A single trip on a bus in the ner city costs €2.10 (two zones), and ight-trip cards sell for €9.20.

ONTACTS TEC. 🌐 *www.infotec.be.*

AR

he most convenient way of getting round the Meuse valley and the Liège egion is by car, especially since public ansportation services are scant. The 411 highway cuts through the region. lsewhere, you travel chiefly on pleasant, wo-lane roads through lovely scenery. etting lost on the back roads of Wallonia a true pleasure.

 the Meuse valley, Rochefort is close to e E411 highway, which links Brussels ith Luxembourg and runs south and ast. Namur is close to the intersection f the E411 with the E42, which links iège with Charleroi, Mons, and Paris, as ell as with Tournai, Lille, and Calais. To et to Tongeren from Brussels take the 40 to Exit 29 for the N69.

iège is almost halfway to Cologne om Brussels on the E40. The city is so linked with Paris by the E42, which erges with E19 from Brussels near lons; with Antwerp by the E313; and ith Maastricht and the Dutch highway ystem by E25, which continues south to in the E411 to Luxembourg.

 you want to rent a car, most car-rental gencies in Liège and Namur are open eekdays and Saturday morning. In iège, the majority of agencies have ffices either on boulevard de la Saveniée boulevard d'Avroy. In Namur there are gencies on avenue des Combattants nd avenue de Luxembourg.

RAIN

wo NMBS/SNCB trains an hour link russels with Namur (one hour from russels's Gare du Midi, 50 minutes from e Gare du Nord). They connect with a cal service to Dinant (25 minutes). Two ains run every hour from Brussels to Liège's Gare des Guillemins (one hour by express train from Brussels Nord, 1 hour and 10 minutes from Brussels Midi; local trains are 10 minutes slower). Thalys high-speed trains cut 15 minutes off travel time from Brussels Midi, but must be prebooked.

All express trains from Ostend to Cologne stop at Liège, as do international trains from Copenhagen and Hamburg to Paris. Direct trains run hourly to Tongeren. There are local train services from Liège via Verviers to Eupen, and to Trois-Ponts (near Stavelot).

The high-speed TGV train runs from points in France and Germany to Liège.

CONTACTS NMBS/SNCB. ☎ *02/528–2828* 🌐 *www.belgiantrain.be/en.*

Hotels

Hotel rooms in this region tend to be low-price, even if there's an outstanding restaurant downstairs. They often fill up on weekends and during high season, June–August. In smaller towns and villages, if you prefer to eat somewhere other than in the hotel you've booked, clear it with the management: you're often expected (and sometimes obliged) to eat in their restaurant. Many hotels offer *demi-pension* (half-board) arrangements, as well as *les weekends gastronomiques*, which include a few elaborate meals for a set rate. Farmhouse accommodations and B&Bs are widely available and especially popular with families.

Restaurants

This part of Belgium is full of atmospheric gray-stone inns serving dishes redolent of forest and farm. Game meats, like venison and wild boar, figure prominently on restaurant menus, especially in fall. Autumn is also a good time for attractive hotel-restaurant packages, and many city dwellers venture into the country for *les weekends gastronomiques*, which may include two or three lavish meals with two nights' lodging. Chefs dabble with various ingredients and cuisines, but most tend toward the French tradition and rely on fresh regional produce. Restaurants generally begin serving lunch at 12:30 and dinner at 7:30 or 8, and casual attire is the norm.

HOTEL AND RESTAURANT PRICES

Hotel prices in the reviews are the lowest cost of a standard double room in high season. Restaurant prices in the reviews are the average cost of a main course at dinner, or if dinner is not served, at lunch.

What It Costs in Euros

	$	$$	$$$	$$$$
RESTAURANTS				
	under €12	€12-€22	€23-€30	over €30
HOTELS				
	under €100	€100-€150	€151-€220	over €220

Safety

Liège is a safe city during the day, and—for the most part—night. Nevertheless, be alert after dark in the central Le Carré district, a nightlife hub full of bars and dimly lit narrow alleys, as this is an area where thieves and pickpockets congregate. Be especially cautious around bank ATMs.

Women are advised not to walk alone late at night in central Liège, as harassment and assaults do occur, albeit rarely. Verbal abuse is the most common issue you may encounter. If traveling alone after 10 pm, taking a cab is advised.

In comparison to Liège, the other towns and cities in the region are very safe. You are highly unlikely to encounter any problems.

Visitor Information

CONTACTS Wallonie Belgique Tourisme. ✉ *Av. Comte de Smet de Nayer 14, Namur* 🌐 *walloniebelgiquetourisme.be.*

Liège

97 km (58 miles) east of Brussels.

The bustling city of Liège—Luik to the Flemish and Dutch, Lüttich to the Germans—sits deep in the Meuse valley at the confluence of the Meuse and Ourthe rivers. After Belgian independence in 1830, Liège was a leader in a countrywide upsurge of industrial activity, and that has marked its character ever since. The first European locomotive was built in Liège, and the Bessemer steel production method was developed here; it is to the burning furnaces that Liège owes its nickname, *la cité ardente* (the Fiery City). Liège's outskirts are still lined with industrial facilities—some operational, some transformed into innovative museums. Although the views may not be beautiful, you shouldn't let this deter you. A soot-covered old building may house a historic treasure, while an inconspicuous cobblestone alley could be home to busy cafés and architectural gems. And, every Sunday morning, as has happened for centuries, the quai is transformed into **La Batte**, one of Europe's biggest weekly street markets.

GETTING HERE AND AROUND

Trains to Liège run from Brussels at least twice every hour, taking between an hour and an hour and a half, depending on the number of interim stops. Hourly regional trains run directly between Antwerp Central and Liège, taking 2¼ hours to complete the journey. However, you can shave 30 minutes off this trip by taking the faster intercity trains in the direction of Brussels, and connecting in Brussels North.

.n extensive network of buses operated y TEC (*www.letec.be*) runs from the nain railway station, the ultramodern Calatrava-designed Liège-Guillemins, o all parts of the city. Although not ommonly used in the other towns, taxis re plentiful in Liège. They can be picked p at cab stands in the principal squares r summoned by phone. Fares are €2.40 lus €1.65 per km in the city and €3.30 er km when you leave the city.

'ISITOR INFORMATION

ONTACTS Maison du Tourisme du Pays e Liège. ✉ *Quai de la Goffe 13, Liège* ☎ *04/221–9221* 🌐 *www.visitezliege.be.*

Sights

athédrale St-Paul

HURCH | Liége's imposing Gothic cathe-ral houses handsome statues by Jean Delcour, including one of St. Paul. (Other raceful works by this 18th-century culptor dot the old city.) The cathedral's nost prized possessions, however, re to be found in the **Treasury** (enter ia rue Bonne Fortune 6), especially ne *Reliquaire de Charles le Téméraire* Reliquary of Charles the Bold), with gold nd enamel figures of St. George and the old duke himself on his knees; curious-, their faces are identical. This reliquary vas presented to Liège by Charles the old in 1471 in penance for having had ne city razed three years earlier. ✉ *Pl. le la Cathédrale, Liège* ☎ *04/232–6132* 🌐 *www.tresordeliege.be* 🎫 *Cathedral: ree. Treasury €6* ⏲ *Treasury closed Mon.*

omplexe Touristique de Blegny

IINE | The highlight of a visit to this omplex east of Liège is a trip down ne former Blegny Coal Mine, which roduced 1,000 tons of coal a day at its eak. Liège's wealth was based on coal, vhich was mined from the Middle Ages ntil 1980. An audiovisual presentation ustrates this history, and former miners ead tours of the surface and under-round facilities. Make an appointment to take the tour in English. A coal mine tour takes two hours, though you can spend at least half a day here with the kids because there's also a museum, playground, restaurant, and café. ✉ *Rue Lambert Marlet 23, Blegny* ✥ *15 km (9 miles) northeast of Liège* ☎ *04/387–4333* 🌐 *www.blegnymine.be* 🎫 *€13.*

Cour St-Antoine

PLAZA/SQUARE | In a clever example of urban renewal, what was formerly a slum is now a beautifully restored residential square with a small-village feel. The facade of the red house at the north end of the square resembles a church and is connected by a small channel to a pyramidlike structure replicating Tikal, a Mayan ruin in Guatemala. ✉ *Between rue des Brasseurs and rue Hors-Château, Liège* 🎫 *Free.*

★ Eglise St-Barthélemy

CHURCH | This church contains Liège's greatest treasure and one of the Seven Religious Wonders of Belgium: the Baptismal Font of Renier de Huy, which dates from between 1107 and 1118. The brass masterpiece of Art Mosan, weighing half a ton, is decorated in high relief with figures of the five biblical baptismal scenes. They're depicted with an extraordinary suppleness, and the font rests on 10 oxen, which are also varied and interesting. ✉ *Pl. St-Barthélemy, Liège* 🌐 *www.visitezliege.be* 🎫 *€2.*

Eglise St-Denis

CHURCH | This is one of the oldest churches in Liège; its outer walls once formed part of the city's defenses. It has a handsome reredos portraying the suffering of Christ. ✉ *Pl. St-Denis, rue de la Cathédrale, Liège* ☎ *04/223–5756* 🌐 *www.visitezliege.be* 🎫 *Free.*

Eglise St-Jacques

CHURCH | The grimy exterior of this mini-cathedral a few blocks south-west of Liège's center, near the place St-Jacques, belies a wonderful interior. Marble, stained glass, and polished wood

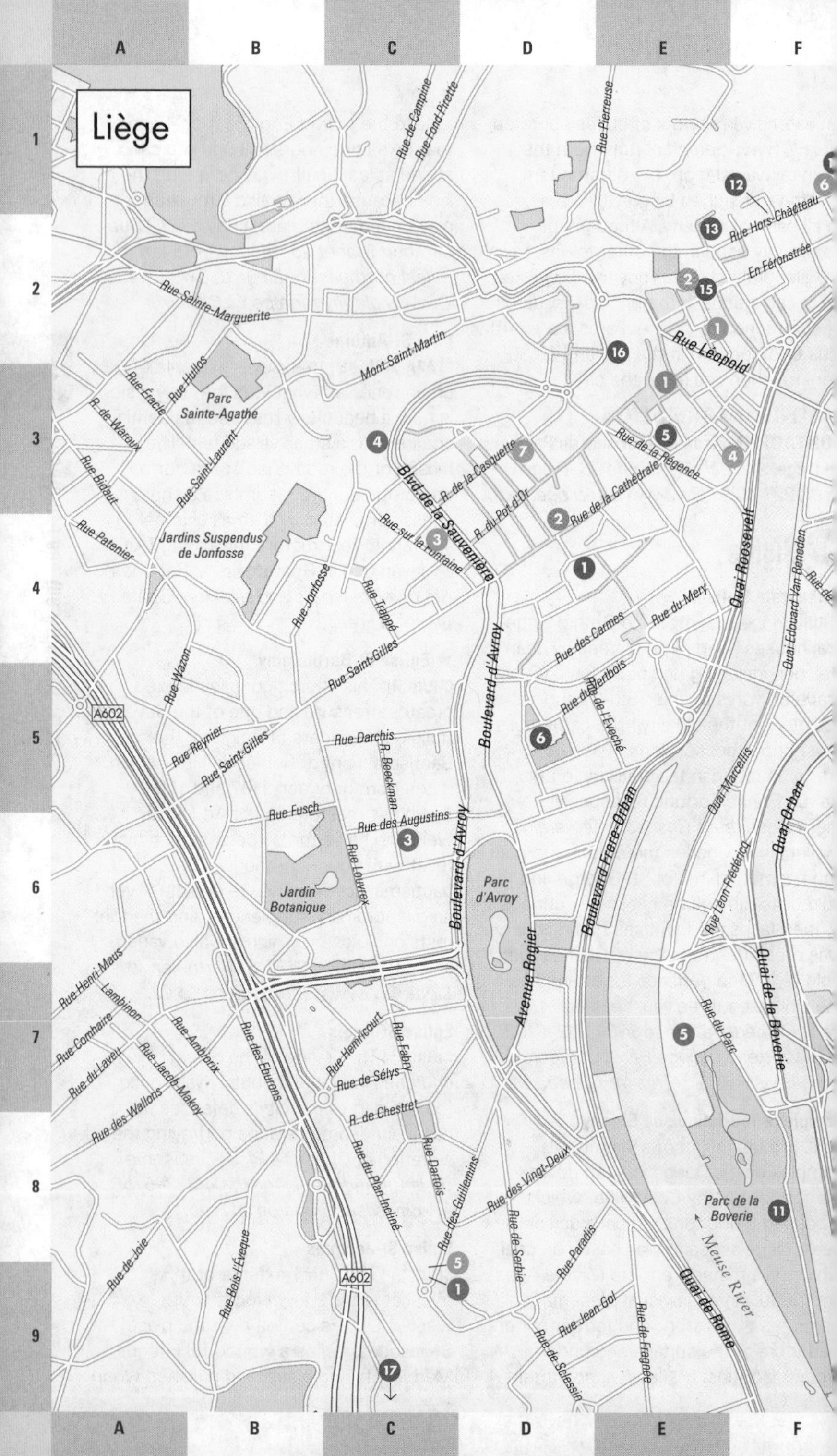

A
B
C
D
E
F
1
2
3
4
5
6
7
8
9
Liège
Rue de Campine
Rue Fond Pirette
Rue Pierreuse
Rue Hors-Château
En Féronstrée
Rue Sainte-Marguerite
Mont Saint-Martin
Rue Léopold
Rue Eracle
Rue Hullos
Parc Sainte-Agathe
R. de Waroux
Rue Saint-Laurent
Rue Bidaut
Rue de la Régence
R. de la Casquette
Blvd de la Sauvenière
R. du Pot d'Or
Rue de la Cathédrale
Rue Patenier
Jardins Suspendus de Jonfosse
Rue sur la Fontaine
Quai Roosevelt
Quai Edouard Van Beneden
Rue Jonfosse
Rue Trappé
Boulevard d'Avroy
Rue du Mery
Rue des Carmes
Rue Saint-Gilles
Rue du Vertbois
Rue de l'Evêché
Rue Wazon
A602
Rue Darchis
R. Beeckman
Rue Reynier
Rue Saint-Gilles
Quai Marcellis
Quai Orban
Rue Fusch
Rue des Augustins
Boulevard Frère-Orban
Rue Louvrex
Rue Léon Frédéricq
Parc d'Avroy
Jardin Botanique
Avenue Rogier
Quai de la Boverie
Rue Henri Maus
Lambinon
Rue Combaire
Rue Ambiorix
Rue des Eburons
Rue Hemricourt
Rue Fabry
Rue du Parc
Rue du Laveu
Rue Jacob-Makoy
Rue de Sélys
Rue des Wallons
R. de Chestret
Rue Dartois
Rue du Plan Incliné
Rue des Guillemins
Rue des Vingt-Deux
Rue de Serbie
Parc de la Boverie
Meuse River
Rue Paradis
Rue de Joie
Rue Bois l'Evêque
Quai de Rome
Rue Jean Gol
Rue de Fragnée
Rue de Sclessin
1
2
3
4
5
6
7
11
12
13
15
16
17

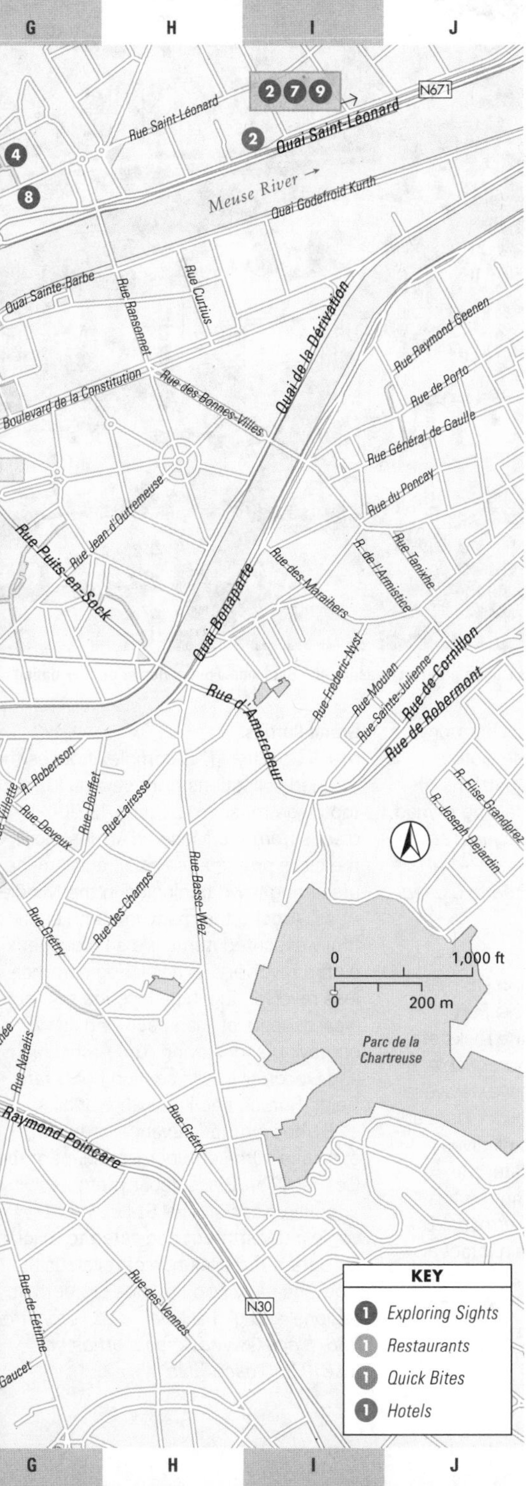

Sights

1 Cathédrale St-Paul **D4**
2 Complexe Touristique de Blegny................................ **I1**
3 Cour St-Antoine...................... **F1**
4 Eglise St-Barthélemy.............. **G1**
5 Eglise St-Denis....................... **E3**
6 Eglise St-Jacques **D5**
7 Fort Eben-Emael **I1**
8 Grand Curtius **G1**
9 Henri-Chapelle Cemetery.......... **I1**
10 Impasses **F1**
11 La Boverie........................... **F8**
12 Montagne de Bueren **F1**
13 Musée de la Vie Wallonne......... **E2**
14 Musée Tchantchès................. **G4**
15 Place du Marché **E2**
16 Place St-Lambert................... **E2**
17 Préhistomuseum..................... **C9**

Restaurants

1 Amon Nanesse **E2**
2 As Ouhès **E2**
3 Bruit Qui Court **C4**
4 Café Lequet........................... **F3**
5 Concordia.............................. **C9**
6 Le Thème **F1**
7 L'Enoteca **D3**

Quick Bites

1 Ma Ferme en Ville **E3**
2 Pollux.................................. **D4**

Hotels

1 Hôtel de l'Univers................... **C9**
2 Hotel Mercure Liège City Centre.................... **I1**
3 Le Cygne D'Argent.................. **C6**
4 Pentahotel Liège..................... **C3**
5 Van der Valk Hotel Liège Congres........................ **E7**

The Eglise St-Barthélemy contains Liege's greatest treasure–the Baptismal Font of Renier de Huy, dating back to the 12th century.

achieve an outstanding visual harmony. The glory of the church is the Gothic vault, decorated in intricate patterns of vivid blue and gold and containing myriad sculpted figures. ✉ *Pl. St-Jacques, south of Nouvelle Ville, Liège* ☎ *04/222–1441* 🌐 *www.visitezliege.be* 🎫 *Free* 🕐 *Closed weekends.*

Fort Eben-Emael

MILITARY SIGHT | Around 24 km (15 miles) north of Liège, the impressive Fort Eben-Emael was built into the rocks after World War I. Supposedly impregnable, it was almost invisible to the eye. However, on May 10, 1940, German gliders landed on the plateau and threw explosives down the air shafts. A day later the 700 Belgian soldiers guarding the fort surrendered to a mere 55 Germans. The fort and its equipment remain intact and can be visited. There's also a museum containing photographs and weaponry. ✉ *Rue du Fort 40, Bassenge* ✣ *24 km (15 miles) north of Liège* ☎ *04/286–2861* 🌐 *www.fort-eben-emael.be* 🎫 *€10* 🕐 *Closed Mon.–Thurs.*

Grand Curtius

OTHER MUSEUM | This complex houses the merged collections from several former top Liège museums. Some 13,000 pieces from the Musée d'Armes recall the city's prominence as an arms-manufacturing town beginning in the Middle Ages. Among the many rare and beautifully executed items are a Lefaucheux pinfire revolver and a Velodog hammerless revolver. Exhibits describe the technical aspects of manufacturing as well as engraving and inlaying. The Archaeology and Decorative Arts section holds rare Belgo-Roman and Frankish works, such as Bishop Notger's Evangelistery, an exquisite 10th-century manuscript of the Gospels. The Glass department exhibits Venetian glass and Val St-Lambert crystal, while a department dedicated to religious art details the evolution of religious art from the early Middle Ages on, both at regional and global level. ✉ *Féronstrée 136, Liège* 🌐 *www.grandcurtius.be* 🎫 *€10* 🕐 *Closed Tues.*

Henri-Chapelle Cemetery
CEMETERY | Twenty-eight kilometers (18 miles) east of Liège is Henri-Chapelle, the largest American military cemetery in Belgium. It is the resting place of 7,989 American soldiers who fell in the Battle of the Bulge. The crosses and stelae are arranged in arcs converging on the central monument, which also contains a small museum and provides a striking view over the plateau of Herve. Ceremonies are held here on American Memorial Day in late May. ✉ *Rte. du Mémorial Américain 159, Hombourg ✣ 28 km (18 miles) east of Liège ☎ 087/687–173 🌐 www.abmc.gov 🎫 Free.*

Impasses
HISTORIC DISTRICT | These narrow mews were where servants had their tiny houses in the days of the prince-bishops. Prominent citizens lived along neighboring En Hors-Château. As late as the 1970s, it was believed that the best approach to urban redevelopment was to tear down these houses. Luckily, common sense prevailed. The Impasse de l'Ange and Impasse de la Couronne are two examples of the six such well-restored impasses in town. Duck under the *årvô*, the bridge over the alleyway, to discover lush gardens, finely restored Tudor homes, and a number of *potales* (wall chapels), devoted mostly to the Virgin or to St. Roch, who was venerated as the protector against disease epidemics. ✉ *Off En Hors- Château, Liège 🎫 Free.*

La Boverie
ART MUSEUM | Almost all the big names of modern and contemporary are represented in this collection of 700-odd French and Belgian paintings dating from the 1850s on. Some of the stars are Emile Claus' *Le Vieux Jardinier* (The Old Gardener) and Paul Gauguin's *Le Sorcier de Hiva-Oa* (The Sorcerer of Hiva-Oa). The museum stands in the attractive Parc de la Boverie, about 3 km (2 miles) southeast of the town center, favored by the Liègeois for a stroll far away from the traffic. You can walk partway along the riverfront to get there. ✉ *Parc de la Boverie 3, Liège 🌐 www.laboverie.com 🎫 €8 ⏲ Closed Mon.*

Montagne de Bueren
HISTORIC SIGHT | This stairway of 374 steps ascends from Hors-Château toward Liège's Citadelle. It honors the memory of Vincent van Bueren, a leader of the resistance against Charles the Bold. In 1468 he climbed the hill with 600 men, intending to ambush the duke and kill him. Betrayed by their Liègeois accents, they lost their lives and the city was pillaged and burned. Charles the Bold, a superstitious man, made sure the churches remained untouched while the city was in flames so he wouldn't be sent to hell. At the base of the stairs is a former nunnery, now a compound for antiques dealers. ✉ *Hors-Château, Liège 🎫 Free.*

Musée de la Vie Wallonne
HISTORY MUSEUM | In an old Franciscan convent, carefully reconstructed interiors give a vivid and varied idea of life in old Wallonia, from coal mines to farm kitchens to the workshops of many different crafts. The museum even includes a court of law, complete with a guillotine. Life-size statues in carnival costumes greet you in the entrance hall. And one gallery is populated by the irreverent marionette Tchantchès and his band, who represent the Liège spirit. ✉ *Cour des Mineurs 1, Liège 🌐 www.provincedeliege.be/en/viewallonne 🎫 €5 ⏲ Closed Mon.*

Musée Tchantchès
OTHER MUSEUM | **FAMILY** | Discover the mystique and mishaps of Liège's most beloved marionette at this museum in the Outremeuse district. Here you can learn the answers to such burning questions as: How did Tchantchès meet his girlfriend Nanesse? Why did he have to eat an iron shoe to fight the measles at the age of three? Was he really designed by an Italian puppeteer? See Tchantchès

in action October through April at the Sunday-morning puppet shows at 10:30, or Wednesday afternoon at 2:30. Note that the museum itself is only open on Tuesday and Thursday afternoon from 2 to 4 pm. There's no explanatory information available in English. ✉ *Rue Surlet 56, Liège* 🌐 *www.tchantches.be* 🎫 *Puppet shows €4* 🕒 *Closed Mon., Wed., and Fri.*

Place du Marché

PLAZA/SQUARE | This bustling square is as old as Liège itself. For centuries it was where the city's commercial and political life was concentrated. The 18th-century Hôtel de Ville is here, with its two entrances: one for the wealthy and one for the common people. A number of the old buildings surrounding it were among the 23,000 destroyed by German bombs. In the center stands the Perron, a large fountain sculpted by Jean Delcour, topped with an acorn—the symbol of Liège's liberty. ✉ *Pl. du Marché, Liège* 🎫 *Free.*

Place St-Lambert

PLAZA/SQUARE | Now a vibrant, bustling focal point, this square went through a long period of neglect after the Cathedral of St. Lambert, the largest cathedral in Europe, was destroyed during the French Revolution. At its center proudly stands a sculpture honoring both the murdered 8th-century saint and the future of Liège. ✉ *Pl. St-Lambert, Liège* ☎ *04/250–9370 Archéoforum* 🌐 *www.archeoforumdeliege.be* 🎫 *Free* 🕒 *Archéoforum: closed Sun. and Mon.*

Préhistomuseum

OTHER MUSEUM | **FAMILY** | The world of early humans is on display at this speculative re-creation of prehistoric dwellings. You can get a sense of your ancestors' technical aptitude while trying your own hand at making pots and polishing stones. The museum is next to the cave of Ramioul, where the lighting system brings out the beauty of the rock formations. Guides explain in English the cave's animal life and its use by humans. Tours are led April–October on weekends at 2. ✉ *Rue de la Grotte 128, Flémalle* ✥ *15 km (9 miles) south of Liège* ☎ *04/275–4975* 🌐 *www.prehisto.museum* 🎫 *€15* 🕒 *Closed Mon.*

Restaurants

Amon Nanesse

$$ | **BELGIAN** | Playful like the puppet Tchantchès, the bar La Maison du Pèkèt concocts cocktails using *pèkèt*—Liège's local liquor—in every way imaginable. When you've had your fill of pèkèts with passion fruit, head next door to the attached restaurant, Amon Nanesse. **Known for:** local Liégeoise and Ardenne specialties; cozy historic ambience; flambéed pèkèt digestifs. 💲 *Average main: €18* ✉ *Rue du Stalon 1–3, Liège* ☎ *04/250–6783* 🌐 *www.maisondupeket.be/amonnanesse* 🕒 *Closed Tues. and Wed.*

As Ouhès

$$ | **BELGIAN** | This stylish spot and long-standing local favorite on the place du Marché serves up large portions of Walloon specialties, such as rabbit stewed in beer, and succulent *boulets* (traditional Liège pork-and-beef meatballs flavored with a fruit syrup) served with mounds of frites. Its original name, As Ohès ("To the Bones" in local dialect), was a nod to the fact that the building sits on the site of an old cemetery—the addition of a "u" transformed it into the more customer-friendly "To the Birds." **Known for:** good mussels and frites; hearty portion sizes; local Liége meatballs. 💲 *Average main: €15* ✉ *Pl. du Marché 21, Liège* ☎ *04/223–3225.*

Bruit Qui Court

$$ | **CONTEMPORARY** | This regal restaurant, discreetly tucked in a handsome courtyard, has a chic dining room with high ceilings, a mezzanine above, and striking arty photographs adorning the walls. The menu offers French-inspired contemporary cuisine, including modern takes on nagret de canard and foie gras, but the main specialties are meal-size salads—y the warm chicken salad or the surf n' turf salad with chicken and scampi. **nown for:** early dinners before a night at the nearby opera; all-day kitchen serving om midmorning until late; informal ining in chic surrounds. *Average main: '16 Bd. de la Sauvenière 142, Liège 04/232–1818 bruitquicourt.be.*

afé Lequet

| **BELGIAN** | Known as a favorite hangout f Georges Simenon and his family, this vood-paneled neighborhood standby erves unbeatable boulets (meatballs) mothered in Liège's special date-and-pple syrup and classic *moules* piled high vith the inevitable frites. Also known as Chez Stockis, the timeworn place—with :s peeling paint and battered wooden urniture—is often filled with regulars, 'oung and old. **Known for:** sharing stories vith local residents; the best boulets in own; a timeless interior, unchanged in a entury. *Average main: €10 Quai Sur Meuse 17, Liège 04/222–2134 www.acebook.com/debruyn.be No credit :ards Closed Tues. No dinner Sun.*

Concordia

;$ | **BELGIAN** | A block from the train station, this dinerlike Liège institution has been here and run by the same family since 1943. Its long and varied menu has various fish, pastas, and salads, but does end to favor lovers of beef and veal. **Known for:** meat-heavy menu, vegetarians nay struggle; mussels served in a dozen different ways; food served all day. *Average main: €21 Rue des Guillemins 114, Liège Near Liège-Guillemins train station 04/252–2915 le-concordia.be.*

Le Thème

$$$ | **FRENCH** | You'll always be surprised and seldom disappointed at this whimsical, colorful den, which changes its nterior styling to a new theme every two years—past examples have ranged from farmyard barn to Alice in Wonderland. The fixed-price menu (with or without wine) changes on a monthly basis; duck usually appears in hunting season. **Known for:** excellent food-wine pairings; constant reinvention of both interior decor and menu; refined high-end modern cooking. *Average main: €25 Impasse de la Couronne 9, Liège 04/222–0202 letheme.com Closed Sun. and Mon. No lunch.*

L'Enoteca

$$$ | **ITALIAN** | Just steps from the opera house, this stylish joint is *the*place in Liège to come for Italian fine dining. Choose from the two-, three- or four-course fixed-price menu (five-course tasting menu only on Friday evening and Saturday). **Known for:** inspired wine-food pairings; modern Mediterranean-inspired cuisine; weekly changing menus. *Average main: €25 Rue de la Casquette 5, Liège 04/222–2464 enoteca.be Closed Sun. and Mon. No lunch Sat.*

Coffee and Quick Bites

Ma Ferme en Ville

$ | **EUROPEAN** | This basic canteen adjoins a central deli with a simple philosophy: seasonal fare sourced from around 100 small-scale suppliers, all located within a 50-km (31-mile) radius. Dishes prepared using ingredients from the store range from an all-day breakfast of fruit muesli and yogurt, via omelets, to burgers. **Known for:** supporting local producers; monthly brunch buffet; strictly seasonal produce. *Average main: €9 Rue Souverain Pont 34, Liège 04/222–1660 www.mafermeenville.be Closed Sun. and Mon. No dinner.*

Pollux

$ | **BAKERY** | This popular bakery is the place to pick up a hot *gaufre* (Belgian waffle), topped with powdered sugar—or, for a little extra, stuffed with chunks of chocolate that will melt as you eat. For those with less sweet teeth, they also offer an extensive range of filled sandwiches and rolls for a light lunch.

For Meat Lovers

Eating in the Ardennes is one of the most straightforward pleasures Belgium has to offer. The region's charcuterie is some of the best in Europe. Ardennes sausage, neat and plump, is made with a blend of veal and pork and is smoked over smoldering oak; its flavor is somewhere between simple American summer sausage and the milder Italian salamis. The real charcuterie star is *jambon d'Ardennes*, ham that is salt-cured and delicately smoked so that its meat—as succulent as its Parma and Westphalian competitors—slices up thin, moist, and tender, more like a superior roast beef than ham. Restaurants offer generous platters of it, garnished with crisp little gherkins and pickled onions or, if you're lucky, a savory onion marmalade. Native river trout makes a slightly lighter meal, though once poached in a pool of butter and heaped with toasted almonds, it may be as rich as red-meat alternatives. One pleasant low-fat alternative, though not always available, is *truite au bleu* (blue trout). Plunged freshly killed into a boiling vinegar stock, the trout turns steely blue and retains its delicate flavor.

Known for: terrace views of the cathedral and square; locals' favorite; waffles fresh-baked to order. *Average main: €5 ✉ Pl. de la Cathédrale 2, Liège ☎ 04/223–6781 ⏲ Closed Sun. No dinner.*

Hotels

Hotel de l'Univers

$ | **HOTEL** | In business in one form or other, this landmark property on a bright, busy street in the town center has smart contemporary furnishings and caters primarily to the modern-day needs of business travelers. **Pros:** on-site brasserie; close to train station; good-value breakfast. **Cons:** can be noisy; proximity to station means surroundings can feel intimidating at night; 20-minute walk from city center. *Rooms from: €89 ✉ Rue des Guillemins 116, Liège ✣ Near Liège-Guillemins train station ☎ 04/254–5555 ⊕ www.hotelunivers.be ⇨ 50 rooms 🍽 No Meals.*

Hotel Mercure Liège City Centre

$ | **HOTEL** | This property on the banks of the Meuse is housed in a 17th-century former convent, and the brick-vaulted ceilings in some public areas add a charming touch of antiquity to what is otherwise a businesslike chain hotel, with well-appointed if characterless rooms. **Pros:** rear garden is a quiet retreat; good breakfast; on-site parking available (for a fee). **Cons:** a 15-minute walk from the main sights; being part of a chain means rooms lack individual character; road at the front is often busy and noisy. *Rooms from: €85 ✉ Rue St-Léonard 182, Liège ☎ 04/228–8111 ⊕ all.accor.com ⇨ 149 rooms 🍽 No Meals.*

★ Le Cygne D'Argent

$ | **HOTEL** | A quiet air of calm hangs over this welcoming, family-run boutique hotel. **Pros:** some rooms have kitchenettes; good, quiet location; clean, individually styled rooms. **Cons:** a 15-minute walk from the main sights; some bathrooms on the small side; no free parking in the vicinity. *Rooms from: €92 ✉ Rue Beeckman 49, Liège ☎ 04/223–7001 ⊕ le-cygne-dargent.webnode.be ⇨ 23 rooms 🍽 No Meals.*

Pentahotel Liège

$$ | **HOTEL** | In the center of town, this modern, full-service hotel is near to all of

iège's ultra-modern train station was designed by famed architect Santiago Calatrava in 2009.

.iège's major sights. **Pros:** good on-site estaurant and bar; close to city center; pacious rooms. **Cons:** some bathrooms ieed modernizing; free Wi-Fi on the slow ide; proximity to several bars means ront rooms can be noisy. $ *Rooms from: €110 ✉ Bd. de la Sauvenière 100, Liège ☎ 04/221–7711 🌐 www.pentahotels.com ⇨ 105 rooms 🍽 No Meals.*

/an der Valk Hotel Liège Congres
$$ | HOTEL | Next to the Palais des Congrès, this modern, well-maintained otel is a favorite choice for European Congress delegates and businesspeople. **Pros:** quiet at night; clean rooms; inviting ool and sauna. **Cons:** slightly dated feel; some carpets could be cleaner; 20-minute walk from city center. $ *Rooms from: €120 ✉ Esplanade de l'Europe 2, Liège ☎ 04/244–1200 🌐 www.congreshotel-iege.be ⇨ 219 rooms 🍽 No Meals.*

Nightlife

The Liègeois have an amazing ability to stay up until all hours, and nightlife is booming on both sides of the Meuse. Le Carré quarter, southwest of the opera house, is favored by students and those who go to a show first and out afterward. In the narrow, cobble-laned Roture quarter in Outremeuse there's hardly a building without a café, club, ethnic restaurant, or jazz hangout.

BARS & CLUBS

Aux Olivettes
BARS | This specialty-beer bar is also a *café chantant*, which means locals will often have the tendency to get up and sing in front of everyone else. *✉ Rue Pied-du-Pont des Arches 6, Liège ☎ 0485/529–995 🌐 www.auxolivettes.com.*

BeerLovers
PUBS | This cozy, central bar beside the city hall serves around 250 international craft and local Wallonian ales, while the range in the adjacent shop stretches to

over 750. ✉ *Rue de la Violette 9, Liège* ☎ *04/221–3977* 🌐 *beer-lovers.be.*

Brasserie {C}
BREWPUBS | Located at the foot of the Montagne de Bueren stairway, the city's only brewpub serves its own Curtius beers and a full food menu, best enjoyed on the summer garden terrace. ✉ *Impasse des Ursulines, Liège* ☎ *04/266–0692* 🌐 *brasseriec.com.*

Café Tchantchès
BARS | This true Liège institution offers evenings of puppet entertainment along with its beer and cocktails. ✉ *Rue Grande-Beche 35, Liège* ☎ *0475/583–691* 🌐 *www.taverne-tchantches.be.*

Performing Arts

Musée Tchantchès
PUPPET SHOWS | **FAMILY** | From October through April, on Wednesday at 2:30 and Sunday morning at 10:30, you can see traditional, informal puppet shows starring the irrepressible Tchantchès. ✉ *Rue Surlet 56, Liège* ☎ *04/342–7575* 🌐 *www.tchantches.be* 🎫 *€4.*

Opéra Royal de Wallonie-Liège
OPERA | Liège's excellent opera company is widely considered to be the country's best and most innovative. ✉ *Pl. de l'Opéra, Liège* ☎ *04/221–4722* 🌐 *www.operaliege.be.*

Orchestre Philharmonique Royal de Liège
CONCERTS | The city's symphony orchestra has recorded prizewinning CDs and tours internationally with a largely contemporary repertoire. The ticket office and reservation line are open weekdays 1–6. ✉ *Bd. Piercot 25–27, Liège* ☎ *04/220–0000* 🌐 *www.oprl.be.*

Shopping

La Batte Market
MARKET | By far the most exciting shopping experience Liège has to offer is at La Batte, one of Europe's biggest weekly street markets, and Belgium's oldest—stallholders have been gathering here for over 400 years. Traffic is diverted away from the quai de la Batte every Sunday from 8–2:30, when vendors and shoppers pour onto the quai for a day of serious browsing. ✉ *Quai de la Batte, Liège.*

Spa

38 km (23 miles) southeast of Liège, 13 km (83 miles) southeast of Brussels.

The Romans came here to take the waters, and they were followed over the centuries by crowned heads, such as Marguerite de Valois, Christina of Sweden, and Peter the Great. Less welcome was Kaiser Wilhelm II, who established his general headquarters in Spa before fleeing to Holland in November 1918 to abdicate control of Germany. By then the town was already past its prime. During the 18th and 19th centuries, it had been the watering place of international high society, and many gracious houses remain from that period. The pleasures of "taking the cure" in beautiful surroundings were heightened in those days by high-stakes gambling, playing *pharaon* or *biribi* for rubles, ducats, piastres, or francs. The casino dates from 1763, but is only one of many architectural gems that line the streets, many of which have been lovingly restored, restoring this small city to its former glory.

GETTING HERE AND AROUND

To reach Spa from Liège, take the hourly train in the direction of Verviers and change in Pepinster. The total journey time is about 45 minutes.

VISITOR INFORMATION

CONTACTS Maison Du Tourisme De Spa - Hautes Fagnes. ✉ *Rue du Marché 1a, Spa* ☎ *087/795–353* 🌐 *www.spa-hautesfagnes.be.*

Sights

Casino de Spa

CASINO | First opened in 1763, Spa's magnificent casino is the oldest in the world. Heads of state from across Europe once flocked here to gamble away their wealth in between bouts of "taking the cure," and it was a meeting place of choice for international high society for more than a century. Today, the casino's glamorous gaming rooms support a number of cultural activities in addition to gambling, and there is also an on-site restaurant. ✉ *Rue Royale 4, Spa* ☎ *087/772–052* 🌐 *casinodespa.be* 🎫 *Free* ⏲ *Restaurant: closed Wed.* ☞ *Minimum age 21.*

L'Eaudyssée de Spa

OTHER ATTRACTION | Located at the **Spa Monopole** bottling plant, which produces the famous Spa brand mineral water, this interactive exhibit details the water's long underground journey of purification. There are also viewing points where you can watch the clattering bottling lines in full flow, and a small museum with exhibits of old bottles and crates. ✉ *Rue Auguste Laporte 34, Spa* ☎ *087/794–111* 🌐 *www.spa.be* 🎫 *€5* ⏲ *Closed weekends.*

Musée de Cheval et Musée de la Ville D'eaux

OTHER MUSEUM | The Musée de Cheval et Musée de la Ville D'eaux are two institutions in one. The first hosts a permanent exhibit on Spa's waters and fountains, and includes a collection of *jolites*, painted figurines fashioned from local wood. The Horse Museum contains an extensive display of equestrian paraphernalia. ✉ *Av. Reine Astrid 77b, Spa* ☎ *087/774–486* 🌐 *www.spavillaroyale.be* 🎫 *€6* ⏲ *Closed mid-Nov.–Feb. Musée de Cheval: closed weekdays.*

Musée de la Lessive

OTHER MUSEUM | The charming Laundry Museum is dedicated to the art and science of keeping clothes clean—not a task to be taken lightly, particularly when royalty and nobility come to town to sweat away their maladies. ✉ *Rue Hanster 10, Spa* ☎ *087/771–418* 🌐 *museedelalessivespa.be* 🎫 *€4* ⏲ *Mar.–June, Sept. and Oct.: closed weekdays. Nov.–Feb.: closed Mon.–Sat.*

Pouhon Pierre le Grand

HOT SPRING | The best-known of Spa's water sources—locally known as *pouhons*—is the Pouhon Pierre Le Grand, which can be visited by tourists as well as *curistes* (people taking the cure). In past times, pregnant women came to drink the iron-rich water. Nowadays, the source draws those with poor circulation, anemia, and arthritis. The building housing the spring dates from 1880, although is was given a major face-lift in 2012. ✉ *Rue du Marché 1A, Spa* ☎ *087/795–353* 🌐 *www.spatourisme.be* 🎫 *€1.*

Restaurants

Brasserie du Grand Maur

$$$ | BELGIAN | In a quiet suburb a 10-minute walk south from the center, this graceful mansion houses a lovely restaurant with a loyal clientele, all in a fabulous setting of polished wood and antiques. The food is classic French-Belgian, with scallops, lobster, and fillet steak all regulars on the monthly changing menu, alongside locally hunted venison in season. **Known for:** Ardenne game in fall hunting season; rear garden terrace; old-world charming atmosphere. [$] *Average main: €25* ✉ *Rue de Barisart 209, Spa* ☎ *087/773–616* 🌐 *www.legrandmaur.com* ⏲ *Closed Sun. and Mon. No lunch.*

Café de l'Europe

$$ | BELGIAN | Serving up hearty portions of Belgian classics and crowd-pleasing favorites in informal surrounds, this modern, airy, diner-style restaurant is popular with local customers. Ardennes ham and *filet américain* (steak tartare) are menu standards, while *biche* (doe) appears during the fall hunting season. **Known for:** simple but hearty local and Belgian classics; informal dining; game in season. $ *Average main: €16* ✉ *Pl. Royale 4, Spa* ☎ *087/221–127* 🌐 *www.cafedeleurope.be* ⏲ *Closed Mon.*

L'Art de Vivre

$$$$ | BELGIAN | Jean-François Douffet's fresh approach in the kitchen contrasts pleasantly with the old-fashioned gentility of many of his local competitors. Sautéed goose liver accompanied by a potato pancake, pike perch with deep-fried basil leaves, roast pigeon with a balsamic vinegar sauce, and ice cream with figs are typical of his creations. **Known for:** top-quality fresh produce; refined high-end dining; peaceful rear summer terrace with water feature. $ *Average main: €35* ✉ *Av. Reine Astrid 53, Spa* ☎ *087/770–444* 🌐 *www.artdevivre.be* ⏲ *Closed Mon. and Tues. No lunch Wed.–Sat.*

Coffee and Quick Bites

La Gâterie

$ | BAKERY | Settle into a booth at this bakery and tearoom for waffles, crepes, homemade ice cream, or a fresh-baked tart. **Known for:** prompt service; excellent waffles; good value. $ *Average main: €4* ✉ *Pl. du Monument 18, Spa* ☎ *087/774–880* ⏲ *Closed Mon. and Fri.*

Hôtel Cardinal

$$ | HOTEL | Offering a real taste of old Spa, this grand urban resort hotel first opened its doors in 1924. **Pros:** bedrooms are modern and comfortable; proximity to thermal center and casino; common areas have old-world charm. **Cons:** need to check in before 8:30 pm; no staff on reception at night; some rooms lack character. $ *Rooms from: €105* ✉ *Pl. Royale 21–23, Spa* ☎ *087/771–064* 🌐 *www.hotel-cardinal.be* *29 rooms* *No Meals.*

Radisson Blu Balmoral Hotel

$$$$ | HOTEL | Up the hill from downtown Spa, this handsome 1905 landmark was where King Leopold II routinely hosted opulent banquets. **Pros:** free parking; on-site wellness center with pool; quiet countryside setting. **Cons:** modern renovations have eroded some old-world charm; can feel somewhat impersonal; a 30-minute walk or short shuttle ride from the center. $ *Rooms from: €232* ✉ *Av. Leopold II 40, Spa* ☎ *087/792–141* 🌐 *www.radissonhotels.com* *89 rooms* *No Meals.*

Radisson Blu Palace Hotel

$$$ | HOTEL | Unlike its sister the Balmoral, the Palace was built in 2003 specifically to accommodate visitors to the Thermes de Spa, to which the hotel has a direct link via a funicular. **Pros:** on-site wellness facilities; convenient access to Thermes de Spa; centrally located, close to shops and restaurants. **Cons:** can feel a little impersonal; funicular is sometimes out of operation; parking expensive and difficult to access. $ *Rooms from: €200* ✉ *Pl. Royale 39, Spa* ☎ *087/792–154* 🌐 *www.radissonhotels.com* *126 rooms* *No Meals.*

★ **Villa des Fleurs**

$ | HOTEL | A sense of elegance abounds in this splendid 1880 Beaux Arts mansion, once the private home of the director of the Spa Casino. **Pros:** free parking; ideally centrally situated; small size means personalized service. **Cons:** no hot breakfast; no on-site bar or restaurant; only some rooms have garden views. $ *Rooms from: €92* ✉ *Rue Albin Body 31, Spa* ☎ *087/795–050* 🌐 *villadesfleurs.be* *12 rooms* *No Meals.*

Circuit de Spa-Francorchamps

AUTO RACING | Motor-sports fans know **Francorchamps** (near Spa) as the site of one of the world's top racing circuits, where Formula 1 drivers zig and zag with astounding speed and precision. The annual Grand Prix race takes place in late August, but there are occasional tours of the circuit and other events throughout the year. ✉ *Rte. du Circuit 55, between Spa and Stavelot* ☎ *087/293–700* 🌐 *www.spa-francorchamps.be* 🎫 *Guided tours: €12. Other prices vary according to event.*

Les Thermes de Spa

SPAS | Les Thermes de Spa is a testament to Spa's recent rejuvenation. The ultramodern thermal center has a full menu of relaxation treatments, plus fitness facilities, hot tubs, two swimming pools, a sauna, and even a funicular link to the city and the Radisson Blu Palace Hotel. A slew of restaurants, shops, and terrace lounges leave nothing to be desired. ✉ *Colline d'Annette et Lubin, Spa* ☎ *087/772–560* 🌐 *www.thermesdespa.com* 🎫 *From €22 (3 hrs)* ☞ *No children under 15; reservations essential.*

Huy

55 km (35 miles) west from Spa, 33 km (20 miles) southwest of Liège, 83 km (50 miles) southeast of Brussels.

Huy (pronounced we), where the Hoyoux joins the Meuse, is a workers' town, and the main employer is the local power industry. It does, however, date all the way back to 1066 and contains some sights of historical interest.

GETTING HERE AND AROUND

Two trains an hour run from Liège, taking 20 minutes. Three trains every hour make the trip between Namur and Huy. The fastest ones also cover the distance in 20 minutes.

VISITOR INFORMATION

CONTACTS Maison du Tourisme Terres-de-Meuse. ✉ *Quai de Namur 1, Huy* ☎ *085/212–915* 🌐 *www.terres-de-meuse.be.*

Sights

Citadelle de Huy

CASTLE/PALACE | For a great view of the town and the surrounding countryside, take the short but steep walk uphill from the Meuse to the cliff-top Citadelle—also known as Fort de Huy—part of the defenses built by the Dutch in the early 19th century. During World War II, the Germans used it as a prison for resistance members and hostages. It now contains an exhibition about the the living conditions of the more than 7,000 prisoners held captive here, and of the general Belgian population during the four years of Nazi occupation. ✉ *Chau. Napoléon, Huy* ☎ *085/215–334* 🌐 *www.huy.be* 🎫 *€4* ⏲ *Closed Nov.–Easter weekend.*

Eglise Collégiale de Notre-Dame

CHURCH | The first stone of the Gothic Eglise Collégiale de Notre-Dame (Collegiate Church of Our Lady) was laid in 1311, although the site was first consecrated in 1066. One of Belgium's finest medieval churches, it has a rose window, the so-called Rondia, 30 feet in diameter. Its treasury contains several magnificent reliquaries, two of them attributed to Godefroid de Huy, who followed in the footsteps of Renier, also a native of Huy and a master of the Mosan style. ✉ *Parvis Théoduin de Bavière, Huy* ☎ *0496/027–065 Treasury* 🌐 *www.tresordehuy.com* 🎫 *Church: free. Treasury: €3* ⏲ *Closed Mon. Treasury: closed mid-Sept.–Mar.; Apr.–mid-Sept. closed weekdays, except July and Aug.*

Grand-Place

PLAZA/SQUARE | Huy's main market square centers on a remarkable fountain, the **Bassinia**, a bronze cistern decorated with saints that dates from 1406. In the 18th century, the Austrians topped it with their double eagle. In the northeast corner of the square, the impressive facade of the **Hôtel de Ville** (town hall) dates from 1766. ✉ *Grand-Place, Huy* 🎫 *Free.*

The massive Citadel in Huy makes for an ideal spot for sweeping views of the town and surrounding countryside.

Musée Communal

HISTORY MUSEUM | From the main square it's a short walk through winding alleys to the Huy's 17th-century Franciscan monastery, a grand building constructed around a central colonnaded cloister. Today it houses the Musée Communal, a mine of local folklore and history from prehistoric to modern times, with an exceptional Art Mosan oak carving of Christ. ✉ *Rue Vankeerberghen 20, Huy* ☎ *085/232–435* 🌐 *www.huy.be* 🎫 *Free* 🕒 *Closed Mon.*

Hautes Fagnes

72 km (45 miles) east from Huy, 20 km (13 miles) northeast of Spa, 40 km (25 miles) east of Liège.

Twenty-one kilometers (13 miles) northeast of Spa sits Eupen, the gateway town for the Hautes Fagnes (High Fens). Here, in the heart of the German-speaking part of Belgium, is a marvelous 45-square-km (17-square-mile) ecological expanse of peat bogs, heath, and marshland—the western part of the German-Belgian Hautes Fagnes-Eifel natural park. This is Belgium's largest area of protected wilderness, and it also happens to be the country's wettest, coldest, and most bizarre terrain. Foggy mists, sometimes dense, make navigating a path through the park's wilderness difficult. The saturated bogs hide quagmires just waiting to pull down unsuspecting feet—thus, explorations are confined to wooden boardwalks. Don't let the somewhat forbidding circumstances deter you; the Hautes Fagnes is one of Belgium's natural wonders.

GETTING HERE AND AROUND

To fully appreciate the wilds of the Hautes Fagnes you'll need your own transport. Driving from Liège via Eupen, it takes approximately 30 minutes to reach the northern edge of the park. The park can also be reached from Spa in about 15 minutes by heading northeast.

Sights

a Maison du Parc-Botrange

IATURE PRESERVE | Parts of the surrounding area can only be visited with a guide, articularly the peat bogs and the feeding reas of the *capercaillies* (large and ery rare woodland grouse—the park's ymbol). At the park's nature and visitor enter, you can book an individual guide, nd you can rent bikes and e-bikes. Inside he center itself, the **Fania** exhibition is an mmersive introduction to the local flora, auna, and landscapes. Part of the visit akes you through a "sensory tunnel" in vhich you can listen to birdsong, peek nto a fox's den, and walk barefoot over eaves and tree bark. ✉ *Rte. de Botrange 131, Waimes, Hautes Fagnes* ☎ *080/440–300* 🌐 *botrange.be* 🎫 *Fania exhibition: €6* 🕑 *Restaurant: closed Mon.*

einhardstein

ASTLE/PALACE | Reinhardstein, the loftiest nd possibly the best-preserved medieval ortress in the country, dating originally rom 1354, is reached by a mile-long hike hrough the Hautes Fagnes. It sits on a spur of rock overlooking the river Warche nd has been in the hands of such illusrious families as the Metternichs, ancesors of Prince Metternich, the architect of he Congress of Vienna in 1815. The Hall of Knights and the Chapel are particular gems. Guided tours, lasting a little over n hour, depart hourly. They are mostly given in French, Dutch, or German, ut guides are usually happy to offer some English explanation upon request. ✉ *Chemin du Cheneux 50, Ovifat, Hautes Fagnes* ☎ *080/446–868* 🌐 *www.reinhardstein.net* 🎫 *€10 (guided tour only)* 🕑 *Closed except during Belgian national and school holidays (see website).*

Malmedy

16 km (10 miles) south from Haute Fagnes, 57 km (34 miles) southeast of Liège.

Malmedy and its neighbor, Stavelot, formed a separate, peaceful principality, ruled by abbots, for 11 centuries before the French Revolution. The Congress of Vienna, redrawing the borders of Europe, handed it to Germany, and it was not reunited with Belgium until 1925. In a scene straight out of *Catch 22,* the center of Malmedy was destroyed by American bombers in 1944—after the town had already been liberated. Still, there's enough left of the old town for an interesting walk. And either of the twin towns is an ideal place to stay while exploring the Hautes Fagnes.

GETTING HERE AND AROUND

The nearest railway station to Malmedy is Trois-Ponts. There are around a dozen daily departures from Liège-Guillemins (50 minutes to one hour). Bus No. 745 connects with train arrivals and takes a further 25 minutes to reach Malmedy, passing through Stavelot en route. A slightly faster route is to take the hourly train from Liège-Guillemins to the town of Verviers, then switch to the connecting express bus No. E21. The total journey time is around 1 hour, 5 minutes, but this bus does not pass through Stavelot.

VISITOR INFORMATION

CONTACTS Malmedy Tourist Office. ✉ *Pl. du Châtelet 9, Malmedy* ☎ *080/799–668* 🌐 *www.malmedy-tourisme.be.*

Sights

Baugnez 44 Historical Museum

MILITARY SIGHT | Around 5 km (3 miles) southeast from central Malmedy (accessible via bus No. 745), this extensive museum is dedicated to the Battle of the Bulge winter offensive of 1944–45,

A hike through the Hautes Fagnes wilderness brings you to Reinhardstein, a beautifully preserved medieval castle.

taking you through the major events that occurred and depicting the daily life of soldiers with audiovisual effects. Particular attention is given to the "Malmedy Massacre" of December 17, 1944, during which soldiers from the Waffen-SS executed 84 American POWs at a crossroads just 100 meters north of the museum—if you want to pay your respects in person there is a **memorial** on that spot. Museum visits include English-language audio guides. ✉ *Rte. de Luxembourg 10, Malmedy* ☎ *080/440–482* 🌐 *www.baugnez44.be* 🎫 *€9* ⏲ *Sept.–June: closed Mon. and Tues. July and Aug.: closed Mon.*

Malmundarium

OTHER MUSEUM | Located in a former Benedictine abbey, the Malmundarium is part cultural center, part museum. The latter often focuses on changing temporary exhibitions, but also includes permanent displays on local history, the paper-making and leather industries, and the *Cwarmê*, Malmedy's colorful local Lent carnival. Adjoining the Malmandarium, the former abbey church became **Cathédrale Saint Pierre** in the 1920s. ✉ *Pl. du Châtelet, 9, Malmedy* ☎ *080/799–668* 🌐 *www.malmundarium.be* 🎫 *€6* ⏲ *Closed Mon.*

Restaurants

A La Truite Argentée

$$ | **BELGIAN** | Food really can't get any fresher than at this friendly family-run inn on the southeast edge of town—order one of the several trout options on offer and fish will be taken directly from the restaurant's own ponds, located steps away in the rear garden. It's a 15-minute walk from the center of Malmedy, but worth it for great food in lovely surrounds. **Known for:** great seafood; peaceful semirural location; hearty Belgian classic dishes. [$] *Average main: €22* ✉ *Bellevue 3, Malmedy* ☎ *080/786–173* 🌐 *www.alatruiteargentee.be* ⏲ *Closed Wed. and Thurs.*

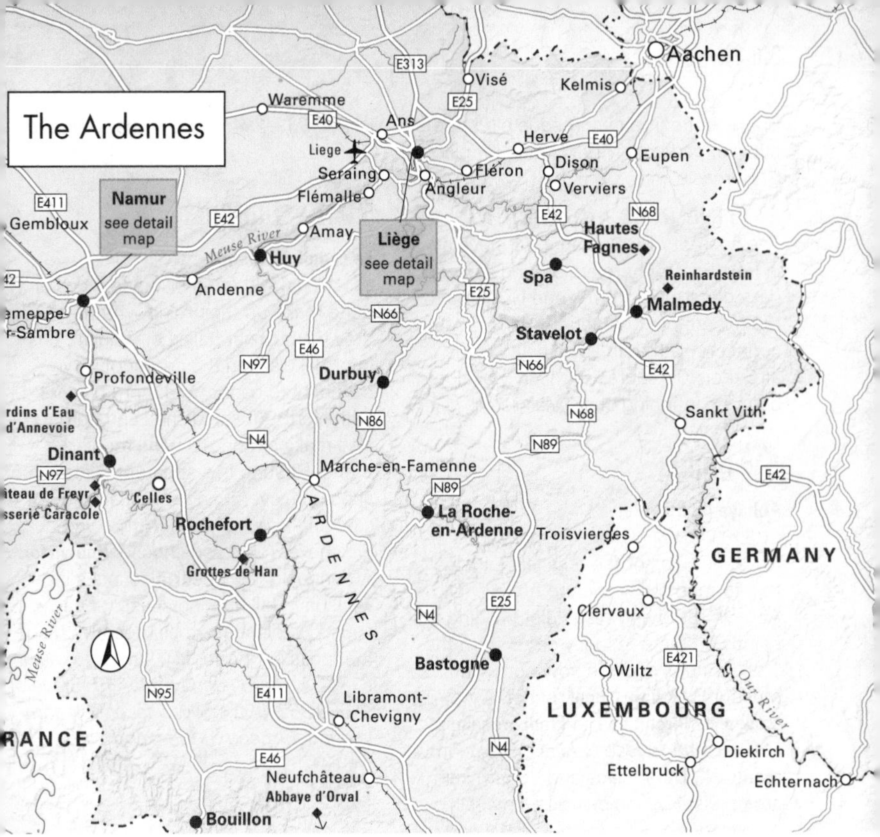

Hotels

My Hotel
$$ | **HOTEL** | The name may be a little ɔdd to English speakers, but all else s very much in order at this gleaming modern hotel just a few minutes' walk 'rom downtown Malmedy. **Pros:** on-site wellness facilities and pool; some rooms have balcony terraces; quiet semirural ocation. **Cons:** modern building lacks charm; wellness treatments are not cheap; restaurant menu could have more regional emphasis. *Rooms from: €150* *Rue Devant les Grands Moulins 25, Malmedy* *080/780–000* *myhotel.be* *84 rooms* *No Meals.*

Stavelot

15 km (9 miles) southwest from Malmedy, 59 km (37 miles) southeast from Liège.

Although Stavelot is practically a twin town of Malmedy, its traditions differ. Here Carnival is celebrated on the fourth Sunday in Lent and is animated by about 2,000 *Blancs-Moussis* (White Monks), dressed in white with long capes and long bright-red noses, who swoop and rush through the streets. The Blancs-Moussis commemorate the monks of Stavelot, who in 1499 were forbidden to participate in Carnival but got around it by celebrating Laetare Sunday (three weeks before Easter). Stavelot was badly damaged in the Battle of the

Bulge, but some picturesque old streets survive, particularly rue Haute, off place St-Remacle.

GETTING HERE AND AROUND

The nearest railway station to Stavelot is Trois-Ponts. There are around a dozen daily departures from Liège Guillemins (50 minutes to one hour). Bus No. 745 connects with train arrivals and takes a further 10 minutes to reach Stavelot, before continuing on to Malmedy.

Sights

Abbaye de Stavelot

OTHER MUSEUM | Only a Romanesque tower remains of the original buildings that formed the *Ancienne Abbaye* (Old Abbey). The grand rose-color building that stands on the site today dates from the 18th century, and it is now home to three museums and the local tourist office. The **Musée du Circuit de Spa-Francorchamps** is dedicated to race cars and the nearby racetrack. Monoplace and Brigatti cars are on display, and one of several films on racing draws you into a virtual ride on the track. The high-tech **Musée Historique de la Principauté de Stavelot-Malmedy** displays archaeological remains and religious objects found in and around the region. The **Musée Guillaume Apollinaire** is devoted to the life and work of the French poet and essayist, who spent time here during his youth. Some of his original manuscripts are on display. ✉ *Pl. St-Remacle, Stavelot* ☎ *080/880–878* 🌐 *www.abbayedestavelot.be* 🎫 *€10 for a visit to all three museums.*

Eglise St-Sébastien

CHURCH | Stavelot's main square is named for St. Remacle, who founded a local abbey in 647. His reliquary, now in the Eglise St-Sébastien, is one of the wonders of Art Mosan. Dating from the 13th century, it is 6½ feet long and decorated with statuettes, of the apostles on the sides and of Christ and the Virgin on the ends. ✉ *Rue de l'Eglise 7, Stavelot* ☎ *080/862–284* 🌐 *tourismestavelot.be* 🎫 *Free.*

Restaurants

Le Loup Gourmand

$$ | **INTERNATIONAL** | For those who can't quite make up their mind whether they want to eat Italian or Belgian, this informal place in the center of town covers both bases, and more besides, with North African dishes and burgers also making it onto a wide-ranging menu. Despite this apparent scatter-gun approach, everything is prepared with care and love, so you can't go wrong whichever route you choose. **Known for:** Ardennes game specialties including venison in fall hunting season; hearty couscous dishes; simple decor putting the focus on the food. $ *Average main: €18* ✉ *Av. Ferdinand Nicolay 19, Stavelot* ☎ *080/862–995* 🌐 *www.facebook.com/leloupgourmand* ⊙ *Tues. and Wed.*

Hotels

★ **Romantik Hotel Le Val d'Amblève**

$$$ | **HOTEL** | Spread across three buildings, including a lovely whitewashed main house, spacious, plush, traditional-contemporary guest rooms look out on gorgeous grounds with century-old trees. **Pros:** romantic setting; free breakfast; free parking. **Cons:** a 10-minute walk from the center; no elevator in villa annex; restaurant is expensive. $ *Rooms from: €165* ✉ *Rte. de Malmedy 7, Stavelot* ☎ *080/281–440* 🌐 *www.levaldambleve.com* ⊙ *Closed mid-Dec.–mid-Jan.* *24 rooms* *Free Breakfast.*

Namur

92 km (57 miles) west from Stavelot, 64 km (38 miles) southeast of Brussels, 61 km (37 miles) southwest of Liège.

In Namur, remnants of the Roman empire stand side by side with the contemporary regional seat of government. The majority of the city's points of interests lie in the historic center, and the best way to discover them is on foot. However, no visit to Namur is complete without a trip up to the Citadelle. It overlooks Namur's characteristic 17th-century mansard rooftops (made from *pierre de Namur*, a bluish-gray stone quarried in the area) and the river valleys beyond. At sunset, the view is magical. From this vantage point you can observe Namur's rapid growth since it was designated the seat of government for Wallonia in 1986.

GETTING HERE AND AROUND

Trains run twice every hour from Brussels to Namur. The journey time is about one hour from Gare du Midi, or 50 minutes from Gare du Nord.

Since 2021, the easiest way to reach the Citadelle from the city center has been to ride the **cable car** (closed Monday October–March). It takes around five minutes to lift passengers around 300 feet above river level, and costs €4.50 one way, €6.50 return.

VISITOR INFORMATION

CONTACTS Office du Tourisme de Namur. ✉ *Pl. de la Station, Namur* ☎ *081/246-449* 🌐 *www.namurtourisme.be.*

Sights

Cathédrale St-Aubain

CHURCH | After floodwaters from the Sambre receded out of Namur in 1751, construction began on this Italian Baroque–style cathedral, made from Belgian marble. Inside, a statue of Notre Dame de la Paix protects the city, and St. Aubain is discreetly represented at the base of the altar, holding his head in his hands. If you're interested in religious relics, take note of the double cross atop the church dome, signifying that a piece of the holy cross is stored on the premises. ✉ *Pl. St-Aubain, Namur* 🌐 *www.namurtourisme.be* 🎫 *Free.*

★ Citadelle de Namur

CASTLE/PALACE | Over the past 1,000 years, this fortification overlooking Namur has been besieged and occupied more than 20 times. Today you can reach it by the cobblestone, cherry tree–lined route Merveilleuse; each curve in the road affords a magnificent view of the city. Alternatively, ride the **cable car** from rue des Brasseurs in the city center. Napoléon famously once described the site as the "anthill of Europe" because of the dense network of **underground tunnels** that crisscross the site. ✉ *Rte. Merveilleuse 64, Namur* ☎ *081/247-370* 🌐 *citadelle.namur.be* 🎫 *Underground galleries €10; visitor center €4; tourist train €6; combi ticket €15* ⏲ *Closed Mon. Oct.–Feb.*

Computer Museum NAM-IP

OTHER MUSEUM | Belgium's first museum dedicated to the evolution of IT takes you on a journey through time, from the earliest abacuses through to the current age of smartphones and beyond, with special emphasis given to Belgians who have been pioneers in the field. You can also watch the exhibits shrink, as they develop from huge electromechanical calculating devices, via bulky mainframes, to tiny microchips. ✉ *Rue Henri Blès 192A, Namur* ☎ *081/346-499* 🌐 *www.nam-ip.be* 🎫 *€8* ⏲ *Closed Mon.*

Eglise St-Loup

CHURCH | Designed by Brother Pierre Huyssens and built in the late 16th century by the Jesuits, this formidable building, now used as a cultural center, is considered part of Wallonia's "Grand Heritage." The marble for the impressive black-and-red columns was quarried from the Ardennes, and the limestone for the carved ceiling is from Maastricht. ✉ *Rue du Collège 17, Namur* 🌐 *www.eglise-saint-loup.be* 🎫 *Free* ⏲ *Closed Mon.*

L'Abbaye de Maredsous

RELIGIOUS BUILDING | Take the N92 to Yvoir and go east on N971 for about 10 km (6 miles) to reach this abbey, built

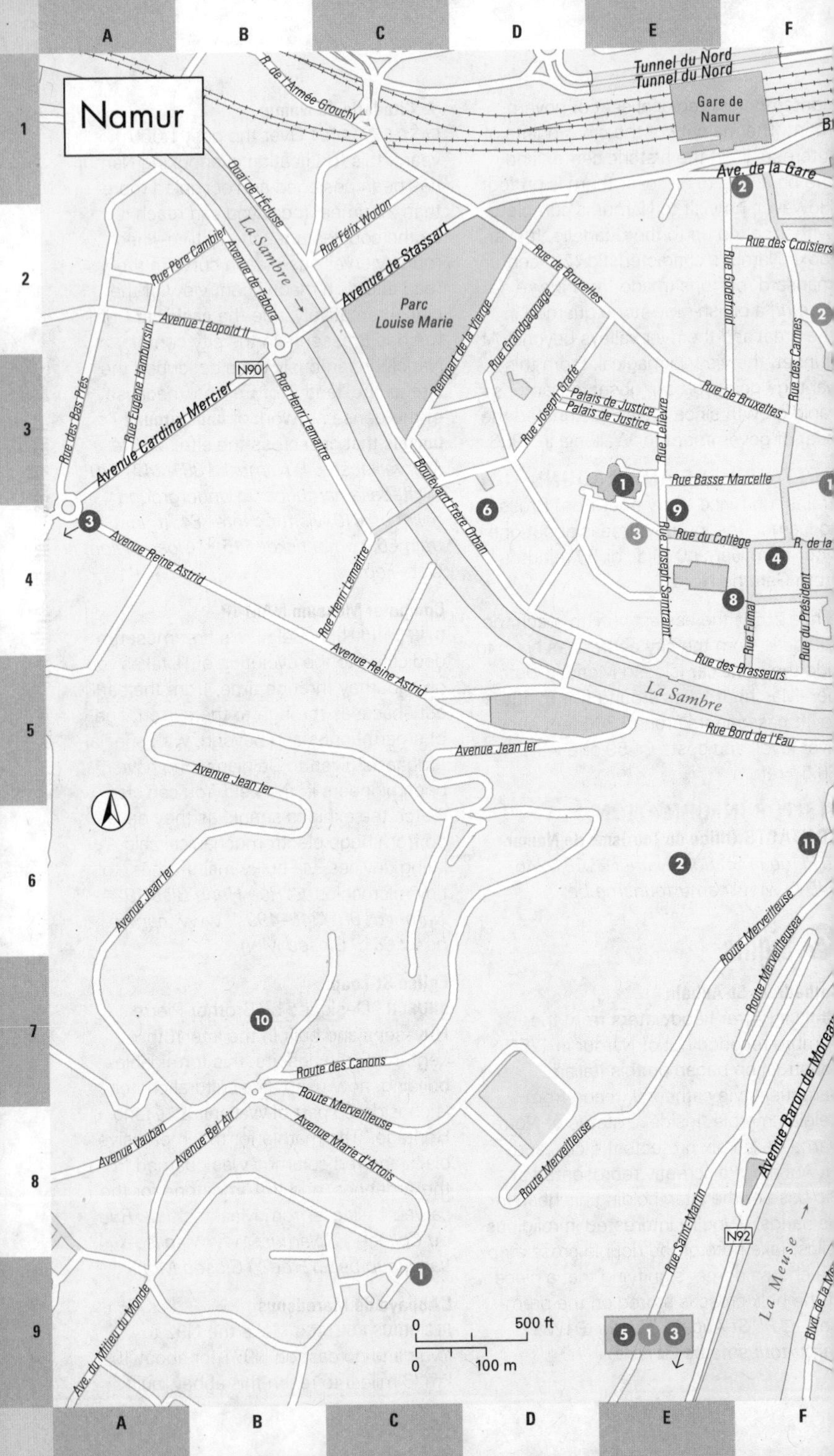
Namur
A
B
C
D
E
F
1
2
3
4
5
6
7
8
9
R. de l'Armée Grouchy
Tunnel du Nord
Tunnel du Nord
Gare de Namur
Ave. de la Gare
Quai de l'Écluse
Rue Félix Wodon
La Sambre
Avenue de Stassart
Rue des Croisiers
Rue de Bruxelles
Rue Godefroid
Rue Père Cambier
Avenue de Tabora
Parc Louise Marie
Rue Grandgagnage
Rue des Carmes
Avenue Léopold II
Rue Eugène Hambursin
N90
Rempart de la Vierge
Rue de Bruxelles
Rue des Bas Prés
Avenue Cardinal Mercier
Rue Henri Lemaître
Rue Joseph Grafé
Palais de Justice
Palais de Justice
Rue Lelièvre
Boulevard Frère Orban
Rue Basse Marcelle
Rue du Collège
R. de la
Avenue Reine Astrid
Rue Henri Lemaître
Rue Joseph Saintraint
Rue du Président
Rue Fumal
Avenue Reine Astrid
Rue des Brasseurs
La Sambre
Rue Bord de l'Eau
Avenue Jean Ier
Avenue Jean Ier
Avenue Jean Ier
Route Merveilleuse
Route Merveilleusea
Route des Canons
Route Merveilleuse
Avenue Marie d'Artois
Avenue Vauban
Avenue Bel Air
Route Merveilleuse
Avenue Baron de Moreau
N92
Rue Saint-Martin
La Meuse
Ave. du Milieu du Monde
Blvd. de la M
0
500 ft
0
100 m

Sights

1 Cathédrale St-Aubain E3
2 Citadelle de Namur E6
3 Computer Museum NAM-IP A4
4 Eglise St-Loup F4
5 L'Abbaye de Maredsous E9
6 L'Arsenal D4
7 Musée des Arts Anciens (TreM.a) G3
8 Musée Félicien Rops F4
9 Palais Provincial E4
10 Parc Attractif Reine Fabiola B7
11 Parfumerie Guy Delforge F6
12 Place d'Armes G4

Restaurants

1 Attablez Vous E9
2 Bistro Belgo Belge F2
3 Brasserie François E4
4 La Petite Fugue F4
5 Le Temps des Cerises G5

Quick Bites

1 Cup'inn F3

Hotels

1 Château de Namur C9
2 Grand Hôtel de Flandre F1
3 La Villa Gracia E9
4 Les Tanneurs I4

KEY
1 Exploring Sights
1 Restaurants
1 Quick Bites
1 Hotels

in the late 19th century as a cloister for a small order. A school, library, fromagerie, brewery, ceramics studio, and farm were eventually added. Now the sprawling complex dominates the hill, but it remains an idyllic spot for picnics, meditative walks, or evening vespers. The visitor center has exhibitions about the abbey, a snack bar serving the abbey's famous beers and cheeses, and a gift shop selling the ceramics and other products that are made by the monks in residence. There is also a small cheese museum, where you can learn about the cheese-making process. ✉ *Rue de Maredsous 11, Denée* 🌐 *www.maredsous.com* 🎫 *Free.*

L'Arsenal

HISTORIC SIGHT | The Arsenal is perhaps the best-preserved work of French architect Sébastien Vauban in all of Europe. Originally built under orders from Louis XIV in 1692 as a munitions depot, the building was restored in the early 1980s and now houses a student center for Namur's university. ✉ *Rue Bruno 11, Namur* 🌐 *www.namurtourisme.be* 🎫 *Free.*

★ **Musée des Arts Anciens (TreM.a)**

ART MUSEUM | Located in a handsome 18th-century town house, this museum contains a large collection of medieval and Renaissance art, the undoubted highlight of which is the **Trésor Hugo d'Oignies**. When you enter the small exhibition room containing these pieces, you will be immediately engaged by the sight of glowing glass cases of brightly lit gold and bejeweled objets d'art. This prize collection of crosses, medallions, reliquaries, and other religious artifacts is considered one of the seven treasures of Belgium. The relics were created by Brother Hugo d'Oignies for the monastery in nearby Oignies in the first half of the 13th century. Between the French Revolution and World War II, the collection was protected by the Sisters of Notre Dame. Look for a tiny portable altar, once belonging to Cardinal Jacques de Vitry, and a book of gospels containing parchment painted with gold leaf. ✉ *Rue de Fer 24, Namur* ☎ *081/776–754* 🌐 *www.museedesartsanciens.be* 🎫 *€3* 🕙 *Closed Mon.*

Musée Félicien Rops

ART MUSEUM | Considered a scandal in his day, Surrealist artist and Namur native Félicien Rops (1833–98) is now heralded as an artistic treasure. This museum houses a large collection of his drawings, engravings, and prints, which are by turns surreal, erotic, and whimsical. Rops spent time in Paris, mingling with the likes of Charles Baudelaire and Stéphane Mallarmé. ✉ *Rue Fumal 12, Namur* ☎ *081/776–755* 🌐 *www.museerops.be* 🎫 *€5* 🕙 *Closed Mon.*

Palais Provincial

GOVERNMENT BUILDING | This lovely 18th-century manor house was built by Namur's Bishop de Strickland; nowadays the Walloon Parliament meets in what was once the bishop's private chapel, and the interior is only open to visitors by appointment. Inside, the walls are lined with art, including an Italian stucco of the four seasons in the foyer, and in the receiving room, which was originally the billiard hall, a portrait of the bishop himself. ✉ *Pl. St-Aubain 2, Namur* 🌐 *www.province.namur.be* 🎫 *Free* 🕙 *By appointment only.*

Parc Attractif Reine Fabiola

AMUSEMENT PARK/CARNIVAL | **FAMILY** | Also located on the Citadelle grounds, this spacious park includes a large playground with miniature golf, a climbing circuit, go-carts, and electric cars. ✉ *Rond Point Thonar 1, Namur* ☎ *081/738–413* 🌐 *www.parf.be* 🎫 *€4* 🕙 *Closed Nov.–Ap*

Parfumerie Guy Delforge

STORE/MALL | Among the nonmilitary sights within the Citadelle, the former officers' mess hall is now a fragrance factory that allows you to witness the steps of isolating and combining the aromas ıvolved in creating a fine perfume. actory visits are by tour only, but a shop ostairs exhibits the work of local artists nd sells the factory's products. ✉ *Rte. 1erveilleuse 60, Namur* ☎ *081/221–219* *www.delforge.com* 🎫 *€4* ⏲ *Guided ours at 3:30, Sat. only, daily during chool holidays.*

lace d'Armes

LAZA/SQUARE | This square has played a art in the economic history of Belgium, or here during the 18th century, when ne city was under Austrian rule, the epartment of Commerce met and noney was minted. It has also felt the runt of Belgium's position as a European attleground—it was leveled in World Var I and again in World War II. Today ne square consists of an immense, ardwood platform—a sunny local neeting place—surrounded by modern uildings containing a conference center nd shops. The annual Christmas Market akes over the square in early December. ust off the north end of the square is ne 18th-century **Beffroi**, a stone tower nat was never actually a belfry, despite s name. ✉ *Pl. d'Armes, Namur* 🎫 *Free.*

Restaurants

Attablez Vous

$$$ | **FRENCH** | Eating is serious business ı the elegant dining room of this grand uburban house in Les Plantes, a suburb km (2 miles) south of central Namur. ward-winning chef Charles Jeandrain ocuses his attention on flavor in his ontemporary French-inspired creations, vith foams and flashy gimmicks taking back seat to good old taste. **Known r:** excellent wine list; attentive service; legantly chic surrounds. $ *Average nain: €35* ✉ *Tienne Maquet 16, Namur* *081/201–023* 🌐 *www.attablezvous.be* *Closed Wed. and Thurs. No lunch Sat.*

istro Belgo Belge

$ | **BELGIAN** | The focus in this simply ırnished, informal bistro is on hearty portions of Belgian classics, with bases covered from *bouchée à la reine* (chicken vol-au-vent) to *boulettes* (meatballs). Also worthy of more than a second glace is the beer list, which tops 100, with plenty of Trappist and lambic choices. **Known for:** good-value mussels in season; dishes cooked in beer; beer and food pairings. $ *Average main: €16* ✉ *Rue Saint Joseph 20, Namur* ☎ *081/810–082* 🌐 *www.estaminetbbb.be* ⏲ *Closed Sun.–Tues. No lunch Wed.–Fri.*

Brasserie François

$$ | **BELGIAN** | In a 200-year-old building with stucco columns and shiny brass everywhere, creating an appropriately elegant setting, this old-school brasserie serves up generous amounts of classic French and Belgian fare all day long (tellingly, the menu includes both steak tartare *and* its Belgian counterpart, filet americain), brought to you by immaculately attired waiters. Other seasonally variable fare includes mussels and game, both at their relevant times of year. **Known for:** Sunday brunches 11–3; freshly shucked oysters; secluded rear garden terrace. $ *Average main: €22* ✉ *Pl. Saint-Aubain 3, Namur* ☎ *081/221–123* 🌐 *www.brasseriefrancois.be.*

La Petite Fugue

$$$ | **FRENCH** | In an unassuming redbrick house on a quiet street off the place du Marché-aux-Légumes, this classy restaurant with quietly understated modern decor lives up to its name—in addition to being a musical term, *le petit fugue* also means "the little escape." The regularly changing menu promises haute cuisine emphasizing regional ingredients, such as locally caught trout and locally raised lamb. **Known for:** game dishes including doe in season; attentive service; fine dining without breaking the bank. $ *Average main: €28* ✉ *Pl. Chanoine Descamps 5, Namur* ☎ *081/231–320* 🌐 *www.lapetitefugue.be* ⏲ *Closed Mon. No dinner Sun.*

Le Temps des Cerises

$$$ | **BELGIAN** | On a narrow street in the city center, this cozy, Old Belgium–theme café serves hearty regional food amid cherry-red furniture, lace curtains, and lots of antique bric-a-brac. A long-established city institution, the graffiti writings and drawings of celebrity visitors who have dined here over the years cover the walls. **Known for:** friendly service; good wine list; longtime signature dish of ham with mustard or beer sauce. *Average main: €23 ✉ Rue des Brasseurs 22, Namur ☎ 081/225–326 ⊕ cerises.be ⊙ Closed Sun. and Mon. No lunch Tues. and Wed. No dinner Sat.*

Coffee and Quick Bites

Cup'inn

$ | **BAKERY** | This centrally located café and bakery specializes in delicious homemade cupcakes, served in all manner of creative guises, just right for washing down with a wide selection of coffees, teas, and infusions. And while these colorful little starlets may hog the limelight, it's worth noting that the cheesecakes and brownies are equally good at turning heads. **Known for:** regular brunch events adding a savory note; good-value sweet treats; friendly service. *Average main: €3 ✉ Rue Haute Marcelle 11, Namur ☎ 081/411–013 ⊕ www.lescupinn.be ⊙ Closed Sun. No dinner.*

Hotels

Château de Namur

$$ | **HOTEL** | Some of the spacious rooms in this lovely 1930s mansion atop the Citadelle's bluff have balconies and splendid views, and all have been beautifully styled with period hints amid the modern fittings. **Pros:** most rooms have river or garden views; impressive setting; restaurant has garden terrace in good weather. **Cons:** some rooms on the small side; no shuttle service into the city; a little out of the center. *Rooms from: €140 ✉ Av. de l'Ermitage 1, Namur ☎ 081/729–900 ⊕ www.chateaudenamur.com 29 rooms No Meals.*

Grand Hotel de Flandre

$ | **HOTEL** | Family run for more than a century, Namur's oldest hotel has been in business since 1904, and its grand entrance celebrates its heritage. **Pros:** affordable parking nearby; good value; friendly service. **Cons:** guest rooms lack historic character; no lounge or bar; few facilities besides bed and breakfast. *Rooms from: €75 ✉ Pl. de la Station 14, Namur ☎ 081/231–868 ⊕ www.hotelflandre.be 33 rooms No Meals.*

★ **La Villa Gracia**

$$$ | **HOTEL** | This small, luxurious, countryside inn beside the River Meuse occupies an early-20th-century mansion a few miles south of Namur. **Pros:** on bu[s] route to Namur; river views; spacious rooms. **Cons:** no a/c; far from the center; no dinner service. *Rooms from: €160 ✉ Chau. de Dinant 1445, Namur ✥ In Wépion, 8 km (5 miles) south of Namur ☎ 081/414–343 ⊕ www.villagracia.com 8 rooms No Meals.*

Les Tanneurs

$$ | **HOTEL** | This exquisite boutique hotel is the creation of Christian Bouvier, who defied developers prepared to redevelop a row of ancient buildings in the heart of Namur—it's a complex web of 15 interconnected former houses. **Pros:** good central location; uniquely styled rooms; quality dining. **Cons:** cheapest rooms are quite plainly decorated; some rooms have no a/c; some rooms inaccessible by elevator. *Rooms from: €140 ✉ Rue des Tanneries 13, Namur ☎ 081/240–02[4] ⊕ www.tanneurs.com 37 rooms No Meals.*

Nightlife

Barnabeer

PUBS | With 30 on tap and around 300 more in bottles and cans, this lively central bar has arguably the best selection of Belgian beers in town. ✉ *Rue de Bruxelles 39, Namur* 🌐 *barnabeer.be.*

Le Chapitre

PUBS | This lovely candlelit bar beside the cathedral is the most atmospheric place to drink in town, and the menu of 80 or so well-chosen beers will give you plenty of reasons to linger. ✉ *Rue du Séminaire 4, Namur* ☎ *0499/844–457* 🌐 *www.facebook.com/lechapitrenamur.*

Le Piano Bar

LIVE MUSIC | This basic central piano bar has a good selection of beers and hosts live jazz, blues, and rock concerts Saturday night, and has karaoke evenings on Monday and Tuesday. ✉ *Pl. du Marché Aux Légumes 10, Namur* ☎ *081/230–633* 🌐 *www.facebook.com/lepianobarnamur.*

Shopping

The heart of Namur's shopping district is along rue de l'Ange and rue de Fer, which are lined with clothing boutiques, music stores, and other shops catering to a predominantly student crowd.

La Cave de Wallonie

FOOD | If you are in search of a gift unique to the Walloon region, look no further—this small store's shelves are lined with regional food products such as pâtés, sausages, jams, honey, and liqueurs. There are also more than 300 Belgian beers in stock, plus stemware from each of the breweries. ✉ *Rue de la Halle 6, Namur* ☎ *0478/565–715* 🌐 *cavedewallonie-coteterroir.business.site.*

Dinant

29 km (17 miles) south of Namur, 93 km (56 miles) southeast of Brussels, 80 km (48 miles) southwest of Liège.

Simultaneously hanging off and tucked under spectacular cliffs on the Meuse, Dinant's dramatic setting has been the stage for a turbulent history. The town has been attacked more than 200 times in the course of eight centuries—one of the more notable assaults occurred when Charles the Bold sacked the town in 1466 and threw 600 men, tied in pairs, into the river. Dinant also has a rich industrial past. Between the 12th and 15th centuries, copper production, known as *dinanderie*, boomed. Eventually the metalworking industry gave way to mining and textiles. Now Dinant (population 13,500) caters to the tourists who flock here to discover the city's historic ruins, natural beauty, and culinary pleasures. Jazz lovers have an additional reason to visit Dinant. Its most famous son is Adolphe Sax (born here in 1814), inventor of the saxophone.

GETTING HERE AND AROUND

Two trains every hour snake along the Meuse river valley between Namur and Dinant. This picturesque trip takes approximately 30 minutes.

VISITOR INFORMATION

CONTACTS Maison du Tourisme Dinant. ✉ *Av. Colonel Cadoux 8, Dinant* ☎ *082/222–870* 🌐 *www.dinant-tourisme.be.*

Sights

Brasserie Caracole

BREWERY | In an old mill 7 km (4 miles) south of Dinant, this brewery heats its brews using a traditional wood stove. Its signature snail mascot is a whimsical allusion to Namur province's reputation for being slow-paced. Even if you don't drink, the distinctive cavernous tasting room lined with old brewing equipment is worth a visit; tours of the brewery include a tasting of four beers. In addition to the normal weekend afternoon opening times, the brewery is also open Wednesday afternoon in July and August. ✉ *Côte Marie-Thérèse 86, Falmignoul, Dinant* 🌐 *www.brasseriecaracole.be* 🎫 *€10* ⏲ *Closed weekdays and Jan.*

The postcard-perfect town of Dinant, tucked under spectacular cliffs and on the Meuse River, is seemingly out of a fairy tale.

Celles

TOWN | Nestled in a small valley surrounded by low hills, this ultracute village 10 km (6 miles) east from Dinant on the N94 has retained a lot of its old-world charm and is among the prettiest in Belgium. The streets are lined with traditional stone houses and the Romanesque **Eglise St-Hadelin** sits at the center of everything. ✉ *Celles, Dinant* 🎫 *Free.*

Château de Freyr

HISTORIC HOME | Beside the river, around 6 km (4 miles) south from Dinant, this impressive Renaissance building has beautiful interiors decorated with 17th-century woodwork and furniture, including a restored children's coach. Louis XIV visited here during the siege of Dinant in 1675. Its park has been laid out in accordance with the design principles of Le Nôtre, the French landscape architect. ✉ *Domaine de Freyr, Waulsort, Dinant* ✣ *6 km (4 miles) south from Dinant* ☎ *082/222–200* 🌐 *www.freyr.be* 🎫 *€9* 🕒 *Closed Mon., July and Aug.; closed weekdays Sept.–June.*

Citadelle de Dinant

MILITARY SIGHT | The Citadelle is on the cliff top, towering directly over Dinant's city center. You can reach it by cable car, or by climbing the 408 steps that were cut into the rock face in the 16th century. The fortress is not as old as you might suspect—the ancient fortification was razed in 1818 by the Dutch, who replaced it with the current structure before being ousted. The view is splendid, and there is an arms museum with cannons and cannonballs. ✉ *Chemin de la Citadelle 1, Dinant* ☎ *082/223–670* 🌐 *www.citadelledinant.be* 🎫 *€11, including cable car* 🕒 *Closed Fri. mid-Nov.–Mar. (cable car weekends only).*

Eglise Collégiale Notre-Dame de Dinant

CHURCH | The town's keystone is its Gothic main church, which dominates the riverfront below the Citadelle. Parts of it date from the 13th century; its distinctive gray onion-dome bell tower, a 16th-century addition following a fire, was originally designed to grace roof of the town hall. The interior is particularly noteworthy for its impressive stained-glass windows, the largest of which was created by the 20th-century artist Gustave Ladon. ✉ *Rue Adolphe Sax 1, Dinant* 🌐 *walloniebelgiquetourisme.be* 🎫 *Free.*

Grotte La Merveilleuse

CAVE | La Merveilleuse, a cave system discovered in 1904 and filled with numerous remarkably white stalactites, is on Dinant's left bank, about 490 yards from the bridge, on the road toward Philippeville. Tours depart hourly and a visit takes about 50 minutes. ✉ *Rte. de Philippeville 142, Dinant* ☎ *082/222–210* 🎫 *€9.*

Jardins d'Eau d'Annevoie

GARDEN | Some 12 km (7½ miles) north of Dinant, just off the road to Namur, the delightful Annevoie Water Gardens present a happy blend of 18th-century French landscaping and romantic Italian garden design. The grounds are particularly remarkable for their naturally occurring, spring-fed waterfalls, fountains, and ponds, interspersed among flower beds, lawns, grottoes, and statues. The water displays function without mechanical aids and have remained in working order for more than two centuries. The adjacent Château d'Annevoie (not open to the public), an impressive 18th-century manor house, blends perfectly with the gardens. ✉ *Rue des Jardins 37a, Annevoie, Dinant* ☎ *082/679–797* 🌐 *www.annevoie.be* 🎫 *€10* ⏲ *Closed Nov.–Mar.*

Maison de la Pataphonie

CHILDREN'S MUSEUM | **FAMILY** | Cofounded by the Association Internationale Adolphe Sax and the city's Maison de la Culture, this wonderful museum invites children to explore, invent, and make music as part of a 75-minute guided tour. Demonstrations show you how to make music without professional instruments, simply using ordinary items like water and bits of copper and wood. At the end of the session, would-be musicians compose their own symphony. Tours start at 2 pm and 4 pm on Sunday and school holidays, more often in summer. ✉ *Rue en Rhée 51, Dinant* ☎ *082/213–939* 🌐 *www.pataphonie.be* 🎫 *€6* ⏲ *Closed Sat. Other hrs vary* ✍ *Reservations advised.*

Maison de Monsieur Sax

OTHER MUSEUM | This small interpretation center dedicated to the life and work of Adolphe Sax, inventor of the saxophone, occupies a building on the very spot where the great man was born in 1814, and contains some of his original creations. Holding sway over the scene, a life-size statue of Sax himself relaxes on a bench directly outside. ✉ *Rue Adolphe Sax 37, Dinant* 🌐 *sax.dinant.be* 🎫 *Free.*

Restaurants

CFP Mosan

$ | **FRENCH** | In a grand mansion overlooking the Meuse, this cooking school where the next generation of Belgian chefs learn the art of cuisine serves a fortnightly changing three-course menu, usually featuring fine traditional French food. Though the dining room is rather plain, it has a beautiful view of the river, and both a garden and a riverside terrace, open in fine weather. **Known for:** great-value set menu; impeccable formal service; two outdoor scenic terraces. [$] *Average main: €9* ✉ *Av. Winston Churchill 36, Dinant* ☎ *082/213–053* 🌐 *www.cfpmosan.be* ⏲ *Closed Sat.–Mon. No dinner.*

La Table d'Antonio

$$$ | **BELGIAN** | The modest red-painted brick facade of this popular restaurant gives little away about what lies within: a smart tiled-floor dining room with a ship-shape bar that leads back to a rear garden terrace, opened up in fine weather. The food is distinctly Belgian with French influences, and it sticks to seasonal, locally sourced produce where possible, but scallops also feature regularly and never disappoint. **Known for:** generous portion sizes; game dishes served in fall hunting season; good seafood. [$] *Average main: €25* ✉ *Rue Alexandre Daoust*

49, Dinant ☎ 082/222–249 🌐 www.table-antonio.be ⏲ Closed Wed. No dinner Mon. and Tues.

Le Jardin de Fiorine

$$$ | CONTEMPORARY | An unassuming gray facade belies the elegant interior of this restaurant in a sprawling old house, with its sharp modern furnishings offset by original features such as fireplaces and tiled floors, and a pretty garden terrace if weather permits. The menu features some apparently simple European dishes such as quiche, elevated to fine-dining levels. **Known for:** good wine list; beautiful rear garden with river views; attentive service. *$ Average main: €24 ✉ Rue Georges Cousot 3, Dinant ☎ 082/227–474 🌐 www.jardindefiorine.be ⏲ Oct.–Mar.: closed Tues.–Thurs. No dinner Sun.*

Hotels

Hotel ibis Dinant Centre

$ | HOTEL | A 10-minute walk south from central Dinant, this modern, new-build hotel enjoys a superb location right by the banks of the Meuse. **Pros:** friendly service; free on-site parking; some rooms have river views. **Cons:** away from the center despite the name; part of a chain; modern rooms lack character. *$ Rooms from: €69 ✉ Rempart d'Albeau 16, Dinant ☎ 082/211–500 🌐 all.accor.com 58 rooms 🍽 No Meals.*

La Merveilleuse by Infiniti Resorts

$$ | HOTEL | In two neo-Gothic buildings dating from the late 19th century, this converted former monastery enjoys superb views of Dinant and the Meuse. **Pros:** some rooms have river views; free breakfast; on-site wellness center with swimming pool. **Cons:** some beds quite narrow; some rooms are small; a short but steep walk uphill from the center. *$ Rooms from: €114 ✉ Charreau Des Capucins 23, Dinant ☎ 082/229–191 🌐 infiniti-resort.be 12 rooms 🍽 Free Breakfast.*

Activities

Kayaking or boating on the Meuse, or its lively tributary, the Lesse, is a great way to see the landscape: forested valleys, rocky cliffs, and countless streams. To tackle the lower Lesse, try the 12-km (8-mile) or 21-km (13-mile) ride from Houyet, through two rapids and past the high cliffs holding Walzin Castle, to Anseremme on the Meuse, south of Dinant. The season runs April–October. Rentals start at around €20 per person.

Dinant évasion - Lesse Kayaks

KAYAKING | FAMILY | This outdoor sports company offers guided kayak trips from Houyet to Anseremme (about five hours, 21 km [13 miles]), from Gendron to Anseremme (about three hours, 12 km [7½ miles]), and from Houyet to Gendron (about two hours, 9 km [5½ miles]). Rental prices for a single-seat kayak start from around €26, including transport—two- and three-seater canoes work out slightly cheaper per person. The same company also offers rock climbing, and "aerial" or "bridge-walking" tours. You can combine two different tours for a full day of activities. *✉ Rue du Vélodrome 15, Dinant ☎ 082/224–397 🌐 www.dinant-evasion.be From €21 ⏲ Closed Nov.–Mar.*

Rochefort

35 km (22 miles) southeast of Dinant, 128 km (79 miles) southeast of Brussels, 55 km (34 miles) southwest of Liège.

In the 12th century, the Count of Rochefort had the most important feudal estate in the province of Liège. Today, Rochefort is a quiet tourist town on the border of Namur and Luxembourg provinces. The name Rochefort means "strong rock" and comes from the prominent rock castle, the Château Comtal, which anchors the town center. Rochefort is known for its delicious Trappist beer and cheese, plus a number of interesting sights in town and in the vicinity, most notably the Grottes de Han. Unfortunately, the **Abbaye de St-Remy** (about 3 km [2 miles] north of Rochefort), where the delicious 6°, 8°, 10°, and Triple Extra Trappist beers are brewed, isn't open to the public, and visitors are not welcome—the few remaining monks are firm about this.

GETTING HERE AND AROUND

The nearest railway station to Rochefort is in Rochefort-Jemelle, about 3 km (2 miles) east. Direct trains run hourly to Jemelle from Namur (40 minutes), and every two hours from Liège (75 minutes). From Jemelle, Bus No. 29 and No. 166a make the short journey to Rochefort in about five minutes. Both run approximately once each hour. Bus No. 29 continues on to the Grottes de Han caves, a further 5 km (3 miles) west. If you are driving, the trip from Namur takes about 45 minutes, or 75 minutes from Liège.

Sights

Château Comtal

CASTLE/PALACE | **FAMILY** | Come for the majestic view and explore ruins dating from the 11th through the 19th centuries at the Castle of the Counts, situated on a rise overlooking Rochefort's town center. To visit, you'll need to join a one-hour tour in the company of your guide, "Emelyne the Witch." Tours depart from the castle gate at 2 pm from April to November, only during Belgian school holidays—the website has a calendar of open days. ✉ *Rue Jacquet, Rochefort* ☎ *0496/617–145* 🌐 *chateaurochefort.be* 🎫 *€4* 🕐 *Closed Dec.–Mar.; Apr.–Nov. only open during school holidays.*

Grotte de Lorette-Rochefort

CAVE | In the woods just above the town center, this cave system was carved by the Lomme River, and it maintains a constantly warm temperature. The most remarkable of its many halls is the Salle de Sabat (Hall of the Witches' Sabbath), which is more than 250 feet high. Visits are by guided tour only (lasting one hour)—tours leave every 45 minutes. While in the area, be sure to take a peek into the adjacent **Chapelle de Lorette**. Josine de la March, Countess of Rochefort, built this tiny chapel in 1620 in the hope that it would hasten the return of her son—who, so the story goes, had been kidnapped by a monkey, and was returned upon the chapel's completion. ✉ *Drève de Lorette, Rochefort* ☎ *084/212–080* 🌐 *www.grotte-de-lorette.be* 🎫 *€11* 🕐 *Closed mid-Nov.–May; June–mid-July and mid-Aug.–mid-Nov., closed Thurs. and Sat.–Tues., except during school holidays.*

★ **Grottes de Han**

CAVE | The magnificent Han Caves, which had provided refuge for threatened tribes since Neolithic times, were only rediscovered in the mid-19th century. To tour them, board an ancient tram in the center of Han-sur-Lesse that carries you to the mouth of the caves. There multilingual guides take over, leading groups on foot through 3 km (2 miles) of dimly lighted chambers. You get occasional glimpses of the underground River Lesse as you pass giant stalagmites and eventually enter the vast cavern called the Dome, 475 feet high, where a single torchbearer dramatically descends the sloping cave wall. The final part of the journey is by boat on the underground river. The trip takes about 75 minutes, and involves a total of 365 steps. The cave is 9°C (48°F), with 90% humidity, all year long, so consider bringing a sweater with you. Your ticket also includes entry to **PrehistoHan** (*Rue des Grottes 46, Han-sur-Lesse*), an exhibition of the many archaeological finds unearthed within the cave system over the past 60 years. ✉ *Rue Joseph Lamotte 2, Han-sur-Lesse* ✣ *6 km (4 miles) southeast of Rochefort* ☎ *084/377–213* 🌐 *grotte-de-han.be* 🎫 *€23* 🕐 *Closed mid-Nov.–mid-Dec. and mid-Jan.–Mar.*

Malagne - Archéoparc de Rochefort
NATURE PRESERVE | Built to incorporate the ruins of a Gallo-Roman villa, the 1,240-acre Malagne has nature trails, regional exhibits, historical re-enactments, and an abundance of events specifically for kids. See website for a schedule of events. ✉ *Rue du Coirbois 85, Rochefort* ☏ *084/222–103* 🌐 *www.malagne.be* *€8* 🕑 *Closed Nov.–Mar.*

L'Inattendu
$$ | **EUROPEAN** | L'Inattendu translates as "The Unexpected," but what you can reliably expect at this cozy bar and restaurant with restrained, almost monochrome, wood-theme decor, is fine French and pan-European food at affordable prices. The homemade Black Angus burgers are especially recommended. **Known for:** good cocktails; excellent crepes for dessert; friendly, attentive service. $ *Average main: €22* ✉ *Rue behogne 34b, Rochefort* ☏ *084/445–987* 🌐 *www.facebook.com/linattenduroche-fort* 🕑 *Closed Mon. and Tues.*

Hotel La Malle Poste
$ | **HOTEL** | Ideally located in the heart of Rochefort, this hotel occupies a beautifully restored 17th-century mansion, with romantically decorated rooms that offer modern conveniences while reflecting the history of the building. **Pros:** good restaurant; free parking; swimming pool and fitness center. **Cons:** rooms in annex have no free Wi-Fi; rooms with bathtubs cost extra; restaurant hours limited. $ *Rooms from: €95* ✉ *Rue de Behogne 46, Rochefort* ☏ *084/210–986* 🌐 *www.malleposte.net* 🕑 *Closed Jan.* *24 rooms* *No Meals.*

Bastogne

50 km (31 miles) southeast from Rochefort, 88 km (53 miles) south of Liège.

Bastogne is where General McAuliffe delivered World War II's most famous response to a surrender request: "Nuts!" Although a number of Ardennes towns were destroyed during the Battle of the Bulge, Bastogne was the epicenter. McAuliffe's American 101st division reached Bastogne on December 19, 1944, one day before General Von Manteuffel's tanks surrounded it. The town was under constant attack, and the miserable weather made it impossible for supplies to be flown in. On December 22, the Germans asked the U.S. forces to surrender. They refused. On Christmas Eve, the defenders were close to a defeat, but relief was near. The American 42nd tank division, led by Major General Gaffey, broke through the German lines. The next day, General Patton managed to safeguard a small corridor through the German lines toward the town. On December 26 the skies cleared and supplies were flown in, but it was another month before the last German stronghold was destroyed. To this day, a Sherman tank occupies a place of honor in the town square, named after General McAuliffe himself.

GETTING HERE AND AROUND

The nearest train station to Bastogne is Marloie, near Marche-en-Famenne, reachable from Namur in 35 minutes. From there, express bus No. E78 takes a further 40 minutes to reach Bastogne. There is also an hourly direct express bus No. E69 from Liège-Guillemins train station, taking around 90 minutes.

There is no public transportation from the city center to the Mardasson Memorial and the Bastogne War Museum. If you don't have a car, you can take a taxi or walk about 1½ miles.

The Battle of the Bulge

It was Hitler himself who came up with the plan for *Wacht am Rhein*, as the Germans call the Battle of the Bulge. Three German armies were to surprise the Allied troops in southeastern Belgium with a blitz offensive through the supposedly impenetrable Ardennes forests. Their goal was to prevent the transport of troop reinforcements and supplies, cut off the British army from the American army, force their surrender, and obtain a peace treaty on the western front. German troops would then move to Russia to concentrate on the eastern front. The plan was to reach Liège within 48 hours, move on toward Brussels, and eventually take the port of Antwerp.

The attack started at 5:30 am on December 16, 1944, and came as a complete surprise to outnumbered Allied forces. American units were shattered and defenses penetrated. To make things worse, about 1,500 Germans disguised as Americans caused confusion, and bad weather made Allied air strikes impossible. The city of Bastogne became a turning point in the battle. German tanks surrounded it on December 20, trapping civilians and American soldiers. General Eisenhower ordered a counterattack, and within eight days 240,000 men were deployed, eventually turning the tide. The weather cleared, allowing the Allies to bomb German strongholds and deliver supplies. By the end of December, the German tank divisions began their withdrawal, but it was another month before the battle was finally won.

VISITOR INFORMATION

CONTACTS Bastogne Tourisme. ✉ *Pl. McAuliffe 60, Bastogne* ☎ *061/212–711* 🌐 *www.bastogne-tourisme.be.*

Sights

Bastogne Barracks

MILITARY SIGHT | This former Belgian army barracks dating from 1936 is where, on December 22nd, 1944, Brigadier General Anthony McAuliffe, Commander of the 101st Airborne Division in Bastogne, uttered the immortal word "Nuts!" in response to a German call for his surrender. Today, the barracks mostly houses an extensive collection of military vehicles from the period. ✉ *Rue de La Roche 40, Bastogne* ☎ *0478/782–498* 🌐 *www.warheritage.be* 🎫 *€10* ⏲ *Closed Dec.–May; June–Sept. closed Mon. and Tues.; Oct.–Nov. closed weekdays.*

★ **Bastogne War Museum**

HISTORY MUSEUM | One of Belgium's best and most moving museums, this huge exhibition space looks at the causes and events of World War II in general, but has a particular focus on the events that happened in and around Bastogne in late 1944, when German troops reoccupied the town for a month. Visits include an audio tour guided by four very different but very real people who lived through the ordeal: a local Belgian boy, a school teacher, an American GI, and a German foot soldier all recount their own experiences of some very dark days. ✉ *Colline du Mardasson 5, Bastogne* ☎ *061/210–220* 🌐 *www.bastognewarmuseum.be* 🎫 *€16* ⏲ *Closed mid-Jan.–late Feb.; late Feb.–mid-Mar. and mid.-Nov.–mid.-Jan. closed Mon.*

At the Bastogne War Museum, you can learn about the Battle of the Bulge that took place here between 1944-45.

Mémorial du Mardasson
MILITARY SIGHT | Standing solemnly beside the Bastogne War Museum, this huge star-shape memorial honors the Americans lost in the Battle of the Bulge. The names of all U.S. Army units and the history of the battle are inscribed on the wall, along with a simple phrase in Latin: "The Belgian people remember their American liberators." Mosaics by Fernand Léger decorate the crypt's Protestant, Catholic, and Jewish chapels. From the top of the memorial you have a magnificent view of the former battlegrounds. The memorial is open all year. ✉ *Rte. de Bizory 1, Bastogne* 🎫 *Free.*

101st Airborne Museum
MILITARY SIGHT | Also known informally as "Le Mess," this museum in the former Belgian army's officers' mess contains dioramas based on actual photos that depict the lives of U.S. 101st Airborne Division troops as they defended the town in 1944. Make sure you take time to check out the "bomb shelter" in the basement: a very loud and very immersive surround-sound reenactment of an air raid—a definite eye-opener, even though there is no actual danger involved. ✉ *Av. de la Gare 11, Bastogne* ☎ *061/501–200* 🌐 *www.101airbornemuseumbastogne.com* 🎫 *€10* 🕒 *Closed Mon. Apr.–Sept.; closed weekdays Oct.–Mar.*

Porte de Trèves
HISTORIC SIGHT | Originally constructed in the 14th century, Trier Gate is the last remaining evidence of the medieval city wall that once encircled Bastogne. The ramparts kept the city safe until 1688, when they were demolished on the orders of French king Louis XIV, and the gate was converted into a prison—a role it performed until 1914. The German offensive in 1944–45 almost destroyed the building, but it has since been restored. Today it occasionally hosts temporary exhibitions—you'll need an appointment to look inside at other times. ✉ *Pl. de la Porte de Trèves, Bastogne* 🌐 *www.bastogne-tourisme.be* 🎫 *Free* 🕒 *Open by appointment only.*

Restaurants

Brasserie Lamborelle

$$ | **BELGIAN** | This quirky tavern-style corner café a block from the main square, partially decorated with cowhide wallpaper, serves an extensive menu of hearty Belgian and pan-European dishes ranging from raclette (grilled cheese), via pasta, to steak. The house special, however, is *croûte au fromage* (sauerkraut with cheese), served in a variety of ways. **Known for:** food menu available all day; excellent beer list; house "Airbourne" beer served in a porcelain GI helmet. *Average main: €15 ✉ Rue Lamborelle 19, Bastogne ☎ 061/218–055 ⊕ wallux.com/brasserie-lamborelle-bastogne ⊙ Closed Mon. and Tues.*

Hotels

Hôtel Léo Station

$$ | **HOTEL** | In business since 1946, this place has come a long way since, and a series of modern extensions and renovations have rendered it virtually unrecognizable from its original form, save for the deceptively drab facade. **Pros:** large rooms; good value; centrally located on the main square. **Cons:** no on-site parking; some rooms are in an annex, a 10-minute walk from the center; front rooms can be noisy. *Rooms from: €140 ✉ Pl. McAuliffe 52, Bastogne ☎ 061/211–441 ⊕ www.wagon-leo.com 34 rooms No Meals.*

Durbuy

52 km (32 miles) north from Bastogne, 51 km (31 miles) south of Liège, 119 km (71 miles) southeast of Brussels.

Surrounded by deep forests in the Ourthe river valley, an 11th-century castle towers over this tiny, picture-perfect town. Ever since John the Blind deemed it a city in 1331, Durbuy has taken pride in promoting itself as "the smallest city in the world," but we are using the term "city" quite loosely here. In reality it is no more than a village, and a small one at that. Allegedly, Durbuy derives its name from a pre-Latin dialect in which *duro bodions* translates as "dwellings near the fortress." The castle is not open to the public, but Durbuy's narrow streets, never more than a stone's throw from the main square, are lined with amazingly well-preserved 16th- and 17th-century architecture. During the summer season they fill with tourists.

One striking geological feature that you won't fail to spot is **La Falize**, a dramatic anticlinal fold or rock that looms large over the northern end of town.

For such a small place, Durbuy hosts a surprising number of festivals and markets. In March, chocoholics flock to the **marché du chocolat**. The last Sunday in August is the **marché des fleurs**, where florists carpet the main square in vibrant blossoms, and on the second Saturday of the month between April and September, a **marché des antiquités** comes to town, setting out all kinds of vintage and antique wares.

GETTING HERE AND AROUND

Getting to Durbuy via public transport can be problematic. The nearest railway station is in Barvaux, 4 km (2 miles) to the east, and if you don't fancy walking from there, bus and taxi options are very limited. Things are a little easier if you have a car; the drive from Liège should take around 50 minutes, but be warned: finding a parking space can be difficult in peak season.

VISITOR INFORMATION

CONTACTS Durbuy Tourist Information. *✉ Pl. aux Foires 25, Durbuy ☎ 086/212–428 ⊕ durbuytourisme.be.*

Sights

Parc des Topiaries

GARDEN | This small park on the bank of the Ourthe offers a lighthearted variation on the concept of a formal European garden. Here, more than 250 box trees have been patiently pruned into a variety of shapes and sizes. Look for the dancing elephant, and the re-creation of Brussels's Manneken Pis. The café terrace commands an excellent view of the village. ✉ *Rue Haie Himbe 1, Durbuy* ☎ *086/219–075* 🌐 *www.topiaires.be* 🎫 *€5.*

Restaurants

La Canette

$$ | **FRENCH** | Candlelit tables and rustic touches characterize the welcoming little bistro, which serves a regularly changing menu of French food with global influences, in homey surrounds. To really soak up Durbuy's enchanting atmosphere, try to snag a table on the front terrace, beside a lovely cobbled lane. **Known for:** good steaks; friendly service; hearty portions. $ *Average main: €18* ✉ *Rue Alphonse Eloy 1, Durbuy* ☎ *086/212–668* 🌐 *www.facebook.com/lacanettedurbuy* ⏲ *Closed Wed. and Thurs. No lunch except Sun.*

Le Clos Des Récollets

$$$ | **BELGIAN** | Although this 17th-century home in the heart of Durbuy is all low ceilings and oak beams, the off-white color scheme in the candlelit dining room keeps things light and airy. The food is exquisite modern Belgian, using mostly local, seasonal produce, but the seafood is truly special—unsurprising as chef Frédéric Bruneel learned his trade at the SAS Sea Grill in Brussels. **Known for:** friendly, welcoming service; romantic fine dining; beautiful outdoor terrace. $ *Average main: €28* ✉ *Rue de la Prévôté 9, Durbuy* ☎ *086/212–969* 🌐 *www.closdesrecollets.be* ⏲ *Closed Tues. and Wed.*

Hotels

Le Sanglier des Ardennes

$$$ | **HOTEL** | Dominating the center of town, this luxury retreat has a stone fireplace, wood beams, and public spaces punctuated by glass cases with perfume, leather, and French scarves for sale. **Pros:** rear rooms have river views; highly regarded restaurant; central location. **Cons:** modern rooms lack the historical charm of the surrounding town; breakfast is expensive; no minibar or refrigerators in rooms. $ *Rooms from: €165* ✉ *Rue Comte d'Ursel 14, Durbuy* ☎ *086/213–262* 🌐 *www.sanglier-durbuy.be* 🛏 *96 rooms* 🍽 *No Meals.*

La Roche-en-Ardenne

30 km (19 miles) south from Durbuy, 77 km (46 miles) south from Liège, 127 km (76 miles) southeast from Brussels.

The nickname "Pearl of the Ardennes" refers to La Roche's beautiful surroundings, not to the town itself. It was leveled by 70,000 shells during the Battle of the Bulge. La Roche was rebuilt quickly after the war and has become a busy tourist resort. Cafés, restaurants, and hotels line the street along the Ourthe river. On weekends and in summer they're filled with tourists taking a break from hiking, biking, skiing, or kayaking in the area. The town shelters below the ruins of the 9th-century medieval château that stands on the hill above it.

A walk through the town, which is no more than a handful of small streets, immediately reminds you of La Roche's violent past. A British M-10 Achilles tank stands at the entrance of the town, and a moving plaque sits at the intersection of rue de la Gare and rue Cielle, the spot where American and British troops met.

, bird's-eye view of the pretty little town of La Roche-en-Ardenne, located along the Ourthe River.

;ETTING HERE AND AROUND

;etting to La Roche-en-Ardenne using ublic transport can be problematic. 'he nearest train station is in Marche-n-Famenne, 20 km (12½ miles) to the vest. There is a regular direct train serice from both Namur and Liège, but the us connection onward to La Roche-en-rdenne (No. 15) only runs a few times ach day.

driving from Liège, take the E25 oward Luxembourg and get off at Exit 0. La Roche is another 17 km (11 miles) long the charming N89. From Brussels, ake the E411 in the direction of Namur nd Luxembourg; jump on the N4 at Exit 8 and drive to Marche-en-Famenne; here follow the bendy N888, which will ake you through the woods to La Roche.

'ISITOR INFORMATION

:ONTACTS Maison du Tourisme Coeur de Ardenne. ✉ *Pl. du Marché 15, La Roche-n-Ardenne* ☎ *084/367–736* 🌐 *www. oeurdelardenne.be.*

Sights

Château de La Roche-en-Ardenne
CASTLE/PALACE | Looming large on a hill above the the town are the ruins of the 11th-century feudal castle. A tiny cobblestone alley from place du Marché takes you there. Throughout the year, occasional medieval-themed events are held here, such as displays of archery or falconry. In summer, the ghost of Berthe, a woman of local legend, supposedly appears at sunset. ✉ *Rue Du Vieux Château 4, La Roche-en-Ardenne* ☎ *084/411–342* 🌐 *www.chateaudelaroche.be* *€7.*

Musée de la Bataille des Ardennes
OTHER MUSEUM | This somewhat dusty museum contains an extensive selection of American, English, and German war relics, including an authentic code-deciphering enigma machine. Numerous photographs re-create life in the Ardennes during the war. ✉ *Rue Châmont 5, La Roche-en-Ardenne* ☎ *084/411–725* 🌐 *www.batarden.be* *€8* ⏲ *Closed weekdays Oct.–Mar.*

Restaurants

Chez Henri

$$$ | **BELGIAN** | This long-standing local favorite right in the center of town has been serving hearty traditional Belgian and regional Ardennes dishes in cozy surrounds for more than half a century. Locally caught trout and Ardennes ham are menu staples, as are mussels and fries in season. **Known for:** friendly service; game dishes in fall season; generous portions. *Average main: €24* ✉ *Rue Chamont 8, La Roche-en-Ardenne* ☎ *084/411–564* ⊕ *www.restaurantardennais.be* ⊙ *Closed Tues. and Wed.*

Hotels

Hostellerie La Claire Fontaine

$$ | **HOTEL** | Set on a gorgeous bluff 1½ km (1 mile) west of town, this family-run hotel has spacious, modern rooms with supercomfy beds—those at the rear have magnificent views of the garden and the forest beyond. **Pros:** most rooms have balconies; free breakfast; free parking. **Cons:** front rooms overlook main highway; a 20-minute from the center; restaurant is expensive. *Rooms from: €125* ✉ *Rue de Vecpré 64, La Roche-en-Ardenne* ☎ *084/412–470* ⊕ *clairefontaine.be* *31 rooms* *Free Breakfast.*

Bouillon

65 km (41 miles) southwest from La Roche-en-Ardenne, 85 km (53 miles) south from Namur.

Sitting close to Belgium's southern border (the nearest large town, Charleville-Mézières, is in France), Bouillon feels an oddly remote place, but it can trace its history back more than 1,000 years. Hemmed in on three sides by a tight bend in the Semois River, and dominated by its superb medieval castle, the strategic importance of Bouillon's location is plain to see.

GETTING HERE AND AROUND

The nearest station to Bouillon is Libramont, which is served by hourly fast trains from Namur (taking around 65 minutes). From Libramont, bus No. 8 takes a further 45 minutes to reach the center of Boullion. Driving from Namur cuts the total journey time by about half.

VISITOR INFORMATION

CONTACTS Maison du Tourisme - Pays de Bouillon en Ardenne. ✉ *Quai des Saulx 12, Bouillon* ☎ *061/465–211* ⊕ *www.paysdebouillon.be.*

Sights

★ **Abbaye d'Orval**

RELIGIOUS BUILDING | Around 29 km (18 miles) southeast of Bouillon, this magnificent abbey is known throughout the world for its famous Trappist beer, but you will need your own transport to reach this remote corner of the country. Founded by Italian Benedictines in 1070, and once one of Europe's richest and most famous monasteries, the abbey flourished for 700 years before being destroyed by French troops in the aftermath of the French Revolution. It was rebuilt between 1926 and 1948 under the supervision of Marie-Albert Van der Cruyssen, a monk and builder from Ghent who started the brewery in 1931 in order to finance the rebuilding project. Sadly, the brewery and most of the monastery's buildings are closed to the public, but you can visit the grounds and tour the ruins of the original abbey. The gardens contain the spring where Mathilde, Duchess of Lorraine, once dropped her wedding band, only to have it miraculously returned by a trout—the magical fish is now the abbey's trademark symbol. A film in English describes life in the monastery, and the 18th-century cellars house a small museum. ✉ *Orval 1, Villers-devant-Orval* ☎ *061/311–060* ⊕ *www.orval.be* *€7.*

High above the Semois River is Château Fort de Bouillon, one of Belgium's largest and oldest remaining castles.

Archéoscope Godefroid de Bouillon
OTHER ATTRACTION | This multimedia show invites you into the world of the castle's most notable occupant, Godfrey (Godefroid) of Bouillon, who ruled here in the late 11th century when the area was still a part of France. It tells the story of Godfrey's biggest—if somewhat dubious—claim to notoriety: he led an army of thousands on the First Crusade, and from 1099 until his death just one year later, he was installed as the first ruler of the Kingdom of Jerusalem. ✉ *Quai des Saulx 14, Bouillon* ☎ *061/468–303* 🌐 *archeoscopebouillon.be* 🎫 *€11* 🕐 *Closed weekdays in Jan.*

★ Château Fort de Bouillon
CASTLE/PALACE | Dominating the surrounding area from atop its rocky spur above the Semois River is one of Belgium's largest and oldest remaining castles. It was first documented in the 10th century, but it may be even older. In 1082, then-owner Godfrey of Bouillon sold the castle to the bishop of Liège in order to raise money to finance the First Crusade. Much of the building's current appearance is down to the French military engineer Vauban, who strengthened the walls in the 17th century on the orders of Louis XIV. You enter the main courtyard by first passing over three drawbridges. Once inside, climb to the top of the 16th-century Tour d'Autriche and you'll be rewarded with stunning views of the town and the Semois River. Kids will particularly enjoy a visit to the torture chamber and the dungeons. ✉ *Esplanade Godefroy 1, Bouillon* ☎ *061/464–202* 🌐 *www.bouilloninitiative.be* 🎫 *€11 (including entry to Musée Ducal)* 🕐 *Closed weekdays in Jan.*

Musée Ducal
HISTORY MUSEUM | This small museum has exhibits explaining the rich history of both the town and its castle. Your entrance ticket to the castle also covers your entry here. ✉ *Rue du Petit 1, Bouillon* ☎ *061/464–189* 🌐 *www.museeducalbouillon.be* 🎫 *€11 (including entry to castle)* 🕐 *Closed weekdays in Jan.*

Restaurants

L'Aristide

$$ | **BELGIAN** | Enjoying a prime riverside spot below the castle, L'Aristide stands out immediately for its bold and bright red color scheme. Food, on the other hand, is more a story of restrained elegance, with a simple but very tasty French-inspired menu that reflects the town's proximity to the border. **Known for:** food served all day; freshly shucked oysters; friendly service. *Average main: €20* ✉ *Quai du Rempart 1, Bouillon* ☎ *061/314–159* 🌐 *wallux.com/laristide* ⊙ *Closed Wed. and Thurs.*

Hotels

Hôtel Panorama

$$ | **HOTEL** | A big selling point at this large hotel is its location: on a hill across the river from the castle, with magnificent views from most rooms and from the expansive front terrace. **Pros:** free breakfast; views of the castle from the front rooms; spacious rooms. **Cons:** wellness center costs extra; cheaper rooms are quite small; hotel is a short but stiff walk uphill from the center. *Rooms from: €120* ✉ *Rue au-dessus de la ville 25, Bouillon* ☎ *061/466–138* 🌐 *www.panoramahotel.be* ⊙ *Closed Jan.; closed Wed. and Thurs. Apr.–Oct.; closed weekdays Nov., Dec., and Feb.–Mar.* *24 rooms* *Free Breakfast.*

Chapter 9

LUXEMBOURG

Updated by
Gareth Clark

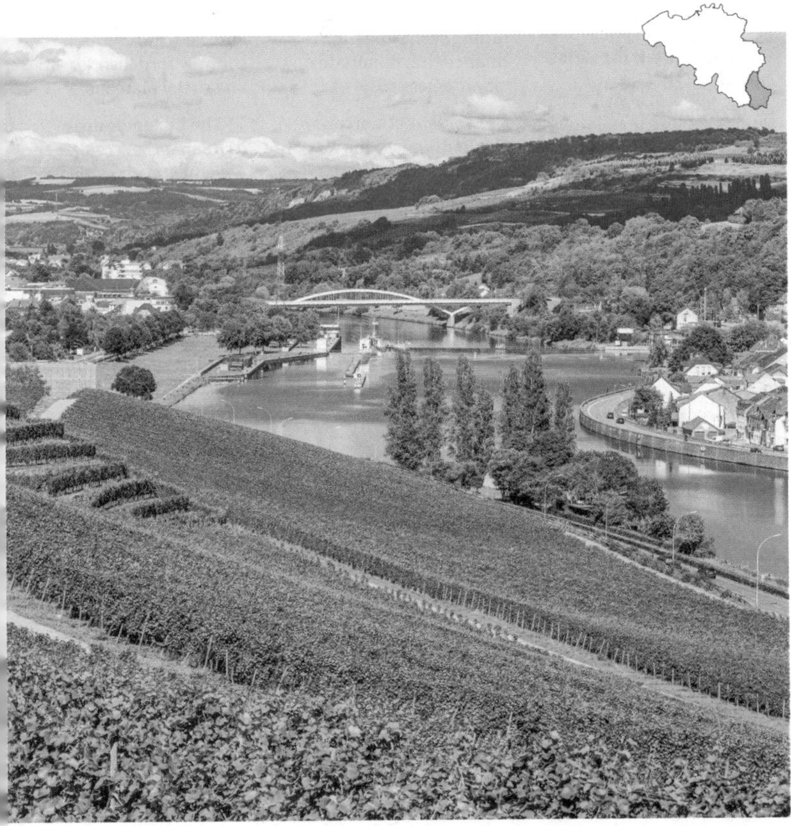

Sights	Restaurants	Hotels	Shopping	Nightlife
★★★★☆	★★★★★	★★★☆☆	★★★☆☆	★★★☆☆

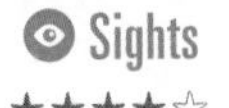

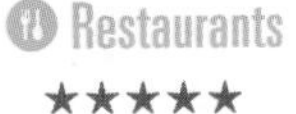

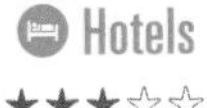

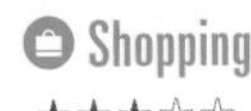

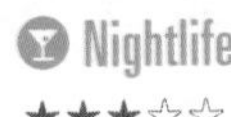

WELCOME TO LUXEMBOURG

TOP REASONS TO GO

★ **Wander the rock-topped capital.** The historic center of Luxembourg City made good use of its setting, turning a rock into an impenetrable fortress. Its walls might be mostly gone, but incredible relics survive.

★ **Explore fairy-tale castles.** More than 70 castles scatter Luxembourg, filled with history, art, and museums. Hikes let you take in these medieval wonders in their full glory.

★ **Walk incredible trails.** The Ardennes and "Little Switzerland" (Mullerthal) regions are riddled with beautiful walks wrapping riverine valleys, rocky plateaus, and wild woodlands.

★ **Visit World War II sites.** The country was scarred by its experiences in the mid-1940s, as the Battle of the Bulge raged. Explore museums and monuments.

★ **Sip Moselle wines.** The vineyards of the Moselle Valley are rightly famous. Visits to their wineries are both delicious and fascinating.

1 Luxembourg City. Raised high on a bluff over the gorges below, there are few more dramatic settings for a capital in Europe. Sadly, many of its medieval defenses were torn down in the mid-1800s, but a scattering of forts, casements, and thrilling nooks survive, making a fascinating contrast with the lively dining scene and high finance that dominates city life here now.

2 Esch-sur-Alzette and the Redlands. This was the industrial heartland of Luxembourg, and when the steel boom crashed in the 1960s, towns like Esch-sur-Alzette faced a stark future. But, instead of folding, this area was revived, as its old mines and pit villages were turned into living museums, like Fond-de-Gras.

3 Remich and the Moselle. These are the winelands of Luxembourg. Villages and vineyards scatter the banks of the Moselle, which runs the border with Germany. Explore them on the Route du Vin trail, or simply catch a boat at Remich and sail between Schengen, Ehnen, and Grevenmacher before heading to the nearby spa town of Mondorf-les-Bains to soak in its waters.

4 Echternach and Little Switzerland. This rocky land on the German border is riddled with spectacular castles, caves, walks, and history. In Echternach, you can glimpse the only traditional religious dancing festival left in Europe, or just wander its magnificent basilica in peace. From there, some of the wildest trails in the country ford lush forests and rocky plateaus.

5 The Luxembourg Ardennes. Few realize the Ardennes even spreads from France and Belgium into Luxembourg, but it covers most of its northern half. Discover river-wrapped villages such as Esch-sur-Sûre and its lakelands, or the historic Vianden where one of the finest castles in Luxembourg looms over the town, then finish high up in Clervaux, home to arguably the finest art treasure in the country. In between, you'll find endless walks through beautiful countryside.

BELGIUM
GERMANY
FRANCE
Troisvierges
Clervaux
Clerve River
Wiltz
Bastogne
Buderscheid
Pronsfeld
Bitburg
Vianden
Our River
Diekirch
Ettelbruck
Schieren
Colmar-Berg
Mertzig
Koetschette
Grosbous
Bissen
Reichlange
Echternach
Larochette
Mersch
Graulinster
Wasserbillig
Oberpallen
Saeul
Lintgen
Junglinster
Gonderange
Grevenmacher
Roodt-sur-Syre
Steinfort
Bridel
Bereldange
Capellen
Senningerberg
Luxembourg
Mamer
LUXEMBOURG
Bertrange
Howald
Hesperange
Bascharage
Pétange
Leudelange
Remich
Niederkorn
Bettembourg
Frisange
Differdange
Belvaux
Mondorf-les-Bains
Esch-sur-Alzette
Kayl
Dudelange
Rumelange
N68
E421
E42
N12
N18
E25
N30
410
N10
E29
51
N15
N14
N23
N22
N4
N8
E44
E411
N2
A4
407
31
A13
N52
E153
1
2
3
4
5
0
5 mi
0
5 km

Tiny Luxembourg, nestled between Germany, France, and Belgium, has been a pawn of world powers for much of its 1,000 years. Yet, from its history of siege and invasion, you would think it was filled with gold. In fact, it was the very defenses against these centuries of attacks that made it so desirable. An impregnable gem that all of Europe wanted—until they no longer did.

Today, Luxembourg is the little country that could: a world financial powerhouse filled with more Michelin-starred restaurants per capita than any nation outside Japan, and surrounded by winelands, medieval villages, hilltop castles, World War II sites, and huge swathes of the Ardennes. All this is packed into a country smaller in size than the state of Rhode Island. But it didn't come easy.

The region was first inhabited more than 3,000 years ago by pre-Celtic tribes, though its modern history didn't start until AD 963, when Charlemagne's descendant Siegfried, Count of the Ardennes, choose a meander on the Alzette River to fortify into the capital of his domain. Then, over the following centuries, everyone wanted a piece of Luxembourg: France, the Habsburgs, the Burgundians, the Netherlands, Prussia, Germany. There were few centuries when it didn't change hands.

By 1815, the country had become a Grand Duchy, albeit beholden to the Netherlands. Its lands were trimmed over various treaties (which is why you have a province called "Luxembourg" in Belgium) in return for more autonomy, finall achieving full independence in 1867. Iron cally, it would then spend the latter parts of the following century becoming one of the founders of the European Union (E.U.). Wearied by its experiences in World War II, Luxembourg's rulers sough to make sure it never happened again. In turn, its financial center grew and, along with its newfound political clout, it now has the third-highest per capita income ir the world.

Planning

Getting Here and Around

AIR

If you're arriving from Belgium, it makes no sense to fly here. But if you're coming internationally, then Luxembourg International, just 7 km (4¼ miles) to the east of the capital, is the country's only major airport. It is well connected, as you'd expect from any large financial center, and handles flights from most of Europe's capitals and major cities. Upon arrival, free buses (No. 16) connect to the downtown area of Luxembourg City every 10 to 30 minutes.

CONTACTS Luxembourg International Airport. ✉ *Rue de Trèves, Luxembourg City* ☎ *24/640* 🌐 *www.lux-airport.lu.*

BUS

Luxembourg's national bus system is extensive and reliable, with every village served at least hourly on weekdays, and often more regularly. Additionally, given the rail network is quite limited in its coverage, buses are the only way to reach certain villages without having a car. Connections for the south can be found in the capital, but for the Mullerthal and Éislek regions, you'll need to get the train to Ettelbruck, where you can catch bus services to most villages, or all the way up to Clervaux. Luxembourg City also has its own efficient internal bus system in addition to a new tram network. Remember that all buses are free to use.

CONTACTS Mobiliteit.lu. 🌐 *www.mobiliteit.lu/en.*

CAR

Despite the high ratio of drivers here (the highest per capita in Europe), a car is very useful for getting around outside the capital. Castles and villages are scattered far apart and connected by pleasant, well-maintained country roads. Even with the dawn of free public transport, it's just easier. Roads are generally in a good condition, signage is excellent, and gas prices are low (for Europe).

CONTACTS Europcar. ✉ *Rte. de Thionville 116, Luxembourg City* ☎ *40/4228* 🌐 *www.europcar.lu.*

TAXI

There is no Uber in Luxembourg. In the capital, you can call for a cab or pick one up at stands by the train station. Taxis are harder to find in the villages.

CONTACTS Taxi Colux. ✉ *Dernier Sol 24, Luxembourg City* ☎ *48/2233* 🌐 *www.colux.lu.*

TRAIN

Train is the best way to reach Luxembourg City if you're coming from Belgium. Regular services to and from Brussels run via Namur, Liège, and Arlon (on the Belgium-Lux border), taking around 3½ hours and costing €22. Direct services run every hour at peak times. Lines from Luxembourg City also connect to France (via Metz, Nancy, Strasbourg, Paris) and Germany (Koblenz). When traveling within the country, all services are free to use, but the network can be a little limited, with bus connections needed to reach certain villages. Everything runs via the capital, with the most useful lines linking Clervaux (via Ettelbruck) and Esch-sur-Alzette (on the Pétange line).

CONTACTS Société Nationale des Chemins de Fer Luxembourgeois (CFL). ✉ *Luxembourg Gare, pl. de la Gare 11, Luxembourg City* ☎ *24/892–489* 🌐 *www.cfl.lu.*

Hotels

Hotels in Luxembourg are mostly tidy and comfortable, rarely reaching the heights of luxury but often quite expensive for what they are. Most stays in Luxembourg City are relatively modern and range from big international chains, found near the airport and around Kirchberg, to family-run grande dames in the old town, to the cheaper new-builds around the train station. The older buildings are often more charming but tend to be restricted in their facilities by planning laws. Most hotels are packed with business travelers on weekdays, and offer reduced rates on weekends when their midweek clientele disappears. Outside the capital, particularly among the villages, hotels often take the form of inns, and the better ones typically double as the finer places to eat in town. Rates here are considerably lower than in the city, where you will rarely find a night's stay for less than €120, even in low season, and there are few to no Airbnb options. Youth hostels can be an appealingly wallet-friendly alternative in the cities and are mostly very modern, while those in the villages often rent bikes, kayaks, and outdoor equipment in summer. Alternatively, the Grand Duchy is well organized for campsites, especially in and around the Ardennes and Mullerthal regions where walkers are more prominent.

Restaurants

Luxembourg has more Michelin-star-starred restaurants per capita than any other European country. It is a haven for fine eateries, usually of the French variety, but it comes at a cost. It's not cheap to dine here, with restaurants in the capital regularly topping €30 and €40 for a main, which is why the city's more moderately priced luncheon menus are a boon to the budget traveler. Non-French restaurants present less expensive alternatives and, given the country's sizable population of people of Italian descent, pasta and pizza have almost acquired the status of "national cuisine." Fast-food eateries are also present in force, especially in the capital, as are, increasingly, vegan alternatives.

When it comes to what's served: "French quality, German quantity" goes the apt and common description. Most stick to the standard brasserie fare, dishing out beef entrecôte with peppercorn sauce and veal cordon bleu (stuffed with ham and cheese) by the dozen and heaped with frites (French fries). Yet this tiny country has its own earthy, heavily pork-focused cuisine, fresh off the farm and mixing French and German influences. Try local dishes such as *judd mat gaardebounen* (smoked pork shoulder with broad beans), *jambon d'Ardennes* (ham served cold with pickled onions), *choucroute* (sauerkraut and sausage), *gromperekichelcher* (fried potato patties), and the beloved *kniddelen* (fried gnocchi-like dumplings usually scattered with lardons or speck).

Lunch takes place mostly between noon and 2. Dinner, except in the fanciest restaurants, tends to be earlier than the European norm, generally between 7 and 9, though the capital, in particular, has an increasing number of bar-restaurants that continue serving long into the small hours.

HOTEL AND RESTAURANT PRICES

Hotel prices in the reviews are the lowest cost of a standard double room in high season. Restaurant prices in the reviews are the average cost of a main course at dinner, or if dinner is not served, at lunch.

What It Costs in Euros

	$	$$	$$$	$$$$
RESTAURANTS				
	under €12	€12–€22	€23–€30	over €30
HOTELS				
	under €100	€100–€150	€151–€220	over €220

When to Go

High Season: June, July, and August are peak tourist months for Luxembourg, when the weather is at its best. Airfares and hotel rates are also at their highest, and crowds at their thickest. Many restaurants close for a week or two in August.

Low Season: November through March is Luxembourg's low season, when both temperatures and prices are lower. In December they spike again for the holidays. Outside the capital, many museums and attractions are closed from October to Easter.

Value Season: The springtime months of April and May and the autumn months of September and October are lovely for visiting Luxembourg. Temperatures are lower than at their summer peaks, but so are crowd levels and prices.

Visitor Information

Unlike most city discount cards, the Luxembourg Card is valid for the entire country, affording free or reduced entry to most sights and a number of tours. They are valid for one (€13), two (€20), or three (€28) days for one person, or can be bought for a pair or a group. Cards are available from tourist information offices and online (*www.luxembourgcard.lu*).

CONTACTS Visit Luxembourg. ✉ *Luxembourg City* ☎ *42/82–821* 🌐 *www.visitluxembourg.com/en.*

Luxembourg City

391 km (243 miles) southeast of Amsterdam, 219 km (136 miles) southeast of Brussels, 29 km (18 miles) east of Arlon.

The capital, perched on a bluff at the confluence of the Pétrusse and Alzette rivers, goes by the same name as the country—*Lëtzebuerg* in Luxembourgish. And when Luxembourgers themselves refer to it, they merely say they are going *en ville* (to the city). But what a city it is.

The UNESCO-listed old town of Luxembourg is of necessity small, bound by the same rock walls that once made it so impregnable and coveted. Recent years have seen a transport revolution transform the city. A new funicular up to Kirchberg and an expanding tram system have both been introduced; and like the trains and well-established bus network, they're all free to use since 2020. But because of its size, the capital is eminently walkable, and this is a city that rewards those who see it on two feet.

Like the rest of Luxembourg, this is a city of transient workers. And of those that do live here, some 70% are foreigners. This has given the capital a cosmopolitan sheen, and there is often a discrepancy between the cozy café bars you'll find locals in and the noisy late-nighters the lively expat community frequent. But there's room for all in this tiny, unique capital of compromise.

GETTING HERE AND AROUND

AIR

Luxembourg International Airport, just 7 km (4¼ miles) to the east of the capital, is well-placed for access to the city. Free buses (No. 16) connect to the downtown area of the capital every 10 to 30 minutes. Currently, the tram doesn't connect to the airport, though plans are that it will by 2024.

BUS AND TRAM

An excellent network of free buses and trams services the capital. The tram line (T1) runs between Gare Central and Luxexpo (Kirchberg), making 15 stops along the way. For the center, get off at Hamlius; to visit the museums at Kirchberg, get off at Philharmonie.

Buses connect just about everywhere in the city, with services running every few minutes at important stops. Useful stops include: Gare Centrale (station), Hamilius (city center), Philharmonie (MUDAM), Pfaffenthal (panoramic elevator), and Grund (bars and restaurants). The light-green Gare-Rocade line services most of the major stops around the city center.

CAR

Cars are a burden in the capital. If possible, don't bring one. Luxembourg City has several major car parks, the largest being Stade de Lux, Gare, Hamilius, and Glacis. They are not free and charges mount up quickly. Roadside parking and outdoor bays are charged according to five zones, but most are free to use on weekends. Alternatively, park-and-ride car parks are found on the outskirts at

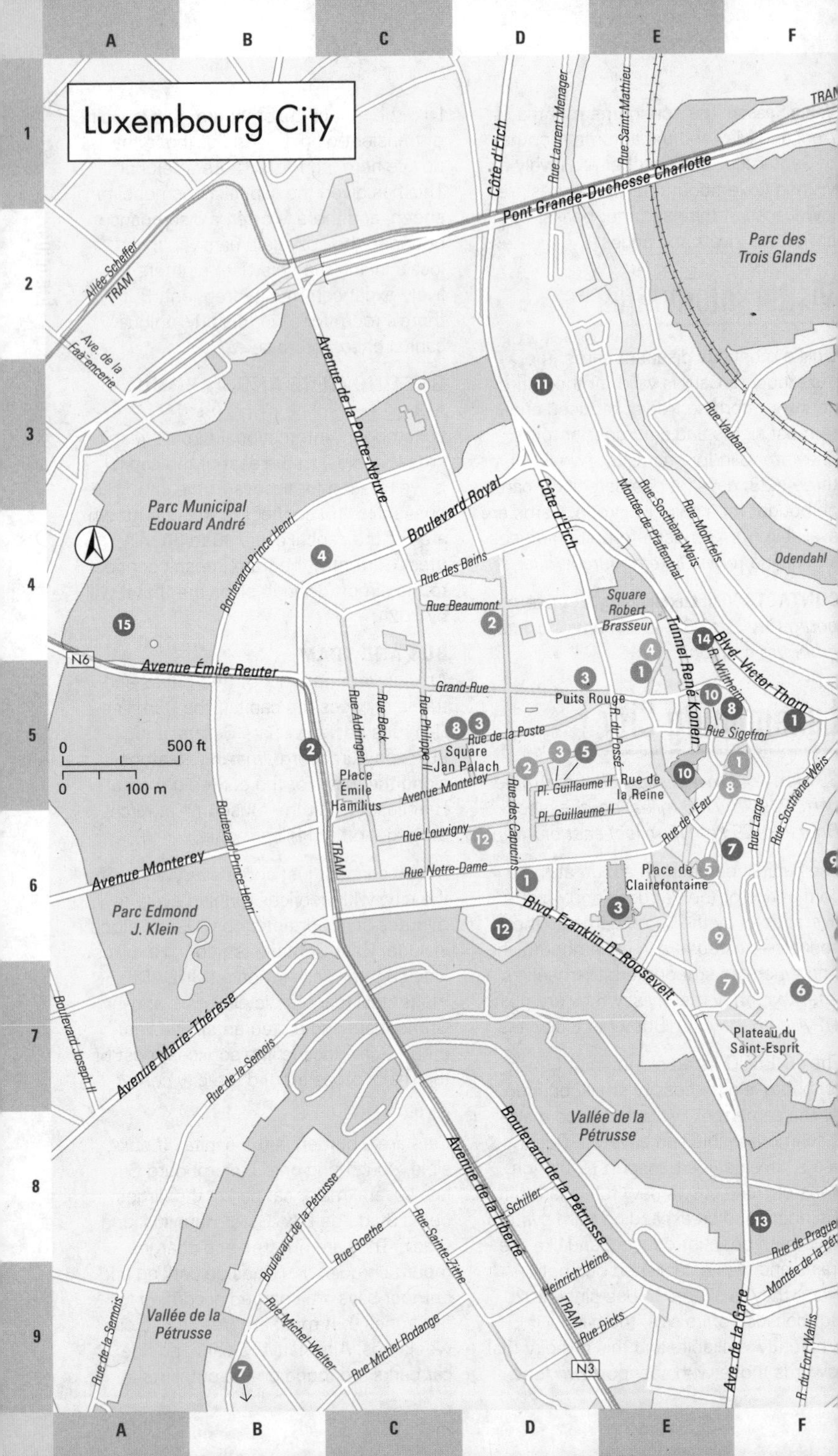
Luxembourg City
A
B
C
D
E
F
1
2
3
4
5
6
7
8
9
Pont Grande-Duchesse Charlotte
Côte d'Eich
Rue Laurent Menager
Rue Saint-Mathieu
TRAM
Parc des Trois Glands
Allée Scheffer
Ave. de la Faïencerie
Avenue de la Porte-Neuve
Rue Vauban
Parc Municipal Edouard André
Boulevard Royal
Montée de Pfaffenthal
Rue Sosthène Weis
Rue Mohrfels
Odendahl
Boulevard Prince Henri
Rue des Bains
Rue Beaumont
Square Robert Brasseur
Tunnel René Konen
Blvd. Victor Thorn
R. Wiltheim
N6
Avenue Émile Reuter
Grand-Rue
Puits Rouge
Rue Aldringen
Rue Beck
Rue Philippe II
R. du Fossé
Rue Sigefroi
Rue de la Poste
Square Jan Palach
0
500 ft
100 m
Place Émile Hamilius
Avenue Monterey
Rue des Capucins
Pl. Guillaume II
Rue de la Reine
Rue de l'Eau
Rue Large
Rue Louvigny
Rue Notre-Dame
Place de Clairefontaine
Parc Edmond J. Klein
Blvd. Franklin D. Roosevelt
Plateau du Saint-Esprit
Boulevard Joseph II
Avenue Marie-Thérèse
Rue de la Semois
Vallée de la Pétrusse
Avenue de la Liberté
Boulevard de la Pétrusse
Schiller
Rue Goethe
Rue Sainte-Zithe
Heinrich Heine
Rue de Prague
Montée de la Pétrusse
Rue Michel Welter
Rue Michel Rodange
Rue Dicks
N3
Ave. de la Gare
R. du Fort Wallis
1
2
3
4
5
6
7
8
9
10
11
12
13
14
15

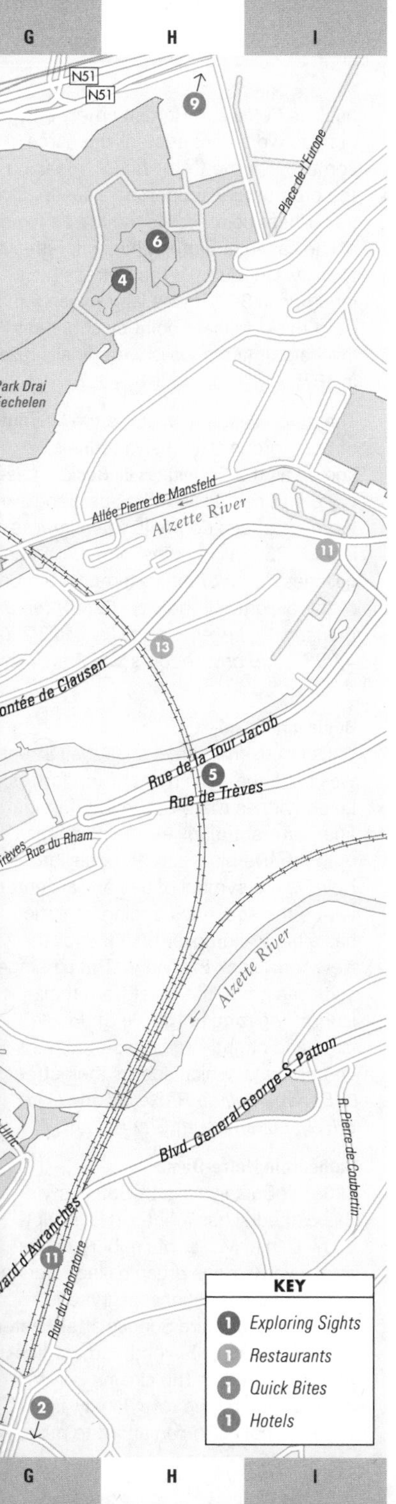

Sights

1 Bock.......................F5
2 Boulevard Royal........B5
3 Cathédrale Notre-Dame..............E6
4 Fort Thungun / Musée Draï Eechelen.................H2
5 Grund.....................H5
6 Musée d'Art Moderne Grand-Duc Jean (MUDAM)................H2
7 Musée d'Histoire de la Ville de Luxembourg.....E6
8 Musée National d'Histoire et d'Art........F5
9 Musée National d'Histoire Naturelle..................F6
10 Palais Grand-Ducal......E5
11 Panoramic Glass Elevator of Pfaffenthal..............D3
12 Place de la Constitution.............D6
13 Pont Viaduc F8
14 Porte des Trois Tours....E4
15 Villa Vauban.............A4

Restaurants

1 Am Tiirmschen...........F5
2 Beet/Seed D5
3 Brasserie Guillaume....D5
4 Chiggeri..................E4
5 Clairefontaine E6
6 Kamakura.................F6
7 L'Annexe..................E7
8 Les Copains D'Abord....E5
9 Mesa Verde E6
10 Mosconi F6
11 Mousel's Cantine I4
12 Roma.....................D6
13 Um Plateau.............H4

Quick Bites

1 Konrad E5
2 Namur....................D4
3 Oberweis D5

Hotels

1 Cravat....................D6
2 Graace Hotel............G9
3 Hôtel Français...........D5
4 Hôtel Le Royal............C4
5 Hôtel Vauban............D5
6 La Pipistrelle B&B.......F7
7 Le Châtelet B9
8 Le Place d'Armes........C5
9 Mama Shelter...........H1
10 Parc Beaux-Arts.........E5
11 Sofitel Le Grand Ducal.............G8

Bouillon, Kockelscheuer, Luxembourg Sud A and B, and Beggen. These are free for the first 24 hours, after which they cost €10 per day.

TAXI

Taxis can be easily found at Gare Centrale, place de la Constitution, place du Théâtre, rue de Willy Goergen, near Philharmonie, and on rue de la Tour Jacob (Clausen). Fares generally start at €2.50 and go up steeply from there (around €2.20 per kilometer). If you can, it's better to stick to public transport.

CONTACTS My Taxi Luxembourg. ✉ *Rte. d'Esch 39, Luxembourg City* ☎ *621/693–014* 🌐 *www.mytaxiluxembourg.lu.* **Alo Taxi.** ✉ *Bd. Prince Henri 29, Luxembourg City* ☎ *28/371–873* 🌐 *alotaxi.lu.*

TRAIN

The city has two major train stops: Gare Centrale, which is south of the center, and Pfaffenthal-Kirchberg, where you can catch the funicular that takes you up to the Kirchberg plateau. Trains coming from Belgium (IC) and France (TGV) will stop at Gare Centrale. From there, you can catch internal trains to the rest of the country, with useful direct lines to Clervaux and Esch-sur-Alzette.

VISITOR INFORMATION

CONTACTS Luxembourg City Tourist Information. ✉ *Pl. Guillaume II 30* ☎ *22/2809* 🌐 *www.visitluxembourg.com* Ⓜ *Tram: T1.*

Sights

If you aren't inclined to get a City Card, then it's worth bearing in mind that a number museums in the capital open till 8 or 9 pm on some days, when there's free entry for the last couple of hours of opening. Most attractions also close their doors on Monday.

★ Bock

MILITARY SIGHT | Luxembourg's raison d'être juts dramatically out over the Alzette river valley. This cliff served as the principal approach to the town as far back as Celtic and Roman times, until bridges were constructed. The name comes from the Celtic *büück,* meaning the promontory supporting a castle. Ove its farthest point looms the ruined towe of the castle of Sigfried himself, father o the city. He founded the fortress Lucilinburhuc in 963; it was later expanded from this dominant point by countless invaders until the walls were finally raze in 1875.

The main reason to visit are the labyrint of underground defensive tunnels, known as the **Casemates du Bock.** These were first built in 1644 by Spain and were expanded some 40 years later to include 23 km (14 miles) of undergrounc galleries. Tours of the casements are on of the delights of the city. ✉ *Montée de Clausen 10, Luxembourg City* ☎ *22/280 47/962–709 private tours* 💳 *€7* Ⓜ *Bus: 4, 10.*

Boulevard Royal

STREET | Luxembourg's mini–Wall Street was once the main moat of the fortress. Lined with as many of the 225 foreign financial institutions as could squeeze onto the five-block street, boulevard Royal is the symbol of a financial center where the securities-trading operation has a higher turnover than that of the New York Stock Exchange. The pinstripe suits can get some relief from their labors by gazing at Niki de St. Phalle's large and brightly colored statue, *La Tempérance,* which adorns their street. ✉ *Between pl. de Bruxelles and Côte d'Eich, Luxembourg City* Ⓜ *Tram: T1.*

Cathédrale Notre-Dame

CHURCH | Built in the late-Gothic style, this cathedral has a fine portal sculpted by Daniel Muller of Freiburg and an attractive Baroque organ gallery. During the fortnight of national pilgrimage starting on the third Sunday after Easter large numbers of Luxembourgers flock to their cathedral. The closing ceremony, attended by the royal family, is an event no politician can afford to miss,

ɔrt Thungen once protected Luxembourg City; today it houses a museum that details the structure's history.

ɘgardless of party and persuasion. The ʳypt, down a broad staircase, contains ɪe tomb of John the Blind, the gallant 4th-century king of Bohemia and Count f Luxembourg, who fell at the Battle f Crécy in France during the Hundred ears' War. Here, too, are the tombs of ɪe grand-ducal dynasty. ✉ *Rue Notre-ɔame, Luxembourg City* ☎ *44/743–401* ⊕ *www.cathol.lu* 🎫 *Free* Ⓜ *Bus: 4, 10.*

ort Thungun / Musée Draï Eechelen

ISTORY MUSEUM | In 1732, the Austri-n rulers of the city strengthened the runewald Front, expanding the original ɔrtifications to the northeast. They built ɔrt Thungen, which was enlarged and ɘinforced a century later. Today, its asements, tunnels, and mines host ɪe excellent Musée Draï Eechelen that etails the building's history and eventual emolition along with the rest of the ity's defenses in the 1867 Treaty of ondon. ✉ *Park Dräi Eechelen 5, Lux-mbourg City* ☎ *26/4335* ⊕ *m3e.public.ɩ* 🎫 *Free; €7 for temporary exhibitions* ⊙ *Museum closed Mon.* Ⓜ *Tram: T1.*

Grund

HISTORIC SIGHT | Once considered dank and squalid, this is one of the oldest parts of the city. Historically, it was where the capital's craftsmen once lived. Today, its houses demand enormous sums—even by Luxembourg standards. In recent years, it has become a popular going-out area. You'll find chic restau-rants and exclusive clubs among the skylighted, renovated town houses and what used to be tumbledown laborers' homes. If you don't fancy the steep walk, an elevator goes to the Upper Town's Plateau du Saint-Esprit. ✉ *Luxembourg City* ✥ *Alzette River Valley: R. Munster, R. de Trèves, Bisserwée* Ⓜ *Bus: 15, 23.*

★ **Musée d'Art Moderne Grand-Duc Jean (MUDAM)** (*Modern Art Museum*)

ART MUSEUM | This gem of a gallery, on the western edge of the Kirchberg plateau, is as much an architectural landmark as it is a museum. The designs of architect I.M. Pei make this stunning edifice as eye-catching as the works of modern art on show within. The building is a mix of limestone and glass—the latter formed into pyramids that both mimic the church spires of the old city across the Alzette valley, and echo Pei's similar work for the Louvre in Paris. The museum's interior is light and airy and the perfect foil for the changing exhibitions by internationally renowned contemporary artists. There are no permanent displays, so repeat visits are always rewarding. Entrance is free between 6 and 9 pm on Wednesday. ✉ *Park Dräi Eechelen 3, Luxembourg City* ☎ *45/37851* 🌐 *www.mudam.lu* 🎫 *€8* 🕒 *Closed Tues.* Ⓜ *Tram: T1.*

Musée d'Histoire de la Ville de Luxembourg (*Luxembourg City Historical Museum*)
HISTORY MUSEUM | Partially underground, this clever museum traces the development of the city over 1,000 years, working its way up through the centuries as you ascend floors. Its lowest levels show the town's preserved ancient stonework. From a glass-wall elevator, you can also enjoy a wonderful view of the ravine from the upper floors. There's free entry every Thursday from 6 to 8. ✉ *Rue du St-Esprit 14, Luxembourg City* ☎ *47/964–500* 🌐 *www.citymuseum.lu* 🎫 *€5* 🕒 *Closed Mon.* Ⓜ *Bus: 2, 4.*

Musée National d'Histoire et d'Art (*National Museum of History and Art*)
ART MUSEUM | The museum lies in one of the oldest parts of town, on the site of the old fish market that once formed the crossroads between two Roman roads. Inside, it has some outstanding paintings by the Expressionist Joseph Kutter, probably Luxembourg's greatest artist. The art gallery includes a fine Cranach and two Turner watercolors of the Luxembourg fortress. It also hosts the spectacular Bentinck-Thyssen collection of 15th- to 19th-century art, including works by Bruegel, Rembrandt, Canaletto, and other masters. The lower floors have been excavated from the rock and are given over to archaeological discoveries, including some fine Roman mosaics, though their descriptions are sadly not signed in English. ✉ *Marché-aux-Poissons, Luxembourg City* ☎ *47/93–301* 🌐 *www.mnha.lu* 🎫 *Free; temporary exhibitions €7* 🕒 *Closed Mon.* Ⓜ *Bus: 4, 10.*

Musée National d'Histoire Naturelle (*National Museum of Natural History*)
SCIENCE MUSEUM | Housed in a converted women's prison in the Grund, this museum has thought-provoking interactive exhibits and dioramas, with an environmental message aimed at both a local and global level. There's free entry on Tuesday from 5.30 until 8. ✉ *Rue Münster 25, Luxembourg City* ☎ *46/22–331* 🌐 *www.mnhn.lu* 🎫 *€5* 🕒 *Closed Mon.* Ⓜ *Bus: 23.*

Palais Grand-Ducal (*Grand-Ducal Palace*)
CASTLE/PALACE | The city's finest building dates from the 16th century. Its elaborate facade shows a Flemish Renaissance influence, with ornate balconies and a symmetrical exterior, and it was formerly the home to the Grand Ducal royal family. It is now mainly used for business and entertaining, though in July and August it opens its doors to visitors, offering the chance to explore its extensive art collection, which was dispersed during World War II before being returned, and the Hall of Kings where foreign envoys are officially received. ✉ *Rue du Marché-aux Herbes 17, Luxembourg City* ☎ *22/2809* 🎫 *€7* 🕒 *Closed Sept.–June* Ⓜ *Bus: 4, 10*

Panoramic Glass Elevator of Pfaffenthal
VIEWPOINT | Pfaffenthal, like the Grund, lingers on the Alzette River at the foot of the great rock on which the Upper City perches. This was always a place for the city's have-nots. It used to be home to a large number of tanneries; dirty, smelly work purposefully kept downstream of the rest. In more recent times, while its near neighbor filled with bars and hip restaurants, this sleepy area went forgotten until in 2016 a glass elevator to the Upper Town was unveiled, followed by a funicular to the Kirchberg plateau (Pfaffenthal-Kirchberg railway station). There's still little else to do here, but bo

ɪxembourg City's finest building, the Palais Grand-Ducal, has an elaborate Flemish Renaissance facade.

ffer magnificent views, and it's worth ɪe stroll down from Fort Thungen or the earby bars of Rives du Clausen just to de either. ✉ *Rue du Pont 2, Luxembourg City* Ⓜ *Bus: 4, 18.*

lace de la Constitution

LAZA/SQUARE | This square, which is ome to a bustling fairground during vinter, is marked by the gilt *Gëlle Fra* Golden Woman), set atop a tall column. his was originally erected to commemoate soldiers lost during World War I. But, 1940, it was torn down by the occupyɪg Nazi forces amid local protests. Plans ɔ rebuild the monument were put on old after the war when the gold-plated tatue went missing. It wasn't found gain until 1980, when fragments of it vere mysteriously discovered beneath a ports stadium. No one knows how it got ɪere. The current version was rebuilt in 984 incorporating pieces of the original nd has become a powerful symbol for ɪe city. ✉ *Bd. F.D. Roosevelt and rue Chimay, Luxembourg City* Ⓜ *Bus: 10.*

Pont Viaduc (*Luxembourg Viaduct*)

BRIDGE | The best views are to be found from atop the **Pont Viaduc** (or la Passerelle). Built in the mid-19th century, this 290-meter-long bridge spans the valley and offers magnificent glimpses of the rocky ledges—partly natural, partly manmade—on which the city was founded. Below you can see the (normally) beautiful **Vallée de la Pétrusse,** a broad park full of willows that lies in the canyon of the Pétrusse River. ✉ *Between av. de la Gare and bd. F.D. Roosevelt, Luxembourg City* Ⓜ *Bus: 29.*

Porte des Trois Tours (*Gate of the Three Towers*)

NOTABLE BUILDING | These three turrets, remains of the fortress, are among the city's most romantic sights. The oldest of the towers was built around 1050. During the French Revolution, this was the location of the guillotine. From here you can clearly see the source of Luxembourg's strength as a fortress: the Bock. ✉ *Bd. Victor Thorn, Luxembourg City* Ⓜ *Tram: T1.*

A view of Luxembourg City's Place de la Constitution and the Adolphe Bridge in the background.

Villa Vauban

ART GALLERY | Also billed as the Musée d'Art de la Ville de Luxembourg (City of Luxembourg Art Gallery), this lovely white mansion house is surrounded by perfectly tended gardens and feels like a haven of peace in the heart of the bustling city. Having undergone several face-lifts and changes of use since it was first built by the wealthy owner of a glove factory in 1873, major renovation work has given the building a new life as a permanent home for Luxembourg City's collection of Old Masters. Works by Canaletto and Van Dyck, to name but two, are juxtaposed with new pieces on matching themes by contemporary artists. Entry is free between 6 and 9 pm on Friday. ✉ *Av. Emile Reuter 18, Luxembourg City* ☎ *47/964–900* 🌐 *www.villavauban.lu* 🎫 *€5* ⏲ *Closed Tues.* Ⓜ *Tram: T1.*

Restaurants

It's no surprise that a city as wealthy as Luxembourg has some excellent fine dining options, with prices to match. Bookings are a must, especially mid-week. Hordes of suits snap up the most prestigious tables, especially at lunch-time, where you'll find some good-value prix-fixe deals at the higher-end eateries. Some of the best meals are to be found in the cobbled byways around the Grand Ducal Palace, particularly on rue de l'Eau and off place de Clairefontaine.

Am Tiirmschen

$$$ | **BRASSERIE** | Those after good Luxembourgish food inevitably boil their choice down to Am Tiirmschen or Um Dierfgen (on Côte d'Eich). Neither restaurant will let you down, but this old hand gets the nod because of its setting. **Known for:** good, swift service; a romantic setting in a building wonderfully hidden off a side street; Luxembourgish classics you need to try at least once. 💲 *Average main: €2*

Rue de l'Eau 32, Luxembourg City 26/270–733 www.amtiirmschen.lu Closed Sun. and Mon. Bus: 2, 4.

eet/Seed

$ | **VEGETARIAN** | This vegan restau-
nt-café has two levels. Downstairs, the afé (Seed) is more of a juice and cocktail ar; above, Beet conjures an upmarket ist-food vibe, dishing up plant-based urgers and soups. **Known for:** it's great alue for the city center; lip-smacking egan treats that don't skimp on the cal-ries; service is quick (if haughty). *Av-rage main: €15 Pl. Guillaume II 26, uxembourg City 26/201–375 www.eet.lu Closed Mon. Tram: T1.*

rasserie Guillaume

$$ | **SEAFOOD** | As you might expect om a city 300 km (186 miles) from e nearest coastline, Luxembourg isn't nown for its seafood. Yet this friendly rasserie on place Guillaume II bucks e trend. **Known for:** a pleasant terrace n one of the nicer squares in the city; ere just aren't many rivals for good eafood in the capital; late-night service ill 1 am nightly) for those not in a rush. *Average main: €25 Pl. Guillaume 12, Luxembourg City 26/202–020 brasserieguillaume.lu Tram: T1.*

higgeri

$$ | **CONTEMPORARY** | The name means chicory" in Luxembourgish but also anslates colloquially as "a funny urprise," which is exactly what this staurant is. The menu features gourmet od with a twist—such as the dinner-in-e-dark option where taste takes over om sight. **Known for:** an experimental enu that is never short of culinary hocks; the bar is a charming hangout; e twice-weekly (Tuesday and Thursday) dark" dinners are a hoot. *Average ain: €26 Rue du Nord 15, Luxem-ourg City 22/9936 www.chiggeri.lu Closed Sun. and Mon. Tram: T1.*

★ Clairefontaine

$$$$ | **FRENCH** | Having always been the go-to for government ministers and visiting dignitaries, long-standing own-er-chef Arnaud Magnier has attempted to shake things up a bit. Out went the old red leather, in came a bolder new look. **Known for:** a spot on one of the city's most attractive squares; the terrace is delightful in summer; simply some of the best cooking in Luxembourg. *Average main: €105 Pl. de Clairefontaine 9, Luxembourg City 46/2211 www.restaurantclairefontaine.lu Closed weekends Jacket and tie Bus: 4, 10.*

Kamakura

$$$$ | **JAPANESE** | If heavy Western cuisine palls, take the elevator down from St-Esprit to the Grund and try this elegant Japanese restaurant. It's a long-standing favorite among locals, with a number of fixed-price menus (from €65) offering delicate, nouvelle-accented dishes, artfully presented and graciously served. À la carte specialties, considerably more expensive, include impeccably fresh sashimi and light tempura vegetables. **Known for:** the best sushi in the country; a menu that changes with the seasons; impeccable service. *Average main: €34 Rue Münster 4, Luxembourg City 47/0604 www.kamakura.lu Closed Sun. Bus: 23.*

L'Annexe

$$$$ | **FRENCH** | The annex of nearby Clairefontaine in both name and nature, this is altogether a more down-to-earth (and cheaper) dining experience, especially at lunchtime where you'll find a good three-course prix fixe for €30. The modern and simply furnished restaurant has a terrace out front and panoramic windows—both provide spectacular views over the Grund as you enjoy delicious bistro-style French food. **Known for:** Michelin-quality food at a cheaper price than its sister restaurant; good-value lunch menus; a quiet setting, away from the city bustle.

Ⓢ *Average main: €32 ✉ Rue du Saint Esprit 7, Luxembourg City ☎ 26/262–507 ⊕ www.lannexe.lu ⊙ Closed Sun. and Mon. Ⓜ Bus: 23.*

Les Copains D'Abord

$$$ | FRENCH | Its name ("Friends First") quotes a popular 1960s song by French *chanteur* George Brassens. It's a coziness replicated on a warm hug of a menu that fixes its ambitions on burgers and the comfier corners of French cuisine. **Known for:** big portions, draft beer, and a solid wine selection; romantic setting on a quiet street; good value for what you get. Ⓢ *Average main: €25 ✉ Rue de l'Eau 24, Luxembourg City ☎ 26/200–273 ⊕ restaurantlescopainsdabordlux.lu ⊙ Closed Sun. Ⓜ Bus: 2, 4.*

Mesa Verde

$$$ | VEGETARIAN | This was the first meat-free restaurant in Luxembourg back in 1990. Today, its vegetarian, vegan, and seafood menu typically piles on myriad flavors (some more successfully than others) as tofu, seitan, spring rolls, veggies, samosas, rice, vol-au-vents, and creamy Thai curry sauces spill across the plate. **Known for:** a nice tree-shaded terrace opens up across the street in summer; veggie comfort food to bring a smile to your face; the occasional band livens up the evening. Ⓢ *Average main: €24 ✉ Rue du St. Esprit 11, Luxembourg City ☎ 46/4126 ⊙ Closed Sun. and Mon. Ⓜ Bus: 2, 4.*

★ Mosconi

$$$$ | ITALIAN | It might have lost one of its Michelin stars but there's no doubting the quality of this excellent eatery—still, arguably, one of the best in the Grand Duchy. It enjoys a perfect setting on the banks of the Alzette River in the heart of the Grund district. **Known for:** a sensuous dining experience of magnificent flavors; the menu is pure indulgence; superlative selection of Italian wines. Ⓢ *Average main: €37 ✉ Rue Münster 13, Luxembourg City ☎ 54/6994 ⊕ www.mosconi.lu ⊙ Closed Sun. and Mon. Jacket required Ⓜ Bus: 23.*

Mousel's Cantine

$$ | EUROPEAN | Directly adjoining the former Mousel brewery, now the Rives de Clausen entertainment district, this comfortable, wood-paneled café serves up heaping platters of local specialties—braised and grilled ham, sausage, broad beans, and fried potatoes—to be washe[d] down with crockery steins of Clausel and unfiltered Gezwickelte beers. New owners have taken over in the last coup[le] of years, but the menu remains very much the same. **Known for:** good-value Luxembourgish dishes; refreshing local beer in a popular going-out area; big portions. Ⓢ *Average main: €22 ✉ Montée d[e] Clausen 46, Luxembourg City ☎ 47/019[…] ⊙ Closed Sun.*

Roma

$$$ | ITALIAN | History courses through th[e] menu here. The first Italian restaurant to open in Luxembourg (back in 1950) is st[ill] arguably the best loved in the city. **Know[n] for:** friendly professional service; it's an institution among locals, and worthy of their love; seasonal menus keep things fresh. Ⓢ *Average main: €30 ✉ Rue Louvigny 5, Luxembourg City ☎ 22/369[…] ⊕ roma.lu ⊙ Closed Sun. and Mon. Ⓜ Tram: T1.*

Um Plateau

$$$ | BRASSERIE | A number of eateries here skewer that middle ground betwee[n] bar and restaurant; this does it better than most. Chic, cozy, and with one of the more packed terraces in the city, Um Plateau sits aside from the rest of the Grund. **Known for:** open late; fun terrace; good small plates. Ⓢ *Average main: €29 ✉ Plateau Altmunster 6, Luxembourg City ☎ 22/3692 ⊕ umplateau.lu ⊙ Close[d] Sun. Ⓜ Bus: 23.*

Coffee and Quick Bites

onrad

$ | **CAFÉ** | A slightly eccentric café bar set ı a vaulted cellar. There are homemade akes, organic snacks, decent coffee, nd not a single piece of matching furni- ure. **Known for:** hang around for the live nusic and shows; the cakes are pretty ood; it's a charming little spot to rest our feet. *Average main: €12 ✉ Rue du Nord 7, Luxembourg City ☎ 26/201–894 Bus: 2, 4.*

lamur

| **CAFÉ** | A Luxembourg favorite since 863, this classic café (there are a pair f locations in the city) attracts everyone rom shoppers to young professionals. ts city-center branch specializes in hocolates, delicious pastries, and coffee nd sandwiches. **Known for:** a caffeinated aven while shopping; if you aren't in the nood for something sweet, the sand- viches are good; perfect for pastries, akes, and snacks. *Average main: €10 ✉ Rue des Capucins 27, Luxembourg City ☎ 352/223–408 🌐 www.namur.lu Closed Sun. Tram: T1.*

berweis

$ | **CAFÉ** | **FAMILY** | Arguably Luxembourg's nost famous patisserie-café is also the nventor of the "*bamkuch*," a strange, ibbed pipe of biscuity almond sponge overed in icing. Light lunches are avail- ble, with the likes of quiche Lorraine nd spinach pie on offer, and there's a uiet terrace on the street. **Known for:** uperb cakes and chocolates to try; their ot chocolate is a must in winter; the astries make for a good post-break- ast pick-me-up. *Average main: €12 ✉ Grand Rue 16, Luxembourg City ☎ 47/0703 🌐 www.oberweis.lu Closed Sun. Tram: T1.*

Hotels

Cravat

$$$ | **HOTEL** | This hotel has been in the Cravat family for over a century, battling modernity every step of the way—the phrase "grande dame" was coined for places like this. **Pros:** it's a living, breathing slice of old Luxembourg; even the bar is like stepping back into the 1950s; the elevators are works of art. **Cons:** rooms can be rather basic; there are few modern facilities, so there's not much luxury for the price; there's a fine line between vintage and dated. *Rooms from: €176 ✉ Bd. F.D. Roosevelt 29, Luxembourg City ☎ 22/1975 🌐 www.hotelcravat.lu 59 rooms Free Breakfast Bus: 4, 10.*

Graace Hotel

$$ | **HOTEL** | Your appreciation of sustainable design may determine your affection for this clever hotel in the hip Bonnevoie area. **Pros:** rooms come with a small terrace area; there's nothing else like it in Luxembourg; expect tasty organic breakfasts (€17 per person). **Cons:** it's a bit of a walk (plus a 10-minute tram ride) to the center; standard rooms are perfect for one, but moving around is Tetris-like for two; you're directly under a noisy flight path. *Rooms from: €150 ✉ Rue Sigismond 10, Luxembourg City ☎ 26/684–343 🌐 www.graacehotel.com 30 rooms No Meals Bus: 2.*

Hôtel Français

$$ | **HOTEL** | Set in an enviable location in the city, on the historic place d'Armes, this small, smart boutique stay offers decent value for its prestigious setting. **Pros:** family-owned stay with lots of character and history; central stay with a sumptuous café-restaurant; free use of a public computer and printer. **Cons:** there are few to no facilities; there's no parking in this part of the city; rooms on the square can be noisy. *Rooms from: €140 ✉ Pl. d'Armes 14, Luxembourg City*

☎ 47/4534 🌐 www.hotelfrancais.lu 🛏 22 rooms 🍴 Free Breakfast Ⓜ Tram: T1.

★ Hôtel Le Royal

$$$$ | HOTEL | There's no grander stay in the city. **Pros:** check-in is 1 pm and checkout is noon; excellent wellness facilities and rooms are pet friendly; the breakfast spread befits the grand setting. **Cons:** it's not as historical as stays in the old town; the hotel lies on a busy main road; its one of the more expensive stays in the city. *$ Rooms from: €260 ✉ Bd. Royal 12, Luxembourg City ☎ 24/161–61 🌐 www.leroyal.com 🛏 210 rooms 🍴 Free Breakfast.*

Hôtel Vauban

$$ | HOTEL | A decent-value city-center stay on the bustling, likeable place Guillaume II. **Pros:** the dining options downstairs are really good; breakfasts are impressive and can be taken on the terrace; quiet efficiency and a good location in the city. **Cons:** there's little remarkable about the basic rooms; it has the feel of a business stay—brisk and useful; the square is pretty noisy on market days. *$ Rooms from: €140 ✉ Pl. Guillaume II 10, Luxembourg City ☎ 22/0493 🌐 hotelvauban.lu 🛏 21 rooms 🍴 Free Breakfast Ⓜ Bus: 2, 5.*

★ La Pipistrelle B&B

$$$ | B&B/INN | This historic B&B of just four rooms lies on the fringes of the Grund, next to Cafe des Artistes and only a steep, five-minute walk up to the city (or just take the handy elevator). **Pros:** great setting on the edge of the Grund; you've got a wealth of drinking and dining close by; it's living history. **Cons:** no parking; it's a B&B, so there are few facilities; there's no elevator or disabled access to rooms and the staircase is narrow. *$ Rooms from: €215 ✉ Montée du Grund 26, Luxembourg City ☎ 621/300–351 🌐 www.pipistrelle.lu 🛏 4 rooms 🍴 Free Breakfast Ⓜ Bus: 23.*

Le Châtelet

$$ | HOTEL | Set on the edge of a quiet residential area but within easy reach of the train station and the center, this pleasant hotel makes the most of its small setting. **Pros:** free use of sauna and gym; a glorious terrace that's a real sun trap; the Cantine restaurant has a glowing reputation. **Cons:** parking costs €15 per night, though this is relatively cheap for Luxembourg; rooms are simple affairs; the area isn't the most charming in the city. *$ Rooms from: €145 ✉ Bd. de la Pétrusse 2, Luxembourg City ☎ 40/2101 🌐 www.chatelet.lu 🛏 39 rooms 🍴 Free Breakfast Ⓜ Tram: T1.*

★ Le Place d'Armes

$$$$ | HOTEL | Simply the nicest-looking rooms in the city. **Pros:** the rooms really are something special; you're in the shopping heart of the city; guests have access to a digital magazine subscription. **Cons:** none of it comes cheap; no pool or wellness facilities; the square outside can be noisy for overlooking rooms. *$ Rooms from: €280 ✉ Pl. d'Armes 18, Luxembourg City ☎ 27/4737 🌐 www.hotel-leplacedarmes.com 🛏 28 rooms 🍴 Free Breakfast Ⓜ Tram: T1.*

Mama Shelter

$$$ | HOTEL | "Mama" likes to make an impression. **Pros:** the rooftop has petanque, table tennis, and nightly DJs; a place in the pantheon of great hotel pillows and mattresses awaits; all films are free on your TV. **Cons:** all the talk of "free porn" on the TVs isn't very family-friendly; the branding can get a bit much and parking costs €17 a night; Kirchberg is pretty removed from the old center. *$ Rooms from: €179 ✉ Rue du Fort Niedergruenewald 2, Kirchberg, Luxembourg City ☎ 20/804–400 🌐 mamashelter.com/luxembourg 🛏 146 rooms 🍴 No Meals Ⓜ Tram: T1.*

Parc Beaux-Arts

$$$$ | HOTEL | The owners run a collection of stays around the city (including Parc Bel Air and Parc Belvue), though neither olds a candle to this historic boutique otel. **Pros:** the location couldn't be more entral; having just 11 suites makes it eel unique; the history of the building nsures any stay is just that little bit speial. **Cons:** its UNESCO-protected status neans it lacks the facilities of its sister otels; there is a lift but it is reached via tairs, so it's not disability friendly; overight parking in the garage is a crazy €45 er night. *Rooms from: €229 ✉ Rue de igefroi 1, Luxembourg City ☎ 26/86–761 www.parcbeauxarts.lu 11 rooms No Meals Ⓜ Bus: 4, 10.*

ofitel Le Grand Ducal

$$$ | HOTEL | What it lacks in setting ying beside one of the busier roads in ne city), Le Grand Ducal makes up for n spectacular views: gazing over the 'étrusse Valley and across to the rockopped center. **Pros:** great full-English reakfast spread; those wonderful views ever get old; there's a 24-hour fitness enter. **Cons:** it's one of the pricier stays n the city; you're not in the historical art of town; some road noise. *Rooms rom: €284 ✉ Rue du Laboratoire 35, uxembourg City ☎ 24/8771 🌐 all.accor. om 128 rooms Free Breakfast Bus: 29.*

Nightlife

here's a lively bar scene in each of uxembourg City's neighborhoods, with laces staying open until 1 am most venings. Midweek, bars tend to flood vith city workers after 6, and Wednesday for reasons known to no one) tends to e the most popular night out.

BARS AND CAFÉS

raft Corner

REWPUBS | The lack of a decent brewpub n the city was evident before this plucky ar opened in the up-and-coming Bonnevoie area, south of the railway tracks. t styles itself as a gastro bar, but the ure here is the beer: around a dozen on ap, all from its own brewery. These run the gamut from IPAs and German-style wheat beers to the obligatory porter and less-common spelt brews. *✉ Rue de Bonnevoie 112 🌐 craftcorner.lu Ⓜ Bus: 2.*

De Gudde Wëllen

LIVE MUSIC | A colorful two-floor music bar on the peaceful cobbles of rue du St. Esprit. On weekends, it focuses on live bands (of the fuzzy-guitar, alt-rock variety), with the second floor turning into a blur of dancing youths. In warmer weather, they open a terrace a short walk away that has proved just as popular in recent years. *✉ Rue du St. Esprit 17, Luxembourg City ☎ 26/202–886 🌐 www.deguddewellen.lu Ⓜ Bus: 4, 10.*

Ënnert de Steiler

BARS | The building of the oldest café-bar in the city dates back to the 14th century. It is a work of art, with stone arches framing the exterior. Inside, you're as likely to find besuited twentysomething city types belting out Oasis songs, dancing on the spot to '90s dance music, or a live salsa band. It's a real pick 'n' mix. *✉ Rue de la Loge 2, Luxembourg City ☎ 20/202–196 🌐 www.facebook.com/EnnertdeSteiler Ⓜ Bus: 2, 4.*

Go Ten

BARS | The decor and snacks in this stylish city center bar are both Japanese inspired. Inside, it's fleshed out in colorful floral blinds and foliage, though the cooler kids stick to the terrace outside. *✉ Rue du Marché-aux-Herbes 10, Luxembourg City ☎ 26/203–652 🌐 www.facebook.com/gotenbar Ⓜ Bus: 2, 5.*

Scott's Pub

PUBS | Scott's Pub, at the bottom of the valley, is a popular gathering place for English-speakers, where outdoor tables line the picturesque Alzette. Flooding in 2021 destroyed much of the terrace and interior, but it has had a refurb and is as good as new. Still the best place to have a pint of bitter in the Grund. *✉ Bisserwée 4, Luxembourg City ☎ 26/226-475 🌐 www.scotts.lu Ⓜ Bus: 23.*

Urban

BARS | Lying in the maw of the lively rue du Marché-aux-Herbes bar street, this enduringly cool spot has always been a step ahead of its noisier, more louche competitors. A long bar, good cocktails, and a busy terrace in the warmer months ensure its popularity among the international-set regulars. ✉ *Rue de la Boucherie 2, Luxembourg City* ☎ *26/478–578* 🌐 *www.urban.lu* Ⓜ *Tram: T1.*

Vinoteca

WINE BARS | The hidden terrace at this popular wine bar and shop, near the old fish market, is a rare find. It has superb views across to the forts of Kirchberg. The collection of local wines is naturally excellent, with a decent selection by the glass accompanied by some rather pricey tapas. ✉ *Rue Wiltheim 6, Luxembourg City* ☎ *26/864–434* 🌐 *barvinoteca.lu* Ⓜ *Bus: 4, 10.*

Vis-à-vis

CAFÉS | A welcome stop for a postshopping drink. This café-bar spans that happy divide between local hangout and tourist-friendly escape. It has made looking unintimidating into an art form, and the small tables outside are prized real estate in summer. ✉ *Rue Beaumont 2, Luxembourg City* Ⓜ *Bus: 10, 14.*

Performing Arts

MUSIC

Philharmonie

MUSIC | Luxembourg is home to the Orchestre Philharmonique du Luxembourg. It performs regular concerts in the Philharmonie concert hall in Kirchberg, a striking building encircled by 823 slender white columns. Lunchtime concerts are often free. ✉ *Pl. de l'Europe 1, Luxembourg City* ☎ *26/322–632* 🌐 *www.philharmonie.lu* Ⓜ *Tram: T1.*

THEATER

Grand Théâtre

THEATER | Good traveling plays (mostly in French and German) pass through the municipal theater, as do a number of operas, ballets, and dance recitals. You can always catch something interesting. ✉ *Rond-Point Robert Schuman 1, Luxembourg City* ☎ *47/963–900* 🌐 *www.theatres.lu* 🎫 *From €20* Ⓜ *Bus: 4, 18.*

Théâtre des Capucins

THEATER | This renovated 17th-century monastery hosts both local troupes and traveling companies spanning opera, dance, and theater. ✉ *Pl. de Thèâtre 9, Luxembourg City* ☎ *47/963–900* 🌐 *www.theatres.lu* 🎫 *From €15* Ⓜ *Tram: T1.*

VISUAL ARTS

Abbaye de Neumünster (*Neumünster Abbey Cultural Center*)

ARTS CENTERS | Since the Benedictine monks were expelled from Luxembourg during the French Revolution, this former abbey has had many owners. For much of the 20th century it served as a men's prison, but has since been transformed into a cultural center, hosting a variety of temporary exhibitions, lectures, and jazz performances. ✉ *Rue Münster 28, Luxembourg City* ☎ *26/205–2444* 🌐 *www.neimenster.lu* Ⓜ *Bus: 23.*

Casino Luxembourg

ARTS CENTERS | In addition to a number of art galleries, Luxembourg has a permanent space for modern and contemporary art exhibits, the Casino. This is where the Hungarian composer Franz Liszt reputedly played his last public concert, and in 1995 it was converted into an exemplary exhibition venue. ✉ *Rue Notre-Dame 41, Luxembourg City* ☎ *22/5045* 🌐 *www.casino-luxembourg.lu* Ⓜ *Tram: T1.*

Shopping

The bulk of the high-end shopping is on the pedestrian-only **Grand Rue** and streets radiating out from it. Shops along **avenue de la Gare** and **avenue de la Liberté,** both forking north from the train station, offer more affordable goods.

PECIALTY SHOPS

HINA

illeroy & Boch

OUSEWARES | Villeroy & Boch porcelain nd glassware had been manufactured in uxembourg since 1767 until production ransferred to China in 2010. Yet locals till flock here for its housewares. In he center of town you'll find its flagship hop on rue du Fossé, though bargain unters will prefer to head for the city utskirts where the factory outlet in impertsberg promises discounts on lder lines and slightly flawed "seconds" t bargain prices. ✉ *Rue du Fossé 2, uxembourg City* ☎ *46/3343* 🌐 *www. illeroy-boch.com.*

HOCOLATES

hocolate House by Nathalie Bonn

HOCOLATE | A local family-run choco- aterie that always delights. Chocolate ralines, truffles, spreads, mediants, nd wooden spoons sunk Excaliber-like nto elaborately decorated chunks of hocolate are all on show. ✉ *Rue du Marché-aux-Herbes 20, Luxembourg City* ☎ *26/262–006* 🌐 *chocolate-house-bonn. u* Ⓜ *Bus: 2, 5.*

LOTHING

ol(t)age

WOMEN'S CLOTHING | Hip boutique with focus on slogan V-necks, cashmere weaters, and bouclé-style scarves. It lso has an atelier shop south of the tation on rue Michel Welter. ✉ *Rue Philippe II 18* ☎ *26/187–579* 🌐 *www. yvoltage.com* Ⓜ *Tram: T1.*

STREET MARKETS

Place d'Armes Antique and Flea Markets

ANTIQUES & COLLECTIBLES | In fine weather, his square's cafés and benches are full f both locals and visitors, while the andstand hosts concerts on summer venings. Best of all, in addition to a flea narket being held on the first Sunday f the month (April–October), you'll lso find a *brocante* (antiques) market illing its center every second and fourth Saturday. In winter, it is also home to a yearly Christmas market. ✉ *Pl. d'Armes, Luxembourg City* ✥ *Rues des Capucins, Génistre, du Curé, de Chimay, and Philippe II; and av. Monterey.*

Place Guillaume II Farmers' Market

MARKET | This square is known locally as the *Knuedler*, a name derived from the knotted belts worn by the Franciscan monks who once had a monastery on this site. On market days (Wednesday and Saturday mornings), beneath the statue of Grand Duke Guillaume II, it fills with fruit and vegetable stands, flower vendors, cheese- and fishmongers, and a few farmers who bring in their personal crops as well as homemade jam, sauerkraut, and goat's cheese. Before you leave, take a moment to soak in the lavish 19th-century Hôtel de Ville (Town Hall), its stairs flanked by two magnificent bronze lions. ✉ *Pl. Guillaume II, Luxembourg City.*

Esch-sur-Alzette and the Redlands

The southern region of Luxembourg has a long history. Both Celts and Romans once founded villages here, but by the 19th and 20th centuries, the area was known for one thing only: its iron and mineral deposits, which gifted the region its nickname, the Redlands (for its red-tinted, iron-rich soils).

In 1798 Esch-sur-Alzette it was just a small village; today, it's Luxembourg's second-largest city, a metropolitan area home to some 60,000. Its old mining sites were rewilded, creating a string of nature reserves. Old pits became museums, and the plants of the industrial Belval area were converted into a university, music venue, and visitor center. This even won the city the European Capital of Culture title for 2022. For visitors, the city is something of a base. You'll not spend much time in its center with so many interesting villages and sights on the outskirts.

GETTING HERE AND AROUND

Esch-sur-Alzette is well connected by rail, with trains going every 30 minutes from the capital. Thereafter, you'll need to take buses to reach Dudelange (No. 4) or Fond-de-Gras (Nos. 1, 6), which are a lot less convenient. So it often pays to have a car if you're intent on exploring the region further. Alzette is just a 20-minute drive from Luxembourg City, following the A4 and A13, and surrounding day trips are rarely more than 15 minutes' drive away.

VISITOR INFORMATION

CONTACTS Esch-sur-Alzette Tourism Information. ✉ *Rue de l'Alzette 85, Esch-sur-Alzette* ☎ *54/1637* 🌐 *citylife.esch.lu.*

Sights

Architectural Walk

HISTORIC SIGHT | FAMILY | You can pick up the map for this architectural walk (free) at the tourism office in town. The route is a breezy 5 km (3 miles) and is a great way to explore a city that, on the surface at least, doesn't appear all that attractive at first. Much of the center was built at the turn of the 20th century, as the iron-ore industry gathered steam. Architects were shipped in from France, Belgium, and Germany, with the era's dominating styles of neo-Gothic, Art Deco, and Art Nouveau seen across magnificent turreted corner houses, the stately town hall, and imperious mansions built for the moguls of the era. ✉ *City Center, Esch-sur-Alzette.*

Blast Furnace Belval

FACTORY | In the early 1900s, the town's Belval neighborhood was home to the biggest ironworks site in Luxembourg. The last furnace was decommissioned in 1997 and the complex now houses a university and the country's biggest music venue, **Rockhal**. The renovated Furnace A is now open to the public. ✉ *Av. du Rock'n'Roll, opposite the Rockhal, Esch-sur-Alzette* ☎ *26/8401* 🌐 *www.minetttou.lu* *€5; guided tours €10* *Closed Mon and Tues.* Ⓜ *Bus: 3, 332.*

★ Dudelange

TOWN | Just 7 km (4½ miles) east of Esch-sur-Alzette, Dudelange is known as the most "Mediterranean" town in Luxembourg. It's certainly not for the weather. It stems from the fact that around 70% of its 17,000 residents are of Italian or Portuguese heritage, as the descendants of immigrant workers who came here at the height of the mining boom. At the heart of its Little Italy neighborhood, in an old railway station, you can seek out the **Centré de Documentation sur les Migrations Humaines** (*www.cdmh.lu*), one of the more enlightening exhibitions and tours in the Grand Duchy, exploring the country's rich history of migration and occupation. This town certainly has a long history of visitors. Romans first set up camp here at the base of what is now **Mt. St.-Jean**. The site was later a stop during the Crusades, and by the 12th century it was the location of a church built for the Order of the Brethren of St. Jean of Jerusalem. The current castle ruins—which include the foundation, a small chapel, and a tower—date from the 1550s. Atop Mt. St.-Jean, the commanding view south stares deep into France. ✉ *Dudelange, Dudelange* Ⓜ *Bus: 4.*

Eglise Saint-Joseph (*St. Joseph's Church*)

CHURCH | The largest and oldest church in Esch-sur-Alzette was built in neo-Gothic style by Charles Arendt, a truly prolific state architect who designed and restored many buildings across Luxembourg in the prewar years. Inside you'll find some impressive murals. ✉ *Rue d'Église, Esch-sur-Alzette* *Free.*

Ellergron Reserve

NATURE PRESERVE | Around 2 km (1 mile) south of the city lies the nature reserve of Ellergron, a former ore extraction zone ıat has been rewilded. The best way to ɛt there is to walk. Take the lift next to ıe railway station to the bridge over the ·acks and you'll find yourself in Gaalgebi-rg park. From there, the reserve is well ·gned. Once you arrive, a visitor center utlines the surrounding trails. You'll also nd the **Musée Mine Cockerill** (Cockerill Mining Museum), which is set in the ld mine workings that date back to 887, now mostly inhabited by bats. By 929, it was hauling 422,000 tons of ore ut of the ground, fueling the country's conomic boom. Interesting displays and elics scatter the old mine, dissecting s history. ✉ *Rue Jean-Pierre Bausch, Esch-sur-Alzette* ☎ *26/544–21* 🌐 *www.minetttour.lu* 🎫 *Free* 🕑 *Reception closed weekends* Ⓜ *Bus: 12.*

scher Déierepark

ARM/RANCH | **FAMILY** | This cheerful gov-ernment-run animal sanctuary perches high in the Gaalgebierg hills above the own. The walk up is a bracing plod hrough the forest park, and once there, ou'll find an array of ancient domestic pecies, including deer, big-horned heep, goats, and cattle. The tree-house afé, in particular, is a congenial spot to vhile away a lunch hour. Note: there's o public transport here that doesn't equire a 20-minute walk. ✉ *Gaalgebierg 64, Esch-sur-Alzette* ☎ *27/543–750* 🌐 *deierepark.esch.lu* 🎫 *Free.*

★ **Fond-de-Gras**

MINE | **FAMILY** | This small valley lies round 10 km (6 miles) northwest of Esch-sur-Alzette, and was once the heart of the country's mining industry, connect-ed via a pair of railway lines: one to ship equipment and ore in and out of nearby Pétange; another to transport the work-ers to the mining village of Lasauvage or into France. It was still operating by he 1960s. In summer, visitors can ride rains into the old mining tunnels, pedal a "draisine" (€10) along the tracks, see ail and mining museums, and tour the old villages where the miners once lived. July also sees the arrival of blues and steampunk festivals. ✉ *Fond-de-Gras 2* ✣ *South of Pétange* ☎ *26/582–069* 🌐 *minettpark.lu* 🎫 *Museum: free; mining train: €7; train 1900: €14* 🕑 *Closed Oct.–Apr.* Ⓜ *Bus: 2 and 6 (change at Differdange).*

★ **Musée National de la Résistance** (*Museum of Resistance*)

HISTORY MUSEUM | Luxembourg was deeply scarred by World War II. The Musée de la Résistance honors its Resistance fighters and is the home of the country's Tomb of the Unknown Soldier. Exhibits focus on the plight of Luxembourg's Jewish population and other communities that were lost during the war. It has recently been renovated in time for its 2022 reopening. ✉ *Pl. de la Résistance, Esch-sur-Alzette* ☎ *54/8472* 🌐 *mnr.lu* 🎫 *Free* 🕑 *Closed Mon.*

Restaurants

Bosque FeVi

$$$ | **SPANISH** | This well-regarded Spanish restaurant, up in the parkland hills of the Gaalgebierg, makes quite the impression. Inside, its wavy walls and blazing fire set a modern tone that the menu picks up and runs with in its focus on refined tapas and tasting menus that veer from foie gras and quince to falafel and crispy noodles. **Known for:** an excellent choice of Spanish wines; inventive tapas to put a smile on your face; beautiful parkland setting. 💲 *Average main: €29* ✉ *Park Gaalgebierg, Esch-sur-Alzette* ✣ *Near the Hotel Seven* ☎ *52/0228* 🌐 *thesevenhotel.lu* 🕑 *Closed Mon.*

★ **Como**

$$$ | **ITALIAN** | The scruffy street on which Como sits might not conjure the kind of memories you can expect to make inside this fine Italian eatery, but therein lies the surprise. Chef Renato Favaro dives into his Lombardy roots with dishes of osso buco, buckwheat tagliatelle-style *pizzoccheri*, and polenta with wild shrimp—all culinary staples of Northern Italy. **Known for:** exceptional service; a fine escape into regional Italian cooking; great produce sourced from Italy. $ *Average main: €28* ✉ *Rue des Remparts 19, Esch-sur-Alzette* ☎ *54/27–231* 🌐 *comoresto.lu* ⏲ *Closed Sun. and Mon.*

Mise en scène

$$ | **ITALIAN** | A pleasant spot for lunch or a quick meal, just next to the theater. It claims to specialize in pizza but, in truth, it does a little bit of everything, usually to a good standard. **Known for:** quick service; lunchtime set meals are good value; a nice spot to try some Luxembourgish food. $ *Average main: €20* ✉ *Rue du Brill 60, next to theater, Esch-sur-Alzette* ☎ *26/532–189* 🌐 *mise-en-scene.lu* ⏲ *Closed Mon. and Wed. evening.*

Restaurant Postkutsch

$$$$ | **FRENCH** | French cuisine in all its decadent glory is the order of the day at chef Claude Magnin's Alzette staple. Special mention goes to the magnificent cheese cart, whose wares can be ordered for takeaway outside of service hours and account for no less that two courses in the decadent tasting menu. **Known for:** we have to mention the cheese again!; assured French cooking with an elegant touch; great service and exquisite presentation. $ *Average main: €64* ✉ *Rue Xavier Brasseur 8, Esch-sur-Alzette* ☎ *54/5169* 🌐 *www.postkutsch.lu* ⏲ *Closed Mon.*

Coffee and Quick Bites

SimpliciThé

$ | **CAFÉ** | This café extension of the famous local tea shop makes for a peaceful break. A selection of soups, from curry and lentil to vegan ramens, make it a good spot for a quick snack. **Known for:** hearty soups to warm you up; the choice of teas is naturally superb; great people-watching spot from the window stools. $ *Average main: €10* ✉ *Rue de la Libération 49, Esch-sur-Alzette* 🌐 *simplicithe.eu* ⏲ *Closed Mon. and Tues.*

Hotels

There is an astonishing lack of accommodation in the main city. Precious few hotels or B&Bs operate there, and those that do aren't all that charming. A better option is up in the pretty park area of Gaalgebierg, which rises south of the railway. It's a 15-minute walk into town, but worth it for the views and the quiet.

★ **Escher Bamhaiser**

$$ | **APARTMENT** | This trio of duplex tree houses (for four or six people) lies on the edge of the deer park, high in the Gaalgebierg area is simply one of the best stays in Luxembourg. **Pros:** the café serves nice food if you can't be bothered to find a restaurant nearby; there's no other sleep quite like it in Luxembourg; great views from the private terraces. **Cons:** breakfast is an extra €15; the sound of the animals can be quite noisy; it's a bit of a walk into town. $ *Rooms from: €120* ✉ *Gaalgebierg 64, Esch-sur-Alzette* ☎ *27/542–233* 🌐 *bamhaiser.esch.lu* *3 tree houses* *No Meals.*

The Seven Hotel

$$ | **HOTEL** | **FAMILY** | This cozy boutique stay, nestled among the muddy paths of the Gaalgebierg hills, has two restaurants, a wellness center (including hammam and small gym), and lodgelike duplex suites that offer grand views—it's a rare dose of luxury on the edge of town. **Pros:** free parking; a lush setting and excellent facilities; Spanish restaurant BosqueFevi is an excellent pick. **Cons:** it's an extra €12 for breakfast; you're a 15-minute walk from the city center; one of the pricer stays in town. $ *Rooms from: €139* ✉ *Galgebierg 50, Esch-sur-Alzette* ☎ *54/0228* 🌐 *theseven-hotel.lu* *15 rooms* *No Meals.*

Valley of the Seven Châteaux

The signposted Valley of the Seven Châteaux can be visited on a road tour from just outside Mersch, 17 km (10 miles) north of the capital, cutting southwest to Hollenfels, Marienthal, and Ansembourg (which has an old castle in the heights and a new one in the valley below), then working west to Septfontaines and south to Koerich and finishing on the border. The castles, in various stages of repair and representing a broad historical spectrum, have often not been restored for visitors, but they loom above forests and over valleys much as they did in Luxembourg's grander days. Follow the road signs marked "Vallée des Sept Châteaux": this rather obscure and never-direct itinerary takes you through farmlands, woods, and—just outside Koerich, at Goeblange—to the foundations of two 4th-century Roman villas, their underground heating and plumbing systems exposed. The rough cobbles leading into the woods are original, too, and if you have the stamina to walk 37 km (23 miles), the route is also a national hiking trail.

Remich and the Moselle

22 km (14 miles) west of Luxembourg City.

Legend has it that the vineyards of the fertile Moselle Valley were originally developed to satisfy the wine-drinking habits of Roman legions. (Antiquities still occasionally surface in the well-cultivated soil.) Today, the Moselle river serves as the border between Luxembourg and Germany, with graceful vineyards still seaming the valley, luring visitors with their promise of fine wines.

GETTING HERE AND AROUND

By car, Remich is just a half-hour drive from Luxembourg City along the E29. From there, the Route du Vin (or N10) runs alongside the Moselle between Schengen (15 minutes) and Grevenmacher (30 minutes). In between are a slew of vineyards and villages. Mondorf-les-Bain is reached via the N16, which connects with the E29 just before Remich.

No trains operate in this area. The No. 175 bus connects both Mondorf-les-Bains and Remich directly to Luxembourg City. From Remich, the Nos. 309, 450, and 451 run the villages alongside the river up to Grevenmacher. This stretch can also be easily explored by boat on the many river tours.

BICYCLE RENTAL

The alternative is to walk or cycle the Route du Vin. A bicycle-rental service offering mountain and city bikes (both €12) and e-bikes (€20) for 24 hours can be found at hire stations in Remich, Schengen, Ehnen, Grevenmacher, and other towns. This only operates between March and October and deposits are required.

CONTACTS Rent-a-Bike Miselerland Center. ✉ *Centre Visit Remich, rte. du Vin 11, Remich* ☎ *621/356–137* 🌐 *www.entente-moselle.lu.*

TOURS

BOAT TOURS

★ MS Princesse Marie-Astrid

BOAT TOURS | A predecessor of the *Princesse Marie-Astrid* hosted the signing of the Schengen agreement, which ratified free cross-border travel across Europe. To capitalize on this, the municipality of the city recently finalized the purchase of the boat. Between Easter and September, it plows the wine villages along the Moselle (Schengen, Remich, Wormeldange, Grevenmacher, etc.), while its restaurant dishes up a fine spread. Tickets can be bought in the office opposite Remich docks. ✉ *Rte. du Vin 10, Grevenmacher* ☎ *75/8275* 🌐 *www.entente-moselle.lu* 🎟 *€18.*

Navitours

BOAT TOURS | Daily boat tours of the Moselle run throughout the year, north and south of Remich, with Navitours. On Sundays, look out for the four-hour gourmet cruise, with a buffet meal included. Also, under their "WaterAdventures" banner, you can rent boats (without a license), kayaks, and a variety of SUPs to explore the river under your own steam. ✉ *Quai de la Moselle, Remich* ☎ *75/8489* 🌐 *navitours.lu* 🎟 *From €10.*

WINE WALKS

Vineyard Hikes

WALKING TOURS | **FAMILY** | The local tourism authority offer free self-guided routes and guided group tours (€130) to the lesser-seen vineyards at Scheierbierg in Remich or those between Stadtbredimus and Greiveldange. Guided hikes start in Remich, Ahn, Ehnen, or Greiveldange and typically end with tastings. ✉ *Rte. du Vin 52, Bech-Kleinmacher* ☎ *26/747–874* 🌐 *www.visitmoselle.lu.*

VISITOR INFORMATION

On the ground floor of the Remich Tourist Information building you'll also find the ticket office for Navitours and MS *Princesse Marie-Astrid.* To the rear of the building is the office for Rent-a-bike Misereland.

CONTACTS Remich Tourist Information. ✉ *Centre Visit Remich, rte. du Vin 1, Remich* ☎ *27/075–416* 🌐 *visitremich.lu.*

Sights

Caves de Wellenstein

WINERY | About 2 km (1 mile) up the hill from Bech-Kleinmacher, in the tiny villag of Wellenstein, is the visitor center for the Vinsmoselle company, a collection of cooperatives that bring together a huge number of the small wineries in th Moselle area. The cellars have been in continual use for over 100 years and are surrounded by 2,223 acres of vineyards. Tours of the facility and tastings take about one hour; it's a good opportunity to try the local ice and straw wines. ✉ *Rue des Caves 37, Bech-Kleinmacher* ☎ *26/661–440* 🌐 *www.vinsmoselle.lu* 🎟 *€8* ⏲ *Closed Sun.* Ⓜ *Bus: 175, 185.*

Caves Lucien Gloden

WINERY | Because of its small production, this is one of the few places where you can try the sweet white wines of this small independent producer. Their tastin room is open on Sunday (3–7) and by appointment during the week. ✉ *Rte. du Vin 9–30, Schengen* ☎ *26/665–704* 🌐 *vin gloden.lu* Ⓜ *Bus: 185.*

Caves St-Martin

WINERY | Caves St-Martin is a small independent vinter producing white wines, sparkling wines, and grape juices. You can tour the facilities and taste some of the products in the lovely pavilion. ✉ *Rte de Stadtbredimus 53, Remich* ☎ *23/699-774 guided tours* 🌐 *www.cavesstmartin.lu* 🎟 *From €7* ⏲ *Closed Mon.; Dec.–Mar.* Ⓜ *Bus: 450, 451.*

Mondorf Domaine Thermal

HOT SPRING | The beginnings of Le Domaine Thermal date back to 1840; nov it's a state-of-the-art, full-service health and sports facility and hotel. You'll find classic spa treatments, including therma baths, massages, manicures, aromatherapy, and mud baths, as well as a health club. Day passes are available. ✉ *Av. de Bains, Mondorf-les-Bains* ☎ *23/666–800*

Luxembourg's Wine Country

Like much about this small country, Luxembourg's wines are little known outside its borders. Yet the Moselle Valley has been producing wine for over 2,000 years—good enough to be celebrated in verse by the Roman poet Decimus Magnus Ausonius and to inspire Celtic burial objects with grape and vine motifs.

While the German vineyards on the eastern side of the river take all the credit, the lack of exports outside Luxembourg's borders (or at least beyond Germany or Belgium) mean that Luxembourg's growers have stayed a well-kept secret for years. It's also kept down prices for a public unwilling to pay the French or German equivalent for locally made wine.

Pretty much all the country's wine is produced within an area of around 3,212 acres, smaller even than the average commercial California vineyard. Within this are squeezed some 450 winegrowers and producers, pumping out 20 million bottles a year. When you think that Italy or France produces 7½ billion bottles annually, it really is just a tiny drop in the ocean. Yet, for all that, Luxembourg wine is worth celebrating.

The south-facing slopes on the local side of the Moselle Valley have mineral deposits and microclimates ideal for growing a variety of wine grapes, including riesling, pinot gris, pinot blanc, auxerrois, pinot noir, gewürztraminer, rivaner, and elbling. The resulting wines are primarily white and dry (unlike their sweeter German counterparts), though many vintners are now experimenting with red, orange, and rosé wine production.

Most winemakers also produce *crémant*, a high-quality sparkling white wine that is often drunk as an aperitif in the Grand Duchy. If you're lucky, you'll also find an ice wine (*ä iswäin*), harvested in winter in temperatures of -7°C, and also *stréiwäin* (straw wine), made from mature grapes laid out to dry on straw mats, and the supersweet late-season *spätlese* wines. Basic quality standards are established by a 1932 national law and by the *Marque Nationale* certification, created in 1935.

About two-thirds of Luxembourg's wine production is controlled by Les Domaines de Vinsmoselle, a collection of six cooperatives that dates back to the 1920s. There are also some 50 independent vintners who sell primarily to private clients. Many of the wineries' caves (both Vinmoselle and independent) are open for tastings and as departure points for vineyard tours—just look for signs along the road as you travel the Route du Vin that runs through the valley.

www.mondorf.lu *Spa access from €22* *Reservations required* *Bus: 175, 309.*

Musée du Vin (*Wine Museum*)

OTHER MUSEUM | Ehnen, with its narrow old streets, carved wooded doors, and unusual circular church, makes a peaceful escape. It's also home to the Musée du Vin, set in a typical group of Luxembourgish farm buildings, with pink stucco and cobbled courts. Its rooms are full of tools, equipment, and photographs of the wine-making industry, with a

The fertile Moselle Valley has been producing wine for over 2,000 years.

demonstration vineyard planted with samples of each of the local varietals. The museum has also been recently renovated and is scheduled to reopen in 2022. ✉ *Rte. du Vin 115, Ehnen* ☎ *75/8888* 🌐 *www.entente-moselle.lu* 🎟 *€4* Ⓜ *Bus: 450.*

Restaurants

Bistro Brasserie Koeppchen
$$ | **BRASSERIE** | Despite originally opening in 1907, this restaurant only improves with age. Seasonal specials accompany a fine selection of Luxembourgish dishes, from the classic *kniddelen*, fried gnocchi-style dumplings with lashings of speck ham or Berdorf cheese, to the typical *wäinzoossiss*, a thick local sausage in a creamy mustard and wine sauce. **Known for:** charming old-world setting; hearty Luxembourgish cooking at a good prices; great wine selection. $ *Average main: €19* ✉ *Berreggaass 9, Wormeldingen, Ehnen* ☎ *76/0046* 🌐 *www.koeppchen.lu* 🕒 *Closed Mon.* Ⓜ *Bus: 450.*

★ La Peniche VINtage
$$ | **EUROPEAN** | This floating restaurant on the quay is something of a new concept (or at least a couple of old ones muddled together): a tasting boat. Degustation menus are filled with local produce and wines that you can buy on board afterwards, and even the furnishings are for sale. **Known for:** you can take away some tasty souvenirs; dinner with a (moving) view; interesting local dishes. $ *Average main: €21* ✉ *Rte. du Vin 1, Remich* ☎ *691/917–630* 🌐 *www.vintageboat.lu* 🕒 *Closed Mon. and Tues.*

Hotels

★ Hôtel de L'Ecluse
$$ | **HOTEL** | This family-run hotel holds more than a few surprises, including a huge green space to its rear complete with outdoor pool (closed in winter), putting green, and views over the

eighboring vineyard. **Pros:** free covered arking area; a peaceful quiet stay; it's eally good value. **Cons:** you really need a ar to get here; you're not near any of the etter-equipped towns or villages; the ont is on a rather busy road. $ *Rooms rom: €105 ✉ Waistrooss 29, 4 km (2½ niles) north of Remich, Wormeldange ☎ 23/619–191 🌐 www.hotel-ecluse.lu 35 rooms 🍽 Free Breakfast Ⓜ Bus: 60, 450.*

Hotel-Restaurant Domaine La Forêt

$ | **HOTEL** | Given the sheer volume of etrol stations lining the road to this xcellent restaurant and spa-hotel, you'd e forgiven for turning around—but that vould be a mistake, because the hotel self is actually rather pretty, wrapped by seasonal garden. **Pros:** the restaurant is vorth booking even if you're not staying; ne spa is far better than in most gas-o-stays and only open to guests; there's pretty garden to relax in. **Cons:** it's a retty steep walk up from the riverbank; ne road leading up to it is one of the ugliest in Luxembourg; it's one of the pricer tays in the area. $ *Rooms from: €150 ✉ Rte. de l'Europe 36, Remich ☎ 23/699–99 🌐 www.foret.lu 16 rooms 🍽 Free Breakfast.*

otel St-Nicholas

$ | **HOTEL** | Located next to the St. Nichos Gate on the Esplanade, this charming verside hotel is something of an old and. **Pros:** it's well-placed for riverboat ips; a great all-rounder in Remich, which thin on the ground for stays; friendly, elpful staff. **Cons:** it's showing its age in laces; it's both roadside and riverside; ne pools aren't huge. $ *Rooms from: €127 ✉ Esplanade 31, Remich ☎ 26/663 🌐 www.saint-nicolas.lu 40 rooms 🍽 No Meals.*

Echternach and Little Switzerland

Echternach is 35 km (22 miles) northeast of Luxembourg City.

The eastern fringe of Luxembourg—a hilly terrain of dense fir and beech forests, high limestone bluffs, and twisting brooks—goes by two names: Mullerthal, and the more playful *Le Petit Suisse.*The latter derives from the area's resemblance to the rugged, rocky mountain valleys of Switzerland, and it's no surprise that it has become a popular spot for European hikers, spelunkers, and climbers.

The region's oldest and largest town is **Echternach.** In the 7th century, a Northumbrian-born missionary, known as St. Willibrord, founded a church here around which the town grew.

GETTING HERE AND AROUND

Car is the best way to get around the Mullerthal. It's a collection of small villages and towns, and while there is a decent bus service, it's still easier to drive, especially as most of the better stays are outside of town. From Luxembourg City, take the E29 northeast; it runs direct to Echternach. From there, Route 364 connects both Berdorf and Beaufort.

The region is not connected by rail, but you can find direct buses (No. 110) from Kirchberg in Luxembourg City to Echternach. From there, the No. 502 connects both Berdorf and Beaufort.

VISITOR INFORMATION

CONTACTS Berdorf Tourist Information. *✉ Beim Martbusch 3, Berdorf ☎ 28/671–521 🌐 www.visitberdorf.lu.* **Echternach Tourist Information.** *✉ Parvis de la Basilique 9–10, Echternach ☎ 72/0230 🌐 www.mullerthal.lu.*

Beaufort is home to two castles, including this 17th-century Renaissance-style chateau.

Sights

Berdorf

TOWN | FAMILY | Berdorf is a small town just 6 km (4 miles) west of Echternach. It has built up a name for itself as a vibrant center for rock climbing and hiking and is surrounded by interesting trails rising up from the plateau and passing through gorges, grottoes, rocks, and fissures. It's a popular base for hikes, with maps and guides to the area found in the local Tourism Information. If you still crave sights, the 55-meter-high **Aquatower** (*www.aquatower-berdorf.lu*) overlooking the town ironically contains a rather dry museum on drinking water, but the view from the top is worth the visit. ✉ *Berdorf* Ⓜ *Bus: 111, 502.*

★ **Châteaux de Beaufort** (*Castles of Beaufort*)

CASTLE/PALACE | Around 15 km (9 miles) west of Echternach, at the top of the Ernz Noire valley, a short detour leads to Beaufort. Near the village stand two splendid castles, side by side: a magnificently imposing medieval shell only partially restored after World War II bombing left it in ruins, and a Renaissance-style chateau dating from the 17th century. ✉ *Rue du Château, Beaufort* ☎ *83/6601* 🌐 *www.visitbeaufort.lu* 🎫 *€5; €10 with a guided tour* 🕒 *Renaissance castle: closed to tours Mon.–Wed. (Apr.–Oct.); Nov.–Mar. by appt. only; the medieval castle is closed Nov.–Mar.* Ⓜ *Bus: 502.*

Echternach Lake

BODY OF WATER | Less than a mile south of the town center lies an artificial lake. Visitors can't swim in the water, but it is surrounded by trails, making it good for cycling (you can rent a bike next to the youth hostel) or a pleasant stroll. In summer, it often hosts an open-air cinema. The remains of a **Roman villa** (free) can also be found just north of the water. ✉ *Echternach Lake, Echternach.*

Église Sts. Pierre et Paul (*Church of St. Peter and St. Paul*)

CHURCH | On a hill just behind the basilica a church stands on the remains of a ƚoman castellum and shows, in its pare architecture, signs of Merovingi-ın, Romanesque, and Gothic influence. ɫour-long private tours (€60) of it can ɔe booked at the tourism office. ✉ *Rue ʲean-Pierre Probst 10, Echternach* ☎ *72/0457.*

ʍusée de l'Abbaye (*Abbey Museum*)
ʀRT MUSEUM | In the Middle Ages, Echter-ıach was known throughout the Western ʋorld for the exquisite illumination ʼminiature illustrations) that accompanied he hand-copied texts produced by the ʒenedictine abbey's scriptorium. The orig-ıal abbey is long gone, but a quadrant ɔf abbey buildings from the 18th century emains. The books displayed here are ɔainstakingly executed reproductions of he originals, down to their gem-stud-ɫed covers. ✉ *Parvis de la Basilique 11, Echternach* ☎ *72/7472* 🌐 *abteimuseum. ɔrg* 🎫 *€3.*

ʼlace du Marché
LAZA/SQUARE | Echternach's cobbled ɔlace du Marché, in the old town center, ɔffers a charming mix of Gothic arcades ınd restored medieval houses, festooned ʋith wrought-iron signs and sculpted ɫrain spouts. The arched and turreted 3th-century **Hôtel de Ville** (Town Hall) ƨ its centerpiece. ✉ *Pl. du Marché, Echternach.*

★ **St. Willibrord Basilica**
ᴄHURCH | Echternach was founded in ʒ98 by St. Willibrord, who came from ɴorthumbria. He established a Bene-ɫictine abbey, which thrived until it was azed during the French invasion of 1794. ː was rebuilt twice thereafter: first in he 19th century, and then again after ː was destroyed in World War II. All the ʋhile, the relics of the saint remained ıafe in the crypt. Beneath the carving of he tomb's neoclassical marble canopy, ou can still glimpse the simple tooled tone sarcophagus cut in the 7th century. ✉ *Echternach, Echternach* ☎ *72/0230* 🎫 *Free.*

Restaurants

Au Vieux Moulin
$$$$ | FRENCH | A few miles south of town, this family-run inn is set within an old mill that was converted in the 1960s. It has simple country decor and pleasant rooms, but the main attraction is the restaurant, which serves delicate, exquisitely presented French cooking paired with Luxembourgish wine. **Known for:** if you're too full to move, the rooms upstairs are worth a stopover; a charming country setting; the dame blanche is duly famous. 💲 *Average main: €35* ✉ *Maison 6, Lauterborn, Echternach* ☎ *72/00–681* 🌐 *www.hotel-au-vieux-moulin.lu* 🕓 *Closed Mon.*

La Grappe d'Or
$$$ | FRENCH | French cuisine with a sea-sonal bias and a gift for flair. Dishes arrive like tiny works of art, painted with the broad strokes of classical French cooking. **Known for:** a solid wine selection; friendly, efficient service; immaculately prepared dishes. 💲 *Average main: €29* ✉ *Rte. de Luxembourg 7, Echternach* ☎ *72/04–571* 🌐 *www.lagrappedorechternach.com* 🕓 *Closed Tues.*

Hotels

Berdorfer Eck
$$ | B&B/INN | This new stay in Berdorf is a jack of all trades: a friendly B&B, artisanal food shop, and bistro. **Pros:** free parking; the little shop is perfect for souvenirs; the breakfasts are huge and delicious. **Cons:** Berdorf is a slightly remote loca-tion; it fills up fast; you're on the edge of town. 💲 *Rooms from: €125* ✉ *Rue d'Echternach 53, Berdorf* ☎ *26/784–434* 🌐 *berdorfer-eck.lu* *7 rooms* 🍽 *Free Breakfast.*

Hôtel Bel-Air
$$$ | HOTEL | Perched on a hilltop over-looking expansive gardens, this grand hotel dates back to 1927. **Pros:** a pristine parkland setting; great wellness facilities;

you can rent bikes from reception. **Cons:** there aren't many months it's warm enough to use the outdoor pool; you're a little far from town, so you need a car; breakfast costs €18. *Rooms from: €166* ✉ *Rte. de Berdorf 1, Echternach* ☎ *72/9383* 🌐 *www.belair-hotel.lu* *38 rooms* *No Meals.*

Nightlife

Cafe de la Poste – Beim Wohli

BARS | Echternach isn't a town with a thriving nightlife, but this raggedy café-bar overlooking the basilica is a cheerful spot for an evening. Board games, good music, and a giant, sci-fi-looking fountain centerpiece that the owner claims "cost as much as a car" makes for a fun night. ✉ *Pl. du Marché 3, Echternach* ☎ *72/0231.*

De Philosoff

BARS | This decades-old bar was lovingly raised from the ashes after it was sadly left vacant. A leafy terrace, a brasserie that dishes up giant burgers, and a decent selection of beers on tap make this a go-to drinking hole once again. ✉ *Rue de La Gare 31, Echternach, Echternach* ☎ *691/774–744* 🌐 *www.philosoff.lu.*

Activities

HIKING TRAILS

Gorge du Loup

HIKING & WALKING | On the way from Echternach to Berdorf, you can squeeze between the cliffs at the Gorge du Loup (Wolf's Throat), a lush, mossy canyon carved between a sandstone plateau, where hidden treasures are said to be guarded by a legendary black dog. The gorge is a popular side trip and easily reached from town on the E1 Trail, a 13.5-km (8-mile) hike that starts at the basilica and loops northwest to take in the gorge in a brisk four hours. ✉ *Gorge du Loup, Echternach* *Free.*

★ **Mullerthal Trail**

HIKING & WALKING | The crowning glory of the Mullerthal region (aka Little Switzerland) is its legendary hiking trail. It stretches 112 km (69½ miles) across three different looped routes, spanning rocky canyons, mossy forests, and quiet riverine valleys. Route 1 (36 km/22 miles) encircles Echternach, the tougher Route 2 (38 km/23 miles) lies just south of Berdorf, and Route 3 (38 km/23 miles) is next to Beaufort. Maps can be found online and at local tourism offices. ✉ *Echternach, Echternach* *Free.*

Luxembourg Ardennes

Vast, rolling green hills and dense fir forests alternate across the country's northern highlands, forming Luxembourg's portion of the great forested Ardennes region. Castles and river-wrapped villages punctuate its hills and valleys, while rocky rivers and streams pour off the slopes, making this a popular walking area.

Esch-sur-Sûre

27 km (17 miles) southwest of Clervaux, 43 km (27 miles) northwest of Luxembourg City.

There are few prettier spots in all of Luxembourg than the little village of Esch-sur-Sûre. Wrapped by densely forested hills, this tiny gooseneck on the River Sûre was once an impenetrable stronghold, and its ruined fortress-castle (unrestored but open to the public) still towers over the small hamlet below, with striking views from the ramparts.

GETTING HERE AND AROUND

Driving is the easiest way to reach Esch-sur-Sûre from Luxembourg City. Routes typically follow the A7 motorway up to Ettelbruck before heading west along the N15, or take a slight detour up to

Bourscheid Castle, complete with turreted towers and massive stone walls, lies just east of Esch-sur-Sûre.

Bourscheid, where the Route d-Esch (308) connects back to the national road.

No trains connect to Esch-sur-Sûre. But it can easily be reached by bus from Ettelbruck, which is a part of the national rail network. From there, take the No. 535, which also makes a stop at Insenborn, a 15-minute walk from the facilities at Upper Sûre Lake.

TOURS

Boat / Amphibian Tour

BOAT TOURS | Try a two-hour solar-powered boat tour on Upper Sûre Lake, or combine a boat trip with a nature hike (about 8 km [5 miles]) back along the left shore of the reservoir lake on the four-hour Amphibian Tour. Trips start in Insenborn or—upon special request—Liefrange and take place from May until the start of October. ✉ *Naturpark Öewersauer, Insenborn, Esch-sur-Sûre* ☎ *89/93–311* 🌐 *www.naturpark-sure.lu* 🎫 *From €10* 🕓 *Closed Oct.–Apr.*

The Mysteries of Esch-sur-Sûre

WALKING TOURS | This free audio guide is available as part of the Éislek tourism app. It's a fun, if theatrical, two-hour journey through the sagas and legends of the town, beginning at the Naturpark Öewersauer Visitor Center. ✉ *Naturpark Öewersauer, 15 Rue de Lultzhausen, Esch-sur-Sûre* 🌐 *www.visit-eislek.lu/en/eislek-app.*

VISITOR INFORMATION

CONTACTS Naturpark Öewersauer Visitor Center. ✉ *Rue de Lultzhausen 15, Esch-sur-Sûre* ☎ *89/93–311* 🌐 *www.naturpark-sure.lu/en.*

Sights

Ancient Cloth Factory

HISTORY MUSEUM | Set within the Natuurpark Visitor Center, this former cloth mill has an exhibition about wool spinning and cloth making. Textiles have been made at this site since the 16th century, though the current factory dates from hundreds of years later, and has been thoroughly restored. Visits include demonstrations of the old textile machinery, and you can buy the fruits of their labor in the shop, though they aren't cheap. ✉ *Naturpark Öewersauer Visitor Center, rte. de Lultzhausen 15, Esch-sur-Sûre* ☎ *89/93–311* 🌐 *www.naturpark-sure.lu* 🎫 *€3.*

★ Bourscheid Castle

CASTLE/PALACE | Around 16 km (10 miles) east of Esch-sur-Sûre, you'll encounter the small town of **Bourscheid**. You'll likely drive through en route, so make sure to detour along the quiet, winding road up to the ruins of Bourscheid Castle. The building dates back to 1000 AD and was ruled by the Lords of Bourscheid for four centuries. ✉ *Schlasswee 1, Bourscheid* ☎ *99/0570* 🌐 *www.castle-bourscheid.lu* 🎫 *€7* Ⓜ *Bus: 535 and 545.*

Esch-sur-Sûre Castle

CASTLE/PALACE | Building began on the castle around 927 AD and it later passed down through the Counts of Esch, who gradually expanded its fortifications. At one point their kingdom stretched to Diekirch, but by 1330 their light had been extinguished, with many of their number lost to the Crusades. Today, visitors can scrabble the two main sections left standing, including what remains of the original keep and the 15th-century round watchtower. ✉ *Rue de Lultzhausen 4–6, Esch-sur-Sûre* 🎫 *Free.*

★ Upper Sûre Lake

NATIONAL PARK | **FAMILY** | The reservoir was dammed in 1961 to create a long-term source of drinking water for Luxembourg. Chunks of it are still off-limits because of this, but there's plenty to explore. In summer, solar-powered boats (May–October) take you on two-hour tours of the water. Mercifully, no motorboats are allowed here, but on warm days the lake fills with windsurfers, paddlers, and wild swimmers. You can rent canoes, kayaks, and SUPs from the youth hostel in Lultzhausen in July and August, and for walkers, there are some 90 km (56 miles) of trails to explore (maps are at the visitor center). But if you'd rather relax, several beaches line the shores at **Insenborn, Lultzhausen,** and across the water at **Liefrange,** with a more secluded stretch found just past the Burfelt viewing platform. This is where locals come to escape for the day. ✉ *Upper Sûre Lake, Esch-sur-Sûre* 🎫 *Free.*

Restaurants

Restaurant Comte Godefroy

$$ | **BRASSERIE** | The restaurant of the Hôtel de la Sûre also has the best food in town. It's solid brasserie cooking at a decent price (for Luxembourg), where hearty portions of cordon bleu, schnitzel, and steaks slathered in pepper sauce please the belly as much as the senses. **Known for:** a nice choice of local beers; hefty portions of classic crowd-pleasers; the faux-stone medeival setting is charming. 💲 *Average main: €21* ✉ *Rue du Pont 1, Esch-sur-Sûre* ☎ *83/9110* 🌐 *www.hotel-de-la-sure.lu.*

Coffee and Quick Bites

Flux

$ | **BURGER** | Hear us out. The location isn't all that promising (next to a petrol station), but this takeaway burger joint is popular for good reason: it's good. **Known for:** the burgers are just huge; it's one for the road; the chili-cheese fries are a decadence to savor. 💲 *Average main: €9* ✉ *Bousserstrooss 5, Hierheck, Esch-sur-Sûre* ☎ *26/889–543.*

Hotels

Hôtel de la Sûre

$$ | **HOTEL** | There aren't a lot of options this far out west, but this sprawling hotel is an assured presence. **Pros:** easy parking and a special garage for motorbikes; can arrange just about anything in the area; good hotel restaurant serving one of the better meals in the area. **Cons:**

service can be a little brusque; a little old-fashioned in parts; limited choice—it's one of only a couple of stays in town. *Rooms from: €136* *Rue du Pont 1, Esch-sur-Sûre* *83/9110* *hotel-de-la-sure.lu* *23 rooms* *Free Breakfast.*

Cicuit du Lac

HIKING & WALKING | If you're after something strenuous, head west to the lake. The 43-km (26-mile) national hiking trail Circuit du Lac is divided into western and eastern sections. Either could be done in a day and are a good way to see the area, though there are plenty of shorter walks here, too. A series of theme trails scatter the shores, with maps available at the Naturpark Öewersauer Visitor Center (from €3.50). *Naturpark Öewersauer, Esch-sur-Sûre* *Free.*

Vianden

11 km (7 miles) northeast of Diekirch, 44 km (27½ miles) north of Luxembourg City.

Walking the peaceful cobbled main street of Vianden today, it's hard to believe that this small, rural town was once at the heart of a powerful dynasty. In the 11th century, this was the seat of Counts of Vianden before being passed on to the Orange-Nassau, a line that includes kings of the Netherlands, England, Scotland, and Ireland. It was one of the region's first "cities" and the capital of a medieval county that spanned 136 villages, as big as Luxembourg is today. The great legacy of that era looms above the town center, a magnificent castle that still draws visitors from near and far.

GETTING HERE AND AROUND

If driving from Luxembourg City, follow the A7 and E421 up to Diekirch where you can pick up the N7 to Vianden. It takes around 50 minutes and avoids the windy roads you find throughout much of the Ardennes.

Vianden doesn't have a railway. The closest station is Ettelbruck, which you can reach by rail from the capital, then pick up the No. 570 bus direct to Vianden. In total, the journey from Luxembourg City takes about 90 minutes. You can also find direct buses (No. 664) from Vianden to Clervaux.

VISITOR INFORMATION

CONTACTS Vianden Tourist Information. *Rue du Vieux Marché 1a, Vianden* *83/4257* *www.visit-vianden.lu/en.*

★ **Château de Vianden** (*Vianden Castle*)

CASTLE/PALACE | Driving around the last bend into Vianden, you're greeted by a full-length view of Vianden Castle rearing up on the hill, replete with conical spires, crenellation, step gables, and massive bulwarks. The castle was built on Roman foundations at the turn of the first millennium, though its most spectacular portions date from the 11th, 12th, and 15th centuries. Its near-pristine appearance is the result of massive restoration in the 20th century. *Mnt. du Château, Vianden* *83/41081 Castle* *www.castle-vianden.lu* *€10.*

Église Trinitaire (*Trinitarian Church*)

CHURCH | The 13th-century Gothic Eglise Trinitaire once functioned as a Trinitarian monastery. Its ancient cloisters have since been restored to sparkling modernity. Inside the church, the main altar is a dazzling affair, made in 1758 in the Rococo style, with every inch of its gilt and marble put to good use. Meanwhile, the recumbent effigy of Marie de Spanheim (who died around 1400) preserves the memory of the last descendant of the Counts of Vianden. *Grand-Rue 49–55, Vianden* *83/42–571* *Free.*

Maison de Victor Hugo (*House of Victor Hugo*)

HISTORIC HOME | In 1870, the French novelist Victor Hugo was still living in exile from his country, after openly criticizing the autocratic rule of Napoléon III. The bulk of his 19 years in the wilderness was spent in the Channel Islands, where he wrote his best-known works. But before he finally returned to France, he spent three months in Vianden, and the town has never forgotten it. The Maison de Victor Hugo is set within the house in which he lived, and celebrates his life with photos, documents, tall tales (it is claimed he stopped a house burning down), and other memorabilia. His writings and works are in French, but an excellent free audio guide narrates the story of his home and the objects found here in English, so it's well worth a visit. ✉ *Rue de la Gare 37, Vianden* ☎ *26/874–088* 🌐 *www.victor-hugo.lu* 🎫 *€5* ⏲ *Closed Mon.*

Ourdall Promenade

TRAIL | Between Stolzembourg and Vianden stretches a pretty promenade. This 8.5-km (5-mile) boardwalk trail parades the edge of the lower basin of the river north of town, away from the road. It's a breathtaking stroll and not too difficult to walk or cycle. It takes around two hours to complete, and if you want, you can always get the No. 570 bus back. Its starting point is opposite the Tourist Information Office. ✉ *Rue du Vieux Marché 1a, Vianden* 🎫 *Free.*

Télésiège de Vianden *(Chairlift)*

VIEWPOINT | From the banks of the river Our, a chairlift carries visitors up for a remarkable view of the valley. It's the only one of its kind in the Grand Duchy, though it isn't always in use and is only in service between April and mid-October. For the more outdoorsy, a woodland path heads down from the upper station to the castle below. ✉ *Rue du Sanatorium 39, Vianden* ☎ *83/4323* 🎫 *€5 single; €6 return* ⏲ *Closed mid-Oct.–Mar.*

Restaurants

There isn't a huge choice when it comes to dining in Vianden. There are few independent eateries and the best restaurants tend to belong to the hotels (and sometimes vice versa), so be sure to check our hotel reviews for extra tips.

Aal Veinen Beim Hunn

$$$ | **BRASSERIE** | Dark, cozy, and casual, this 1683 inn serves simple brasserie fare—schnitzels, cordon bleu, fondue—and a wide selection of grilled meats cooked in full view of the dining area over a sizzling wood fire. If you've given up on pork chops, this is the place to get reacquainted. **Known for:** a likeable spot to overnight; churning out meaty classics on demand; cheery and quick service. $ *Average main: €24* ✉ *Grand-Rue 114, Vianden* ☎ *83/4368* 🌐 *beimhunn.lu* ⏲ *Closed Tues.*

Café Du Pont

$$ | **BRASSERIE** | The service might be among the more lethargic in town, but where this café-restaurant truly shines is its setting: perched directly above the waters of the River Our. The menu is pretty standard stuff, with an array of schnitzels catching the eye. **Known for:** a sumptuous setting over the water's edge; the weekly menus are decent value; a good spot to rest up for a walk. $ *Average main: €18* ✉ *Grand Rue 1, Vianden* ☎ *83/4061* 🌐 *www.cafedupont.lu* ⏲ *Closed Tues.*

Hotels

Hotel Petry

$ | **HOTEL** | One of a pair of local hotels run by the same family—the other (Belle Vue) has impressive wellness facilities, but is farther out, larger, and often frequented by tour groups. **Pros:** try the pancake maker at the buffet breakfast; try to bag a balcony room overlooking the river; the pizzeria is much loved by locals. **Cons:** doesn't have the historic charm of other hotels in the area; you're on the main road; lacks its own pool facilities. $ *Rooms from: €97* ✉ *Rue de la Gare 15, Vianden* ☎ *83/4122* 🌐 *www.hotel-petry.com* 🛏 *30 rooms* 🍽 *Free Breakfast.*

Hôtel-Restaurant Victor Hugo
$ | HOTEL | At the bottom of the hill and perched on the river, this comfortable hotel pays homage to Vianden's most famous visitor, who settled across the road during his short exile in the area. **Pros:** free garage for bicycles and motorbikes; great food and dining terrace; there's a small sauna for guests. **Cons:** no parking for cars; there's not much to do in the area; rooms are largely quite basic. $ *Rooms from: €89* ✉ *Rue Victor Hugo 3, Vianden* ☎ *83/41601* 🌐 *www.hotelvictorhugo.lu* 🛏 *24 rooms* 🍽 *No Meals.*

Nightlife

★ **Ancien Cinéma Café Club**
THEMED ENTERTAINMENT | An absolute gem. This bar-café doubles up as both a gig venue and fully fledged cinema. The clues are littered all over the walls, as stars of the silver screen peer down at you. Most of the time, it's just flickering silent films as background detail, but it shows the odd classic or documentary. Add to that friendly service, a decent choice of beers, solid pub food, and the occasional live band, and you have the best night out in the Ardennes. ✉ *Grand Rue 23, Vianden* ☎ *26/874–532.*

Clervaux

31 km (19 miles) northwest of Vianden, 62 km (38½ miles) north of Luxembourg City.

This small forest town, surrounded by deep-cleft hills and nestled in a loop of the Clerve river, suffered greatly during World War II. By the end of the fighting, it was reduced to rubble and even the 12th-century castle was burned to a shell. But Clervaux was raised from the ashes. Now travelers come here to hike its hills, listen to Gregorian plainchant at the Benedictine abbey, and see what is, arguably, the most compelling art exhibit in the country.

GETTING HERE AND AROUND

Clervaux is one of the few places in Luxembourg where it's as easy to take the free public transport as to drive. The route by car is pretty simple, following the A7 and E421 up from Luxembourg City, taking just one hour. The train (every 30 minutes) from the capital takes the same amount of time, though it's worth noting that Clervaux station is around a 15-minute walk from town. From the center, you can take direct buses to the towns of Wiltz (No. 642) and Vianden (No. 664).

VISITOR INFORMATION

CONTACTS Clervaux Tourist Information. ✉ *Grand-Rue 11, Clervaux* ☎ *92/0072* 🌐 *www.visit-clervaux.lu/en.*

Sights

Abbaye de Clervaux (*Clervaux Abbey*)
RELIGIOUS BUILDING | The Benedictine Abbey of Sts. Maurice and Maur was built in 1910 in the neo-Gothic style of France's famous Abbey of Cluny. It sits perched high above the town and the monks here lead a life of strict prayer and meditation. The abbey is best known for its Gregorian plainchant, which has even been released on albums. Daily visits are limited, though you can see a museum on abbey life in the crypt and visit the friendly shop (2:30–5:30 weekdays; 11:30–5:30 weekends), which sells apple juice made by the monks. ✉ *Pl. de l'Abbaye 1, Clervaux* ☎ *92/0072 guided tour* 🌐 *www.abbaye-clervaux.lu* 🎟 *Free.*

★ **Château de Clervaux / The Family of Man**
ART MUSEUM | The oldest parts of Clervaux Castle date back to the 12th century, when it was built on the order of Count Gerhard von Sponheim, a brother of the Count of Vianden. Over the centuries it

Clervaux Castle is home to the famous Family of Man photography exhibit assembled by Luxembourg-born photographer Edward Steichen.

expanded greatly, and it was from here that Philip de Lannoi (the ascendant of Franklin Delano Roosevelt) set forth in 1621 to make his fortune in America. But in the dying days of World War II, the first engagements of Germany's Ardennes Counteroffensive (Battle of the Bulge) saw the town and its historic buildings destroyed, as the tanks rolled in. The burned ruins of the castle fell into state hands thereafter, and it was heavily rebuilt. Inside, you'll now find a number of museums and exhibits, including the tiny **Museum of the Battle of the Bulge**, though this is little signed and is mostly a collection of weapons and shrapnel, and a museum of **1/100 scale models** of Luxembourg's castle. But pride of place goes to **The Family of Man** exhibition of photography, the greatest artistic sight in the country. Two entire floors are taken up by this UNESCO-listed exhibition that was curated and assembled by the Luxembourg-born photographer Edward J. Steichen (1879–1973). In 1951, he invited entries for a collection of images that would record mankind in all its flawed wonder and mystery. He whittled the entries down from 2 million to around 500 and toured them around the world. Since 1994, it has been exhibited in Clervaux and remains one of the world's great cultural sights, charting war, life, death, happiness, sadness, family, and everything in between in simple black-and-white prints. A must-see. ✉ *Montée du Château 6, Clervaux* ☎ *27/8001* 🌐 *www.clervaux.lu* 🎫 *€6* ⏲ *Closed Mon. and Tues.*

Restaurants

La Table de Clervaux

$$$ | BRASSERIE | FAMILY | The restaurant of the Hotel du Commerce has had a revamp in recent years, but remains an eminently reliable spot for a bit of brasserie fare, with a menu steeped in the French classics and the odd Luxembourgish aside. Think *Bouchée à la Reine* (creamy chicken-stuffed vol-au-vents) and the usual array of steaks, cordon bleus, and carpaccios, all pulled off with no little flair. **Known for:** its family-friendly fare,

Wartime Luxembourg

Luxembourg stayed neutral during both World Wars in the 20th century, yet it didn't stop Germany from occupying its land (1914–18; 1940–45) and sending its men off to die as cannon fodder on the Russian front.

It also witnessed one of the last big dice throws by the Axis forces, for whom the writing was on the wall after the United States entered World War II. The Ardennes Counteroffensive (or Battle of the Bulge) was designed to quickly split the Allied armies along the Western Front, so Germany could encircle them and force a peace treaty in its favor. Instead, it devolved into one of the war's bloodiest battles, as the deep winter snows ran red. It's one that locals here will never forget.

The Cemeteries

In Hamm, just beyond the eastern fringes of Luxembourg City, you'll find the World War II **American Military Cemetery** (*www.abmc.gov/luxembourg*) where General George Patton chose to be buried with his men. More than 5,000 soldiers of the Third Army were buried here, having died on Luxembourg soil; there are also 117 graves of unknown soldiers. Each is marked with either a Star of David or a simple cross, but they are not separated by race, rank, religion, or origin—except for the 22 pairs of brothers, who lie side by side.

From here, a small road, about 1 km (½ mile) long, leads to Sandweiler, where the **German Military Cemetery** shelters more than twice as many war dead. Blunt stone crosses identify multiple burial sites, some marked with names and serial numbers; others simply say *Ein Deutscher Soldat* (a German soldier).

The Museums

Ettelbruck, a short train ride from Luxembourg City, has several spots of interest to World War II buffs, including a life-size statue of General Patton, in full combat gear, just outside of town. Its **General Patton Memorial Museum** (*www.patton.lu*) is also dedicated to the man who liberated the city on Christmas Day 1944 and is filled with photographs and relics from World War II.

In neighboring Diekirch, in the **Musee National d'Histoire Militaire** (*mnhm.business.site*), you'll find life-size dioramas depicting the Battle of the Bulge as well as discussion of other wars and eras. It eschews focusing on strategies and fronts for more human stories, delving into everything from K rations to the propaganda flyers—both German and American—scattered to demoralize already homesick soldiers at Christmas.

In **Wiltz** and **Clervaux**, you'll find two small museums, both housed in their respective castles, each dedicated to the Battle of the Bulge. The latter (see Clervaux) is more of a collection of shrapnel and weapons with little elaboration, while the Wiltz museum (*www.wiltz.lu*) tells the story of the battle from a local perspective.

Leave the Ardennes and head south to Esch-sur-Alzette, where the newly refurbished **Musée National de la Résistance** (*see Esch-sur-Alzette*) delves imaginatively into Luxembourg's occupation during World War II (1940–45), documenting local resistance groups and life in the camps.

with burgers for the kids; classic French food to savor; an impressive wine selection. *Average main: €24 ✉ Hotel du Commerce, rte. de Marnach 2, Clervaux ☎ 92/1032 🌐 www.latabledeclervaux.com ⏲ Closed Mon.*

★ Restaurant du Château

$$$$ | **FRENCH** | The culinary gem of the city. The setting, nestled within the courtyard of the castle, is a peach, and its terrace makes a grand alfresco escape on a summer's evening. **Known for:** a beautiful castle garden setting; elaborate gastronomy in a town sorely lacking high-end alternatives; excellent wine menu. *Average main: €56 ✉ Montée du Château 4, Clervaux ☎ 26/904–857 🌐 www.rdcc.lu ⏲ Closed Mon. and Tues.*

Hotels

Hotel Du Commerce

$$ | **HOTEL** | Below the castle and slightly apart from the center, this spacious hotel has been in the same family for three generations and combines slick, spare modernity—tile, stucco, polished oak—with homey old details (fringed lamps, heavy upholstery). **Pros:** ample parking; great pool and sauna; a good price for what you get. **Cons:** there's a €12 fee for bringing your pets; you have to pay extra to use some of the wellness facilities; it's just off the noisy main road into town. *Rooms from: €124 ✉ Rte. de Marnach 2, Clervaux ☎ 92/1032 🌐 www.hoteldu-commerce.lu 50 rooms Free Breakfast.*

★ Le Clervaux Boutique & Design Hotel

$$$ | **HOTEL** | **FAMILY** | This is actually two hotels, which have been attached via a walkway—the older of the two is the 90-room Koener, complete with a pair of restaurants (steak house and French), a large wellness center, and cocktail bar—but guests at the 22-suite Le Clervaux opposite also share these facilities for free, so there's little excuse not to opt for the slightly more interesting stay. **Pros:** access to a small gym and great wellness facilities; you're right in the very center of Clervaux; the Cabana bar is one of the better nights out in town. **Cons:** private parking is €15 per night; breakfast isn't included; it's the priciest stay here (the Koener is about €30 a night cheaper). *Rooms from: €170 ✉ Grand-Rue 9, Clervaux ☎ 92/1105 🌐 www.inter-clervaux.lu 22 suites No Meals.*

Index

A

bbaye d'Aulne, *286*
bbaye de Clervaux, *373*
bbaye de St-Remy, *327*
bbaye de Stavelot, *316*
bbaye d'Orval, *334*
bbaye Notre-Dame de la Paix (Chimay Abbey), *290*
bbaye Notre-Dame de Scourmont, *291*
bdijmuseum Ten Duinen, *239*
bdijsite Herkenrode, *159–160*
ir travel, *32, 43*
ntwerp and the Northeast, 125
ruges and the Coast, 211
russels, 61
hent and the Leie, 166
uxembourg, 340–341
leuse and the Ardennes, 296
Vestern Wallonia, 249
irspace Indoor Skydiving, *286*
merican Military Cemetery, *375*
ncien Cinéma Café Club, *373*
ncient Cloth Factory, *369–370*
ncient Wall Ramparts, *283*
nnevoie Castle, *23*
nno *1465, 237*
ntwerp and the Northeast, *14, 122–162*
ining, 126–127, 134–137, 147–148, 153–154, 157–158, 159, 160, 162
dging, 126, 137–138, 148, 154–155, 158, 161, 162
ightlife and the arts, 139–140, 148–149, 155, 158
rices, 127
afety, 127
hopping, 140–141, 149–150, 155
urs, 127
ansportation, 125–126
sitor information, 127
ntwerp Story, The, *129*
ntwerp Zoo, *141*
quatower, *366*
rchéoscope Godefroid de Bouillon, *335*
rchitectural Walk (Esch-sur-Alzette), *358*
rdennes, The. ⇨ **See Meuse and the Ardennes**
rentshuis, *213*
rt Nouveau Walk (Charleroi), *286*
scenseur Funiculaire de Strépy-Thieu, *279–280*
th, *246, 248, 267–270*
tlantikwall Rayverside, *237*
tomium, *104*
ttablez Vous ✕ , *321*
ugust ▣ , *154*
ugustijnenbrug, *221*
ugustijnenrei, *221*
uto racing, *310–311*
utoworld, *88*

B

B&B A Côté du Cinquantenaire ▣ , *94*
Bassinia, *311*
Bastion VIII, *193*
Bastogne, *294, 328–331*
Bastogne Barracks, *329*
Bastogne War Museum, *25, 329*
Battle of the Bulge, *329*
Baugnez *44 Historical Museum, 313–314*
Beaches
Bruges and the Coast, 234, 236, 238, 240
Luxembourg, 370
Beaux-Arts Mons, *254*
Beer, *20–21*
Antwerp, 139
Bruges and the Coast, 241
Brussels, 76
Ghent, 172
Western Wallonia, 267
Beersel, *61, 117–118*
Beersel Castle, *22*
Beffroi (Mons), *254*
Beffroi (Namur), *321*
Beffroi (Tournai), *262*
Beffroi et l'Hôtel de Ville (Binche), *283–284*
Beffroi et l'Hôtel de Ville (Charleroi), *286*
Begijnhof, *172*
Begijnhof (Antwerp), *141*
Begijnhof (Lier), *158*
Begijnhof van Kortrijk, *203*
Belfort (Bruges), *219*
Belfort van Gent, *172*
Belgian Coast, *210*
Beloeil Castle, *22*
Berdorf, *366*
Bicycling, *32, 43*
Antwerp and the Northeast, 125, 127
Bruges and the Coast, 211, 213
Brussels, 61
Ghent and the Leie, 168, 197
Luxembourg, 361
Western Wallonia, 271
Billie's Bier Kafétaria, *139*
Binche, *247, 248, 282–285*
Binche Palace Ruins, *284*
Blast Furnace Belval, *358*
Boat tours
Antwerp and the Northeast, 127
Ghent and the Leie, 168, 169, 172
Luxembourg, 361–362, 369
Boat travel, *211*
Bock, *346*
Boentje Café ✕ , *109*
Bois du Cazier, *286–287*
Bois-du-Luc, *279*
Bonnefooi (bar), *75*
Books and films about Belgium, *26–27*
Botte du Hainaut, *290*
Boucle Noire (GR412), *287*
Bouillon, *294, 334–336*
Bouillon Castle, *22*
Boulevard Leopold ▣ , *154*
Bourscheid, *370*
Bourscheid Castle, *370*
BOZAR: Centre for Fine Arts, *86*
BPS *22, 287*
Brasserie à Vapeur, *267*
Brasserie Caracole, *323*
Brasserie de l'Abbaye d'Aulne, *286*
Brasserie la Binchoise ✕ , *284*
Brewery Bourgogne de Flandres, *213*
Brouwerij Het Anker, *156*
Bruges and the Coast, *14–15, 208–244*
beaches, 234, 236, 238, 240
cuisine, 223
dining, 212, 221–224, 233, 234–235, 236, 238, 240, 243–244
lodging, 212, 224–225, 228, 235, 236, 238–239, 244
nightlife and the arts, 228–230, 239
prices, 212
shopping, 230–231
tours, 213
transportation, 211–212
visitor information, 213
Bruges Beer Experience, *213, 216*
Brugs Bierfestival, *49*
Brusselpoort, *156*
Brussels, *14, 58–120*
dining, 64, 71–73, 84–85, 92–94, 95, 98–101, 107–109, 112–114, 116–117, 118–119, 120
discounts and deals, 65
festivals and seasonal events, 63, 68
lodging, 63, 73–74, 85–86, 94, 100–101, 109, 114
nightlife and the arts, 63–64, 75–77, 86–87, 94, 101–102, 104, 109–110, 114–115
prices, 63, 64
shopping, 64, 77–79, 87–88, 102, 104, 115
timing the visit, 65
tours, 64–65
transportation, 61–63
visitor information, 65
Brussels International Film Festival, *49*
Brussels Jazz Festival, *63*
Brussels side trips, *59, 110–120*
Brussels Summer Festival, *63*
Brusselse Forten, *193*
Buda island, *203*
Burg (Bruges), *216*
Bus travel, *32, 43*
Antwerp and the Northeast, 125
Bruges and the Coast, 211
Brussels, 61–62
Ghent and the Leie, 166–167
Luxembourg, 341
Meuse and the Ardennes, 296–297
Western Wallonia, 249
Butte du Lion, *274*

C

Cable car (Namur), *317*
Café des Spores ✕ , *98*
Canal du Center and Boat Lifts, *279–280*
Car travel and rentals, *33–35, 43*
Antwerp and the Northeast, 125
Bruges and the Coast, 211–212
Brussels, 62
Ghent and the Leie, 167
Luxembourg, 341

Meuse and the Ardennes, 297
Western Wallonia, 249
Carnaval de Binche, *283*
Carnival, *49*
Carpet of Flowers, *68*
Casemates du Bock, *346*
Casino de Spa, *309*
Castle of the Counts (Gravensteen), *23, 173*
Castles, *22–23*
Cathédrale Notre-Dame (Luxembourg City), *346–347*
Cathédrale Notre-Dame de Tournai, *262*
Cathédrale St-Aubain, *317*
Cathédrale St-Michel et Ste-Gudula, *79*
Cathédrale St-Paul, *299*
Cavalcade de Jemappes, *49*
Caves de Wellenstein, *362*
Caves Lucien Gloden, *362*
Caves St-Martin, *362*
Celles, *324*
Céma Passion ✕, *281*
Centraal Station (Antwerp), *141–142*
Centre Belge de la Bande Dessinée, *65, 68*
Centré de Documentation sur les Migrations Humaines, *358*
Centre de la Gravure et de l'Image Imprimée, *280*
Chabrol ✕, *107*
Chairlift (Télésiège de Vianden), *372*
Chapelle de Lorette, *327*
Charleroi, *247, 248, 285–290*
Charlier Museum, *104*
Château Comtal, *327*
Château d'Attre, *268*
Château de Beloeil, *268*
Château de Chimay, *291*
Château de Clervaux / The Family of Man, *373–374*
Château de Freyr, *324*
Château de la Roche-en-Ardenne, *333*
Château de Seneffe, *280*
Château de Vianden, *371*
Château Fort de Bouillon, *335*
Châteaux de Beaufort, *366*
Chez Duche ✕, *288*
Children, travel with, *28*
Chimay, *247, 248, 290–292*
Chimay Abbey (Abbaye Notre-Dame de la Paix), *290*
Chocolate, *103*
Chocolate Nation, *25, 142–143*
Choco-Story, *216*
Cinquantenaire and Schuman (Brussels), *58, 88–94*
Citadelle de Dinant, *324*
Citadelle de Huy, *311*
Citadelle de Namur, *317*
Clairefontaine ✕, *351*
Classissimo, *63*
Clervaux, *373–376*
Climate, *42, 65, 342–343*
Coast, The. ⇨ **See Bruges and the Coast**
Collégiale Sainte-Gertrude, *272*
Collégiale Sainte-Waudru de Mons, *254*
Combat de la Lumeçon, *259*
Comic-strip murals (Brussels), *68*
Comme Chez Soi ✕, *71*
Como ✕, *359–360*
Complexe Touristique de Blegny, *299*
Computer Museum NAM-IP, *317*
Contacts, *43*
Coudenberg, *23*
Coudenberg/Musée BELvue, *79*
Cour St-Antoine (Liège), *299*
Cuisine, *18–19, 223, 306*

D

Damme, *208, 231–233*
De Haan, *208, 235–236*
De Haan Beach, *236*
De Halve Maan, *216*
De Heilig Bloedprocessie, *49*
De Koninck Brewery, *152*
De Noordzee | Mer du Nord ✕, *71*
De Ruien (Underground Antwerp), *128*
De Wereld van Kina (The World of Kina), *172–173*
De Witte Lelie 🏨, *148*
Deinze, *191–192*
Dendermonde, *164, 192–196*
Dendre Valley RaVel Cycling Route, *271*
Deurle, *186, 188–191*
Diamond industry, *142*
Diamond Quarter (Antwerp), *143*
Dinant, *294, 323–326*
Dining, *37–38.* ⇨ *See also under specific locations*
Discounts and deals, *38, 65, 169*
DIVA, *128*
Dodengang, *242*
D'Oude Schuur ✕, *187*
Ducasse de Mons, *49, 259*
Dudelange, *358*
Durbuy, *294, 331–332*

E

Echternach and Little Switzerland, *338, 365–368*
Echternach Lake, *366*
Ecopark Adventures, *262*
Eerste Korenmetershuis, *173*
Eglise Collégiale de Notre-Dame (Huy), *311*
Eglise Collégiale Notre-Dame de Dinant, *324–325*
Église Collégiale Saint-Ursmer, *284*
Église Notre Dame du Sablon, *81*
Eglise St-Barthélemy, *299*
Église Saint-Christophe de Charleroi, *287*
Eglise St-Denis, *299*
Eglise St-Jacques, *299, 302*
Eglise Saint-Joseph, *358*
Eglise St-Loup, *317*
Église Saint-Pierre (Lessines), *271*
Église Saint-Quentin, *263*
Eglise St-Sébastien, *316*
Église Sts. Pierre et Paul (Echternach), *366–367*
Église Trinitaire, *371*
1898 The Post 🏨, *181*
Ellergron Reserve, *358–359*
Embassies, *42, 43*
Emergencies, *34*
Erfgoeddag, *49*
Escher Bamhaiser 🏨, *360*
Escher Déierepark, *359*
Esch-sur-Alzette and the Redlands, *338, 357–360*
Esch-sur-Sûre, *368–371*
Esch-sur-Sûre Castle, *370*
European Union Quarter (Brussels), *88*

F

Family of Man exhibition, *373–374*
Fania exhibition, *313*
Festivals and seasonal events, *49–51* ⇨ *See also under specific locations*
Fête Médiévale de Bouillon, *50*
Film Fest Ghent, *51*
Fiskebar ✕, *153–154*
Flemish Brabant, *61*
Flemish language, *54–55*
Flemish Primitives, *220*
Floralia Brussels, *49*
Fond-de-Gras, *359*
F*1 Belgian Grand Prix, 50*
For Freedom Museum, *234*
Fort Eben-Emael, *302*
Fort Thungun / Musée Draï Eechelen, *347*
Fotomuseum (FOMU), *152*
French language, *52–53*
Freyr Castle, *22*
FunKey Hotel 🏨, *109*

G

Gaasbeek, *61, 118–119*
Gaasbeek Castle, *22*
Gallo-Romeins Museum, *162*
Garderobe Manneken Pis, *25*
Gare Maritime ✕, *108*
General Patton Memorial Museum, *375*
Gentse Feesten, *50*
Gentse Floraliën, *185*
Geraardsbergen, *200–202*
German Military Cemetery, *375*
Gevert-Minne Museum, *187*
Ghent and the Leie, *14, 164–206*
dining, 167–168, 178–180, 187, 190, 192, 194–195, 198–199, 201–202, 205–206
discounts and deals, 169
festivals and seasonal events, 185
lodging, 167, 180–182, 187–188, 190–191, 195, 199, 202, 206
nightlife and the arts, 182–184, 195–196, 199–200, 206
prices, 168
shopping, 184–186, 188, 191, 196
tours, 168, 169, 172, 197
transportation, 166–167
visitor information, 169

odshuizen de Pelikaan, *220*
raanmarkt 13 (shop), *149*
rand Curtius, *302*
rand-Hornu, *254*
rand Place (Brussels), *68*
rand Place (Mons), *254*
rand Place (Tournai), *262–263*
rand-Place (Huy), *311*
raslei, *173*
ravensteen (Castle of the Counts), *23, 173*
reat Mosque, *92*
reenhouses of Laeken, *104*
roeningemuseum, *216*
root Begijnhof (Leuven), *111*
root Strand (Oostende), *238*
rote Markt (Antwerp), *128*
rote Markt (Geraardsbergen), *200*
rote Markt (Kortrijk), *203*
rote Markt (Leuven), *111*
rote Markt (Mechelen), *156*
rotte de Lorette-Rochefort, *327*
rotte La Merveilleuse, *325*
rottes de Han, *327*
rund (Luxembourg City), *347*
ruut (brewpub), *183*
ruuthusemuseum, *216–217*
UM – Ghent University Museum, *173, 176*
us ✕, *84–85*

allerbos Forest, *117*
apje-Tapje, *50*
asselt, *159–161*
autes Fagnes, *294, 312–313*
avenhuis, *129*
ealth and safety, *38–39*
ntwerp and the Northeast, 127
euse and the Ardennes, 298
eilig Bloed Basiliek, *217–218*
enri-Chapelle Cemetery, *303*
ergé Museum, *25*
et Eilandje (Antwerp), *128–141*
et Steen, *129*
iking, *368, 371*
ill '*62 - Sanctuary Wood Museum, 242*
istorical Houses (Tournai), *263*
istorium Brugge, *218*
ooge Crater Museum, *242*
ôpital Notre-Dame à la Rose, *271–272*
orta Museum, *24*
ôtel Amigo, *73–74*
ôtel de l'Ecluse, *364–365*
otel de Orangerie, *225*
ôtel de Ville (Brussels), *68*
ôtel de Ville (Echternach), *367*
ôtel de Ville (Huy), *311*
ôtel de Ville (Mons), *254*
ôtel des Galeries, *74*
ôtel Du Parc, *270*
otel Dukes' Palace, *225*
otel Grupello, *202*
otel Julien, *138*
otel le Côté Vert, *277*

Hôtel Le Royal, *354*
Hotel Messeyne, *206*
Hotel-Restaurant Domaine La Forêt, *365*
Hotels. ⇨ See Lodging
Hougoumont Farm, *274–275*
Huidenvettersplein, *220*
Huis Arnold Vander Haeghen, *176*
Huis de Lailing, *198*
Huis van Alijn, *176*
Huy, *294, 311–312*

I

IJzertoren, *243*
Immunizations, *39*
Impasses (Liège), *303*
In Flanders Fields Museum, *24, 242*
In 't Spinnekopke ✕, *71*
Indoor skydiving, *286*
Insenborn, *370*
Itineraries, *44–48*
Ixelles and Saint-Gilles (Brussels), *58–59, 95–104*

J

James Ensorhuis, *237*
Jan van Eyckplein (Bruges), *218*
Jane, The ✕, *154*
Japanse Tuin, *160*
Jardins d'Eau d'Annevoie, *325*
Jenevermuseum, *160*
Jezuietenplein 21, *199*
Jiggers (bar), *183*
Juliana Hotel Brussels, *74*

K

Kantcentrum, *218–219*
Kasteel Ooidonk, *191*
Kasteel van Beersel, *117*
Kasteel van Gaasbeek, *118*
Kayaking, *326*
Kazerne Dossin, *156*
Keramis Center of Ceramics, *280*
Klein Strand, *238*
Knokke-Heist, *208, 233–235*
Knokke-Heist Beach, *234*
Koksijde, *208, 239–240*
Koksijde Beach, *240*
Koninklijk Museum voor Schone Kunsten (KMSKA), *152–153*
Koornstapelhuis, *173*
Korenlei, *173*
Korenmarkt (Ghent), *176*
Kortrijk, *165, 202–206*
Kunstenfestivaldesarts, *49, 63*

L

La Boverie, *303*
La Collégiale Saints-Pierre-et-Paul, *291*
La Falize, *331*
La Louvière, *247, 248, 278–281*
La Maison Cauchie, *88*
La Maison du Parc-Botrange, *313*
La Malterie ✕, *292*

La Peniche VINtage ✕, *364*
La Petite Madeleine ✕, *265*
La Pipistrelle B&B, *354*
La Régate Internationale de Baignoires, *50*
La Roche-en-Ardenne, *294, 332–334*
La Table de La Manufacture Urbaine ✕, *288*
La Tramasure ✕, *272*
La Villa Gracia, *322*
L'Abbaye de Maredsous, *317, 320*
Laeken and Schaerbeek (Brussels), *59, 104–110*
Lake Virelles, *291*
Lambic beer, *76*
Lange Wapper, *135*
Language, *52–55*
L'Arsenal, *320*
L'Artotheque, *255*
Last Post, *243*
Latem School, *189*
Le Clervaux Boutique & Design Hotel, *376*
Le Cygne D'Argent, *306*
Le Place d'Armes, *354*
L'Eaudyssée de Spa, *309*
Leie, The. ⇨ See Ghent and the Leie
Leiestreek Villages, *164, 186–192*
L'Envers ✕, *257–258*
Leopold Café Presse ✕, *93*
Les Ancien Abattoirs, *255*
Les Gribaumonts ✕, *258*
Les Marolles (Brussels), *68*
L'Espace Chimay ✕, *291*
l'Espace Gallo-Romain, *268*
Lessines, *246, 271–272*
Leuven, *61, 111–115*
Liefmans Brewery, *197*
Liefrange, *370*
Liège, *294, 296, 298–308*
Lier, *122, 158–159*
Limburg Province, *122, 159–162*
Little Paris ✕, *277*
Little Switzerland, *338, 365–368*
Lodging, *39–40, 43.* ⇨ *See also under specific locations*
Louvain-la-Neuve, *246, 248, 277–278*
Lower Town (Brussels), *58, 65–79*
Lucie et les Papillions, *255*
Lultzhausen, *370*
Luxembourg, *15, 338–376*
beaches, 370
dining, 342, 350–353, 359–360, 364, 367, 370, 372, 374, 376
history, 375
lodging, 341–342, 353–355, 360, 364–365, 367–368, 370–371, 372–373, 376
nightlife and the arts, 355–356, 368, 373
prices, 342
shopping, 356–357
sports and the outdoors, 361, 368, 371
timing the visit, 342–343
tours, 361–362, 369
transportation, 340–341
visitor information, 343
Luxembourg Ardennes, *338, 368–376*
Luxembourg City, *338, 343–357*

M

M Leuven, *111–112*
MA Festival, *50*
Maagdendale Abbey, *198*
Maagdenhuis, *143, 146*
Made in Louise , *100*
Main Street Hotel , *244*
Maison Antoine ✕, *92*
Maison Autrique, *105*
Maison de la Pataphonie, *325*
Maison de l'Histoire Européenne, *89*
Maison de Monsieur Sax, *325*
Maison de Victor Hugo, *372*
Maison Des Anges , *272*
Maison des Géants, *268–269*
Maison Tournaisienne: Musée de Folklore, *263*
Maison Van Gogh, *255*
Malagne - Archéoparc de Rochefort, *328*
Malmedy, *294, 313–315*
Malmundarium, *314*
Màloma ✕, *108–109*
Manneken Pis, *68, 201*
Marché des antiquités, *331*
Marché des fleurs, *331*
Marché du chocolat, *331*
Markt (Bruges), *219*
Marktplein (Damme), *232*
Martin's Dream Hotel , *260*
Martin's Klooster , *114*
Martin's Louvain-La-Neuve , *278*
Masters Expo, *49*
Mechelen, *122, 155–159*
Meebrug, *220*
Meir, Diamond Quarter, and Centraal Station (Antwerp), *141–150*
Meise, *61, 119–120*
Memorial (Malmedy), *314*
Mémorial du Mardasson, *330*
Memorial Museum Passchendaele *1917, 242–243*
Menenpoort, *243*
Mercator, *238*
Metselaars, *173*
Meuse and the Ardennes, *15, 294–336*
cuisine, 306
dining, 297–298, 304–306, 309–310, 314, 316, 321–322, 325–326, 328, 331, 332, 334, 336
festivals and seasonal events, 331
lodging, 297, 306–307, 310, 315, 316, 322, 326, 328, 331, 332, 334, 336
nightlife and the arts, 307–308, 322–323
prices, 298
safety, 298
shopping, 308, 320–321, 323
sports and the outdoors, 310–311, 326
transportation, 296–297
visitor information, 298
MiLL, *280*
Mini-Europe, *105*
Minnewater Park, *219*
Mitraillette ✕, *258*
Mode Museum (MoMu), *129, 132*
Modern Alchemist, The (bar), *102*
Mondorf Domaine Thermal, *362–363*
Money matters, *40–41*
Mons, *246, 248, 251–261*
Mons Memorial Museum, *255–256*
Montagne de Bueren, *303*
MOOF (Museum of Original Figurines), *68–69*
Mosconi ✕, *352*
Moselle, The, *338, 361–365*
Motel One , *85–86*
MOU – Museum Oudenaarde and the Flemish Ardennes, *198*
Mt. St.-Jean, *358*
MS Princesse Marie-Astrid (boat tours), *361–362*
MSK – Museum of Fine Arts Ghent, *176*
Mullerthal Trail, *368*
MUMONS, *256*
Mundaneum, *256*
Musée Art et Histoire, *89*
Musée Communal (Huy), *312*
Musée Communal de Nivelles, *273*
Musée Constantin Meunier, *95*
Musée d'Art Moderne Grand-Duc Jean (MUDAM), *347–348*
Musée d'Art Spontané, *105*
Musée de Cheval et Musée de la Ville D'eaux, *309*
Musée de la Banque Nationale de Belgique, *69*
Musée de la Bataille des Ardennes, *333*
Musée de la Lessive, *309*
Musée de la Photographie, *287*
Musée de la Tapisserie, *263–264*
Musée de la Vie Wallonne, *303*
Musée de la Ville de Bruxelles, *69*
Musée de l'Abbaye, *367*
Musée des Arts Anciens (TreM.a), *320*
Musée des Arts Décoratifs François Duesberg, *256*
Musée des Beaux-Arts (Charleroi), *287*
Musée des Beaux-Arts (Tournai), *264*
Musée des Instruments de Musique (MIM), *80*
Musée des Sciences Naturelles, *89*
Musée d'Histoire de la Ville de Luxembourg, *348*
Musée d'Histoire Militaire, *264*
Musée d'Histoire Naturelle, *264*
Musée Draï Eechelen, *347*
Musée du Circuit de Spa-Francorchamps, *316*
Musée du Doudou, *257*
Musée du Mémorial *1815, 275*
Musée du Tram, *89*
Musée du Vin, *363–364*
Musée Ducal, *335*
Musée Félicien Rops, *320*
Musée Fin-de-Siècle, *80*
Musée Guillaume Apollinaire, *316*
Musée Hergé, *278*
Musée Historique de la Principauté de Stavelot-Malmedy, *316*
Musée Horta, *95*
Musée International du Carnaval et du Masque, *284*
Musée Juif de Belgique, *81*
Musée L, *278*
Musée Magritte, *81*
Musée Mine Cockerill, *359*
Musée Mode and Dentelle, *69–70*
Musée National de la Résistance, *359, 375*
Musée National d'Histoire et d'Art, *348*
Musee National d'Histoire Militaire *375*
Musée National d'Histoire Naturell *348*
Musée Oldmasters, *81*
Musée Royal de l'Afrique Centrale, *116*
Musée Royal de l'Armée et d'Histoire Militaire, *89*
Musée Royal de Mariemont, *280*
Musée Schaerbeekois de la Bière, *105, 107*
Musée Tchantchès, *303–304*
Musée Wellington, *275*
Musée Wiertz, *95*
Museum Aan de IJzer, *243*
Museum aan de Stroom, *132*
Museum Dhondt-Dhaenens, *190*
Museum Gust de Smet, *190*
Museum Hof van Busleyden, *156*
Museum Mayer Van den Bergh, *146*
Museum of Modern Art (MuHKA), *15*
Museum of the Battle of the Bulge, *374*
Museum Of Walloon Life, *24*
Museum van Deinze en de Leiestreek (MUDEL), *191–192*
Museums, *24–25*
Muur van Geraardsbergen, *201*
mu.ZEE, *238*

N

Namur, *294, 296, 316–323*
Napoléon, *276*
National Day, *50*
Nightlife and the arts. ⇨ **See unde specific locations**
Nivelles, *246, 248, 272–273*
Northeast, The. ⇨ **See Antwerp ar the Northeast**
Novotel Charleroi Centre , *289*
Nüetnigenough ✕, *72*
Nuit Blanche, *51*

O

Oak ✕, *179*
Omer Vander Ghinste Brewery, *204*
Ommegang, *50, 68*
101st Airborne Museum, *330*
1/100 scale models, *374*
Onze-Lieve-Vrouw ter Duinenkerk (Oostende), *239*
Onze-Lieve-Vrouwe Kerk (Kortrijk), *2*
Onze-Lieve-Vrouwebasiliek (Tongeren), *162*
Onze-Lieve-Vrouwekathedraal (Antwerp), *132*
Onze-Lieve-Vrouwekerk (Bruges), *219–220*

nze-Lieve-Vrouwekerk van Pamele, *198*
nze-Lieve-Vrouw-Hemelvaartkerk (Damme), *232–233*
oidonk Castle, *22*
ostende, *208, 236–239*
ostkerke, *233*
penluchtmuseum Bokrijk, *160*
rigine ✕, *92–93*
ud Beersel Brewery, *117–118*
ude Stad and Het Eilandje (Antwerp), *128–141*
udenaarde, *197–200*
ur Lady ter Hoyen, *172*
urdall Promenade, *372*

airi Daiza, *269*
alais Grand-Ducal, *348*
alais Provincial, *320*
alais Royale, *81*
AM – Provincial Archeological Museum, *198*
and, The, *228*
anorama, The, *275*
anoramic Glass Elevator of Pfaffenthal, *348–349*
arc Attractif Reine Fabiola, *320*
arc des Topiaries, *332*
arc du Cinquantenaire, *92*
arc Josephat, *107*
arc Léopold, *92*
arfumerie Guy Delforge, *320–321*
ark van Tervuren, *116*
arliamentarium, *88*
assports and visas, *41*
aul Delvaux Museum, *240*
paix, *267*
ixel Museum, *107*
ace d'Armes (Namur), *321*
ace de la Constitution (Luxembourg City), *349*
ace du Grand Sablon (Brussels), *81, 84*
ace du Marché (Echternach), *367*
ace du Marché (Liège), *304*
ace du Petit Sablon (Brussels), *81, 84*
ace Royale (Brussels), *84*
ace Ste-Catherine (Brussels), *70*
ace St-Lambert (Liège), *304*
ane travel. ⇨ See Air travel
antentuin Meise, *120*
antin-Moretus Museum/Prentenkabinet, *24, 132*
ont des Trous, *264*
ont Viaduc, *349*
oortersloge, *218*
orte de Hal, *95*
orte de Trèves, *330*
orte des Trois Tours, *349*
ouhon Pierre le Grand, *309*
rehistoHan, *327*
éhistomuseum, *304*
ices
twerp and the Northeast, 127
uges and the Coast, 212
ussels, 63, 64
Ghent and the Leie, 168
Luxembourg, 342
Meuse and the Ardennes, 298
Western Wallonia, 250
Public transportation, *62, 125–126*
Publiek ✕, *180*

Q

Quai No. 4 ✕, *270*
Quartier de l'Ilôt Sacré (Brussels), *70*

R

Rebelle ✕, *205*
Red Star Line Museum, *132*
Redlands, The, *338, 357–360*
Reien, *220*
Reinhardstein, *313*
Remich and the Moselle, *338, 361–365*
Restaurant du Château ✕, *376*
Restaurants. ⇨ **See Dining under specific locations**
Ride-sharing, *35, 43, 62*
Rochefort, *294, 326–328*
Rock Werchter, *50*
Rockhal, *358*
Roman villa, *366*
Romantik Hotel le Val d'Amblève, *316*
Royal Greenhouses of Laeken, The, *49*
Royal Museums Of Fine Arts, *25*
Rozenhoedkaai, *220*
Rubenshuis, *146*

S

Safety, *38–39*
Antwerp and the Northeast, 127
Meuse and the Ardennes, 298
St. Symphorien Military Cemetery, *257*
St. Willibrord Basilica, *367*
Saint-Gilles (Brussels), *58–59, 95–104*
Saint-James Quarter (Nivelles), *273*
Schaerbeek (Brussels), *59, 104–110*
Schuman (Brussels), *58, 88–94*
Scooters, *61*
Shopping. ⇨ **See under specific locations**
SILEX'S: Neolithic Flint Mines at Spiennes, *257*
Sint Anna's Tunnel (Underpass; Antwerp), *132–133*
Sint-Alexius Begijnhof and Museum, *193*
Sint-Andrieskerk, *133*
Sint-Baafs Kathedraal, *176–177*
Sint-Batholomeuskerk, *201*
Sint-Carolus Borromeuskerk, *133*
Sint-Gummaruskerk, *158*
Sint-Jacobskerk, *146*
Sint-Janshospitaal Museum, *220*
Sint-Janshuismolen and Koelewei-molen, *221*
Sint-Maartenskerk, *205*
Sint-Martens-Latem, *186–188*
Sint-Martinuskerk, *187*
Sint-Niklaaskerk, *177*
Sint-Pauluskerk, *133–134*
Sint-Pieters en Paulus Abbey, *194*
Sint-Pietersabdij, *178*
Sint-Pieterskerk, *112*
Sint-Romboutskathedraal, *156–157*
Sint-Servaasbasiliek Grimbergen, *120*
SMAK - Municipal Museum of Contemporary Art, *178*
Snijders & Rockoxhuis, *146–147*
South of the Center (Antwerp), *150–155*
Spa (Meuse and the Ardennes), *294, 308–311*
Spa Monopole, *309*
Spanjaardstraat (Bruges), *221*
Spas, *311*
Sports and the outdoors. ⇨ **See under specific locations**
Stadhuis (Ghent), *178*
Stadhuis (Leuven), *112*
Stadhuis (Mechelen), *156*
Stadhuis and Belfort (Dendermonde), *194*
STAM - Ghent City Museum, *178*
Stavelot, *294, 315–316*
Steamtrain Dendermonde–Puurs, *194*
Steenhouwersdijk, *220*
Stella Artois Brewery, *112*

T

'T Fornuis ✕, *137*
Taxes, *41, 43*
Taxis, *35, 43*
Antwerp and the Northeast, 126
Bruges and the Coast, 212
Brussels, 62
Luxembourg, 341
Teasers by Rock-Fort ✕, *224*
Télésiège de Vianden (Chairlift), *372*
Tervuren, *61, 115–117*
Teseum, *162*
Texture Museum, *205*
T'Grof Zout ✕, *201–202*
Théâtre Royal de Toone, *71*
Timing the visit, *42, 65, 342–343*
Tipping, *41–42*
Tolhuis (Bruges), *218*
Tolhuis (Ghent), *173*
Tomorrowland, *50*
Tongeren, *159, 161–162*
Torenhof, *188*
Tour Burbant, *269*
Tour Henry VIII, *264–265*
Tour of Flanders Museum, *198*
Tournai, *246, 248, 261–267*
Tours. ⇨ **See under specific locations**
Train travel, *35–36, 43*
Antwerp and the Northeast, 126
Bruges and the Coast, 212
Brussels, 62–63
Ghent and the Leie, 167
Luxembourg, 341
Meuse and the Ardennes, 297
Western Wallonia, 249–250
Train World, *107*

Transportation, *32–36.* ⇨ *See also under specific locations*
Treasury (Liège), *299*
Trésor Hugo d'Oignies, *320*
Tweede Korenmetershuis, *173*
Twin towers, *203*
Tyne Cot Cemetery, *243*

U

U.S. embassies, *42, 43*
Underground Antwerp (De Ruien), *128*
Underground tunnels (Namur), *317*
Underpass (Sint Anna's Tunnel; Antwerp), *132–133*
Universiteitsbibliotheek, *112*
Upper Sûre Lake, *370*
Upper Town (Brussels), *58, 79–88*

V

Vallée de la Paix, *286*
Vallée de la Pétrusse, *349*
Valley of the Seven Châteaux, *361*
Vanhaegen B&B, The , *182*
Vianden, *371–376*
Villa des Fleurs , *310*
Villa Vauban, *350*
Visas, *41*
Visitor information, *42, 43.* ⇨ *See also under specific locations*
Vismarkt (Bruges), *220*
Vismet (Brussels), *70*
Vlaamse Ardennen, *164, 196–202*
Vlaeykensgang (Antwerp), *134*
Vleeshuis, *134*
Vleeshuis Museum, *194*
Vocabulary, *52–55*
Volkskundemuseum, *221*
Vrije Schippers, *173*

W

Walking tours, *127, 362, 369*
Walloon Brabant, *248*
Waterloo, *246, 248, 273–277*
Weather, *42, 65, 342–343*
Western Wallonia, *15, 246–292*
dining, 250, 257–259, 265, 270, 272, 273, 276–277, 278, 280–281, 284–285, 288, 291–292
festivals and seasonal events, 259, 283
lodging, 250, 259–260, 265–266, 270, 272, 273, 277, 278, 281, 288–289, 292
nightlife and the arts, 260–261, 266–267, 289, 292
prices, 250
shopping, 261, 267, 289–290
sports and the outdoors, 286
tours, 274
transportation, 249–250
visitor information, 250
Wiltz, *375*
Wine Country (Luxembourg), *363*
Wine tours, *362*
Winter Wonders, *51*
World of Kina, The (De Wereld van Kina), *172–173*

Y

Yamato ×, *99*
Ypres, *208, 210, 240–244*

Z

Zimmertoren, *158–159*
Zurenborg (Antwerp), *153*
Zwin Natuur Park, *234*
Zythos Bierfestival (ZBF), *49*

Photo Credits

Front Cover: Grant Faint [Description: View of canal, Brugge, Damme village, canal. **Back cover, from left to right:** Freeartist/iStock, adisa/iStockphoto, sorincolac/iStock. **Spine:** Catarina Belova/Shutterstock. **Interior, from left to right:** Kisa_Markiza/iStockphoto (1). Boerescul/Dreamstime (2-3). **Chapter 1: Experience Belgium:** Cge2010/Shutterstock (6-7). Sorincolac/iStockphoto (8-9). T.w. Van Urk/ Dreamstime (9). Museum/Piet De Kersgieter (9). Paul Daniels/Shutterstock (10). Jean-Paul Remy/Visit.brussels (10). Toerismevlaanderen/ Milo Profi Fotografie (10). Inge Kinnet i.o.v/Musea Brugge (10). WBT/Olivier Polet (11). Kobby_dagan/Dreamstime (11). Tomas1111 / Dreamstime (12). Michael Mulkens/Dreamstime (12). Brewery/Milo-Profi/Arthur Los (12). Cuteideasforlife/Dreamstime (12). Thomas Dekiere Shutterstock (13). Ismishko/Shutterstock (18). Fanfo/Shutterstock (18). Jonny Allen/ Shutterstock (18). Vezzani Photography/Shutterstock (19 Wut_Moppie/Shutterstock (19). Alexandros Michailidis/Shutterstock (20). Shawn Hamilton/Shutterstock (20). Annavee/Shutterstock (20). Alexandros Michailidis/Shutterstock (21). GlennV/Shutterstock (21). Ieoks/Shutterstock (22). Klodien/Dreamstime (22). WBT/J.P. Remy (22). Thomas Dekiere/ Shutterstock (22). Krysek/Shutterstock (23). Paul Louis/ Courtesy of Musée Horta - Horta Museum (24). AnnDcs/Shutterstock (24). Radiokafka/Dreamstime (24). Chris Lawrence Travel/Shutterstock (24). Jean Marc Pierard/Dreamstime (25). Chantal de Bruijne/ Shutterstock (25). Radiokafka/Shutterstock (25). Richair/Dreamstime (25). **Chapter 3: Brussels:** Sorincolac/iStockphoto (57). Radiokafka/ Dreamstime (69). Danileon/Dreamstime (70). Jasmine Van Hevel/Coudenberg (80). Tatiana Popova/Shutterstock (84). Skyfish/Shutterstock (87). Trabantos/Shutterstock (93). Adam Zoltan/iStockphoto (99). Orpheus26/iStockphoto (105). Warner Lerooy/Dreamstime (108). Mistervla Shutterstock (113). Tatiana Popova/Shutterstock (119). **Chapter 4: Antwerp and the Northeast:** Ixuskmitl/Dreamstime (121). James Byard/ Dreamstime (129). B-hide the scene/Shutterstock (133). Radiokafka/Dreamstime.com (134). Ekinyalgin/Dreamstime (136). Catarina Belova/Shutterstock (143). Siraanamwong/Dreamstime (147). Radiokafka/Dreamstime (152). Boerescu/Shutterstock (157). Elly Mens/Shutterstock (161). **Chapter 5: Ghent and the Leie:** Ekaterinabelova/Dreamstime (163). Huysman Geert/Shutterstock (173). Ekaterinabelova/ Dreamstime (174-175). 22tomtom/Dreamstime (177). Khaled Louis Fazely/Shutterstock (188). Wirestock Creators/Shutterstock (192). Kiev. Victor/Shutterstock (204). **Chapter 6: Bruges and the Coast:** Cge2010/Shutterstock (207). Dmitry Rukhlenko/Shutterstock (217). Michae Mulkens/Shutterstock (218). Piith Hant/Shutterstock (221). KavalenkavaVolha/iStockphoto (226-227). SL-Photography/ Shutterstock (237). **Chapter 7: Western Wallonia:** Kobby Dagan/Shutterstock (245). NAPA/Shutterstock (251). Milosk50/Dreamstime (256). Vadim Nefedoff Shutterstock (263). Jean-Paul Remy_WBT (269). Jean-Philippe Van Damme_Waterloo Tourism Board (275). **Chapter 8: The Meuse and the Ardennes:** Allard1/Dreamstime (293). Leonid Andronov/ iStockphoto (302). Boarding1now/Dreamstime (307). Traveller70/Shutterstoc (312). Ivanderbiesen/Dreamstime (314). Sergey Novikov/Dreamstime (324). Bastogne War Museum (330). Sergey Dzyuba/Shutterstock (333 Tatif55/Shutterstock (335). **Chapter 9: Luxembourg:** Ciwoa/Shutterstock (337). Roberto La Rosa/Shutterstock (347). Marcin Krzyzak/ Shutterstock (349). Frantic00/Shutterstock (350). Ciwoa/Shutterstock (364). Nikolai Sorokin/Dreamstime (366). Menno Schaefer/Shuttersto (369). World Wander/iStockphoto (374). **About Our Writers:** All photos are courtesy of the writers.

*Every effort has been made to trace the copyright holders, and we apologize in advance for any accidental errors. We would be happy to apply the corrections in the following edition of this publication.

Fodor's ESSENTIAL BELGIUM

Publisher: Stephen Horowitz, *General Manager*

Editorial: Douglas Stallings, *Editorial Director*; Jill Fergus, Amanda Sadlowski, Caroline Trefler, *Senior Editors*; Kayla Becker, Alexis Kelly, *Editors;* Angelique Kennedy-Chavannes, *Assistant Editor*

Design: Tina Malaney, *Director of Design and Production*; Jessica Gonzalez, *Graphic Designer*

Production: Jennifer DePrima, *Editorial Production Manager*; Elyse Rozelle, *Senior Production Editor;* Monica White, *Production Editor*

Maps: Rebecca Baer, *Senior Map Editor*; David Lindroth, Mark Stroud (Moon Street Cartography), *Cartographers*

Photography: Viviane Teles, *Senior Photo Editor;* Namrata Aggarwal, Payal Gupta, Ashok Kumar, *Photo Editors;* Rebecca Rimmer, *Photo Production Associate;* Eddie Aldrete, *Photo Production Intern*

Business and Operations: Chuck Hoover, *Chief Marketing Officer*; Robert Ames, *Group General Manager*; Devin Duckworth, *Director of Print Publishing*

Public Relations and Marketing: Joe Ewaskiw, *Senior Director of Communications and Public Relations*

Fodors.com: Jeremy Tarr, *Editorial Director;* Rachael Levitt, *Managing Editor*

Technology: Jon Atkinson, *Director of Technology;* Rudresh Teotia, *Lead Developer*; Jacob Ashpis, *Content Operations Manager*

Writers: Gareth Clark, Tim Skelton

Editor: Jill Fergus

Production Editor: Jennifer DePrima

1st Edition

ISBN 978-1-64097-515-6

ISSN 2831-8382

All details in this book are based on information supplied to us at press time. Always confirm information when it matters, especially if you're making a detour to visit a specific place. Fodor's expressly disclaims any liability, loss, or risk, personal or otherwise, that is incurred as a consequence of the use of any of the contents of this book.

SPECIAL SALES
This book is available at special discounts for bulk purchases for sales promotions or premiums. For more information, e-mail SpecialMarkets@fodors.com.

PRINTED IN CANADA

10 9 8 7 6 5 4 3 2 1

About Our Writers

After tentatively venturing out from his native North-East England, **Gareth Clark** has worked in publishing all over the world, editing *Time Out* magazines in the UAE and China before returning to the U.K. to work on long-running travel magazine *Wanderlust*. Along the way, he has written or edited guidebooks on China, the UAE, Malta, Greece, Belgium, and Luxembourg. He updated the Brussels, Ghent and the Leie, Western Wallonia, Experience, and Luxembourg chapters.

Having lived for more than 30 years in the Netherlands, British-born Dutchman **Tim Skelton** spends much of his free time venturing south across the Belgian border to indulge his passion for the local beers. He is also the author of two essential Dutch beer guides—*Beer in the Netherlands* (2nd edition 2020) and *Around Amsterdam in 80 Beers* (2nd edition 2015), available from *www.skeltonink.eu*—and has written four editions of a guidebook to Luxembourg for Bradt Travel Guides. For this edition he updated the Travel Smart, Antwerp and the Northeast, Bruges and the Coast, and The Meuse and the Ardennes chapters.